Optical Networks:
A Practical Perspective

Wen Li

The Morgan Kaufmann Series in Networking
Series Editor, David Clark

Optical Networks: A Practical Perspective
Rajiv Ramaswami and Kumar N. Sivarajan

Practical Computer Network Analysis and Design
James D. McCabe

Frame Relay Applications: Business and Technology Case Studies
James P. Cavanagh

High-Performance Communication Networks
Jean Walrand and Pravin Varaiya

Computer Networks: A Systems Approach
Larry L. Peterson and Bruce S. Davie

Forthcoming:

Wide Area Network Design: Concepts and Tools for Optimization
Robert S. Cahn

Switching in IP Networks: IP Switching, Tag Switching, and Related Technologies
Bruce S. Davie, Paul Doolan, and Yakov Rekhter

Gigabit Workstations
Jonathan M. Smith, Bruce S. Davie, and C. Brendan Traw

Internet Payment Systems
Mark H. Linehan and Dan Schutzer

Advanced Cable Television Technology
Walter S. Ciciora, James O. Farmer, and David J. Large

ATM Applications: Business and Technology Case Studies
James P. Cavanagh

Multicasting
Lixia Zhang

Electronic Commerce: The Wired Corporation
Dan Schutzer

Internet Infrastructure and its Enterprise Deployment
Ken Tachibana and Bruce Bartolf

Optical Networks:
A Practical Perspective

Rajiv Ramaswami
Tellabs, Inc.

Kumar N. Sivarajan
Indian Institute of Science

Morgan Kaufmann Publishers, Inc.
San Francisco, California

Senior Editor Jennifer Mann
Production Manager Yonie Overton
Production Editor Cheri Palmer
Editorial Assistant Karyn Johnson
Cover Design Martin Heirakuji

Text Design Windfall Software
Copyeditor Robert Fiske
Proofreader Jennifer McClain
Printer Courier Corporation

This book has been author-typeset using LaTeX.

Morgan Kaufmann Publishers, Inc.
Editorial and Sales Office
340 Pine Street, Sixth Floor
San Francisco, CA 94104-3205
USA
Telephone 415/392-2665
Facsimile 415/982-2665
Internet mkp@mkp.com
Order toll free 800/745-7323

02 01 00 99   5 4 3 2

Library of Congress Cataloging-in-Publication Data

Ramaswami, Rajiv
    Optical networks : a practical perspective / Rajiv Ramaswami,
Kumar N. Sivarajan.
       p. cm.
    Includes bibliographical references and index.
    ISBN 1-55860-445-6
    1. Optical communications. 2. Fiber optics. I. Sivarajan, Kumar
N.
TK5103.59.R36   1998
621.382'75–dc31
                                      97-46057
                                        CIP

To our parents.

Foreword

by Paul E. Green, Jr.
Director, Optical Network Technology
Tellabs, Inc.

Not too many years ago, whenever one wanted to send messages effectively, there were really only two choices—send them by wire or send them by radio. This situation lasted for decades until the mid-1960s, when the fiber optics revolution began, quietly at first, and then with increasing force as people began to appreciate that sending pulses of light through tiny strands of glass wasn't so crazy after all. This revolution is now in full cry, with 4000 strand miles of fiber being installed per day, just in the United States alone. Fiber has been displacing wire in many applications, and gradually it is emerging as one of the two dominant Cinderella transmission technologies of today, wireless being the other. One of these (wireless) goes anywhere but doesn't do much when it gets there, whereas the other (fiber) will never go everywhere but does a great deal indeed wherever it reaches. From the earliest days of fiber communication, people realized that this simple glass medium has incredible amounts of untapped bandwidth capacity waiting to be mined, should the day come when we would actually need it, and should we be able to figure out how to tap it. That day has now come. The demand is here and so are the solutions.

This book describes a revolution within a revolution, the opening up of the capacity of the now-familiar optical fiber to carry more messages, handle a wider variety of transmission types, and provide improved reliabilities and ease of use. In many places where fiber has been installed simply as a better form of copper, even the gigabit capacities that result have not proved adequate to keep up with the demand. The inborn human voracity for more and more bandwidth, plus the growing realization that there are other flexibilities to be had by imaginative use of the fiber, have led people to explore all-optical networks, the subject of this book.

Such networks are those in which either wavelength division or time division is used in new ways to form entire network structures where the messages travel in purely optical form all the way from one user location to another.

When I attempted the same kind of book in 1993, nobody was quite sure whether optical networking would be a roaring success or disappear into the annals of "whatever happened to . . ." stories of technology that had once sounded great on paper, but that had somehow never panned out in the real world. My book (*Fiber Optic Networks,* Prentice Hall) spent most of its pages talking about technology building blocks and lamenting their limitations since there was little to say about real networks, the architectural considerations underlying them, and what good they had ever done anybody.

In the last four years, optical networking has indeed really happened, essentially all of it based on wavelength division multiplexing, and with this book Ramaswami and Sivarajan, two of the principal architects of this success, have redressed the insufficiencies of earlier books such as mine. Today, hundreds of millions of dollars of wavelength division networking systems are being sold annually, major new businesses have been created that produce nothing but optical networks, and bandwidth bottlenecks are being relieved and proliferating protocol zoos tamed by this remarkably transparent new way of doing networking; what's more, there is a rich architectural understanding of where to go next. Network experts, fresh from the novelties of such excitements as the Web, now have still another wonderful toy shop to play in. The whole optical networking idea is endlessly fascinating in itself—based on a medium with thousands of gigabits of capacity yet so small as to be almost invisible, transmitters no larger than a grain of salt, amplifiers that amplify vast chunks of bandwidth purely as light, transmission designs that bypass 50 years of hard-won but complex coding, modulation and equalization insights, network architectures that subsume many functions usually done more clumsily in the lower layers of classical layered architectures—these are all fresh and interesting topics that await the reader of this book.

To understand this new networking revolution within a revolution, it is necessary to be led with a sure hand through territory that to many will be unfamiliar. The present authors, with their rare mixture of physics and network architecture expertise, are eminently qualified to serve as guides. After spending some time with this book, you will be more thoroughly conversant with all the important issues that today affect how optical networks are made, what their limitations and potentialities are, and how they fit in with more classical forms of communication networks based on electronic time division. Whether you are a computer network expert wondering how to use fiber to break the bandwidth bottlenecks that are limiting your system capabilities, a planner or implementer trying to future-proof your telephone network, a teacher planning a truly up-to-date communication engineering curriculum, a student looking for a fun lucrative career, or a midcareer person in need of a retread, this volume will provide the help you need.

The authors have captured what is going on and what is going to be going on in this field in a completely up-to-date treatment unavailable elsewhere. I learned a lot from reading it and expect that you will too.

Contents

III Appendices 553

Preface

Fiber optics has become the core of our telecommunications and data networking infrastructures. Optical fiber is the preferred means of transmission for any data over a few tens of megabits per second and over anything from a kilometer and upwards. The first generation of fiber optic networks used optical fiber predominantly as a replacement for copper cable for transmission at higher bit rates over longer distances. The second generation of fiber optic networks is just emerging. These networks really exploit the capacity of fiber to achieve overall transmission capacities of several tens of gigabits per second to terabits per second. Moreover, they exploit routing and switching of signals in the optical domain. The rapid evolution of technology, coupled with the insatiable demand for bandwidth, is resulting in a rapid transition of these networks from research laboratories into the marketplace.

The fundamentals of optical fiber transmission are covered well in several books. There is, however, a need for a book that covers the transmission aspects of second-generation fiber optic networks, and focuses on the *networking* aspects such as architectures, and control and management issues. Such a book would not be complete without describing the components needed to build these networks, particularly since the network architectures strongly depend on these components, and a person designing optical networks will need to be familiar with their capabilities. Thus this book attempts to cover components, transmission, and networking issues related to second-generation optical networks. It is targeted at professionals who are network planners, designers or operators, graduate students in electrical engineering and computer science, and engineers wanting to learn about optical networks.

Teaching and Learning from This Book

This book can be used as a textbook for graduate courses in electrical engineering or computer science. Much of the material in this book has been covered in courses taught by us. Part I covers components and transmission technology aspects of optical networking, and Part II deals with the networking aspects. To understand the networking issues in Part II, students will require a basic undergraduate-level knowledge of communication networks and probability. We have tried to make the transmission-related chapters in Part I of the book accessible to networking professionals. For example, components are treated first in a simple qualitative manner from the viewpoint of a network designer, but their principle of operation is then explained in detail. Some prior knowledge of electromagnetics will be useful in understanding the detailed quantitative treatment in some of the sections. Advanced sections are marked by an asterisk; these sections can be omitted without loss of continuity.

With this background, the book can be the basis for a graduate course in an electrical engineering curriculum. Alternatively, a graduate course in a computer science department might emphasize network architectures and control and management, by focusing on Part II, and skim over the technology portions of the book in Part I. Likewise, a course on optical transmission in an electrical engineering department might instead focus on Part I and omit the remaining chapters. Each chapter is accompanied by a number of problems, and instructors may obtain a solution manual by contacting the publisher at *orders@mkp.com*.

Second, we have attempted to provide an overview of much recent work in this emerging field, so as to make the book useful to researchers in the field as an up-to-date reference. Each chapter includes an extensive list of references for those who might wish to explore further. The problems include some research topics for further exploration as well. Finally, we hope that the book will also serve as an introduction to people working in other areas who wish to become familiar with fiber optics.

Overview of the Book

Chapter 1 offers an introduction to optical networks. Part I of the book is devoted to the technology underlying optical networks. Chapter 2 describes how light propagates in optical fiber, and deals with the phenomena of loss, dispersion, and fiber nonlinearities, which play a major role in the design of transmission systems. Chapter 3 provides an overview of the different components needed to build a network, such as transmitters, receivers, multiplexers, and switches. Chapter 4 describes how electrical signals are converted to light signals (the modulation process) at the transmitter and how they are recovered at the receiver (demodulation). Chapter 5 focuses on the physical layer design of the latest generation of transmission systems and networks, and the factors limiting the system performance.

Part II is devoted to a variety of networking aspects of optical networks. Chapter 6 describes the different first-generation optical networks that are deployed widely today. Chapter 7 covers broadcast and select WDM networks that are suitable for LANs and MANs. Different topologies, media-access, and scheduling methods will be described and compared in a uniform framework. Chapter 8 describes networks using wavelength routing. These networks are emerging from the laboratories into commercial deployment. The chapter covers the architectural aspects of these networks and focuses on the key design issues. Chapter 9 describes how to overlay virtual networks, for example, IP or ATM networks over an underlying second-generation optical network. Chapter 10 covers control and management, including connection management, fault management, and safety management. Chapter 11 describes several significant experimental wavelength routing demonstrations, field trials, and prototypes. Chapter 12 describes passive optical network solutions for fiber-to-the-curb and fiber-to-the-home access network applications. Chapter 13 covers the issues associated with deploying the new second generation technology in different types of telecommunications networks. Chapter 14 covers optical time division multiplexed networks, which are today in the research labs but offer future potential for transmission at very high rates on each WDM channel.

The appendices cover some of the basics of stochastic processes and graph theory for readers as background material for the book. The large number of symbols and parameters used in Part I (Technology) is also summarized in an appendix.

Acknowledgments

First and foremost, we would like to thank Paul Green for introducing us to this field and being our mentor over the years, as well as for writing the foreword to this book. We would like to acknowledge, in particular, Rick Barry, Ori Gerstel, Ashish Vengsarkar, Weyl-Kuo Wang, and Chaoyu Yue for their detailed reviews and discussions of part or all of the material in the book. In addition, we would like to thank Venkat Anatharam, Dan Blumenthal, Kamal Goel, Karen Liu, Roger Merel, Rick Neuner, and Niall Robinson for their comments. We would also like to thank Rajesh M. Krishnaswamy for performing one of the simulations in Section 8.5, A. Selvarajan for answering some of our technology-related questions, and Chandrika Sridhar for helping with the preparation of the solutions manual.

We would also like to thank the folks at Morgan Kaufmann; in particular, our editor, Jennifer Mann, for guiding us through the entire process from start to finish and for her efforts to improve the quality of our book, and our production editor, Cheri Palmer, for orchestrating the production of the book.

Finally, we'd like to acknowledge the invaluable support given to us by our wives, Uma and Vinu, during this endeavor, and to Uma for drawing many of the figures in the book.

Introduction to Optical Networks

IN THE INFORMATION AGE, we are seeing a relentless demand for networks of higher and higher capacities, at lower and lower costs. This demand is fueled by many different factors. The tremendous growth of the Internet and the World Wide Web has brought more and more users online, consuming large amounts of bandwidth due to data transfers involving video and images. Moreover, a telephone call from a user logging into the Internet lasts much longer than a voice call, resulting in a significant increase in the load that the telephone network must support. At the same time, businesses are relying increasingly on intranets and extranets—essentially, high-speed networks—for their day-to-day operations. Furthermore, the ultimate vision of the information age is that information can be located anywhere but is accessible from everywhere as if it were located locally. Networks of enormous capacity will be required to provide the infrastructure to realize this vision. All these factors are driving the need for more bandwidth in networks as well as new network services.

To fulfill the demands for bandwidth and to deploy new services, network operators must deploy new technologies, and optical networking is one such key technology. New technologies invariably result in reducing the cost of bandwidth. This reduced cost of bandwidth in turn spurs the development of a new set of applications that make use of more and more bandwidth, which in turn drives the need for more bandwidth in the network. This positive feedback cycle shows no sign of abating in the near future.

At the same time that we are witnessing this tremendous growth in network traffic and the demand for new services, the world's telecommunications markets are being deregulated. Large telephone monopolies that in the past could take their time to plan network upgrades are now faced with increasing competition in local as well as long-distance services. The new entrants to this game are actively building new networks. The old players must rapidly incorporate new technology in their networks to maintain a competitive edge. Competitive pressures are likely to result in a significant reduction in the price of bandwidth to end users, and will at the same time, force network operators to run their networks more efficiently.

All this is driving the development of high-capacity optical networks and their remarkably rapid transition from the research laboratories into commercial deployment. This book aims to cover optical network technologies, systems, and networking issues, as well as economic and other deployment considerations.

1.1 Telecommunications Networks

Before we discuss the role of optical networks in the telecommunications infrastructure, let us classify the different types of telecommunications networks present today. First we have networks that are deployed in private enterprises. The equipment, as well as the communication links within their sites in these networks, is typically owned by the enterprise. Links that cross public land are usually leased from a telecommunications carrier. We refer to these networks as (private) *enterprise networks*. Networks within buildings are called *local-area networks* (LANs), those that span a campus or metropolitan area are called *metropolitan-area networks* (MANs), and networks that span even longer distances are called *wide-area networks* (WANs).

Then we have networks that are owned by the telecommunications carriers. These carriers operate the network and provide services to other users. Among these services are the leased lines offered to enterprises, but the carriers offer more sophisticated services as well. These networks are called *public networks*. We will classify public networks into four categories (see Figure 1.1). A carrier has a *central office* in every neighborhood in the regions where it operates. An *access network* is the part of the network that reaches out from a carrier's central office into individual homes and businesses. A *local-exchange network* is the part of the network that interconnects the carrier's central offices in a metropolitan area. An *interexchange network* is typically a long-haul network that interconnects cities or major traffic hubs. Note that these different networks may be owned and operated by different entities. Finally, there are the *undersea networks*, not shown in the figure, that typically connect continents with undersea optical fiber cable whose length, in many cases, is several thousand kilometers.

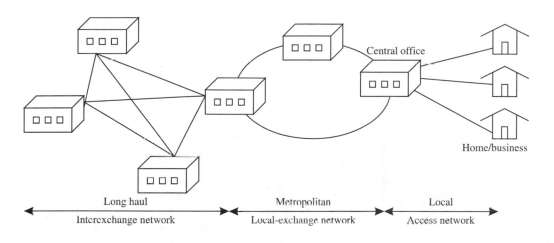

Figure 1.1   Different parts of a public network.

1.2   First-Generation Optical Networks

Optical fiber transmission has played a key role in increasing the bandwidth of telecommunications networks. Optical fiber offers much higher bandwidths than copper cables and is less susceptible to various kinds of electromagnetic interferences and other undesirable effects. As a result, it is the preferred medium for transmission of data at anything more than a few tens of megabits per second over any distance more than a kilometer. In some cases, it is being used for short-distance (a few meters) interconnections inside computers as well. For many years, the main thrust was to develop technologies to transmit at higher and higher bit rates over longer and longer distances. Figure 1.2 plots the growth in bandwidth over time of different types of networks, using data from [Fra93]. This tremendous growth in bandwidth is primarily due to the deployment of optical fiber communication systems. The latest statistics from the Federal Communications Commission [Kra97] indicate that as of the end of 1996, the local-exchange carriers in the United States had deployed more than 360,000 sheath (cable) miles of fiber, containing more than 12 million fiber miles. More than 106,000 route miles of fiber had been deployed by the interexchange carriers in the United States containing more than 2.9 million miles of optical fiber [Kra97]. (Each route comprises many fiber cables. Each cable contains many fibers. A 10-mile-long route using 3 fiber cables is said to have 10 route miles and 30 sheath miles. If each cable has 20 fibers, the same route is said to have 600 fiber miles.)

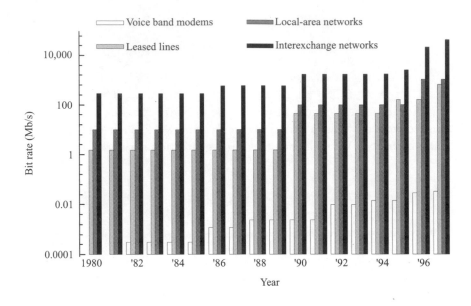

Figure 1.2   Bandwidth growth over time in different types of networks.

On average, more than half of these miles are *lit*—that is, the fibers are in use. The remaining fibers are *dark*—that is, the fibers are currently unused. The types of technologies that will be needed to provide upgrades to the network capacity along a desired route will depend very much on whether dark fibers are available or not on that route. Laying new fiber is an expensive proposition unless space is available in existing ducts, in which case, it is relatively easy to pull additional fiber through. However, even if dark fibers are available, significant economic benefits can be obtained by realizing higher capacities over a single fiber rather than using multiple fibers at lower capacities, particularly over long distances. This subject will be treated in Chapter 13.

In all these networks, optical fiber is used purely as a transmission medium, serving as a replacement for copper cable, and all the switching and processing of the bits is handled by electronics. We refer to these networks as *first-generation* optical networks, and they are widely deployed today in all kinds of telecommunications networks, except perhaps in residential access networks. Although fiber is provided to several businesses today, it has yet to reach individual homes, due to the huge cost of wiring the infrastructure and the questionable rate of return on this investment seen by the service providers. Note from Figure 1.2 that the bandwidths into our homes are still limited by the bandwidth available on our phone line, which is made of twisted-pair copper cable. These lines are capable of carrying data at a few Mb/s using digital subscriber loop (DSL) technology, but voice-grade lines are limited at the central office to 4 kHz of bandwidth.

Examples of first-generation optical networks are SONET (*synchronous optical network*) and SDH (*synchronous digital hierarchy*) networks, which form the core of the telecommunications infrastructure in North America and in Europe and Asia, respectively, as well as a variety of enterprise networks such as FDDI (*fiber distributed data interface*). We will study these first-generation networks in Chapter 6.

1.3   Multiplexing Techniques

The increasing demand for bandwidth, along with the fact that it is relatively expensive in many cases to lay new fiber, implies that we must find ways to increase the capacity on existing fiber. There are fundamentally two ways of increasing the transmission capacity on a fiber, as shown in Figure 1.3. The first is to increase the bit rate. This requires higher-speed electronics. Many lower-speed data streams are multiplexed into a higher-speed stream at the transmission bit rate by means of electronic *time division multiplexing* (TDM). Today, the highest transmission rate in commercially available systems is around 10 Gb/s; 40 Gb/s TDM technology is being developed in research laboratories. To push TDM technology beyond these rates, researchers are working on methods to perform the multiplexing and demultiplexing functions *optically*. This approach is called *optical time division multiplexing* (OTDM). Laboratory experiments have demonstrated the multiplexing/demultiplexing of several 10 Gb/s streams into/from a 250 Gb/s stream, although commercial implementation of OTDM is still several years away. We will study OTDM systems in Chapter 14. However, multiplexing and demultiplexing high-speed streams by itself is not sufficient to realize practical networks. We need to contend with the various impairments that arise as these very high-speed streams are transmitted over a fiber. For a variety of reasons that we will discuss in Chapters 5 and 13, it appears to be quite difficult to sustain a bit rate of much beyond 10 Gb/s over a fiber with TDM over significant distances.

Another way to increase the capacity is by a technique called *wavelength division multiplexing* (WDM). WDM is essentially the same as frequency division multiplexing, which has been used in radio systems for more than a century. The idea is to transmit data simultaneously at multiple carrier wavelengths (or, equivalently, frequencies) over a fiber. To first order, these wavelengths do not interfere with each other provided they are kept sufficiently far apart. There are several undesirable second-order effects where wavelengths do interfere with each other, and we will study these in Chapters 2 and 5. WDM transmission systems employing up to 32

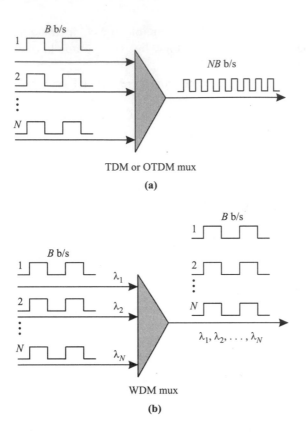

Figure 1.3   Different multiplexing techniques for increasing the transmission capacity on an optical fiber. (a) Electronic or optical time division multiplexing, and (b) wavelength division multiplexing. Both multiplexing techniques take in N data streams, each of B b/s, and multiplex them into a single fiber with a total aggregate rate of NB b/s.

wavelengths at 2.5 Gb/s each over a single fiber are commercially available today, and systems with fewer wavelengths at 10 Gb/s are becoming available. WDM links are being deployed today in interexchange and enterprise networks, and they have been deployed in undersea networks as well.

WDM provides a way to increase the transmission capacity by using multiple channels at different wavelengths. TDM provides a way to increase the bit rates on each channel. Thus TDM and WDM are complementary approaches. The question of what combination of TDM and WDM to use in systems is an important one facing network operators today, and we will discuss this issue in Chapter 13. Using a combination of TDM and WDM, transmission capacities of more than 2 Tb/s over a single fiber have been demonstrated by several research laboratories. Commercially available transmission systems offer about 80 Gb/s of capacity today, and these research experiments indicate what will be feasible commercially in a few years.

1.4   Second-Generation Optical Networks

In recent years, researchers have realized that optical networks are capable of providing more functions than just point-to-point transmission. Major advantages are to be gained by incorporating some of the switching and routing functions that were performed by electronics into the optical part of the network. For example, as data rates get higher and higher, it becomes more difficult for electronics to process data. Suppose the electronics must process data in blocks of 53 bytes each. In a 100 Mb/s data stream, we have 4.24 μs to process a block, whereas at 10 Gb/s, the same block must be processed within 42.4 ns. In first-generation networks, the electronics at a node must not only handle all the data intended for that node, but also all the data that is being passed through that node on to other nodes in the network. If the latter data could be routed through in the optical domain, the burden on the underlying electronics at the node would be significantly reduced. This is one of the key drivers for second-generation optical networks. Both OTDM and WDM networks based on this paradigm are being developed. WDM networks are expected to be deployed in the next few years, not only in interexchange networks and undersea networks, but also in local-exchange and access networks. Thus the main focus of the book will be on WDM. OTDM networks constitute a longer-term approach, and we will cover them in Chapter 14.

1.4.1   Services

In order to understand the role of second-generation optical networks, it is important to understand the types of services that they can potentially offer to their users. To do so, it is useful to think of the second-generation optical network as constituting an optical layer that offers services to higher layers in the network. Any network can be visualized as consisting of many layers, with each layer performing possibly different functions. For example, the internet protocol (IP) can be thought of as a network layer that uses several possible underlying layers (such as an ethernet or a token ring local-area network) to provide services in turn to layers that reside above it in the layered hierarchy.

Second-generation optical networks may offer three types of services to higher network layers, as shown in Figure 1.4. The first service is a *lightpath* service, applicable for WDM networks. A lightpath is a connection between two nodes

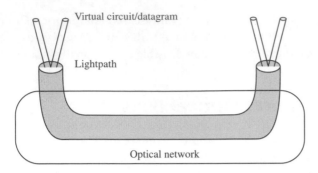

Figure 1.4   Different services offered by a second-generation optical network.

in the network, and it is set up by assigning a dedicated wavelength to it on each link in its path. Note that individual wavelengths are likely to carry data at fairly high bit rates (a few Gb/s), and this entire bandwidth is provided to the higher layer by a lightpath. Depending on the capabilities of the network, this lightpath could be set up or taken down upon request of the higher layer. This can be thought of as a *circuit-switched* service, akin to the service provided by today's telephone network: the network sets up or takes down calls upon request of the user. Alternatively, the network may provide only *permanent* lightpaths, which are set up at the time the network is deployed. This lightpath service is likely to be the most commonly used service to start with, and can be used to support high-speed connections for a variety of overlying networks.

Another service is the so-called *virtual circuit* service. Here the network offers a circuit-switched connection between two nodes. However, the bandwidth offered on the connection can be smaller than the full bandwidth available on a link or wavelength. For instance, a user may request a connection with 1 Mb/s of bandwidth, and the network links may operate at 10 Gb/s. Thus the network must incorporate some form of time division multiplexing to combine multiple virtual circuits onto a wavelength in WDM links or onto the transmission bit rate in the case of OTDM links. This form of multiplexing may be *fixed* or *statistical*. The difference between these is shown in Figure 1.5.

Fixed multiplexing allocates a guaranteed amount of bandwidth to each virtual circuit. The bandwidth of all the virtual circuits on a link must equal the link bandwidth. Statistical multiplexing attempts to use the link bandwidth more efficiently by supporting a larger number of virtual circuits on the link. It makes use of the statistical properties of the virtual circuits. At any given time, some circuits may

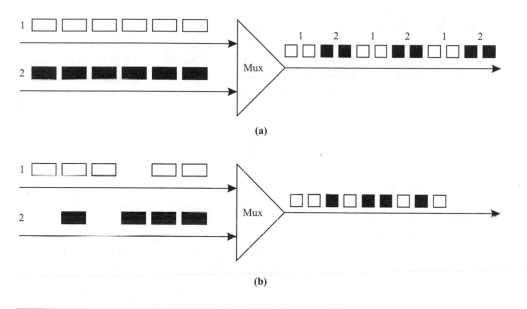

Figure 1.5 Different types of time division multiplexing : (a) fixed, (b) statistical.

be idle and others busy. Statistical multiplexing is implemented by breaking up the data on each circuit into short packets, and multiplexing and switching packets from different virtual circuits on a link. This is called *packet switching*. It is possible to exploit the "bursty" nature of packet arrivals to support more virtual circuits on a link, compared to fixed multiplexing. The tradeoff is that it is not possible to guarantee a certain amount of bandwidth or other quality-of-service measure to each circuit. Statistical multiplexing is used widely in almost all computer networks today, such as the Internet. There is no attempt at present to provide any guaranteed quality of service in such networks—these networks provide services on a best-effort basis.

The telephone network, on the other hand, was designed primarily to support voice traffic, which is not as bursty as computer data, and thus primarily uses fixed multiplexing. As a consequence, it provides a guaranteed amount of bandwidth once a call is established, but is not as efficient at supporting data traffic.

There is a great deal of effort today to design networks that use statistical multiplexing so as to make efficient use of the available bandwidth while providing some guarantees on the quality of service that they offer. The asynchronous transfer mode (ATM) network is a consequence of this thinking. The internet protocol is also evolving to provide similar services.

Finally, the network may also support a *datagram* service, which allows short packets or messages of information to be transmitted between the nodes in the network, without the overhead of setting up explicit connections. The internet protocol is an example of a protocol that provides only datagram services. Also, each of these services may be offered as a point-to-point service, or as a point-to-multipoint (multicast) service. The latter service may be useful for applications such as video broadcasting.

1.4.2   Transparency

A major feature of second-generation networks that relates to the circuit-switched lightpath service is that this type of service can be *transparent* to the actual data being sent over the lightpath once it is set up. For instance, a certain maximum bit rate or bandwidth might be specified, and the service may accept data at any bit rate and any protocol format. It may also be able to carry analog data.

An example of a transparent network of this sort is the telephone network. Once a call is established in the telephone network, it provides 4 kHz of bandwidth over which a user can send a variety of different types of traffic such as voice, data, or fax. There is no question that transparency in the telephone network today has had a far-reaching impact on our lifestyles. Chapter 13 describes how transparency has become a useful feature of second-generation optical networks as well.

The levels of transparency achievable in an optical network depend on several parameters of the physical layer, such as bandwidth and signal-to-noise ratios. If the signal remains in optical form from its source to its destination, a higher degree of transparency may be obtained. Even here, analog signals require much higher signal-to-noise ratios than digital signals. The actual requirements depend on the modulation format used as well as the bit rate. This is studied further in Chapter 5.

However, in some cases, the signal may not be able to remain in optical form all the way to its destination and may have to be regenerated in between. This involves converting the signal from optical form to electronic form and back again to optical form. Having these electronic regenerators in the path of the signal reduces the transparency of that path. There are three types of regeneration techniques for digital data. The standard one is called regeneration *with* retiming and reshaping, also called 3R. Here the bit clock is extracted from the signal, and the signal is reclocked. This technique essentially produces a "fresh" copy of the signal at each regeneration step, allowing the signal to go through a very large number of regenerators. However, it eliminates transparency to bit rates and frame formats, since acquiring the clock usually requires knowledge of both of these. Some limited form of bit rate transparency is possible by making use of programmable clock recovery chips that can work at a set of bit rates that are multiples of one another. For example, chipsets that perform clock recovery at either 2.4 Gb/s or 622 Mb/s are commercially available today.

An implementation using regeneration of the optical signal *without* retiming, also called 2R, offers transparency to bit rates, without supporting analog data or different modulation formats [GJR96]. However, this approach limits the number of regeneration steps allowed, particularly at higher bit rates, over a few hundred Mb/s. The limitation is due to the jitter, which accumulates at each regeneration step.

The final form of regeneration is 1R, where the signal is simply received and retransmitted without retiming or reshaping. This form of regeneration can handle analog data as well, but its performance is significantly poorer than the other two forms of regeneration.

1.4.3 Competing Technologies

The alternative to using second-generation optical networks is to continue developing the technologies underlying first-generation optical networks. This means increasing the transmission speeds on the fiber, as well as increasing the speeds, number of ports, and processing power of electronic switches. As transmission speeds increase beyond the few gigabits per second achieved today to several tens of gigabits per second, it becomes more and more difficult to perform all the switching and processing functions electronically. However, electronic switching is a mature technology highly suited for integration. Optical switching and routing, on the other hand, is a developing technology. Today, it is possible to incorporate circuit-switching, or *crossconnect,* capabilities in the network by using optical switches. However, as we will see later in this chapter and in Chapter 14, we are still far away from being able to offer optical packet switching at prices that will be competitive with electronic packet switching.

Thus, second-generation optical networks are starting out by offering the circuit-switched lightpath service, primarily because that is where the current state of technology allows competitive provisioning of services. The more advanced virtual circuit and datagram services, which require packet switching to be provided by the network, will become feasible as the technology improves over the next several years.

1.4.4 WDM Architectures

If we look at today's network architectures, we find that most local- and metropolitan-area networks (for example, ethernet and token ring) use very simple broadcast topologies such as rings or buses. All nodes in the network share a single channel for transmitting and receiving data. In contrast, wide-area networks use a mesh topology, with nodes having switches to forward data coming in from

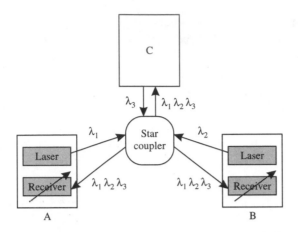

Figure 1.6   A WDM broadcast and select network.

a node to another node. These networks are usually sparsely connected, due to the cost of the links and the switches at the nodes. They provide spatial reuse of the network capacity, which is not usually the case for local-area networks.

WDM network architectures can be classified into two broad categories: *broadcast and select* architectures and *wavelength routing* architectures. A broadcast and select WDM network is shown in Figure 1.6. In the example shown, different nodes transmit at different wavelengths. Their signals are *broadcast* by a passive device in the middle of the network to all the nodes. In this case, the device is a passive *optical star coupler*. The coupler combines the signals from all the nodes and delivers a fraction of the power from each signal on to each output port. Each node employs a tunable optical filter to *select* the desired wavelength for reception. This form of a network is simple and suitable for use in local- or metropolitan-area networks, such as access networks. The number of nodes in these networks is limited because the wavelengths cannot be reused in the network—there can be at most one simultaneous transmission on a given wavelength—and because the transmitted power from a node must be split among all the receivers in the network. We will explore these networks in Chapter 7.

A more sophisticated and practical architecture today is one that employs wavelength routing. Such a network is shown in Figure 1.7. The nodes in the network are capable of routing different wavelengths at an input port to different output ports. This enables us to set up many simultaneous *lightpaths* using the same wavelength in the network; that is, the capacity can be reused spatially. For example, Figure 1.7 shows three lightpaths. The lightpath between A and D and the lightpath between

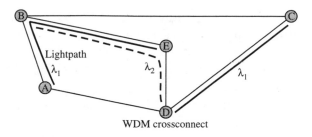

Figure 1.7   A WDM wavelength routing network.

C and D do not share any links in the network and can therefore be set up using the same wavelength λ_1. At the same time, the lightpath between B and D shares a link with the lightpath between A and D, and must therefore use a different wavelength. Note that these lightpaths all use the same wavelength on every link in their path. This is a constraint that we must deal with if we do not have *wavelength conversion* capabilities within the network. Suppose we had only two wavelengths available in the network and wanted to set up a new lightpath between nodes C and E via node D. Without wavelength conversion, we would not be able to set up this lightpath. On the other hand, if node D can perform wavelength conversion, then we can set up this lightpath using wavelength λ_2 on link CD and wavelength λ_1 on link DE.

This architecture also avoids broadcasting the power to unwanted receivers in the network. Thus these networks are suitable for deployment in metropolitan- and wide-area networks, such as local-exhange and interexchange networks. Wavelength routing networks will be explored in Chapter 8.

1.4.5   The Optical Layer

The term *optical layer* is now commonly used to denote the functionality of a second-generation WDM optical network that provides lightpaths to its users. This layer resides under existing layers such as SONET. To a SONET network, the lightpaths are simply replacements for hard-wired fiber connections between SONET terminals. SONET networks today incorporate a variety of functions. These include point-to-point connections, as well as *add/drop* functions wherein part of a traffic stream is dropped at a node and the remaining passed through. This function is particularly important because individual nodes may terminate only a small fraction of the total traffic flowing through them. SONET networks also include crossconnects, which switch multiple traffic streams. Finally, they are able to handle equipment and link failures in the network without disrupting the service they provide.

The optical layer performs a similar range of functions. It supports point-to-point WDM links as well as an add/drop function wherein a node drops some wavelengths and passes the remaining ones through.

So why have multiple layers in the network that perform similar functions? The answer is that this form of layering significantly reduces network equipment costs. Different layers are more efficient at performing functions at different bit rates. For example, the SONET layer can efficiently (that is, cost effectively) switch and process traffic streams up to, say, 2.5 Gb/s today. However, it is very expensive to have this layer process 32 2.5 Gb/s streams coming in on a WDM link. The optical layer, on the other hand, is particularly efficient at processing traffic on a wavelength-by-wavelength basis, but not particularly good at processing traffic streams at lower granularities, for example, 155 Mb/s. Therefore, it makes sense to use the optical layer to process large amounts of bandwidth at a relatively coarse level, and the SONET layer to process smaller amounts of bandwidth at a relatively finer level. This fundamental observation is the key driver to providing such functions in multiple layers, and we will study this in detail in Chapter 8. A similar observation also holds for the service restoration function of these networks. Certain failures are better handled by the optical layer and certain others by the SONET layer. We will study this aspect in Chapter 10.

1.4.6   OTDM Architectures

As in the case of WDM networks, the simplest form of an OTDM network is a broadcast and select network. Instead of wavelengths, different nodes get different time slots to transmit their data. These networks suffer from the same problems as WDM broadcast and select networks, but may eventually become suitable for deployment in local-area networks. Another form of an OTDM network is an optical packet-switched network, shown in Figure 1.8. This network attempts to perform all the functions that are performed by packet-switched networks today. Instead of the electronic packet switches used at the nodes today, the OTDM approach uses high-speed optical packet switches at the nodes. A node takes a packet coming in, reads its header, and switches it to the appropriate output port. The node may also impose a new header on the packet. It must also handle *contention* for output ports. If two packets coming in on different ports need to go out on the same output port, one of the packets must be buffered, or sent out on another port.

Ideally, all the functions inside the node would be performed in the optical domain, but in practice, certain functions, such as processing the header and controlling the switch, get relegated to the electronic domain. This is because of the very limited processing capabilities in the optical domain. The header itself could be sent at a lower bit rate than the data so that it can be processed electronically. The mission of

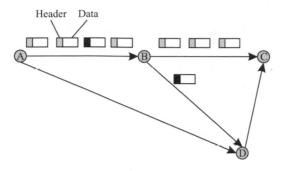

Figure 1.8 An optical packet-switched network.

optical packet switching is to perform all these functions at much higher bit rates than electronic packet switching. However, designers are handicapped by several factors. One important factor is the lack of optical buffering. Optical buffers are realized by using a length of fiber and are just simple delay lines, not real memories. Another factor is the relatively primitive state of optical-switching technology, compared to electronics. Note that OTDM can be combined with WDM in the same network. Chapter 14 covers all these aspects in detail.

1.5 System and Network Evolution

We conclude this chapter by outlining the trends and factors that have shaped the evolution of optical fiber transmission systems and networks. In the process, we will also describe the major roadblocks that had to be overcome along the way and introduce the factors inhibiting further increases in transmission capacity. We will study these factors in detail in the remainder of the book.

Figure 1.9 shows the evolution of optical fiber transmission systems, both terrestrial and undersea systems. Early experiments in the 1960s demonstrated the capability of waveguides to transport information encoded in light signals. But it was not until the invention of low-loss optical fiber in the early 1970s that optical fiber transmission systems really took off. This silica-based optical fiber has three low-loss windows in the 0.8, 1.3, and 1.55 μm wavelength bands with the lowest loss being around 0.25 dB/km in the 1.55 μm band. These fibers enabled transmission of light signals over distances of several tens of kilometers before they needed to be *regenerated*. A regenerator converts the light signal into an electrical signal and retransmits a fresh copy of the data as a new light signal.

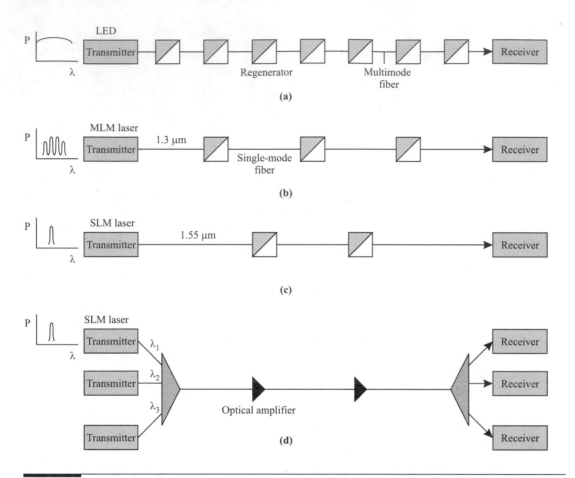

Figure 1.9   Evolution of optical fiber transmission systems. (a) An early system using LEDs over multimode fiber. (b) A system using MLM lasers over single-mode fiber in the 1.3 μm band to overcome modal dispersion in multimode fiber. (c) A later system using the 1.55 μm band for lower loss, and using SLM lasers to overcome chromatic dispersion limits. (d) A current-generation WDM system using multiple wavelengths at 1.55 μm and optical amplifiers instead of regenerators.

The early fibers were the so-called *multimode* fibers. Multimode fibers have core diameters of about 50 to 85 μm. Light propagates in these fibers in the form of multiple *modes*, each taking a slightly different path through the fiber and thus effectively traveling at a slightly different velocity, for a given fiber length. The early telecommunication systems used multimode fibers along with light-emitting diodes (LEDs) or *multilongitudinal mode* (MLM) Fabry-Perot laser transmitters in the 0.8 and 1.3 μm wavelength bands. These transmitters were relatively low-cost devices that emitted light over a fairly wide spectrum of several nanometers to tens of nanometers. These early systems had to have regenerators every few km to regenerate the signal, which was degraded primarily due to a phenomenon known as *modal dispersion*. In a multimode fiber, the energy in a pulse travels in different modes, each with a different velocity. As a result, the pulse gets smeared after it has traveled some distance along the fiber. This smearing in general is called *dispersion*, and this specific form is called modal dispersion. Such systems are still used for low-cost computer interconnection at a few hundred Mb/s over a few km.

The next generation of systems deployed in the early 1980s used *single-mode* fiber as a means of eliminating modal dispersion, along with MLM Fabry-Perot lasers in the 1.3 μm wavelength band. Single-mode fiber has a relatively small core diameter of about 8 to 10 μm, which forces all the energy in a light signal to travel in the form of a single mode. This effectively eliminated modal dispersion and enabled a dramatic increase in the bit rates and distances possible between regenerators. These systems typically had regenerator spacings of about 40 km and operated at bit rates of a few hundred Mb/s. The distance between regenerators was determined primarily by the fiber loss. The next step in this evolution in the late 1980s was to deploy systems in the 1.55 μm wavelength window to take advantage of the lower loss in this window relative to the 1.3 μm window, so as to have longer spans between regenerators. At this point, another impairment, namely, *chromatic dispersion*, started becoming a limiting factor as far as increasing the bit rates was concerned. Even in a single-mode fiber, different frequency components of a pulse propagate with different velocities. This effect is called chromatic dispersion. It turns out that without any special effort, silica-based optical fiber has essentially no chromatic dispersion in the 1.3 μm band, but has significant dispersion in the 1.55 μm band. Such fiber is called *standard single-mode fiber*.

The high chromatic dispersion at 1.55 μm motivated the development of *dispersion-shifted fiber*. Dispersion-shifted fiber is carefully designed to have zero dispersion in the 1.55 μm wavelength window so that one need not worry about chromatic dispersion in this window. However, by this time there was already a large installed base of standard single-mode fiber deployed for which this solution could not be applied. Luckily, there was another way to overcome chromatic dispersion. The wider the spectrum of the transmitted pulse, the greater the smearing due to chromatic dispersion. The MLM Fabry-Perot lasers, as we said earlier, emitted over a fairly wide spectrum of several nanometers (or, equivalently, hundreds of gigahertz). If we reduce the spectrum of the transmitted pulse to something close to its modulation bandwidth (for example, about 2.5 GHz for a 2.5 Gb/s data stream), the penalty due to chromatic dispersion is significantly reduced. This motivated the development of the narrow spectral-width *single-longitudinal mode (SLM)* distributed-feedback (DFB) laser, which spurred further increases in the bit rate to more than a Gb/s.

The next major milestone in the evolution of optical fiber transmission systems was the development of *Erbium-doped fiber amplifiers* (EDFAs) in the late 1980s and early 1990s. EDFAs spurred the deployment of yet another new generation of systems. Significant cost reductions became possible by replacing the regenerators with EDFAs. The EDFA provides another major benefit: being transparent to bit rates and modulation formats, it effectively allows the system to be upgraded in bit rates at a later date by changing only the equipment at the ends of the link. Another major advantage of EDFAs is that they are capable of amplifying signals at many wavelengths simultaneously. This provided another way of increasing the system capacity: rather than increasing the bit rate, keep the bit rate the same and use more than one wavelength, that is, use wavelength division multiplexing (WDM). Adding more wavelengths can prove to be more economical than adding more fibers and regenerators or amplifiers that would be needed for each of these fibers. In the late 1990s, we are now seeing the deployment of high-capacity WDM systems operating with 8–32 wavelengths, each carrying traffic at 2.5 Gb/s. At the same time, conventional time division multiplexing (TDM) technology is pushing bit rates up to 10 Gb/s and beyond. Meanwhile, research laboratories are already demonstrating transmission experiments with more than 2 Tb/s total capacity. We will look at the considerations underlying the choice of TDM or WDM technology in Chapter 13. Chromatic dispersion is still a major factor affecting the design of these systems. In addition, nonlinear effects in fiber, the nonflat gain spectrum of EDFAs, and polarization-related effects are now becoming significant impairments preventing further increases in transmission capacity. Chapter 5 is devoted to the study of these impairments and how they can be overcome; the origin of many of these effects is studied in Chapter 2.

The late 1980s also witnessed the emergence of a variety of first-generation optical networks. In the data communications world, we saw the deployment of metropolitan-area networks, such as the 100 Mb/s fiber distributed data interface (FDDI), and networks to interconnect mainframe computers, such as the 200 Mb/s enterprise serial connection (ESCON). In the telecommunications world, standardization and mass deployment began of the synchronous optical network (SONET) in North America and the similar synchronous digital hierarchy (SDH) network in Europe and Japan. All these networks are widely deployed today.

As these first-generation networks were being deployed in the late 1980s and early 1990s, people started thinking about innovative network architectures that would use fiber for more than just transmission. Most of the early experimental efforts were focused on broadcast and select WDM networks, and similar OTDM networks, but both are still solutions awaiting a problem! Major advances in component technology are needed to make them commercially viable. Research activity on OTDM packet-switched networks and broadcast and select WDM continues today.

Meanwhile, wavelength-routed networks became a major focus area for several researchers in the early 1990s as people realized the benefits of having an optical layer, and they are now being rapidly introduced as commercial products, in interexchange and local-exchange networks.

There was also a major effort to promote the concept of *fiber to the home* (FTTH) and its many variants, such as *fiber to the curb* (FTTC), in the late 1980s and early 1990s. The problems with this concept were the high infrastructure cost and the questionable return on investment resulting from customers' reluctance to pay for a bevy of new services such as video to the home. However, telecommunications deregulation, coupled with the increasing demand for broadband services such as Internet access and video on demand, is accelerating the deployment of such networks by the major operators today, and we are seeing an increasingly important role for fiber in the access part of the network.

Summary

We described two generations of optical networks in this chapter: first-generation networks and second-generation networks. First-generation networks use optical fiber as a replacement for copper cable to get higher capacities. Second-generation networks attempt to perform more functions in the optical domain, such as routing and switching wavelengths, and eventually routing and switching packets in optical form. We saw that there were two complementary approaches to increasing transmission capacity: using more wavelengths on the fiber (WDM) and increasing the bit rate (TDM). Second-generation WDM networks using wavelength routing are emerging from the research laboratories today. Optical packet switching is still in its infancy and is limited by the lack of optical buffers and the current state of optical switching technology. These second-generation networks need to overcome a new set of transmission impairments in the fiber, such as dispersion, nonlinear effects in fiber, the nonflat gain spectrum of the optical amplifiers, and polarization-related effects, all of which we will study in subsequent chapters.

Further Reading

For a good introduction to the field of optical networks, we recommend the 1993 book by Green [Gre93]. A number of journal and magazine special issues focus on this emerging field [HSS98, CHK+96, FGO+96, HD97, Bar96, NO94, KLHN93, CNW90, Pru89, Bra89]. Some additional tutorial articles appear in [Ram93a, Ram93b, Muk92a, Muk92b, Gre91]. Experiments reporting more than

1 Tb/s transmission over a single fiber were reported at the Optical Fiber Communication Conference in 1996, and the numbers are being improved upon constantly. See, for example, [Ona96, Gna96b, Gna96a, Yan96], and of course, ... the rest of this book.

Several conferences cover optical networks. The main ones include the Optical Fiber Communication Conference, European Conference on Optical Communication, Infocom, and the IEEE's International Conference on Communication. New system and networking products are demonstrated at Supercomm and the National Fiber-Optic Engineers' Conference. Archival journals such as the IEEE's *Journal of Lightwave Technology, Transactions on Networking,* and *Journal of Selected Areas in Communication* along with the *IEEE Communications Magazine* provide good coverage of this subject as well.

References

[Bar96]   R. A. Barry, editor. *IEEE Network: Special Issue on Optical Networks*, volume 10, Nov. 1996.

[Bra89]   C. A. Brackett, editor. *IEEE Communications Magazine: Special Issue on Lightwave Systems and Components*, volume 27, Oct. 1989.

[CHK+96]   R. L. Cruz, G. R. Hill, A. L. Kellner, R. Ramaswami, and G. H. Sasaki, editors. *IEEE JSAC/JLT Special Issue on Optical Networks*, volume 14, June 1996.

[CNW90]   N. K. Cheung, G. Nosu, and G. Winzer, editors. *IEEE JSAC: Special Issue on Dense WDM Networks*, volume 8, Aug. 1990.

[FGO+96]   M. Fujiwara, M. S. Goodman, M. J. O'Mahony, O. K. Tonguez, and A. E. Willner, editors. *IEEE/OSA JLT/JSAC Special Issue on Multiwavelength Optical Technology and Networks*, volume 14, June 1996.

[Fra93]   A. G. Fraser. Banquet speech. In *Proceedings of Workshop on High-Performance Communication Subsystems*, Williamsburg, VA, Sept. 1993.

[GJR96]   P. E. Green, F. J. Janniello, and R. Ramaswami. Multichannel protocol-transparent WDM distance extension using remodulation. *IEEE JSAC/JLT Special Issue on Optical Networks*, 14(6):962–967, June 1996.

[Gna96a]   A. H. Gnauck et al. 100 Gb/s × 10 channel OTDM/WDM transmission using a single supercontinuum WDM source. In *OFC'96 Technical Digest*, 1996. Postdeadline paper PD21.

[Gna96b]   A. H. Gnauck et al. One terabit/s transmission experiment. In *OFC'96 Technical Digest*, 1996. Postdeadline paper PD20.

[Gre91]   P. E. Green. The future of fiber-optic computer networks. *IEEE Computer*, 24(9):78–89, Sept. 1991.

[Gre93]   P. E. Green. *Fiber-Optic Networks*. Prentice Hall, Englewood Cliffs, NJ, 1993.

[HD97]   G. R. Hill and P. Diemeester, editors. *IEEE Communications Magazine: Special Issue on Photonic Networks in Europe*, volume 35, April 1997.

[HSS98]   A. M. Hill, A. A. M. Saleh, and K. Sato, editors. *IEEE JSAC: Special Issue on High-Capacity Optical Transport Networks*, 1998. To appear.

[KLHN93] M. J. Karol, C. Lin, G. Hill, and K. Nosu, editors. *IEEE/OSA Journal of Lightwave Technology: Special Issue on Broadband Optical Networks*, May/June 1993.

[Kra97]   J. M. Kraushaar. *Fiber Deployment Update*. Federal Communications Commission, Aug. 1997. Available from *http://www.fcc.gov*.

[Muk92a] B. Mukherjee. WDM-based local lightwave networks—Part I: Single-hop systems. *IEEE Network*, 6(3):12–27, May 1992.

[Muk92b] B. Mukherjee. WDM-based local lightwave networks—Part II: Multihop systems. *IEEE Network*, 6(4):20–32, July 1992.

[NO94]   K. Nosu and M. J. O'Mahony, editors. *IEEE Communications Magazine: Special Issue on Optically Multiplexed Networks*, volume 32, Dec. 1994.

[Ona96]   H. Onaka et al. 1.1 Tb/s WDM transmission over a 150 km 1.3 μm zero-dispersion single-mode fiber. In *OFC'96 Technical Digest*, 1996. Postdeadline paper PD19.

[Pru89]   P. R. Prucnal, editor. *IEEE Network: Special Issue on Optical Multiaccess Networks*, volume 3, March 1989.

[Ram93a] R. Ramaswami. Multi-wavelength lightwave networks for computer communication. *IEEE Communications Magazine*, 31(2):78–88, Feb. 1993.

[Ram93b] R. Ramaswami. Systems issues in multi-wavelength optical networks. In *Proceedings of 31st Annual Allerton Conference on Communications, Control and Computing*, Sept. 1993.

[Yan96]   Y. Yano et al. 2.6 Tb/s WDM transmission experiment using optical duobinary coding. In *ECOC'96 Technical Digest*, 1996. Postdeadline paper Th.B.3.1.

Technology

2
chapter

Propagation of Signals in Optical Fiber

O PTICAL FIBER IS A REMARKABLE communication medium, compared to other media such as copper or free space. An optical fiber provides low-loss transmission over an enormous frequency range of about 25 THz, which is orders of magnitude more than the bandwidth available in copper cables or any other transmission medium. This property allows signals to be transmitted over long distances at high speeds before they need to be amplified or regenerated. It is due to this property that optical fiber communication systems are so widely used today.

As transmission systems evolved to longer distances and higher bit rates, the phenomenon of *dispersion* became an important limiting factor. Dispersion refers to the phenomenon where different components of the signal travel at different velocities in the fiber. In particular, *chromatic* dispersion refers to the phenomenon where different frequency components of the signal travel with different velocities in the fiber. As today's systems evolve to multiple wavelengths and even higher bit rates and distances, *nonlinear effects* in the fiber are beginning to present serious limitations. As we will see, there is a complex interplay of nonlinear effects with chromatic dispersion as well.

We start this chapter by discussing the basics of light propagation in optical fiber, starting from a simple geometrical optics model to the more general wave theory model based on solving Maxwell's equations. We then devote the rest of the chapter to understanding the basics of chromatic dispersion and fiber nonlinearities. Designing advanced systems optimized with respect to these parameters is treated in Chapter 5.

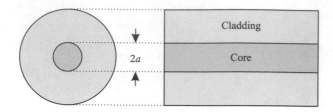

Figure 2.1   Cross section and longitudinal section of an optical fiber showing the core and cladding regions.

2.1   Light Propagation in Optical Fiber

An optical fiber consists of a cylindrical *core* surrounded by a *cladding*. The cross section of an optical fiber is shown in Figure 2.1. Both the core and the cladding are made primarily of silica (SiO_2), which has a *refractive index* of approximately 1.45. The *refractive index* of a material is the ratio of the speed of light in vacuum to the speed of light in that material. During the manufacturing of the fiber, certain impurities (or dopants) are introduced in the core and/or the cladding so that the refractive index is slightly higher in the core than in the cladding.

2.1.1   Geometrical Optics Approach

We can obtain a simplified understanding of light propagation in optical fiber using the so-called *ray theory* or *geometrical optics* approach. This approach is valid when the fiber that is used has a core radius a that is much larger than the operating wavelength λ. Such fibers are termed *multimode*, and first-generation optical communication links were built using such fibers with a in the range of 25–100 μm and λ around 0.85 μm.

In the geometrical optics approach, light can be thought of as consisting of a number of "rays" propagating in straight lines within a material (or medium) and getting reflected and/or refracted at the interfaces between two materials. Figure 2.2 shows the interface between two media of refractive index n_1 and n_2. A light ray from medium 1 is incident on the interface of medium 1 with medium 2. The *angle of incidence* is the angle between the *incident ray* and the normal to the interface between the two media, and is denoted by θ_1. Part of the energy is reflected into medium 1 as a *reflected ray*, and the remainder (neglecting absorption) passes into medium 2 as a *refracted ray*. The *angle of reflection* θ_{1r} is the angle between the reflected ray and the normal to the interface; similarly, the *angle of refraction* θ_2 is

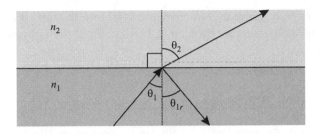

Figure 2.2   Reflection and refraction of light rays at the interface between two media.

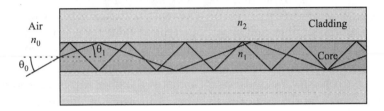

Figure 2.3   Propagation of light rays in optical fiber by total internal reflection.

the angle between the refracted ray and the normal. The laws of geometrical optics state that

$$\theta_{1r} = \theta_1$$

and

$$n_1 \sin \theta_1 = n_2 \sin \theta_2. \tag{2.1}$$

Equation 2.1 is known as *Snell's law*.

As the angle of incidence θ_1 increases, the angle of refraction θ_2 also increases. If $n_1 > n_2$, there comes a time when $\theta_2 = \pi/2$ radians. This happens when $\theta_1 = \sin^{-1} n_2/n_1$. For larger values of θ_1, there is no refracted ray, and all the energy from the incident ray is reflected. This phenomenon is called *total internal reflection*. The smallest angle of incidence for which we get total internal reflection is called the *critical angle* and equals $\sin^{-1} n_2/n_1$.

Simply stated, from the geometrical optics viewpoint, light propagates in optical fiber due to a series of total internal reflections that occur at the core–cladding interface. This is depicted in Figure 2.3. In this figure, the coupling of light from the medium outside (taken to be air with refractive index n_0) into the fiber is also shown. It can be shown using Snell's law (see Problem 2.1) that only those light rays that are incident at an angle

$$\theta_0 < \theta_0^{\max} = \sin^{-1} \frac{\sqrt{n_1^2 - n_2^2}}{n_0}$$

at the air–core interface will undergo total internal reflection at the core–cladding interface and will thus propagate. Such rays are called *guided rays*. The quantity $n_0 \sin \theta_0^{\max}$ is a measure of the light-gathering capacity of the fiber and is called the *numerical aperture* (NA). The refractive index difference $n_1 - n_2$ is usually small, and it is convenient to denote the fractional refractive index difference $(n_1 - n_2)/n_1$ by Δ. For small Δ, NA $\approx n_1\sqrt{2\Delta}$. As an example, if $\Delta = 0.01$, which is a typical value for (multimode) fiber, and $n_1 = 1.5$, a typical value for silica, assuming we are coupling from air, so that $n_0 = 1$, we obtain NA ≈ 0.212 and thus $\theta_0^{\max} \approx 12°$.

Owing to the different lengths of the paths taken by different guided rays, the energy in a narrow (in time) pulse at the input of the fiber will be spread out over a larger time interval at the output of the fiber. A measure of this time spread, which is called *modal dispersion*, is obtained by taking the difference in time, δT, between the fastest and the slowest guided rays. We will see later that by suitably designing the fiber, modal dispersion can be significantly reduced (graded-index fiber) and even eliminated (single-mode fiber).

We now derive an approximate measure of the time spread due to modal dispersion. Consider a fiber of length L. The fastest guided ray is the one that travels along the center of the core and takes a time $T_f = Ln_1/c$ to traverse the fiber, c being the speed of light in vacuum. The slowest guided ray is incident at the critical angle on the core–cladding interface, and it can be shown that it takes a time $T_s = Ln_1^2/cn_2$ to propagate through the fiber. Thus

$$\delta T = T_s - T_f = \frac{L}{c} \frac{n_1^2}{n_2} \Delta.$$

How large can δT be before it begins to matter? That depends on the bit rate used. A rough measure of the delay variation δT that can be tolerated at a bit rate of B b/s is half the bit period $1/2B$ s. Thus modal dispersion sets the following limit:

$$\delta T = \frac{L}{c} \frac{n_1^2}{n_2} \Delta < \frac{1}{2B}. \tag{2.2}$$

The capacity of an optical communication system is frequently measured in terms of the *bit rate–distance product*. If a system is capable of transmitting x Mb/s over a distance of y km, it is said to have a bit rate–distance product of xy (Mb/s)-km.

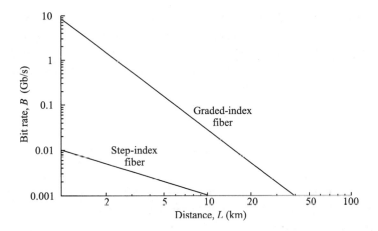

Figure 2.4 Limit on the bit rate–distance product due to modal dispersion in a step-index and a graded-index fiber. In both cases, $\Delta = 0.01$ and $n_1 = 1.5$.

The reason for doing this is that usually the same system is capable of transmitting x' Mb/s over y' km providing $x'y' < xy$; thus only the product of the bit rate and the distance is constrained. (This is true for simple systems that are limited by loss, but is no longer true for systems that are limited by dispersion and nonlinear effects in the fiber.) From (2.2), the modal dispersion constrains the bit rate–distance product of an optical communication link to

$$BL < \frac{1}{2}\frac{n_2}{n_1^2}\frac{c}{\Delta}.$$

For example, if $\Delta = 0.01$ and $n_1 = 1.5 (\approx n_2)$, we get $BL < 10$ (Mb/s)-km. This limit is plotted in Figure 2.4.

Note that NA increases with increasing Δ, whereas the limit on the bit rate–distance product decreases with increasing Δ. Δ is typically chosen to be a fraction of 1% so as to minimize the effects of modal dispersion, and since the NA is consequently small, lenses or other suitable mechanisms are used to couple light into the fiber.

The fiber we have described is a *step-index* fiber since the variation of the refractive index along the fiber cross section can be represented as a function with a step at the core–cladding interface. However, almost all multimode fibers used today are *graded-index* fibers, and the refractive index decreases gradually, or continuously, from its maximum value at the center of the core to the value in the cladding at the core–cladding interface. This has the effect of reducing δT because the rays traversing the shortest path through the center of the core encounter the highest refractive index and travel slowest, whereas rays traversing longer paths encounter regions of lower refractive index and travel faster. For the optimum graded-index profile (which is very nearly a quadratic decrease of the refractive index in the core from its maximum value at the center to its value in the cladding), it can be shown that δT, the time difference between the fastest and slowest rays to travel a length L of the fiber, is given by

$$\delta T = \frac{L}{c} \frac{n_1 \Delta^2}{8}.$$

Assuming that the condition $\delta T < 1/2B$, where B is the bit rate, must be satisfied, we get the following limit on the bit rate–distance product of a communication system employing graded-index fiber:

$$BL < \frac{4c}{n_1 \Delta^2}.$$

For example, if $\Delta = 0.01$ and $n_1 = 1.5$, we get $BL < 8$ (Gb/s)-km. This limit is also plotted in Figure 2.4. For instance, there are commercial systems operating at 200 Mb/s over a few km using multimode fibers today.

Graded-index fibers significantly reduce the effects of modal dispersion. But in order to overcome modal dispersion completely, one must use fibers whose core radius is appreciably smaller and of the order of the operating wavelength. Such fibers are called *single-mode* fibers (the precise reason for this term will become clear later). Roughly speaking, the different paths that light rays can take in a multimode fiber can be termed as different *modes* in which light can propagate. In a single-mode fiber, there is only one mode in which light can propagate.

The physical reason for the confinement of the light within the fiber core can no longer be attributed to total internal reflection since this picture is invalid when the fiber core radius is comparable to the light wavelength, as is the case for single-mode fiber. The following physical explanation for the propagation of light in single-mode fiber is based on [Neu88]. In any medium with a constant refractive index, a narrow light beam tends to spread due to a phenomenon called *diffraction*. Thus in such a medium, the beam width will increase as light propagates. This effect can be counteracted by using an inhomogeneous medium in which the refractive index near the beam center is appropriately larger than the refractive index at the beam periphery. In such a medium, the beam center travels slightly slower than the beam periphery so that the medium effectively provides continuous focusing of the light to offset the spreading effect of diffraction. This allows the beam to be *guided* in the medium and go long distances with low loss, which would not be the case if the beam were allowed to spread out. A step-index optical fiber is an example of such an inhomogeneous medium since the refractive index in the core (beam center) is larger than that in the cladding (beam periphery).

In the following sections, we will provide a more quantitative description of the propagation of light in single-mode fibers using the wave theory approach. The wave theory is more general and is applicable for all values of the fiber radius. The ray theory is an approximation that holds when the optical wavelength is much smaller than the radius of the fiber core. Our objective is to gain a quantitative understanding of two phenomena that are important in the design of fiber optic communication systems: chromatic dispersion and fiber nonlinearities.

2.1.2   Wave Theory Approach

Light is an electromagnetic wave, and its propagation in any medium is governed by *Maxwell's equations*. These equations are stated later in this section. The propagation of light can be described by specifying the evolution of the associated electric and magnetic field vectors in space and time, denoted by $\mathbf{E}(\mathbf{r}, t)$ and $\mathbf{H}(\mathbf{r}, t)$, respectively. Here $\mathbf{r}$ denotes the position vector and t denotes time. Sometimes it will be more convenient to deal with the Fourier transforms of these vectors. The Fourier transform of $\mathbf{E}$ is defined as

$$\tilde{\mathbf{E}}(\mathbf{r}, \omega) = \int_{-\infty}^{\infty} \mathbf{E}(\mathbf{r}, t) \exp(i\omega t) \, dt. \tag{2.3}$$

The Fourier transform of $\mathbf{H}$ and other vectors that we will encounter later are defined similarly. Note that even when $E(\mathbf{r}, t)$ is real, $\tilde{\mathbf{E}}(\mathbf{r}, \omega)$ can be complex. It turns out to be quite convenient, in many cases, to allow $\mathbf{E}(\mathbf{r}, t)$ to be complex valued as well. But it is understood that we should consider only the real part of the solutions obtained.

The electrons in an atom are negatively charged, and the nucleus carries a positive charge. Thus when an electric field is applied to a material such as silica, the forces experienced by the nuclei and the electrons are in opposite directions. These forces result in the atoms being *polarized* or distorted. The *induced electric polarization* of the material, or simply *polarization*, can be described by a vector $\mathbf{P}$, which depends both on the material properties and the applied field. The induced polarization can be viewed as the response of the medium to the applied electric field. We will shortly discuss the relationship between $\mathbf{P}$ and $\mathbf{E}$ in detail. It is convenient to define another vector $\mathbf{D}$ called the *electric flux density*, which is simply related to the electric field $\mathbf{E}$ and electric polarization $\mathbf{P}$ by

$$\mathbf{D} = \epsilon_0 \mathbf{E} + \mathbf{P} \tag{2.4}$$

where ϵ_0 is a constant called the *permittivity of vacuum*. The flux density in vacuum is simply $\epsilon_0 E$. The *magnetic polarization* **M** and the *magnetic flux density* **B** can be defined in an analogous fashion as

$$\mathbf{B} = \mu_0(\mathbf{H} + \mathbf{M}). \tag{2.5}$$

However, since silica is a nonmagnetic material, $\mathbf{B} = \mu_0\mathbf{H}$, where μ_0 is a constant called the *permeability of vacuum*. Maxwell's equations take into account the effect of material properties on the propagation of electromagnetic waves, since they not only involve **E** and **H** but also the flux densities **D** and the magnetic flux density **B**.

The relationship between **P** and **E** in optical fiber due to the nature of silica is the origin of two important effects related to the propagation of light in fiber, namely, dispersion and nonlinearities. These two effects set limits on the performance of optical communication systems today. We will understand the origin of these effects in this chapter. Methods of dealing with these effects in optical communication systems will be discussed in Chapter 5.

The relationship between the vectors **P** and **E** depends on the nature of the medium. Next, we discuss five characteristics of a medium and their effect on the relationship between the induced polarization **P** in the medium and the applied electric field **E**.

Locality of Response. In a medium whose response to the applied electric field is local, $\mathbf{P}(\mathbf{r})$ at $\mathbf{r} = \mathbf{r}_1$ depends only on $\mathbf{E}(\mathbf{r}_1)$. The values of $\mathbf{E}(\mathbf{r})$ for $\mathbf{r} \neq \mathbf{r}_1$ have no effect on $\mathbf{P}(\mathbf{r}_1)$. This property holds to a good degree of approximation for silica fibers in the 0.5–2 μm wavelength range that is of interest in optical communication systems.

Isotropy. An isotropic medium is one whose electromagnetic properties such as the refractive index are the same in all directions. In an isotropic medium, **E** and **P** are vectors with the same orientation. Silica is an isotropic medium, and a perfectly cylindrical optical fiber is also isotropic. However, this is not exactly true if the cylindrical symmetry of fiber is destroyed. A medium whose refractive indices along two different directions, for example, the x and y axes in an appropriate coordinate system, are different, is said to *birefringent*. An optical fiber that does not possess cylindrical symmetry is also said to be birefringent. Birefringence of materials such as lithium niobate is exploited in designing certain components such as modulators, isolators, and tunable filters. We will discuss these components in Chapter 3.

Linearity. In a linear, isotropic medium,

$$\mathbf{P}(\mathbf{r}, t) = \epsilon_0 \int_{-\infty}^{t} \chi(\mathbf{r}, t - t')\mathbf{E}(\mathbf{r}, t')\, dt', \tag{2.6}$$

where χ is called the *susceptibility,* or more accurately, *linear susceptibility,* of the medium. Thus the induced polarization is obtained by convolving the applied electric field with (ϵ_0 times) the susceptibility of the medium. If $\tilde{P}$ and $\tilde{\chi}$ denote the Fourier transforms of P and χ, respectively, (2.6) can be written in terms of Fourier transforms as

$$\tilde{P}(r, \omega) = \epsilon_0 \tilde{\chi}(r, \omega)\tilde{E}(r, \omega). \tag{2.7}$$

Electrical engineers will note that in this linear case, the induced polarization can be viewed as the output of a linear system with impulse response $\epsilon_0 \chi(r, t)$, or transfer function $\epsilon_0 \tilde{\chi}(r, \omega)$, and input $E(r, t)$ (or $\tilde{E}(r, \omega)$). It is important to note that the value of P at time t depends not only on the value of E at time t but also on the values of E before time t. Thus the response of the medium to the applied electric field is not instantaneous. (In other words, $\tilde{\chi}(r, \omega)$ is not independent of ω.) This is the origin of an important type of dispersion known as *chromatic dispersion,* which sets a fundamental limit on the performance of optical communication systems. If the medium response is instantaneous so that the susceptibility (impulse response) is a Dirac delta function, its Fourier transform would be a constant, independent of ω, and chromatic dispersion would vanish. Thus the origin of chromatic dispersion lies in the delayed response of the induced polarization in the silica medium to the applied electric field.

This linear relationship between P and E does not hold exactly for silica but is a good approximation at moderate signal powers and bit rates. The effects of nonlinearities on the propagation of light will be discussed in Section 2.4.

Homogeneity. A homogeneous medium has the same electromagnetic properties at all points within it. In such a medium, χ, and hence $\tilde{\chi}$, are independent of the position vector r, and we can write $\chi(t)$ for $\chi(r, t)$. Whereas silica is a homogeneous medium, optical fiber is not, since the refractive indices in the core and cladding are different. However, individually, the core and cladding regions in a step-index fiber are homogeneous. The core of a graded-index fiber is inhomogeneous. A discussion of the propagation of light in graded-index fiber is beyond the scope of this book.

Losslessness. Although silica fiber is certainly not lossless, the loss is negligible and can be assumed to be zero in the discussion of *propagation modes.* These modes would not change significantly if the nonzero loss of silica fiber were included in their derivation.

In this section, we assume that the core and the cladding regions of the silica fiber are *locally responsive, isotropic, linear, homogeneous,* and *lossless.* These assumptions are equivalent to assuming the appropriate properties for P, E, and χ in the fiber according to the preceding discussion.

Recall that the refractive index of a material n is the ratio of the speed of light in vacuum to the speed of light in that material. The susceptibility is a more fundamental material property, and the refractive index is actually defined in terms of the susceptibility as

$$n^2(\omega) \stackrel{\text{def}}{=} 1 + \tilde{\chi}(\omega). \tag{2.8}$$

Since the susceptibility $\tilde{\chi}$ is a function of the angular frequency ω, so is the refractive index. Hence we have written $n(\omega)$ for n is (2.8). This dependence of the refractive index on frequency is the origin of chromatic dispersion in optical fibers as we noted. For optical fibers, the value of $\tilde{\chi} \approx 1.25$, and the refractive index $n \approx 1.5$.

With these assumptions, starting from Maxwell's equations, we derive the following *wave equations* for $\tilde{\mathbf{E}}$ and $\tilde{\mathbf{H}}$ in the next section, which may be omitted without loss of continuity.

$$\nabla^2 \tilde{\mathbf{E}} + \frac{\omega^2 n^2(\omega)}{c^2} \tilde{\mathbf{E}} = 0 \tag{2.9}$$

$$\nabla^2 \tilde{\mathbf{H}} + \frac{\omega^2 n^2(\omega)}{c^2} \tilde{\mathbf{H}} = 0. \tag{2.10}$$

Here ∇^2 denotes the Laplacian operator, which is given in Cartesian coordinates by $\frac{\partial^2}{\partial x^2} + \frac{\partial^2}{\partial y^2} + \frac{\partial^2}{\partial z^2}$. Thus the wave equations are second-order, linear, partial differential equations for the Fourier transforms of the electric and magnetic field vectors. Note that each wave equation actually represents three equations—one for each component of the corresponding field vector.

Wave Equations *

The propagation of electromagnetic waves is governed by the following *Maxwell's equations*:

$$\nabla \cdot \mathbf{D} \;=\; \rho \tag{2.11}$$

$$\nabla \cdot \mathbf{B} \;=\; 0 \tag{2.12}$$

$$\nabla \times \mathbf{E} \;=\; -\frac{\partial \mathbf{B}}{\partial t} \tag{2.13}$$

$$\nabla \times \mathbf{H} \;=\; \mathbf{J} + \frac{\partial \mathbf{D}}{\partial t} \tag{2.14}$$

Here, ρ is the charge density, and $\mathbf{J}$ is the current density. We assume that there are no free charges in the medium so that $\rho = 0$. For such a medium, $\mathbf{J} = \sigma \mathbf{E}$, where σ is the conductivity of the medium. Since the conductivity of silica is extremely low ($\sigma \approx 0$), we assume that $\mathbf{J} = 0$; this amounts to assuming a lossless medium.

In any medium, we also have, from (2.4) and (2.5),

$$\mathbf{D} = \epsilon_0 \mathbf{E} + \mathbf{P},$$

where $\mathbf{P}$ is the electric polarization of the medium and

$$\mathbf{B} = \mu_0(\mathbf{H} + \mathbf{M}),$$

where $\mathbf{M}$ is the magnetic polarization of the medium. Since silica is a nonmagnetic material, we set $\mathbf{M} = 0$.

Using these relations, we can eliminate the flux densities from Maxwell's curl equations (2.13) and (2.14) and write them only in terms of the field vectors $\mathbf{E}$ and $\mathbf{H}$, and the electric polarization $\mathbf{P}$. For example,

$$\nabla \times \nabla \times \mathbf{E} = -\mu_0\epsilon_0 \frac{\partial^2 \mathbf{E}}{\partial t^2} - \mu_0 \frac{\partial^2 \mathbf{P}}{\partial t^2}. \tag{2.15}$$

To solve this equation for $\mathbf{E}$, we have to relate $\mathbf{P}$ to $\mathbf{E}$. If we neglect nonlinear effects, we can assume the linear relation between $\mathbf{P}$ and $\mathbf{E}$ given by (2.6) and further, because of the homogeneity assumption, we can write $\chi(t)$ for $\chi(\mathbf{r}, t)$. We will relax this assumption when we discuss nonlinear effects in Section 2.4.

We can solve (2.15) for $\mathbf{E}$ most conveniently by using Fourier transforms. The Fourier transform $\tilde{\mathbf{E}}$ of $\mathbf{E}$ is defined by (2.3); $\tilde{\mathbf{P}}$ and $\tilde{\mathbf{H}}$ are defined similarly. It follows from the properties of Fourier transforms that

$$\mathbf{E}(\mathbf{r}, t) = \frac{1}{2\pi} \int_{-\infty}^{\infty} \tilde{\mathbf{E}}(\mathbf{r}, \omega) \exp(-i\omega t)\, d\omega.$$

By differentiating this equation with respect to t, we obtain the Fourier transform of $\partial\mathbf{E}/\partial t$ as $-i\omega\tilde{\mathbf{E}}$.

Taking the Fourier transform of (2.15), we get

$$\nabla \times \nabla \times \tilde{\mathbf{E}} = \mu_0\epsilon_0\omega^2\tilde{\mathbf{E}} + \mu_0\omega^2\tilde{\mathbf{P}}.$$

Using (2.7) to express $\tilde{\mathbf{P}}$ in terms of $\tilde{\mathbf{E}}$, this reduces to

$$\nabla \times \nabla \times \tilde{\mathbf{E}} = \mu_0\epsilon_0\omega^2\tilde{\mathbf{E}} + \mu_0\epsilon_0\omega^2\tilde{\chi}\tilde{\mathbf{E}}.$$

We denote $c = 1/\sqrt{\mu_0\epsilon_0}$; c is the speed of light in vacuum. When losses are neglected, as we have neglected them, $\tilde{\chi}$ is real, and we can write $n(\omega) = \sqrt{1 + \tilde{\chi}(\omega)}$, where n is the refractive index. Note that this is the same as (2.8), which we used as the definition for the refractive index. With this notation,

$$\nabla \times \nabla \times \tilde{\mathbf{E}} = \frac{\omega^2 n^2}{c^2} \tilde{\mathbf{E}}. \tag{2.16}$$

By using the identity,

$$\nabla \times \nabla \times \tilde{\mathbf{E}} = \nabla(\nabla \cdot \tilde{\mathbf{E}}) - \nabla^2 \tilde{\mathbf{E}},$$

(2.16) can be rewritten as

$$\nabla^2 \tilde{\mathbf{E}} + \frac{\omega^2 n^2}{c^2} \tilde{\mathbf{E}} = \nabla(\nabla \cdot \tilde{\mathbf{E}}). \tag{2.17}$$

Owing to our assumption of a homogeneous medium (χ independent of $\mathbf{r}$) and using (2.11) and (2.8), we get

$$0 = \nabla \cdot \tilde{\mathbf{D}} = \epsilon_0 \nabla \cdot (1 + \tilde{\chi}) \tilde{\mathbf{E}} = \epsilon_0 n^2 \nabla \cdot \tilde{\mathbf{E}}. \tag{2.18}$$

This enables us to simplify (2.17) and obtain the *wave equation* (2.9) for $\tilde{\mathbf{E}}$. Following similar steps, the wave equation (2.10) can be derived for $\tilde{\mathbf{H}}$.

Fiber Modes

The electric and magnetic field vectors in the core $\tilde{\mathbf{E}}_{core}$ and $\tilde{\mathbf{H}}_{core}$, and the electric and magnetic field vectors in the cladding $\tilde{\mathbf{E}}_{cladding}$ and $\tilde{\mathbf{H}}_{cladding}$, must satisfy the wave equations, (2.9) and (2.10), respectively. However, the solutions in the core and the cladding *are not independent;* they are related by boundary conditions on $\tilde{\mathbf{E}}$ and $\tilde{\mathbf{H}}$ at the core–cladding interface. Quite simply, every pair of solutions of these wave equations that satisfies these boundary conditions is a *fiber mode*.

Assume the direction of propagation of the electromagnetic wave (light) is z. Also assume that the fiber properties such as the core diameter and the core and cladding refractive indices are independent of z. Then it turns out that the z-dependence of the electric and magnetic fields of each fiber mode is of the form $e^{i\beta z}$. The quantity β is called the *propagation constant* of the mode. Each (nondegenerate) fiber mode has a different *propagation constant β* associated with it. The propagation constant is measured in units of radians per unit length. It determines the speed at which pulse energy in a mode propagates in the fiber. (Note that this concept of different propagation speeds for different modes has an analog in the geometrical optics approach. We can think of a "mode" as one possible path that a guided ray can take. Since the path lengths are different, the propagation speeds of the modes are different.) We will discuss this further in Section 2.3. The light energy propagating in the fiber will be divided among the modes supported by the fiber and since the modes travel at different speeds in the fiber, the energy in a narrow pulse at the input of a length of fiber will be spread out at the output. Thus it is desirable to *design the fiber such that it supports only a single mode*. Such a fiber is called a *single-mode fiber*, and the mode that it supports is termed the *fundamental mode*. We had already come to a similar conclusion at the end of Section 2.1.1, but the wave theory approach enables us to get a clearer understanding of the concept of modes.

To better understand the notion of a propagation constant of a mode, consider the propagation of an electromagnetic wave in a homogeneous medium with refractive index n. Further assume that the wave is *monochromatic*, that is, all its energy is concentrated at a single angular frequency ω or free-space wavelength λ. In this case, the propagation constant is $\omega n/c = 2\pi n/\lambda$. In terms of the *wave number* $k = 2\pi/\lambda$, the propagation constant is kn. Thus for a wave propagating purely in the core, the propagation constant is kn_1, and for a wave propagating only in the cladding, the propagation constant is kn_2. The fiber modes propagate partly in the cladding and partly in the core, and thus their propagation constants β satisfy $kn_2 < \beta < kn_1$. Instead of the propagation constant of a mode, we can consider its *effective index* $n_{eff} = \beta/k$. The effective index of a mode thus lies between the refractive indices of the cladding and the core. For a monochromatic wave in a single-mode fiber, the effective index is analogous to the refractive index: the speed at which the wave propagates is c/n_{eff}. We will discuss the propagation constant further in Section 2.3.

The solution of (2.9) and (2.10) is discussed in [Agr92, Jeu90]. We only state some important properties of the solution here and in Section 2.1.2.

It can be shown that the core radius a, the core refractive index n_1, and the cladding refractive index n_2 must satisfy the cutoff condition

$$V \stackrel{\text{def}}{=} \frac{2\pi}{\lambda} a \sqrt{n_1^2 - n_2^2} < 2.405 \qquad (2.19)$$

in order for a fiber to be *single moded at wavelength* λ. The smallest wavelength λ for which a given fiber is single moded is called the *cutoff wavelength* and denoted by λ_{cutoff}. Note that V decreases with a and $\Delta = (n_1 - n_2)/n_1$. Thus single-mode fibers tend to have small radii and small core–cladding refractive index differences. Typical values are $a = 4\ \mu$m and $\Delta = 0.003$, giving a V value close to 2 at 1.55 μm. The calculation of the cutoff wavelength λ_{cutoff} for these parameters is left as an exercise (Problem 2.4).

Since the value of Δ is typically small, the refractive indices of the core and cladding are nearly equal, and the light energy is not strictly confined to the fiber core. In fact, a significant portion of the light energy can propagate in the fiber cladding. For this reason, the fiber modes are said to be *weakly guided*. For a given mode, for example, the fundamental mode, the proportion of light energy that propagates in the core depends on the wavelength. This gives rise to spreading of pulses through a phenomenon called *waveguide dispersion*, which we will discuss in Section 2.3.

A fiber with a large value of the V parameter is called a *multimode fiber* and supports several modes. For large V, the number of modes can be approximated by $V^2/2$. For multimode fibers, typical values are $a = 25\ \mu$m and $\Delta = 0.005$, giving a V

value of about 28 at 0.8 μm. Thus a typical multimode fiber supports a few hundred propagation modes.

The parameter V can be viewed as a normalized wave number since for a given fiber (fixed a, n_1, and n_2), it is proportional to the wave number. It is useful to know the propagation constant β of the fundamental mode supported by a fiber as a function of wavelength. This is needed to design components such as filters whose operation depends on coupling energy from one mode to another, as will become clear in Chapter 3. For example, such an expression can be used to calculate the velocity with which pulses at different wavelengths propagate in the fiber. The exact determination of β must be done numerically. But, analogous to the normalized wave number, we can define a normalized propagation constant, or normalized effective index, b by

$$b \stackrel{\text{def}}{=} \frac{\beta^2 - k^2 n_2^2}{k^2 n_1^2 - k^2 n_2^2} = \frac{n_{\text{eff}}^2 - n_2^2}{n_1^2 - n_2^2}.$$

This normalized propagation constant can be approximated with a relative error less than 0.2% by the equation

$$b(V) \approx (1.1428 - 0.9960/V)^2$$

for V in the interval (1.5, 2.5); see [Neu88, p. 71], or [Jeu90, p. 25], where the result is attributed to [RN76]. This is the range of V that is of interest in the design of single-mode optical fibers.

Polarization

We defined a fiber mode as a solution of the wave equations that satisfies the boundary conditions at the core–cladding interface. Two linearly independent solutions of the wave equations exist for all λ, however large. Both these solutions correspond to the fundamental mode and have the same propagation constant. The other solutions exist only for $\lambda < \lambda_{\text{cutoff}}$.

Assume that the electric field $\tilde{\mathbf{E}}(\mathbf{r}, t)$ is written as $\tilde{\mathbf{E}}(\mathbf{r}, t) = \tilde{E}_x \hat{e}_x + \tilde{E}_y \hat{e}_y + \tilde{E}_z \hat{e}_z$, where $\hat{e}_x$, $\hat{e}_y$, and $\hat{e}_z$ are the unit vectors along the x, y, and z directions, respectively. Note that each of E_x, E_y, and E_z can depend, in general, on x, y, and z. We take the direction of propagation (fiber axis) as z and consider the two linearly independent solutions to (2.9) that correspond to the fundamental mode. It can be shown (see [Jeu90]) that one of these solutions has $\tilde{E}_x = 0$ but $\tilde{E}_y$, $\tilde{E}_z \neq 0$, whereas the other has $\tilde{E}_y = 0$ but $\tilde{E}_x$, $\tilde{E}_z \neq 0$. Since z is also the direction of propagation, E_z is called the *longitudinal* component. The other nonzero component, which is either E_x or E_y, is called the *transverse* component. For the fundamental mode, the longitudinal component is of the form $E_z = 2\pi J_l(x, y) \exp(i\beta z)$. Here $J_l(x, y)$ is a function only of $\rho = \sqrt{x^2 + y^2}$ due to the cylindrical symmetry of the fiber and is expressible in terms of Bessel functions. The transverse component of the fundamental mode is of the form $E_x(E_y) = 2\pi J_t(x, y) \exp(i\beta z)$, where again $J_t(x, y)$ depends only on $\sqrt{x^2 + y^2}$ and can be expressed in terms of Bessel functions. Thus, for each of the solutions corresponding to the fundamental mode, we can write

$$\tilde{\mathbf{E}}(\mathbf{r}, \omega) = 2\pi J(x, y) e^{i\beta(\omega)z} \hat{e}(x, y), \qquad (2.20)$$

where $J(x, y) = \sqrt{J_l(x, y)^2 + J_t(x, y)^2}$ and the $\hat{e}$ is the unit vector along the direction of $\tilde{\mathbf{E}}(\mathbf{r}, \omega)$. In this equation, we have explicitly written β as a function of ω to emphasize this dependence. In general, $J()$ and $\hat{e}()$ are also functions of ω, but this dependence can be neglected for pulses whose spectral width is much smaller than their center frequency. This condition is satisfied by pulses used in optical communication systems.

Before we discuss the electric field distributions of the fundamental mode further, we need to understand the concept of *polarization* of an electric field. Since the electric field is a vector, for a time-varying electric field, both the magnitude and the direction can vary with time. A time-varying electric field is said to be *linearly polarized* if its direction is a constant, independent of time. If the electric field associated with an electromagnetic wave has no component along the direction of propagation of the wave, the electric field is said to be *transverse*. For the fundamental mode of a single-mode fiber, the magnitude of the longitudinal component E_z is much smaller than the magnitude of the transverse component, E_x or E_y. Thus the electric field associated with the fundamental mode can effectively be assumed to be a transverse field.

With this assumption, the two linearly independent solutions of the wave equations for the electric field are linearly polarized along the x and y directions. Since these two directions are perpendicular to each other, the two solutions are said to be *orthogonally polarized*. Since the wave equations are linear, any linear combination of these two linearly polarized fields is also a solution, and thus a fundamental mode. The *state of polarization* (SOP) refers to the distribution of light energy among the two polarization modes. The reason the fiber is still termed *single mode* is that these two polarization modes have the same propagation constant, at least in an ideal, perfectly circularly symmetric fiber. Thus, though the energy of a pulse is divided between these two polarization modes, since they have the same propagation constant, it does not give rise to pulse spreading by the phenomenon of dispersion.

In practice, fibers are not perfectly circularly symmetric, and the two orthogonally polarized modes have slightly different propagation constants. Since the light energy of a pulse propagating in a fiber will usually be split between these two modes, this difference in propagation constant gives rise to pulse spreading. This phenomenon is called *polarization-mode dispersion* (PMD). This is similar, in principle, to pulse spreading in the case of multimode fibers, but the effect is much weaker. We will study the effects of PMD on optical communication systems in Section 5.7.4.

Many optical materials and components constructed using them respond differently to the different polarization components in the input light. Some components where these polarization effects are used include isolators, circulators, and acousto-optic tunable filters, which we will study in Chapter 3.

Light Propagation in Dielectric Waveguides

A *dielectric* is a material whose conductivity is very small; silica is a dielectric material. Any dielectric region of higher refractive index placed in another dielectric of lower refractive index for the purpose of guiding (optical) waves can be called a *dielectric waveguide*. Thus an optical fiber is also a dielectric waveguide. However, the term is more often used to refer to a device where the guiding occurs in some region of a glass or dielectric slab. In most applications, the guiding region has a rectangular cross section. In contrast, the guiding region of an optical fiber is its core, which has a circular cross section.

The propagation of light in waveguides can be analyzed in a fashion similar to that of propagation in optical fiber. In the ray theory approach, which is applicable when the dimensions of the guiding region are much larger than the wavelength, the guiding process is due to total internal reflection; light that is launched into the waveguide at one end is confined to the guiding region. When we use the wave theory approach, we again find that only certain distributions of the electromagnetic fields are supported or guided by the waveguide, and these are called the *modes* of the waveguide. Furthermore, the dimensions of the waveguide can be chosen so that the waveguide supports only a single mode, the *fundamental mode*, above a certain *cutoff wavelength*, just as in the case of optical fiber.

However, the modes of a rectangular waveguide are quite different from the fiber modes. For most rectangular waveguides, their width is much larger than their depth. For these waveguides, the modes can be classified into two groups: one for which the electric field is approximately transverse called the *TE modes*, and the other for which the magnetic field is approximately transverse called the *TM modes*. (The transverse approximation holds exactly if the waveguides have infinite width; such waveguides are called *slab waveguides*.) If the width of the waveguide is along the x direction (and much larger than the depth), the TE modes have an electric field that is approximately linearly polarized along the x direction. The same is true for the magnetic fields of TM modes.

The fundamental mode of a rectangular waveguide is a TE mode. But in some applications, for example, in the design of isolators and circulators (Section 3.2.1), the waveguide is designed to support two modes: the fundamental TE mode and the lowest-order TM mode. For most waveguides, for example, those made of silica, the propagation constants of the fundamental TE mode and lowest-order TM mode are very close to each other. The electric field vector of a lightwave propagating in such a waveguide can be expressed as a linear combination of the TE and TM modes. In other words, the energy of the lightwave is split between the TE and TM modes. The proportion of light energy in the two modes depends on the input excitation. This proportion also changes when gradual or abrupt discontinuities are present in the waveguide.

In some applications, for example, in the design of acousto-optic tunable filters (Section 3.3.8), it is desirable for the propagation constants of the fundamental TE mode and lowest-order TM mode to have a significant difference. This can be arranged by constructing the waveguide using a *birefringent material*, such as lithium niobate. For such a material, the refractive indices along different axes are quite different, resulting in the effective indices of the TE and TM modes being quite different.

2.2   Loss and Bandwidth

Although we neglected the attenuation loss in the fiber in the derivation of propagation modes, its effect can be modeled easily as follows: the output power P_{out} at the end of a fiber of length L is related to the input power P_{in} by

$$P_{out} = P_{in} e^{-\alpha L}.$$

Here the parameter α represents the fiber attenuation. It is customary to express the loss in units of dB/km; thus a loss of α_{dB} dB/km means that the ratio P_{out}/P_{in} for $L = 1$ km satisfies

$$10 \log_{10} \frac{P_{out}}{P_{in}} = -\alpha_{dB}$$

or

$$\alpha_{dB} = (10 \log_{10} e)\alpha \approx 4.343\alpha.$$

The two main loss mechanisms in an optical fiber are *material absorption* and *Rayleigh scattering*. Material absorption includes absorption by silica as well as the impurities in the fiber. The material absorption of pure silica is negligible in the entire 0.8–1.6 μm band that is used for optical communication systems. The reduction of the loss due to material absorption by the impurities in silica has been very important in making optical fiber the remarkable communication medium that

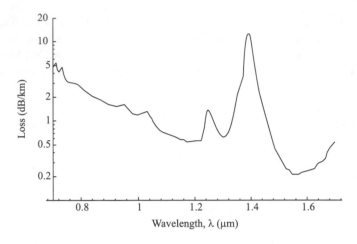

Figure 2.5   Attenuation loss in silica as a function of wavelength. After [Agr92].

it is today. The loss has now been reduced to negligible levels at the wavelengths of interest for optical communication. So much so that the loss due to Rayleigh scattering is the dominant component in today's fibers in all the three wavelength bands used for optical communication: 0.8 μm, 1.3 μm, and 1.55 μm. Figure 2.5 shows the attenuation loss in silica as a function of wavelength. We see that the loss has local minima at these three wavelength bands with typical losses of 2.5, 0.4, and 0.25 dB/km. (In a typical optical communication system, a signal can undergo a loss of about 20–30 dB before it needs to be amplified or regenerated. At 0.25 dB/km, this corresponds to a distance of 80–120 km.) The attenuation peaks separating these bands are primarily due to absorption by the residual water vapor in the silica fiber.

The bandwidth can be measured either in terms of wavelength $\Delta\lambda$ or in terms of frequency Δf. These are related by the equation

$$\Delta f \approx \frac{c}{\lambda^2}\Delta\lambda.$$

This equation can be derived by expanding the relation $f = c/\lambda$ in a Taylor's series and keeping only the term with the first derivative. Consider the long wavelength 1.3 and 1.5 μm bands, which are the primary bands used today for optical communication. The usable bandwidth of optical fiber in these bands, which we can take as the bandwidth over which the loss in dB/km is within a factor of 2 of its minimum, is approximately 80 nm at 1.3 μm and 180 nm at 1.55 μm. In terms of optical frequency, these bandwidths correspond to about 35,000 GHz! This is an enormous amount of bandwidth indeed, considering that the bit rate needed for most user applications today is no more than a few tens of Mb/s.

As we saw, the dominant loss mechanism in optical fiber is Rayleigh scattering. Rayleigh scattering arises because of fluctuations in the density of the medium (silica) at the microscopic level. We refer to [BW80] for a detailed description of the scattering mechanism. The loss due to Rayleigh scattering is a fundamental one and decreases with increasing wavelength. The loss coefficient α_R due to Rayleigh scattering at a wavelength λ can be written as $\alpha_R = A/\lambda^4$, where A is called the Rayleigh scattering coefficient. Note that the Rayleigh scattering loss decreases rapidly with increasing wavelength due to the λ^{-4} dependence. Glasses with substantially lower Rayleigh attenuation coefficients at 1.55 μm are not known. In order to reduce the fiber loss below the current best value of about 0.2 dB/km, one possibility is to operate at higher wavelengths, so as to reduce the loss due to Rayleigh scattering. However, at such higher wavelengths, the material absorption of silica is quite significant. Other materials such as fluorozirconate (ZiFr$_4$) are being explored in order to realize the low loss that is potentially possible by operating at these wavelengths.

2.3   Chromatic Dispersion

Dispersion is the name given to any effect wherein different components of the transmitted signal travel at different velocities in the fiber, arriving at different times at the receiver. We already discussed the phenomenon of modal dispersion in Section 2.1 and polarization-mode dispersion in Section 2.1.2. Our main goal in this section will be to understand the phenomenon of *chromatic dispersion* and the system limitations imposed by it. Other forms of dispersion and their effect on the design of the system are discussed in Section 5.7.

Chromatic dispersion is the term given to the phenomenon by which different *spectral* components of a pulse travel at different velocities. To understand the effect of chromatic dispersion, we must understand the significance of the propagation constant. We will restrict our discussion to single-mode fiber since in the case of multimode fiber, the effects of modal dispersion usually overshadow that of chromatic dispersion. So the propagation constant in our discussions will be that associated with the fundamental mode of the fiber.

Chromatic dispersion arises for two reasons. The first is that the refractive index of silica, the material used to make optical fiber, is frequency dependent. Thus different frequency components travel at different speeds in silica. This component of chromatic dispersion is termed *material dispersion*. Although this is the principal component of chromatic dispersion for most fibers, there is a second component called *waveguide dispersion*. To understand the physical origin of waveguide dispersion, recall from Section 2.1.2 that the light energy of a mode propagates partly in the core and partly in the cladding. Also recall that the effective index of a mode lies between the refractive indices of the cladding and the core. The actual value of the effective index between these two limits depends on the proportion of power that is contained in the cladding and the core. If most of the power is contained in the core, the effective index is closer to the core refractive index; if most of it propagates in the cladding, the effective index is closer to the cladding refractive index. The power distribution of a mode between the core and cladding of the fiber is itself a function of the wavelength. Thus, even in the absence of material dispersion—so that the refractive indices of the core and cladding are independent of wavelength—if the wavelength changes, this power distribution changes, causing the effective index or propagation constant of the mode to change. This is the physical explanation for waveguide dispersion.

In mathematical terms, chromatic dispersion arises because the propagation constant β is not proportional to the angular frequency ω, that is, $d\beta/d\omega \neq$ constant (independent of ω). $d\beta/d\omega$ is denoted by β_1, and β_1^{-1} is called the *group velocity*. As we will see, this is the velocity with which a pulse propagates through the fiber (in the absence of dispersion). Chromatic dispersion is also called *group velocity dispersion*.

If we were to launch a pure monochromatic wave at frequency ω_0 into a length of optical fiber, the magnitude of the (real) electric field vector associated with the wave would be given by

$$|\mathbf{E}(\mathbf{r}, t)| = J(x, y) \cos(\omega_0 t - \beta(\omega_0)z). \tag{2.21}$$

Here the z coordinate is taken to be along the fiber axis. This equation can be derived from (2.20) by taking the inverse Fourier transform. Recall that $J(x, y)$ is the distribution of the electric field along the fiber cross section and is determined by solving the wave equation. This pure monochromatic wave propagates at a velocity $\omega_0/\beta(\omega_0)$. This is called the *phase velocity of the wave*. In practice, signals used for optical communication are not monochromatic waves but pulses having a nonzero spectral width. To understand how such pulses propagate, consider a pulse consisting of just two spectral components: one at $\omega_0 + \Delta\omega$ and the other at $\omega_0 - \Delta\omega$. Further assume that $\Delta\omega$ is small so that we may approximate

$$\beta(\omega_0 \pm \Delta\omega) \approx \beta_0 \pm \beta_1 \Delta\omega,$$

where $\beta_0 = \beta(\omega_0)$ and

$$\beta_1 = \left.\frac{d\beta}{d\omega}\right|_{\omega=\omega_0}.$$

The magnitude of the electric field vector associated with such a pulse would be given by

$$
\begin{aligned}
|\mathbf{E}(\mathbf{r}, t)| \quad = \quad & J(x, y)\,[\cos\left((\omega_0 + \Delta\omega)t - \beta(\omega_0 + \Delta\omega)z\right) + \\
& \cos\left((\omega_0 - \Delta\omega)t - \beta(\omega_0 - \Delta\omega)z\right)] \\
\approx \quad & 2J(x, y)\cos(\Delta\omega t - \beta_1\Delta\omega z)\cos(\omega_0 t - \beta_0 z).
\end{aligned}
$$

This pulse can be viewed in time t and space z as the product of a very rapidly varying sinusoid, namely, $\cos(\omega_0 t - \beta_0 z)$, which is also called the *phase* of the pulse, and a much more slowly varying *envelope*, namely, $\cos(\Delta\omega t - \beta_1\Delta\omega z)$. Note that in this case the phase of the pulse travels at a velocity of ω_0/β_0, whereas the envelope of the pulse travels at a velocity of $1/\beta_1$. The quantity ω_0/β_0 is called the *phase velocity* of the pulse, and $1/\beta_1$ is called the *group velocity*.

In general, pulses used for optical communication can be represented in this manner as the product of a slowly varying envelope function (of z and t), which is usually not a sinusoid, and a sinusoid of the form $\cos(\omega_0 t - \beta_0 z)$, where ω_0 is termed the *center frequency* of the pulse. And just as in the preceding case, the envelope of the pulse propagates at the group velocity, $1/\beta_1$. This concept can be stated more precisely as follows.

Consider a pulse whose shape, or envelope, is described by $A(z, t)$, and whose center frequency is ω_0. Assume that the pulses have *narrow spectral width*. By this we mean that most of the energy of the pulse is concentrated in a frequency band whose width is negligible compared to the center frequency ω_0 of the pulse. This assumption is usually satisfied for most pulses used in optical communication systems. With this assumption, it can be shown that the magnitude of the (real) electric field vector associated with such a pulse is (see, for example, [Agr92])

$$
|\mathbf{E}(\mathbf{r}, t)| = J(x, y)\Re[A(z, t)e^{-i(\omega_0 t - \beta_0 z)}], \tag{2.22}
$$

where $\Re[q]$ denotes the real part of q. Here β_0 is the value of the propagation constant β at the frequency ω_0. $J(x, y)$ has the same significance as before. It is mathematically convenient to allow the pulse envelope $A(z, t)$ to be complex valued so that it captures not only the change in the pulse shape during propagation but also any induced phase shifts. Thus if $A(z, t) = |A(z, t)| \exp(i\phi_A(z, t))$, the *phase of the pulse* is given by

$$
\phi(t) = \omega_0 t - \beta_0 z - \phi_A(z, t). \tag{2.23}
$$

To get the description of the actual pulse, we must multiply $A(z, t)$ by $\exp(-i(\omega_0 t - \beta_0 z))$ and take the real part. We will illustrate this in (2.26).

Here we have also assumed that the pulse is obtained by modulating a nearly monochromatic source at frequency ω_0. This means that the frequency spectrum of the optical source has negligible width compared to the frequency spectrum of the pulse. We will consider the effect of relaxing this assumption later in this section.

By assuming that the higher derivatives of β with respect to ω are negligible, we can derive (see [Agr92]) the following partial differential equation for the evolution of the pulse shape $A(z, t)$:

$$\frac{\partial A}{\partial z} + \beta_1 \frac{\partial A}{\partial t} + \frac{i}{2}\beta_2 \frac{\partial^2 A}{\partial t^2} = 0. \tag{2.24}$$

Here,

$$\beta_2 = \left. \frac{d^2\beta}{d\omega^2} \right|_{\omega=\omega_0}.$$

Note that if β were a linear function of ω, that is, $\beta_2 = 0$, then $A(z, t) = F(t - \beta_1 z)$, where F is an arbitrary function that satisfies (2.24). Then $A(z, t) = A(0, t - \beta_1 z)$ for all z and t, and arbitrary pulse shapes propagate without change in shape (and at velocity $1/\beta_1$). In other words, *if the group velocity is independent of ω, no broadening of the pulse occurs.* Thus β_2 is the key parameter governing group velocity or chromatic dispersion. It is termed the *group velocity dispersion parameter* or, simply, *GVD parameter.*

2.3.1 Chirped Gaussian Pulses

We next discuss how a specific family of pulses changes shape as they propagate along a length of single-mode optical fiber. The pulses we consider are called *chirped Gaussian pulses*. An example is shown in Figure 2.6. The term *Gaussian* refers to the envelope of the launched pulse. *Chirped* means that the frequency of the launched pulse changes with time. Both aspects are illustrated in Figure 2.6, where the center frequency ω_0 has been vastly diminished for the purposes of illustration.

We consider chirped pulses for two reasons. First, the pulses emitted by semiconductor lasers when they are directly modulated are considerably chirped, and such transmitters are widely used in practice. As we will see in Chapter 5, this chirp has a significant effect on the design of optical communication systems. The second reason is that some nonlinear effects that we will study in Section 2.4 can cause otherwise unchirped pulses to acquire a chirp. It then becomes important to study the effect of chromatic dispersion on such pulses.

The assumption of a Gaussian envelope is mostly for mathematical convenience. Pulses used in practice tend to be more rectangular than Gaussian. However, the

Figure 2.6 A chirped Gaussian pulse.

results we derive will be qualitatively valid for most pulse envelopes. In the next section, we will briefly describe quantitatively how chirped Gaussian pulses propagate in optical fiber. The key result that we will use in subsequent discussions is that after a pulse with initial width T_0 has propagated a distance z, its width T_z is given by

$$\frac{|T_z|}{T_0} = \sqrt{\left(1 + \frac{\kappa \beta_2 z}{T_0^2}\right)^2 + \left(\frac{\beta_2 z}{T_0^2}\right)^2}. \tag{2.25}$$

Here κ is called the *chirp factor* of the pulse and is proportional to the rate of change of the pulse frequency with time.

Propagation of Chirped Gaussian Pulses *

Mathematically, a chirped Gaussian pulse at $z = 0$ is described by the equation

$$
\begin{aligned}
G(t) &= \Re\left[A_0 e^{-\frac{1+i\kappa}{2}\left(\frac{t}{T_0}\right)^2} e^{-i\omega_0 t}\right] \\
&= A_0 e^{-\frac{1}{2}\left(\frac{t}{T_0}\right)^2} \cos\left(\omega_0 t + \frac{\kappa}{2}\left(\frac{t}{T_0}\right)^2\right).
\end{aligned} \tag{2.26}
$$

The peak amplitude of the pulse is A_0. The parameter T_0 determines the width of the pulse. It has the interpretation that it is the half-width of the pulse at the $1/e$-intensity point. (The intensity of a pulse is the square of its amplitude.) The *chirp factor* κ determines the degree of chirp of the pulse. From (2.23), the phase of this pulse is

$$\phi(t) = \omega_0 t + \frac{\kappa t^2}{2T_0^2}.$$

The instantaneous angular frequency of the pulse is the derivative of the phase and is given by

$$\frac{d}{dt}\left(\omega_0 t + \frac{\kappa}{2}\frac{t^2}{T_0^2}\right) = \omega_0 + \frac{\kappa}{T_0^2}t.$$

We define the *chirp factor* of a Gaussian pulse as T_0^2 times the derivative of its instantaneous angular frequency. Thus the chirp factor of the pulse described by (2.26) is κ. This pulse is said to be *linearly chirped* since the instantaneous angular frequency of the pulse increases or decreases *linearly* with time t, depending on the sign of the chirp factor κ. In other words, the chirp factor κ is a constant, independent of time t, for linearly chirped pulses.

Let $A(z, t)$ denote a chirped Gaussian pulse as a function of time and distance. At $z = 0$,

$$A(0, t) = A_0 e^{-\frac{1+i\kappa}{2}\left(\frac{t}{T_0}\right)^2}. \tag{2.27}$$

If we solve (2.24) for a chirped Gaussian pulse (so the initial condition for this differential equation is that $A(0, t)$ is given by (2.27)), we get

$$A(z, t) = \frac{A_0 T_0}{\sqrt{T_0^2 - i\beta_2 z(1 + i\kappa)}} \exp\left(-\frac{(1 + i\kappa)(t - \beta_1 z)^2}{2\left(T_0^2 - i\beta_2 z(1 + i\kappa)\right)}\right). \tag{2.28}$$

The key point to note here is that $A(z, t)$ is also the envelope of a chirped Gaussian pulse for all $z > 0$, but the width of this pulse increases as z increases if $\beta_2\kappa > 0$. This happens because the parameter governing the pulse width is now $T_z^2 = T_0^2 - i\beta_2 z(1 + i\kappa)$, and the magnitude of T_z monotonically increases with increasing z if $\beta_2\kappa > 0$. A measure of the pulse broadening at distance z is the ratio $|T_z|/T_0$. The analytical expression (2.25) for this ratio can be derived from (2.28).

Broadening of Chirped Gaussian Pulses

Figure 2.7 shows the pulse broadening effect of chromatic dispersion graphically. In these figures, the center or carrier frequency of the pulse, ω_0, has deliberately been shown vastly diminished for the purposes of illustration. We assume β_2 is negative; this is true for standard single-mode fiber in the 1.55 μm band. Figure 2.7(a) shows an unchirped ($\kappa = 0$) Gaussian pulse, and Figure 2.7(b) shows the same pulse after it has propagated a distance $2T_0^2/|\beta_2|$ along the fiber. Figure 2.7(c) shows a chirped Gaussian pulse with $\kappa = -3$, and Figure 2.7(d) shows the same pulse after it has propagated a distance of only $0.4T_0^2/|\beta_2|$ along the fiber. The amount of broadening

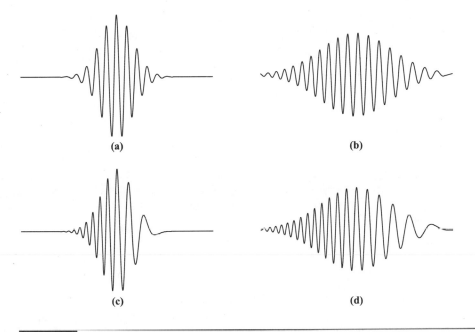

Figure 2.7   Illustration of the pulse broadening effect of chromatic dispersion on unchirped and chirped Gaussian pulses (for $\beta_2 < 0$). (a) An unchirped Gaussian pulse at $z = 0$. (b) The pulse in (a) at $z = 2L_D$. (c) A chirped Gaussian pulse with $\kappa = -3$ at $z = 0$. (d) The pulse in (c) at $z = 0.4L_D$. For systems operating over standard single-mode fiber at 1.55 μm, $L_D \approx 1800$ km at 2.5 Gb/s, whereas $L_D \approx 115$ km at 10 Gb/s.

can be seen to be about the same as that of the unchirped Gaussian pulse, but the distance traveled is only a fifth. This shows that the presence of chirp significantly enhances the pulse broadening due to chromatic dispersion (when the product $\kappa\beta_2$ is positive).

The quantity $T_0^2/|\beta_2|$ is called the *dispersion length* and is denoted by L_D. It serves as a convenient normalizing measure for the distance z in discussing the effects of dispersion. For example, the effects of dispersion can be neglected if $z \ll L_D$ since in that case, from (2.25), $|T_z|/T_0 \approx 1$. It also has the interpretation that the width of an unchirped pulse at the $1/e$-intensity point increases by a factor of $\sqrt{2}$ after it has propagated a distance equal to the dispersion length. The dispersion length for a 2.5 Gb/s system operating over standard single-mode fiber at 1.55 μm is approximately 1800 km, assuming $T_0 = 0.2$ ns, which is half the bit interval. If the bit rate of the system is increased to 10 Gb/s with $T_0 = 0.05$ ns, again half the

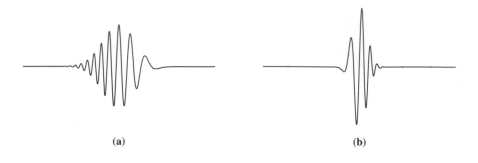

(a)   (b)

Figure 2.8 Illustration of the pulse compression effect of chromatic dispersion when $\kappa\beta_2 < 0$. (a) A chirped Gaussian pulse with $\kappa = -3$ at $z = 0$. (b) The pulse in (a) at $z = 0.4L_D$.

bit interval, the dispersion length decreases to approximately 115 km. This indicates that the limitations on systems due to chromatic dispersion are much more severe at 10 Gb/s than at 2.5 Gb/s. We will discuss the system limitations of chromatic dispersion in Section 2.3.2.

For $\kappa = 0$ and $z = 2L_D$, (2.25) yields $|T_z|/T_0 = \sqrt{5} \approx 2.24$. For $\kappa = -3$ and $z = 0.4L_D$, (2.25) yields $|T_z|/T_0 = \sqrt{5} \approx 2.24$. Thus both pulses broaden to the same extent, and these values are in agreement with Figure 2.7.

An interesting phenomenon occurs when the product $\kappa\beta_2$ is negative. The pulse initially undergoes compression up to a certain distance and then undergoes broadening. This is illustrated in Figure 2.8. The pulse in Figure 2.8(a) is the same chirped Gaussian pulse shown in Figure 2.7(c) and has the chirp parameter $\kappa = -3$. But the sign of β_2 is now positive (which is the case, for example, in the lower portion of the 1.3 μm band), and the pulse, after it has propagated a distance $z = 0.4L_D$, is shown in Figure 2.8(b). The pulse has now undergone compression rather than broadening. This can also be seen from (2.25) since we now get $|T_z|/T_0 = 1/\sqrt{5} \approx 0.45$. However, as z increases further, the pulse will start to broaden quite rapidly. This can be seen from Figure 2.9, where we plot the pulse width evolution as a function of distance for different chirp parameters. (Also see Problem 2.12.) We will discuss this phenomenon further in Sections 2.4.1 and 2.4.3.

A careful observation of Figure 2.7(b) shows that the unchirped Gaussian pulse acquires chirp when it has propagated some distance along the fiber. Furthermore, the acquired chirp is negative since the frequency of the pulse decreases with increasing time, t. The derivation of an expression for the acquired chirp is left as an exercise (Problem 2.9).

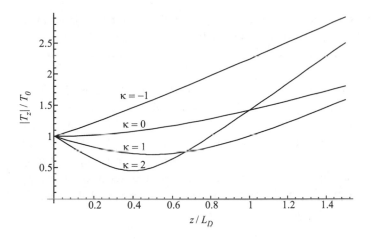

Figure 2.9   Evolution of pulse width as a function of distance (z/L_D) for chirped and unchirped pulses in the presence of dispersion. We assume $\beta_2 < 0$, which is the case for 1.55 μm systems operating over standard single-mode fiber. Note that for positive chirp the pulse width initially decreases but subsequently broadens more rapidly. For systems operating over standard single-mode fiber at 1.55 μm, $L_D \approx 1800$ km at 2.5 Gb/s, whereas $L_D \approx 115$ km at 10 Gb/s.

2.3.2   System Limitations

The pulse broadening effect of chromatic dispersion causes the signals in adjacent bit periods to overlap. This phenomenon is called *intersymbol interference* (ISI). We next derive the system limitations imposed by chromatic dispersion for unchirped Gaussian pulses. The results can be extended in a straightforward manner to pulses with chirp.

Consider a fiber of length L. From (2.25), the width of the output pulse is given by

$$T_L = \sqrt{T_0^2 + \left(\frac{\beta_2 L}{T_0}\right)^2}.$$

This is the half-width of the pulse at the $1/e$-intensity point. A different, and more commonly used, measure of the width of a pulse is its *root-mean square (rms) width* T^{rms}. For a pulse, $A(t)$, this is defined as

$$T^{\text{rms}} = \sqrt{\frac{\int_{-\infty}^{\infty} t^2 |A(t)|^2\, dt}{\int_{-\infty}^{\infty} |A(t)|^2\, dt}}. \tag{2.29}$$

We leave it as an exercise (Problem 2.10) to show that for Gaussian pulses whose half-width at the $1/e$-intensity point is T_0,

$$T^{\text{rms}} = T_0/\sqrt{2}.$$

If we are communicating at a bit rate of B bits/s, the bit period is $1/B$ s. We will assume that satisfactory communication is possible only if the width of the pulse as measured by its rms width T^{rms} is less than a specified fraction ϵ of the bit period. The value of ϵ depends on the allowable *power penalty*. The *power penalty* for chromatic dispersion is the additional signal-to-noise ratio needed to overcome the ISI effects caused by it; see Section 5.2 for a precise description. For a power penalty of 2 dB, in a typical system we are allowed to have $\epsilon = 0.491$ [Bel95]. Therefore, $T_L^{\text{rms}} = T_L/\sqrt{2} < \epsilon/B$ or

$$BT_L < \epsilon\sqrt{2}.$$

Through this condition, chromatic dispersion sets a limit on the length of the communication link we can use at bit rate B without regenerative repeaters. T_L is a function of T_0 and can be minimized by choosing T_0 suitably. We leave it as an exercise (Problem 2.13) to show that the optimum choice of T_0 is

$$T_0^{\text{opt}} = \sqrt{\beta_2 L},$$

and for this choice of T_0, the optimum value of T_L is

$$T_L^{\text{opt}} = \sqrt{2|\beta_2|L}.$$

The physical reason there is an optimum pulse width is as follows. If the pulse is made too narrow in time, it will have a wide spectral width and hence greater dispersion and more spreading. However, if the pulse occupies a large fraction of the bit interval, it has less room to spread. The optimum pulse width arises from a tradeoff between these two factors. For this optimum choice of T_0, the condition $BT_L < \epsilon\sqrt{2}$ becomes

$$B\sqrt{2|\beta_2|L} < \epsilon\sqrt{2}. \tag{2.30}$$

The key point to note here is that the bit rate B scales as $1/\sqrt{L}$. Usually, the value of β_2 is specified indirectly through the *dispersion parameter* D, which is related to β_2 by the equation

$$D = -\frac{2\pi c}{\lambda^2}\beta_2. \tag{2.31}$$

Thus (2.30) can be written as

$$B\lambda\sqrt{\frac{|D|L}{2\pi c}} < \epsilon. \tag{2.32}$$

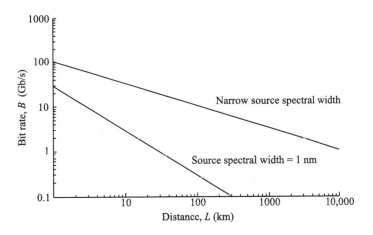

Figure 2.10 Chromatic dispersion limits on the simultaneously achievable bit rates and distances. A chromatic dispersion penalty of 2 dB has been assumed; alternatively, the rms width of the dispersion-broadened pulse must lie within a fraction 0.491 of the bit period.

D is usually specified in units of ps/km-nm. For standard single-mode fiber, the typical value of D in the 1.55 μm band is 17 ps/km-nm. For this value of D, (2.32) yields the condition $B^2 L < 11126$ (Gb/s)^2-km. This limit is plotted in Figure 2.10.

Note that we derived the dispersion limits for unchirped pulses. The situation is much less favorable in the presence of frequency chirp. A typical value of the chirp parameter κ of a directly modulated semiconductor laser at 1.55 μm is -6, and β_2 is also negative so that monotone pulse broadening occurs. We leave it as an exercise to the reader (Problem 2.11) to calculate the chromatic dispersion limit with this value of κ and compare it to the dispersion limit for an unchirped pulse at a bit rate of 2.5 Gb/s.

Large Source Spectral Width

We derived (2.25) for the width of the output pulse by assuming a nearly monochromatic source, such as a DFB laser. In practice, this assumption is not satisfied for many sources such as MLM Fabry-Perot lasers. This formula must be modified to account for the finite spectral width of the optical source. Assume that the frequency spectrum of the source is given by

$$F(\omega) = B_0 W_0 e^{-(\omega-\omega_0)^2/2W_0^2}.$$

Thus the spectrum of the source has a Gaussian profile around the center frequency ω_0, and W_0 is a measure of the frequency spread or bandwidth of the pulse. The *rms spectral width* W^{rms}, which is defined in a fashion similar to that of the rms temporal width (2.29), is given by $W^{\text{rms}} = W_0/\sqrt{2}$. As in the case of Gaussian pulses, the assumption of a Gaussian profile is chiefly for mathematical convenience; however, the results derived hold qualitatively for other source spectral profiles. From this spectrum, in the limit as $W_0 \to 0$, we obtain a monochromatic source at frequency ω_0. Equation (2.25) for the width of the output pulse is obtained under the assumption $W_0 << 1/T_0$. If this assumption does not hold, it must be modified to read

$$\frac{|T_z|}{T_0} = \sqrt{\left(1 + \frac{\kappa \beta_2 z}{T_0^2}\right)^2 + (1 + W_0^2 T_0^2)\left(\frac{\beta_2 z}{T_0^2}\right)^2}. \tag{2.33}$$

From this formula, we can derive the limitation imposed by chromatic dispersion on the bit rate B and the link length L. We have already examined this limitation for the case $W_0 \ll 1/T_0$. We now consider the case $W_0 \gg 1/T_0$ and again neglect chirp.

Consider a fiber of length L. With these assumptions, from (2.33), the width of the output pulse is given by

$$T_L = \sqrt{T_0^2 + (W_0 \beta_2 L)^2}.$$

In this case, since the spectral width of the pulse is dominated by the spectral width of the source and not by the temporal width of the pulse ($W_0 \gg 1/T_0$), we can make T_0 much smaller than the bit period $1/B$ provided the condition $W_0 \gg 1/T_0$ is still satisfied. For such short input pulses, we can approximate T_L by

$$T_L = W_0 |\beta_2| L.$$

Therefore, the condition $BT_L < \epsilon \sqrt{2}$ translates to

$$BL\beta_2 W^{\text{rms}} < \epsilon.$$

The key difference from the case of small source spectral width is that the bit rate B scales *linearly* with L. Thus chromatic dispersion is much more of a problem in communication systems that use sources with nonnegligible spectral widths.

The spectral width of a source is commonly expressed in wavelength units rather than in angular frequency units. A spectral width of W in radial frequency units corresponds to a spectral width in wavelength units of $(\Delta\lambda) = -2\pi c W/\lambda^2$. Using this and the relation $D = -2\pi c \beta_2/\lambda^2$, the chromatic dispersion limit becomes

$$BL|D|(\Delta\lambda) < \epsilon. \tag{2.34}$$

For $D = 17$ ps/km-nm and source spectral width of 1 nm, the chromatic dispersion limit $BL < 30$ (Gb/s)-km. This limit is also plotted in Figure 2.10. Thus at a bit rate of 1 Gb/s, the link length is limited to < 30 km, which is a severe limitation. This illustrates the importance of (a) using nearly monochromatic sources, for example, DFB lasers, for high-speed optical communication systems, and (b) devising methods of overcoming dispersion.

As we have seen, the parameter β_2 is the key to group velocity or chromatic dispersion. For a given pulse, the magnitude of β_2 governs the extent of pulse broadening due to chromatic dispersion and determines the system limitations. In Section 2.3.3, we will study how its effects can be minimized.

2.3.3   Controlling the Dispersion Profile

As we have already seen, group velocity dispersion is commonly expressed in terms of the *dispersion parameter* D that is related to β_2 as $D = -(2\pi c/\lambda^2)\beta_2$. D can be written as $D = D_M + D_W$, where D_M is the material dispersion, and D_W is the waveguide dispersion, both of which we have discussed earlier. Figure 2.11 shows D_M, D_W, and D for standard single-mode fiber. D_M increases monotonically with λ and equals 0 for $\lambda = 1.276$ μm. On the other hand, D_W decreases monotonically with λ and is always negative. The total dispersion D is zero around $\lambda = 1.31$ μm;

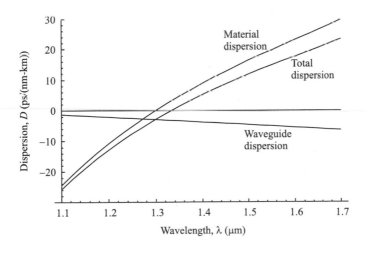

Figure 2.11   Material, waveguide, and total dispersion in standard single-mode optical fiber. After [Agr92].

thus the waveguide dispersion shifts the zero-dispersion wavelength by a few tens of nm.

For standard single-mode fiber, the dispersion effects are small in the 1.3 μm band, and systems operating in this wavelength range are loss limited. On the other hand, there is considerable interest in optical communication systems operating in the 1.55 μm band today because of the low loss in this region and the well-developed Erbium-doped fiber amplifier technology. But as we have already seen, optical communication systems in this band are chromatic dispersion limited. This limitation can be reduced if somehow the zero-dispersion wavelength were shifted to the 1.55 μm band. We do not have much control over the material dispersion D_M though it can be varied slightly by doping the core and cladding regions of the fiber. However, we can vary the waveguide dispersion D_W considerably so as to shift the zero-dispersion wavelength into the 1.55 μm band. Fibers with this property are called *dispersion-shifted* fibers. This and other kinds of optical fiber are discussed in Section 5.7 in the context of transmission system design.

2.4   Nonlinear Effects

Our description of optical communication systems under the linearity assumption we made in Section 2.1.2 is adequate to understand the behavior of these systems when they are operated at moderate power (a few mW) and at bit rates up to about 2.5 Gb/s. However, at higher bit rates such as 10 Gb/s and above and/or at higher transmitted powers, it is important to consider the effect of nonlinearities. In the case of WDM systems, nonlinear effects can become important even at moderate powers and bit rates.

The nonlinear effects that we consider in this section arise owing to the dependence of the refractive index on the *intensity* of the applied electric field, which in turn is proportional to the square of the field amplitude. The most important nonlinear effects in this category are *self-phase modulation* (SPM) and *four-wave mixing* (FWM). Two other nonlinear effects that do not fall in this category are *stimulated Raman scattering* (SRS) and *stimulated Brillouin scattering* (SBS). We will discuss these effects in Chapter 5.

In the case of self-phase modulation, the transmitted pulses undergo chirping. This induced chirp factor becomes significant at high power levels. We have already seen in Section 2.3 that the pulse broadening effects of dispersion can be enhanced in the presence of chirp if the chirp factor κ and the GVD parameter β_2 have the same sign. Thus the SPM-induced chirp can significantly increase the dispersion penalty for these systems. For high bit rate systems, the SPM-induced chirp can significantly increase the dispersion penalty even at moderate power levels. The precise effects of

SPM are critically dependent not only on the sign of the GVD parameter β_2 but also on the length of the system.

Note that the induced chirp in a channel depends on the variation of the refractive index with the intensity on that channel. This effect is categorized as SPM. In a WDM system with multiple channels, the induced chirp in one channel depends on the variation of the refractive index with the intensity on that channel. This latter effect is called CPM.

In the case of WDM systems, another important nonlinear effect is that of four-wave mixing. If the WDM system consists of frequencies $f_1, \ldots, f_n$, four-wave mixing gives rise to new signals at frequencies such as $2f_i - f_j$ and $f_i + f_j - f_k$. These signals appear as crosstalk to the existing signals in the system. These crosstalk effects are particularly severe when the channel spacing is tight. Reduced dispersion enhances the crosstalk induced by four-wave mixing. Thus systems using dispersion-shifted fibers are much more affected by four-wave mixing effects than systems using standard single-mode fiber.

In this section, we will investigate these nonlinear effects by relaxing the linearity assumption we made in Section 2.1.2. We will continue, however, to make the other assumptions of local responsivity, isotropy, homogeneity, and losslessness on the silica medium. The losslessness assumption can be removed by carrying out the remaining discussion using complex variables for the following fields and susceptibilities, as is done, for example, in [Agr95]. However, to keep the discussion simple, we use real variables for all the fields and neglect the effect of fiber loss.

For a linear medium, as we saw in Section 2.1.2, we have the relation (2.7):

$$\tilde{\mathbf{P}}(\mathbf{r}, \omega) = \epsilon_0 \tilde{\chi}(\mathbf{r}, \omega) \tilde{\mathbf{E}}(\mathbf{r}, \omega)$$

between the Fourier transforms $\tilde{\mathbf{P}}$ and $\tilde{\mathbf{E}}$ of the induced polarizations and applied electric fields, respectively. Since we are considering nonlinearities in this section, it is no longer as convenient to work in the Fourier transform domain. By taking inverse Fourier transforms, this relation can be written in the time domain as (2.6):

$$\mathbf{P}_L(\mathbf{r}, t) = \epsilon_0 \int_{-\infty}^{t} \chi^{(1)}(t - t') \mathbf{E}(\mathbf{r}, t') \, dt', \tag{2.35}$$

where we have dropped the dependence of the susceptibility on $\mathbf{r}$ due to the homogeneity assumption, written $\mathbf{P}_L$ instead of $\mathbf{P}$ to emphasize the linearity assumption used in obtaining this relation, and used $\chi^{(1)}(,)$ instead of $\chi(,)$ for convenience in what follows.

In discussing the effect of nonlinearities, we will assume that the electric field of the fundamental mode is linearly polarized along the x direction. Recall from Section 2.1.2 that the electric field in a single-mode fiber is a linear combination of two modes, linearly polarized along the x and y directions. The following results can be generalized to this case, but the resulting expressions are significantly more complex. Hence we make the assumption of linearly polarized fields.

Because of the isotropy assumption, even in the presence of nonlinearities, the induced polarization is along the same direction as the electric field, which is the x direction, by assumption. Thus the vector functions $\mathbf{E}(\mathbf{r}, t)$ and $\mathbf{P}(\mathbf{r}, t)$ have only one component, which we will denote by the scalar functions $E(\mathbf{r}, t)$ and $P(\mathbf{r}, t)$, respectively. With this assumption, in the presence of nonlinearities, we show in Appendix C that we can write

$$P(\mathbf{r}, t) = \mathcal{P}_L(\mathbf{r}, t) + \mathcal{P}_{NL}(\mathbf{r}, t).$$

Here $\mathcal{P}_L(\mathbf{r}, t)$ is the *linear polarization* given by (2.35) with the vectors $\mathbf{P}_L(,)$ and $\mathbf{E}(,)$ replaced by the scalars $\mathcal{P}_L(,)$ and $E(,)$, respectively, due to the linear polarization assumption. The *nonlinear polarization* $\mathcal{P}_{NL}(\mathbf{r}, t)$ is given by

$$\mathcal{P}_{NL}(\mathbf{r}, t) = \epsilon_0 \chi^{(3)} E^3(\mathbf{r}, t), \tag{2.36}$$

where $\chi^{(3)}$ is called the *third-order nonlinear susceptibility* and is assumed to be a constant (independent of t). Recall that the refractive index is related to the susceptibility by (2.8). Thus the nonlinear polarization causes the refractive index to become intensity dependent, which is the root cause of these nonlinear effects. We will use this equation (2.36) as the starting point in understanding three important nonlinear phenomena affecting the propagation of signals in optical fiber: *self-phase modulation* (SPM), *cross-phase modulation* (CPM), and *four-wave mixing* (FWM). For simplicity, we will assume that the signals used are *monochromatic plane waves*; that is, the electric field is of the form

$$E(\mathbf{r}, t) = E(z, t) = E \cos(\omega_0 t - \beta_0 z),$$

where E is a constant. The term *monochromatic* implies the electric field has a single frequency component, namely, ω_0, and the term *plane wave* indicates that the electric field is constant in the plane perpendicular to the direction of propagation, z. Hence we have also written $E(z, t)$ for $E(\mathbf{r}, t)$. In the case of wavelength division multiplexed (WDM) signals, we assume that the signal in each wavelength channel is a monochromatic plane wave. Thus if there are n wavelength channels at the angular frequencies $\omega_1, \ldots, \omega_n$, with the corresponding propagation constants $\beta_1, \ldots, \beta_n$, the electric field of the composite WDM signal is

$$E(\mathbf{r}, t) = E(z, t) = \sum_{i=1}^{n} E_i \cos(\omega_i t - \beta_i z).$$

(Since the signals on each WDM channel are not necessarily in phase, we should add an arbitrary phase ϕ_i to each of the sinusoids, but we omit this in order to keep the expressions simple.)

2.4.1   Self-Phase Modulation

SPM arises because the refractive index of the fiber has an intensity-dependent component. This nonlinear refractive index causes an induced phase shift that is proportional to the intensity of the pulse. Thus different parts of the pulse undergo different phase shifts, which gives rise to chirping of the pulses. Pulse chirping in turn enhances the pulse broadening effects of dispersion. This chirping effect is proportional to the transmitted signal power so that SPM effects are more pronounced in systems using high transmitted powers. The SPM-induced chirp affects the pulse broadening effects of dispersion and thus is important to consider for high bit rate systems that already have significant dispersion limitations. For systems operating at 10 Gb/s and above, or for lower bit rate systems that use high transmitted powers, SPM can significantly increase the system penalty due to dispersion because of increased ISI.

In order to understand the effects of SPM, consider a single-channel system where the electric field is of the form

$$E(z, t) = E \cos(\omega_0 t - \beta_0 z).$$

In the presence of fiber nonlinearities, we want to find how this field evolves along the fiber. For the monochromatic plane wave we have assumed, this means finding the propagation constant β_0. Using (2.36), the nonlinear polarization is given by

$$
\begin{aligned}
\mathcal{P}_{NL}(\mathbf{r}, t) &= \epsilon_0 \chi^{(3)} E^3 \cos^3(\omega_0 t - \beta_0 z) \\
&= \epsilon_0 \chi^{(3)} E^3 \left(\frac{3}{4} \cos(\omega_0 t - \beta_0 z) + \frac{1}{4} \cos(3\omega_0 t - 3\beta_0 z) \right).
\end{aligned}
\tag{2.37}
$$

Thus the nonlinear polarization has a new frequency component at $3\omega_0$. The wave equation for the electric field (2.9) is derived assuming only the linear component of the induced polarization is present. In the presence of a nonlinear polarization component, it must be modified. We omit the details of how it should be modified but just remark that the solution of the modified equation will have, in general, electric fields at the new frequencies generated as a result of nonlinear polarization. Thus in this case, the electric field will have a component at $3\omega_0$.

The fiber has a propagation constant at the angular frequency $3\omega_0$ of the generated field, which we will denote by $\beta(3\omega_0)$. From (2.37), the electric field generated as a result of nonlinear polarization at $3\omega_0$ has a propagation constant $3\beta_0$, where

$\beta_0 = \beta(\omega_0)$ is the propagation constant at the angular frequency ω_0. In an ideal, dispersionless fiber $\beta = \omega n/c$, where the refractive index n is a constant independent of ω so that $\beta(3\omega_0) = 3\beta(\omega_0)$. But in real fibers that have dispersion, n is not a constant, and $\beta(3\omega_0)$ will be very different from $3\beta(\omega_0)$. Because of this mismatch between the two propagation constants—which is usually described as a lack of *phase match*— the electric field component at $3\omega_0$ becomes negligible. This phase-matching condition will be important in our discussion of four-wave mixing in Section 2.4.5.

Neglecting the component at $3\omega_0$, the nonlinear polarization can be written as

$$P_{NL}(\mathbf{r}, t) = \left(\frac{3}{4} \epsilon_0 \chi^{(3)} E^2 \right) E \cos(\omega_0 t - \beta_0 z). \tag{2.38}$$

When the wave equation (2.9) is modified to include the effect of nonlinear polarization and solved for β_0 with this expression for the nonlinear polarization, we get

$$\beta_0 = \frac{\omega_0}{c} \sqrt{1 + \tilde{\chi}^{(1)} + \frac{3}{4} \chi^{(3)} E^2}.$$

From (2.8), $n^2 = 1 + \tilde{\chi}^{(1)}$. Hence

$$\beta_0 = \frac{\omega_0 n}{c} \sqrt{1 + \frac{3}{4n^2} \chi^{(3)} E^2}.$$

Since $\chi^{(3)}$ is very small for silica fibers (as we will see), we can approximate this by

$$\beta_0 = \frac{\omega_0}{c} \left(n + \frac{3}{8n} \chi^{(3)} E^2 \right). \tag{2.39}$$

Thus the electric field $E(z, t) = E \cos(\omega_0 t - \beta_0 z)$ is a sinusoid whose phase changes as $E^2 z$. This phenomenon is referred to as *self-phase modulation* (SPM). The *intensity* of the electric field corresponding to a plane wave with amplitude E is $I = \frac{1}{2} \epsilon_0 c n E^2$. Thus the phase change due to SPM is proportional to the intensity of the electric field. Note that this phase change increases as the propagation distance z increases. Since the relation between β and the refractive index n in the linear regime is $\beta = \omega n/c$, we can also interpret (2.39) as specifying an *intensity-dependent refractive index*

$$\hat{n}(E) = n + \bar{n} E^2 \tag{2.40}$$

for the fiber, in the presence of nonlinearities. The quantity $\bar{n} = \frac{3}{8n} \chi^{(3)}$ is called the *nonlinear index coefficient* and varies in the range 2.2–3.4×10^{-8} $\mu m^2/W$ in silica fiber. We will assume the value 3.2×10^{-8} $\mu m^2/W$ in the numerical examples we compute. In using this value, we assume that E^2 is expressed in units of $W/\mu m^2$. Strictly speaking, it is the *intensity* of the field $I = \frac{1}{2} \epsilon_0 c n |E|^2$, which is measured in units of $W/\mu m^2$. Thus when we express $\bar{n}$ in units of $\mu m^2/W$, we have already incorporated a multiplicative factor of $2/\epsilon_0 c n$ into this value.

Pulses used in optical communication systems have finite temporal widths, and hence are nonmonochromatic. They are also not plane waves—that is, they have a transverse ((x, y) plane) distribution of the electric field that is not constant but dictated by the geometry of the fiber. Nevertheless, the same qualitative effect of self-phase modulation holds for these pulses. In this section, we will give an intuitive explanation of the effect of SPM on pulses. In Section 2.4.3, we will undertake a more quantitative explanation.

Owing to SPM, the phase of the electric field contains a term that is proportional to the intensity of the electric field. However, because of their finite temporal extent, such pulses do not have a constant intensity for the electric field. Thus the phase shift undergone by different parts of the pulse is different. Note that the sign of the phase shift due to SPM is negative because of the minus sign in the expression for the phase, namely, $\omega_0 t - \beta_0 z$. The peak of the pulse undergoes the maximum phase shift in absolute value, and its leading and trailing edges undergo progressively smaller phase shifts. Since the frequency is the derivative of the phase, the trailing edges of the pulse undergo a negative frequency shift and the leading edges a positive frequency shift. Since the chirp is proportional to the derivative of the frequency, this implies that the chirp factor κ is positive. Thus *SPM causes positive chirping* of pulses.

Owing to the relatively small value of the nonlinear susceptibility $\chi^{(3)}$ in optical fiber, the effects of SPM become important only when high powers are used (since E^2 then becomes large). Since the SPM-induced chirp changes the dispersion effects, at the same power levels, it becomes important to consider SPM effects for shorter pulses (higher bit rates) that are already severely affected by dispersion. These two points must be kept in mind during the following discussion. We will quantify the required powers and pulse durations in Section 2.4.3.

The effect of this positive chirping depends on the sign of the GVD parameter β_2. If $\beta_2 > 0$, the dispersion is said to be *normal*. Pulses in silica fiber experience normal dispersion below the zero-dispersion wavelength, which is around 1.3 μm for standard single-mode fiber. When $\beta_2 < 0$, the dispersion is said to be *anomalous*; this is the case for pulses in the entire 1.55 μm band in standard single-mode fiber. For dispersion-shifted fiber, the dispersion zero lies in the 1.55 μm band. As a result, pulses in one part of the 1.55 μm band experience normal dispersion, and pulses in the other part of the band experience anomalous dispersion. We have seen in Section 2.3 that if the product $\kappa \beta_2 > 0$, the chirp significantly enhances the pulse broadening effects of dispersion. Thus *SPM causes enhanced, monotone, pulse broadening in the normal dispersion regime.*

Even the qualitative effect of SPM in the anomalous dispersion regime depends critically on the amount of dispersion present. When the effects of SPM and dispersion are nearly equal, but dispersion dominates, SPM can actually reduce the pulse broadening effect of dispersion. This phenomenon can be understood from Figure 2.8, where we saw that a positively chirped pulse undergoes initial compression in the anomalous dispersion regime. The reason the pulse doesn't broaden considerably after this initial compression as described in Problem 2.12 is that the chirp factor is not constant for the entire pulse but dependent on the pulse amplitude (or intensity). This intensity dependence of the chirp factor is what leads to qualitatively different behaviors in the anomalous dispersion regime, depending on the amount of dispersion present. When the effects of dispersion and SPM are equal (we make this notion precise in Section 2.4.3), the pulse remains stable, that is, doesn't broaden further, after undergoing some initial broadening. When the amount of dispersion is negligible, say, around the zero-dispersion wavelength, SPM leads to amplitude modulation of the pulse.

2.4.2 Cross-Phase Modulation

In WDM systems, the intensity-dependent nonlinear effects are enhanced since the combined signal from all the channels can be quite intense, even when individual channels are operated at moderate powers. Thus the intensity-dependent phase shift, and consequent chirping, induced by SPM alone is enhanced because of the intensities of the signals in the other channels. This effect is referred to as *cross-phase modulation* (CPM).

To understand the effects of CPM, it is sufficient to consider a WDM system with two channels. For such a system,

$$E(\mathbf{r}, t) = E_1 \cos(\omega_1 t - \beta_1 z) + E_2 \cos(\omega_2 t - \beta_2 z).$$

Using (2.36), the nonlinear polarization is given by

$$
\begin{aligned}
\mathcal{P}_{NL}(\mathbf{r}, t) =&\ \epsilon_0 \chi^{(3)} \left(E_1 \cos(\omega_1 t - \beta_1 z) + E_2 \cos(\omega_2 t - \beta_2 z) \right)^3 \\
=&\ \epsilon_0 \chi^{(3)} \left[\left(\frac{3E_1^3}{4} + \frac{3E_2^2 E_1}{2} \right) \cos(\omega_1 t - \beta_1 z) \right. \\
&\ + \left(\frac{3E_2^3}{4} + \frac{3E_1^2 E_2}{2} \right) \cos(\omega_2 t - \beta_2 z) \\
&\ + \frac{3E_1^2 E_2}{4} \cos((2\omega_1 - \omega_2)t - (2\beta_1 - \beta_2)z) \\
&\ + \frac{3E_2^2 E_1}{4} \cos((2\omega_2 - \omega_1)t - (2\beta_2 - \beta_1)z) \\
&\ + \frac{3E_1^2 E_2}{4} \cos((2\omega_1 + \omega_2)t - (2\beta_1 + \beta_2)z)
\end{aligned}
$$

$$+ \frac{3E_2^2 E_1}{4} \cos((2\omega_2 + \omega_1)t - (2\beta_2 + \beta_1)z)$$

$$+ \frac{E_1^3}{4} \cos(3\omega_1 t - 3\beta_1 z)$$

$$+ \frac{E_2^3}{4} \cos(3\omega_1 t - 3\beta_1 z) \Bigg].$$

$$(2.41)$$

The terms at $2\omega_1 + \omega_2$, $2\omega_2 + \omega_1$, $3\omega_1$, and $3\omega_2$ can be neglected since the phase-matching condition will not be satisfied for these terms owing to the presence of fiber dispersion. We will discuss the terms at $2\omega_1 - \omega_2$ and $2\omega_2 - \omega_1$ in Section 2.4.5 when we consider four-wave mixing. The component of the nonlinear polarization at the frequency ω_1 is

$$\frac{3}{4}\epsilon_0 \chi^{(3)} \left(E_1^2 + 2E_1 E_2 \right) E_1 \cos(\omega_1 t - \beta_1 t).$$

$$(2.42)$$

When the wave equation (2.9) is modified to include the effect of nonlinear polarization and solved for the resulting electric field, this field has a sinusoidal component at ω_1 whose phase changes in proportion to $(E_1^2 + 2E_2 E_1)z$. The first term is due to SPM, whereas the effect of the second term is called *cross-phase modulation* or CPM. Note that if $E_1 = E_2$ so that the two fields have the same intensity, the effect of CPM appears to be twice as bad as that of SPM. Since the effect of CPM is qualitatively similar to that of SPM, we expect CPM to exacerbate the chirping and consequent pulse spreading effects of SPM in WDM systems, which we discussed in Section 2.4.1.

In practice, the effect of CPM in WDM systems operating over standard single-mode fiber can be significantly reduced by increasing the wavelength spacing between the individual channels. Owing to fiber dispersion, the propagation constants β_i of these channels then become sufficiently different so that the pulses corresponding to individual channels *walk away* from each other. This is the case, for example, with channel spacings of 100 GHz. Owing to this *pulse walk-off* phenomenon, the pulses, which were initially temporally coincident, cease to be so after propagating for some distance, and cannot interact further. Thus the effect of CPM is reduced. In general, all nonlinear effects in optical fiber are weak and depend on long interaction lengths to build up to significant levels. So any mechanism that reduces the interaction length decreases the effect of the nonlinearity. Note, however, that in dispersion-shifted fiber, the pulses in different channels do not walk away from each other since they travel with approximately the same group velocities. Thus CPM can be a significant problem in high-speed (10 Gb/s and higher) WDM systems operating over dispersion-shifted fiber.

2.4.3   Nonlinear Effects on Pulse Propagation *

So far, we have understood the origins of SPM and CPM and the fact that these effects result in changing the phase of the pulse as a function of its intensity (and the intensity of other pulses at different wavelengths in the case of CPM). To understand the magnitude of this phase change or chirping and how it interacts with dispersion, we will need to go back and look at the differential equation governing the evolution of the pulse shape as it propagates in the fiber. We will also find that this relationship is important in understanding the fundamentals of *solitons* in Section 2.5.

We will consider pulses for which the magnitude of the associated (real) electric field vector is given by (2.22), which is

$$|\mathbf{E}(\mathbf{r}, t)| = J(x, y)\Re[A(z, t)e^{-i(\omega_0 t - \beta_0 z)}].$$

Recall that $J(x, y)$ is the transverse distribution of the electric field of the fundamental mode dictated by the geometry of the fiber, $A(z, t)$ is the complex envelope of the pulse, ω_0 is its center frequency, and $\Re[\cdot]$ denotes the real part of its argument. Let A_0 denote the peak amplitude of the pulse, and $P_0 = A_0^2$ its peak power.

We have seen that the refractive index becomes intensity dependent in the presence of SPM, and is given by (2.40) for a plane monochromatic wave. For non-monochromatic pulses with envelope A propagating in optical fiber, this relation must be modified so that the frequency *and* intensity-dependent refractive index is now given by

$$\hat{n}(\omega, E) = n(\omega) + \bar{n}|A|^2/A_e. \tag{2.43}$$

Here, $n(\omega)$ is the linear refractive index, which is frequency dependent because of dispersion, but also intensity independent, and A_e is the effective cross-sectional area of the fiber, which is typically $50 \ \mu m^2$ (see Figure 5.28 in Chapter 5 and the accompanying explanation). The expression for the propagation constant (2.39) must also be similarly modified, and the frequency and intensity-dependent propagation constant is now given by

$$\hat{\beta}(\omega, E) = \beta(\omega) + \frac{\omega \, \bar{n}|A|^2}{c \ A_e}. \tag{2.44}$$

Note that in (2.43) and (2.44) when we use the value $\bar{n} = 3.2 \times 10^{-8} \ \mu m^2/W$, the intensity of the pulse $|A|^2$ must be expressed in watts (W). We assume this is the case in what follows and will refer to $|A|^2$ as the power of the pulse (though, strictly speaking, it is only proportional to the power).

For convenience, we denote

$$\gamma = \frac{\omega \ \bar{n}}{c \ A_e} = \frac{2\pi \ \bar{n}}{\lambda \ A_e}$$

and thus $\hat{\beta} = \beta + \gamma|A|^2$. Comparing this with (2.43), we see that γ bears the same relationship to the propagation constant β as the nonlinear index coefficient $\bar{n}$ does to the refractive index n. Hence, we call γ the *nonlinear propagation coefficient*. At a wavelength $\lambda = 1.55 \ \mu$m and taking $A_e = 50 \ \mu$m^2, $\gamma = 2.6$ /W-km.

To take into account the intensity dependence of the propagation constant, (2.24) must be modified to read

$$\frac{\partial A}{\partial z} + \beta_1 \frac{\partial A}{\partial t} + \frac{i}{2}\beta_2 \frac{\partial^2 A}{\partial t^2} = i\gamma|A|^2 A. \tag{2.45}$$

In this equation, the term $\frac{i}{2}\beta_2 \frac{\partial^2 A}{\partial t^2}$ incorporates the effect of dispersion, as discussed in Section 2.3, and the term $i\gamma|A|^2 A$ incorporates the intensity-dependent phase shift.

Note that this equation incorporates the effect of dispersion also. The combined effects of dispersion and SPM on pulse propagation can thus be analyzed using this equation as the starting point. These effects are qualitatively different from that of dispersion or SPM acting alone.

In order to understand the relative effects of dispersion and SPM, it is convenient to introduce the following change of variables:

$$\tau = \frac{t - \beta_1 z}{T_0}, \qquad \xi = \frac{z}{L_D} = \frac{z|\beta_2|}{T_0^2}, \qquad \text{and} \qquad U = \frac{A}{\sqrt{P_0}}. \tag{2.46}$$

In these new variables, (2.45) can be written as

$$i\frac{\partial U}{\partial \xi} - \frac{\text{sgn}(\beta_2)}{2}\frac{\partial^2 U}{\partial \tau^2} + N^2|U|^2 U = 0, \tag{2.47}$$

where

$$N^2 = \gamma P_0 L_D = \frac{\gamma P_0}{|\beta_2|/T_0^2}.$$

This equation (2.47) is called the Nonlinear Schrödinger equation (NLSE).

The change of variables introduced by (2.46) has the following interpretation. Since the pulse propagates with velocity β_1 (in the absence of dispersion), $t - \beta_1 z$ is the time axis in a reference frame moving with the pulse. The variable τ is the time in this reference frame but in units of T_0, which is a measure of the pulse width. The variable ξ measures distance in units of the *dispersion length* $L_D = T_0^2/|\beta_2|$, which we already encountered in Section 2.3. The quantity P_0 represents the peak power of the pulse, and thus U is the envelope of the pulse normalized to have unit peak power.

Note that the quantity $1/\gamma P_0$ also has the dimensions of length; we call it the *nonlinear length* and denote it by L_{NL}. Using $\gamma = 2.6$ /W-km and $P_0 = 1$ mW, we get $L_{NL} = 384$ km. If the pulse power P_0 is increased to 10 mW, the nonlinear length decreases to 38 km. The nonlinear length serves as a convenient normalizing measure for the distance z in discussing nonlinear effects, just as the dispersion length does for the effects of dispersion. Thus the effect of SPM on pulses can be neglected for pulses propagating over distances $z \ll L_{NL}$. Then we can write the quantity N introduced in the NLSE as $N^2 = L_D/L_{NL}$. Thus it is the ratio of the dispersion and nonlinear lengths. When $N \ll 1$, the nonlinear length is much larger than the dispersion length so that the nonlinear effects can be neglected compared to those of dispersion. This amounts to saying that the third term (the one involving N) in the NLSE can be neglected. In this case, the NLSE reduces to the equation (2.24) for the evolution of pulses in the presence of dispersion alone, with the change of variables given by (2.46).

The NLSE serves as the starting point for the discussion of the combined effects of GVD and SPM. For arbitrary values of N, the NLSE has to be solved numerically. These numerical solutions are important tools for the understanding of the combined effects of dispersion and nonlinearities on pulses and are discussed extensively in [Agr95]. The qualitative description of these solutions in both the normal and anomalous dispersion regimes is discussed in Section 2.4.1.

We can use (2.45) to estimate the SPM-induced chirp for Gaussian pulses. To do this, we neglect the dispersion term and consider the equation

$$\frac{\partial A}{\partial z} + \beta_1 \frac{\partial A}{\partial t} = i\gamma |A|^2 A. \tag{2.48}$$

By using the variables τ and U introduced in (2.46) instead of t and A, and $L_{NL} = (\gamma P_0)^{-1}$, this reduces to

$$\frac{\partial U}{\partial z} = \frac{i}{L_{NL}} |U|^2 U. \tag{2.49}$$

Note that we have not used the change of variable ξ for z since L_D is infinite when dispersion is neglected. This equation has the solution

$$U(z, \tau) = U(0, \tau) e^{iz|U(0,\tau)|^2/L_{NL}}. \tag{2.50}$$

Thus the SPM causes a phase change but no change in the envelope of the pulse. Note that the initial pulse envelope $U(0, \tau)$ is arbitrary; so this is true for all pulse shapes. Thus *SPM by itself leads only to chirping, regardless of the pulse shape*; it is dispersion that is responsible for pulse broadening. The SPM-induced chirp, however, modifies the pulse broadening effects of dispersion.

2.4.4 SPM-Induced Chirp for Gaussian Pulses

Consider an initially unchirped Gaussian pulse with envelope $U(0, \tau) = e^{-\tau^2/2}$. We have assumed a normalized envelope so that the pulse has unit peak amplitude and $1/e$-width $T_0 = 1$. For such a pulse, the parameter

$$L_{NL} = \frac{\lambda A_e}{2\pi \bar{n} P_0}$$

is called the nonlinear length. Here P_0 is the peak power of the pulse, assumed to be unity in this case. If the link length is comparable to the nonlinear length, the effect of the nonlinearity can be quite severe.

In the presence of SPM alone (neglecting dispersion), this pulse acquires a distance-dependent chirp. The initially unchirped pulse and the same pulse with an SPM-induced chirp after the pulse has propagated a distance $L = 3L_{NL}$ are shown in Figure 2.12. In this figure, the center frequency of the pulse is vastly diminished for the purposes of illustration.

Using (2.50), the SPM-induced phase change can be calculated to be $-(L/L_{NL})e^{-\tau^2}$. Using the definition of the instantaneous frequency and chirp factor from Section 2.3, we can calculate the instantaneous frequency of this pulse to be

$$\omega = \omega_0 + \frac{2L}{L_{NL}} \tau e^{-\tau^2}$$

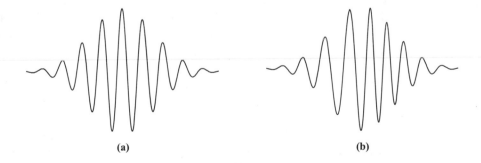

(a) (b)

Figure 2.12 Illustration of the SPM-induced chirp. (a) An unchirped Gaussian pulse. (b) The pulse in (a) after it has propagated a distance $L = 3L_{NL}$ under the effect of SPM. (Dispersion has been neglected.)

and the chirp factor of this pulse to be

$$\kappa_{\text{SPM}} = \frac{2L}{L_{NL}} e^{-\tau^2} (1 - 2\tau^2). \tag{2.51}$$

Here ω_0 is the center frequency of the pulse. The SPM-induced phase change, the change, $\omega - \omega_0$, in the instantaneous frequency from the center frequency, and the chirp factor are plotted in Figure 2.13, for $L = L_{NL}$. Note that the SPM-induced chirp is not linear since it depends on τ. Near the center of the pulse when $\tau \approx 0$, $\kappa_{\text{SPM}} \approx 2L/L_{NL}$. The SPM-induced chirp is thus positive around the center of the pulse and is significant if L is comparable to L_{NL}. For example, if $L = L_{NL}$, the chirp factor at the pulse center is equal to 2.

The SPM-induced chirp appears to increase linearly with distance from (2.51). However, this is true only when losses are neglected. To take into account the effect of fiber loss, the expression (2.51) for the SPM-induced chirp should be modified by replacing L by the *effective length* L_e defined by

$$L_e \stackrel{\text{def}}{=} \frac{1 - e^{-\alpha L}}{\alpha}. \tag{2.52}$$

Note that $L_e < 1/\alpha$ and $L_e \to 1/\alpha$ for large L. Thus the SPM-induced chirp at the pulse center is bounded above by $2/L_{NL}\alpha$. At 1.55 μm, $\alpha \approx 0.22$ dB/km and $1/\alpha \approx 20$ km. Thus, regardless of the propagated distance L, the SPM-induced chirp is significant only if L_{NL} is comparable to 20 km. Since we calculated that the nonlinear length $L_{NL} = 384$ km for a transmitted power of 1 mW, the SPM-induced effects can be neglected at these power levels. At a transmitted power level of 10 mW, $L_{NL} = 38$ km so that SPM effects cannot be neglected.

The combined effects of SPM-induced chirp and dispersion can be studied by numerically solving the NLSE (2.47). For simplicity, we consider the following approximate expression for the width $|T_L|$ of an initially unchirped Gaussian pulse after it has propagated a distance L:

$$\frac{|T_L|}{T_0} = \sqrt{1 + \sqrt{2}\frac{L_e}{L_{NL}}\frac{L}{L_D} + \left(1 + \frac{4}{3\sqrt{3}}\frac{L_e^2}{L_{NL}^2}\right)\frac{L^2}{L_D^2}}. \tag{2.53}$$

This expression is derived in [PAP86] starting from the NLSE and is also discussed in [Agr95]. Note the similarity of this expression to the broadening factor for chirped Gaussian pulses (2.25); L_e/L_{NL} in (2.53) serves the role of the chirp factor in (2.25).

Consider a 10 Gb/s system operating over standard single-mode fiber at 1.55 μm. Since $\beta_2 < 0$ and the SPM-induced chirp is positive, from Figure 2.9 we expect that pulses will initially undergo compression and subsequently broaden. Since the SPM-induced chirp increases with the transmitted power, we expect both the extent

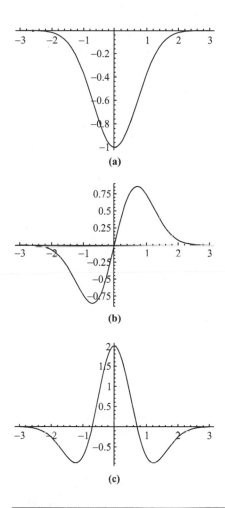

Figure 2.13 The phase (a), instantaneous frequency (b), and chirp (c) of an initially unchirped Gaussian pulse after it has propagated a distance $L = L_{NL}$.

of initial compression and the rate of subsequent broadening to increase with the transmitted power. This is indeed the case as can be seen from Figure 2.14, where we use (2.53) to plot the evolution of the pulse width as a function of the link length, taking into account the chirp induced by SPM. We consider an initially unchirped Gaussian pulse of width (half-width at $1/e$-intensity point) 50 ps, which is half the bit period. Three different transmitted powers, 1 mW, 10 mW, and 20 mW, are considered. As expected, for a transmit power of 20 mW, the pulse compresses more

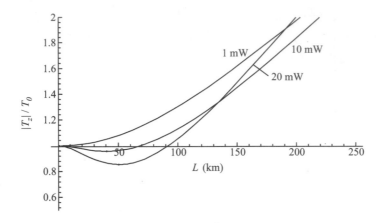

Figure 2.14 Evolution of pulse width as a function of the link length L for transmitted powers of 1 mW, 10 mW, and 20 mW, taking into account the chirp induced by SPM. A 10 Gb/s system operating over standard single-mode fiber at 1.55 μm with an initial pulse width of 50 ps is considered.

initially but subsequently broadens more rapidly so that the pulse width exceeds that of a system operating at 10 mW or even 1 mW. The optimal transmit power therefore depends on the link length and the amount of dispersion present. For standard single-mode fiber in the 1.55 μm band, the optimal power is limited to the 2–10 mW range for link lengths of the order of 100 km and is a real limit today for 10 Gb/s systems. We can use higher transmit powers to optimize other system parameters such as the signal-to-noise ratio (SNR) but at the cost of increasing the pulse broadening due to the combined effects of SPM and dispersion.

In amplified systems, as we will see in Chapter 5, two things happen: the effective length L_e is multiplied by the number of amplifier spans as the amplifier resets the power after each span, and in general, higher output powers are possible. Both of these serve to exacerbate the effects of nonlinearities.

In WDM systems, CPM aids the SPM-induced intensity dependence of the refractive index. Thus in WDM systems, these effects may become important even at lower power levels particularly when dispersion-shifted fiber is used so that the dispersion-induced walk-off effects on CPM are minimized.

2.4.5   Four-Wave Mixing

In a WDM system using the angular frequencies $\omega_1, \ldots, \omega_n$, the intensity dependence of the refractive index not only induces phase shifts within a channel but also gives rise to signals at new frequencies such as $2\omega_i - \omega_j$ and $\omega_i + \omega_j - \omega_k$. This phenomenon is called *four-wave mixing*. In contrast to SPM and CPM, which are significant mainly for high bit rate systems, the four-wave mixing effect is independent of the bit rate but is critically dependent on the channel spacing and fiber dispersion. Decreasing the channel spacing increases the four-wave mixing effect, and so does decreasing the dispersion. Thus the effects of FWM must be considered even for moderate bit rate systems when the channels are closely spaced and/or dispersion-shifted fibers are used.

To understand the effects of four-wave mixing, consider a WDM signal that is the sum of n monochromatic plane waves. Thus the electric field of this signal can be written as

$$E(\mathbf{r}, t) = \sum_{i=1}^{n} E_i \cos(\omega_i t - \beta_i z)$$

Using (2.36), the nonlinear polarization is given by

$$
\begin{aligned}
\mathcal{P}_{NL}(\mathbf{r}, t) \;=\;& \epsilon_0 \chi^{(3)} \sum_{i=1}^{n} \sum_{j=1}^{n} \sum_{k=1}^{n} E_i \cos(\omega_i t - \beta_i z) E_j \cos(\omega_j t - \beta_j z) E_k \cos(\omega_k t - \beta_k z) \\[2mm]
=\;& \frac{3\epsilon_0 \chi^{(3)}}{4} \sum_{i=1}^{n} \left(E_i^2 + 2\sum_{j \neq i} E_i E_j \right) E_i \cos(\omega_i t - \beta_i z) & (2.54)
\end{aligned}
$$

$$+ \frac{\epsilon_0 \chi^{(3)}}{4} \sum_{i=1}^{n} E_i^3 \cos(3\omega_i t - 3\beta_i z) \qquad\qquad\qquad (2.55)$$

$$+ \frac{3\epsilon_0 \chi^{(3)}}{4} \sum_{i=1}^{n} \sum_{j \neq i} E_i^2 E_j \cos((2\omega_i - \omega_j)t - (2\beta_i - \beta_j)z) \qquad (2.56)$$

$$+ \frac{3\epsilon_0 \chi^{(3)}}{4} \sum_{i=1}^{n} \sum_{j \neq i} E_i^2 E_j \cos((2\omega_i + \omega_j)t - (2\beta_i + \beta_j)z) \qquad (2.57)$$

$$+ \frac{6\epsilon_0 \chi^{(3)}}{4} \sum_{i=1}^{n} \sum_{j>i} \sum_{k>j} E_i E_j E_k$$

$$\Big(\cos((\omega_i + \omega_j + \omega_k)t - (\beta_i + \beta_j + \beta_k)z) \qquad (2.58)$$

$$+ \cos((\omega_i + \omega_j - \omega_k)t - (\beta_i + \beta_j - \beta_k)z) \qquad (2.59)$$

$$+ \cos((\omega_i - \omega_j + \omega_k)t - (\beta_i - \beta_j + \beta_k)z) \qquad (2.60)$$

$$+ \cos((\omega_i - \omega_j - \omega_k)t - (\beta_i - \beta_j - \beta_k)z)\bigg). \qquad (2.61)$$

Thus the nonlinear susceptibility of the fiber generates new fields (waves) at the frequencies $\omega_i \pm \omega_j \pm \omega_k$ (ω_i, ω_j, ω_k not necessarily distinct). This phenomenon is termed *four-wave mixing*. The reason for this term is that three *waves* with the frequencies ω_i, ω_j, and ω_k combine to generate a *fourth* wave at a frequency $\omega_i \pm \omega_j \pm \omega_k$.

The term (2.54) represents the effect of SPM and CPM that we have discussed in Sections 2.4.1 and 2.4.2. The terms (2.55), (2.57), and (2.58) can be neglected because of lack of phase matching. Under suitable circumstances, it is possible to approximately satisfy the phase-matching condition for the remaining terms, which are all of the form $\omega_i + \omega_j - \omega_k$, i, $j \neq k$ (ω_i, ω_j not necessarily distinct). For example, if the wavelengths in the WDM system are closely spaced, or are spaced near the dispersion zero of the fiber, then β is nearly constant over these frequencies and the phase-matching condition is nearly satisfied. When this is so, the power generated at these frequencies can be quite significant.

There is a compact way to express these four-wave mixing terms of the form $\omega_i + \omega_j - \omega_k$, i, $j \neq k$, that is frequently used in the literature. Define $\omega_{ijk} = \omega_i + \omega_j - \omega_k$ and the *degeneracy factor*

$$d_{ijk} = \begin{cases} 3, & i = j, \\ 6, & i \neq j. \end{cases}$$

Then the nonlinear polarization term at ω_{ijk} can be written as

$$\mathcal{P}_{ijk}(z, t) = \frac{\epsilon_0 \chi^{(3)}}{4} d_{ijk} E_i E_j E_k \cos((\omega_i + \omega_j - \omega_k)t - (\beta_i + \beta_j - \beta_k)z). \qquad (2.62)$$

If we assume that the optical signals propagate as plane waves over an effective cross-sectional area A_e within the fiber (see Figure 5.28) using (2.62), it can be shown that the power of the signal generated at the frequency ω_{ijk} after traversing a fiber length of L is

$$P_{ijk} = \left(\frac{\omega_{ijk} d_{ijk} \chi^{(3)}}{8 A_e n_{\text{eff}} c} \right)^2 P_i P_j P_k L^2,$$

where P_i, P_j, and P_k are the input powers at ω_i, ω_j, and ω_k. Note that the refractive index n is replaced by the effective index n_{eff} of the fundamental mode. In terms of the nonlinear refractive index $\bar{n}$, this can be written as

$$P_{ijk} = \left(\frac{\omega_{ijk} \bar{n} d_{ijk}}{3 c A_e} \right)^2 P_i P_j P_k L^2. \qquad (2.63)$$

We now consider a numerical example. We assume that each of the optical signals at $\omega_i, \omega_j,$ and ω_k has a power 1 mW and the effective cross-sectional area of the fiber is $A_e = 50 \ \mu\text{m}^2$. We also assume $\omega_i \neq \omega_j$ so that $d_{ijk} = 6$. Using $\bar{n} = 3.0 \times 10^{-8} \ \mu\text{m}^2/\text{W}$, and taking the propagation distance $L = 20$ km, we calculate that the power P_{ijk} of the signal at the frequency ω_{ijk} generated by the four-wave mixing process is about 9.5 μW. Note that this is only about 20 dB below the signal power of 1 mW. In a WDM system, if another channel happens to be located at ω_{ijk}, the four-wave mixing process can produce significant degradation of that channel.

In practice, the signals generated by four-wave mixing have lower powers due to the lack of perfect phase matching and the attenuation of signals due to fiber loss. We will consider some numerical examples that include these effects in Chapter 5.

2.5 Solitons

Solitons are narrow pulses with high peak powers and special shapes. The most commonly used soliton pulses are called *fundamental solitons*, and the shape of these pulses is shown in Figure 2.15. As we have seen in Section 2.3, most pulses undergo broadening (spreading in time) due to group velocity dispersion when propagating through optical fiber. However, the soliton pulses take advantage of nonlinear effects in silica, specifically self-phase modulation (SPM) discussed in Section 2.4.1, to overcome the pulse broadening effects of group velocity dispersion. Thus these pulses can propagate for long distances with no change in shape.

We saw in Section 2.3 that the pulse envelope propagates with the group velocity $1/\beta_1$ along the fiber and that, in general, owing to the effects of group velocity dispersion, the pulse progressively broadens as it propagates. If $\beta_2 = 0$, all pulse shapes propagate without broadening, but if $\beta_2 \neq 0$, is there any pulse shape that propagates without broadening? The key to the answer lies in the one exception to this pulse broadening effect that we already encountered in Section 2.3, namely, that if the chirp parameter of the pulse has the right sign (opposite to that of β_2), the pulse initially undergoes compression. But we have seen that even in this case (Problem 2.12), the pulse subsequently broadens. This happens in all cases where the chirp is *independent* of the pulse envelope. However, when the chirp is induced by SPM, the degree of chirp depends on the pulse envelope. If the relative effects of SPM and GVD are controlled just right, and the appropriate pulse shape is chosen, the pulse compression effect undergone by chirped pulses can exactly offset the pulse broadening effect of dispersion. The pulse shapes for which this balance between pulse compression and broadening occurs so that the pulse either undergoes no change in shape or undergoes periodic changes in shape only are called *solitons*. The

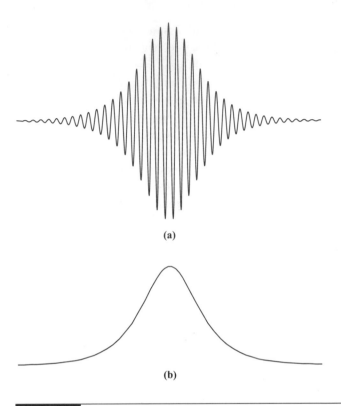

Figure 2.15   (a) A fundamental soliton pulse and (b) its envelope.

family of pulses that undergo no change in shape are called *fundamental solitons*, and those that undergo periodic changes in shape are called *higher-order solitons*.

The significance of solitons for optical communication is that they overcome the detrimental effects of chromatic dispersion completely. Optical amplifiers can be used at periodic intervals along the fiber so that the attenuation undergone by the pulses is not significant. Solitons and optical amplifiers, when used together, offer the promise of very high bit rate, repeaterless, data transmission over very large distances. By the combined use of solitons and Erbium-doped fiber amplifiers (Section 3.4.3), repeaterless data transmission at a bit rate of 20 Gb/s over a distance of 7150 km has been demonstrated in the laboratory [Big97].

Soliton transmission systems are being actively researched today. Their main advantage is their relative immunity to fiber dispersion, which in turn allows transmission at high speeds of a few tens of Gb/s. On the other hand, there are other, simpler methods to manage dispersion in a conventional on–off-keyed system, as we will study in Chapter 5. Solitons can also be used in conjunction with WDM, but significant impairments arise when two pulses at different wavelengths overlap in time and position in the fiber. Such collisions, which occur frequently in the fiber, add timing jitter to the pulses. For these reasons, soliton systems are not yet commercially deployed.

As for optical networks, solitons primarily find application in time division multiplexed networks. The use of soliton pulses is key to the realization of the very high bit rates required in OTDM systems. These aspects of solitons will be explored in Chapter 14.

In the next section, we will undertake a brief quantitative discussion of soliton propagation in optical fiber.

2.6   Soliton Pulse Propagation *

In the anomalous dispersion regime (1.55 μm band for standard single-mode fiber and most dispersion-shifted fibers), the GVD parameter β_2 is negative. Thus $\text{sgn}(\beta_2) = -1$, and the NLSE of (2.47) can be written as

$$i\frac{\partial U}{\partial \xi} + \frac{1}{2}\frac{\partial^2 U}{\partial \tau^2} + N^2 |U|^2 U = 0. \tag{2.64}$$

An interesting phenomenon occurs in this anomalous dispersion regime when N is an integer. In this case, the modified NLSE (2.64) can be solved analytically, and the resulting pulse envelope has an amplitude that is independent of ξ (for $N = 1$) or periodic in ξ (for $N \geq 2$). This implies that these pulses propagate with no change in their widths or with a periodic change in their widths. The solutions of this equation are termed *solitons*, and N is called the *order* of the soliton.

It can be verified that the solution of (2.64) corresponding to $N = 1$ is

$$U(\xi, \tau) = e^{i\xi/2}\text{sech}\tau. \tag{2.65}$$

The pulse corresponding to this envelope is called the *fundamental soliton*. The fundamental soliton pulse and its envelope are sketched in Figure 2.15(a) and (b), respectively. (As in the case of chirped Gaussian pulses in Section 2.3, the frequency of the pulse is shown vastly diminished for the purposes of illustration.)

Note that (in a reference frame moving with the pulse) the magnitude of the fundamental soliton pulse envelope, or the pulse shape, does not change with the distance coordinate z. However, the pulse acquires a phase shift that is linear in z as it propagates.

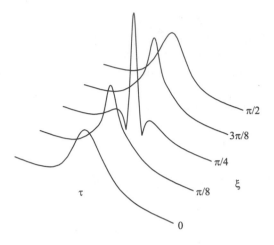

Figure 2.16   The magnitude of the pulse envelope of the second-order soliton.

Recall that the order of the soliton, N, is defined by

$$N^2 = \gamma P_0 L_D = \frac{\gamma P_0}{|\beta_2|/T_0^2}.$$

Since γ and β_2 are fixed for a given fiber and operating wavelength, for a fixed soliton order, the peak power P_0 of the pulse increases as the pulse width T_0 decreases. Since operation at very high bit rates requires narrow pulses, this also implies that large peak powers are necessary in soliton communication systems.

It can also be verified that the solution of (2.64) corresponding to $N = 2$ is

$$U(\xi, \tau) = 4e^{i\xi/2} \frac{\cosh 3\tau + 3\cosh \tau e^{i4\xi}}{\cosh 4\tau + 4\cosh 2\tau + 3\cos 4\xi}. \tag{2.66}$$

The magnitude of this normalized pulse envelope is sketched in Figure 2.16 as a function of ξ and τ. The periodicity of the pulse envelope with respect to ξ can be clearly seen from this plot. In each period, the pulse envelope first undergoes compression due to the positive chirping induced by SPM and then undergoes broadening, finally regaining its original shape.

Summary

The understanding of light propagation in optical fiber is key to the appreciation of not only the significant advantages of using optical fiber as a propagation medium but also of the problems that we must tackle in designing high bit rate WDM systems. We started by understanding how light propagates in multimode fibers using a simple ray theory approach. This introduced the concept of pulse broadening due to multimode dispersion and motivated the use of single-mode fibers. After describing the elements of light propagation in single-mode fibers, we studied the limitations imposed on optical communication systems due to the pulse broadening effects of chromatic dispersion. Although dispersion is the most important phenomenon limiting the performance of systems at bit rates of 2.5 Gb/s and below, nonlinear effects become important at higher bit rates. Hence we studied the origin of these nonlinear effects and briefly outlined the constraints on optical communication systems imposed by them. We will return to the system limitations of both dispersion and nonlinearities when we discuss the design of optical transmission systems in Chapter 5.

Further Reading

The propagation of light in optical fiber is treated in several books at varying levels of detail. One of the earliest books on this subject is the one by Marcuse [Mar74]. The book by Green [Gre93] starts with the fundamentals of both geometrical optics and electromagnetics and describes the propagation of light using both the ray and wave theory approaches. The concepts of polarization and birefringence are also treated in some detail. However, the effects of dispersion and nonlinearities are described only qualitatively. The book on fiber optic communication by Agrawal [Agr92] focuses on the wave theory approach and treats the evolution of chirped Gaussian pulses in optical fiber and the pulse broadening effects of chromatic dispersion in detail. Chromatic dispersion and modal dispersion are also treated at length in the books by Miller and Kaminow [MK88] and Lin [Lin89]. We recommend the book by Ramo, Whinnery, and van Duzer [RWv84] for an in-depth study of electromagnetic theory leading up to the description of light propagation in fiber. The books by Jeunhomme [Jeu90] and Neumann [Neu88] are devoted to the propagation of light in single-mode fibers. Jeunhomme treats fiber modes in detail and has a more mathematical treatment. We recommend Neumann's book for its physical explanations of the phenomena involved.

In all these books, nonlinear effects are only briefly mentioned. The book by Agrawal [Agr95] is devoted to nonlinear fiber optics and contains a very detailed description of light propagation in optical fiber, including all the nonlinear effects we have discussed. Soliton propagation is also discussed. One of the earliest papers on four-wave mixing is [HJKM78]. Note that cgs units are used in this paper. The units used in the description of nonlinear effects are a source of confusion. The relationships between the various units and terminologies used in the description of nonlinear effects are described in the book by Butcher and Cotter [BC90]. This book also contains a particularly clear exposition of the fundamentals of nonlinear effects. The system impact of dispersion and nonlinearities and their interplay is discussed in detail in [KK97]. A nice treatment of the basics of solitons appears in [KBW96].

Problems

2.1 Show that the numerical aperture NA of a step-index multimode fiber is

$$NA = \sqrt{n_1^2 - n_2^2}.$$

2.2 A standard multimode glass fiber has a core diameter of 50 μm and cladding refractive index of 1.45. If it is to have a limiting modal dispersion δT of 10 ns/km, find its numerical aperture. Also calculate the maximum bit rate for transmission over a distance of 20 km.

2.3 Derive equation (2.10) for the evolution of the magnetic field vector $\tilde{\mathbf{H}}$.

2.4 Derive an expression for the cutoff wavelength λ_{cutoff} of a step-index fiber with core radius a, core refractive index n_1, and cladding refractive index n_2. Calculate the cutoff wavelength of a fiber with core radius $a = 4$ μm and $\Delta = 0.003$.

2.5 Consider a step-index fiber with a core radius of 4 μm and a cladding refractive index of 1.45.
   (a) For what range of values of the core refractive index will the fiber be single moded for all wavelengths in the 1.2–1.6 μm range?
   (b) What is the value of the core refractive index for which the V parameter is 2.0 at $\lambda = 1.55$ μm? What is the propagation constant of the single mode supported by the fiber for this value of the core refractive index?

2.6 Assume that, in the manufacture of single-mode fiber, the tolerance in the core radius a is $\pm 5\%$ and the tolerance in the normalized refractive index difference Δ is $\pm 10\%$, from their respective nominal values. If the nominal value of Δ is specified to be 0.005, what is the largest nominal value that you can specify for a while ensuring that the resulting fiber will be single moded for $\lambda > 1.2$ μm even in the presence of the worst-case (but within the specified tolerances) deviations of a and Δ from their nominal values? Assume that the refractive index of the core is 1.5.

2.7 In a reference frame moving with the pulse, the basic propagation equation that governs pulse evolution inside a dispersive fiber is

$$\frac{\partial A}{\partial z} + \frac{i}{2}\beta_2 \frac{\partial^2 A}{\partial t^2} = 0,$$

where $A(z, t)$ is the pulse envelope. If $A(0, t) = A_0 \exp(-t^2/2T_0^2)$ for some constants A_0 and T_0, solve this propagation equation to find an expression for $A(z, t)$.

Note: You may use the following result without proof:

$$\int_{-\infty}^{\infty} \exp(-(x - m)^2/2\alpha)\, dx = \sqrt{2\pi\alpha}$$

for all *complex* m and α provided $\Re(\alpha) > 0$.

Hint: Consider the Fourier transform $\tilde{A}(z, \omega)$ of $A(z, t)$.

2.8 Starting from (2.28), derive the expression (2.25) for the width T_z of a chirped Gaussian pulse with initial width T_0 after it has propagated a distance z.

2.9 Show that an unchirped Gaussian pulse launched at $z = 0$ remains Gaussian for all z but acquires a distance-dependent chirp factor

$$\kappa(z) = \frac{\mathrm{sgn}(\beta_2)z/L_D}{1 + (z/L_D)^2}.$$

2.10 Show that the rms width of a Gaussian pulse whose half-width at the $1/e$-intensity point is T_0 is given by $T_0/\sqrt{2}$.

2.11 For a narrow but chirped Gaussian pulse with chirp factor $\kappa = -6$, calculate the chromatic dispersion limit at a bit rate of 1 Gb/s, in the 1.55 μm band, for a penalty of 2 dB. Compare this with the chromatic dispersion limit for unchirped pulses plotted in Figure 2.10.

2.12 Consider a chirped Gaussian pulse for which the product $\kappa\beta_2$ is negative that is launched at $z = 0$. Let $\kappa = 5$.
   (a) For what value of z (as a multiple of L_D) does the launched pulse attain its minimum width?
   (b) For what value of z is the width of the pulse equal to that of an unchirped pulse, for the same value of z? (Assume the chirped and unchirped pulses have the same initial pulse width.)

2.13 Show that the optimum choice of the pulse width of an unchirped Gaussian pulse (with narrow spectral width) that minimizes the pulse broadening effects of chromatic dispersion over a fiber of length L is

$$T_0^{\mathrm{opt}} = \sqrt{\beta_2 L}.$$

2.14 In discussing the chromatic dispersion penalty, the Bellcore standard for SONET systems [Bel95] specifies the spectral width of a pulse, for *single-longitudinal mode* (SLM) lasers, as its 20-dB spectral width divided by 6.07. We will study these lasers in Section 3.5.1. Show that for SLM lasers whose spectra have a Gaussian profile, this is equivalent to the rms spectral width.

2.15 Show that in the case of four-wave mixing, the nonlinear polarization is given by (2.54)–(2.58).

2.16 You want to design a soliton communication system at 1.55 μm at which wavelength the fiber has $\beta_2 = -2$ ps^2/km and $\gamma = 1$/W-km. The peak power of the pulses you can generate is limited to 50 mW. If you must use fundamental solitons and the bit period must be at least 10 times the full width at half-maximum (T_{FWHM}) of the soliton pulses, what is the largest bit rate you can use?

References

[Agr92]   G. P. Agrawal. *Fiber-Optic Communication Systems*. John Wiley, New York, 1992.

[Agr95]   G. P. Agrawal. *Nonlinear Fiber Optics, 2nd edition*. Academic Press, San Diego, CA, 1995.

[BC90]   P. N. Butcher and D. Cotter. *The Elements of Nonlinear Optics*, volume 9 of *Cambridge Studies in Modern Optics*. Cambridge University Press, Cambridge, 1990.

[Bel95]   Bellcore. *SONET transport systems: Common generic criteria*, 1995. GR-253-CORE.

[Big97]   S. Bigo et al. Error-free 20-Gbit/s soliton transmission over 7150 km through all-optical synchronous phase modulation. In *OFC'97 Technical Digest*, pages 143–144, 1997.

[BW80]   M. Born and E. Wolf. *Principles of Optics*. Pergamon Press, Oxford, 1980.

[Gre93]   P. E. Green. *Fiber-Optic Networks*. Prentice Hall, Englewood Cliffs, NJ, 1993.

[HJKM78]   K. O. Hill, D. C. Johnson, B. S. Kawasaki, and R. I. MacDonald. CW three-wave mixing in single-mode optical fibers. *Journal of Applied Physics*, 49(10):5098–5106, Oct. 1978.

[Jeu90]   L. B. Jeunhomme. *Single-Mode Fiber Optics*. Marcel Dekker, New York, 1990.

[KBW96]   L. G. Kazovsky, S. Benedetto, and A. E. Willner. *Optical Fiber Communication Systems*. Artech House, Boston, 1996.

[KK97]   I. P. Kaminow and T. L. Koch, editors. *Optical Fiber Telecommunications III*. Academic Press, San Diego, CA, 1997.

[Lin89]   C. Lin, editor. *Optoelectronic Technology and Lightwave Communications Systems*. Van Nostrand Reinhold, New York, 1989.

[Mar74]   D. Marcuse. *Theory of Dielectric Optical Waveguides*. Academic Press, New York, 1974.

[MK88]   S. D. Miller and I. P. Kaminow, editors. *Optical Fiber Telecommunications II.* Academic Press, San Diego, CA, 1988.

[Neu88] E.-G. Neumann. *Single-Mode Fibers.* Springer-Verlag, Berlin, 1988.

[PAP86] M. J. Potasek, G. P. Agrawal, and S. C. Pinault. Analytic and numerical study of pulse broadening in nonlinear dispersive optical fibers. *Journal of Optical Society of America B*, 3(2):205–211, Feb. 1986.

[RN76]   H.-D. Rudolph and E.-G. Neumann. Approximations for the eigenvalues of the fundamental mode of a step-index glass fiber waveguide. *Nachrichtentechnische Zeitschrift*, 29(14):328–329, 1976.

[RWv84] S. Ramo, J. R. Whinnery, and T. van Duzer. *Fields and Waves in Communication Electronics.* John Wiley, New York, 1984.

3
chapter

Components

IN THIS CHAPTER, we will discuss the physical principles behind the operation of the most important components of optical communication systems. For each component, we will give a simple descriptive treatment followed by a more detailed mathematical treatment.

The components used in modern optical communication systems include couplers, lasers, photodetectors, optical amplifiers, optical switches, and filters and multiplexers. After describing couplers, which are the simplest components, we will cover filters and multiplexers, which are important components in WDM systems. This will be followed by optical amplifiers. Understanding filters and optical amplifiers is essential to understanding the operation of lasers, which comes next. Then we discuss photodetectors, followed by optical switches, and finally wavelength converters.

3.1 Couplers

A *directional coupler* is used to combine and split signals in an optical network. A 2×2 coupler consists of two input ports and two output ports, and is shown in Figure 3.1. One possible construction for a directional coupler is to fuse two fibers together in the middle; another possibility is to fabricate it using waveguides in integrated optics. By careful design, the coupler can be made wavelength independent over a usefully wide range. Such a coupler, shown in Figure 3.1, takes a fraction α of the power from input 1 and places it on output 1 and the remaining fraction $1 - \alpha$ on output 2. Likewise, a fraction $1 - \alpha$ of the power from input 2 is distributed to output 1 and the remaining power to output 2.

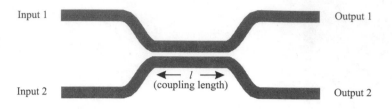

Figure 3.1   A directional coupler.

A coupler can be used as a power splitter if the coupling length, l in Figure 3.1, is adjusted such that half the power from each input appears at each output. Such a coupler is called a 3-dB coupler. An $n \times n$ star coupler is a natural generalization of the 3-dB 2×2 coupler. It is an n-input, n-output device with the property that the power from each input is divided equally among all the outputs. An $n \times n$ star coupler can be constructed by suitably interconnecting a number of 3-dB couplers, as will be seen in Chapter 7 (Figure 7.3). However, other constructions of an $n \times n$ coupler in integrated optics are also possible; see, for example, [Dra89].

Couplers are also used to tap off a small portion of the power from a light stream for monitoring purposes or other reasons. Such couplers are also called taps and are designed with values of α close to 1, typically 0.90–0.95.

Couplers are the building blocks for several other optical devices. We will explore the use of 3-dB directional couplers to construct optical switches in Section 3.7. Couplers are also the principal components used to construct *Mach-Zehnder interferometers*, which can be used as optical filters and multiplexers/demultiplexers. We will study these devices in Section 3.3.6.

So far, we have looked at wavelength-independent couplers. A coupler can be made wavelength selective, meaning its coupling coefficient will then depend on the wavelength of the signal. Such couplers are widely used to combine signals at 1310 nm and 1550 nm into a single fiber without loss. In this case, the 1310 nm signal on input 1 is passed through to output 1, whereas the 1550 nm signal on input 2 is passed through also to output 1. The same coupler can also be used to separate the two signals coming in on a common fiber. Such couplers are also used to combine 980 nm or 1480 nm pump signals along with a 1550 nm signal into an Erbium-doped fiber amplifier; see Figures 3.29 and 3.31.

3.1.1   Principle of Operation

When two waveguides are placed in proximity to each other, as shown in Figure 3.1, light "couples" from one waveguide to the other. This is because the propagation modes of the combined waveguide are quite different from the propagation modes of a single waveguide due to the presence of the other waveguide. When the two waveguides are identical, which is the only case we consider in this book, light launched into one waveguide couples to the other waveguide completely and then back to the first waveguide in a periodic manner. A quantitative analysis of this coupling phenomenon must be made using *coupled mode theory* [Yar85] and is beyond the scope of this book. The net result of this analysis is that the electric fields, E_{o1} and E_{o2}, at the outputs of a directional coupler may be expressed in terms of the electric fields at the inputs E_{i1} and E_{i2} as follows:

$$\begin{pmatrix} E_{o1}(f) \\ E_{o2}(f) \end{pmatrix} = e^{-i\beta l} \begin{pmatrix} \cos(\kappa l) & i\sin(\kappa l) \\ i\sin(\kappa l) & \cos(\kappa l) \end{pmatrix} \begin{pmatrix} E_{i1}(f) \\ E_{i2}(f) \end{pmatrix}. \tag{3.1}$$

Here, l denotes the coupling length (see Figure 3.1), and β is the propagation constant in each of the two waveguides of the directional coupler. The quantity κ is called the *coupling coefficient* and is a function of the width of the waveguides, the refractive indices of the waveguiding region (core) and the substrate, and the proximity of the two waveguides. Equation (3.1) will prove useful in deriving the transfer functions of more complex devices built using directional couplers (see Problem 3.1).

Though the directional coupler is a 2-input, 2-output device, it is often used with only one active input, say, input 1. In this case, the power transfer function of the directional coupler is

$$\begin{pmatrix} T_{11}(f) \\ T_{12}(f) \end{pmatrix} = \begin{pmatrix} \cos^2(\kappa l) \\ \sin^2(\kappa l) \end{pmatrix}. \tag{3.2}$$

Here, $T_{ij}(f)$ represents the power transfer function from input i to output j and is defined by $T_{ij}(f) = |E_{oj}|^2/|E_{ii}|^2$. Equation (3.2) can be derived from (3.1) by setting $E_{i2} = 0$.

Note from (3.2) that for a 3-dB coupler the coupling length must be chosen to satisfy $\kappa l = (2k + 1)\pi/4$, where k is a nonnegative integer.

3.1.2 Conservation of Energy

The general form of (3.1) can be derived merely by assuming that the directional coupler is lossless. Assume that the input and output electric fields are related by a general equation of the form

$$\begin{pmatrix} E_{o1} \\ E_{o2} \end{pmatrix} = \begin{pmatrix} s_{11} & s_{12} \\ s_{21} & s_{22} \end{pmatrix} \begin{pmatrix} E_{i1} \\ E_{i2} \end{pmatrix}. \tag{3.3}$$

The matrix

$$S = \begin{pmatrix} s_{11} & s_{12} \\ s_{21} & s_{22} \end{pmatrix}$$

is the transfer function of the device relating the input and output electric fields, and is called the *scattering matrix*. We use complex representations for the input and output electric fields, and thus the s_{ij} are also complex. It is understood that we must consider the real part of these complex fields in applications. This complex representation for the s_{ij} allows us to conveniently represent any induced phase shifts.

For convenience, we denote $\mathbf{E}_o = (E_{o1}, E_{o2})^T$ and $\mathbf{E}_i = (E_{i1}, E_{i2})^T$, where the superscript T denotes the transpose of the vector/matrix. In this notation, (3.3) can be written compactly as $\mathbf{E}_o = S\mathbf{E}_i$.

The sum of the powers of the input fields is proportional to $\mathbf{E}_i^T \mathbf{E}_i^* = |E_{i1}|^2 + |E_{i2}|^2$. Similarly, the sum of the powers of the output fields is proportional to $\mathbf{E}_o^T \mathbf{E}_o^* = |E_{o1}|^2 + |E_{o2}|^2$. If the directional coupler is lossless, the power in the output fields must equal the power in the input fields so that

$$\begin{aligned} \mathbf{E}_o^T \mathbf{E}_o &= (S\mathbf{E}_i)^T (S\mathbf{E}_i)^* \\ &= \mathbf{E}_i^T (S^T S^*) \mathbf{E}_i^* \\ &= \mathbf{E}_i^T \mathbf{E}_i^*. \end{aligned}$$

Since this relationship must hold for arbitrary $\mathbf{E}_i$, we must have

$$S^T S^* = I, \tag{3.4}$$

where I is the identity matrix. Note that this relation follows merely from conservation of energy and can be readily generalized to a device with an arbitrary number of inputs and outputs.

For a 2×2 directional coupler, by the symmetry of the device, we can set $s_{21} = s_{12} = a$ and $s_{22} = s_{11} = b$. Applying (3.4) to this simplified scattering matrix, we get

$$|a|^2 + |b|^2 = 1 \tag{3.5}$$

and

$$ab^* + ba^* = 0. \tag{3.6}$$

From (3.5), we can write

$$|a| = \cos(x) \text{ and } |b| = \sin(x). \tag{3.7}$$

If we write $a = \cos(x)e^{i\phi_a}$ and $b = \sin(x)e^{i\phi_b}$, (3.6) yields

$$\cos(\phi_a - \phi_b) = 0. \tag{3.8}$$

Thus ϕ_a and ϕ_b must differ by an odd multiple of $\pi/2$. The general form of (3.1) now follows from (3.7) and (3.8).

The conservation of energy has some important consequences for the kinds of optical components that we can build. First note that for a 3-dB coupler, though the electric fields at the two outputs have the same magnitude, they have a relative phase shift of $\pi/2$. This relative phase shift, which follows from the conservation of energy as we saw earlier, plays a crucial role in the design of devices such as the Mach-Zehnder interferometer that we will study in Section 3.3.6.

Another consequence of the conservation of energy is that *lossless combining* is not possible. Thus we cannot design a device with three ports where the power input at two of the ports is completely delivered to the third port. This result is demonstrated in Problem 3.2.

3.2   Isolators and Circulators

Couplers and most other passive optical devices are *reciprocal* devices, in that the devices work exactly the same way if their inputs and outputs are reversed. However, in many systems there is a need for a passive nonreciprocal device. An isolator is an example of such a device. Its main function is to allow transmission in one direction through it but block all transmission in the other direction. Isolators are used in systems in front of optical amplifiers and lasers primarily to prevent reflections from entering these devices, which would otherwise degrade their performance. The two key parameters of an isolator are its *insertion loss*, which is the loss in the forward direction, and which should be as small as possible, and its *isolation*, which is the loss in the reverse direction, and which should be as large as possible. The typical insertion loss is around 1 dB, and the isolation is around 40 to 50 dB.

3.2.1   Principle of Operation

In order to understand the operation of an isolator, we need to understand the notion of *polarization*. Recall from Section 2.1.2 that the *state of polarization* (SOP) of light propagating in a single-mode fiber refers to the orientation of its electric field vector on a plane that is orthogonal to its direction of propagation. At any time, the electric field vector can be expressed as a linear combination of the two orthogonal linear polarizations supported by the fiber. We will call these two polarization modes the horizontal and vertical modes.

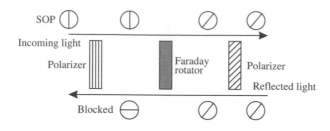

Figure 3.2   Principle of operation of an isolator that works only for a particular state of polarization of the input signal.

The principle of operation of an isolator is shown in Figure 3.2. Assume that the input light signal has the vertical SOP shown in the figure. It is passed through a *polarizer*, which passes only light energy in the vertical SOP and blocks light energy in the horizontal SOP. The polarizer is followed by a *Faraday rotator*. A Faraday rotator is an asymmetric device, made of a crystal that rotates the SOP, say, clockwise, by 45°, regardless of the direction of propagation. The Faraday rotator is followed by another polarizer that passes only SOPs with this 45° orientation. Thus the light signal from left to right is passed through the device without any loss. On the other hand, light entering the device from the right due to a reflection, with the same 45° SOP orientation, is rotated another 45° by the Faraday rotator, and thus blocked by the first polarizer.

Note that the preceding explanation above assumes a particular SOP for the input light signal. In practice we cannot control the SOP of the input, and so the isolator must work regardless of the input SOP. This requires a more complicated design, and many different designs exist. One such design for a miniature polarization-independent isolator is shown in Figure 3.3. The input signal with an arbitrary SOP is first sent through a *spatial walk-off polarizer* (SWP). The SWP splits the signal into its two orthogonally polarized components. The vertical component goes through while the horizontal component is deflected. Each component goes through a Faraday rotator, which rotates the SOPs by 45°. The Faraday rotator is followed by a *half-wave plate*. The half-wave plate rotates the SOPs by 45° in the clockwise direction for signals propagating from left to right, and by 45° in the counterclockwise direction for signals propagating from right to left. Therefore, the combination of the Faraday rotator and the half-wave plate converts the horizontal polarization into a vertical polarization and vice versa, and the two signals are combined by another SWP at the output. For reflected signals in the reverse direction, the half-wave plate and Faraday rotator cancel each other's effects, and the SOPs remain

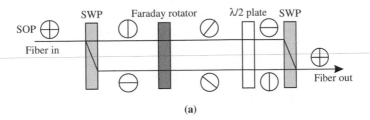

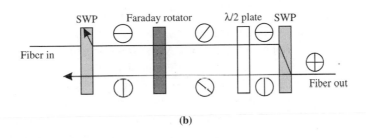

(a)

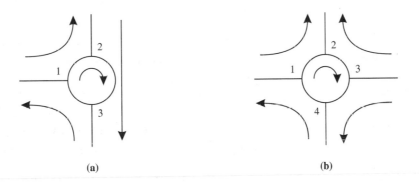

(b)

Figure 3.3 A polarization-independent isolator.

Figure 3.4 Circulators: (a) three-port, and (b) four-port.

unchanged as they pass through these two devices and are thus not recombined by the SWP at the input.

The principle of operation of a *circulator* is similar to that of an isolator, except that it has multiple ports, typically three or four, as shown in Figure 3.4. In a three-port circulator, an input signal on port 1 is sent out on port 2, an input signal on port 2 is sent out on port 3, and an input signal on port 3 is sent out on port 1. Circulators are useful to construct optical add/drop elements, as we will see in Section 3.3.3.

3.3   Multiplexers and Filters

In this section, we will study the principles underlying the operation of a variety of wavelength selection technologies. Optical filters are essential components in transmission systems for at least two applications: to multiplex and demultiplex wavelengths in a WDM system—these devices are called multiplexers/demultiplexers—and to provide equalization of the gain and filtering of noise in optical amplifiers. Further, understanding optical filtering is essential to understanding the operation of lasers later in this chapter.

The different applications of optical filters are shown in Figure 3.5. A simple filter selects one wavelength and rejects all others. A multiplexer combines signals at different wavelengths on its input ports onto a common output port, and a demultiplexer performs the opposite function.

Multiplexers and demultiplexers are used in WDM terminals as well as in larger *wavelength routers* and *wavelength add/drop* elements. A *wavelength router* is the key component for a class of optical networks called *wavelength routing networks*. The function of a wavelength router is shown in Figure 3.5. This is a 2-input, 2-output device with each input carrying a WDM signal consisting of the *same set of wavelengths*, $\lambda_1, \lambda_2, \lambda_3, \lambda_4$. Of course, the signals modulating the same wavelengths on the two inputs can be, and are usually, different. We let λ_j^i denote wavelength λ_j on input link i; thus the wavelengths on input 1 to the router are denoted $\lambda_1^1, \lambda_2^1, \lambda_3^1, \lambda_4^1$. From input 1, the wavelengths λ_2^1 and λ_3^1 are routed to output 1, whereas the other two wavelengths are routed to output 2. The opposite is true of input 2, from which the wavelengths λ_2^2 and λ_3^2 are routed to output 2, whereas the other two wavelengths are routed to output 1. Another way to view this is that the router *exchanges* wavelengths λ_1 and λ_4 between the two inputs, and the signals resulting from this exchange are routed to the outputs.

Although the router illustrated in Figure 3.5 has two inputs and outputs with four wavelengths on each of them, the generalization to an arbitrary number of inputs and outputs with an arbitrary number of wavelengths on each of them is straightforward. The same set of wavelengths must be used on each input/output. A wavelength on any input can be routed to any output. But—and this is the key restriction—the same wavelength from two different inputs cannot be routed to the same output. We will study the implications of this restriction imposed by a router on the performance of wavelength routing optical networks in Chapter 8.

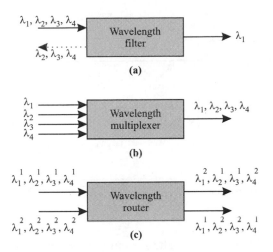

Figure 3.5   Different applications for optical filters in optical networks. (a) A simple filter. (b) A multiplexer or a demultiplexer. (c) A wavelength router.

If the routing pattern of a wavelength router is fixed in time, we term the router *static*. If the routing pattern can be changed, for example, by the application of appropriate control signals, the router is termed *dynamic*. Static routers can be constructed using wavelength multiplexers and demultiplexers. Such a possible construction for the router of Figure 3.5 is illustrated in Figure 3.6. Dynamic routers can be constructed using optical switches in addition to multiplexers and demultiplexers. We will study different dynamic router architectures in Chapter 8.

An add/drop multiplexer is essentially a simple form of a wavelength router with one input port and one output port with an additional local port wherein wavelengths are added to/dropped from the incoming light stream.

A variety of optical filtering technologies are available. Their key characteristics for use in systems are the following:

1. Good optical filters should have low *insertion losses*. The insertion loss is the input-to-output loss of the filter.

2. The loss should be independent of the state of polarization of the input signals. The state of polarization varies randomly with time in most systems, and if the filter has a *polarization-dependent loss* (PDL), the output power will vary with time as well—an undesirable feature.

3. The passband of a filter should be insensitive to variations in ambient temperature. The *temperature coefficient* is measured by the amount of wavelength shift

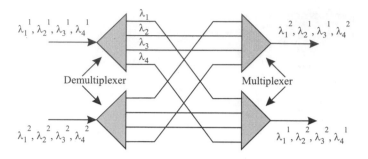

Figure 3.6   A static wavelength router.

per unit degree change in temperature. The system requirement is that over the entire operating temperature range (about 100°C typically), the wavelength shift should be much less than the wavelength spacing between adjacent channels in a WDM system.

4. As more and more filters are cascaded in a WDM system, the passband becomes progressively narrower. To ensure reasonably broad passbands at the end of the cascade, the individual filters should have very flat passbands, so as to accommodate small changes in operating wavelengths of the lasers. This is measured by the 1-dB bandwidth, as shown in Figure 3.7.

5. At the same time, the passband skirts should be sharp to reduce the amount of energy passed through from adjacent channels. This energy is seen as *crosstalk* and degrades the system performance. The crosstalk suppression, or *isolation* of the filter, which is defined as the relative power passed through from the adjacent channels, is an important parameter as well.

In addition to all the performance parameters described, perhaps the most important consideration is cost. Technologies that require careful hand assembly tend to be more expensive. There are two ways of reducing the cost of optical filters. The first is to fabricate them using integrated-optic waveguide technology. This is analogous to semiconductor chips, although the state of integration achieved with optics is significantly less. These waveguides can be made on many substrates, including silica, silicon, InGaAs, and polymers. Waveguide devices tend to be inherently polarization dependent due to the geometry of the waveguides, and care must be taken to reduce the PDL in these devices. The second method is to realize all-fiber devices. Such devices are amenable to mass production and inherently polarization independent. It is also easy to couple light in and out of these devices from/into other fibers. Both of these approaches are being pursued today.

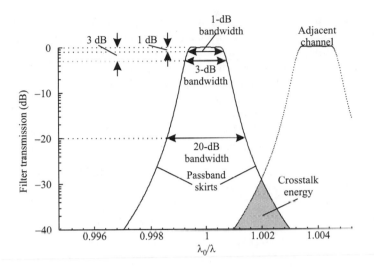

Figure 3.7   Characterization of some important spectral-shape parameters of optical filters. λ_0 is the center wavelength of the filter, and λ denotes the wavelength of the light signal.

All the filters and multiplexers we study use the property of *interference* among optical waves. In addition, some filters, for example, gratings, use the *diffraction* property. This is the property by which light from a source tends to spread in all directions. Table 3.1 compares the performance of different filtering technologies.

3.3.1   Gratings

The term *grating* is used to describe almost any device whose operation involves interference among multiple optical signals originating from the same source but with different relative *phase shifts*. An exception is a device where the multiple optical signals are generated by repeated traversals of a single cavity; such devices are called *etalons*. An electromagnetic wave (light) of angular frequency ω propagating, say, in the z direction has a dependence on z and t of the form $\cos(\omega t - \beta z)$. Here, β is the propagation constant and depends on the medium. The *phase* of the wave is $\omega t - \beta z$. Thus a relative phase shift between two waves from the same source can be achieved if they traverse two paths of different lengths.

Two examples of gratings are shown in Figure 3.8(a) and (b). Gratings have been widely used for decades in optics to separate light into its constituent wavelengths. In WDM communication systems, gratings are used as demultiplexers to separate

Table 3.1 Comparison of passive wavelength multiplexing/demultiplexing technologies. A 16-channel system with 100 GHz channel spacing is assumed. Other key considerations include center wavelength accuracy and manufacturability. All these approaches face problems in scaling with the number of wavelengths. DTMF is the thin-film multicavity filter, and AWG is the arrayed waveguide grating. For the fiber grating, the temperature coefficient is after passive temperature compensation.

Filter Property	Fiber Bragg Grating	DTMF	AWG	Stimax Grating
1 dB BW (nm)		0.4	0.4	0.09
20 dB BW (nm)		1.2		
Isolation (dB)	40	25	22	30
Loss (dB)	0.2	7	9	6
PDL (dB)	0	0.2	0.8	
Temp. coeff. (nm/°C)	0.0007	0.0005	0.01	0.01

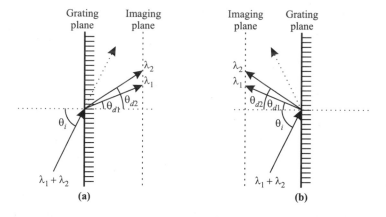

Figure 3.8   (a) A transmission grating and (b) a reflection grating.

the individual wavelengths. The Stimax grating of Table 3.1 is a grating of the type we describe in this section.

Consider the grating shown in Figure 3.8(a). Multiple narrow slits are spaced equally apart on a plane, called the *grating plane*. The spacing between two adjacent slits is called the *pitch* of the grating. Light incident from a source on one side of the grating is transmitted through these slits. Since each slit is narrow, by the phenomenon known as *diffraction*, the light transmitted through each slit spreads out in all directions. Thus each slit acts as a secondary source of light. Consider some other plane parallel to the grating plane at which the transmitted light from all the slits interferes. We will call this plane the *imaging plane*. Consider any point on this imaging plane. For wavelengths for which the individual interfering waves at this point are in phase, we have constructive interference and an enhancement of the light intensity at these wavelengths. For a large number of slits, which is the case usually encountered in practice, the interference is not constructive at other wavelengths, and there is little light intensity at this point from these wavelengths. Since different wavelengths interfere constructively at different points on the imaging plane, the grating effectively separates a WDM signal into its constituent wavelengths. In a fiber optic system, optical fibers could be placed at different imaging points to collect light at the different wavelengths.

Note that if there were no diffraction, we would simply have light transmitted or reflected along the directed dotted lines in Figure 3.8(a) and (b). Thus the phenomenon of diffraction is key to the operation of these devices, and for this reason they are called *diffraction gratings*. Since multiple *transmissions* occur in the grating of Figure 3.8(a), this grating is called a *transmission grating*. If the transmission slits are replaced by narrow reflecting surfaces, with the rest of the grating surface being nonreflecting, we get the reflection grating of Figure 3.8(b). The principle of operation of this device is exactly analogous to that of the transmission grating. A majority of the gratings used in practice are reflection gratings since they are somewhat easier to fabricate. In addition to the plane geometry we have considered, gratings are fabricated in a concave geometry. In this case, the slits (for a transmission grating) are located on the arc of a circle. In many applications, a concave geometry leads to fewer auxiliary parts like lenses and mirrors needed to construct the overall device, say, a WDM demultiplexer, and is thus preferred.

The Stimax grating listed in Table 3.1 [LL84] is a reflection grating that is integrated with a concave mirror and the input and output fibers. Its characteristics are described in Table 3.1, and it has been used in commercially available WDM transmission systems. However, it is a bulk device not amenable to easy fabrication and hence very expensive. Attempts have been made to realize similar gratings in optical waveguide technology but these devices are yet to achieve loss, PDL, and isolation comparable to the bulk version.

Principle of Operation

To understand quantitatively the principle of operation of a (transmission) grating, consider the light transmitted through adjacent slits as shown in Figure 3.9. The distance between adjacent slits—the *pitch* of the grating—is denoted by a. We assume that the light source is far enough away from the grating plane compared to a so

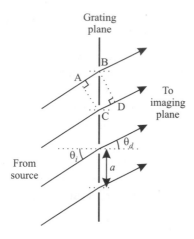

Figure 3.9   Principle of operation of a transmission grating. The reflection grating works in an analogous manner. The path length difference between rays diffracted at angle θ_d from adjacent slits is $\overline{AB} - \overline{CD} = a[\sin(\theta_i) - \sin(\theta_d)]$.

that the light can be assumed to be incident at the same angle θ_i to the plane of the grating at each slit. We consider the light rays diffracted at an angle θ_d from the grating plane. The imaging plane, like the source, is assumed to be far away from the grating plane compared to the grating pitch. It can be shown (Problem 3.4) that the path length difference between the rays traversing through adjacent slits is the difference in lengths between the line segments $\overline{AB}$ and $\overline{CD}$, and is given approximately by $a[\sin(\theta_i) - \sin(\theta_d)]$. Thus constructive interference at a wavelength λ occurs at the imaging plane among the rays diffracted at angle θ_d if the following *grating equation* is satisfied:

$$a[\sin(\theta_i) - \sin(\theta_d)] = m\lambda, \tag{3.9}$$

for some integer m, called the *order* of the grating. The grating effects the separation of the individual wavelengths in a WDM signal since the grating equation is satisfied at different points in the imaging plane for different wavelengths. This is illustrated in Figure 3.8 where different wavelengths are shown being diffracted at the angles at which the grating equation is satisfied for that wavelength. For example, θ_{d1} is the angle at which the grating equation is satisfied for λ_1.

Note that the energy at a single wavelength is distributed over all the discrete angles that satisfy the grating equation (3.9) at this wavelength. When the grating is used as a demultiplexer in a WDM system, light is collected from only one of these angles, and the remaining energy is lost. In fact, most of the energy will be concentrated in the zeroth order ($m = 0$) interference maximum, which occurs at $\theta_i = \theta_d$ for all wavelengths. The light energy in this zeroth order interference maximum is wasted since the wavelengths are not separated. Thus gratings must be designed so that the light energy is maximum at one of the interference maxima of nonzero order so that the lost energy is negligible. This can be done using a technique called *blazing* [KF86, p. 386].

3.3.2 Bragg Gratings

Bragg gratings are widely used in fiber optic communication systems. In general, any periodic perturbation in the propagating medium serves as a Bragg grating. This perturbation is usually a periodic variation of the refractive index of the medium. We will see in Section 3.5.1 that lasers use Bragg gratings to achieve single frequency operation. In this case, the Bragg gratings are written in waveguides. Bragg gratings written in fiber can be used to make a variety of devices such as filters, add/drop multiplexers, and dispersion compensators. We will see later that the Bragg grating principle also underlies the operation of the acousto-optic tunable filter. In this case, the Bragg grating is formed by the propagation of an acoustic wave in the medium.

Principle of Operation

Consider two waves propagating in the same direction with propagation constants β_0 and β_1. Energy is coupled from one wave to the other if they satisfy the Bragg *phase-matching* condition

$$|\beta_0 - \beta_1| = \frac{2\pi}{\Lambda},$$

where Λ is the period of the grating. In a reflective filter, we have light with propagation constant β_1 propagating from the left to right. The energy from this wave is coupled onto a scattered wave traveling in the opposite direction at the same wavelength provided

$$|\beta_0 - (-\beta_0)| = 2\beta_0 = \frac{2\pi}{\Lambda}.$$

Letting $\beta_0 = 2\pi n_{\text{eff}}/\lambda_0$, λ_0 being the wavelength of the incident wave and n_{eff} the effective refractive index of the waveguide or fiber, the wave is reflected provided

$$\lambda_0 = 2n_{\text{eff}}\Lambda.$$

This wavelength λ_0 is called the Bragg wavelength. In practice, the reflection efficiency decreases as the wavelength of the incident wave is detuned from the Bragg

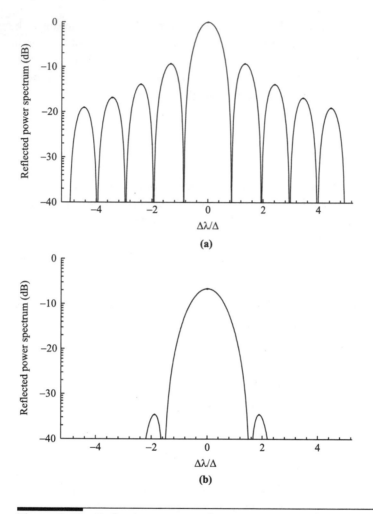

Figure 3.10   Reflection spectra of Bragg gratings with (a) uniform index profile, and (b) apodized index profile. $\Delta\lambda/\Delta$ is a normalized measure of the detuning from the phase-matching wavelength.

wavelength, and is plotted in Figure 3.10(a). Thus if several wavelengths are transmitted into a fiber Bragg grating, the Bragg wavelength is reflected while the other wavelengths are transmitted.

The reflection spectrum shown in Figure 3.10(a) is for a grating with a uniform refractive index pattern change across its length. In order to eliminate the undesirable side lobes, it is possible to obtain an *apodized* grating where the refractive index change is made smaller toward the edges of the grating. (The term *apodized* means "to cut off the feet.") The reflection spectrum of an apodized grating is shown in Figure 3.10(b). Note that, for the apodized grating, the side lobes have been drastically reduced but at the expense of increasing the main lobe width.

3.3.3   Fiber Gratings

Fiber gratings are attractive devices that can be used for a variety of applications, including filtering, add/drop functions, and for compensating for accumulated dispersion in the system. Being all-fiber devices, their main advantages are their low loss, ease of coupling (with other fibers), polarization insensitivity, low temperature coefficient, and simple packaging. As a result, they can be extremely low-cost devices.

Gratings are written in fibers by making use of the *photosensitivity* of certain types of optical fibers. A conventional silica fiber doped with germanium becomes extremely photosensitive. Exposing this fiber to ultraviolet (UV) light causes changes in the refractive index within the fiber core. A grating can be written in such a fiber by exposing its core to two interfering UV beams. This causes the radiation intensity to vary periodically along the length of the fiber. Where the intensity is high, the refractive index is increased and where it is low, the refractive index is unchanged. The change in refractive index needed to obtain gratings is quite small—around 10^{-4}. Other techniques, such as phase masks, can also be used to produce gratings. A phase mask is a diffractive optical element. When it is illuminated by a light beam, it splits the beams into different diffractive orders, which then interfere with one another to write the grating into the fiber.

Fiber gratings are classified as either *short-period* or *long-period* gratings, based on the period of the grating. Short-period gratings are also called Bragg gratings and have periods that are comparable to the wavelength, typically around 0.5 μm. We discussed the behavior of Bragg gratings in Section 3.3.2. Long-period gratings, on the other hand, have periods that are much higher than the wavelength, ranging from a few hundred μm to a few mm.

Fiber Bragg Gratings

Fiber Bragg gratings can be fabricated with extremely low loss (0.1 dB), high wavelength accuracy (± 0.05 nm is easily achieved), high adjacent channel crosstalk suppression (40 dB), as well as flat tops.

The temperature coefficient of a fiber Bragg grating is typically 1.25×10^{-2} nm/$^\circ$C due to the variation in fiber length with temperature. However, it is possible to compensate for this change by packaging the grating with a material that has a negative thermal expansion coefficient. These passively temperature-compensated

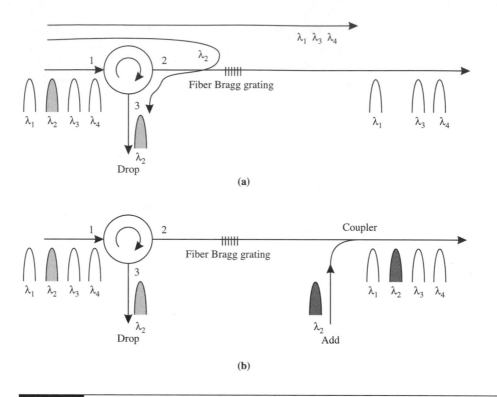

Figure 3.11   Optical add/drop elements based on fiber Bragg gratings. (a) A drop element. (b) A combined add/drop element.

gratings have temperature coefficients of around 0.07×10^{-2} nm/°C. This implies a very small 0.07 nm center wavelength shift over an operating temperature range of 100°C, which means that they can be operated without any active temperature control.

These properties of fiber Bragg gratings make them very useful devices for system applications. Fiber Bragg gratings are finding a variety of uses in WDM systems, ranging from filters and optical add/drop elements to dispersion compensators. A simple optical drop element based on fiber Bragg gratings is shown in Figure 3.11(a). It consists of a three-port circulator with a fiber Bragg grating. The circulator transmits light coming in on port 1 out on port 2 and transmits light coming in on port 2 out on port 3. In this case, the grating reflects the desired wavelength λ_2, which is then dropped at port 3. The remaining three wavelengths are passed through. It is possible to implement an add/drop function along the same lines, by introducing a coupler to add the same wavelength that was dropped, as shown in Figure 3.11(b).

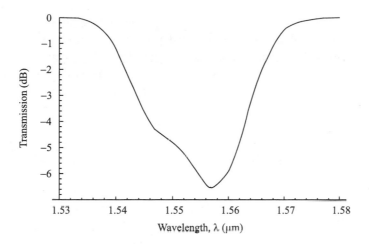

Figure 3.12 Transmission spectrum of a long-period fiber Bragg grating used as a gain equalizer for Erbium-doped fiber amplifiers. After [Ven96a].

Many variations of this simple add/drop element can be realized by using gratings in combination with couplers and circulators. A major concern in these designs is that the reflection of these gratings is not perfect, and as a result, some power at the selected wavelength leaks through the grating. This can cause undesirable crosstalk, and we will study this effect in Chapter 5.

Fiber Bragg gratings can also be used to compensate for dispersion accumulated along the link. We will study this application in Chapter 5 in the context of dispersion compensation.

Long-Period Fiber Gratings

Long-period fiber gratings are fabricated in the same manner as fiber Bragg gratings and are used today primarily as filters inside Erbium-doped fiber amplifiers to compensate for their nonflat gain spectrum. As we will see, these devices serve as very efficient band rejection filters, and can be tailored to provide almost exact equalization of the Erbium gain spectrum. Figure 3.12 shows the transmission spectrum of such a grating. These gratings retain all the attractive properties of fiber gratings and are expected to become widely used for several filtering applications.

Principle of Operation

These gratings operate on somewhat different principles compared to Bragg gratings. In fiber Bragg gratings, energy from the forward propagating mode in the fiber core at the right wavelength is coupled into a backward propagating mode. In long-period gratings, energy is coupled from the forward propagating mode in the fiber core onto other forward propagating modes in the cladding. These cladding modes are extremely lossy, and their energy decays rapidly as they propagate along the fiber, due to losses at the cladding-to-air interface and due to microbends in the fiber. There are many cladding modes, and coupling occurs between a core mode at a given wavelength and a cladding mode depending on the pitch of the grating Λ, as follows: if β denotes the propagation constant of the mode in the core (assuming a single-mode fiber) and β_{cl}^p that of the pth-order cladding mode, then the phase-matching condition dictates that

$$\beta - \beta_{cl}^p = \frac{2\pi}{\Lambda}.$$

In general, the difference in propagation constants between two forward propagating modes is quite small, leading to a fairly large value of Λ in order for coupling to occur. This value is usually a few hundred μm. (Note that in Bragg gratings, the difference in propagation constants between the forward and backward propagating modes is quite large, leading to a small value for Λ, typically around 0.5 μm.) If n_{eff} and n_{eff}^p denote the effective refractive indices of the core and pth-order cladding modes, then the wavelength at which energy is coupled from the core mode to the cladding mode can be obtained as

$$\lambda = \Lambda(n_{eff} - n_{eff}^p),$$

where we have used the relation $\beta = 2\pi n_{eff}/\lambda$.

Therefore, once we know the effective indices of the core and cladding modes, we can design the grating with a suitable value of Λ so as to cause coupling of energy out of a desired wavelength band. This causes the grating to act as a wavelength-dependent loss element. Methods for calculating the propagation constants for the cladding modes are discussed in [Ven96b]. The amount of wavelength-dependent loss can be controlled during fabrication by controlling the UV exposure time. Complicated transmission spectra can be obtained by cascading multiple gratings with different center wavelengths and different exposures. The example shown in Figure 3.12 was obtained by cascading two such gratings [Ven96a].

3.3.4 Fabry-Perot Filters

A Fabry-Perot filter consists of the cavity formed by two highly reflective mirrors placed parallel to each other as shown in Figure 3.13. This filter is also called a Fabry-Perot interferometer or etalon. The input light beam to the filter enters the

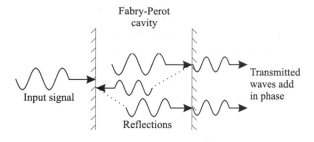

Figure 3.13   A Fabry-Perot filter.

first mirror at right angles to its surface. The output of the filter is the light beam leaving the second mirror.

This is a classical device that has been used widely in interferometric applications. They have been used as filters for WDM applications in several optical network testbeds. There are better filters today, such as the thin-film resonant multicavity filter that we will study in Section 3.3.5. These latter filters can be viewed as Fabry-Perot filters with wavelength-dependent mirror reflectivities. Thus the fundamental principle of operation of these filters is the same as that of the Fabry-Perot filter. The Fabry-Perot cavity is also used in lasers (see Section 3.5.1).

Compact Fabry-Perot filters are commercially available components. Their main advantage over some of the other devices is that they can be tuned to select different channels in a WDM system, as discussed later.

Principle of Operation

The principle of operation of the device is illustrated in Figure 3.13. The input signal is incident on the left surface of the cavity. After one pass through the cavity, as shown in Figure 3.13, a part of the light leaves the cavity through the right facet and a part is reflected. A part of the reflected wave is again reflected by the left facet to the right facet. For those wavelengths for which the cavity length is an integral multiple of half the wavelength in the cavity—so that a round trip through the cavity is an integral multiple of the wavelength—all the light waves transmitted through the right facet *add in phase*. Such wavelengths are called the *resonant wavelengths* of the cavity. The determination of the resonant wavelengths of the cavity is discussed in Problem 3.5.

The power transfer function of a filter is the fraction of input light power that is transmitted by the filter as a function of optical frequency f, or wavelength. For the Fabry-Perot filter, this function is given by

$$T_{FP}(f) = \frac{\left(1 - \frac{A}{1-R}\right)^2}{\left(1 + \left(\frac{2\sqrt{R}}{1-R}\sin(2\pi f\tau)\right)^2\right)}. \tag{3.10}$$

This can also be expressed in terms of the optical free-space wavelength λ as

$$T_{FP}(\lambda) = \frac{\left(1 - \frac{A}{1-R}\right)^2}{\left(1 + \left(\frac{2\sqrt{R}}{1-R}\sin(2\pi nl/\lambda)\right)^2\right)}.$$

(By a slight abuse of notation, we use the same symbol for the power transfer function in both cases.) Here A denotes the absorption loss of each mirror, which is the fraction of incident light that is absorbed by the mirror. The quantity R denotes the *reflectivity* of each mirror (assumed to be identical), which is the fraction of incident light that is reflected by the mirror. The one-way propagation delay across the cavity is denoted by τ. The refractive index of the cavity is denoted by n and its length by l. Thus $\tau = nl/c$, where c is the velocity of light in vacuum. This transfer function can be derived by considering the sum of the waves transmitted by the filter after an odd number of passes through the cavity. This is left as an exercise (Problem 3.6).

The power transfer function of the Fabry-Perot filter is plotted in Figure 3.14 for $A = 0$ and $R = 0.75$, 0.9, and 0.99. Note that very high mirror reflectivities are required to obtain good isolation of adjacent channels.

The power transfer function $T_{FP}(f)$ is periodic in f, and the peaks, or *passbands*, of the transfer function occur at frequencies f that satisfy $f\tau = k/2$ for some positive integer k. Thus in a WDM system, even if the wavelengths are spaced sufficiently far apart compared to the width of each passband of the filter transfer function, several frequencies (or wavelengths) may be transmitted by the filter if they coincide with different passbands. In order for a single wavelength to be selected by the filter, all the wavelengths must lie between some two successive passbands of the filter transfer function. The spectral range between two successive passbands of the filter is called the *free spectral range* or FSR. A measure of the width of each passband is its *full width* at the point where the transfer function is *half* of its *maximum* (FWHM). In WDM systems, one is interested in the number of wavelengths that can be used. As we have seen, these wavelengths must lie within one FSR of the filter. Thus the ratio FSR/FWHM is an approximate (order-of-magnitude) measure of the number

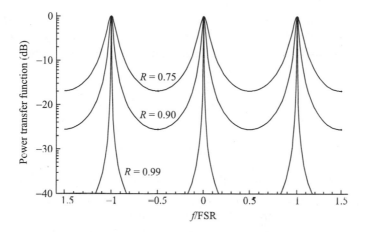

Figure 3.14 The transfer function of a Fabry-Perot filter. FSR denotes the free spectral range, f the frequency, and R the reflectivity.

of wavelengths that can be accommodated by the system. This ratio is called the *finesse*, F, of the filter, and is given by

$$F = \frac{\pi \sqrt{R}}{1 - R}. \tag{3.11}$$

This expression can be derived from (3.10) and is left as an exercise (Problem 3.7).

Tunability

A Fabry-Perot filter can be tuned to select different wavelengths in one of several ways. The simplest approach is to change the cavity length. The same effect can be achieved by varying the refractive index within the cavity. Consider a WDM system, all of whose wavelengths lie within one FSR of the Fabry-Perot filter. The frequency f_0 that is selected by the filter satisfies $f_0 \tau = k/2$ for some positive integer k. Thus f_0 can be changed by changing τ, which is the one-way propagation time for the light beam across the cavity. If we denote the length of the cavity by l and its refractive index by n, $\tau = ln/c$, where c is the speed of light in vacuum. Thus τ can be changed by changing either l or n.

Mechanical tuning of the filter can be effected by moving one of the mirrors so that the cavity length changes. This permits tunability only in times of the order of a few milliseconds. For a mechanically tuned Fabry-Perot filter, a precise mechanism is needed in order to keep the mirrors parallel to each other in spite of their relative movement. The reliability of mechanical tuning mechanisms is also relatively poor.

Another approach to tuning is to use a piezoelectric material within the cavity. A piezoelectric filter undergoes compression on the application of a voltage. Thus the length of the cavity filled with such a material can be changed by the application of a voltage, thereby effecting a change in the resonant frequency of the cavity. The piezo material, however, introduces undesirable effects such as thermal instability and hysteresis, making such a filter difficult to use in practical systems.

3.3.5   Multilayer Dielectric Thin-Film Filters

A thin-film resonant cavity filter (TFF) is a Fabry-Perot interferometer, or etalon, (see Section 3.3.4) where the mirrors surrounding the cavity are realized by using multiple reflective dielectric thin-film layers (see Problem 3.10). This device acts as a bandpass filter, passing through a particular wavelength and reflecting all the other wavelengths. The wavelength that is passed through is determined by the cavity length.

A thin-film resonant multicavity filter (TFMF) consists of two or more cavities separated by reflective dielectric thin-film layers, as shown in Figure 3.15. The effect of having multiple cavities on the response of the filter is illustrated in Figure 3.16. As more cavities are added, the top of the passband becomes flatter and the skirts become sharper, both very desirable filter features.

In order to obtain a multiplexer or a demultiplexer, a number of these filters can be cascaded, as shown in Figure 3.17. Each filter passes a different wavelength and

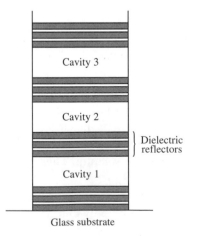

Figure 3.15   A three-cavity thin-film resonant dielectric thin-film filter. After [SS96].

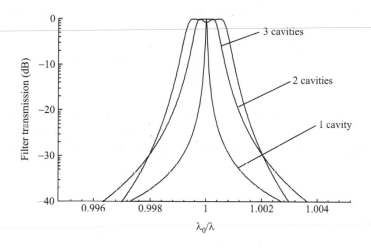

Figure 3.16   Transfer functions of single-cavity, two-cavity, and three-cavity dielectric thin-film filters. Note how the use of multiple cavities leads to a flatter passband and a sharper transition from the passband to the stop band.

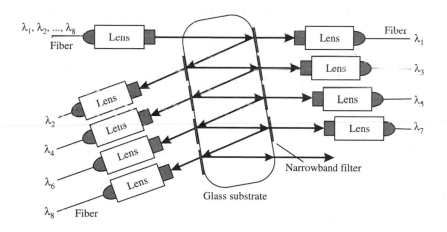

Figure 3.17   A wavelength multiplexer/demultiplexer using multilayer dielectric thin-film filters. After [SS96].

reflects all the others. When used as a demultiplexer, the first filter in the cascade passes one wavelength and reflects all the others onto the second filter. The second filter passes another wavelength and reflects the remaining ones, and so on.

This device has many features that make it attractive for system applications. It is possible to have a very flat top on the passband and very sharp skirts. The device is extremely stable with regard to temperature variations, has low loss, and is insensitive to the polarization of the signal. Typical parameters for a 16-channel multiplexer are shown in Table 3.1. For these reasons, TFMFs are becoming widely used in commercial systems today. Understanding the principle of operation of these devices requires some knowledge of electromagnetic theory, and so we defer this to Appendix E.

3.3.6   Mach-Zehnder Interferometers

A Mach-Zehnder interferometer (MZI) is an interferometric device that makes use of two interfering paths of different lengths to resolve different wavelengths. Devices constructed on this principle have been around for some decades. Today, Mach-Zehnder interferometers are typically constructed in integrated optics and consist of two 3-dB directional couplers interconnected through two paths of differing lengths, as shown in Figure 3.18(a). The substrate is usually silicon, and the waveguide regions are silica (SiO_2), which has a higher refractive index.

Mach-Zehnder interferometers are useful as both filters and (de)multiplexers. Even though there are better technologies for making narrow band filters, for example, dielectric multicavity thin-film filters, MZIs are still useful in realizing wide band filters. For example, MZIs can be used to separate the wavelengths in the 1.3 μm and 1.55 μm bands. Narrow band MZI filters are fabricated by cascading a number of stages, as we will see, and this leads to larger losses. In principle, very good crosstalk performance can be achieved using MZIs if the wavelengths are spaced such that the undesired wavelengths occur at, or close to, the nulls of the power transfer function. However, in practice, the wavelengths cannot be fixed precisely (for example, the wavelengths drift owing to temperature variations or age), and the crosstalk performance is far from the ideal situation. Also the passband of narrow band MZIs is not flat. In contrast, the dielectric multicavity thin-film filters have flat passbands and stop bands.

MZIs are useful as 2-input, 2-output multiplexers and demultiplexers. They can also be used as tunable filters, where the tuning is achieved by varying the temperature of one of the arms of the device. This causes the refractive index of that arm to change, which in turn affects the phase relationship between the two arms and causes a different wavelength to be coupled out. The tuning time required is of the order of several ms. For larger multiplexers and demultiplexers, better technologies

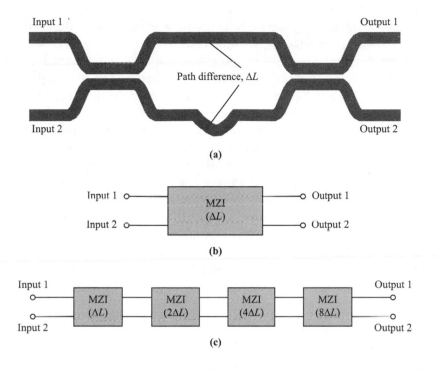

Figure 3.18   (a) A Mach-Zehnder interferometer constructed by interconnecting two 3-dB directional couplers. (b) A block diagram representation of the MZI in (a). ΔL denotes the path difference between the two arms. (c) A block diagram of a four-stage Mach-Zehnder interferometer.

are available today. One example is the *arrayed waveguide grating* (AWG) described in the next section. Since the understanding of the MZI is essential to understanding the AWG, we will now describe the principle of operation of MZIs.

Principle of Operation

Consider the operation of the MZI as a demultiplexer; so only one input, say, input 1, has a signal (see Figure 3.18(a)). After the first directional coupler, the input signal power is divided equally between the two arms of the MZI, but the signal in one arm has a phase shift of $\pi/2$ with respect to the other. Specifically, the signal in the lower arm lags the one in the upper arm in phase by $\pi/2$, as discussed in Section 3.1. This is best understood from (3.1). Since there is a length difference of ΔL between the two arms, there is a further phase lag of $\beta \Delta L$ introduced in the signal in the lower arm. In the second directional coupler, the signal from the lower arm undergoes another phase delay of $\pi/2$ in going to the first output relative to the signal from the upper arm. Thus the total relative phase difference at the first or upper *output* between the two signals is $\pi/2 + \beta \Delta L + \pi/2$. At the output directional coupler, in going to the second *output,* the signal from the upper arm lags the signal from the lower arm in phase by $\pi/2$. Thus the total relative phase difference at the second or lower output between the two signals is $\pi/2 + \beta \Delta L - \pi/2 = \beta \Delta L$.

If $\beta \Delta L = k\pi$ and k is odd, the signals at the first output add in phase, whereas the signals at the second output add with opposite phases and thus cancel each other. Thus the wavelengths passed from the first input to the first output are those wavelengths for which $\beta \Delta L = k\pi$ and k is odd. The wavelengths passed from the first input to the second output are those wavelengths for which $\beta \Delta L = k\pi$ and k is even. This could have been easily deduced from the transfer function of the MZI (3.12), but this detailed explanation will help in the understanding of the arrayed waveguide grating (Section 3.3.7).

Assume that the difference between these path lengths is ΔL and that only one input, say, input 1, is active. Then it can be shown (see Problem 3.11) that the power transfer function of the Mach-Zehnder interferometer is given by

$$\begin{pmatrix} T_{11}(f) \\ T_{12}(f) \end{pmatrix} = \begin{pmatrix} \sin^2(\beta \Delta L/2) \\ \cos^2(\beta \Delta L/2) \end{pmatrix}. \tag{3.12}$$

Thus the path difference between the two arms, ΔL, is the key parameter characterizing the transfer function of the MZI. We will represent the MZI of Figure 3.18(a) using the block diagram of Figure 3.18(b).

Now consider k MZIs interconnected, as shown in Figure 3.18(c) for $k = 4$. Such a device is termed a *multistage Mach-Zehnder interferometer.* The path length difference for the kth MZI in the cascade is assumed to be $2^{k-1} \Delta L$. The transfer function of each MZI in this multistage MZI together with the power transfer function of the entire filter is shown in Figure 3.19. The power transfer function of the multistage MZI is also shown on a dB scale in Figure 3.20.

We will now describe how an MZI can be used as a 1×2 demultiplexer. Since the device is reciprocal, it follows from the principles of electromagnetics that if the inputs and outputs are interchanged, it will act as a 2×1 multiplexer.

Consider a single MZI with a fixed value of the path difference ΔL. Let one of the inputs, say, input 1, be a wavelength division multiplexed signal with all the wavelengths chosen to coincide with the peaks or troughs of the transfer function. For concreteness, assume the propagation constant $\beta = 2\pi n_{\text{eff}}/\lambda$, where n_{eff} is the effective refractive index of the waveguide. The input wavelengths λ_i would have to be chosen such that $n_{\text{eff}} \Delta L/\lambda_i = m_i/2$ for some positive integer m_i. The wavelengths λ_i for which m is odd would then appear at the first output (since the transfer

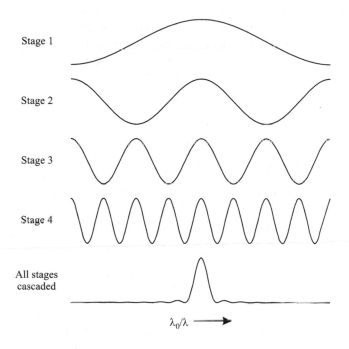

Figure 3.19   Transfer functions of each stage of a multistage MZI.

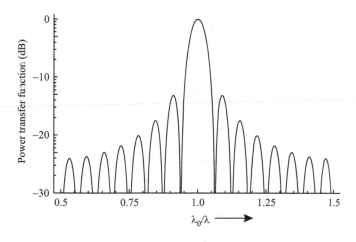

Figure 3.20   Transfer function of a multistage Mach-Zehnder interferometer.

function is $\sin^2(m_i\pi/2)$), and the wavelengths for which m_i is even would appear at the second output (since the transfer function is $\cos^2(m_i\pi/2)$).

If there are only two wavelengths, one for which m_i is odd and the other for which m_i is even, we have a 1×2 demultiplexer. The construction of a $1 \times n$ demultiplexer when n is a power of two, using $n - 1$ MZIs, is left as an exercise (Problem 3.12). But there is a better method of constructing larger demultiplexers, which we describe next.

3.3.7   Arrayed Waveguide Grating

An *arrayed waveguide grating* (AWG) is a generalization of the Mach-Zehnder interferometer. This device is illustrated in Figure 3.21. It consists of two multiport couplers interconnected by an array of waveguides. The MZI can be viewed as a device where *two* copies of the same signal, but shifted in phase by different amounts, are added together. The AWG is a device where *several* copies of the same signal, but shifted in phase by different amounts, are added together.

The AWG has several uses. It can be used as an $n \times 1$ *wavelength multiplexer*. In this capacity, it is an n-input, 1-output device where the n inputs are signals at different wavelengths that are combined onto the single output. The inverse of this function, namely, $1 \times n$ *wavelength demultiplexing*, can also be performed using an AWG. Although these wavelength multiplexers and demultiplexers can also be built using MZI interconnected in a suitable fashion, it is preferable to use an AWG. Relative to an MZI chain, an AWG has lower loss, flatter passband, and is easier to realize on an integrated-optic substrate. The input and output waveguides, the multiport couplers, and the arrayed waveguides are all fabricated on a single substrate. The substrate material is usually silicon, and the waveguides are silica, Ge-doped silica, or SiO_2-Ta_2O_5. 32-channel AWGs are commercially available, and

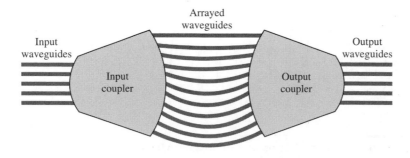

Figure 3.21   An arrayed waveguide grating (AWG).

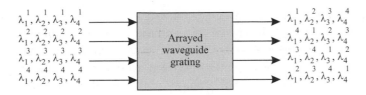

Figure 3.22   The routing pattern of a static router constructed from an arrayed wave-guide grating.

smaller AWGs are being used in WDM transmission systems. Their temperature co-efficient (0.01 nm/°C) is not as low as those of some other competing technologies such as fiber gratings and multilayer thin-film filters. So we will need to use active temperature control for these devices.

The AWG can also be used as a static router. However, this router is not capable of achieving an arbitrary routing pattern. Although several interconnection patterns can be achieved by a suitable choice of the wavelengths and the free spectral range (FSR) of the device, the most useful one is illustrated in Figure 3.22. This figure shows a 4 × 4 router using four wavelengths with one wavelength routed from each of the inputs to each of the outputs. Such a device may be useful to interconnect broadcast-star networks, as we will discuss in Section 7.1.

In order to achieve this interconnection pattern, the operating wavelengths and the free spectral range (FSR) of the AWG must be chosen suitably. The FSR of the AWG is derived in Problem 3.14. Given the FSR, we leave the determination of the wavelengths to be used to achieve this interconnection pattern as another exercise (Problem 3.15).

Principle of Operation

Consider the AWG shown in Figure 3.21. Let the number of inputs and outputs of the AWG be denoted by n. Let the couplers at the input and output be $n \times m$ and $m \times n$ in size, respectively. Thus the couplers are interconnected by m waveguides. We will call these waveguides *arrayed waveguides* to distinguish them from the input and output waveguides. The lengths of these waveguides are chosen such that the difference in length between consecutive waveguides is a constant denoted by ΔL. The MZI is a special case of the AWG, where $n = m = 2$. We will now determine which wavelengths will be transmitted from a given input to a given output. The first coupler splits the signal into m parts. The relative phases of these parts are determined by the distances traveled in the coupler from the input waveguides to the arrayed waveguides. Denote the differences in the distances traveled (relative to any one of the input waveguides and any one of the arrayed waveguides) between input waveguide i and arrayed waveguide k by d_{ik}^{in}. Assume that arrayed waveguide k has a path length larger than arrayed waveguide $k-1$ by ΔL. Similarly, denote the differences in the distances traveled (relative to any one of the arrayed waveguides and any one of the output waveguides) between arrayed waveguide k and output waveguide j by d_{kj}^{out}. Then, the relative phases of the signals from input i to output j traversing the m different paths between them are given by

$$\phi_{ijk} = \frac{2\pi}{\lambda}(n_1 d_{ik}^{\text{in}} + n_2 k \Delta L + n_1 d_{kj}^{\text{out}}), \qquad k = 1, \ldots, m. \tag{3.13}$$

Here, n_1 is the refractive index in the input and output directional couplers, and n_2 is the refractive index in the arrayed waveguides. From input i, those wavelengths λ, for which $\phi_{ijk}, k = 1, \ldots, m$, differ by a multiple of 2π will add in phase at output j. The question is are there any such wavelengths?

If the input and output couplers are designed such that $d_{ik}^{\text{in}} = d_i^{\text{in}} + k\delta_i^{\text{in}}$ and $d_{kj}^{\text{out}} = d_j^{\text{out}} + k\delta_j^{\text{out}}$, then (3.13) can be written as

$$\begin{aligned}
\phi_{ijk} &= \frac{2\pi}{\lambda}(n_1 d_i^{\text{in}} + n_1 d_j^{\text{out}}) \\
&+ \frac{2\pi k}{\lambda}(n_1 \delta_i^{\text{in}} + n_2 \Delta L + n_1 \delta_j^{\text{out}}), \qquad k = 1, \ldots, m.
\end{aligned} \tag{3.14}$$

Such a construction is possible and is called the *Rowland circle* construction. It is illustrated in Figure 3.23 and discussed further in Problem 3.13. Thus wavelengths

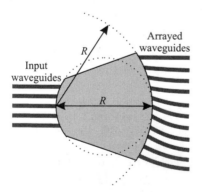

Figure 3.23 The Rowland circle construction for the couplers used in the AWG. The arrayed waveguides are located on the arc of a circle, called the *grating circle*, whose center is at the end of the central input (output) waveguide. Let the *radius* of this circle be denoted by R. The other input (output) waveguides are located on the arc of a circle whose *diameter* is equal to R; this circle is called the *Rowland circle*. The vertical spacing between the arrayed waveguides is chosen to be constant.

λ that are present at input i and that satisfy $n_1 \delta_i^{\text{in}} + n_2 \Delta L + n_1 \delta_j^{\text{out}} = p\lambda$ for some integer p add in phase at output j.

For use as a demultiplexer, all the wavelengths are present at the same input, say, input i. Therefore, if the wavelengths, $\lambda_1, \lambda_2, \ldots, \lambda_n$ in the WDM system satisfy $n_1 \delta_i^{\text{in}} + n_2 \Delta L + n_1 \delta_j^{\text{out}} = p\lambda_j$ for some integer p, we infer from (3.14) that these wavelengths are demultiplexed by the AWG. Note that though Δd_i^{in} and ΔL are necessary to define the precise set of wavelengths that are demultiplexed, the spacing between them is independent of Δd_i^{in} and ΔL, and determined primarily by Δd_j^{out}.

Note in the preceding example that if wavelength λ_j' satisfies $n_1 \delta_i^{\text{in}} + n_2 \Delta L + n_1 \delta_j^{\text{out}} = (p+1)\lambda_j'$, then both λ_j and λ_j' are "demultiplexed" to output j from input i. Thus like many of the other filter and multiplexer/demultiplexer structures we have studied, the AWG has a periodic response (in frequency), and all the wavelengths must lie within one free spectral range (FSR). The derivation of an expression for this FSR is left as an exercise (Problem 3.14).

3.3.8 Acousto-Optic Tunable Filter

The acousto-optic tunable filter is a versatile device. It is probably the only known *tunable* filter that is capable of selecting several wavelengths simultaneously. This capability can be used to construct a (multi)wavelength router, as we will explain later in this section.

The acousto-optic tunable filter (AOTF) is one example of several optical devices whose construction is based on the interaction of sound and light. The basic principles of this interaction are dealt with in the references. Figure 3.24 shows the various parts of an AOTF. This is an integrated-optics version of the AOTF and is the one we will discuss.

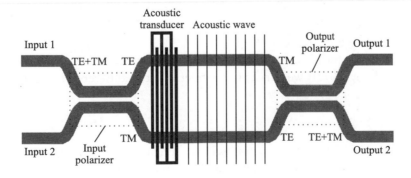

Figure 3.24 An integrated-optics AOTF.

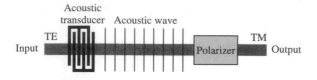

Figure 3.25   A simple AOTF.

Principle of Operation

Consider the device shown in Figure 3.25. It consists of a waveguide constructed from a birefringent material and supporting only the lowest-order TE and TM modes (see Section 2.1.2). We assume that the input light energy is entirely in the TE mode. A *polarizer*, which selects only the light energy in the TM mode, is placed at the other end of the channel waveguide. If, somehow, the light energy in a narrow spectral range around the wavelength to be selected is converted to the TM mode, while the rest of the light energy remains in the TE mode, we have a wavelength-selective filter. This conversion is effected in an AOTF by launching an acoustic wave along, or opposite to, the direction of propagation of the light wave.

As a result of the propagation of the acoustic wave, the density of the medium varies in a periodic manner. The period of this density variation is equal to the wavelength of the acoustic wave. This periodic density variation acts as a *Bragg grating*. From the discussion of such gratings in Section 3.3.2, it follows that if the refractive indices n_{TE} and n_{TM} of the TE and TM modes satisfy the *Bragg condition*

$$\frac{n_{TM}}{\lambda} = \frac{n_{TE}}{\lambda} \pm \frac{1}{\Lambda},$$
(3.15)

then light couples from one mode to the other. Thus light energy in a narrow spectral range around the wavelength λ that satisfies (3.15) undergoes TE to TM mode conversion. Thus the device acts as a narrow bandwidth filter when only light energy in the TE mode is input and only the light energy in the TM mode is selected at the output, as shown in Figure 3.25.

In LiNbO$_3$, the TE and TM modes have refractive indices n_{TE} and n_{TM} that differ by about 0.07. If we denote this refractive index difference by (Δn), the Bragg condition (3.15) can be written as

$$\lambda = \Lambda(\Delta n).$$
(3.16)

The wavelength that undergoes mode conversion and thus lies in the passband of the AOTF can be selected, or tuned, by suitably choosing the acoustic wavelength Λ. In order to select a wavelength of 1.55 μm, for (Δn) = 0.07, using (3.16) the acoustic wavelength is about 22 μm. Since the velocity of sound in LiNbO$_3$ is about 3.75 km/s, the corresponding RF frequency is about 170 MHz. Since the RF frequency is easily tuned, the wavelength selected by the filter can also be easily tuned.

The AOTF considered here is a polarization-dependent device since the input light energy is assumed to be entirely in the TE mode. A polarization-independent AOTF, shown in Figure 3.24, can be realized in exactly the same manner as a polarization-independent isolator by decomposing the input light signal into its TE and TM constituents and sending each constituent separately through the AOTF and recombining them at the output.

Transfer Function

Whereas the Bragg condition determines the wavelength that is selected, the width of the filter passband is determined by the length of the acousto-optic interaction. The longer this interaction, and hence the device, the narrower the passband. It can be shown that the wavelength dependence of the fraction of the power transmitted by the AOTF is given by

$$T(\lambda) = \frac{\sin^2\left((\pi/2)\sqrt{1 + (2\Delta\lambda/\Delta)^2}\right)}{1 + (2\Delta\lambda/\Delta)^2}.$$

This is plotted in Figure 3.26. Here $\Delta\lambda = \lambda - \lambda_0$, where λ_0 is the optical wavelength that satisfies the Bragg condition, and $\Delta = \lambda_0^2/l\Delta n$ is a measure of the filter passband width. Here, l is the length of the device (or, more correctly, the length of the acousto-optic interaction). It can be shown that the full width at half-maximum (FWHM) bandwidth of the filter is $\approx 0.8\Delta$ (Problem 3.17). This equation clearly shows that the longer the device, the narrower the passband. However, there is a tradeoff here: the tuning speed is inversely proportional to l. This is because the tuning speed is essentially determined by the time it takes for a sound wave to travel the length of the filter.

AOTF as a Router

The polarization-independent AOTF illustrated in Figure 3.24 can be used as a 2-input, 2-output wavelength router. We studied the operation of this device as a filter in Section 3.3.8; in this case, only one of the inputs was active. We leave it as an exercise (Problem 3.18) to show that when the second input is also active, the energy at the wavelength λ satisfying the Bragg phase-matching condition (3.16) is *exchanged* between the two ports. This is illustrated in Figure 3.27(a), where the wavelength λ_1 satisfies the Bragg condition and is exchanged between the ports.

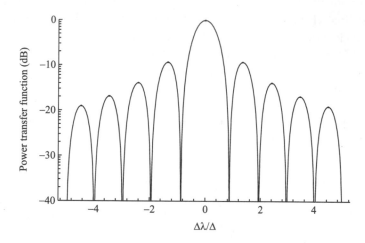

Figure 3.26   The power transfer function of the acousto-optic tunable filter.

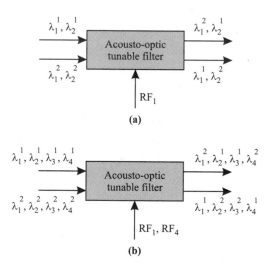

Figure 3.27   Wavelength routers constructed from acousto-optic tunable filters. (a) The wavelength λ_1 is exchanged between the two ports. (b) The wavelengths λ_1 and λ_4 are simultaneously exchanged between the two ports by the simultaneous launching of two appropriate acoustic waves.

Now the AOTF has one remarkable property that is not shared by any other tunable filter structure we know. By launching multiple acoustic waves *simultaneously*, the Bragg condition (3.16) can be satisfied for multiple optical wavelengths simultaneously. Thus multiple wavelength exchanges can be accomplished simultaneously between two ports with a single device of the form shown in Figure 3.24. This is illustrated in Figure 3.27(b), where the wavelengths λ_1 and λ_4 are exchanged between the ports. Thus this device performs the same routing function as the static router of Figure 3.6. However, the AOTF is a completely general 2-input, 2-output *dynamic* router since the routing pattern, or the set of wavelengths to be exchanged, can be changed easily by varying the frequencies of the acoustic waves launched in the device. In principle, larger dimensional dynamic routers (with more input and output ports) can be built by suitably cascading 2×2 routers.

As of this writing, the AOTF has not yet lived up to its promise either as a versatile tunable filter or a wavelength router. One reason for this is the high level of crosstalk that is present in the device. As can be seen from Figure 3.26, the first side lobe in its power transfer function is not even 10 dB below the peak transmission. This problem can be alleviated to some extent by cascading two such filters. In fact, the cascade can even be built on a single substrate. But even then the first side lobe would be less than 20 dB below the peak transmission. It is harder to cascade more such devices without facing other problems such as an unacceptably high transmission loss. Another reason for the comparative failure of the AOTF today is that the passband width is fairly large (1 nm or more) even when the acousto-optic interaction length is around 1 inch (Problem 3.19). Devices with larger interaction lengths are more difficult to fabricate. However, some recent theoretical work [Son95] indicates that some of these problems, particularly crosstalk, may be solvable. The crosstalk problems that arise in AOTFs when used as multiwavelength routers are discussed in detail in [Jac96].

$\underline{3.4}$ Optical Amplifiers

In an optical communication system, the optical signals from the transmitter are attenuated by the optical fiber as they propagate through it. After some distance, the cumulative loss of signal strength causes the signal to become too weak to be detected. Before this happens, the signal strength has to be restored. Prior to the advent of optical amplifiers over the last decade, the only option was to regenerate the signal, that is, receive the signal and retransmit it. This process is accomplished by *regenerators*. A regenerator converts the optical signal to an electrical signal, cleans it up, and converts it back into an optical signal for onward transmission.

Optical amplifiers offer several advantages compared to regenerators. Regenerators are specific to the bit rate and modulation format used by the communication system. On the other hand, optical amplifiers are insensitive to the bit rate or signal formats. Thus a system using optical amplifiers can be more easily upgraded, for example, to a higher bit rate, without replacing the amplifiers. In contrast, in a system using regenerators, such an upgrade would require all the regenerators to be replaced. Furthermore, optical amplifiers have fairly large gain bandwidths, and as a consequence, a single amplifier can simultaneously amplify several wavelength division multiplexed (WDM) signals. In contrast, we would need a regenerator for each wavelength. Thus optical amplifiers have become essential components in high-performance optical communication systems. We will explore the principles behind the operation of these devices. The impact of optical amplifiers on the physical layer design of the system will be discussed in Chapters 4 and 5.

We will consider three different types of amplifiers: *Erbium-doped fiber amplifiers* (EDFAs), *Praseodymium-doped fiber amplifiers* (PDFAs), and *semiconductor optical amplifiers* (SOAs).

3.4.1   Stimulated Emission

In all the amplifiers we consider, the key physical phenomenon behind signal amplification is *stimulated emission* of radiation by atoms in the presence of an electromagnetic field. (This is not true of fiber Raman or fiber Brillouin amplifiers, which make use of fiber nonlinearities, but we do not treat these here.) This field is an optical signal in the case of optical amplifiers. Stimulated emission is the principle underlying the operation of lasers as well; we will study lasers in Section 3.5.1.

According to the principles of quantum mechanics, any physical system (for example, an atom) is found in one of a discrete number of energy levels. Accordingly, consider an atom and two of its energy levels, E_1 and E_2, with $E_2 > E_1$. An electromagnetic field whose frequency f_c satisfies $hf_c = E_2 - E_1$ induces transitions of atoms between the energy levels E_1 and E_2. Here, h is Planck's constant (6.63 × 10^{-34} J s). This process is depicted in Figure 3.28. Both kinds of transitions, $E_1 \rightarrow E_2$ and $E_2 \rightarrow E_1$, occur. $E_1 \rightarrow E_2$ transitions are accompanied by *absorption* of photons from the incident electromagnetic field. $E_2 \rightarrow E_1$ transitions are accompanied by the *emission* of photons of energy hf_c, the same energy as that of the incident photons. This emission process is termed *stimulated emission* to distinguish it from another kind of emission called *spontaneous emission*, which we will discuss later. Thus if stimulated emission were to dominate over absorption—that is, the incident signal causes more $E_2 \rightarrow E_1$ transitions than $E_1 \rightarrow E_2$ transitions—we would have a net increase in the number of photons of energy hf_c and an amplification of the signal. Otherwise, the signal will be attenuated.

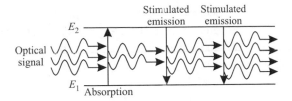

Figure 3.28   Stimulated emission and absorption in an atomic system with two energy levels.

It follows from the theory of quantum mechanics that the rate of the $E_1 \rightarrow E_2$ transitions per atom *equals* the rate of the $E_2 \rightarrow E_1$ transitions *per atom*. Let this common rate be denoted by r. If the populations (number of atoms) in the energy levels E_1 and E_2 are N_1 and N_2, respectively, we have a net increase in power (energy per unit time) of $(N_2 - N_1)rhf_c$. Clearly, for amplification to occur, this must be positive, that is, $N_2 > N_1$. This condition is known as *population inversion*. The reason for this term is that, at thermal equilibrium, lower energy levels are more highly populated, that is, $N_2 < N_1$. Therefore, at thermal equilibrium, we have only absorption of the input signal. In order for amplification to occur, we must *invert* the relationship between the populations of levels E_1 and E_2 that prevails under thermal equilibrium.

Population inversion can be achieved by supplying additional energy in a suitable form to pump the electrons to the higher energy level. This additional energy can be in optical or electrical form.

3.4.2   Spontaneous Emission

Before describing the operation of the different types of amplifiers, it is important to understand the impact of spontaneous emission. Consider again the atomic system with the two energy levels discussed earlier. Independent of any external radiation that may be present, atoms in energy level E_2 transit to the lower energy level E_1 emitting a photon of energy hf_c. The spontaneous emission rate per atom from level E_2 to level E_1 is a characteristic of the system, and its reciprocal, denoted by τ_{21}, is called the *spontaneous emission lifetime*. Thus if there are N_2 atoms in level E_2, the rate of spontaneous emission is N_2/τ_{21}, and the spontaneous emission power is $hf_c N_2/\tau_{21}$.

The spontaneous emission process does not contribute to the gain of the amplifier (to first order). Although the emitted photons have the same energy hf_c as the incident optical signal, they are emitted in random directions, polarizations, and phase. This is unlike the stimulated emission process where the emitted photons not only have the same energy as the incident photons but also the same direction of propagation, phase, and polarization. This phenomenon is usually described by saying that the stimulated emission process is *coherent*, whereas the spontaneous emission process is *incoherent*.

Spontaneous emission has a deleterious effect on the system. The amplifier treats spontaneous emission radiation as another electromagnetic field at the frequency hf_c and the spontaneous emission also gets amplified, in addition to the incident optical signal. This *amplified spontaneous emission* (ASE) appears as noise at the output of the amplifier. The implications of ASE on the design of optical communication systems are discussed in Chapters 4 and 5. In addition, in some amplifier designs, the ASE can be large enough so as to *saturate* the amplifier. Saturation effects are explored in Chapter 5.

3.4.3   Erbium-Doped Fiber Amplifiers

An Erbium-doped fiber amplifier (EDFA) is shown in Figure 3.29. It consists of a length of silica fiber whose core is doped with ionized atoms, Er^{3+}, of the rare earth element Erbium. This fiber is pumped using a pump signal from a laser, typically at a wavelength of 980 nm or 1480 nm. So around the doped fiber is a wavelength selective coupler to combine the output of the pump laser with the input signal. At the output, another coupler separates the amplified signal from any remaining pump signal power. Usually, an isolator is used at the input and/or output of any amplifier to prevent reflections into the amplifier—we will see in Section 3.5 that reflections can convert the amplifier into a laser, making it unusable as an amplifier.

A combination of several factors has made the EDFA the amplifier of choice in today's optical communication systems. This includes (a) the availability of compact and reliable high-power semiconductor pump lasers, (b) the fact that it is an all-fiber device, making it polarization independent and easy to couple light in and out of it, (c) the simplicity of the device, and (d) the fact that it introduces no crosstalk

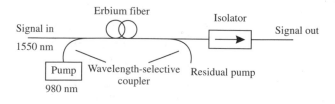

Figure 3.29   An Erbium-doped fiber amplifier.

when amplifying WDM signals. This last aspect is discussed later in the context of semiconductor optical amplifiers.

Principle of Operation

Three of the energy levels of Erbium ions in silica glass are shown in Figure 3.30 and are labeled E_1, E_2, and E_3 in order of increasing energy. Several other levels in Er^{3+} are not shown. Each energy level that appears as a discrete line in an isolated ion of Erbium is split into multiple energy levels when these ions are introduced into silica glass. This process is termed *Stark splitting*. Moreover, glass is not a crystal and thus does not have a regular structure. Thus the Stark splitting levels introduced are slightly different for different Erbium ions, depending on the local surroundings seen by those ions. Macroscopically, that is, when viewed as a collection of ions, this has the effect of spreading each discrete energy level of an Erbium ion into a continuous *energy band*. This spreading of energy levels is a useful characteristic for optical amplifiers since they increase the frequency or wavelength range of the signals that can be amplified. Within each energy band, the Erbium ions are distributed in the various levels within that band in a nonuniform manner by a process known as *thermalization*. It is due to this thermalization process that an amplifier is capable of amplifying several wavelengths simultaneously. Note that Stark splitting denotes the phenomenon by which the energy levels of free Erbium ions are split into a number of levels, or into an energy band, when the ion is introduced into silica glass.

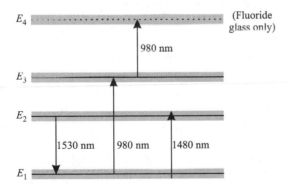

Figure 3.30   Three energy levels E_1, E_2, and E_3 of Er^{3+} ions in silica glass. The fourth energy level, E_4, is present in fluoride glass but not in silica glass. The energy levels are spread into bands by the Stark splitting process. The difference between the energy levels is labeled with the wavelength in nm of the photon corresponding to it.

Thermalization refers to the process by which the Erbium ions are distributed within the various (split) levels constituting an energy band.

Recall from our discussion of the two energy level atomic system that only an optical signal at the frequency f_c satisfying $hf_c = E_2 - E_1$ could be amplified in that case. If these levels are spread into bands, all frequencies that correspond to the energy difference between some energy in the E_2 band and some energy in the E_1 band can be amplified. In the case of Erbium ions in silica glass, the set of frequencies that can be amplified by stimulated emission from the E_2 band to the E_1 band corresponds to the wavelength range 1525–1570 nm, a bandwidth of 50 nm, with a peak around 1532 nm. By a lucky coincidence, this is exactly one of the low attenuation windows of standard optical fiber that optical communication systems use.

Denote the atomic (or ionic) population in level E_i by N_i, $i = 1, 2, 3$. In thermal equilibrium, $N_1 > N_2 > N_3$. The population inversion condition for stimulated emission from E_2 to E_1 is $N_2 > N_1$ and can be achieved by a combination of absorption and spontaneous emission as follows. The energy difference between the E_1 and E_3 levels corresponds to a wavelength of 980 nm. So if optical power at 980 nm—called the *pump power*—is injected into the amplifier, it will cause transitions from E_1 to E_3 and vice versa. Since $N_1 > N_3$, there will be a net absorption of the 980 nm power. This process is called *pumping*.

The atoms that have been raised to level E_3 by this process will quickly transit to level E_2 by the spontaneous emission process. The lifetime for this process, τ_{32}, is about 1 μs. Atoms from level E_2 will also transit to level E_1 by the spontaneous emission process, but the lifetime for this process, τ_{21}, is about 10 ms, which is much larger than the E_3 to E_2 lifetime. Moreover, if the pump power is sufficiently large, atoms that transit to the E_1 level are rapidly raised again to the E_3 level only to transit to the E_2 level again. The net effect is that most of the atoms are found in level E_2, and thus we have population inversion between the E_2 and E_1 levels. Therefore, if simultaneously a signal in the 1525–1570 nm band is injected into the fiber, it will be amplified by stimulated emission from the E_2 to the E_1 level.

Several levels other than E_3 are higher than E_2 and, in principle, can be used for pumping the amplifier. But the pumping process is more efficient, that is, uses less pump power for a given gain, at 980 nm than these other wavelengths. Another possible choice for the pump wavelength is 1480 nm. This choice corresponds to absorption from the bottom sublevel of the E_1 band to the top sublevel of the E_2 band itself. Pumping at 1480 nm is not as efficient as 980 nm pumping. Moreover, the degree of population inversion that can be achieved by 1480 nm pumping is lower. The higher the population inversion, the lower the ASE introduced by the amplifier. Thus 980 nm pumping is preferred to realize low-noise amplifiers. However, higher-power pump lasers are available at 1480 nm, compared to 980 nm, and thus

1480 nm pumps find applications in amplifiers designed to yield high output powers. Another advantage of the 1480 nm pump is that the pump power can also propagate with low loss in the silica fiber that is used to carry the signals. Therefore, the pump laser can be located remotely from the amplifier itself. This feature is used in some systems to avoid placing any active components in the middle of the link.

Gain Flatness

Since the population levels at the various levels within a band are different, the gain of an EDFA becomes a function of the wavelength. Thus in a WDM communication system, different WDM channels undergo different degrees of amplification. This is a critical issue, particularly in WDM systems with cascaded amplifiers, and is discussed in Section 5.5.2.

One way to improve the flatness of the amplifier gain profile is to use fluoride glass fiber instead of silica fiber, doped with Erbium [Cle94]. Such amplifiers are called EDFFAs, or Erbium-doped fluoride fiber amplifiers. The fluoride glass produces a naturally flatter gain spectrum compared to silica glass. However, there are a few drawbacks to using fluoride glass. The noise performance of EDFFAs is poorer than EDFAs. One reason is that they must be pumped at 1480 nm and cannot be pumped at 980 nm. This is because fluoride glass has an additional higher energy level E_4 above the E_3 level, as shown in Figure 3.30, with the difference in energies between these two levels corresponding to 980 nm. This causes the 980 nm pump power to be absorbed for transitions from the E_3 to E_4 level, which does not produce useful gain. This phenomenon is called *excited state absorption*.

In addition to this drawback, fluoride fiber itself is difficult to handle. It is brittle, difficult to splice with conventional fiber, and susceptible to moisture. Nevertheless, EDFFAs are now commercially available devices.

Another approach to flatten the EDFA gain is to use a filter inside the amplifier. The EDFA has a relatively high gain at 1532 nm, which can be reduced by using a notch filter in that wavelength region inside the amplifier. Some of the filters described in Section 3.3 can be used for this purpose. Long-period fiber gratings and dielectric thin-film filters are currently the leading candidates for this application.

Multistage Designs

In practice, most amplifiers deployed in real systems are more complicated than the simple structure shown in Figure 3.29. Figure 3.31 shows a more commonly used two-stage design. The two stages are optimized differently. The first stage is designed to provide high gain and low noise, and the second stage is designed to produce high output power. As we will see in Problem 4.4 in Chapter 4, the noise performance of the whole amplifier is determined primarily by the first stage.

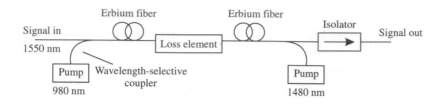

Figure 3.31   A two-stage Erbium-doped fiber amplifier.

Thus this combination produces a high-performance amplifier with low noise and high output power. Another important consideration in the design is to provide redundancy in the event of the failure of a pump, the only active component of the amplifier. The amplifier shown in the figure uses two pumps and is designed so that the failure of one pump has only a small impact on the system performance. Another feature of the two-stage design that we will address in Problem 4.4 is that a loss element can be placed between the two stages with negligible impact on the performance. This loss element may be a gain flattening filter, a simple optical add/drop multiplexer, or a dispersion compensation module used to compensate for accumulated dispersion along the link.

3.4.4   Praseodymium-Doped Fiber Amplifiers

The success of the EDFA led to the quest for a similar device to amplify signals in the 1.3 μm wavelength band, which is another important band used by optical communication systems. A perfect device is yet to be found, although the Praseodymium-doped fiber amplifier (PDFA) offers some promise. The principle of operation of this amplifier is very similar to the EDFA. The pump wavelength for PDFAs is 1017 nm, where pump lasers are not yet well developed. They use fluoride fiber instead of silica fiber, which leads to the problems described in the context of EDFFAs. However, these difficulties are beginning to be overcome, and PDFAs may become commercially available in the next few years.

3.4.5   Semiconductor Optical Amplifiers

Semiconductor optical amplifiers (SOAs) actually preceded EDFAs, although we will see that they are not as good as EDFAs for use as amplifiers. However they are finding other applications in switches and wavelength converter devices. Moreover, the understanding of SOAs is key to the understanding of semiconductor lasers, the most widely used transmitters today.

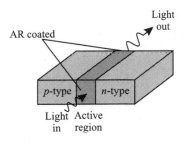

Figure 3.32   Block diagram of a semiconductor optical amplifier. Amplification occurs when light propagates through the active region.

Figure 3.32 shows the block diagram of a semiconductor optical amplifier. The SOA is essentially a *pn*-junction. As we will explain shortly, the depletion layer that is formed at the junction acts as the *active region*. Light is amplified through stimulated emission when it propagates through the active region. For an amplifier, the two ends of the active region are given an antireflection (AR) coating to eliminate ripples in the amplifier gain as a function of wavelength. In the case of a semiconductor laser, there would be no AR coating.

Semiconductor optical amplifiers (SOAs) differ from EDFAs in the manner in which population inversion is achieved. First, the populations are not those of atoms in various energy states but of carriers—electrons or holes—in a semiconductor material. A semiconductor consists of two bands of electron energy levels: a band of low mobility levels called the *valence band* and a band of high mobility levels called the *conduction band*. These bands are separated by an energy difference called the *bandgap* and denoted by E_g. No energy levels exist in the bandgap. Consider a *p*-type semiconductor material. At thermal equilibrium, there is only a very small concentration of electrons in the conduction band of the material, as shown in Figure 3.33(a). With reference to the previous discussion of EDFAs, it is convenient to think of the conduction band as the higher energy band E_2, and the valence band as the lower energy band E_1. The terms *higher* and *lower* refer to the electron energy in these bands. (Note that if we were considering an *n*-type semiconductor, we would be considering hole energies rather than electron energies, the conduction band would be the lower energy band E_1, and the valence band, the higher energy band E_2.) In the population inversion condition, the electron concentration in the conduction band is much higher, as shown in Figure 3.33(b). This increased concentration is such that in the presence of an optical signal, there are more electrons transiting from the conduction band to the valence band by the process of stimulated emission than there are electrons transiting from the valence band to the conduction band

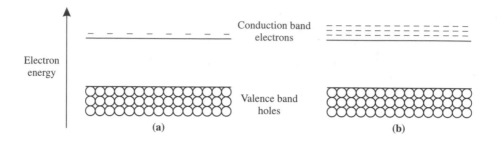

Figure 3.33   The energy bands in a *p*-type semiconductor and the electron concentration at (a) thermal equilibrium, and (b) population inversion.

by the process of absorption. In fact, for SOAs, this condition must be used as the defining one for population inversion, or optical gain.

Population inversion in an SOA is achieved by *forward biasing* a *pn-junction*. A *pn-junction* consists of two semiconductors: a *p*-type semiconductor that is doped with suitable impurity atoms so as to have an excess concentration of holes, and an *n*-type semiconductor that has an excess concentration of electrons. To understand the operation of a *pn*-junction, it is convenient to think of holes also as charge carriers similar to electrons except that they have positive charge. When the two semiconductors are in juxtaposition, as in Figure 3.34(a), holes diffuse from the *p*-type semiconductor to the *n*-type semiconductor, and electrons diffuse from the *n*-type semiconductor to the *p*-type semiconductor. This creates a region with net negative charge in the *p*-type semiconductor and a region with net positive charge in the *n*-type semiconductor, as shown in Figure 3.34(b). These regions are devoid of free charge carriers and are together termed the *depletion region*. When no voltage (bias) is applied to the *pn*-junction, the minority carrier concentrations (electrons in the *p*-type region and holes in the *n*-type region) remain at their thermal equilibrium values. When the junction is *forward biased*—positive bias is applied to the *p*-type and negative bias to the *n*-type—as shown in Figure 3.34(c), the width of the depletion region is reduced, and there is a drift of electrons from the *n*-type region to the *p*-type region. This drift increases the electron concentration in the conduction band of the *p*-type region. Similarly, there is a drift of holes from the *p*-type to the *n*-type region that increases the hole concentration in the valence band of the *n*-type region. When the forward bias voltage is sufficiently high, these increased minority carrier concentrations result in population inversion, and the *pn*-junction acts as an optical amplifier.

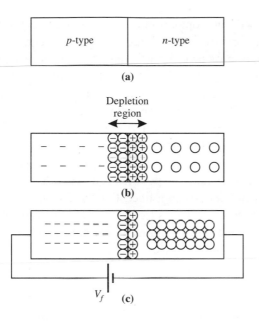

Figure 3.34 A forward-biased *pn*-junction used as an amplifier. (a) A *pn*-junction. (b) Minority carrier concentrations and depletion region with no bias voltage applied. (c) Minority carrier concentrations and depletion region with a forward bias voltage, V_f.

In practice, a simple *pn*-junction is not used, but a thin layer of a different semiconductor material is sandwiched between the *p*-type and *n*-type regions. Such a device is called a *heterostructure*. This semiconductor material then forms the *active region* or *layer*. The material used for the active layer has a slightly smaller bandgap and a higher refractive index than the surrounding *p*-type and *n*-type regions. The smaller bandgap helps to confine the carriers injected into the active region (electrons from the *n*-type region and holes from the *p*-type region). The larger refractive index helps to confine the light during amplification since the structure now forms a dielectric waveguide (see Section 2.1.2).

In semiconductor optical amplifiers, the population inversion condition (stimulated emission exceeds absorption) must be evaluated as a function of optical frequency or wavelength. Consider an optical frequency f_c such that $hf_c > E_g$, where E_g is the bandgap of the semiconductor material. The lowest optical frequency (or largest wavelength) that can be amplified corresponds to this bandgap. As the forward bias voltage is increased, the population inversion condition for this wavelength is reached first. As the forward bias voltage increases further, the electrons injected into the p-type region occupy progressively higher energy levels, and signals with smaller wavelengths can be amplified. In practice, bandwidths of the order of 100 nm can be achieved with SOAs. This is much larger than what is achievable with EDFAs. Signals in the 1.3 and 1.55 μm bands can even be simultaneously amplified using SOAs. Nevertheless, EDFAs are widely preferred to SOAs for several reasons. The main reason is that SOAs introduce severe crosstalk when they are used in WDM systems. This is discussed next. The gains and output powers achievable with EDFAs are higher. The coupling losses and the polarization-dependent losses are also lower with EDFAs since the amplifier is also a fiber. Finally, the SOA requires very high-quality antireflective coatings on its facets (reflectivity of less than 10^{-4}), which is not easy to achieve. Higher values create ripples in the gain spectrum and cause gain variations due to temperature fluctuations.

3.4.6   Crosstalk in SOAs

Consider an SOA to which is input the sum of two optical signals at different wavelengths. Assume that both wavelengths are within the bandwidth of the SOA. The presence of one signal will deplete the minority carrier concentration by the stimulated emission process so that the population inversion seen by the other signal is reduced. Thus the other signal will not be amplified to the same extent and, if the minority carrier concentrations are not very large, may even be absorbed! (Recall that if the population inversion condition is not achieved, there is net absorption of the signal.) Thus for wavelength division multiplexed networks, the gain seen by the signal in one channel varies with the presence or absence of signals in the other channels. This phenomenon is called *crosstalk*, and it has a detrimental effect on the system performance.

This crosstalk phenomenon depends on the spontaneous emission lifetime from the high-energy to the low-energy state. If the lifetime is large enough compared to the rate of fluctuations of power in the input signals, the electrons cannot make the transition from the high-energy state to the lower-energy state in response to these fluctuations. Thus there is no crosstalk whatsoever. In the case of SOAs, this lifetime is of the order of ns. Thus the electrons can easily respond to fluctuations in power of signals modulated at gigabit/second rates, resulting in a major system impairment due to crosstalk. In contrast, the spontaneous emission lifetime in an EDFA is about 10 ms. Thus crosstalk is introduced only if the modulation rates of the input signals are less than a few kHz, which is not usually the case. Thus EDFAs are better suited for use in WDM systems than SOAs.

The crosstalk effect is not without its uses. We will see in Section 3.8.2 that it can be used to make a *wavelength converter.*

3.5   Transmitters

3.5.1   Lasers

Lasers are the most widely used light sources in optical communication systems. A laser is essentially an optical amplifier enclosed within a reflective cavity that causes it to oscillate via positive feedback. *Semiconductor* lasers use semiconductors as the gain medium, whereas *fiber* lasers typically use Erbium-doped fiber as the gain medium. Semiconductor lasers are by far the most popular light sources for optical communication systems. They are compact, usually only a few hundred μm in size. Since they are essentially *pn*-junctions, they can be fabricated in large volumes using highly advanced integrated semiconductor technology. The lack of any need for optical pumping, unlike fiber lasers, is another advantage. In fact, a fiber laser typically uses a semiconductor laser as a pump! Semiconductor lasers are also highly efficient in converting input electrical (pump) energy into output optical energy.

Both semiconductor and Erbium fiber lasers are capable of achieving high output powers, typically between 0 and 10 dBm. Fiber lasers are used mostly to generate periodic trains of very short pulses (by using a technique called mode locking, discussed later in this section).

Principle of Operation

Consider any of the optical amplifiers described, and assume that a part of the optical energy is reflected at the ends of the amplifying or *gain medium,* or *cavity,* as shown in Figure 3.35. Further assume that the two ends of the cavity are plane and parallel to each other. Thus the gain medium is placed in a *Fabry-Perot cavity* (see Section 3.3.4). Such an optical amplifier is called a *Fabry-Perot amplifier.* The two end faces of the cavity (which play the role of the mirrors) are called *facets.*

The result of placing the gain medium in a Fabry-Perot cavity is that the gain is high only for the resonant wavelengths of the cavity. The argument is the same as that which was used in the case of the Fabry-Perot filter (Section 3.3.4). After one pass through the cavity, as shown in Figure 3.35, a part of the light leaves the cavity through the right facet, and a part is reflected. A part of the reflected wave is again reflected by the left facet to the right facet. For the resonant wavelengths of the cavity, all the light waves transmitted through the right facet *add in phase.* As a result of in-phase addition, the amplitude of the transmitted wave is greatly increased for

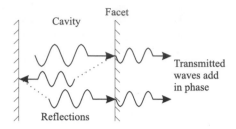

Figure 3.35   Reflection and transmission at the facets of a Fabry-Perot cavity.

these resonant wavelengths compared to other wavelengths. Thus when the facets are at least partially reflecting, the gain of the optical amplifier becomes a function of the wavelength.

If the combination of the amplifier gain and the facet reflectivity is sufficiently large, the amplifier will start to "oscillate," or produce light output, even in the absence of an input signal. For a given device, the point at which this happens is called its *lasing threshold*. Beyond the threshold, the device is no longer an amplifier but an oscillator or *laser*. This occurs because the stray spontaneous emission, which is always present at all wavelengths within the bandwidth of the amplifier, gets amplified even without an input signal, and appears as the light output. This process is quite similar to what happens in an electronic oscillator, which can be viewed as an (electronic) amplifier with positive feedback. (In electronic oscillators, the thermal noise current due to the random motion of electrons serves the same purpose as spontaneous emission.) Since the amplification process is due to stimulated emission, the light output of a laser is *coherent*. In fact, laser is an acronym for *light amplification* by *stimulated emission* of *radiation*.

Longitudinal Modes

For laser oscillation to occur at a particular wavelength, two conditions must be satisfied. First, the wavelength must be within the bandwidth of the gain medium that is used. Thus if a laser is made from Erbium-doped fiber, the wavelength must lie in the range 1525–1560 nm. The second condition is that the length of the cavity must be an integral multiple of half the wavelength in the cavity. For a given laser, all the wavelengths that satisfy this second condition are called the *longitudinal modes* of that laser. The adjective "longitudinal" is used to distinguish these from the waveguide modes (which should strictly be called spatial modes) that we studied in Section 2.1.

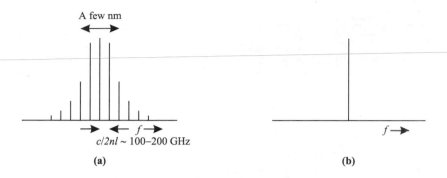

Figure 3.36   The spectrum of the output of (a) an MLM laser, and (b) an SLM laser. The laser cavity length is denoted by l, and its refractive index by n. The frequency spacing between the modes of an MLM laser is then $c/2nl$.

The laser described earlier is called a *Fabry-Perot laser* (FP laser) and will usually oscillate simultaneously in several longitudinal modes. Such a laser is termed a *multiple-longitudinal mode,* or MLM laser. MLM lasers have large spectral widths, typically around 10 nm. A typical spectrum of the output of an MLM laser is shown in Figure 3.36(a). We saw in Section 2.3.2 that for high-speed optical communication systems, the spectral width of the source must be as narrow as possible. Thus it is desirable to design a laser that oscillates in a single-longitudinal mode (SLM) only. The spectrum of the output of an SLM laser is shown in Figure 3.36(b). Single-longitudinal mode oscillation can be achieved by using a filtering mechanism in the laser that selects the desired wavelength and provides loss at the other wavelengths. An important attribute of such a laser is its *side-mode suppression ratio,* which determines the level to which the other longitudinal modes are suppressed, compared to the main mode. This ratio is typically more than 30 dB for practical SLM lasers. We will now consider some mechanisms that are commonly employed for realizing SLM lasers.

Distributed-Feedback Lasers

In the Fabry-Perot laser described earlier, the feedback of the light occurs from the reflecting facets at the ends of the cavity. Thus the feedback can be said to be *localized* at the facets. Light feedback can also be provided in a *distributed* manner by a series of closely spaced reflectors. The most common means of achieving this is by providing a periodic variation in the width of the cavity, as shown in Figure 3.37(a) and (b).

In the corrugated section of the cavity, the incident wave undergoes a series of reflections. The contributions of each of these reflected waves to the resulting

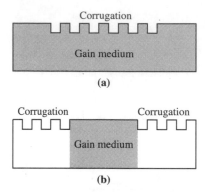

Figure 3.37   The structure of (a) a distributed-feedback (DFB) laser and (b) a distributed Bragg reflector (DBR) laser.

transmitted wave from the cavity add in phase, if the period of the corrugation is an integral multiple of half the wavelength in the cavity. The reasoning for this condition is the same as that used for the Fabry-Perot cavity. This condition is called the Bragg condition and was discussed in Section 3.3.2. The Bragg condition will be satisfied for a number of wavelengths, but the strongest transmitted wave occurs for the wavelength for which the corrugation period is *equal* to half the wavelength, rather than some other integer multiple of it. Thus this wavelength gets preferentially amplified at the expense of the other wavelengths. By suitable design of the device, this effect can be used to suppress all other longitudinal modes so that the laser oscillates in a single-longitudinal mode whose wavelength is equal to twice the corrugation period. By varying the corrugation period at the time of fabrication, different operating wavelengths can be obtained.

Any laser that uses a corrugated waveguide to achieve single-longitudinal mode operation can be termed a distributed-feedback laser. However, the acronym *DFB laser* is used only when the corrugation occurs within the gain region of the cavity, as shown in Figure 3.37(a). When the corrugation is outside the gain region, as in Figure 3.37(b), the laser is called a *distributed Bragg reflector,* or *DBR laser.* The main advantages of DBR lasers are that the gain region is decoupled from the wavelength selection region. Thus it is possible to control both regions independently. For example, by changing the refractive index of the wavelength selection region, the laser can be tuned to a different wavelength without affecting its other operating parameters.

DFB lasers are inherently more complex to fabricate than FP lasers and thus relatively more expensive. However, DFB lasers are used in almost all high-speed transmission systems today. FP lasers are used for shorter-distance data communication applications.

Reflections into a DFB laser cause its wavelength and power to fluctuate and are prevented by packaging the laser with an isolator in front of it. The laser is also usually packaged with a thermoelectric (TE) cooler and a photodetector attached to its rear facet. The TE cooler is necessary to maintain the laser at a constant operating temperature to prevent its wavelength from drifting. The photodetector monitors the optical power leaking out of the rear facet, which is proportional to the optical power coming out of the laser.

The packaging of a DFB laser contributes a significant fraction of the overall cost of the device. For WDM systems, it is very useful to package multiple DFB lasers at different wavelengths inside a single package. This device can then serve as a multiwavelength light source, or alternatively, as a tunable laser (only one of the lasers in the array is turned on, depending on the desired wavelength). These lasers can all be grown on a single substrate in the form of an array. Four and eight wavelength laser arrays have been fabricated in research laboratories, but have not quite progressed to volume manufacturing. The primary reason for this is the relatively low yield of the array as a whole. If one of the lasers doesn't meet specifications, the entire array will have to be discarded.

External Cavity Lasers

Suppression of oscillation at more than one longitudinal mode can also be achieved by using another cavity—called an *external cavity*—following the primary cavity where gain occurs. This is illustrated in Figure 3.38. Just as the primary cavity has resonant wavelengths, so does the external cavity. This effect can be achieved, for example, by using reflecting facets for the external cavity as well. The net result of having an external cavity is that the laser is capable of oscillating only at those wavelengths that are resonant wavelengths of *both* the primary and external cavity. By suitable design of the two cavities, it can be ensured that only one wavelength in the gain bandwidth of the primary cavity satisfies this condition. Thus the laser oscillation can be confined to a single-longitudinal mode.

Instead of another Fabry-Perot cavity, as shown in Figure 3.38, we can use a diffraction grating (see Section 3.3.1) in the external cavity, as shown in Figure 3.39. Such a laser is called a *grating external cavity* laser. In this case, the facet of the gain cavity facing the grating is given an antireflection coating. The wavelengths reflected by the diffraction grating back to the gain cavity are determined by the pitch of the grating (see Section 3.3.1) and its tilt angle (see Figure 3.39) with respect to the gain cavity. An external cavity laser, in general, uses a *wavelength-selective mirror* instead of a wavelength-flat mirror. (A highly polished and/or metal-coated

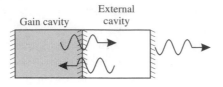

Figure 3.38   The structure of an external cavity laser.

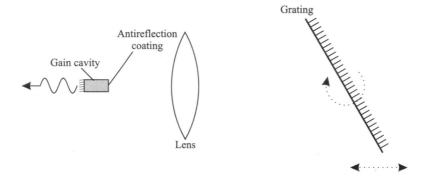

Figure 3.39   The structure of a grating external cavity laser.

facet used in conventional lasers acts as a wavelength-flat mirror.) The reflectivity of a wavelength-selective mirror is a function of the wavelength. Thus only certain wavelengths experience high reflectivities and are capable of lasing. If the wavelength-selective mirror is chosen suitably, only one such wavelength will occur within the gain bandwidth, and we will have a single-mode laser.

Several of the filters discussed in Section 3.3 can be used as wavelength-selective mirrors in external cavity lasers. We have already seen the use of the diffraction grating (Section 3.8) and Fabry-Perot filter (Section 3.3.4) in external cavity lasers. These laser structures are used today primarily in optical test instruments and are not amenable to low-cost volume production as SLM light sources for transmission systems. One version of the external cavity laser, though, appears to be particularly promising for this purpose. This device uses a fiber Bragg grating in front of a conventional FP laser with its front facet AR coated. This device then acts as an SLM DBR laser. It can be fabricated at relatively low cost compared to DFB lasers and is inherently more temperature stable in wavelength due to the low temperature coefficient of the fiber grating.

One disadvantage of external cavity lasers is that they cannot be modulated directly at high speeds. This is related to the fact that the cavity length is large.

Tunable Lasers

So far, we have considered lasers whose operating wavelength is nominally fixed, though it can drift with temperature and age. In many of the networks that we will study in Chapters 7 and 8, there is a need to tune the wavelength of the transmitter. This leads us naturally to consider tunable lasers. Another, more subtle, reason for considering tunable lasers in WDM systems (links as well as networks), even when the transmit wavelength is fixed, is from the inventory point of view. It is more convenient from an operational viewpoint to have a single transmitter part, independent of the operating wavelength, since it reduces the number of different parts that have to be stocked and handled. This is one of the main reasons today for considering tunable lasers. We will briefly outline the main principles used to tune the operating wavelength of a laser.

External cavity lasers(can be tuned if the center wavelength of the grating or other wavelength-selective mirror used can be changed. Consider the grating external cavity laser shown in Figure 3.39. The wavelength selected by the grating for reflection to the gain cavity is determined by the pitch of the diffraction grating, its tilt angle with respect to the gain cavity, and its distance from the gain cavity (see Section 3.3.1, specifically, (3.9)). Thus by varying the tilt angle and the distance of the diffraction grating from the gain cavity (shown by the dotted arrows in Figure 3.39), the laser wavelength can be changed. This is a slow method of tuning since the tilt and position of the diffraction grating have to be changed by mechanical means. However, a very wide tuning range of about 100 nm can be obtained for semiconductor lasers by this method. This method of tuning is appropriate for test instruments but not for a compact light source for communication systems.

A faster method of tuning a semiconductor laser is based on the fact that the refractive index of the semiconductor changes with the injected current density. Owing to this effect, the lasing wavelength of any semiconductor wavelength changes with the injected forward bias current. Of course, the output light power also increases with increase in the injected current, and we would like to have wavelength tuning without a simultaneous change in the output power. Observe that in a DBR laser, the induced index change by increased carrier injection causes the pitch of the Bragg grating to vary and thus the lasing wavelength to change. Thus if we could inject two currents, a current I_g in the gain region and a current I_B in the Bragg region, we would have independent control of the output power and wavelength of the laser. Such a laser is called a two-section DBR laser. These devices hold promise for use as tunable light sources in communication systems. Lasers capable of being tuned over 8 nm and 20 wavelengths have been demonstrated using this approach [Kam96].

Vertical Cavity Surface Emitting Lasers

In this section, we will study another class of lasers that achieve single-longitudinal mode operation in a slightly different manner. As we saw in Figure 3.36, the frequency spacing between the modes of an MLM laser is $c/2nl$, where l is the length of the cavity and n is its refractive index. If we were to make the length of the cavity sufficiently small, the mode spacing increases such that only one longitudinal mode occurs within the gain bandwidth of the laser. It turns out that making a very thin active layer is much easier if the active layer is deposited on a semiconductor substrate, as illustrated in Figure 3.40. This leads to a vertical cavity with the mirrors being formed on the top and bottom surfaces of the semiconductor wafer. The laser output is also taken from one of these (usually top) surfaces. For these reasons, such lasers are called *vertical cavity surface emitting lasers*, or VCSELs. The other lasers that we have been discussing hitherto can thus be referred to as *edge emitting lasers*.

Since the gain region has a very short length, very high mirror reflectivities are required in order for laser oscillation to occur. Such high mirror reflectivities are difficult to obtain with metallic surfaces. A stack of alternating low and high index dielectrics serves as a highly reflective, though wavelength-selective, mirror. The reflectivity of such a mirror is discussed in Problem 3.10. Such dielectric mirrors can be deposited at the time of fabrication of the laser.

One problem with VCSELs is the large ohmic resistance encountered by the injected current. This leads to considerable heating of the device and the need for efficient thermal cooling. Many of the dielectric materials used to make the mirrors have low thermal conductivity. So the use of such dielectric mirrors makes room temperature operation of VCSELs difficult to achieve since the heat generated by the device cannot be dissipated easily. For this reason, for several years after they were

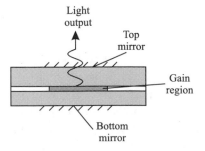

Figure 3.40   The structure of a vertical cavity surface emitting laser (VCSEL).

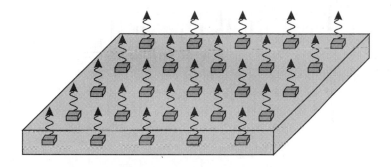

Figure 3.41   A two-dimensional array of vertical cavity surface emitting lasers.

first demonstrated in 1979, VCSELs were not capable of operating at room temperature. However, significant research effort has been expended on new materials and techniques, and as of this writing, VCSELs operating at 1.5 μm at a temperature of 64°C have been demonstrated [MZB97].

In a WDM system, many wavelengths are transmitted simultaneously over each link. Usually, this requires a separate laser for each wavelength. The cost of the transmitters can be significantly reduced if all the lasers can be integrated on a single substrate. This is the main motivation for the development of arrayed lasers such as the DFB laser arrays that we discussed earlier. Moreover, an arrayed laser can be used as a tunable laser simply by turning on only the required one of the lasers in the array. The use of surface emitting lasers enables us to fabricate a two-dimensional array of lasers, as shown in Figure 3.41. Much higher array packing densities can be achieved using surface emitting lasers than edge emitting ones because of this added dimension. However, it is harder to couple light from the lasers in this array onto optical fiber since multiplexers that work conveniently with this two-dimensional geometry are not readily available. These arrayed lasers have the same yield problem as other arrayed laser structures; if one of the lasers doesn't meet specifications, the entire array will have to be discarded.

Mode-Locked Lasers

Mode-locked lasers are used to generate narrow optical pulses that are needed for the high-speed TDM systems that we will study in Chapter 14. Consider a Fabry-Perot laser that oscillates in N longitudinal modes, which are adjacent to each other. This means that if the wavelengths of the modes are $\lambda_0, \lambda_1, \ldots, \lambda_{N-1}$, the cavity length l satisfies $l = (k+i)\lambda_i/2, i = 0, 1, \ldots, N-1$, for some integer k. From this condition, it can be shown (see Problem 3.5) that the corresponding frequencies $f_0, f_1, \ldots, f_{N-1}$

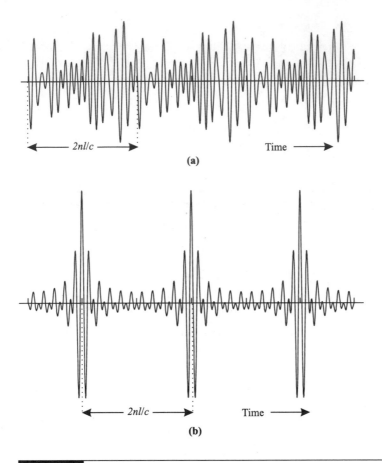

Figure 3.42   Output oscillation of a laser oscillating simultaneously in 10 longitudinal modes. In (a) the phases of the modes are chosen at random. In (b) all the phases are equal to each other; such a laser is said to be mode locked.

of these modes must satisfy $f_i = f_0 + i\Delta f$, $i = 0, 1, \ldots, N - 1$. The oscillation at frequency f_i is of the form $a_i \cos(2\pi f_i t + \phi_i)$, where a_i is the amplitude and ϕ_i the phase of mode i. (Strictly speaking, this is the distribution in time of the electric field associated with the longitudinal mode.) Thus the total laser output oscillation takes the form

$$\sum_{i=0}^{N-1} a_i \cos(2\pi f_i t + \phi_i).$$

This expression is plotted in Figure 3.42 for $N = 10$, for different sets of values of the ϕ_i. In Figure 3.42(a), the ϕ_i are chosen at random, and in Figure 3.42(b), they are chosen to be equal to each other. All the a_i are chosen to be equal in both cases, and the frequency f_0 has been diminished from its typical value for the purpose of illustration.

From Figure 3.42(a), we observe that the output amplitude of an MLM laser varies rapidly with time when it is not mode locked. We have also seen in Figure 3.36(a) that the frequency spacing between adjacent longitudinal modes is $c/2nl$. If $n = 3$ and $l = 200$ μm, which are typical values for semiconductor lasers, this frequency spacing is 250 GHz. Thus these amplitude fluctuations occur extremely rapidly (at a time scale of the order of a few ps) and pose no problems for on–off modulation even at bit rates of a few tens of Gb/s.

We see from Figure 3.42(b) that when the ϕ_i are chosen to be equal to each other, the output oscillation of the laser takes the form of a periodic train of narrow pulses. A laser operating in this manner is called a *mode-locked laser* and is the most common means of generating narrow optical pulses.

The time interval between two pulses of a mode-locked laser is $2nl/c$, as indicated in Figure 3.42(b). For a typical semiconductor laser, as we have seen earlier, this corresponds to a few ps. For modulation in the 1–10 GHz range, the interpulse interval should be in the 0.1–1 ns range. Cavity lengths, l, of the order of 1–10 cm (assuming $n = 1.5$) are required in order to realize mode-locked lasers with interpulse intervals in this range. These large cavity lengths are easily obtained using fiber lasers, which require the length anyway to obtain sufficient gain to induce lasing.

The most common means of achieving mode lock is by modulating the gain of the laser cavity. Either amplitude or frequency modulation can be used. Mode locking using amplitude modulation is illustrated in Figure 3.43. The gain of the cavity is modulated with a period equal to the interpulse interval, namely, $2nl/c$. The amplitude of this modulation is chosen such that the average gain is insufficient for any single mode to oscillate. However, if a large number of modes are in phase, there can be a sufficient buildup in the energy inside the cavity for laser oscillation to occur at the instants of high gain, as illustrated in Figure 3.43.

Gain modulation of the fiber laser can be achieved by introducing an external modulator inside the cavity.

3.5.2   Light-Emitting Diodes

Lasers are expensive devices and not affordable for many applications where the data rates are low and distances are short. This is the case in many data communications applications (see Chapter 6) and in some access networks (Chapter 12). In such cases, *light-emitting diodes* (LEDs) provide a cheaper alternative.

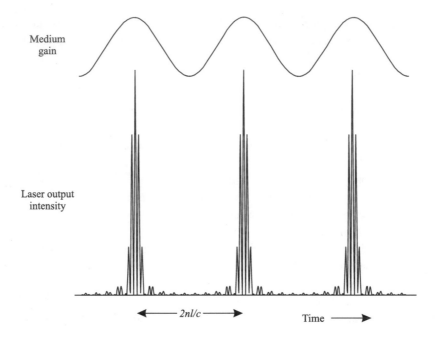

Medium
gain

Laser output
intensity

$2nl/c$

Time

Figure 3.43   Illustration of mode locking by amplitude modulation of the cavity gain.

We already remarked in Section 3.4 that the spontaneous emission that is present in addition to stimulated emission degrades the performance of an optical amplifier. This is also true for lasers, because the spontaneous emission process competes with the stimulated emission process for the higher-energy atoms/ions/carriers. Thus materials like GaAs used to make lasers have the property that stimulated emission dominates over spontaneous emission. Semiconductor materials like Si and Ge for which the opposite is true, that is, spontaneous emission dominates over stimulated emission, are useful for making LEDs.

An LED is a forward-biased *pn*-junction in which the recombination of the injected minority carriers (electrons in the *p*-type region and holes in the *n*-type region) by the spontaneous emission process produces light. (Nonradiative recombination is also possible and is an important factor affecting the performance of LEDs.) Because spontaneous emission occurs within the entire bandwidth of the gain medium (corresponding to all energy differences between the valence and conduction bands for an LED), the light output of an LED has a broad spectrum, unlike that of a laser. LEDs are also not capable of producing high-output powers like lasers, and typical output powers are of the order of −20 dBm. They cannot be directly modulated (see Section 3.5.2) at data rates higher than a few hundred Mb/s.

In some low-speed, low-budget applications, there is a requirement for a source with a narrow spectral width. DFB lasers provide narrow spectral widths but may be too expensive for these applications. In such cases, LED slicing provides a cheaper alternative. An *LED slice* is the output of a narrow passband optical filter placed in front of the LED. The optical filter selects a portion of the LED's output. Different filters can be used to select (almost) nonoverlapping spectral slices of the LED output. Thus one LED can be shared by a number of users. We will see an application for this technique in Chapter 12.

Direct and External Modulation

The process of imposing data on the light stream is called modulation. The simplest and most widely used modulation scheme is called *on–off keying* (OOK), where the light stream is turned on or off, depending on whether the data bit is a 1 or 0. We will study this in more detail in Chapter 4.

OOK modulated signals are usually realized in one of two ways: (a) by *direct modulation* of a semiconductor laser or an LED, or (b) by using an *external modulator*. The direct modulation scheme is illustrated in Figure 3.44. The drive current into the semiconductor laser is set well above threshold for a 1 bit and below (or at) threshold for a 0 bit. The ratio of the output powers for the 1 and 0 bits is called the *extinction ratio*. Direct modulation is simple and inexpensive since no other components are required for modulation other than the light source (laser/LED) itself. In fact, a major advantage of semiconductor lasers is that they can be directly modulated. In contrast, many other lasers are continuous wave sources and cannot be modulated directly at all. These lasers require an external modulator. For example, owing to the long lifetime of the Erbium atoms at the E_2 level in Figure 3.30, Erbium lasers cannot be directly modulated even at speeds of a few kb/s.

The disadvantage of direct modulation is that the resulting pulses are considerably *chirped*. Chirp is a phenomenon wherein the carrier frequency of the transmitted pulse varies with time, and it causes a broadening of the transmitted spectrum. As we saw in Section 2.3, chirped pulses have sharply worse dispersion limits than unchirped pulses. The amount of chirping can be reduced by increasing the power of a 0 bit so that the laser is always kept well above its threshold; the disadvantage is that this reduces the extinction ratio, which in turn, degrades the system performance, as we will see in Section 5.3. This enhanced pulse broadening of chirped pulses is significant enough to warrant the use of *external modulators* in high-speed, dispersion-limited communication systems.

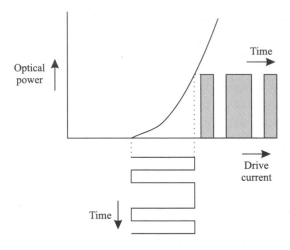

Figure 3.44   Direct modulation of a semiconductor laser.

An OOK external modulator is placed in front of a light source and turns the light signal on or off based on the data to be transmitted. The light source itself is continuously operated. This has the advantage of minimizing undesirable effects such as chirp. Several types of external modulators are commercially available and are increasingly being integrated with the laser itself inside a single package to reduce the packaging cost. In fact, transmitter packages that include a laser, external modulator, and wavelength stabilization circuits are becoming commercially available for use in WDM systems.

An external modulator is essential in soliton communication systems since we can usually realize only a periodic train of unmodulated short pulses and the pulses corresponding to a 0 bit must be blocked by the use of an external modulator. We discussed the generation of short pulses in Section 3.5.1.

3.6   Detectors

A receiver converts an optical signal into a usable electrical signal. Figure 3.45 shows the different components within a receiver. The *photodetector* generates an electrical current proportional to the incident optical power. The *front-end amplifier* increases the power of the generated electrical signal to a usable level. In digital communication systems, the front-end amplifier is followed by a *decision circuit* that estimates the data from the output of the front-end amplifier. The design of this decision circuit

Figure 3.45 Block diagram of a receiver in a digital communication system.

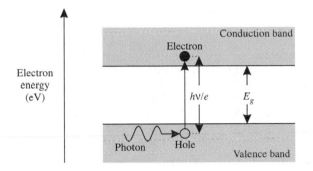

Figure 3.46 The basic principle of photodetection using a semiconductor. Incident photons are absorbed by electrons in the valence band creating a free or mobile electron–hole pair. This electron–hole pair gives rise to a photocurrent when an external voltage is applied.

depends on the modulation scheme used to transmit the data and will be discussed in Section 4.2. An optical amplifier may be optionally placed before the photodetector to act as a *preamplifier*. The performance of optically preamplified receivers will be discussed in Chapter 4. This section covers photodetectors and front-end amplifiers.

3.6.1 Photodetectors

The basic principle of photodetection is illustrated in Figure 3.46. Photodetectors are made of semiconductor materials. Photons incident on a semiconductor are absorbed by electrons in the valence band. As a result, these electrons acquire higher energy and are excited into the conduction band, leaving behind a hole in the valence band. When an external voltage is applied to the semiconductor, these electron–hole pairs give rise to an electrical current, termed the *photocurrent*.

It is a principle of quantum mechanics that each electron can absorb only one photon to transit between energy levels. Thus the energy of the incident photon must be at least equal to the bandgap energy in order for a photocurrent to be generated. This is also illustrated in Figure 3.46. This gives us the following constraint on the

Table 3.2   Bandgap energies and cutoff wavelengths for a number of semiconductor materials. $In_{1-x}Ga_xAs$ is a ternary compound semiconductor material where a fraction $1 - x$ of the Ga atoms in GaAs are replaced by In atoms. $In_{1-x}Ga_xAs_yP_{1-y}$ is a quaternary compound semiconductor material where, in addition, a fraction $1 - y$ of the As atoms are replaced by P atoms. By varying x and y, the bandgap energies and cutoff wavelengths can be varied.

Material	E_g (eV)	λ_{cutoff} (μm)
Si	1.17	1.06
Ge	0.775	1.6
GaAs	1.424	0.87
InP	1.35	0.92
$In_{0.55}Ga_{0.45}As$	0.75	1.65
$In_{1-0.45y}Ga_{0.45y}As_yP_{1-y}$	0.75–1.35	1.65–0.92

frequency f_c or the wavelength λ at which a semiconductor material with bandgap E_g can be used as a photodetector:

$$hf_c = \frac{hc}{\lambda} \geq eE_g. \tag{3.17}$$

Here, c is the velocity of light, and e is the electronic charge.

The largest value of λ for which (3.17) is satisfied is called the *cutoff wavelength* and denoted by λ_{cutoff}. Table 3.2 lists the bandgap energies and the corresponding cutoff wavelengths for a number of semiconductor materials. We see from this table that the well-known semiconductors silicon (Si) and gallium arsenide (GaAs) cannot be used as photodetectors in the 1.3 and 1.55 μm bands. Although germanium (Ge) can be used to make photodetectors in both these bands, it has some disadvantages that reduce its effectiveness for this purpose. The new compounds indium gallium arsenide (InGaAs) and indium gallium arsenide phosphide (InGaAsP) are commonly used to make photodetectors in the 1.3 and 1.55 μm bands. Silicon photodetectors are widely used in the 0.8 μm band.

The fraction of the energy of the optical signal that is absorbed and gives rise to a photocurrent is called the *efficiency* η of the photodetector. For transmission at high bit rates over long distances, optical energy is scarce, and thus it is important to design the photodetector to achieve an efficiency η as close to 1 as possible. This can be achieved by using a semiconductor slab of sufficient thickness. The power absorbed by a semiconductor slab of thickness L μm can be written as

$$P_{\text{abs}} = (1 - e^{-\alpha L}) P_{\text{in}}, \tag{3.18}$$

where P_{in} is the incident optical signal power, and α is the absorption coefficient of the material; therefore,

$$\eta = \frac{P_{\text{abs}}}{P_{\text{in}}} = 1 - e^{-\alpha L}. \tag{3.19}$$

The absorption coefficient depends on the wavelength and is zero for wavelengths $\lambda > \lambda_{\text{cutoff}}$. Thus a semiconductor is transparent to wavelengths greater than its cutoff wavelength. Typical values of α are of the order of 10^4/cm so that to achieve an efficiency $\eta > 0.99$, a slab of thickness of the order of 10 μm is needed. The area of the photodetector is usually chosen to be sufficiently large so that all the incident optical power can be captured by it. Photodetectors have a very wide operating bandwidth since a photodetector at some wavelength can also serve as a photodetector at all smaller wavelengths. Thus a photodetector designed for the 1.55 μm band can also be used in the 1.3 μm band.

Photodetectors are commonly characterized by their *responsivity* $\mathcal{R}$. If a photodetector produces an average current of I_p amperes when the incident optical power is P_{in} watts, the responsivity

$$\mathcal{R} = \frac{I_p}{P_{\text{in}}} \text{ A/W.}$$

Since an incident optical power P_{in} corresponds to an incidence of P_{in}/hf_c photons/s on the average, and a fraction η of these incident photons are absorbed and generate an electron in the external circuit, we can write

$$\mathcal{R} = \frac{e\eta}{hf_c} \text{ A/W.}$$

The responsivity is commonly expressed in terms of λ; thus

$$\mathcal{R} = \frac{e\eta\lambda}{hc} = \frac{\eta\lambda}{1.24} \text{ A/W,}$$

where λ in the last expression is expressed in μm. Since η can be made quite close to 1 in practice, the responsivities achieved are of the order of 1 A/W in the 1.3 μm band and 1.2 A/W in the 1.55 μm band.

In practice, the mere use of a slab of semiconductor as a photodetector does not realize high efficiencies. This is because many of the generated conduction band

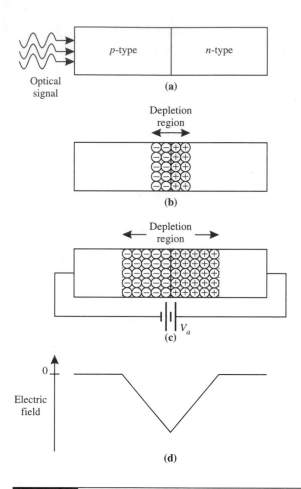

Figure 3.47   A reverse-biased *pn*-junction used as a photodetector. (a) A *pn*-junction photodiode. (b) Depletion region with no bias voltage applied. (c) Depletion region with a reverse bias voltage, V_a. (d) Built-in electric field on reverse bias.

electrons recombine with holes in the valence band before they reach the external circuit. Thus it is necessary to sweep the generated conduction band electrons rapidly out of the semiconductor. This can be done by imposing an electric field of sufficient strength in the region where the electrons are generated. This is best achieved by using a semiconductor *pn*-junction (see Section 3.4.5) instead of a homogeneous slab and applying a reverse bias voltage to it, as shown in Figure 3.47. Such a photodetector is called a *photodiode*.

The depletion region in a *pn*-junction creates a built-in electric field. Both the depletion region and the built-in electric field can be enhanced by the application of a *reverse bias* voltage (positive bias to the *n*-type and negative bias to the *p*-type). In this case, the electrons that are generated by the absorption of photons within or close to the depletion region will be swept into the *n*-type semiconductor before they recombine with the holes in the *p*-type semiconductor. This process is called *drift* and gives rise to a current in the external circuit. Similarly, the generated holes in or close to the depletion region drift into the *p*-type semiconductor owing to the electric field.

Electron–hole pairs that are generated far away from the depletion region travel primarily under the effect of diffusion and may recombine without giving rise to a current in the external circuit. This reduces the efficiency η of the photodetector. More important, since diffusion is a much slower process than drift, the *diffusion current* that is generated by these electron–hole pairs will not respond quickly to changes in the intensity of the incident optical signal, thus reducing the frequency response of the photodiode.

pin Photodiodes

To improve the efficiency of the photodetector, a very lightly doped *intrinsic* semiconductor is introduced between the *p*-type and *n*-type semiconductors. Such photodiodes are called *pin* photodiodes, where the *i* in *pin* is for intrinsic. In these photodiodes, the depletion region extends completely across this intrinsic semiconductor (or region). The width of the *p*-type and *n*-type semiconductors is small compared to the intrinsic region so that much of the light absorption takes place in this region. This increases the efficiency and thus the responsivity of the photodiode.

A more efficient method of achieving this is to use a semiconductor material for these regions that is *transparent* at the wavelength of interest. Thus the wavelength of interest is larger than the cutoff wavelength of this semiconductor, and no absorption of light takes place in these regions. This is illustrated in Figure 3.48, where the material InP is used for the *p*-type and *n*-type regions, and InGaAs for the intrinsic

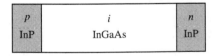

Figure 3.48 A *pin* photodiode based on a heterostructure. The *p*-type and *n*-type regions are made of InP, which is transparent in the 1.3 and 1.55 μm wavelength bands. The intrinsic region is made of InGaAs, which strongly absorbs in both these bands.

region. Such a *pin* photodiode structure is termed a *double heterojunction* or a *heterostructure* since it consists of two junctions of completely different semiconductor materials. From Table 3.2, we see that the cutoff wavelength for InP is 0.92 μm, and that for InGaAs is 1.65 μm. Thus the *p*-type and *n*-type regions are transparent in the 1.3–1.6 μm range, and the diffusion component of the photocurrent is completely eliminated.

Avalanche Photodiodes

The responsivities of the photodetectors we have described thus far has been limited by the fact that one photon can generate only one electron when it is absorbed. However, if the generated electron is subjected to a very high electric field, it can acquire sufficient energy to knock off more electrons from the valence band to the conduction band. These secondary electron–hole pairs can generate even further electron–hole pairs when they are accelerated to sufficient levels. This process is called *avalanche multiplication.* Such a photodiode is called an *avalanche photodiode,* or simply an *APD.*

The number of secondary electron–hole pairs generated by the avalanche multiplication process by a single (primary) electron is random, and the mean value of this number is termed the *multiplicative gain* and denoted by G_m. The multiplicative gain of an APD can be made quite large and even infinite—a condition called *avalanche breakdown.* However, a large value of G_m is also accompanied by a larger variance in the generated photocurrent, which adversely affects the noise performance of the APD. Thus there is a tradeoff between the multiplicative gain and the noise factor. APDs are usually designed to have a moderate value of G_m that optimizes their performance. We will study this issue further in Section 4.2.

3.6.2   Front-End Amplifiers

Two kinds of front-end amplifiers are used in optical communication systems: the *high-impedance* front end and the *transimpedance* front end. The equivalent circuits for these amplifiers are shown in Figure 3.49.

The capacitances C in this figure include the capacitance due to the photodiode, the amplifier input capacitance, and other parasitic capacitances. The main design issue is the choice of the load resistance R_L. We will see in Chapter 4 that the *thermal noise* current that arises due to the random motion of electrons and contaminates the photocurrent is inversely proportional to the load resistance. Thus to minimize the thermal noise, we must make R_L large. However, the bandwidth of the photodiode, which sets the upper limit on the usable bit rate, is inversely proportional to the output load resistance seen by the photodiode, say, R_p. First consider the high-impedance

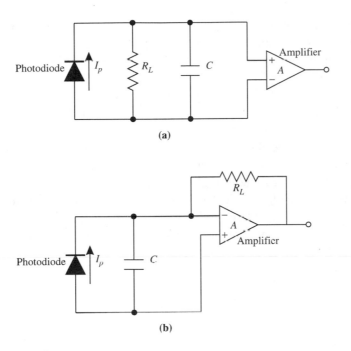

(a)

(b)

Figure 3.49 (a) Equivalent circuit for a high-impedance front-end amplifier. (b) Equivalent circuit for a transimpedance front-end amplifier.

front end. In this case, $R_p = R_L$, and we must choose R_L small enough to accommodate the bit rate of the system. Thus there is a tradeoff between the bandwidth of the photodiode and its noise performance. Now consider the transimpedance front end for which $R_p = R_L/(A+1)$, where A is the gain of the amplifier. The bandwidth is increased by a factor of $A + 1$ for the same load resistance. However, the thermal noise current is also higher than that of a high-impedance amplifier with the same R_L (due to considerations beyond the scope of this book), but this increase is quite moderate—a factor usually less than 2. Thus the transimpedance front end is chosen over the high-impedance one for most optical communication systems.

There is another consideration in the choice of a front-end amplifier: *dynamic range*. This is the difference between the largest and smallest signal levels that the front-end amplifier can handle. This may not be an important consideration for many optical communication links since the power level seen by the receivers is usually more or less fixed. However, dynamic range of the receivers is a very important consideration in the case of networks where the received signal level can vary by a few orders of magnitude. The transimpedance amplifier has a significantly higher dynamic range than the high-impedance one, and this is another factor in favor of choosing the transimpedance amplifier. The higher dynamic range arises because large variations in the photocurrent I_p translate into much smaller variations at the amplifier input, particularly if the amplifier gain is large. This can be understood with reference to Figure 3.49(b). A change ΔI_p in the photocurrent causes a change in voltage $\Delta I_p R_L$ (ignoring the current through the capacitance C) across the resistance R_L. This results in a voltage change across the inputs of the amplifier of only $\Delta I_p R_L/(A+1)$. Thus if the gain, A, is large, this voltage change is small. In the case of the high-impedance amplifier, however, the voltage change across the amplifier inputs would be $\Delta I_p R_L$ (again ignoring the current through the capacitance C).

A *field-effect transistor*, or FET, has a very high input impedance and for this reason is often used as the amplifier in the front end. A *pin* photodiode and an FET are often integrated on the same semiconductor substrate, and the combined device is called a *pinFET*.

3.7 Switches

Optical switches are used in optical networks for a variety of applications. As for the switches, the main distinguishing feature behind these applications is in the switching time required, which varies from a few milliseconds to subnanosecond switching times, as summarized in Table 3.3. One application of optical switches is in *provisioning* of lightpaths. In this application, the switches are used inside optical crossconnects to reconfigure them to support new lightpaths. In this application, the switches are replacements for manual fiber patch panels. Thus for this application, switches with millisecond switching times are acceptable. The challenge here is to realize large switch sizes. Another important application is that of *protection switching*. Here the switches are used to switch the traffic stream from a primary fiber on to another fiber in case the primary fiber fails. This application typically

Table 3.3 Applications for optical switches and their switching time requirements.

Application	Switching Time Required
Provisioning	1–10 ms
Protection switching	1–10 μs
Packet switching	1 ns
External modulation	10 ps

requires switching times of the order of a microsecond to a hundred microseconds. Small 2 × 2 switches are usually sufficient for this purpose. Switches are also important components in high-speed optical *packet-switched* networks. In these networks, switches are used to switch signals on a packet-by-packet basis. For this application, the switching time must be much smaller than a packet duration, and large switches will be needed. For example, a 53-byte packet at 10 Gb/s is 42 ns long, so the switching time required for efficient operation is of the order of a few ns. Yet another use for switches is as external modulators to turn on and off the data in front of a laser source. In this case, the switching time must be a small fraction of the bit duration. So an external modulator for a 10 Gb/s signal (with a bit duration of 100 ps) must have a switching time (or, equivalently, a rise and fall time) of about 10 ps. The state of integration of optical switches is considerably less than that of electronic switches. A 16 × 16 optical switch is considered a "large" switch!

In addition to the switching time, the other important parameters used to characterize the suitability of a switch for optical networking applications are the following:

1. The *extinction ratio* of an on–off switch is the ratio of the output power in the on-state to the output power in the off-state. This ratio should be as large as possible, and is particularly important in external modulators. Whereas simple mechanical switches have extinction ratios of 40–50 dB, high-speed external modulators tend to have extinction ratios of 10–15 dB.

2. The *insertion loss* of a switch is the fraction of power (usually expressed in dB) that is lost because of the presence of the switch and must be as small as possible. Some switches have different losses for different input–output connections. This is an undesirable feature, because it increases the dynamic range of the signals in the network. With such switches, we may need to include variable optical attenuators to equalize the loss across different paths.

3. Switches are not ideal. Even if input x is nominally connected to output y, some power from input x may appear at the other outputs. For a given switching state or interconnection pattern, and output, the *crosstalk* is the ratio of the power at that output from the desired input to the power from all other inputs. Usually, the *crosstalk of a switch* is the worst-case crosstalk over all outputs and interconnection patterns.

4. As with other components, switches should have a low polarization-dependent loss (PDL). When used as external modulators, polarization dependence can be tolerated since the switch is used immediately following the laser, and the laser's output state of polarization can be controlled by using a special

Table 3.4 Comparison of different optical switching technologies. The mechanical and polymer-based switches behave in the same manner for 1.3 and 1.55 μm wavelengths, but other switches are designed to operate at only one of these wavelength bands. The numbers represent parameters for commercially available switches in 1997.

Type	Size	Loss (dB)	Crosstalk (dB)	PDL (dB)	Switching Time
Mechanical	8 × 8	3	55	0.2	10 ms
Thermo-optic					
Silica	8 × 8	10	15	Low	2 ms
Polymer	8 × 8	10	30	Low	2 ms
Electro-optic					
LiNbO$_3$	4 × 4	8	35	1	10 ps
SOA	4 × 4	0	40	Low	1 ns

polarization-preserving fiber to couple the light from the laser into the external modulator.

Many different technologies are available to realize optical switches. These are compared in Table 3.4.

3.7.1 Mechanical Switches

In mechanical switches, the switching function is performed by some mechanical means. One such switch uses a mirror arrangement whereby the switching state is controlled by moving a mirror in and out of the optical path. Another type of mechanical switch uses a directional coupler. Bending or stretching the fiber in the interaction region changes the coupling ratio of the coupler and can be used to switch light from an input port between different output ports.

Mechanical switches have low insertion losses, low PDL, low crosstalk, and are relatively inexpensive devices. However, their switching speeds are of the order of a few ms. For these reasons, they are particularly suited for use in optical crossconnects for provisioning applications but not for the other applications discussed earlier. As with most mechanical components, long-term reliability for these switches is of some concern, but they are still by far more mature than all the other optical switching technologies available today. Larger switches can be realized by cascading small switches, as we will explain in Section 3.7.5, or in some cases, can be directly fabricated.

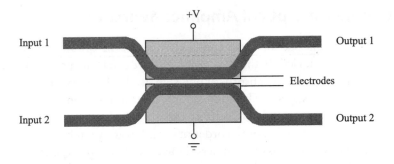

Figure 3.50   An electro-optic directional coupler switch.

3.7.2   Electro-Optic Switches

A 2×2 electro-optic switch uses a directional coupler whose coupling ratio is changed not by varying the coupling length, but by changing the refractive index of the material in the coupling region. One commonly used material is lithium niobate ($LiNbO_3$). A switch constructed on a lithium niobate waveguide is shown in Figure 3.50. Switching is accomplished by applying an appropriate voltage to the electrodes.

An electro-optic switch is capable of changing its state extremely rapidly; typically, in less than 1 ns. This switching time limit is determined by the capacitance of the electrode configuration. Because of this property, such a switch is suitable for use as an external modulator.

Among the advantages of lithium niobate switches are that they allow modest levels of integration, compared to mechanical switches. Larger switches can be realized by integrating several 2×2 switches on a single substrate. However, they tend to have a relatively high loss and PDL, and are more expensive than mechanical switches.

3.7.3   Thermo-Optic Switches

These switches are essentially 2×2 integrated-optic Mach-Zehnder interferometers, constructed on waveguide material whose refractive index is a function of the temperature. By varying the refractive index in one arm of the interferometer, the relative phase difference between the two arms can be changed, resulting in switching an input signal from one output port to another. These devices have been made on silica as well as polymer substrates, but have relatively poor crosstalk. Also the thermo-optic effect is quite slow, and switching speeds are of the order of a few ms.

3.7.4   Semiconductor Optical Amplifier Switches

The SOA described in Section 3.4.5 can be used as an on–off switch by varying the bias voltage to the device. If the bias voltage is reduced, no population inversion is achieved, and the device absorbs input signals. If the bias voltage is present, it amplifies the input signals. The combination of amplification in the on-state and absorption in the off-state makes this device capable of achieving very large extinction ratios. The switching speed is of the order of 1 ns. Larger switches can be fabricated by integrating SOAs with passive couplers. However, this is an expensive component, and it is difficult to make it polarization independent.

3.7.5   *Large Switches*

Switch sizes larger than 2×2 can be realized by appropriately cascading small switches. The main considerations in building large switches are the following:

Number of small switches required. Optical switches are made by cascading 2×2 or 1×2 switches, and thus the cost is to some extent proportional to the number of such switches needed. However, this is only one of the factors that affects the cost. Other factors include packaging, splicing, and ease of fabrication.

Loss uniformity. As we mentioned in the context of switch characteristics earlier, switches may have different losses for different combinations of input and output ports. This situation is exacerbated for large switches. A measure of the loss uniformity can be obtained by considering the minimum and maximum number of switch elements in the optical path, for different input and output combinations.

Number of crossovers. Large optical switches are sometimes fabricated by integrating multiple switch elements on a single substrate. These include the lithium niobate directional coupler switches, the SOA-based switches, and the Mach-Zehnder thermo-optic switches that we studied earlier. Unlike integrated electronic circuits (ICs) where connections between the various components can be made at multiple layers, in integrated optics, all these connections must be made in a single layer by means of waveguides. If the paths of two waveguides cross, two undesirable effects are introduced: power loss and crosstalk. In order to have acceptable loss and crosstalk performance for the switch, it is thus desirable to minimize, or completely eliminate, such waveguide crossovers.

Blocking characteristics. In terms of the switching function achievable, switches are of two types: *blocking* or *nonblocking*. A switch is said to be *nonblocking* if an unused input port can be connected to any unused output port. Thus a nonblocking switch is capable of realizing every interconnection pattern between

Table 3.5 Comparison of different switch architectures. The switch count for the Spanke architecture is made in terms of 1×2 switches, whereas 2×2 switches are used for the other architectures.

Property	Crossbar	Beneš	Spanke-Beneš	Spanke
Nonblocking type	Wide-sense	Rearrangeable	Rearrangeable	Strict-sense
No. of switches	n^2	$\frac{n}{2}(2\log_2 n - 1)$	$\frac{n}{2}(n-1)$	$2n(n-1)$
Crossovers	None	Yes	None	Yes
Maximum loss	$2n-1$	$2\log_2 n - 1$	n	$2\log_2 n$
Minimum loss	1	$2\log_2 n - 1$	$\frac{n}{2}$	$2\log_2 n$

the inputs and the outputs. If some interconnection pattern(s) cannot be realized, the switch is said to be *blocking*. Most applications require nonblocking switches. However, even nonblocking switches can be further distinguished in terms of the effort needed to achieve the nonblocking property. A switch is said to be *wide-sense nonblocking* if any unused input can be connected to any unused output, without requiring any existing connection to be rerouted.

A nonblocking switch that may require rerouting of connections to achieve the nonblocking property is said to be *rearrangeably nonblocking*. Rerouting of connections may or may not be acceptable depending on application since the connection must be interrupted, at least briefly, in order to switch it to a different path. The advantage of rearrangeably nonblocking switch architectures is that they use fewer small switches to build a larger switch of a given size, compared to the wide-sense nonblocking switch architectures.

While rearrangeably nonblocking architectures use fewer switches, they require a more complex control algorithm to set up connections. Since optical switches are not very large (32×32 is already considered a large switch), the increased control complexity may be quite acceptable. The main drawback of rearrangeably nonblocking switches is that many applications will not allow existing connections to be disrupted, even temporarily, to accommodate a new connection.

Usually, there is a tradeoff between these different aspects. We will illustrate this when we study different architectures for building large switches next. Table 3.5 compares the characteristics of these architectures.

Crossbar

A 4×4 crossbar switch is shown in Figure 3.51. This switch uses sixteen 2×2 switches, and the interconnection between inputs and outputs is achieved by appropriately setting the states of these 2×2 switches. The setting of the 2×2 switches required

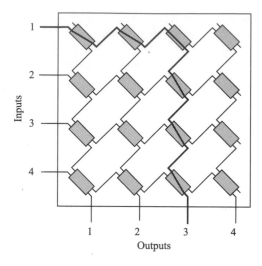

Figure 3.51   A 4 × 4 switch realized using sixteen 2 × 2 switches.

to connect input 1 to output 3 is shown in Figure 3.51. This connection can be viewed as taking a path through the network of 2 × 2 switches making up the 4 × 4 switch. Note that there are other paths from input 1 to output 3; however, this is the preferred path as we will see shortly.

The crossbar architecture is wide-sense nonblocking. To connect input i to output j, the path taken traverses the 2 × 2 switches in row i till it reaches column j and then traverses the switches in column j till it reaches output j. Thus the 2 × 2 switches on this path in row i and column j must be set appropriately for this connection to be made. We leave it to you to be convinced that *if this connection rule is used*, this switch is nonblocking and doesn't require existing connections to be rerouted. (For completeness, we note that a switch that is nonblocking regardless of the connection rule that is used, as long as the rule finds an available path between the input and the output, is said to be *strict-sense nonblocking*.)

In general, an $n \times n$ crossbar requires n^2 2 × 2 switches. The shortest path length is 1 and the longest path length is $2n - 1$, and this is one of the main drawbacks of the crossbar architecture. The switch can be fabricated without any crossovers.

Beneš

The Beneš architecture is a rearrangeably nonblocking switch architecture, and is one of the most efficient switch architectures in terms of the number of 2 × 2 switches it uses to build larger switches. A rearrangeably nonblocking 8 × 8 switch that uses

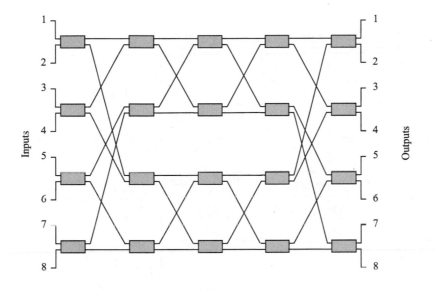

Figure 3.52   A rearrangeably nonblocking 8×8 switch realized using twenty 2×2 switches interconnected in the Beneš architecture.

only twenty 2×2 switches is shown in Figure 3.52. In comparison, an 8×8 crossbar switch requires sixty-four 2×2 switches. In general, an $n \times n$ Beneš switch requires $(n/2)(2 \log_2 n - 1)$ 2×2 switches, n being a power of 2. The loss is the same through every path in the switch—each path goes through $2 \log_2 n - 1$ 2×2 switches. Its two main drawbacks are that it is not wide-sense nonblocking, and that a number of waveguide crossovers are required, making it difficult to fabricate in integrated optics.

Spanke-Beneš

A good compromise between the crossbar and Beneš switch architectures is shown in Figure 3.53, which is a rearrangeably nonblocking switch using twenty-eight 2×2 switches and *no* waveguide crossovers. This switch architecture was discovered by Spanke and Beneš [SB87] and is called the *n-stage planar architecture* since it requires n stages (columns) to realize an $n \times n$ switch. It requires $n(n-1)/2$ switches, the shortest path length is $n/2$, and the longest path length is n. There are no crossovers. Its main drawbacks are that it is not wide-sense nonblocking and the loss is nonuniform.

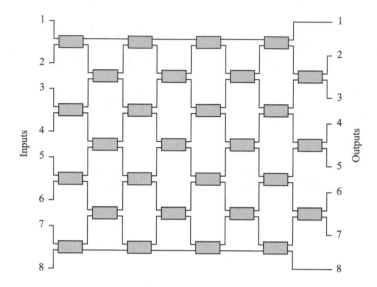

Figure 3.53   A rearrangeably nonblocking 8×8 switch realized using twenty-eight 2×2 switches and no waveguide crossovers interconnected in the n-stage planar architecture.

Spanke

The Spanke architecture shown in Figure 3.54 is turning out to be a popular architecture for building large nonintegrated switches. An $n \times n$ switch is made by combining n $1 \times n$ switches along with n $n \times 1$ switches, as shown in the figure. The architecture is strict-sense nonblocking, requires $2n(n-1)$ 1×2 switches, and each path has length $2 \log_2 n$.

3.8   Wavelength Converters

A wavelength converter is a device that converts data from one incoming wavelength to another outgoing wavelength. Wavelength converters are useful components in WDM networks for three major reasons. First, data may enter the network at a wavelength that is not suitable for use within the network. For example, the first-generation networks of Chapter 6 commonly transmit data in the 1310 nm wavelength window, using LEDs or Fabry-Perot lasers. Neither the wavelength nor the type of lasers is compatible with WDM networks. So at the inputs and outputs of the network, data must be converted from these wavelengths to narrow band WDM signals in the 1550 nm wavelength range.

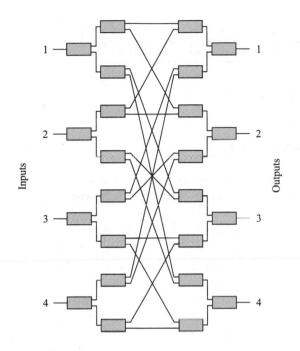

Figure 3.54   A strict-sense nonblocking 4×4 switch realized using twenty-four 1×2/2×1 switches interconnected in the Spanke architecture.

Second, wavelength converters may be needed within the network to improve the utilization of the available wavelengths on the network links. This topic is studied in detail in Chapter 8.

Finally, wavelength converters may be needed at boundaries between different networks if the different networks are managed by different entities and these entities do not coordinate the allocation of wavelengths in their networks.

Wavelength converters can be classified based on the range of wavelengths that they can handle at their inputs and outputs. A fixed-input, fixed-output device always takes in a fixed-input wavelength and converts it to a fixed-output wavelength. A variable-input, fixed-output device takes in a variety of wavelengths but always converts the input signal to a fixed-output wavelength. A fixed-input, variable-output device does the opposite function. Finally, a variable-input, variable-output device can convert any input wavelength to any output wavelength.

There are three fundamental ways of achieving wavelength conversion: (a) optoelectronic, (b) optical gating, and (c) wave mixing. The latter two approaches are all-optical but not yet mature enough for commercial use.

Figure 3.55   Optoelectronic wavelength conversion.

3.8.1   Optoelectronic Approach

This is perhaps the simplest, most obvious, and most practical method today to realize wavelength conversion. As shown in Figure 3.55, the input signal is first converted to electronic form, regenerated, and then retransmitted using a laser at a different wavelength. This is usually a variable-input, fixed-output converter. The receiver does not usually care about the input wavelength, as long as it is in the 1310 or 1550 nm window. The laser is usually a fixed-wavelength laser. A variable output can be obtained by using a tunable laser.

The performance and transparency of the converter depend on the type of regeneration used. In the simplest case, the receiver simply converts the incoming photons to electrons, which get amplified by an analog RF (radio-frequency) amplifier and drive the laser. This is called 1R regeneration. This form of conversion is truly transparent to modulation format (provided the appropriate receiver is used to receive the signal) and can handle analog data as well. However, noise is added at the converter, and the effects of nonlinearities and dispersion (see Chapter 5) are not reset.

Another alternative is to use regeneration with reshaping but without retiming, also called 2R regeneration. This is applicable only to digital data. The signal is reshaped by sending it through a logic gate, but not retimed. Additional phase jitter is introduced owing to this process and will eventually limit the number of stages that can be cascaded. Some transparency is lost because only digital data with a prespecified modulation format can be handled this way.

The final alternative is to use regeneration with reshaping and retiming (3R). This completely resets the effects of nonlinearities, fiber dispersion, and amplifier noise; moreover, it introduces no additional noise. However, retiming is a bit rate specific function, and we lose transparency. If transparency is not very important, this is a very attractive approach.

3.8.2   Optical Gating

Optical gating makes use of an optical device whose characteristics change with the intensity of an input signal. This change can be transferred to another unmodulated *probe* signal at a different wavelength going through the device. At the output, the probe signal contains the information that is on the input signal. Like the optoelectronic approach, these devices are variable-input and either fixed-output or variable-output devices, depending on whether the probe signal is fixed or tunable. The transparency offered by this approach is limited—only intensity-modulated signals can be converted.

We will study two types of conversion based on this principle, cross-gain modulation (CGM) and cross-phase modulation (CPM). Both use nonlinear effects in semiconductor optical amplifiers (SOAs). Both approaches work over a wide range of signal and probe wavelengths, as long as they are within the amplifier gain bandwidth, which is about 100 nm. Early SOAs were polarization sensitive, but by careful fabrication, it is possible to make them polarization insensitive. SOAs also add spontaneous emission noise to the signal (see Section 5.5).

3.8.3   Cross-Gain Modulation

This type of conversion makes use of the dependence of the gain of an SOA on its input power, as shown in Figure 3.56. As the input power increases, the carriers in the gain region of the SOA get depleted, resulting in a reduction in the amplifier gain. What makes this interesting is that the carrier dynamics within the SOA are very fast, happening on a picosecond time scale. Thus the gain responds in tune with the fluctuations in input power on a bit-by-bit basis. The device can handle bit rates as high as 10 Gb/s. If a low-power probe signal at a different wavelength is sent into the SOA, it will experience a low gain when there is a 1 bit in the input signal and a higher gain when there is a 0 bit. This very same effect produces crosstalk when multiple signals at different wavelengths are amplified by a single SOA and makes the SOA unsuitable for amplifying WDM signals.

The advantage of CGM is that it is conceptually simple. However, there are several drawbacks. The achievable extinction ratio is small (< 10) since the gain does not really drop to zero when there is an input 1 bit. The input signal power must be high (around 0 dBm) so that the amplifier is saturated enough to produce a good variation in gain. This high-powered signal must be eliminated at the amplifier output by suitable filtering, unless the signal and probe are counterpropagating. Moreover, as the carrier density within the SOA varies, it changes the refractive index as well, which in turn affects the phase of the probe and creates a large amount of pulse distortion.

3.8.4   Cross-Phase Modulation

The same phase-change effect that creates pulse distortion in CGM can be used to effect wavelength conversion. As the carrier density in the amplifier varies with the

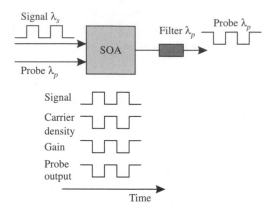

Figure 3.56   Wavelength conversion by cross-gain modulation in a semiconductor optical amplifier.

input signal, it produces a change in refractive index, which in turn modulates the phase of the probe. This phase modulation can be converted into intensity modulation by using an interferometer such as a Mach-Zehnder interferometer (MZI) (see Section 3.3.6). Figure 3.57 shows one possible configuration of a wavelength converter using cross-phase modulation. Both arms of the MZI have exactly the same length and incorporate an SOA. The signal is sent in at one end (A) and the probe at the other end (B). If no signal is present, then the probe signal comes out unmodulated. When the signal is present, it induces a phase change in each amplifier. The couplers in the MZI are designed with an asymmetric coupling ratio $\gamma \neq 0.5$. This makes the phase change in each amplifier different. This results in an intensity-modulated probe signal at the output (A).

The advantage of this approach over CGM is that much less signal power is required to achieve a large phase shift compared to a large gain shift. In fact, a low signal power and a high probe power can be used, making this method more attractive than CGM. This method also produces a better extinction ratio. Depending on where the MZI is operated, the probe can be modulated with the same polarity as the input signal, or the opposite polarity. Referring to Figure 3.57, where we plot the power coupled out at the probe wavelength versus the power at the signal wavelength, depending on the slope of the demultiplexer, a signal power increase can either decrease or increase the power coupled out at the probe wavelength. Like CGM, the bit rate that can be handled is at most 10 Gb/s and is limited by the carrier lifetime.

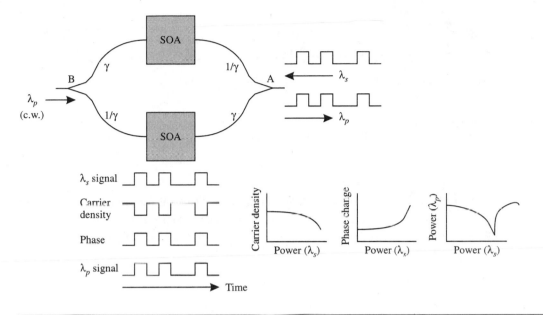

Figure 3.57   Wavelength conversion by cross-phase modulation using semiconductor optical amplifiers embedded inside a Mach-Zehnder interferometer.

3.8.5   Wave Mixing

The four-wave mixing phenomenon that occurs owing to nonlinearities in the transmission medium and that we studied in Section 2.4.5 can also be utilized to realize wavelength conversion. Recall that four-wave mixing causes three waves at frequencies f_1, f_2, and f_3 to produce a fourth wave at the frequency $f_1 + f_2 - f_3$; when $f_1 = f_2$, we get a wave at the frequency $2f_1 - f_3$. What is interesting about four-wave mixing is that the resulting waves can lie in the same band as the interacting waves. As we have seen in Section 2.4.5, in optical fibers, the generated four-wave mixing power is quite small but can lead to crosstalk if present (see Section 5.8.3).

For the purposes of wavelength conversion, the four-wave mixing power can be enhanced by using an SOA because of the higher intensities within the device. If we have a signal at frequency f_s and a probe at frequency f_p, then four-wave mixing will produce signals at frequencies $2f_p - f_s$ and $2f_s - f_p$, as long as all these frequencies lie within the amplifier bandwidth (Figure 3.58).

The main advantage of four-wave mixing is that it is truly transparent, because the effect does not depend on the modulation format (since both amplitude and phase are preserved during the mixing process) and the bit rate. The disadvantages

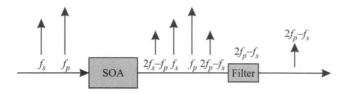

Figure 3.58 Wavelength conversion by four-wave mixing in a semiconductor optical amplifier.

are that the other waves must be filtered out at the SOA output, and the conversion efficiency goes down significantly as the wavelength separation between the signal and probe is increased. We will study the conversion efficiency of four-wave mixing in Section 5.8.3.

Summary

We have studied many different optical components in this chapter. Couplers, isolators, and circulators are all commodity components. Many of the optical filters that we studied are now commercially available, with fiber gratings, thin-film multicavity filters, and arrayed waveguide gratings all competing for use in commercial WDM systems. Semiconductor DFB lasers are used in most high-speed communication systems today although other single-longitudinal mode laser structures may eventually become viable commercially. High-speed APDs and pinFET receivers are both available today. Optical switches are still relatively immature components although there is an increasing need for these devices in optical add/drop multiplexers and crossconnects. All-optical wavelength converters are still in the research laboratories, awaiting significant cost reductions and performance improvements before they can become practical.

Further Reading

The book by Green [Gre93] treats many of the optical components considered in this chapter in more detail, particularly tunable filters and lasers.

The Stimax grating is described in [LL84] and [Gre93]. Gratings are described in detail in several textbooks on optics, for example, [KF86, BW80]. Fiber gratings are now available from several vendors; see [CK94, Ben96] for tutorials on their fabrication and properties, and [Ven96b, Ven96a] for applications of long-period gratings. Dielectric thin-film multicavity filters are commercially available components as well [Opt96]. For a description of how they work, see [SS96] and [Kni76]. The electromagnetics background necessary to understand their operation is provided, for example, by [RWv84]. Early papers on the arrayed waveguide grating are [DEK91] and [VS91]. The principle behind their operation is described in [TSN94, TOTI95, TOT96]. The integrated-optics AOTF is described in [SBJC90], and its systems applications are discussed in [Che90].

There is an extensive literature on optical amplifiers. See [Des94] for EDFAs and [O'M88] for a tutorial on SOAs.

There are several textbooks on the subject of lasers alone; see, for example, [AD86]. Laser oscillation and photodetection are covered in detail in [Yar85]. [JQE91] is a good reference for several laser-related topics, including VCSELs. Other good tutorials on lasers appear in [LZ89, Lee91, SIA92]. Tunable laser diodes are covered in [KM88]. A very readable and up-to-date survey of vertical cavity lasers, including a discussion of the problems encountered in operating them at room temperature, can be found in [MZB97]. A new class of lasers with extremely short cavity dimensions called quantum well lasers has been widely studied over the last decade. See [AY86] for a good introduction to this subject. The mathematical theory behind mode locking is explained in [Yar89] and [Yar65]. There is an extensive discussion of various mode-locking methods for fiber lasers in [Agr95].

A very accessible survey of mechanical switches can be found in [Kas95, Chapter 13]. The tutorial article by Spanke [Spa87] is a good review of large switch architectures for optical switches. See also [MS88] for a good collection of papers on optical switching. The classic book by Beneš [Ben65] is the authoritative reference for the mathematical theory of large switch architectures developed for telephony applications.

Surveys and comparisons of different types of wavelength converters appear in [Yoo96, ISSV96, DMJ+96].

▬ Problems

3.1   Consider the 2×2 3-dB coupler shown in Figure 3.59. Suppose we connect the two outputs with a piece of fiber. Assume that the polarizations are preserved through the device. A light signal is sent in on the first input. What happens? Derive the field transfer function for the device. Assume the coupler used is a reciprocal device so that it works exactly the same way if its inputs and outputs are reversed. *Hint:* This device is called a loop mirror.

Input

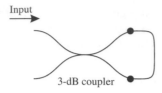

3-dB coupler

Figure 3.59   A 3-dB coupler with the two outputs connected by a piece of fiber.

3.2   Consider a device with three ports where it is desired to send all the energy input at ports 1 and 2 to port 3. We assume, for generality, that all ports can be used as inputs and outputs. The scattering matrix of such a device can be written as

$$\mathbf{S} = \begin{pmatrix} 0 & 0 & s_{13} \\ 0 & 0 & s_{23} \\ s_{31} & s_{32} & s_{33} \end{pmatrix}.$$

Show that a scattering matrix of this form cannot satisfy the conservation of energy condition, (3.4). Thus it is impossible to build a device that combines all the power from two input ports to a third port, without loss.

3.3   Consider an isolator that is a two-port device where power must be transferred from port 1 to port 2, but no power must be transferred from port 2 to port 1. The scattering matrix of such a device can be written as

$$\mathbf{S} = \begin{pmatrix} s_{11} & s_{12} \\ 0 & s_{22} \end{pmatrix}.$$

Show that a scattering matrix of this form cannot satisfy the conservation of energy condition, (3.4). Thus the loss occurs in the isolator because the power input at port 2 must be absorbed by it. However, the power input at port 1 can be transferred to port 2 without loss.

3.4   In Figure 3.9, show that the path length difference between the rays diffracted at angle θ_d and traversing through adjacent slits is approximately $a[\sin(\theta_i) - \sin(\theta_d)]$ when the grating pitch a is small compared to the distance of the source and the imaging plane from the grating plane.

3.5   Show that the resonant frequencies f_n of a Fabry-Perot cavity satisfy $f_n = f_0 + n\Delta f$, n integer, for some fixed f_0 and Δf. Thus these frequencies are spaced equally apart. Note that the corresponding wavelengths are *not* spaced equally apart.

3.6   Derive the power transfer function of the Fabry-Perot filter.

3.7   Derive the expression (3.11) for the finesse of the Fabry-Perot filter. Assume that the mirror reflectivity, R, is close to unity.

3.8   Consider a cascade of two Fabry-Perot filters with cavity lengths l_1 and l_2, respectively. Assume the mirror reflectivities of both filters equal R and the refractive index of their cavities is n. Neglect reflections from the second cavity to the first and vice versa. What is the power transfer function of the cascade? If $l_1/l_2 = k/m$ where k and m are relatively prime integers, find an expression for the FSR of the cascade. Express this FSR in terms of the FSRs of the individual filters.

3.9   Show that the transfer function of the dielectric slab filter shown in Figure E.1(b) is identical to that of a Fabry-Perot filter with facet reflectivity

$$\sqrt{R} - \frac{n_2 - n_1}{n_2 + n_1},$$

assuming $n_3 = n_1$.

3.10 Consider a stack of $2k$ alternating low index (n_L) and high index (n_H) dielectric films. Let each of these films have a quarter wave thickness at λ_0. In the notation of Section 3.3.5, this stack can be denoted by $(HL)^k$. Find the reflectivity of this stack as a function of the optical wavelength λ. Thus a single cavity dielectric thin-film filter can be viewed as a Fabry-Perot filter with wavelength-dependent mirror reflectivities.

3.11 Derive the power transfer function of the Mach-Zehnder interferometer, assuming only one of its two inputs is active.

3.12 Consider the Mach-Zehnder interferometer of Section 3.3.6.
      (a) With the help of a block diagram, show how a $1 \times n$ demultiplexer can be constructed using n 1 MZIs. Assume n is a power of two. You must specify the path length differences ΔL that must be used in each of the MZIs.
      (b) Can you simplify your construction if only a specific one of the signals needs to be separated from the rest of the $n - 1$?

3.13 Consider the Rowland circle construction shown in Figure 3.23. Show that the differences in path lengths between a fixed input waveguide and any two successive arrayed waveguides is a constant. Assume that the length of the arc on which the arrayed waveguides are located is much smaller than the diameter of the Rowland circle. *Hint:* Choose a Cartesian coordinate system whose origin is the point of tangency of the Rowland and grating circles. Now express the Euclidean distance between an arbitrary input (output) waveguide and an arbitrary arrayed waveguide in this coordinate system. Use the assumption stated earlier to simplify your expression. Finally, note that the vertical spacing between the arrayed waveguides is constant. In the notation of the book, this shows that $\delta_i = d \sin\theta_i$, where d is the vertical separation between successive arrayed waveguides, and θ_i is the angular separation of input waveguide i from the central input waveguide, as measured from the origin.

3.14 Derive an expression for the free spectral range (FSR) of an arrayed waveguide grating (AWG) for a fixed-input waveguide i and a fixed-output waveguide j. The FSR depends on the input and output waveguides. But show that if the arc length of the Rowland circle on which the input and output waveguides are located (see Figure 3.23) is small, then the FSR is approximately constant. Use the result from Problem 3.13 that $\delta_i = d \sin \theta_i$.

3.15 Consider an AWG that satisfies the condition given in Problem 3.14 for its FSR to be approximately independent of the input and output waveguides. Given the FSR, determine the set of wavelengths that must be selected in order for the AWG to function as the wavelength router depicted in Figure 3.22. Assume that the angular spacing between the input (and output) waveguides is constant. Use the result from Problem 3.13 that $\delta_i = d \sin \theta_i$.

3.16 Design an AWG that can multiplex/demultiplex 16 WDM signals spaced 100 GHz apart in the 1.55 μm band. Your design must specify, among other things, the spacing between the input/output waveguides, the path length difference between successive arrayed waveguides, the radius R of the grating circle, and the FSR of the AWG. Assume the refractive index of the input/output waveguides and the arrayed waveguides is 1.5. Note that the design may not be unique, and you may have to make reasonable choices for some of the parameters, which will in turn determine the rest of the parameters.

3.17 Show that the FWHM bandwidth of the acousto-optic filter is $\approx 0.8 \lambda_0^2 / l \Delta n$.

3.18 Explain how the polarization-independent acousto-optic tunable filter illustrated in Figure 3.24 acts as a 2-input, 2-output wavelength router when both its inputs are active.

3.19 Calculate the acousto-optic interaction length that would be required for the AOTF to have a passband width (FWHM) of 1 nm at an operating wavelength of 1.55 μm. Assume $\Delta n = 0.07$.

3.20 Consider a 16-channel WDM system where the interchannel spacing is nominally 100 GHz. Assume that one of the channels is to be selected by a filter with a 1-dB bandwidth of 2 GHz. We consider three different filter structures for this purpose.

- Fabry-Perot filter: Assume the center wavelengths of the channels do not drift. What is the required finesse and the corresponding mirror reflectivity of a Fabry-Perot filter that achieves a crosstalk suppression of 30 dB from each adjacent channel? If the center wavelengths of the channels can drift up to ± 20 GHz from their nominal values, what is the required finesse and mirror reflectivity?

- Mach-Zehnder interferometer: Assume a cascade of MZIs, as shown in Figure 3.18(c), is used for this purpose and the same level of crosstalk suppression must be achieved. What is the path length difference ΔL and the number of stages required, when the channel center wavelengths are fixed and when they can drift by ± 20 GHz?

- AOTF: Can an AOTF be used to achieve the same level of crosstalk suppression?

3.21   This problem compares different simple add/drop multiplexer architectures.

(a) First consider the fiber Bragg grating based add/drop element shown in Figure 3.11(b). Suppose a 5% tap is used to couple the added signal in to the output, and the grating induces a loss of 0.5 dB for the transmitted signals and no loss for the reflected signal. Assume that the circulator has a loss of 1 dB per pass. Carefully compute the loss seen by a channel that is dropped, a channel that is added, and a channel that is passed through the device. Suppose the input power per channel is -15 dBm. At what power should the add channel be transmitted so that the powers on all the channels at the output are the same?

(b) Suppose you had to realize an add/drop multiplexer that drops and adds four wavelengths. One possible way to do this is to cascade four add/drop elements of the type shown in Figure 3.11 in series. In this case, compute the best-case and worst-case loss seen by a channel that is dropped, a channel that is added, and a channel that is passed through the device.

(c) Another way to realize a four-channel add/drop multiplexer is shown in Figure 3.60. Repeat the preceding exercise for this architecture. Assume that the losses are as shown in the figure. Which of the two would you prefer from a loss perspective?

(d) Assume that fiber gratings cost $500 each, circulators $3000 each, filters $1000 each, and splitters, combiners and couplers $100 each. Which of the two preceding architectures would you prefer from a cost point of view?

3.22   In a photodetector, why don't the conduction band electrons absorb the incident photons?

3.23   Consider the 4×4 switch shown in Figure 3.51 made up of 2×2 switches. Suppose each 2×2 switch has crosstalk suppression of 50 dB. What is the overall crosstalk suppression of the 4×4 switch? Assume for now that powers can be added and that we do not have to worry about individual electric fields adding in phase. If we wanted an overall crosstalk suppression of 40 dB, what should the crosstalk suppression of each switch be?

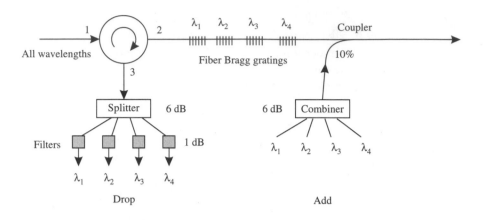

Figure 3.60   A four-channel add/drop multiplexer architecture.

References

[AD86]   G. P. Agrawal and N. K. Dutta. *Long-Wavelength Semiconductor Lasers*. Van Nostrand Reinhold, New York, 1986.

[Agr95]   G. P. Agrawal. *Nonlinear Fiber Optics, 2nd edition*. Academic Press, San Diego, CA, 1995.

[AY86]   Y. Arakawa and A. Yariv. Quantum well lasers—gain, spectra, dynamics. *IEEE Journal of Quantum Electronics*, 22(9):1887–1899, Sept. 1986.

[Ben65]   V. E. Beneš. *Mathematical Theory of Connecting Networks*. Academic Press, New York, 1965.

[Ben96]   I. Bennion et al. UV-written in-fibre Bragg gratings. *Optical Quantum Electronics*, 28(2):93–135, Feb. 1996.

[BW80]   M. Born and E. Wolf. *Principles of Optics*. Pergamon Press, Oxford, 1980.

[Che90]   K-W. Cheung. Acoustooptic tunable filters in narrowband WDM networks: System issues and network applications. *IEEE Journal of Selected Areas in Communications*, 8(6):1015–1025, Aug. 1990.

[CK94]   R. J. Campbell and R. Kashyap. The properties and applications of photosensitive germanosilicate fibre. *International Journal of Optoelectronics*, 9(1):33–57, 1994.

[Cle94]   B. Clesca et al. Gain flatness comparison between Erbium-doped fluoride and silica fiber amplifiers with wavelength-multiplexed signals. *IEEE Photonics Technology Letters*, 6(4):509–512, April 1994.

[DEK91]   C. Dragone, C. A. Edwards, and R. C. Kistler. Integrated optics $N \times N$ multiplexer on silicon. *IEEE Photonics Technology Letters*, 3:896–899, Oct. 1991.

[Des94]   E. Desurvire. *Erbium-Doped Fiber Amplifiers*. John Wiley, New York, 1994.

[DMJ+96] T. Durhuus, B. Mikkelsen, C. Joergensen, S. Lykke Danielsen, and K. E. Stubkjaer. All optical wavelength conversion by semiconductor optical amplifiers. *IEEE/OSA JLT/JSAC Special Issue on Multiwavelength Optical Technology and Networks*, 14(6):942–954, June 1996.

[Dra89]   C. Dragone. Efficient $n \times n$ star couplers using Fourier optics. *IEEE/OSA Journal on Lightwave Technology*, 7(3):479–489, March 1989.

[Gre93]   P. E. Green. *Fiber-Optic Networks*. Prentice Hall, Englewood Cliffs, NJ, 1993.

[ISSV96] E. Iannone, R. Sabella, L. De Stefano, and F. Valeri. All optical wavelength conversion in optical multicarrier networks. *IEEE Transactions on Communications*, 44(6):716–724, June 1996.

[Jac96]   J. L. Jackel et al. Acousto-optic tunable filters (AOTFs) for multiwavelength optical cross-connects: Crosstalk considerations. *IEEE/OSA JLT/JSAC Special Issue on Multiwavelength Optical Technology and Networks*, 14(6):1056–1066, June 1996.

[JQE91]   *IEEE Journal of Quantum Electronics*, June 1991.

[Kam96]   I. P. Kaminow et al. A wideband all-optical WDM network. *IEEE JSAC/JLT Special Issue on Optical Networks*, 14(5):780–799, June 1996.

[Kas95]   N. Kashima. *Passive Optical Components for Optical Fiber Transmission*. Artech House, Boston, 1995.

[KF86]   M. V. Klein and T. E. Furtak. *Optics, 2nd edition*. John Wiley, New York, 1986.

[KM88]   K. Kobayashi and I. Mito. Single frequency and tunable laser diodes. *IEEE/OSA Journal on Lightwave Technology*, 6(11):1623–1633, November 1988.

[Kni76]   Z. Knittl. *Optics of Thin Films*. John Wiley, New York, 1976.

[Lee91]   T. P. Lee. Recent advances in long-wavelength semiconductor lasers for optical fiber communication. *Proceedings of IEEE*, 79(3):253–276, March 1991.

[LL84]   J. P. Laude and J. M. Lerner. Wavelength division multiplexing/demultiplexing (WDM) using diffraction gratings. *SPIE-Application, Theory and Fabrication of Periodic Structures*, 503:22–28, 1984.

[LZ89]   T. P. Lee and C-N. Zah. Wavelength-tunable and single-frequency lasers for photonic communication networks. *IEEE Communications Magazine*, 27(10):42–52, Oct. 1989.

[MS88]   J. E. Midwinter and P. W. Smith, editors. *IEEE JSAC: Special Issue on Photonic Switching*, volume 6, Aug. 1988.

[MZB97]   N. M. Margalit, S. Z. Zhang, and J. E. Bowers. Vertical cavity lasers for telecom applications. *IEEE Communications Magazine*, 35(5):164–170, May 1997.

[O'M88]   M. J. O'Mahony. Semiconductor laser amplifiers for future fiber systems. *IEEE/OSA Journal on Lightwave Technology*, 6(4):531–544, April 1988.

[Opt96]   Optical Corporation of America. *16 Channel Dense Wavelength Division Multiplexer (DWDM)*, 1996. Specification available at *http://www.oca.com*.

[RWv84]   S. Ramo, J. R. Whinnery, and T. van Duzer. *Fields and Waves in Communication Electronics*. John Wiley, New York, 1984.

[SB87]   R. A. Spanke and V. E. Beneš. An *n*-stage planar optical permutation network. *Applied Optics*, 26, April 1987.

[SBJC90]   D. A. Smith, J. E. Baran, J. J. Johnson, and K-W. Cheung. Integrated-optic acoustically-tunable filters for WDM networks. *IEEE Journal of Selected Areas in Communications*, 8(6):1151–1159, Aug. 1990.

[SIA92]   Y. Suematsu, K. Iga, and S. Arai. Advanced semiconductor lasers. *Proceedings of IEEE*, 80:383–397, 1992.

[Son95]   G. H. Song. Toward the ideal codirectional Bragg filter with an acousto-optic-filter design. *IEEE/OSA Journal on Lightwave Technology*, 13(3):470–480, March 1995.

[Spa87]   R. A. Spanke. Architectures for guided-wave optical space switching systems. *IEEE Communications Magazine*, 25(5):42–48, May 1987.

[SS96]   M. A. Scobey and D. E. Spock. Passive DWDM components using microplasma optical interference filters. In *OFC'96 Technical Digest*, pages 242–243, San Jose, Feb. 1996.

[TOT96]   H. Takahashi, K. Oda, and H. Toba. Impact of crosstalk in an arrayed-waveguide multiplexer on $n \times n$ optical interconnection. *IEEE/OSA JLT/JSAC Special Issue on Multiwavelength Optical Technology and Networks*, 14(6):1097–1105, June 1996.

[TOTI95]   H. Takahashi, K. Oda, H. Toba, and Y. Inoue. Transmission characteristics of arrayed $n \times n$ wavelength multiplexer. *IEEE/OSA Journal on Lightwave Technology*, 13(3):447–455, March 1995.

[TSN94]   H. Takahashi, S. Suzuki, and I. Nishi. Wavelength multiplexer based on SiO_2–Ta_2O_5 arrayed-waveguide grating. *IEEE/OSA Journal on Lightwave Technology*, 12(6):989–995, June 1994.

[Ven96a]   A. M. Vengsarkar et al. Long-period fiber-grating-based gain equalizers. *Optics Letters*, 21(5):336–338, 1996.

[Ven96b]   A. M. Vengsarkar et al. Long-period gratings as band-rejection filters. *IEEE/OSA Journal on Lightwave Technology*, 14(1):58–64, Jan. 1996.

[VS91]   A. R. Vellekoop and M. K. Smit. Four-channel integrated-optic wavelength demultiplexer with weak polarization dependence. *IEEE/OSA Journal on Lightwave Technology*, 9:310–314, 1991.

[Yar65] A. Yariv. Internal modulation in multimode laser oscillators. *Journal of Applied Physics*, 36:388, 1965.

[Yar85] A. Yariv. *Optical Electronics, 3rd Edition*. Holt, Rinehart and Winston, New York, 1985.

[Yar89] A. Yariv. *Quantum Electronics, 3rd edition*. John Wiley, New York, 1989.

[Yoo96] S. J. B. Yoo. Wavelength conversion techniques for WDM network applications. *IEEE/OSA JLT/JSAC Special Issue on Multiwavelength Optical Technology and Networks*, 14(6):955–966, June 1996.

4 chapter

Modulation and Demodulation

O UR GOAL IN THIS CHAPTER is to understand the processes of modulation and demodulation of digital signals. We start by discussing *modulation*, which is the process of converting digital data in electronic form to an optical signal that can be transmitted over the fiber. We then study the *demodulation* process, which is the process of converting back the optical signal into electronic form and extracting the data that was transmitted. We will derive expressions for the bit error rate introduced by the whole transmission process. With this background, in the next chapter, we will tackle transmission system engineering, which requires careful attention to a variety of impairments that affect system performance.

4.1 Modulation

For the purpose of transmission over an optical fiber, digital data must be converted into a suitable optical format. This process is called *modulation*. The most commonly used modulation scheme in optical communication is *on–off keying* (OOK). This modulation scheme is illustrated in Figure 4.1. In this modulation scheme, a 1 bit is encoded by the presence of a light pulse in the bit interval or by turning a light source (laser or LED) "on." A 0 bit is encoded (ideally) by the absence of a light pulse in the bit interval or by turning a light source "off." The bit interval is the interval of time available for the transmission of a single bit. For example, at a bit rate of 1 Gb/s, the bit interval is 1 ns. As we saw in Section 3.5.2, we can either *directly* modulate the light source by turning it on or off, or use an external modulator in front of

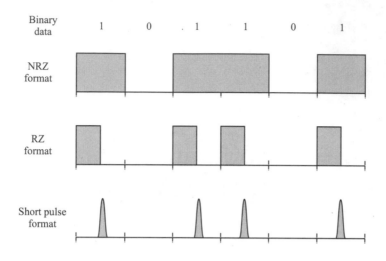

Figure 4.1   On–off keying (OOK) modulation of binary digital data.

the source to perform the same function. Using an external modulator results in less *chirp*, and thus less of a penalty due to dispersion, and is the preferred approach for high-speed transmission over long distances.

4.1.1   Signal Formats

The OOK modulation scheme can use many different signal formats. The most common signal formats are Non-Return-to-Zero (NRZ), Return-to-Zero (RZ), and the short pulse format. These formats are illustrated in Figure 4.1. In the NRZ format, the pulse for a 1 bit occupies the entire bit interval, and no pulse is used for a 0 bit. If there are two successive 1s, the pulse occupies two successive bit intervals. In the RZ format, the pulse for a 1 bit occupies only half the bit interval, and no pulse is used for a 0 bit. The short pulse format is a variation of the RZ format, where the pulse for a 1 bit occupies a small portion of the bit interval, with no pulse being transmitted for a 0 bit.

The major advantage of the NRZ format over the other formats is that the signal occupies a much smaller bandwidth—about half that of the RZ format. The problem with the NRZ format is that long strings of 1s or 0s will result in a total absence of any transitions, making it difficult for the receiver to acquire the bit clock. The RZ format ameliorates this problem somewhat since long strings of 1s (but not strings of 0s) will still produce transitions.

A problem with all these formats is the lack of *DC balance*. An OOK modulation scheme is said to have *DC balance* if, for all sequences of data bits that may have to be transmitted, the average transmitted power is constant. It is important for an OOK modulation scheme to achieve DC balance since this makes it easier to set the decision threshold at the receiver (see Section 5.2).

To ensure sufficient transitions in the signal and to provide DC balance, either *line coding* or *scrambling* is used in the system. There are many different types of line codes. One form of a *binary block line code* encodes a block of k data bits into n bits that are then modulated and sent over the fiber. At the receiver, the n bits are mapped back into the original k data bits (assuming there were no errors). Line codes can be designed so that the encoded bit sequence is DC balanced and provides sufficient transitions irrespective of the input data bit sequence. An example of such a line code is the (8, 10) code that is used in the Fiber Channel standard [WF83, SV96]. This code has $k = 8$ and $n = 10$. The fiber distributed data interface (FDDI) [Ros86] uses a (4, 5) code that is significantly less complex than this (8, 10) code but does not quite achieve DC balance; the worst-case DC imbalance is 10% [Bur86].

An alternative to using line coding is to use *scrambling*. Scrambling is a one-to-one mapping of the data stream into another data stream before it is transmitted on the link. At the transmitter, a scrambler takes the incoming bits and does an EXOR operation with another carefully chosen sequence of bits. The latter sequence is chosen so as to minimize the likelihood of long sequences of 1s or 0s in the transmitted stream. The data is recovered back at the receiver by a descrambler that extracts the data from the scrambled stream. The advantage of scrambling over line coding is that it does not require any additional bandwidth. The disadvantages are that it does not guarantee DC balance, nor does it guarantee a maximum length for a sequence of 1s or 0s. However, the probability of having long run lengths or DC imbalance is made very small by choosing the mapping so that likely input sequences with long run lengths are mapped into sequences with a small run length. However, since the mapping is one-to-one, it is possible to choose an input sequence that results in a bad output sequence. The mapping is chosen so that only very rare input sequences produce bad output sequences. See Problem 4.2 for an example of how scrambling is implemented and its properties.

In practice, the NRZ format is used in most high-speed communication systems. Computer data links use line codes. Most high-speed telecommunications links use scrambling instead.

The short pulse format is similar to the RZ format in that there is a pulse in the bit interval for a 1 bit and no pulse for a 0 bit. However, the pulse occupies only a fraction of the bit interval. The short pulse format is useful in certain high bit rate communications systems for which the pulse width must occupy a fraction of the bit interval in order to minimize the effects of chromatic dispersion (see

Section 2.3.2). The short pulse format is also used in soliton communication systems (see Section 2.5) where the optical pulses must be widely separated in order to realize the dispersion-free propagation properties of solitons.

4.2   Demodulation

The modulated signals are transmitted over the optical fiber where they undergo attenuation and dispersion, have noise added to them from optical amplifiers, and sustain a variety of other impairments that we will discuss in Chapter 5. At the receiver, the transmitted data must be recovered with an acceptable *bit error rate* (BER). The required BER for high-speed optical communication systems today is typically 10^{-12}, that is, one allowed bit error for every terabit of data transmitted, on average. Recovering the transmitted data involves two steps: (a) recovering the *bit clock,* that is, the bit interval boundaries, and (b) determining the bit that was transmitted during each bit interval. The pulse broadening effect of dispersion smears adjacent pulses into one another and affects the bit clock recovery. Techniques for bit clock recovery are discussed in the references. In this section, we will assume that the bit clock has been recovered and focus on the problem of recovering the transmitted bit within a given bit interval.

4.2.1   An Ideal Receiver

In principle, the demodulation process can be quite simple. The receiver looks for the presence or absence of light during a bit interval. If no light is seen, it infers that a 0 bit was transmitted, and if any light is seen, it infers that a 1 bit was transmitted. This is called *direct detection.* Unfortunately, even in the absence of other forms of noise, this will not lead to an ideal error-free system because of the random nature of photon arrivals at the receiver. A light signal arriving with power P can be thought of as a stream of photons arriving at average rate P/hf_c. Here, h is Planck's constant (6.63×10^{-34} J/Hz), f_c is the carrier frequency, and hf_c is the energy of a single photon. This stream can be thought of as a Poisson random process.

Note that our simple receiver does not make any errors when a 0 bit is transmitted. However, when a 1 bit is transmitted, the receiver may decide that a 0 bit was transmitted if no photons were received during that bit interval. If B denotes the bit rate, then the probability that n photons are received during a bit interval $1/B$ is given by

$$e^{-(P/hf_c B)}\frac{\left(\frac{P}{hf_c B}\right)^n}{n!}.$$

Thus the probability of not receiving any photons is $e^{-(P/hf_cB)}$. Assuming equally likely 1s and 0s, the bit error rate of this ideal receiver would be given as

$$\text{BER} = \frac{1}{2}e^{-\frac{P}{hf_cB}}.$$

Let $M = P/hf_cB$. The parameter M represents the average number of photons received during a 1 bit. Then the bit error rate can be expressed as

$$\text{BER} = \frac{1}{2}e^{-M}.$$

This expression represents the error rate of an ideal receiver and is called the *quantum limit*. To get a bit error rate of 10^{-12}, note that we would need an average of $M = 27$ photons per 1 bit.

In practice, most receivers are not ideal, and their performance is not as good as that of the ideal receiver because they must contend with various other forms of noise, as we shall soon see.

4.2.2 A Practical Direct Detection Receiver

As we have seen in Section 3.6, (see Figure 3.45), the optical signal at the receiver is first photodetected to convert it into an electrical current. The main complication in recovering the transmitted bit is that in addition to the photocurrent due to the signal there are usually three other additional noise currents. The first is the *thermal noise* current due to the random motion of electrons that is always present at any finite temperature. The second is the *shot noise* current due to the random distribution of the electrons generated by the photodetection process even when the input light intensity is constant. The shot noise current, unlike the thermal noise current, is not added to the generated photocurrent but is merely a convenient representation of the variability in the generated photocurrent as a separate component. The third source of noise is the spontaneous emission due to optical amplifiers that may be used between the source and the photodetector. The amplifier noise currents are treated in Section 4.2.5 and Appendix F. In this section, we will consider only the thermal and shot noise currents.

The thermal noise current in a resistor R at temperature T can be modeled as a Gaussian random process with zero mean and autocorrelation function $(4k_BT/R)\delta(\tau)$. Here k_B is Boltzmann's constant and has the value 1.38×10^{-23} J/°K, and $\delta(\tau)$ is the Dirac delta function, defined as $\delta(\tau) = 0, \tau \neq 0$ and $\int_{-\infty}^{\infty} \delta(\tau)d\tau = 1$. Thus the noise is white, and in a bandwidth or frequency range B_e, the thermal noise current has the variance

$$\sigma^2_{\text{thermal}} = (4k_BT/R)B_e.$$

This value can be expressed as $I_t^2 B_e$, where I_t is the parameter used to specify the current standard deviation in units of pA/$\sqrt{\text{Hz}}$. Typical values are of the order of 1 pA/$\sqrt{\text{Hz}}$.

The electrical bandwidth of the receiver, B_e, is chosen based on the bit rate of the signal. In practice, B_e varies from $1/2T$ to $1/T$, where T is the bit period. We will also be using the parameter B_o to denote the optical bandwidth seen by the receiver. The optical bandwidth of the receiver itself is very large, but the value of B_o is usually determined by filters placed in the optical path between the transmitter and receiver. By convention, we will measure B_e in baseband units, and B_o in passband units. Therefore, the minimum possible value of $B_o = 2B_e$, to prevent signal distortion.

As we saw in the previous section, the photon arrivals are accurately modeled by a Poisson random process. The photocurrent can thus be modeled as a stream of electronic charge impulses, generated whenever a photon arrives at the photodetector. For signal powers that are usually encountered in optical communication systems, the photocurrent can be modeled as

$$I = \bar{I} + i_s,$$

where $\bar{I}$ is a constant current, and i_s is a Gaussian random process with mean zero and autocorrelation $\sigma_{\text{shot}}^2 \delta(\tau)$. For *pin* diodes, $\sigma_{\text{shot}}^2 = 2e\bar{I}$. This is derived in Appendix F. The constant current $\bar{I} = \mathcal{R}P$, where $\mathcal{R}$ is the responsivity of the photodetector, which was discussed in Section 3.6. Here, we are assuming that the dark current, which is the photocurrent that is present in the absence of an input optical signal, is negligible. Thus the shot noise current is also white and in a bandwidth B_e has the variance

$$\sigma_{\text{shot}}^2 = 2e\bar{I}B_e. \tag{4.1}$$

If we denote the load resistor of the photodetector by R_L, the total current in this resistor can be written as

$$I = \bar{I} + i_s + i_t,$$

where i_t has the variance $\sigma_{\text{thermal}}^2 = (4k_B T/R_L)B_e$. The shot noise and thermal noise currents are assumed to be independent so that, if B_e is the bandwidth of the receiver, this current can be modeled as a Gaussian random process with mean $\bar{I}$ and variance

$$\sigma^2 = \sigma_{\text{shot}}^2 + \sigma_{\text{thermal}}^2.$$

Note that both the shot noise and thermal noise variances are proportional to the bandwidth B_e of the receiver. Thus there is a tradeoff between the bandwidth of a receiver and its noise performance. A receiver is usually designed so as to have just sufficient bandwidth to accommodate the desired bit rate so that its noise performance is optimized. In most practical direct detection receivers, the variance of the thermal noise component is much larger than the variance of the shot noise and determines the performance of the receiver.

4.2.3 Front-End Amplifier Noise

We saw in Chapter 3 (Figure 3.45) that the photodetector is followed by a front-end amplifier. Components within the front-end amplifier, such as the transistor, also contribute to the thermal noise. This noise contribution is usually stated by giving the *noise figure* of the front-end amplifier. The *noise figure* of a front-end amplifier specifies the factor by which the thermal noise present at the input of the amplifier is enhanced at its output. We will denote this quantity by F_n. Thus the thermal noise contribution of the receiver has variance

$$\sigma_{\text{thermal}}^2 = \frac{4k_B T}{R_L} F_n B_e \tag{4.2}$$

when the front-end amplifier noise contribution is included. Typical values of F_n are 3–5 dB.

4.2.4 APD Noise

As we remarked in Section 3.6.1, the avalanche gain process in APDs has the effect of increasing the noise current at its output. This increased noise contribution arises from the random nature of the avalanche multiplicative gain, G_m. This noise contribution is modeled as an increase in the shot noise component at the output of the photodetector. If we denote the responsivity of the APD by $\mathcal{R}_{\text{APD}}$, the average photocurrent is given by $\bar{I} = \mathcal{R}_{\text{APD}} P = G_m \mathcal{R} P$, and the shot noise current at the APD output has variance

$$\sigma_{\text{shot}}^2 = 2e G_m^2 F_A(G_m) \mathcal{R} P B_e. \tag{4.3}$$

The quantity $F_A(G_m)$ is called the *excess noise factor* of the APD and is an increasing function of the gain G_m. It is given by

$$F_A(G_m) = k_A G_m + (1 - k_A)(2 - 1/G_m).$$

The quantity k_A is called the ionization coefficient ratio and is a property of the semiconductor material used to make up the APD. It takes values in the range (0–1). The excess noise factor is an increasing function of k_A, and thus it is desirable to keep k_A small. The value of k_A for silicon (which is used at 0.8 μm wavelength) is $\ll 1$, and for InGaAs (which is used at 1.3 and 1.55 μm wavelength bands) is 0.7.

Note that $F_A(1) = 1$, and thus (4.3) also yields the shot noise variance for a *pin* receiver if we set $G_m = 1$.

4.2.5   Optical Preamplifiers

As we have seen in the previous sections, the performance of simple direct detection receivers is limited primarily by thermal noise generated inside the receiver. The performance can be improved significantly by using an optical (pre)amplifier in front of the receiver, as shown in Figure 4.2. The amplifier provides added gain to the input signal. Unfortunately, as we saw in Section 3.4.2, the spontaneous emission present in the amplifier appears as noise at its output. The spontaneous noise power at the output of the amplifier for each polarization mode is given by

$$P_N = n_{\rm sp} h f_c (G - 1) B_o, \tag{4.4}$$

where $n_{\rm sp}$ is a constant called the spontaneous emission factor, G is the amplifier gain, and B_o is the optical bandwidth. Two fundamental polarization modes are present in a single-mode fiber, as we saw in Chapter 2. Hence the total noise power at the output of the amplifier is $2P_N$.

The value of $n_{\rm sp}$ depends on the level of population inversion within the amplifier. With complete inversion $n_{\rm sp} = 1$, but it is typically higher, around 2–5 for most amplifiers. For convenience, let

$$P_n = n_{\rm sp} h f_c.$$

To understand the impact of amplifier noise on the detection of the received signal, consider the optical preamplifier system shown in Figure 4.2, used in front of a standard *pin* direct detection receiver. The photodetector produces a current that is proportional to the incident power. The signal current is given by

$$I = \mathcal{R} G P, \tag{4.5}$$

where P is the received optical power.

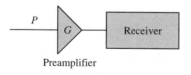

Preamplifier

Figure 4.2   A receiver with an optical preamplifier.

The photodetector produces a current that is proportional to the optical power. The optical power is proportional to the square of the electric field. Thus the noise field beats against the signal and against itself, giving rise to noise components referred to as the *signal-spontaneous* beat noise and *spontaneous-spontaneous* beat noise, respectively. In addition, shot noise and thermal noise components are also present.

The variances of the thermal noise, shot noise, signal-spontaneous noise, and spontaneous-spontaneous noise currents at the receiver are, respectively,

$$\sigma^2_{\text{thermal}} = I_t^2 B_e, \tag{4.6}$$

$$\sigma^2_{\text{shot}} = 2e\mathcal{R}[GP + P_n(G-1)B_o]B_e, \tag{4.7}$$

$$\sigma^2_{\text{sig-spont}} = 4\mathcal{R}^2 G P P_n(G-1)B_e, \tag{4.8}$$

and

$$\sigma^2_{\text{spont-spont}} = 2\mathcal{R}^2[P_n(G-1)]^2(2B_o - B_e)B_e. \tag{4.9}$$

These variances are derived in Appendix F. Here I_t is the receiver thermal noise current. Provided the amplifier gain is reasonably large (> 10 dB), which is usually the case, the shot noise and thermal noise are negligible compared to the signal-spontaneous and spontaneous-spontaneous beat noise. In the bit error rate regime of interest to us (10^{-9} to 10^{-15}), these noise processes can be modeled adequately as Gaussian processes. The spontaneous-spontaneous beat noise can be made very small by reducing the optical bandwidth B_o. This can be done by filtering the amplifier noise before it reaches the receiver. In the limit, B_o can be made as small as $2B_e$. So the dominant noise component is usually signal-spontaneous beat noise.

The amplifier noise is commonly specified by an easily measurable parameter known as the *noise figure*. The noise figure F_n is the ratio of the input signal-to-noise ratio (SNR_i) to the output signal-to-noise ratio. At the amplifier input, assuming that only signal shot noise is present, using (4.5) and (4.1), the SNR is given by

$$\text{SNR}_i = \frac{(\mathcal{R}P)^2}{2\mathcal{R}ePB_e}.$$

At the amplifier output, assuming that the dominant noise term is the signal-spontaneous beat noise, using (4.5) and (4.8), the SNR is given by

$$\text{SNR}_o \approx \frac{(\mathcal{R}GP)^2}{4\mathcal{R}^2 P G(G-1)n_{\text{sp}}hf_c B_e}.$$

The noise figure of the amplifier is then

$$F_n = \frac{\text{SNR}_i}{\text{SNR}_o} \approx 2n_{\text{sp}} \tag{4.10}$$

In the best case, with full population inversion, $n_{\text{sp}} = 1$. Thus the best-case noise figure is 3 dB. Practical amplifiers have a somewhat higher noise figure, typically in the 4 to 7 dB range. This derivation assumed that there are no coupling losses between the amplifier and the input and output fibers. Having an input coupling loss degrades the noise figure of the amplifier (see Problem 4.4).

4.2.6   Bit Error Rates

Earlier, we calculated the bit error rate of an ideal direct detection receiver. Next, we will calculate the bit error rate of the practical receivers already considered, which must deal with a variety of different noise impairments.

The receiver makes decisions as to which bit (0 or 1) was transmitted in each bit interval by sampling the photocurrent. Owing to the presence of noise currents, the receiver could make a wrong decision resulting in an erroneous bit. In order to compute this bit error rate, we must understand the process by which the receiver makes a decision regarding the transmitted bit.

First, consider a *pin* receiver without an optical preamplifier. For a transmitted 1 bit, let the received optical power $P = P_1$, and let the mean photocurrent $\bar{I} = I_1$. Then $I_1 = \mathcal{R}P_1$, and the variance of the photocurrent is

$$\sigma_1^2 = 2eI_1B_e + 4k_BTB_e/R_L.$$

If P_0 and I_0 are the corresponding quantities for a 0 bit, $I_0 = \mathcal{R}P_0$, and the variance of the photocurrent is

$$\sigma_0^2 = 2eI_0B_e + 4k_BTB_e/R_L.$$

For ideal OOK, P_0 and I_0 are zero, but we will see later (Section 5.3) that this is not always the case in practice.

Let I_1 and I_0 denote the photocurrent sampled by the receiver during a 1 bit and a 0 bit, respectively, and let σ_1^2 and σ_0^2 represent the corresponding noise variances. The noise signals are assumed to be Gaussian. The actual variances will depend on the type of receiver, as we saw earlier. So the bit decision problem faced by the receiver has the following mathematical formulation. The photocurrent for a 1 bit is therefore a sample of a Gaussian random variable with mean I_1 and variance σ_1 (and similarly for the 0 bit as well). The receiver must look at this sample and decide whether the transmitted bit is a 0 or a 1. The possible probability density functions

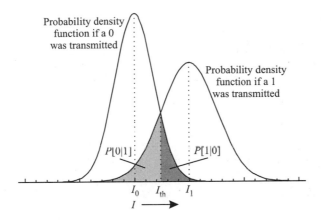

Figure 4.3   Probability density functions for the observed photocurrent.

of the sampled photocurrent are sketched in Figure 4.3. There are many possible *decision rules* that the receiver can use; the receiver's objective is to choose the one that minimizes the bit error rate. This *optimum decision rule* can be shown to be the one that, given the observed photocurrent I, chooses the bit (0 or 1) that was *most likely* to have been transmitted. Furthermore, this optimum decision rule can be implemented as follows. Compare the observed photocurrent to a decision threshold I_{th}. If $I \geq I_{th}$, decide that a 1 bit was transmitted; otherwise, decide that a 0 bit was transmitted.

For the case when 1 and 0 bits are equally likely (which is the only case we consider in this book), the threshold photocurrent is given approximately by

$$I_{th} = \frac{\sigma_0 I_1 + \sigma_1 I_0}{\sigma_0 + \sigma_1}. \tag{4.11}$$

This value is very close but not exactly equal to the optimal value of the threshold. The proof of this result is left as an exercise (Problem 4.6). Geometrically, I_{th} is the value of I for which the two densities sketched in Figure 4.3 cross. The probability of error when a 1 was transmitted is the probability that $I < I_{th}$ and is denoted by $P[0|1]$. Likewise, $P[1|0]$ is the probability of deciding that a 1 was transmitted when actually a 0 was transmitted and is the probability that $I \geq I_{th}$. Both probabilities are indicated in Figure 4.3.

Let $Q(x)$ denote the probability that a zero mean, unit variance Gaussian random variable exceeds the value x. Thus

$$Q(x) = \frac{1}{\sqrt{2\pi}} \int_x^\infty e^{-y^2/2} \, dy. \tag{4.12}$$

It now follows that

$$P[0|1] = Q\left(\frac{I_1 - I_{th}}{\sigma_1}\right)$$

and

$$P[1|0] = Q\left(\frac{I_{th} - I_0}{\sigma_0}\right).$$

Using (4.11), it can then be shown that the BER (see Problem 4.5) is given by

$$\text{BER} = Q\left(\frac{I_1 - I_0}{\sigma_0 + \sigma_1}\right). \tag{4.13}$$

The Q function can be numerically evaluated. Let $\gamma = Q^{-1}(\text{BER})$. For a BER rate of 10^{-12}, we need $\gamma \approx 7$. For a BER rate of 10^{-9}, $\gamma \approx 6$.

Note that it is particularly important to have a variable threshold setting in receivers if they must operate in systems with signal-dependent noise, such as optical amplifier noise. Many high-speed receivers do incorporate such a feature. However, many of the simpler receivers do not have a variable threshold adjustment and set their threshold corresponding to the average received current level, namely, $(I_1 + I_0)/2$. This threshold setting yields a higher bit error rate given by

$$\text{BER} = \frac{1}{2}\left[Q\left(\frac{(I_1 - I_0)}{2\sigma_1}\right) + Q\left(\frac{(I_1 - I_0)}{2\sigma_0}\right)\right].$$

We can use (4.13) to evaluate the BER when the received signal powers for a 0 and a 1 bit and the noise statistics are known. Often, we are interested in the inverse problem, namely, determining what it takes to achieve a specified BER. This leads us to the notion of *receiver sensitivity*. The receiver sensitivity $\bar{P}_{rec}$ is defined as the minimum average optical power necessary to achieve a specified BER, usually 10^{-12} or better. Sometimes the receiver sensitivity is also expressed as the number of photons required per 1 bit M, which is given by

$$M = \frac{2\bar{P}_{rec}}{h f_c B},$$

where B is the bit rate.

In the notation introduced earlier, the receiver sensitivity is obtained by solving (4.13) for the average power per bit $(P_0 + P_1)/2$ for the specified BER, say, 10^{-12}. Assuming $P_0 = 0$, this can be obtained as

$$\bar{P}_{rec} = \frac{(\sigma_0 + \sigma_1)\gamma}{2 G_m \mathcal{R}}. \tag{4.14}$$

Here, G_m is the multiplicative gain for APD receivers and is unity for *pin* photo-diodes.

First consider an APD or a *pin* receiver, with no optical amplifier in the system. The thermal noise current is independent of the received optical power. However, the shot noise variance is a function of $\bar{P}_{rec}$. Assume that no power is transmitted for a 0 bit. Then $\sigma_0^2 = \sigma_{thermal}^2$ and $\sigma_1^2 = \sigma_{thermal}^2 + \sigma_{shot}^2$, where the shot noise variance σ_{shot}^2 must be evaluated for the received optical power $P_1 = 2\bar{P}_{rec}$ that corresponds to a 1 bit. From (4.3),

$$\sigma_{shot}^2 = 4eG_m^2 F_A(G_m)\mathcal{R}\bar{P}_{rec}B_e.$$

Using this and solving (4.14) for the receiver sensitivity $\bar{P}_{rec}$, we get

$$P_{rec} = \frac{\gamma}{\mathcal{R}}\left(eB_e F_A(G_m)\gamma + \frac{\sigma_{thermal}}{G_m}\right). \tag{4.15}$$

Assume that for a bit rate of B b/s, a receiver bandwidth $B_e = B/2$ Hz is required. Let the front-end amplifier noise figure $F_n = 3$ dB and the load resistor $R_L = 100\ \Omega$. Then, assuming the temperature $T = 300°$K, the thermal noise current variance, from (4.2) is

$$\sigma_{thermal}^2 = \frac{4k_B T}{R_L}F_n B_e = 1.656 \times 10^{-22}B\ \text{A}^2. \tag{4.16}$$

Assuming the receiver operates in the 1.55 μm band, the quantum efficiency $\eta = 1$, $\mathcal{R} = 1.55/1.24 = 1.25$ A/W. Using these values, we can compute the sensitivity of a *pin* receiver from (4.15), by setting $G_m = 1$. For BER $= 10^{-12}$ and thus $\gamma \approx 7$, the receiver sensitivity of a *pin* diode is plotted as a function of the bit rate in Figure 4.4. In the same figure, the sensitivity of an APD receiver with $k_A = 0.7$ and an avalanche multiplicative gain $G_m = 10$ is also plotted. It can be seen that the APD receiver has a sensitivity advantage of about 8–10 dB over a *pin* receiver.

We now derive the sensitivity of the optically preamplified receiver shown in Figure 4.2. In amplified systems, the signal-spontaneous beat noise component usually dominates over all the other noise components, unless the optical bandwidth B_o is large, in which case the spontaneous-spontaneous beat noise can also be significant. Making this assumption, the bit error rate can be calculated using (4.13), (4.5), and (4.8), as

$$\text{BER} = Q\left(\frac{\sqrt{GP}}{2\sqrt{(G-1)P_n B_e}}\right). \tag{4.17}$$

Let us see what receiver sensitivity can be obtained for an ideal preamplified receiver. The receiver sensitivity is measured either in terms of the required power at a particular bit rate or in terms of the number of photons per bit required. As before, we

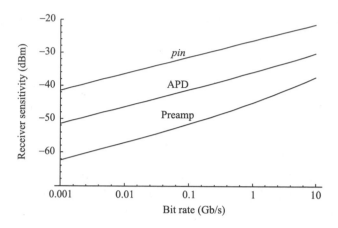

Figure 4.4   Sensitivity plotted as a function of bit rate for typical *pin*, APD, and optically preamplified receivers. The parameters used for the receivers are described in the text.

can assume that $B_e = B/2$. Assuming that the amplifier gain G is large and that the spontaneous emission factor $n_{sp} = 1$, we get

$$\text{BER} = Q\left(\sqrt{\frac{M}{2}}\right).$$

To obtain a BER of 10^{-12}, the argument to the $Q(.)$ function γ must be 7. This yields a receiver sensitivity of $M = 98$ photons per 1 bit. In practice, an optical filter is used between the amplifier and the receiver to limit the optical bandwidth B_o and thus reduce the spontaneous-spontaneous and shot noise components in the receiver. For practical preamplified receivers, receiver sensitivities of a few hundred photons per 1 bit are achievable. In contrast, a direct detection pinFET receiver without a preamplifier has a sensitivity of the order of a few thousand photons per 1 bit.

Figure 4.4 also plots the receiver sensitivity for an optically preamplified receiver, assuming a noise figure of 6 dB for the amplifier and an optical bandwidth $B_o = 50$ GHz that is limited by a filter in front of the amplifier. From Figure 4.4, we see that the sensitivity of a *pin* receiver at a bit rate of 1 Gb/s is -26 dBm and that of an APD receiver is -36 dBm.

In systems with cascades of optical amplifiers, the notion of sensitivity is not very useful because the signal reaching the receiver already has a lot of added amplifier noise. In this case, the two parameters that are measured are the average received signal power, $\bar{P}_{rec}$, and the received optical noise power, P_{ASE}. The *optical signal-to-noise ratio* (OSNR) is defined as $\bar{P}_{rec}/P_{ASE}$. In the case of an optically preamplified receiver, $P_{\text{ASE}} = 2P_n(G - 1)B_o$. A system designer needs to relate the measured OSNR with the bit error rate. Neglecting the receiver thermal noise and shot noise, it can be shown using (4.13), (4.5), (4.8), and (4.9) that the argument to the $Q(.)$ function, γ, is related to the OSNR as follows:

$$\gamma = \frac{2\sqrt{\frac{B_o}{B_e}}\text{OSNR}}{1 + \sqrt{1 + 4\text{OSNR}}}. \tag{4.18}$$

Consider a typical 2.5 Gb/s system with $B_e = 2$ GHz, with an optical filter with bandwidth $B_o = 36$ GHz placed between the amplifier cascade and the receiver. For $\gamma = 7$, this system requires an OSNR = 4.37, or 6.4 dB. However, this is usually not sufficient because the system must deal with a variety of impairments, such as dispersion and nonlinearities. We will study these in Chapter 5. A rough rule of thumb used by system designers is to design the amplifier cascade to obtain an OSNR of at least 20 dB at the receiver, so as to allow sufficient margin to deal with the other impairments.

4.2.7 Subcarrier Modulation and Multiplexing

The optical signal emitted by a laser operating in the 1310 or 1550 nm wavelength band has a center frequency around 10^{14} Hz. This frequency is the *optical carrier* frequency. In what we have studied so far, the data modulates this optical carrier. In other words, with an OOK signal, the optical carrier is simply turned on or off, depending on the bit to be transmitted.

Instead of modulating the optical carrier directly, we can have the data first modulate an electrical carrier in the microwave frequency range, typically ranging from 10 MHz to 10 GHz, as shown in Figure 4.5. The upper limit on the carrier frequency is determined by the modulation bandwidth available from the transmitter. The modulated microwave carrier then modulates the optical transmitter. If the transmitter is directly modulated, then changes in the microwave carrier amplitude get reflected as changes in the transmitted optical power envelope, as shown in Figure 4.5. The microwave carrier can itself be modulated in many different ways, including amplitude, phase, and frequency modulation, and both digital and analog modulation techniques can be employed. The figure shows an example where the microwave carrier is amplitude modulated by a binary digital data signal. The microwave carrier is called the *subcarrier*, with the optical carrier being considered the main carrier. This form of modulation is called *subcarrier modulation*.

The main motivation for using subcarrier modulation is to multiplex multiple data streams onto a single optical signal. This can be done by combining multiple microwave carriers at different frequencies and modulating the optical transmitter

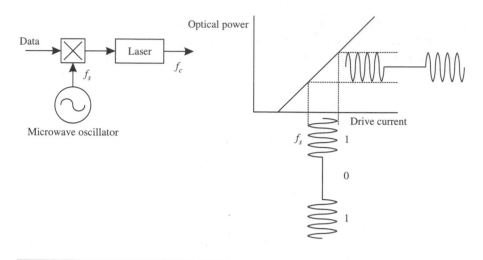

Figure 4.5   Subcarrier modulation. The data stream first modulates a microwave carrier, which, in turn, modulates the optical carrier.

with the combined signal. At the receiver, the signal is detected like any other signal, and the rest of the processing, to separate the subcarriers and extract the data from each subcarrier, is done electronically. This form of multiplexing is called *subcarrier multiplexing* (SCM).

SCM is widely used by cable operators today for transmitting multiple analog video signals using a single optical transmitter. We will study this application further in Chapter 12. SCM is also used sometimes to combine a control data stream along with the actual data stream. This is done in some of the TDM networks that we will explore in Chapter 14.

4.2.8   Coherent Detection

We saw earlier that simple direct detection receivers are limited by thermal noise and do not achieve the shot-noise limited sensitivities of ideal receivers. We saw that the sensitivity could be improved significantly by using an optical preamplifier. Another way to improve the receiver sensitivity is to use a technique called *coherent detection*.

The key idea behind coherent detection is to provide gain to the signal by mixing it with another local light signal from a so-called *local-oscillator* laser. At the same time, the dominant noise in the receiver becomes the shot noise due to the local oscillator, allowing the receiver to achieve the shot-noise limited sensitivity.

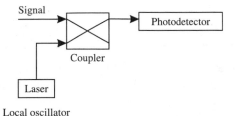

Signal

Photodetector

Coupler

Laser

Local oscillator

Figure 4.6   A simple coherent receiver.

A simple coherent receiver is shown in Figure 4.6. The incoming light signal is mixed with a local-oscillator signal via a 3-dB coupler and sent to the photodetector. (We will ignore the 3-dB splitting loss induced by the coupler since it can be eliminated by a slightly different receiver design—see Problem 4.14.) Assume that the phase and polarization of the two waves are perfectly matched. The power seen by the photodetector is then

$$
\begin{aligned}
P_r(t) &= \left[\sqrt{2aP}\cos(2\pi f_c t) + \sqrt{2P_{\text{LO}}}\cos(2\pi f_{\text{LO}}t)\right]^2 \\
&= aP + P_{\text{LO}} + 2\sqrt{aPP_{\text{LO}}}\cos[2\pi(f_c - f_{\text{LO}})t].
\end{aligned}
\tag{4.19}
$$

Here, P denotes the input signal power, P_{LO} the local-oscillator power, $a = 1$ or 0 depending on whether a 1 or 0 bit is transmitted (for an OOK signal), and f_c and f_{LO} represent the carrier frequencies of the signal and local-oscillator waves. We have neglected the $2f_c$, $2f_{\text{LO}}$, and $f_c + f_{\text{LO}}$ components since they will be filtered out by the receiver. In a *homodyne* receiver, $f_c = f_{\text{LO}}$, and in a *heterodyne* receiver, $f_c - f_{\text{LO}} = f_{\text{IF}} \neq 0$. Here, f_{IF} is called the intermediate frequency (IF), typically a few gigahertz.

To illustrate why coherent detection yields improved receiver sensitivities, consider the case of a homodyne receiver. For a 1 bit, we have

$$
I_1 = \mathcal{R}(P + P_{\text{LO}} + 2\sqrt{PP_{\text{LO}}}),
$$

and for a 0 bit,

$$
I_0 = \mathcal{R}P_{\text{LO}}.
$$

The key thing to note here is that by making the local-oscillator power P_{LO} sufficiently large, we can make the shot noise dominate over all the other noise components in the receiver. Thus the noise variances are

$$
\sigma_1^2 = 2eI_1 B_e
$$

and

$$\sigma_0^2 = 2e I_0 B_e.$$

Usually, P_{LO} is around 0 dBm and P is less than -20 dBm. So we can also neglect P compared to P_{LO} when computing the signal power, and both P and $\sqrt{P P_{LO}}$ compared to P_{LO} when computing the noise variance σ_1^2. With this assumption, using (4.13), the bit error rate is given by

$$\text{BER} = Q\left(\sqrt{\frac{\mathcal{R}P}{2e B_e}}\right).$$

As before, assuming $B_e = B/2$, this expression can be rewritten as

$$\text{BER} = Q(\sqrt{M}),$$

where M is the number of photons per 1 bit as before. For a BER of 10^{-12}, we need the argument of the $Q(.)$ function γ to be 7. This yields a receiver sensitivity of 49 photons per 1 bit, which is significantly better than the sensitivity of a simple direct detection receiver.

However, coherent receivers are generally quite complex to implement and must deal with a variety of impairments. Note that in our derivation we assumed that the phase and polarization of the two waves match perfectly. In practice, this is not the case. If the polarizations are orthogonal, the mixing produces no output. Thus coherent receivers are highly sensitive to variations in the polarizations of the signal and local-oscillator waves as well as any phase noise present in the two signals. There are ways to get around these obstacles by designing more complicated receiver structures [KBW96, Gre93]. However, direct detection receivers with optical preamplifiers, which yield comparable receiver sensitivities, provide a simpler alternative and are widely used today.

There is another advantage to be gained by using coherent receivers in a multi-channel WDM system. Instead of using a demultiplexer or filter to select the desired signal optically, with coherent receivers, this selection can be done in the IF domain using electronic filters, which can be designed to have very sharp skirts. This allows very tight channel spacings to be achieved. In addition, in a WDM system, the receiver can be tuned between channels in the IF domain, allowing for rapid tunability between channels, a desirable feature to support fast packet switching. However, we will require highly wavelength stable and controllable lasers and components to make use of this benefit. These factors may result in the resurrection of coherent receivers when WDM systems with large numbers of channels are designed in the future.

Summary

Modulation is the process of converting data in electronic form to optical form for transmission on the fiber. The simplest form of digital modulation is on–off keying, and most systems use on–off keying today. Direct modulation of the laser or LED source can be used for transmission at low bit rates over short distances, whereas external modulation is needed for transmission at high bit rates over long distances. Some form of line coding or scrambling is needed to prevent long runs of 1s or 0s in the transmitted data stream to allow the clock to be recovered easily at the receiver and to maintain DC balance.

A simple direct detection receiver looks at the energy received during a bit interval to decide whether it is a 1 or 0 bit. The receiver sensitivity is the average power required at the receiver to achieve a certain bit error rate. The sensitivity of a simple direct detection receiver is determined primarily by the thermal noise in the receiver. The sensitivity can be improved by using APDs instead of *pin* photodetectors or by using an optical preamplifier. Another technique to improve the sensitivity as well as the channel selectivity of the receiver is coherent detection. However, coherent detection is susceptible to a large number of impairments, and it requires a significantly more complicated receiver structure to overcome these impairments. For this reason, it is not practically implemented today.

Further Reading

Many books on optical communication cover modulation and detection in greater depth than we have. See, for example, [Gre93, MK88, Agr92]. See also [BL90] for a nice tutorial article on the subject. Subcarrier multiplexing and modulation is treated in depth in [WOe90, OLH89, Dar87, Gre93]. Line coding, scrambling, and bit clock recovery are covered extensively in [LM88]. The principles of signal detection are covered in the classic book by van Trees [vT68]. For a derivation of shot noise statistics, see [Pap84].

The noise introduced by optical amplifiers has been studied extensively in the literature. Amplifier noise statistics have been derived using quantum mechanical approaches [Per73, Yam80, MYK82, Dan95] as well as semiclassical approaches [Ols89, RH90]. There was a great deal of effort devoted to realizing coherent receivers in the 1980s, but the advent of optical amplifiers in the late 1980s and early 1990s provided a simpler alternative. See [BL90, KBW96] for a detailed treatment of coherent receivers.

Problems

4.1 A very simple line code used in early data networks is called *bit stuffing*. The objective of this code is to prevent long runs of 1s or 0s but not necessarily achieve DC balance. The encoding works as follows. Suppose the maximum number of consecutive 1s that we are allowed in the bit stream is k. Then the encoder inserts a 0 bit whenever it sees k consecutive 1 bits in the input sequence.

  (a) Suppose the incoming data to be transmitted is 11111111111001000000. What is the encoded bit stream, assuming $k = 5$?

  (b) What is the algorithm used by the decoder to recover the data? Suppose the received bit stream is 0111110101111100011. What is the decoded bit stream?

4.2 The SONET standard uses scrambling to prevent long runs of 1s and 0s from occurring in the transmitted bit stream. The scrambling is accomplished by a carefully designed feedback shift register shown in Figure 4.7. The shift register consists of flip flops whose operation is controlled by a clock running at the bit rate, and is reset at the beginning of each frame.

  (a) Suppose the incoming data to be transmitted is 11111111111001000000. Assume that the shift register contents are 1111111 at the beginning. What is the scrambled output?

  (b) Write a simulation program to compute the scrambled output as a function of the input. The input is a sequence of bits generated by a pseudo-random sequence with equal probabilities for a 1 and a 0. Plot the longest run length of 1s and the longest run length of 0s observed as a function of the sequence length for sequences up to 10 million bits long. Again assume that the shift register contents are 1111111 at the beginning of the sequence. What do you observe?

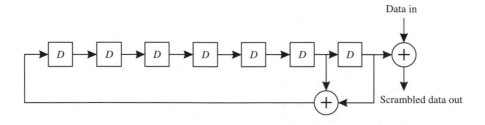

Figure 4.7   The feedback shift register used for scrambling in SONET.

4.3 Consider the SNR of an APD receiver when both shot noise and thermal noise are present. Assuming that the *excess noise factor* of the APD is given by $F_A(G_m) = G_m^x$ for some $x \in (0, 1)$, derive an expression for the optimum value G_m^{opt} of the APD gain G_m that maximizes the SNR.

4.4 This problem deals with the noise figure of a chain of optical amplifiers and placement of loss elements in the amplifier. The loss element may be an optical add/drop multiplexer, or a gain flattening filter, or a dispersion compensation module used to compensate for accumulated dispersion along the link. The question is where should this loss element be placed—in front of the amplifier, after the amplifier, or inside the amplifier.

(a) Consider an optical amplifier with noise figure F. Suppose we introduce a loss element in front of it, with loss $0 < \epsilon \leq 1$ ($\epsilon = 0$ implies no loss, and $\epsilon = 1$ implies 100% loss). Show that the noise figure of the combination is $F/(1 - \epsilon)$. Note that this loss element may also simply reflect the coupling loss into the amplifier. Observe that this combination has a poor noise figure.

(b) Suppose the loss element is placed just after the amplifier. Show that the noise figure of the combination is still F, that is, placing a loss element after the amplifier doesn't affect the noise figure. However, the price we pay in this case is a reduction in optical output power, since the amplifier output is attenuated by the loss element placed after it.

(c) Consider an optical amplifier chain with two amplifiers, with gains G_1 and G_2, respectively, and noise figures F_1 and F_2, respectively, with no loss between the two amplifiers. Assuming $G_1 \gg 1$, show that the noise figure of the combined amplifier chain is

$$F = F_1 + \frac{F_2}{G_1}.$$

In other words, the noise figure of the chain is dominated by the noise figure of the first amplifier, provided its gain is reasonably large, which is usually the case.

(d) Now consider the case where a loss element with loss ϵ is introduced between the first and second amplifier. Assuming $G_1, G_2 \gg 1$, and $(1 - \epsilon)G_1 G_2 \gg 1$, show that the resulting noise figure of the chain is given by

$$F = F_1 + \frac{F_2}{(1 - \epsilon)G_1}.$$

Observe that the loss element doesn't affect the noise figure of the cascade significantly as long as $(1 - \epsilon)G_1 \gg 1$, which is usually the case. This is an important fact that is made use of in designing systems. The amplifier is broken down into two stages, the first stage having high gain and low noise figure, and the loss element is inserted between the two stages. This setup has the advantage that there is no reduction in the noise figure as well as the output power.

4.5 Show that the BER for an OOK direct detection receiver is given by

$$\text{BER} = Q\left(\frac{I_1 - I_0}{\sigma_0 + \sigma_1}\right).$$

4.6 Consider a binary digital communication system with received signal levels m_1 and m_0 for a 1 bit and 0 bit, respectively. Let σ^2 and σ_0^2 denote the noise variances for a 1 and 0 bit, respectively. Assume that the noise is Gaussian and that a 1 and 0 bit are equally likely. In this case, the bit error rate BER is given by

$$\text{BER} = \frac{1}{2}Q\left(\frac{m_1 - T_d}{\sigma_1}\right) + \frac{1}{2}Q\left(\frac{T_d - m_0}{\sigma_0}\right),$$

where T_d is the receiver's decision threshold. Show that the value of T_d that minimizes the bit error rate is given by

$$T_d = \frac{-m_1\sigma_0^2 + m_0\sigma_1^2 + \sqrt{\sigma_0^2\sigma_1^2(m_1 - m_0)^2 + 2(\sigma_1^2 - \sigma_0^2)\ln(\sigma_1/\sigma_0)}}{\sigma_1^2 - \sigma_0^2}. \tag{4.20}$$

For the case of high signal-to-noise ratios, it is reasonable to assume that

$$(m_1 - mo)^2 \gg \frac{2(\sigma_1^2 - \sigma_0^2)\ln(\sigma_1/\sigma_0)}{\sigma_0^2\sigma_1^2}.$$

In this case, (4.20) can be simplified to

$$T = \frac{m_0\sigma_1 + m_1\sigma_0}{\sigma_1 + \sigma_0}.$$

With $m_1 = RP_1$ and $m_0 = RP_0$, this is the same as (4.11).

4.7 Consider a *pin* direct detection receiver where the thermal noise is the main noise component, and its variance has the value given by (4.16). What is the receiver sensitivity expressed in photons per 1 bit at a bit rate of 100 Mb/s and 1 Gb/s for a bit error rate of 10^{-12}? Assume that the operating wavelength is 1.55 μm and the responsivity is 1.25 A/W.

4.8 Consider the receiver sensitivity, P_r (for an arbitrary BER, not necessarily 10^{-9}), of an APD receiver when both shot noise and thermal noise are present but neglecting the dark current, for direct detection of on–off keyed signals. Assume no power is transmitted for a zero bit.

(a) Derive an expression for P_r.

(b) Find the optimum value G_m^{opt} of the APD gain G_m that minimizes P_r.

(c) For $G_m = G_m^{\text{opt}}$, what is the (minimum) value of P_r?

4.9 Derive (4.17).

4.10 Plot the receiver sensitivity as a function of bit rate for an optically preamplified receiver for three different optical bandwidths: (a) the ideal case, $B_o = 2B_e$, (b) $B_o = 100$ GHz, and (c) $B_o = 30$ THz, that is, an unfiltered receiver. Assume an amplifier noise figure of 6 dB, and the electrical bandwidth B_e is half the bit rate, and use the thermal noise variance given by (4.16). What do you observe as the optical bandwidth is increased?

4.11 You are doing an experiment to measure the BER of an optically preamplified receiver. The setup consists of an optical amplifier followed by a variable attenuator to adjust the power going into the receiver, followed by a *pin* receiver. You plot the BER versus the power going into the receiver over a wide range of received powers. Calculate and plot this function. What do you observe regarding the slope of this curve? Assume that $B_o = 100$ GHz, $B_e = 2$ GHz, $B = 2.5$ Gb/s, a noise figure of 6 dB for the optical amplifier, and a noise figure of 3 dB for the front-end amplifier.

4.12 Derive (4.18).

4.13 Another form of digital modulation that can be used in conjunction with coherent reception is *phase-shift keying* (PSK). Here $\sqrt{2P}\cos(2\pi f_c t)$ is received for a 1 bit and $-\sqrt{2P}\cos(2\pi f_c t)$ is received for a 0 bit. Derive an expression for the bit error rate of a PSK homodyne coherent receiver. How many photons per bit are required to obtain a bit error rate of 10^{-9}?

4.14 A balanced coherent receiver is shown in Figure 4.8. The input signal and local oscillator are sent through a 3-dB coupler, and each output of the coupler is connected to a photodetector. This 3-dB coupler is different in that it introduces an additional

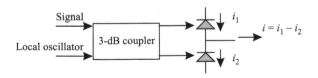

Figure 4.8   A balanced coherent receiver.

phase shift of $\pi/2$ at its second input and second output. The detected current is the difference between the currents generated by the two photodetectors. Show that this receiver structure avoids the 3-dB penalty associated with the receiver we discussed in Section 4.2.8. Use the transfer function for a 3-dB coupler described in Chapter 3 (3.1).

References

[Agr92] G. P. Agrawal. *Fiber-Optic Communication Systems*. John Wiley, New York, 1992.

[BL90] J. R. Barry and E. A. Lee. Performance of coherent optical receivers. *Proceedings of IEEE*, 78(8):1369–1394, Aug. 1990.

[Bur86] W. E. Burr. The FDDI optical data link. *IEEE Communications Magazine*, 24(5):18–23, May 1986.

[Dan95] S. L. Danielsen et al. Detailed noise statistics for an optically preamplified direct detection receiver. *IEEE/OSA Journal on Lightwave Technology*, 13(5):977–981, 1995.

[Dar87] T. E. Darcie. Subcarrier multiplexing for multiple-access lightwave networks. *IEEE/OSA Journal on Lightwave Technology*, LT-5:1103–1110, 1987.

[Gre93] P. E. Green. *Fiber-Optic Networks*. Prentice Hall, Englewood Cliffs, NJ, 1993.

[KBW96] L. G. Kazovsky, S. Benedetto, and A. E. Willner. *Optical Fiber Communication Systems*. Artech House, Boston, 1996.

[LM88] E. A. Lee and D. G. Messerschmitt. *Digital Communication*. Kluwer Academic Publishers, Boston, 1988.

[MK88] S. D. Miller and I. P. Kaminow, editors. *Optical Fiber Telecommunications II*. Academic Press, San Diego, CA, 1988.

[MYK82] T. Mukai, Y. Yamamoto, and T. Kimura. S/N and error-rate performance of AlGaAs semiconductor laser preamplifier and linear repeater systems. *IEEE Transactions on Microwave Theory and Techniques*, 30(10):1548–1554, 1982.

[OLH89] R. Olshanksy, V. A. Lanzisera, and P. M. Hill. Subcarrier multiplexed lightwave systems for broadband distribution. *IEEE/OSA Journal on Lightwave Technology*, 7(9):1329–1342, Sept. 1989.

[Ols89] N. A. Olsson. Lightwave systems with optical amplifiers. *IEEE/OSA Journal on Lightwave Technology*, 7(7):1071–1082, July 1989.

[Pap84] A. Papoulis. *Probability, Random Variables, and Stochastic Processes*. McGraw-Hill, New York, 1984.

[Per73] S. D. Personick. Applications for quantum amplifiers in simple digital optical communication systems. *Bell System Technical Journal*, 52(1):117–133, Jan. 1973.

[RH90] R. Ramaswami and P. A. Humblet. Amplifier induced crosstalk in multi-channel optical networks. *IEEE/OSA Journal on Lightwave Technology*, 8(12):1882–1896, Dec. 1990.

[Ros86] F. E. Ross. FDDI—a tutorial. *IEEE Communications Magazine*, 24(5):10–17, May 1986.

[SV96] M. W. Sachs and A. Varma. Fibre channel and related standards. *IEEE Communications Magazine*, 34(8):40–49, Aug. 1996.

[vT68] H. L. van Trees. *Detection, Estimation, and Modulation Theory. Part I*. John Wiley, New York, 1968.

[WF83] A. X. Widmer and P. A. Franaszek. A DC-balanced, partitioned-block, 8B-10B transmission code. *IBM Journal of Research and Development*, 27(5):440–451, Sept. 1983.

[WOe90] W. I. Way, R. Olshansky, and K. Sato (editors). Special issue on applications of RF and microwave subcarriers to optical fiber transmission in present and future broadband networks. *IEEE Journal of Selected Areas in Communications*, 8(7), Sept. 1990.

[Yam80] Y. Yamamoto. Noise and error-rate performance of semiconductor laser amplifiers in PCM-IM transmission systems. *IEEE Journal of Quantum Electronics*, 16:1073–1081, 1980.

chapter 5

Transmission System Engineering

OUR GOAL IN THIS CHAPTER is to understand how to design the physical layer of an optical network. To this end, we will understand the various impairments that we must deal with, how to allocate margins for each of these impairments, how to reduce the effect of these impairments, and finally all the tradeoffs that are involved between the different design parameters.

5.1 System Model

Figure 5.1 shows a block diagram of the various components of a unidirectional WDM link. The transmitter consists of a set of DFB lasers, one for each wavelength. The signals at the different wavelengths are combined into a single fiber by means of an optical multiplexer. An optical power amplifier may be used to increase the transmission power. After some distance along the fiber, the signal is amplified by an optical in-line amplifier. Depending on the distance, bit rate, and type of fiber used, the signal may also be passed through a dispersion-compensating module, usually at each amplifier stage. At the receiving end, the signal may be amplified by an optical preamplifier before it is passed through a demultiplexer. Each wavelength is then received by a separate photodetector.

Throughout this chapter, we will be focusing on digital systems, although it is possible to transmit analog signals over fiber as well. The physical layer of the system must ensure that bits are transmitted from the source to their destination reliably. The measures of quality are the bit error rate (BER) and the additional margin

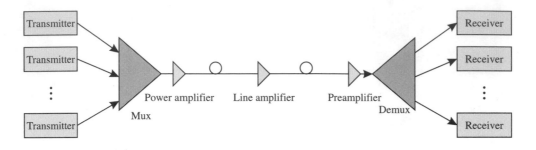

Figure 5.1   Components of a WDM link.

provided in the system. Usually the required bit error rates are of the order of 10^{-9} to 10^{-15}, typically 10^{-12}. The BER depends on the amount of noise as well as other impairments that are present in the system.

The physical layer is also responsible for the link initialization and link take-down procedures, which are necessary to prevent exposure to potentially harmful laser radiation. This aspect is dealt with in Chapter 10.

We will look at the different components that are part of a system, including the transmitters, receivers, optical amplifiers, wavelength multiplexers, demultiplexers and switches, and the fiber itself, and discuss various forms of system impairments that arise from each of these components. Table A.1 in Appendix A summarizes the large number of parameters that are used in this chapter.

5.2   Power Penalty

The physical layer design must take into account the effect of a number of system impairments as previously discussed. Usually each impairment results in a *power penalty* to the system. In the presence of an impairment, a higher signal power will be required at the receiver in order to maintain a desired bit error rate. One way to define the power penalty is as the increase in signal power required (in dB) to maintain the same bit error rate in the presence of impairments. Another way to define the power penalty is as the reduction in signal-to-noise ratio as quantified by the value of γ (the argument to the $Q(.)$ function as defined in Section 4.2.6) due to a specific impairment. We will be using the latter definition since it is easier to calculate and consistent with the way we do system design.

Let P_1 denote the optical power received during a 1 bit, and P_0 the power received during a 0 bit without any system impairments. The corresponding electrical currents are given by $\mathcal{R}P_1$ and $\mathcal{R}P_0$, respectively, where $\mathcal{R}$ is the *responsivity* of the photodetector.

Let σ_1 and σ_0 denote the noise standard deviations during a 1 bit and a 0 bit, respectively. Assume that the noise is Gaussian. The bit error rate, assuming equally likely 1s and 0s, is obtained from (4.13) as

$$\text{BER} = Q\left(\frac{\mathcal{R}(P_1 - P_0)}{\sigma_1 + \sigma_0}\right). \tag{5.1}$$

This expression assumes that the receiver's decision threshold is set to the optimal value indicated by (4.11).

In the presence of impairments, let P_1', P_0', σ_1', σ_0' denote the received powers and noise standard deviations, respectively. Assuming an optimized threshold setting, the power penalty is given by

$$\text{PP} = -10\log\left(\frac{\frac{\mathcal{R}(P_1' - P_0')}{\sigma_1' + \sigma_0'}}{\frac{\mathcal{R}(P_1 - P_0)}{\sigma_1 + \sigma_0}}\right). \tag{5.2}$$

Calculating the power penalty in general for the simple AC-coupled receiver discussed in Section 4.2.6 is somewhat more complicated, but we will see that it is the same as the penalty for the optimized receiver for two important cases of interest.

The first case of interest is when the dominant noise component is receiver thermal noise, for which $\sigma_0 = \sigma_1 = \sigma_{\text{th}}$. This is usually the case in unamplified direct detection *pin* receivers. In this case, or in any situation where the noise is independent of the signal power, the power penalty is given by

$$\text{PP}_{\text{sig indep}} = -10\log\left(\frac{P_1' - P_0'}{P_1 - P_0}\right). \tag{5.3}$$

and the best threshold setting corresponds to the setting of a simple AC-coupled receiver.

The other case of interest is amplified systems, or systems with APD receivers. In amplified systems, the dominant noise component is usually the amplifier signal-spontaneous beat noise (see Section 4.2.5). In APD receivers, the dominant noise component is the shot noise, which is enhanced because of the APD gain (see Section 3.6.1). In both cases, we can assume that $\sigma_1 \propto \sqrt{P_1}$; that is, the noise variance depends on the signal power. Assume also that $P_0 \ll P_1$. In this case, we can assume that $\sigma_1 \gg \sigma_0$. Here an optimized receiver would set its threshold close to the 0 level, whereas the simple receiver would still set its threshold at the average received power

Table 5.1 A typical system design that allocates power penalties for various transmission impairments.

Impairment	Allocation (dB)
Ideal γ	17
Transmitter	1
Crosstalk	1
Dispersion	2
Nonlinearities	1
Polarization-dependent loss	3
Component aging	3
Margin	3
Required γ	31

and would have a somewhat higher bit error rate. However, the power penalties turn out to be the same in both cases. This penalty is given by

$$\text{PP}_{\text{sig-dep}} = -5 \log \left(\frac{P_1'}{P_1} \right). \tag{5.4}$$

Finally, it must be kept in mind that polarization plays an important role in many system impairments where signals interfere with each other. The worst case usually is when the interfering signals have the same state of polarization. However, the state of polarization of each signal varies slowly with time in a random manner, and thus we can expect the power penalties to vary with time as well. The system must be designed, however, to accommodate the worst case, usually identical polarizations.

System design requires careful budgeting of the power penalties for the different impairments. Here we sketch out one way of doing such a design for a transmission system with optical amplifiers. First we determine the ideal value of the parameter γ (see Section 4.2.6) that is needed. For a bit error rate of 10^{-12} typically assumed in high-speed transmission systems, we need $\gamma = 7$, or $20 \log \gamma = 17$ dB. This would be the case if there were no transmission impairments leading to power penalties. In practice, the various impairments result in power penalties that must be added on to this ideal value of γ, as shown in Table 5.1, to obtain the required value of γ that the system must be designed to yield. For instance, in the table, we allocate a 1-dB power penalty for an imperfect transmitter and 2-dB power penalty for dispersion. (We will study these and several other impairments in the rest of this chapter.) The required value of γ after adding all these allocations is 31 dB. This is the value that we must obtain if we assume an ideal system to start with and compute γ based on only optical amplifier noise accumulation. The power penalty due to each impairment is then calculated one at a time assuming that the rest of the system is ideal. In practice, this is an approximate method because the different impairments may be related to each other, and we may not be able to isolate each one by itself. For example, the power penalties due to a nonideal transmitter and crosstalk may be related to each other, whereas dispersion may be treated as an independent penalty.

5.3 Transmitter

The key system design parameters related to the transmitter are its output power, rise/fall time, extinction ratio, modulation type, side-mode suppression ratio, and wavelength stability and accuracy.

The output power depends on the type of transmitter. DFB lasers put out about 1 mW (0 dBm) to 10 mW (10 dBm) of power. An optical power amplifier can be used to boost the power, typically to as much as 50 mW (17 dBm). The upper limits on power are dictated by nonlinearities (Section 5.8) and safety considerations, which we will discuss in Section 10.5.

The extinction ratio is defined as the ratio of the power transmitted when sending a 1 bit, P_1, to the power transmitted when sending a 0 bit, P_0. Assuming that we are limited to an average transmitted power P, we would like to have $P_1 = 2P$ and $P_0 = 0$. This would correspond to an extinction ratio $r = \infty$. Practical transmitters, however, have extinction ratios between 10 and 20. With an extinction ratio r, we have

$$P_0 = \frac{2P}{r+1}$$

and

$$P_1 = \frac{2rP}{r+1}.$$

Reducing the extinction ratio reduces the difference between the 1 and 0 levels at the receiver and thus produces a penalty. The power penalty due to a nonideal extinction ratio in systems limited by signal-independent noise is obtained from (5.3) as

$$PP_{\text{sig-indep}} = -10\log\frac{r-1}{r+1}.$$

Note that this penalty represents the decrease in signal-to-noise ratio performance of a system with a nonideal extinction ratio relative to a system with infinite extinction ratio, assuming the same *average* transmitted power for both systems. On the other hand, if we assume that the two systems have the same peak transmit power, that is, the same power for a 1 bit, then the penalty can be calculated to be

$$PP_{\text{sig-indep}} = -10 \log \frac{r-1}{r}.$$

Lasers tend to be physically limited by peak transmit power; however, upper limits on output power are usually limited by eye safety regulations (see Section 10.5.1), which are stated in terms of limitations on average power. The formula to be used depends on which factor actually limits the power for a particular system.

The penalty is higher when the system is limited by signal-dependent noise, which is typically the case in amplified systems (Section 4.2.5)—see Problem 5.6. This is due to the increased amount of noise present at the 0 level. Other forms of signal-dependent noise may arise in the system, such as laser relative intensity noise (RIN).

The laser at the transmitter may be modulated directly, or a separate external modulator can be used. Direct modulation is cheaper but results in a broader spectral width due to chirp (Section 2.3). This will result in an added power penalty due to chromatic dispersion (see Section 2.3). Broader spectral width may also result in penalties when the signal is passed through optical filters, such as WDM muxes and demuxes. This penalty can be reduced by reducing the extinction ratio.

Wavelength stability of the transmitter is an important issue and is addressed in Sections 5.9 and 5.10.5.

$\underline{5.4}$ Receiver

The key system parameters associated with a receiver are its *sensitivity* and *overload parameter*. The sensitivity is the average optical power required to achieve a certain bit error rate at a particular bit rate. It is usually measured at a bit error rate of 10^{-12} using a pseudo-random $2^{23} - 1$ bit sequence. The overload parameter is the maximum input power that the receiver can accept. Typical sensitivities of different types of receivers for a set of bit rates are shown in Table 5.2 and a more detailed evaluation can be found in Section 4.2.6. APD receivers have higher sensitivities than pinFET receivers and are typically used in high bit rate systems operating at and above 2.5 Gb/s. However, a pinFET receiver with an optical preamplifier has a sensitivity that is comparable to an APD receiver. The overload parameter defines the dynamic range of the receiver and can be as high as 0 dBm for 2.5 Gb/s receivers, regardless of the specific receiver type.

Table 5.2 Typical sensitivities of different types of receivers in the 1.55 μm wavelength band. These receivers also operate in the 1.3 μm band, but the sensitivity is not as good at 1.3 μm.

Bit Rate	Type	Sensitivity	Overload Parameter
155 Mb/s	pinFET	-36 dBm	-7 dBm
622 Mb/s	pinFET	-32 dBm	-7 dBm
2.5 Gb/s	APD	-34 dBm	-8 dBm

5.5 Optical Amplifiers

Optical amplifiers have become an essential component in transmission systems and networks to compensate for system losses. The most commonly used device today is the Erbium-doped fiber amplifier (EDFA) described in Chapter 3, which has a gain bandwidth of about 35 nm in the 1.55 μm wavelength region. The great advantage of EDFAs is that they are capable of simultaneously amplifying many WDM channels. EDFAs have spawned a new generation of transmission systems. Most newly installed optical fiber transmission systems today use EDFAs instead of repeaters.

Amplifiers are used in three different configurations, as shown in Figure 5.2. An optical *preamplifier* is used just in front of a receiver to improve its sensitivity. A *power* amplifier is used in front of a transmitter to increase the output power. A *line* amplifier is used typically in the middle of the link to compensate for link losses. The design of the amplifier depends on the configuration. A power amplifier is designed to provide the maximum possible output power. A preamplifier is designed to provide high gain and the highest possible sensitivity, that is, the least amount of additional noise. A line amplifier is designed to provide a combination of all these.

Unfortunately, the amplifier is not a perfect device. There are several major imperfections that system designers need to worry about when using amplifiers in a system. First, an amplifier introduces noise, in addition to providing gain. Second, the gain of the amplifier depends on the total input power. For high input powers,

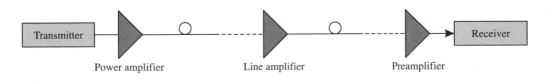

Figure 5.2 Power, line, and preamplifiers.

the amplifier tends to saturate and the gain drops. This can cause undesirable power transients in networks. Finally, although EDFAs are a particularly attractive choice for WDM systems, their gain is not flat over the entire passband. Thus some channels see more gain than the others. This problem gets worse when a number of amplifiers are cascaded. We have studied optically preamplified receivers in Section 4.2.5. In this section, we will study the effect of gain saturation, gain nonflatness, noise, and power transients in systems with cascades of optical amplifiers.

5.5.1   Gain Saturation

An important consideration in designing amplified systems is the saturation of the optical amplifier. Depending on the pump power and the amplifier design itself, the output power of the amplifier is limited. As a result, when the input signal power is increased, the amplifier gain drops. This behavior can be captured approximately by the following equation:

$$G = 1 + \frac{P^{\text{sat}}}{P_{\text{in}}} \ln \frac{G_{\text{max}}}{G}. \tag{5.5}$$

Here, G_{max} is the unsaturated gain, and G the saturated gain of the amplifier, P^{sat} is its internal saturation power, and P_{in} is the input signal power. Figure 5.3 plots the amplifier gain as a function of the input signal power for a typical EDFA. For low input powers, the amplifier gain is at its unsaturated value, and at very high input powers, $G \to 1$ and the output power $P_{\text{out}} = P_{\text{in}}$. The output saturation power $P_{\text{out}}^{\text{sat}}$ is defined to be the output power at which the amplifier gain has dropped by 3 dB. Using (5.5) and the fact that $P_{\text{out}} = G P_{\text{in}}$, and assuming that $G \gg 1$, the output saturation power is given by

$$P_{\text{out}}^{\text{sat}} \approx P^{\text{sat}} \ln 2.$$

The saturation power is a function of the pump power and other amplifier parameters. It is quite common to have output saturation powers of the order of 10 to 100 mW (10 to 20 dBm).

There is no fundamental problem in operating an EDFA in saturation, and power amplifiers usually do operate in saturation. The only thing to keep in mind is that the saturated gain will be less than the unsaturated gain.

5.5.2   Gain Equalization

The flatness of the EDFA passband becomes a critical issue in WDM systems with cascaded amplifiers. The amplifier gain is not exactly the same at each wavelength. Small

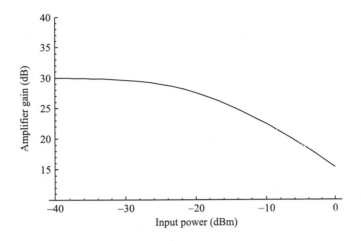

Figure 5.3 Gain saturation in an optical amplifier. Unsaturated gain $G_{max} = 30$ dB and saturation power $P^{sat} = 10$ dBm.

variations in gain between channels in a stage can cause large variations in the power difference between channels at the output of the chain. For example, if the gain variation between the worst channel and the best channel is 1 dB at each stage, after 10 stages it will be 10 dB, and the worst channel will have a much poorer signal-to-noise ratio than the best channel. This effect is shown in Figure 5.4(a). Building amplifiers with flat gain spectra is therefore very important—see Section 3.4.3—and is the best way to solve this problem. In practice, it is possible to design EDFAs to be inherently flat in the 1545–1560 nm wavelength region, and this is where many early WDM systems operate. However, systems with a larger number of channels will need to use the 1530–1545 nm wavelength range, where the gain of the EDFA is not flat.

At the system level, a few approaches have been proposed to overcome this lack of gain flatness. The first approach is to use preequalization, or preemphasis, as shown in Figure 5.4(b). Based on the overall gain shape of the cascade, the transmitted power per channel can be set such that the channels that see low gain are launched with higher powers. The goal of preequalization is to ensure that all channels are received with approximately the same signal-to-noise ratios at the receiver and fall within the receiver's dynamic range. However, the amount of equalization that can be done is limited, and other techniques may be needed to provide further equalization. Also this technique is difficult to implement in a network, as opposed to a point-to-point link.

The second approach is to introduce equalization at each amplifier stage, as shown in Figure 5.4(c). After each stage, the channel powers are equalized.

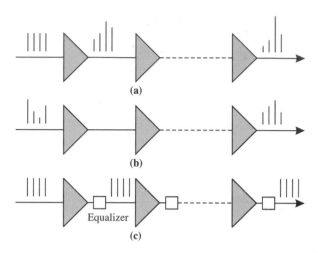

Figure 5.4   Effect of unequal amplifier gains at different wavelengths. (a) A set of channels with equal powers at the input to a cascaded system of amplifiers will have vastly different powers and signal-to-noise ratios at the output. (b) This effect can be reduced by preequalizing the channel powers. (c) Another way to reduce this effect is to introduce equalization at each amplifier stage. The equalization can be done using a filter inside the amplifier as well.

This equalization can be done in many ways. One way is to demultiplex the channels, attenuate each channel differently, and then multiplex them back together. This approach involves using a considerable amount of hardware. It adds wavelength-tolerance penalties due to the added muxes and demuxes (see Section 5.6.6). For these reasons, such an approach is impractical. Another approach is to use a multichannel filter, such as an acousto-optic tunable filter (AOTF). In an AOTF, each channel can be attenuated differently by applying a set of RF signals with different frequencies. Each RF signal controls the attenuation of a particular center wavelength, and by controlling the RF powers of each signal, it is possible to equalize the channel powers. However, an AOTF requires a large amount of RF drive power (of the order of 1 W) to equalize more than a few (2–4) channels. Both approaches introduce several dBs of additional loss and some power penalties due to crosstalk. The preferred solution is to add an optical filter within the amplifier with a carefully designed passband to compensate for the gain spectrum of the amplifier so as to obtain a flat spectrum at its output. Both dielectric thin-film filters (Section 3.3.5) and long-period fiber gratings (Section 3.3.3) appear to be good candidates for this purpose.

5.5.3 Amplifier Cascades

Consider a system of total length L with amplifiers spaced l km apart—see Figure 5.5. The loss between two stages is $e^{-\alpha l}$, where α is the fiber attenuation. Each amplifier adds some spontaneous emission noise. Thus the optical signal-to-noise ratio, OSNR (see Section 4.2.6 for the definition), gradually degrades along the chain.

The amplifier gain must be at least large enough to compensate for the loss between amplifier stages; otherwise, the signal (and hence the OSNR) will degrade rapidly with the number of stages. Consider what happens when we choose the unsaturated amplifier gain to be larger than the loss between stages. For the first few stages, the total input power (signal plus noise from the previous stages) to a stage increases with the number of stages. Consequently, the amplifiers begin to saturate and their gains drop. Farther along the chain, a spatial steady-state condition is reached where the amplifier output power and gain remains the same from stage to stage. These values, $\overline{P}_{\text{out}}$, and $\overline{G}$, respectively, can be computed by observing that

$$(\overline{P}_{\text{out}}e^{-\alpha l})\overline{G} + 2P_n B_o(\overline{G} - 1) = \overline{P}_{\text{out}}. \tag{5.6}$$

Here $\overline{P}_{\text{out}}e^{-\alpha l}$ is the total input power to the amplifier stage, and the second term, from (4.4) is the spontaneous emission noise added at this stage. Also from (5.5) we must have

$$\overline{G} = 1 + \frac{P^{\text{sat}}}{\overline{P}_{\text{out}}e^{-\alpha l}} \ln \frac{G_{\text{max}}}{\overline{G}}. \tag{5.7}$$

Equations (5.6) and (5.7) can be solved simultaneously to compute the values of $\overline{P}_{\text{out}}$ and $\overline{G}$ (Problem 5.7). Observe from (5.6) that $\overline{G}e^{-\alpha l} < 1$, that is, the steady-state gain will be slightly smaller than the loss between stages, due to the added noise at each stage. Thus in designing a cascade, we must try to choose the saturated gain G to be as close to the loss between stages as possible.

Let us consider a simplified model of an amplifier cascade where we assume the saturated gain $G = e^{\alpha l}$. With L/l amplifiers in the system, the total noise power at the output, using (4.4), is

$$2P_n B_o(G - 1)L/l = 2P_n B_o(e^{\alpha l} - 1)L/l.$$

Given a desired OSNR, the launched power P must satisfy

$$P \geq (\text{OSNR})2P_n B_o(e^{\alpha l} - 1)L/l.$$

Figure 5.6 plots the required power P versus amplifier spacing l. If we don't worry about nonlinearities, we would try to maximize l subject to limitations on transmit power and amplifier output power. The story changes in the presence of nonlinearities, as we will see in Section 5.8.

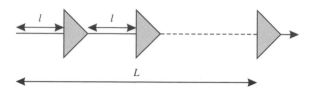

Figure 5.5   A system with cascaded optical amplifiers.

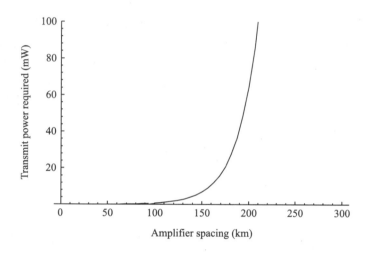

Figure 5.6   Power versus amplifier spacing. Required OSNR $= 50$, $n_{sp} = 2$, $B_o = 20$ GHz, $\alpha = 0.22$ dB/km, and the total link length $L = 1000$ km.

5.5.4   Power Transients and Automatic Gain Control

Power transients are an important effect to consider in WDM links and networks with a number of amplifiers in cascade. If some of the channels fail, the gain of each amplifier will increase because of the reduction in input power to the amplifier. In the worst case, $W - 1$ out of the W channels could fail as shown in Figure 5.7. The surviving channels will then see more gain, and will then arrive at their receivers with higher power. Likewise, the gain seen by existing channels will depend on what other channels are present. Thus setting up or taking down a new channel may affect the power levels in other channels. These factors drive the need for providing automatic gain control (AGC) in the system to keep the output power per channel at each amplifier constant, regardless of the input power.

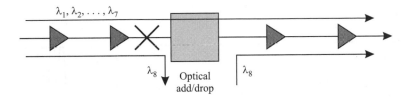

Figure 5.7   Illustrating the impact of failures in a network with optical amplifiers.

With only one amplifier in the cascade, the increase in power due to channel outages occurs rather slowly, in about 100 μs. However, with multiple amplifiers in the chain, the increase in power is much more rapid, with a rise time of a few to tens of μs, and can result in temporary outages in the surviving channels. To prevent this, the AGC system must work very fast, within a few μs, to prevent these power transients from occurring.

Several types of AGC systems have been proposed. A simple AGC circuit monitors the signal power into the amplifier and adjusts the pump power to vary the gain if the input signal power changes. The response time of this method is limited ultimately by the lifetime of the electrons from the third energy level to the second energy level in Erbium (see Section 3.4.3), which is around 1 μs.

Another interesting AGC circuit uses an optical feedback loop, as shown in Figure 5.8. A portion of the amplifier output is tapped off, filtered by a bandpass filter, and fed back into the amplifier. The gain of the loop is controlled carefully by using an attenuator in the loop. This feedback loop causes the amplifier to lase at the wavelength passed by the filter in the loop. This has the effect of clamping the amplifier gain seen by other wavelengths to a fixed value, irrespective of the input signal power. Moreover, it is usually sufficient to have this loop in the first amplifier in the cascade. This is because the output lasing power at the loop wavelength becomes higher as the input signal power decreases, and acts as a compensating signal to amplifiers farther down the cascade. Therefore, amplifiers farther down the cascade do not see a significant variation in the input power. Owing to the additional couplers required for the AGC at the input and output, the amplifier noise figure is slightly increased and its output power is reduced.

Yet another approach is to introduce an additional wavelength on the link to act as a compensating wavelength. This wavelength is introduced at the beginning of the link and tapped off at the end of the link. The power on this wavelength is increased to compensate for any decrease in power seen at the input to the link. This method requires an additional laser and is not as cost effective as the other ones. It can compensate for only a few channels.

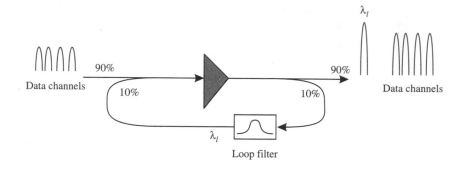

Figure 5.8   Optical automatic gain control circuit for an optical amplifier.

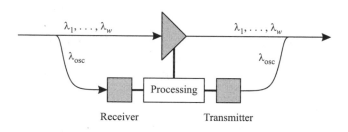

Figure 5.9   The optical supervisory channel.

5.5.5 Optical Supervisory Channel

In systems with line amplifiers, a separate supervisory channel is required to convey information associated with monitoring the state of the amplifiers along the link, particularly if these amplifiers are in remote locations where other direct access is not possible. The supervisory channel could also be used to control the line amplifiers, for example, turning them on or turning them off for test purposes. For these reasons, the supervisory channel must be separated from the other channels at each amplifier stage, and received, processed, and retransmitted, as shown in Figure 5.9. Moreover, we do not want it to fail if the amplifier fails. The supervisory channel can also be used to carry other control information, for example, information used to set up and take down connections in the network—see Chapter 10.

The supervisory channel is carried at a wavelength different from that of the data wavelengths. The choice of the exact wavelength involves a number of tradeoffs. It could be in-band in the sense that it is within the EDFA bandwidth, or out-of-band if it is outside the EDFA bandwidth.

Assuming that the data wavelengths operate in the 1550 nm band, one out-of-band choice is to use the 1310 nm wavelength. This is fine if we do not wish to send data at 1310 nm as well.

Another choice is to use the 1480 nm wavelength, where lasers are easily available. This happens to be one of the wavelengths used to pump an EDFA. If the amplifier happens to be pumped at this wavelength, and a small amount of pump power leaks out, then it will be seen as intrachannel crosstalk (see Section 5.6.1) by the supervisory channel. Moreover, one option with operating an EDFA is to locate the pump laser upstream from the doped fiber (called remote pumping). This option will be precluded if the supervisory channel is at the 1480 nm wavelength.

The in-band approach is to use a wavelength that lies within the EDFA pass-band (1530–1565 nm). However, we may want to use this wavelength to carry data traffic. Another problem with this option is that it is more difficult to separate this wavelength from the data wavelengths at the amplifier input as well as combine it at the amplifier output. The only advantage of this approach might be that some of the amplifier noise can be filtered out at each stage. For instance, if a two-stage amplifier design is used, the in-band supervisory channel can be filtered out after the first stage along with the amplifier noise that is present at this wavelength.

After going through these tradeoffs, the standards bodies have adopted the 1510 nm wavelength as the preferred choice. This wavelength is outside the EDFA passband and does not coincide with a pump wavelength or with a wavelength that would be used for data transmission. This is an appropriate choice for systems with small numbers of wavelengths (8–16) when the wavelengths typically span from 1540 to 1560 nm. However, as we increase the number of wavelengths, we start using the 1530 to 1540 nm band as well, and now it becomes somewhat more difficult to separate the 1510 nm wavelength from these other wavelengths. This requires a more sophisticated filter such as a thin-film device, instead of a simple wavelength-selective coupler, adding some cost and loss.

Yet another choice used by some vendors is the 1610–1620 nm wavelength range, which retains the benefits of the 1510 nm choice but at the same time ensures that the supervisory channel is kept sufficiently far apart from the data channels.

5.6 Crosstalk

Crosstalk is the general term given to the effect of other signals on the desired signal. Almost every component in a WDM system introduces crosstalk of some form or another. The components include filters, wavelength multiplexers/demultiplexers, switches, semiconductor optical amplifiers, and the fiber itself (by way of nonlinearities). Two forms of crosstalk arise in WDM systems: *interchannel crosstalk* and *intrachannel crosstalk*. The first case is when the crosstalk signal is at a wavelength sufficiently different from the desired signal's wavelength that the difference is larger than the receiver's electrical bandwidth. This form of crosstalk is called interchannel crosstalk. Interchannel crosstalk can also occur through more indirect interactions, for example, if one channel affects the gain seen by another channel, as with nonlinearities (Section 5.8). The second case is when the crosstalk signal is at the same wavelength as that of the desired signal or sufficiently close to it that the difference in wavelengths is within the receiver's electrical bandwidth. This form of crosstalk is called intrachannel crosstalk. Intrachannel crosstalk effects can be much more severe than interchannel crosstalk, as we will see. In both cases, crosstalk results in a power penalty.

5.6.1   Intrachannel Crosstalk

Intrachannel crosstalk arises when a signal at a wavelength that is the same as the desired wavelength, or close enough that the difference frequency is within the receiver's electrical bandwidth, leaks into the desired signal's receiver. Intrachannel crosstalk is usually not a major problem in transmission links but can be a major problem in networks. One source of this arises from cascading a wavelength demultiplexer (demux) with a wavelength multiplexer (mux), as shown in Figure 5.10(a). The demux ideally separates the incoming wavelengths to different output fibers. In reality, however, a portion of the signal at one wavelength, say, λ_i, leaks into the adjacent channel λ_{i+1} owing to nonideal suppression within the demux. When the wavelengths are combined back again into a single fiber by the mux, a small portion of the λ_i that leaked into the λ_{i+1} channel will also leak back into the common fiber at the output. Although both signals contain the same data, they are not in phase with each other, due to different delays encountered by them. This causes intrachannel crosstalk. Another source of this type of crosstalk arises from optical switches, as shown in Figure 5.10(b), due to the nonideal isolation of one switch port from the other.

The crosstalk penalty is highest when the state of polarization (SOP) of the crosstalk signal is the same as the SOP of the desired signal. In practice, the SOPs vary slowly with time in a system using standard single-mode fiber (nonpolarization preserving). Similarly, the crosstalk penalty is highest when the crosstalk signal is exactly out of phase with the desired signal. The phase relationship between the two signals can vary over time due to several factors, including temperature variations. We must, however, design the system to work even if the two SOPs happen to match and the signals are exactly out of phase. Thus, for the calculations in this section, we

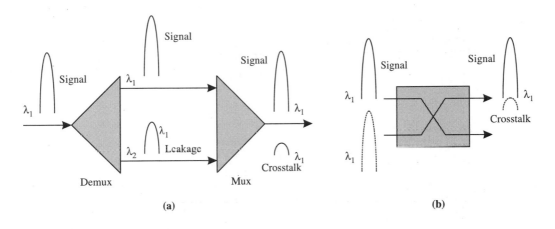

Figure 5.10   Sources of intrachannel crosstalk. (a) A cascaded wavelength demultiplexer and a multiplexer, and (b) an optical switch.

will assume that the SOPs are the same, and compute the penalty when the signals are out of phase, which is the worst-case scenario.

The power penalty due to intrachannel crosstalk can be determined as follows. Let P denote the average received signal power and ϵP the average received crosstalk power from a single other crosstalk channel. Assume that the signal and crosstalk are at the same optical wavelength. The electric field at the receiver can be written as

$$E(t) = \sqrt{2P}d_s(t)\cos[2\pi f_c t + \phi_s(t)] + \sqrt{2\epsilon P}d_x(t)\cos[2\pi f_c t + \phi_x(t)].$$

Here, $d_s(t) = 0, 1$ depending on whether a 0 or 1 is being sent in the desired channel, $d_x(t) = 0, 1$ depending on whether a 0 or 1 is being sent in the crosstalk channel, f_c is the frequency of the optical carrier, and $\phi_s(t)$ and $\phi_x(t)$ are the random phases of the signal and crosstalk channels, respectively. It is assumed that all channels have an ideal extinction ratio of ∞.

The photodetector produces a current that is proportional to the received power within its receiver bandwidth. This received power is given by

$$P_r = Pd_s(t) + \epsilon Pd_x(t) + 2\sqrt{\epsilon}Pd_s(t)d_x(t)\cos[\phi_s(t) - \phi_x(t)]. \tag{5.8}$$

Assuming $\epsilon \ll 1$, we can neglect the ϵ term compared to the $\sqrt{\epsilon}$ term. Also the worst case above is when the $\cos(.) = -1$. Using this, we get the received power during a 1 bit as

$$P_r(1) = P(1 - 2\sqrt{\epsilon})$$

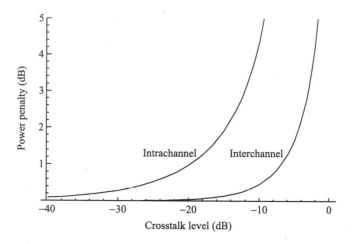

Figure 5.11   Thermal noise limited intrachannel and interchannel crosstalk power penalties as a function of crosstalk level, $-10 \log \epsilon$. Signal-spontaneous noise limited penalties would be reduced by half the values shown in the figure.

and the power during a 0 bit as

$$P_r(0) = 0.$$

First consider the case where the detection is limited by receiver thermal noise, which is independent of the received power. Using (5.3), the power penalty for this case is

$$\text{PP}_{\text{sig-indep}} = -10 \log(1 - 2\sqrt{\epsilon}). \tag{5.9}$$

In amplified systems, or in systems with APD receivers, the dominant noise component is signal dependent (see Section 5.2). For this case, $\sigma_1 \propto \sqrt{P}$ and $\sigma_0 \ll \sigma_1$. Using (5.4), the power penalty in this case becomes

$$\text{PP}_{\text{sig-dep}} = -5 \log(1 - 2\sqrt{\epsilon}). \tag{5.10}$$

If there are N interfering channels, each with average received power $\epsilon_i P$, then ϵ in (5.9) and (5.10) is given by $\sqrt{\epsilon} = \sum_{i=1}^{N} \sqrt{\epsilon_i}$ (see Problem 5.8).

Figure 5.11 shows the crosstalk penalties plotted against the crosstalk level for intrachannel and interchannel crosstalk, which we will consider next. If we allow a 1-dB penalty with signal-independent noise, then the intrachannel crosstalk level should be 20 dB below the desired signal.

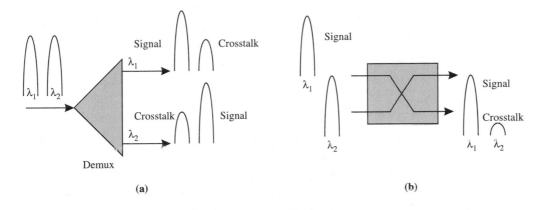

Figure 5.12 Sources of interchannel crosstalk. (a) An optical demultiplexer, and (b) an optical switch with inputs at different wavelengths.

5.6.2 Interchannel Crosstalk

Interchannel crosstalk can arise from a variety of sources. A simple example is an optical filter or demultiplexer that selects one channel and imperfectly rejects the others, as shown in Figure 5.12(a). Another example is in an optical switch switching different wavelengths, shown in Figure 5.12(b), where the crosstalk arises owing to imperfect isolation between the switch ports.

Estimating the power penalty due to interchannel crosstalk is fairly straightforward. If the wavelength spacing between the desired signal and crosstalk signal is large compared to the receiver bandwidth, (5.8) can be written as

$$P_r = P d_s(t) + \epsilon P d_x(t).$$

Therefore, in the worst case, we have

$$P_r(1) = P,$$

and

$$P_r(0) = \epsilon P.$$

Using (5.3), the power penalty for the thermal noise limited case is given by

$$PP_{\text{sig-indep}} = -10 \log(1 - \epsilon). \tag{5.11}$$

For systems dominated by signal-dependent noise, the penalty is obtained from (5.4) as

$$PP_{\text{sig-dep}} = -5 \log(1 - \epsilon). \tag{5.12}$$

If there are N interfering channels, each with average received power $\epsilon_i P$, then ϵ in (5.11) and (5.12) is given by $\epsilon = \sum_{i=1}^{N} \epsilon_i$ (see Problem 5.8).

Example 5.1   Consider an unamplified WDM system with a filter receiving the desired channel and rejecting the others. The main crosstalk component usually comes from the two adjacent channels, and the crosstalk from the other channels is usually negligible. Assuming a 0.5-dB crosstalk penalty requirement, the adjacent channel suppression must be greater than 12.6 dB.

5.6.3   Crosstalk in Networks

Crosstalk suppression becomes particularly important in networks, where a signal propagates through many nodes, and accumulates crosstalk from different elements at each node. In order to obtain an approximate idea of the crosstalk requirements, suppose that a signal accumulates crosstalk from N sources, each with crosstalk level ϵ_s. This neglects the fact that some interfering channels may have higher powers than the desired channel. Networks are very likely to contain amplifiers and be limited by signal-spontaneous beat noise. Figure 5.13 plots the power penalties calculated from (5.10) and (5.12). For example, if we have 10 interfering equal-power crosstalk elements, each producing intrachannel crosstalk, then we must have a crosstalk suppression of below 35 dB in each element, in order to have an overall penalty of less than 1 dB.

5.6.4   Bidirectional Systems

In a bidirectional transmission system, data is transmitted in both directions over a single fiber, as shown in Figure 5.14. Additional crosstalk mechanisms arise in these systems. Although the laws of physics do not prevent the same wavelength from being used for both directions of transmissions, this is not a good idea in practice because of reflections. A back-reflection from a point close to the transmitter at one end, say, end A, will send a lot of power back into A's receiver, creating a large amount of crosstalk. In fact, the reflected power into A may be larger than the signal power received from the other end B. Reflections within the end equipment can be carefully controlled, but it is more difficult to restrict reflections from the fiber link itself. For this reason, bidirectional systems typically use different wavelengths in different directions. The two directions can be separated at the ends either by

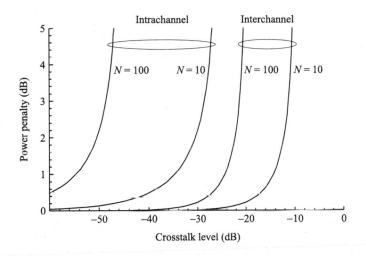

Figure 5.13   Signal-spontaneous noise limited intrachannel and interchannel crosstalk penalties as a function of crosstalk level $-10\log\epsilon_s$ in a network. The parameter N denotes the number of crosstalk elements, all assumed to produce crosstalk at equal powers.

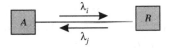

Figure 5.14   A bidirectional transmission system.

using an optical circulator or a WDM mux/demux, as in Figure 5.15. (If the same wavelength must be used in both directions, one alternative that is sometimes used in short-distance access networks is to use time division multiplexing where only one end transmits at a time.)

If a WDM mux/demux is used to handle both directions of transmission, crosstalk can also arise because a signal at a transmitted wavelength is reflected within the mux into a port that is used to receive a signal from the other end, as in Figure 5.15(a). The mux/demux used should have adequate crosstalk suppression to ensure that this is not a problem. Likewise, if an optical circulator is used, crosstalk can arise because of imperfect isolation in the circulator, as shown in Figure 5.15(b). We have to be careful about these effects when designing bidirectional optical amplifiers as well.

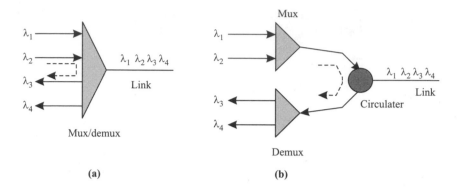

Figure 5.15   Separating the two directions in a bidirectional system: (a) using a wavelength multiplexer/demultiplexer, and (b) using an optical circulator. Both methods can introduce crosstalk, as shown by dashed lines in the figure.

5.6.5   Crosstalk Reduction

The simplest (and preferred) approach toward crosstalk reduction is to improve the crosstalk suppression at the device level; in other words, let the device designer worry about it. The network designer calculates and specifies the crosstalk suppression required for each device based on the number of cascaded such devices in the network and the allowable penalty due to crosstalk. However, there are a few architectural approaches toward reducing specific forms of crosstalk, particularly crosstalk arising in optical switches.

The first approach is to use *spatial dilation*, which is illustrated in Figure 5.16. Figure 5.16(a) shows a 2×2 optical switch with crosstalk ϵ. To improve the crosstalk suppression, we can *dilate* the switch, as shown in Figure 5.16(b), by adding some unused ports to it. Now the crosstalk is reduced to ϵ^2. The drawbacks of dilation are that it cannot be achieved without a significant increase in the number of switches. Usually, the number of switches is doubled.

Another approach to reduce the crosstalk in a WDM network is to use *wavelength dilation* in the switches. This is particularly useful if a single switch is to handle multiple wavelengths, such as the acousto-optic tunable filter (AOTF) of Section 3.3.8. To reduce the interchannel crosstalk, one can use two switches instead of one, as shown in Figure 5.17. The first switch handles the odd-numbered channels, and the second the even-numbered channels. This effectively doubles the channel spacing as far as crosstalk is concerned. Again the cost is that twice as many switches

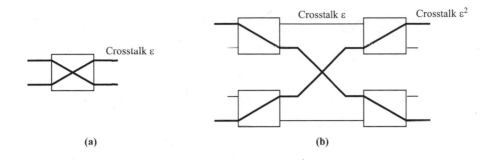

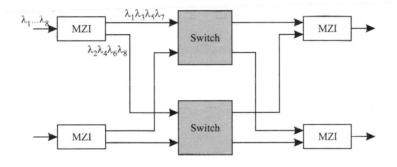

Figure 5.16   Using spatial dilation to reduce switch crosstalk. (a) A simple 2 × 2 switch. (b) A dilated version of a 2 × 2 switch.

Figure 5.17   Using wavelength dilation to reduce switch crosstalk. MZI denotes a Mach-Zehnder interferometer that separates the channels into two groups or combines them.

are required. In the extreme case of wavelength dilation, we can have a separate switch for each wavelength.

A simple method to reduce crosstalk in the mux/demux of Figure 5.10 is to add an additional filter for each wavelength between the demux and mux stages. The extra filter stage produces an additional level of isolation and improves the overall crosstalk performance dramatically, but of course adds to the cost of the unit.

5.6.6   Cascaded Filters

Networks are likely to have several mux/demuxes or filters cascaded. When two mux/demuxes or filters are cascaded, the overall passband is much smaller than

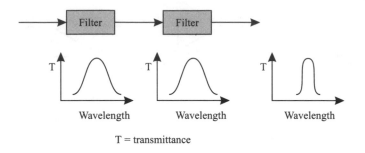

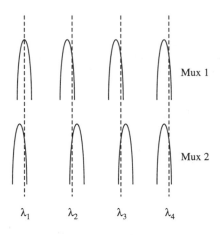

Figure 5.18   Bandwidth narrowing due to cascading of two filters.

Figure 5.19   Wavelength misalignment between two mux/demuxes.

the passbands of the individual filters. Figure 5.18 shows this effect. The required wavelength stability and accuracy in these systems therefore goes up with the number of cascaded stages.

A related problem arises from the accuracy of wavelength registration in these mux/demuxes. If the center wavelengths of two units in a cascade are not identical (see Figure 5.19), the overall loss through the cascade for the desired signal will be higher, and the crosstalk from the adjacent channels could also be higher. If we are concerned only with one channel, we could align the center wavelengths exactly by temperature tuning the individual mux/demuxes. However, other channels could become even more misaligned in the process (tuning one channel tunes the others as well). In addition, the lasers themselves could have a tolerance regarding their center wavelength. In a cascaded system, wavelength inaccuracies cause additional power penalties due to added signal loss and crosstalk (see Problems 5.13 and 5.14).

$\underline{5.7}$ Dispersion

Dispersion is the name given to any effect wherein different components of the transmitted signal travel at different velocities in the fiber, arriving at different times at the receiver. A signal pulse launched into a fiber arrives smeared at the other end as a consequence of this effect. This smearing causes intersymbol interference, which in turn leads to power penalties. The amount of accumulated dispersion depends on the length of the link.

Several forms of dispersion arise in optical communication systems. The important ones are *modal dispersion, polarization-mode dispersion*, and *chromatic dispersion*. Of these, we have already studied modal dispersion and chromatic dispersion in Chapter 2 and quantified the limitations that they impose on the link length and/or bit rate.

Modal dispersion arises only in multimode fiber, where the different modes travel with different velocities. Modal dispersion was discussed in Section 2.1. The link length in a multimode system is usually limited by modal dispersion and not by the loss. Clearly modal dispersion is not a problem with single-mode fiber.

Polarization-mode dispersion (PMD) arises because the fiber core is not perfectly circular, particularly in older installations. Thus different polarizations of the signal travel with different group velocities. PMD is proving to be a serious impediment in very high-speed systems operating at 10 Gb/s bit rates and beyond.

The main form of dispersion that we are concerned with is *chromatic dispersion*, which has a profound impact in the design of single-mode transmission systems (so much so that we often use the term "dispersion" to mean "chromatic dispersion"). Chromatic dispersion and the system limitations posed by it are discussed in detail in Section 2.3. Chromatic dispersion arises because different frequency components of a pulse (and also signals at different wavelengths) travel with different group velocities in the fiber, and thus arrive at different times at the other end. Chromatic dispersion is a characteristic of the fiber, and different fibers have different chromatic dispersion profiles. It is typically measured in units of ps/nm-km, where ps refers to the time spread of the pulse, the nm is the spectral width of the pulse, and km corresponds to the link length. The accumulated dispersion increases with the link length.

5.7.1   Chromatic Dispersion Penalty

The exact calculation of the penalty due to chromatic dispersion is fairly complicated and is discussed in Section 2.3. An idea of the transmission limitations imposed by chromatic dispersion can be obtained by assuming that the pulse spreading due to chromatic dispersion should be less than a fraction ϵ of the bit period. For a penalty of 1 dB, $\epsilon = 0.306$, and for a penalty of 2 dB, $\epsilon = 0.491$ [Bel95]. If D is the fiber chromatic dispersion at the operating wavelength, B the bit rate, $\Delta\lambda$ the spectral width of the transmitted signal, and L the length of the link, this limitation can be expressed as (2.34)

$$|D|LB(\Delta\lambda) < \epsilon. \tag{5.13}$$

This is for the case when the source spectral width is nonnegligible. When this can be neglected, for example, for DFB lasers modulated at a few hundred Mb/s or more, the limit is expressed as (2.32)

$$B\lambda\sqrt{\frac{|D|L}{2\pi c}} < \epsilon. \tag{5.14}$$

The spectral width of the transmitted signal depends on the type of source and whether it is directly modulated or whether an external modulator is used. MLM Fabry-Perot lasers have spectral widths of several nm, whereas SLM DFB lasers have unmodulated spectral widths of typically less than 50 MHz. Directly modulating a DFB laser would ideally cause its spectral width to correspond to the modulation bandwidth (for example, about 2.5 GHz for a 2.5 Gb/s on–off modulated signal). In practice, however, the spectral width can increase owing to chirp. As the modulation current (and thus optical power) varies, it is accompanied by changes in carrier density within the laser cavity, which in turn, changes the refractive index of the cavity, causing frequency variations in its output. The magnitude of the effect depends on the variation in current (or power), but it is not uncommon to observe spectral widths over 10 GHz as a consequence of chirp. Chirp can be reduced by decreasing the extinction ratio. The spectral width can also be increased owing to back-reflections from connectors, splices, and other elements in the optical path. To prevent this effect, high-speed lasers are typically packaged with built-in isolators.

Dispersion management is a very important part of designing WDM transmission systems, since dispersion affects the penalties due to various types of fiber nonlinearities, as we will see in Section 5.8. We can use several techniques to reduce the impact of chromatic dispersion: (a) using external modulation in conjunction with DFB lasers, (b) using fiber with small dispersion, and (c) by dispersion compensation. The first alternative is commonly used today in high-speed systems. Using fiber with small dispersion is possible only in new fiber installations. Dispersion compensation

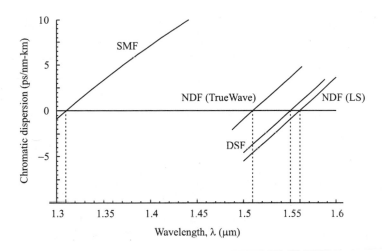

Figure 5.20 Chromatic dispersion characteristics of different types of single-mode fiber. The dispersion profiles are approximate.

can be employed when external modulation alone is not sufficient to reduce the dispersion penalty. The last two options are discussed next.

5.7.2 Single-Mode Fiber Types

There are three types of single-mode fibers, and they differ in their chromatic dispersion profile as a function of wavelength, as shown in Figure 5.20.

Standard single-mode fiber (SMF). This is the most common type of fiber deployed. Most of the installed fiber in the United States and Europe falls into this category. This fiber was designed to provide zero chromatic dispersion at 1310 nm, to support the early long-haul transmission systems operating at this wavelength. It has a chromatic dispersion of at most 20 ps/nm-km in the 1.55 μm wavelength range and usually around 17 ps/nm-km.

Dispersion-shifted fiber (DSF). As transmission systems started using the low-loss 1.55 μm wavelength range, the need for a fiber with zero chromatic dispersion at this wavelength became apparent, leading to the development of DSF. DSF has a chromatic dispersion of at most 3.3 ps/nm-km in the 1.55 μm wavelength range and typically zero dispersion at 1550 nm. A large fraction of the installed base in Japan is DSF.

Nonzero dispersion fiber (NDF). Although DSF overcomes the problems due to chromatic dispersion in the 1.55 μm wavelength window, unfortunately, it is not suitable for use with WDM because of severe penalties due to four-wave mixing and other nonlinearities—see Section 5.8. As we shall see, these penalties are reduced if a little chromatic dispersion is present in the fiber because the different interacting waves then travel with different group velocities. This led to the recent development of NDF fiber. NDF has a chromatic dispersion between 1 and 6 ps/nm-km, or between −1 and −6 ps/nm-km, in the 1.55 μm wavelength window. This reduces the penalties due to nonlinearities while retaining most of the advantages of DSF. This fiber is just beginning to be installed. Examples include the LS fiber from Corning, which has a zero dispersion wavelength of 1560 nm and a small dispersion of 0.092(λ − 1560) ps/nm-km in the 1550 nm wavelength window, and the TrueWave™ fiber from Lucent Technologies.

5.7.3   Dispersion Compensation

Along with the development of different fiber types, researchers have also developed various methods of compensating for chromatic dispersion. The two most popular methods use dispersion compensating fibers and chirped fiber Bragg gratings.

Dispersion Compensating Fibers

Special dispersion compensating fibers (DCFs) have been developed that provide negative dispersion in the 1550 nm wavelength range. For example, DCFs that can provide total dispersion of between −340 and −1360 ps/nm are commercially available. A DCF with −1360 ps/nm can compensate for an 80-km length of standard single-mode fiber (at 17 ps/nm-km) to achieve a net zero dispersion. One disadvantage of this approach is the added loss introduced in the system by the DCF. For instance the −1360 ps/nm DCF has a loss of 9 dB. Thus a commonly used measure for evaluating a DCF is the *figure of merit* (FOM), which is defined as the ratio of the absolute amount of chromatic dispersion per unit wavelength to the loss introduced by the DCF. The FOM is measured in ps/nm-dB, and the higher the FOM, the more efficient the fiber is at compensating for dispersion. The FOM for the DCF in the preceding example is thus 150 ps/nm-dB, and there is intensive research underway to develop DCFs with higher FOMs. The FOM as defined here does not fully characterize the efficiency of the DCF since it does not take into account the added nonlinearities introduced by the DCF. A modified FOM that does take this into account has been proposed in [FTCV96].

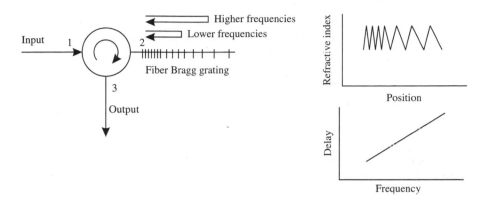

Figure 5.21 Chirped fiber Bragg grating for dispersion compensation.

Chirped Fiber Bragg Gratings

The fiber Bragg grating that we studied in Chapter 3 is a versatile device that can be used to compensate for dispersion. Such a device is shown in Figure 5.21. The grating itself is linearly chirped, in that the period of the grating varies linearly with position, as shown in Figure 5.21. This makes the grating reflect different wavelengths (or frequencies) at different points along its length. Effectively, a chirped Bragg grating introduces different delays at different frequencies.

In a regular fiber, chromatic dispersion introduces larger delays for the lower-frequency components in a pulse. To compensate for this effect, we can design chirped gratings that do exactly the opposite—namely, introduce larger delays for the higher-frequency components, in other words, compress the pulses. The delay as a function of frequency is plotted in Figure 5.21 for a sample grating.

Ideally, we want a grating that introduces a large amount of dispersion over a wide bandwidth so that it can compensate for the fiber dispersion over a large length as well as a wide range of wavelengths. In practice, the total length of the grating is limited by the size of the phase masks available today to about 10 cm [Lam97]. So the maximum delay that can be introduced by the grating is 1 ns. This delay corresponds to the product of the dispersion introduced by the grating and the bandwidth over which it is introduced. Thus we can have gratings that introduce large dispersion over a small bandwidth, for example, 1000 ps/nm over a 1 nm bandwidth, or small dispersion over a wide bandwidth, for example, 100 ps/nm over a 10 nm bandwidth. Note that 100 km of standard single-mode fiber causes a total dispersion of 1700 ps/nm. Therefore, in practice, in order to use chirped gratings to compensate for a few hundred km of fiber dispersion, they must be very narrow band; in other

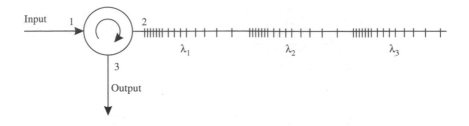

Figure 5.22   Chirped fiber Bragg gratings for compensating three wavelengths in a WDM system.

words, we would need to use a different grating for each wavelength, as shown in Figure 5.22.

Chirped gratings are therefore ideally suited to compensate for individual wavelengths rather than multiple wavelengths. In contrast, dispersion compensating fiber (DCF) is better suited to compensate over a wide range of wavelengths. However, compared to chirped gratings, DCF introduces higher loss and additional penalties because of increased nonlinearities.

The first choice in most systems is to use external modulators to reduce the signal spectral width. If that is not sufficient to limit the chromatic dispersion penalty, then dispersion compensation can be used.

5.7.4   Polarization-Mode Dispersion (PMD)

The origin of PMD lies in the fact that owing to the ellipticity of the fiber core, different polarizations travel with different group velocities. Moreover, the distribution of signal energy over the different state of polarizations (SOPs) changes slowly with time, for example, because of changes in the ambient temperature. This causes the PMD penalty to vary with time as well. In addition to the fiber itself, PMD can arise from individual components used in the network as well.

The time-averaged differential time delay between the two orthogonal SOPs on a link is known to obey the relation

$$\langle \Delta \tau \rangle = D_{\text{PMD}} \sqrt{L},$$

where $\Delta \tau$ is the time-averaged differential time delay, L is the link length, and D_{PMD} is the fiber PMD parameter, measured in ps/$\sqrt{\text{km}}$. The PMD for typical fiber lies between 0.5 and 2 ps/$\sqrt{\text{km}}$. However, carefully constructed new links can have PMD as low as 0.1 ps/$\sqrt{\text{km}}$.

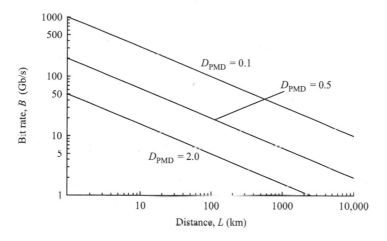

Figure 5.23   Limitations on the simultaneously achievable bit rates and distances imposed by PMD.

In reality, the SOPs vary slowly with time, and the actual differential time delay $\Delta\tau$ is a random variable. It is commonly assumed to have a Maxwellian probability density function (see Appendix D). With this distribution, the probability that the actual delay will be greater than 3 times the average delay is about 4×10^{-5} (see Appendix D). If the differential delay varies significantly once a day, the actual differential delay will exceed 3 times the average delay once every 70 years. However, some cables can have significantly more rapid variations in the differential delay. If the differential delay varies significantly once a minute, the actual differential delay will exceed 3 times the average delay once every 17 days.

For a differential delay of $0.3T$, where T is the bit duration, the power penalty is approximately 0.5 dB for a receiver limited by thermal noise and 1 dB for a receiver with signal-dependent noise [ITU96c]. Given our earlier reasoning, this means that in order to have a penalty of 1 dB or less during normal operation, we must have the average differential delay be less than $0.1T$, that is,

$$\langle\Delta\tau\rangle = D_{\text{PMD}}\sqrt{L} < 0.1T. \tag{5.15}$$

This limit is plotted in Figure 5.23 for a 10 Gb/s system. Observe that for a bad fiber with PMD of 2 ps/$\sqrt{\text{km}}$, the limit is only 25 km. This is an extreme case, but points out that PMD can impose a significant limitation.

The limitations due to modal dispersion, chromatic dispersion, and PMD are compared in Figure 5.24.

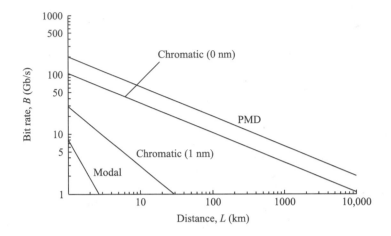

Figure 5.24   Limitations on the simultaneously achievable bit rates and distances imposed by modal dispersion, chromatic dispersion with a source spectral width of 1 nm, chromatic dispersion with negligible source spectral width, and PMD with $D_{\text{PMD}} = 0.5$.

In addition to PMD, some other polarization-dependent effects influence system performance. One of these arises from the fact that many components have a polarization-dependent loss (PDL); that is,the loss through the component depends on the state of polarization. These losses accumulate in a system with many components in the transmission path. Again, since the state of polarization fluctuates with time, the signal-to-noise ratio at the end of the path will also fluctuate with time, and careful attention needs to be paid to maintain the total PDL on the path to within acceptable limits. An example of this is a simple angled-facet connector used in some systems to reduce reflections. This connector can have a PDL of about 0.1 dB, but hundreds of such connectors can be present in the transmission path.

5.8   Fiber Nonlinearities

As long as the optical power within an optical fiber is small, the fiber can be treated as linear medium, that is, the loss and refractive index of the fiber are independent of the signal power. However, when power levels get fairly high in the system, we have to worry about the impact of nonlinear effects, which arise due to the fact that, in reality, both the loss (gain) and index depend on the optical power in the fiber. Nonlinearities can place significant limitations on high-speed systems as well as WDM systems.

Nonlinearities can be classified into two categories. The first occurs owing to scattering effects in the fiber medium due to the interaction of light waves with phonons (molecular vibrations) in the silica medium. The two main effects in this category are *stimulated Brillouin scattering* (SBS) and *stimulated Raman scattering* (SRS). The second set of effects occurs owing to the dependence of refractive index on the optical power. This category includes four-wave mixing (FWM), self-phase modulation (SPM), and cross-phase modulation (CPM). In Chapter 2, we looked at the origins of SPM, CPM, and FWM. Here we will understand both the limitations that all these nonlinearities place on system designers and the origins of SBS and SRS.

Except for SPM and CPM, all these effects provide gains to some channels at the expense of depleting power from other channels. SPM and CPM, on the other hand, affect only the phase of signals and can cause spectral broadening, which in turn, leads to increased dispersion penalties.

The nonlinear interaction depends on the transmission length and the cross-sectional area of the fiber. The longer the link length, the more the interaction and the worse the effect of the nonlinearity. However, as the signal propagates along the link, its power decreases because of fiber attenuation. Modeling this effect can be quite complicated, and in practice, a simple model that assumes that the power is constant over a certain *effective length L_e* has proved to be quite sufficient in understanding the effect of nonlinearities. Suppose P denotes the power transmitted into the fiber and $P(z) = Pe^{-\alpha z}$ denotes the power at distance z along the link, with α being the fiber attenuation. Let L denote the actual link length. Then the effective length (see Figure 5.25) is defined as the length L_e such that

$$PL_e = \int_{z=0}^{L} P(z)dz.$$

This yields

$$L_e = \frac{1 - e^{-\alpha L}}{\alpha}.$$

Typically, $\alpha = 0.22$ dB/km at 1.55 μm wavelength, and for long links where $L \gg 1/\alpha$, we have $L_e \approx 20$ km.

In systems with optical amplifiers, the signal gets amplified at each amplifier stage without resetting the effects due to nonlinearities from the previous span. Thus the effective length in such a system is the sum of the effective lengths of each span. In a link of length L with amplifiers spaced l km apart, the effective length is approximately given by

$$L_e = \frac{1 - e^{-\alpha l}}{\alpha} \frac{L}{l}. \tag{5.16}$$

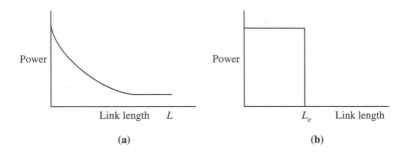

Figure 5.25   Effective transmission length calculation.

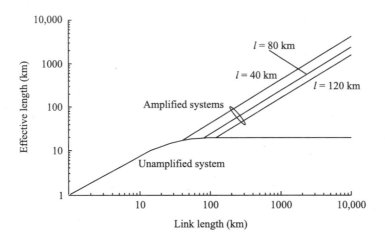

Figure 5.26   Effective transmission length as a function of link length.

Figure 5.26 shows the effective length plotted against the actual length of the transmission link for unamplified and amplified systems. The figure indicates that in order to reduce the effective length, it is better to have fewer amplifiers spaced further apart. However, what matters in terms of the system effects of nonlinearities is not just the effective length; it is the product of the launched power P and the effective length L_e. Figure 5.6 showed how P varies with the amplifier spacing l. Now we are interested in finding out how PL_e grows with the amplifier spacing l. This is shown in Figure 5.27. The figure shows that the effect of nonlinearities can be reduced by reducing the amplifier spacing. Although this may make it easier to design the

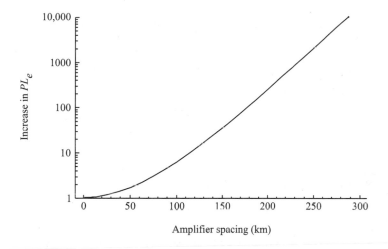

Figure 5.27   Relative value of PL_e versus amplifier spacing. The ordinate is the value relative to an amplifier spacing of 1 km. $\alpha = 0.22$ dB/km.

amplifiers (they need lower gain), we will also need more amplifiers, resulting in an increase in system cost.

The effect of a nonlinearity grows with the intensity in the fiber, which, for a given power, is inversely proportional to the area of the core. Since the power is not uniformly distributed within the cross section of the fiber, it is convenient to use an effective cross-sectional area A_e (see Figure 5.28), related to the actual area A and the cross-sectional distribution of intensity $I(r, \theta)$, as

$$A_e = \frac{[\int_r \int_\theta r\, dr\, d\theta\, I(r, \theta)]^2}{\int_r \int_\theta r\, dr\, d\theta\, I^2(r, \theta)},$$

where r and θ denote the polar coordinates. For the cases of interest here, A_e is just the area of the single-mode fiber core, which is approximately 50 μm^2, assuming a core diameter of 8 μm. The dispersion compensating fibers that we studied in Section 5.7.3 tend to have smaller core areas and hence exhibit higher nonlinearities.

In scattering effects, energy gets transferred from one light wave to another wave at a higher wavelength (or lower energy). The lost energy is absorbed by the molecular vibrations, or phonons, in the medium. (The type of phonon involved is different for SBS and SRS.) This second wave is called the *Stokes wave*. The signal can be thought of as being a "pump" wave that causes amplification of the Stokes wave. As the pump propagates in the fiber, it loses power and the Stokes wave gains power. In our case, the pump wave is the signal wave, and the Stokes wave is the

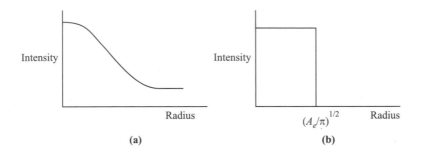

Figure 5.28   Effective cross-sectional area.

unwanted wave that is generated due to the scattering process. In general, scattering effects are characterized by a gain coefficient g, measured in m/W and spectral width Δf over which the gain is present.

The effect of a scattering nonlinearity depends on PL_e and thus increases with an increase in the input power and the link length. The longer the link, the greater is the amount of power that is coupled out from the signal (pump) into the Stokes wave. For a given link length, an approximate measure of the power level at which the effect of a nonlinearity starts becoming significant is the *threshold power*. For a given fiber length, the threshold power of a scattering nonlinearity is defined as the incident optical power per channel into the fiber at which the pump and Stokes powers at the fiber output are equal. In amplified systems, the threshold power is reduced because of the increase in the effective length. This makes amplified systems more susceptible to impairments due to nonlinearities.

5.8.1   *Stimulated Brillouin Scattering*

In the case of SBS, the phonons involved are acoustic phonons, and the interaction occurs over a very narrow line width of $\Delta f_B = 20\,\text{MHz}$ at $1.55\,\mu\text{m}$. Also the Stokes and pump waves propagate in opposite directions. Thus SBS does not cause any interaction between different wavelengths, as long as the wavelength spacing is much greater than 20 MHz, which is typically the case. SBS can, however, create significant distortion within a single channel. SBS produces gain in the direction opposite to the direction of propagation of the signal, in other words, back toward the source. Thus it depletes the transmitted signal as well as generates a potentially strong signal back toward the transmitter, which must be shielded by an isolator. The SBS gain coefficient g_B is approximately 4×10^{-11} m/W, independent of the wavelength.

The intensities of the pump wave I_p and the Stokes wave I_s are related by the coupled wave equations [Buc95]

$$\frac{dI_s}{dz} = -g_B I_p I_s + \alpha I_s, \tag{5.17}$$

and

$$\frac{dI_p}{dz} = -g_B I_p I_s - \alpha I_p. \tag{5.18}$$

The intensities are related to the powers as $P_s = A_e I_s$ and $P_p = A_e I_p$. For the case where the Stokes power is much smaller than the pump power, we can assume that the pump wave is not depleted. This amounts to neglecting the $-g_B I_p I_s$ term on the right-hand side of (5.18). With this assumption, (5.17) and (5.18) can be solved (see Problem 5.17) for a link of length L to yield

$$P_s(0) = P_s(L)e^{-\alpha L} e^{\frac{g_B P_p(0) L_e}{A_e}} \tag{5.19}$$

and

$$P_p(L) = P_p(0)e^{-\alpha L}. \tag{5.20}$$

Note that the output of the pump wave is at $z = L$, but the output of the Stokes wave is at $z = 0$ since the two waves are counterpropagating.

The calculation of the threshold power P_{th} is quite involved, and we simply state the following approximation for it from [Smi72]:

$$P_{\text{th}} \approx \frac{21bA_e}{g_B l_e}.$$

The value of b lies between 1 and 2 depending on the relative polarizations of the pump and Stokes waves. Assuming the worst-case value of $b = 1$, we get $P_{\text{th}} = 1.3$ mW. Since this is a low value, some care must be taken in the design of optical communication systems to reduce the SBS penalty.

The preceding expression assumes that the pump signal has a very narrow line width and lies within the narrow 20 MHz gain bandwidth of SBS. The threshold power is considerably increased if the signal has a broad line width, and thus much of the pump power lies outside the 20 MHz gain bandwidth of SBS. An approximate expression that incorporates this effect is given by

$$P_{\text{th}} \approx \frac{21bA_e}{g_B L_e} \left(1 + \frac{\Delta f_{\text{source}}}{\Delta f_B}\right),$$

where Δf_{source} is the line width of the source. With $\Delta f_{\text{source}} = 200$ MHz, and still assuming $b = 1$, the SBS threshold increases to $P_{\text{th}} = 14.4$ mW.

The SBS penalty can be reduced in several ways:

1. Keep the power per channel to much below the SBS threshold. The tradeoff is that in a long-haul system, we may have to reduce the amplifier spacing.

2. Since the gain bandwidth of SBS is very small, its effect can be decreased by increasing the line width of the source. This can be done by directly modulating the laser, which causes the line width to increase owing to chirp. This may cause a significant dispersion penalty. The dispersion penalty can, however, be reduced by suitable dispersion management, as we will see later. Another approach is to dither the laser slightly in frequency, say, at 200 MHz, which does not cause as high a penalty because of dispersion but increases the SBS threshold power by an order of magnitude, as we saw earlier. This approach is commonly employed in high bit rate systems transmitting at high powers. Irrespective of the bit rate, the use of an external modulator along with a narrow line width source increases the SBS threshold by only a small factor (between 2 and 4) for amplitude-modulated systems. This is because a good fraction of the power is still contained in the optical carrier for such systems.

3. Use phase modulation schemes rather than amplitude modulation schemes. This reduces the power present in the optical carrier, thus reducing the SBS penalty. In this case, the line width of the source can be taken to be proportional to the bit rate. However, this may not be a practical option in most systems.

5.8.2   Stimulated Raman Scattering

If two or more signals at different wavelengths are injected into a fiber, SRS causes power to be transferred from the lower-wavelength channels to the higher-wavelength channels (see Figure 5.29). Unlike SBS, SRS is a broadband effect. Figure 5.30 shows its gain coefficient as a function of wavelength spacing. The peak gain coefficient g_R is approximately 6×10^{-14} m/W at 1.55 μm, which is much smaller than the gain coefficient for SBS. However, channels up to 150 THz (125 nm) apart will be coupled with SRS. Also SRS causes coupling in both the direction of propagation and the reverse direction. Coupling occurs between two channels only if both channels are sending 1 bits (that is, power is present in both channels). Thus the SRS penalty is reduced when dispersion is present because the signals in the different channels travel at different velocities, reducing the probability of overlap between pulses at different wavelengths at any point in the fiber. This is the same *pulse walk-off* phenomenon that we discussed in the case of cross-phase modulation (CPM) in Section 2.4.2. Typically, dispersion reduces the SRS effect by a factor of two.

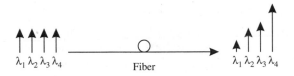

Figure 5.29   The effect of SRS. Power from lower-wavelength channels is transferred to the higher-wavelength channels.

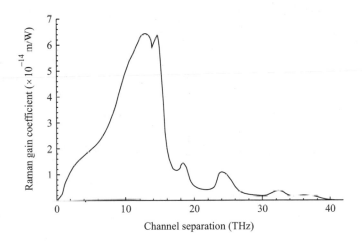

Figure 5.30   SRS gain coefficient as a function of channel separation. After [Agr92].

To calculate the effect of SRS in a multichannel system, following [Chr84], we approximate the Raman gain shape as a triangle, where the Raman gain coefficient as a function of wavelength spacing $\Delta\lambda$ is given by

$$g(\Delta\lambda) = \begin{cases} g_R \frac{\Delta\lambda}{\Delta\lambda_c}, & \text{if } 0 \leq \Delta\lambda \leq \Delta\lambda_c, \\ 0 & \text{otherwise.} \end{cases}$$

Here we choose $\Delta\lambda_c = 125$ nm. Consider a system with W equally spaced channels $0, 1, \ldots, W - 1$ with $\Delta\lambda_s$ denoting the channel spacing. Assume that all the channels fall within the Raman gain bandwidth, that is, the system bandwidth $\Lambda = (W - 1)\Delta\lambda_s \leq \Delta\lambda_c$. This is the case of practical interest given that the Raman gain bandwidth is 125 nm and the channels within a WDM system must usually be spaced within a 30 nm band dictated by the bandwidth of optical amplifiers.

The worst affected channel is the channel corresponding to the lowest wavelength, channel 0, when there is a 1 bit in all the channels. Assume that the transmitted power is the same on all channels. Assume further that there is no interaction between the other channels, and the powers of the other channels remain the same (this approximation yields very small estimation errors). Assume also that the polarizations are scrambled. This is the case in practical systems. In systems that use polarization-maintaining fiber, the Raman interaction is enhanced, and the equation that follows does not have the factor of 2 in the denominator. The fraction of the power coupled from the worst affected channel, channel 0, to channel i is given approximately by [Buc95]

$$P_o(i) = g_R \frac{i \Delta \lambda_s}{\Delta \lambda_c} \frac{P L_e}{2 A_e}.$$

This expression can be derived starting from the coupled wave equations for SRS that are similar in form to (5.17) and (5.18)—see [Buc95] for details. So the fraction of the power coupled out of channel 0 to all the other channels is

$$P_o = \sum_{i=1}^{W-1} P_o(i) = \frac{g_R \Delta \lambda_s P L_e}{2 \Delta \lambda_c A_e} \frac{W(W-1)}{2}. \tag{5.21}$$

The power penalty for this channel is then

$$-10 \log(1 - P_o).$$

In order to keep the penalty below 0.5 dB, we must have $P_o < 0.1$, or, from (5.21),

$$W P(W - 1) \Delta \lambda_s L_e < 40,000 \text{ mW nm km}.$$

Observe that the total system bandwidth is $\Lambda = (W-1)\Delta \lambda_s$ and the total transmitted power is $P_{\text{tot}} = WP$. Thus the result can be restated as

$$P_{\text{tot}} \Lambda L_e < 40,000 \text{ mW nm km}.$$

The preceding formula was derived assuming that no dispersion is present in the system. With dispersion present, the right-hand side can be relaxed to approximately $80,000$ mW nm km.

If the channel spacing is fixed, the power that can be launched decreases with W as $1/W^2$. For example, in a 32-wavelength system with channels spaced 0.8 nm (100 GHz) apart, and $L_e = 20$ km, $P \leq 2.5$ mW. Figure 5.31 plots the maximum allowed transmit power per channel as a function of the link length.

Although SRS is not a significant problem in systems with a small number of channels due to the relatively high threshold power, it can pose a serious problem

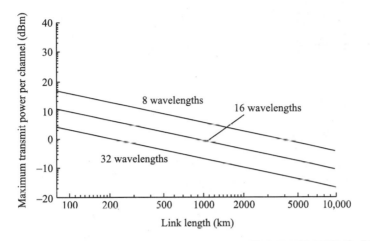

Figure 5.31 Limitation on the maximum transmit power per channel imposed by stimulated Raman scattering. The channel spacing is assumed to be 0.8 nm, and amplifiers are assumed to be spaced 80 km apart.

in systems with a large number of wavelengths. To alleviate the effects of SRS, we can (a) keep the channels spaced as closely together as possible, and/or (b) keep the power levels below the threshold, which will require us to reduce the distance between amplifiers.

5.8.3 Four-Wave Mixing

We saw in Section 2.4 that the nonlinear polarization causes three signals at frequencies ω_i, ω_j, and ω_k to interact to produce signals at frequencies $\omega_i \pm \omega_j \pm \omega_k$. Among these signals, the most troublesome one is the signal corresponding to

$$\omega_{ijk} = \omega_i + \omega_j - \omega_k, \; i \neq k, j \neq k. \tag{5.22}$$

Depending on the individual frequencies, this beat signal may lie on or very close to one of the individual channels in frequency, resulting in significant crosstalk to that channel. In a multichannel system with W channels, this effect results in a large number $(W(W-1)^2)$ of interfering signals corresponding to i, j, k varying from 1 to W in (5.22). In a system with 3 channels, for example, 12 interfering terms are produced, as shown in Figure 5.32.

Interestingly, the effect of four-wave mixing depends on the phase relationship between the interacting signals. If all the interfering signals travel with the same group velocity, as would be the case if there were no dispersion, the effect is reinforced.

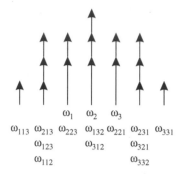

ω_1 ω_2 ω_3

ω_{113} ω_{213} ω_{223} ω_{132} ω_{221} ω_{231} ω_{331}

ω_{123} ω_{312} ω_{321}

ω_{112} ω_{332}

Figure 5.32   Four-wave mixing terms caused by the beating of three equally spaced channels at frequencies ω_1, ω_2, and ω_3.

On the other hand, with dispersion present, the different signals travel with different group velocities. Thus the different waves alternately overlap in and out of phase, and the net effect is to reduce the mixing efficiency. The velocity difference is greater when the channels are spaced farther apart (in systems with dispersion).

To quantify the power penalty due to four-wave mixing, we will use the results of the analysis from [SBW87, SNIA90, TCF+95, OSYZ95]. We start with (2.63) from Section 2.4.5, which is

$$P_{ijk} = \left(\frac{\omega_{ijk}\bar{n}d_{ijk}}{3cA_e}\right)^2 P_i P_j P_k L^2.$$

This equation assumes a link of length L without any loss and dispersion. Here P_i, P_j, and P_k denote the powers of the mixing waves and P_{ijk} the power of the resulting new wave, $\bar{n}$ is the nonlinear refractive index (3.0×10^{-8} μm^2/W), and d_{ijk} is the so-called degeneracy factor.

In a real system, both loss and dispersion are present. To take the loss into account, we replace L with the effective length L_e, which is given by (5.16) for a system of length L with amplifiers spaced l km apart. The presence of dispersion reduces the efficiency of the mixing, and we can model this by assuming a parameter η_{ijk}, which represents the efficiency of mixing of the three waves at frequencies ω_i, ω_j, and ω_k. Taking these two into account, the preceding equation can be modified to

$$P_{ijk} = \eta_{ijk}\left(\frac{\omega_{ijk}\bar{n}d_{ijk}}{3cA_e}\right)^2 P_i P_j P_k L_e^2.$$

For OOK signals, this represents the worst-case power at frequency ω_{ijk} assuming a 1 bit has been transmitted simultaneously on frequencies ω_i, ω_j, and ω_k.

The efficiency η_{ijk} goes down as the phase mismatch $\Delta\beta$ between the interfering signals increases. From [SBW87], we obtain the efficiency as

$$\eta_{ijk} = \frac{\alpha^2}{\alpha^2 + (\Delta\beta)^2}\left[1 + \frac{4e^{-\alpha l}\sin^2(\Delta\beta l/2)}{(1 - e^{-\alpha l})^2}\right].$$

Here, $\Delta\beta$ is the difference in propagation constants between the different waves, and D is the chromatic dispersion. Note that the efficiency has a component that varies periodically with the length as the interfering waves go in and out of phase. In our examples, we will assume the maximum value for this component. The phase mismatch can be calculated as

$$\Delta\beta = \beta_i + \beta_j - \beta_k - \beta_{ijk},$$

where β_r represents the propagation constant at wavelength λ_r.

Four-wave mixing manifests itself as intrachannel crosstalk. The total crosstalk power for a given channel ω_c is given as $\sum_{\omega_i+\omega_j-\omega_k=\omega_c} P_{ijk}$. Assume the amplifier gains are chosen to match the link loss so that the output power per channel is the same as the input power. The crosstalk penalty can therefore be calculated from (5.10).

Assume that the channels are equally spaced and transmitted with equal power, and the maximum allowable penalty due to FWM is 1 dB. Then if the transmitted power in each channel is P, the maximum FWM power in any channel must be $< \epsilon P$, where ϵ can be calculated to be 0.034 for a 1-dB penalty using (5.10). Since the generated FWM power increases with link length, this sets a limit on the transmit power per channel as a function of the link length. This limit is plotted in Figure 5.33 for both standard single-mode fiber (SMF) and dispersion-shifted fiber (DSF) for three cases: (a) 8 channels spaced 100 GHz apart, (b) 32 channels spaced 100 GHz apart, and (c) 32 channels spaced 50 GHz apart. For SMF the dispersion parameter is taken to be $D = 17$ ps/km-nm, and for DSF the dispersion zero is assumed to lie in the middle of the transmitted band of channels. The slope of the dispersion curve, $dD/d\lambda$, is taken to be 0.055 ps/km-nm^2. We leave it as an exercise (Problem 5.20) to compute the power limits in the case of nonzero dispersion fiber.

In Figure 5.33, first note that the limit is significantly worse in the case of dispersion-shifted fiber than it is for standard fiber. This is because the four-wave mixing efficiencies are much higher in dispersion-shifted fiber owing to the low value of the dispersion. Second, the power limit gets worse with an increasing number of channels, as can be seen by comparing the limits for 8-channel and 32-channel

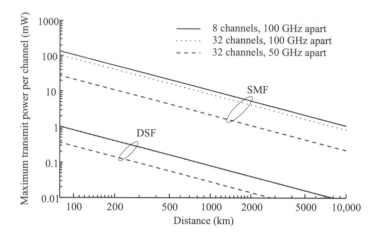

Figure 5.33 Limitation on the maximum transmit power per channel imposed by four-wave mixing for systems operating over standard single-mode fiber and dispersion-shifted fiber. The amplifiers are assumed to be spaced 80 km apart.

systems for the same 100 GHz spacing. This effect is due to the much larger number of four-wave mixing terms that are generated when the number of channels is increased. In the case of dispersion-shifted fiber, this decrease is imperceptible since, even though there are many more terms for the 32-channel case, the same 8 channels around the dispersion zero as in the 8-channel case contribute almost all the four-wave mixing power. The four-wave mixing power contribution from the other channels is small because there is much more dispersion at these wavelengths. Finally, the power limit decreases significantly if the channel spacing is reduced, as can be seen by comparing the curves for the two 32-channel systems with channel spacings of 100 GHz and 50 GHz. This decrease in the allowable transmit power arises because the four-wave mixing efficiency increases with a decrease in the channel spacing since the phase mismatch $\Delta\beta$ is reduced. (For SMF, though the efficiencies at both 50 GHz and 100 GHz are small, the efficiency at 50 GHz is much higher than at 100 GHz.)

Four-wave mixing is a severe problem in WDM systems using dispersion-shifted fiber (DSF) but does not usually pose a major problem in systems using standard fiber. In fact, it motivated the development of nonzero dispersion fiber (NDF)—see Section 5.7. In general, the following actions alleviate the penalty due to four-wave mixing:

1. Unequal channel spacing: The positions of the channels can be chosen carefully so that the beat terms do not overlap with the data channels inside the receiver bandwidth. This may be possible for a small number of channels in some cases, but needs careful computation of the exact channel positions.

2. Increased channel spacing: This increases the group velocity mismatch between channels. This has the drawback of increasing the overall system bandwidth, requiring the optical amplifiers to be flat over a wider bandwidth, and increases the penalty due to SRS.

3. Using higher wavelengths beyond 1560 nm with DSF: The idea behind this is that even with DSF, a significant amount of dispersion is present in this range, which reduces the effect of four-wave mixing. However, the problem is the lack of good amplifiers in this band. The gain of the current EDFAs drops off quite sharply beyond 1560 nm. Research is underway to extend the gain bandwidth of EDFAs so as to make long-distance transmission possible in this band.

4. As with other nonlinearities, reducing transmitter power and the amplifier spacing will decrease the penalty.

5. If the wavelengths can be demultiplexed and multiplexed in the middle of the transmission path, we can introduce different delays for each wavelength. This randomizes the phase relationship between the different wavelengths. Effectively, the FWM powers introduced before and after this point are summed instead of the electric fields being added in phase, resulting in a smaller FWM penalty.

5.8.4 Self-/Cross-Phase Modulation

As we saw in Section 2.4, SPM and CPM also arise out of the intensity dependence of the refractive index. Fluctuations in optical power of the signal causes changes in the phase of the signal. This induces additional chirp, which in turn, leads to higher dispersion penalties. In practice, SPM can be a significant consideration in designing systems at 10 Gb/s and higher, and leads to a restriction that the maximum power per channel should not exceed a few dBm. CPM does not usually pose a problem in WDM systems unless the channel spacings are extremely tight (a few tens of GHz).

5.8.5 Dispersion Management

As we have seen, dispersion plays a key role in reducing the effects of nonlinearities. However, dispersion by itself produces penalties due to pulse smearing, which leads to intersymbol interference. The important thing to note is that we can engineer systems

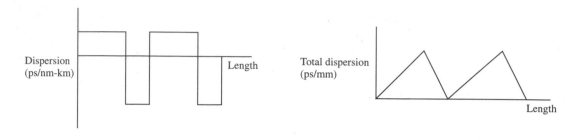

Figure 5.34   Dispersion management in a WDM link.

with zero total dispersion but with dispersion present at all points along the link. The dispersion map of such a system is shown in Figure 5.34. Between amplifier spans is standard single-mode fiber, but at each amplifier location, dispersion compensating fiber is introduced with a negative dispersion slope. This approach ensures that dispersion is present everywhere in the network, leading to reduced penalties due to nonlinearities, but the total dispersion is small so that we need not worry about dispersion-induced penalties. One problem with WDM systems is that since the dispersion varies for each channel, it may not be possible to compensate for the entire system using a common dispersion compensating fiber. An alternative is to provide the appropriate dispersion compensation for each channel separately at the receiver after the channels are demultiplexed.

5.9   Wavelength Stabilization

Luckily for us, it turns out that the wavelength drift due to temperature variations of some of the key components used in WDM systems is quite small. Typical multiplexers and demultiplexers made of silica/silicon have temperature coefficients of 0.01 nm/°C, whereas DFB lasers have a temperature coefficient of 0.1 nm/°C. Some of the other devices that we studied in Chapter 3 have even lower temperature coefficients.

The DFB laser source used in most systems is a key element that must be kept wavelength stabilized. In practice, it may be sufficient to maintain the temperature of the laser fairly constant to within ±0.1°C, which would stabilize the laser to within ±0.01 nm/°C. The laser comes packaged with a thermistor and a thermo-electric (TE) cooler. The temperature can be sensed by monitoring the resistance of the thermistor and can be kept constant by adjusting the drive current of the TE cooler. However, the laser wavelength can also change owing to aging effects over a long period.

Laser manufacturers usually specify this parameter, typically around ±0.1 nm. If this presents a problem, an external feedback loop may be required to stabilize the laser. A small portion of the laser output can be tapped off and sent to a frequency discriminating element, such as an optical filter, and its output can be monitored to establish the laser wavelength, which can then be controlled by adjusting the laser temperature.

Depending on the temperature range needed (typically −10 to 60°C for equipment in telco central offices), it may be necessary to temperature control the multiplexer/demultiplexer as well. For example, even if the multiplexer and demultiplexer are exactly aligned at, say, 25°C, the ambient temperature at the two ends of the link could be different by 70°C, assuming the given numbers. Assuming a temperature coefficient of 0.01 nm/°C, we would get a 0.7 nm difference between the center wavelengths of the multiplexer and demultiplexer, which is clearly intolerable if the interchannel spacing is only 0.8 nm (100 GHz). One problem with temperature control is that it reduces the reliability of the overall component because the TE cooler is often the least reliable component.

An additional factor to be considered is the dependence of laser wavelength on its drive current, typically between 100 MHz/mA and 1 GHz/mA. A laser is typically operated in one of two modes: constant output power or constant drive current, and the drive circuitry incorporates feedback to maintain these parameters at constant values. Keeping the drive current constant ensures that the laser wavelength does not shift because of current changes. However, as the laser ages, it will require more drive current to produce the same output power, so the output power may decrease with time. On the other hand, keeping the power constant may require the drive current to be increased as the laser ages, inducing a small wavelength shift. With typical channel spacings of 100 GHz or thereabouts, this is not a problem, but with tighter channel spacings, it may be desirable to operate the laser in constant current mode and tolerate the penalty (if any) due to the reduced output power.

5.9.1   Dynamic Range Issues in Networks

One of the problems arising specifically in WDM networks as opposed to point-to-point links is that different lightpaths in the network will have different power levels and signal-to-noise ratios. This can make system design particularly difficult. A common approach used to solve this problem is to equalize the powers of each channel at each node individually. Thus at each node, the powers in all the channels are set to a common value. This ensures that all lightpaths reach their receivers with the same power, regardless of where they originated from or their path through the network.

5.10 Overall Design Considerations

We have seen that there is an interplay of many different effects that influence the system design parameters. We will summarize some of these effects in this section. In addition, two key issues in this regard, (a) the tradeoff between higher bit rates per channel versus more channels, and (b) whether to use bidirectional or unidirectional systems, will be discussed in Chapter 13.

5.10.1 Fiber Type

Among the many issues facing system designers is what type of fiber should be deployed in new installations. This very much depends on the type of system that is going to be deployed. For single-channel systems operating at very high bit rates (10 Gb/s and above) over long distances, dispersion-shifted fiber (DSF) is the best choice. However, DSF makes it much harder to use WDM for upgrading the link capacity in the future, primarily due to four-wave mixing. For WDM systems, the choice of fiber type depends on the distance and bit rate per channel. DSF is clearly a bad choice. If the system is not chromatic dispersion limited, then standard single-mode fiber (SMF) is the best choice, because such a system is least susceptible to degradation from nonlinearities. As the distance and bit rate increase in future upgrades, the system will eventually become chromatic dispersion limited (for example, over 600 km at 2.5 Gb/s), and dispersion compensation must be incorporated into the system. For WDM systems operating at high bit rates over long distances, nonzero dispersion fiber (NDF) provides a good alternative to using standard single-mode fiber with dispersion compensation.

5.10.2 Transmit Power and Amplifier Spacing

The upper limit on the transmitted power per channel P is determined by the saturation power of the optical amplifiers, the effect of nonlinearities, and safety considerations. From a cost point of view, we would like to maximize the distance l between amplifier stages, so as to minimize the number of amplifiers. The transmitted power per channel, P, and the total link length L, along with the amplifier noise figure and receiver sensitivity, determines the maximum value of l possible. In addition, as l increases, the penalty due to nonlinearities also increases, which by itself may play a role in limiting the value of l.

5.10.3 Interchannel Spacing and Number of Wavelengths

Another design choice is the interchannel spacing. On the one hand, we would like to make the spacing as large as possible, since it makes it easier to multiplex and demultiplex the channels and relaxes the requirements on component wavelength stability. Larger interchannel spacing also reduces the four-wave mixing penalty if that is an issue (for example, in systems with dispersion-shifted fiber). It also allows future upgrades to higher bit rates per channel, which may not be feasible with very tight channel spacings. For example, today's systems operate with 100 GHz channel spacing with bit rates per channel up to 10 Gb/s. If the channel spacing is reduced to 50 GHz, it becomes much harder to operate the channels at 10 Gb/s.

On the other hand, we would like to have as many channels as possible within the limited amplifier gain bandwidth, which argues for having a channel spacing as tight as possible. For a given number of channels, it is easier to flatten the amplifier gain profile over a smaller total bandwidth. Moreover, the smaller the total system bandwidth, the lesser the penalty due to stimulated Raman scattering (although this is not a limiting factor unless the number of channels is fairly large).

Other factors also limit the number of wavelengths that can be supported in the system. The total amplifier output power that can be obtained is limited typically to 17–20 dBm, and this power must be shared among all the channels in the system. So as the number of wavelengths increases, the power per channel decreases, and this limits the total system span. Another limiting factor is the stability and wavelength selectivity of the multiplexers and demultiplexers. Taking all this into consideration, 32–40 channel systems with 100 GHz spacings appear to be quite feasible in the short term, and larger numbers of channels can be obtained by reducing the channel spacing and improving the stability and selectivity of the wavelength multiplexers and demultiplexers.

5.10.4   All-Optical Networks

All-optical networks consist of optical fiber links between nodes with all-optical switching and routing of signals at the nodes, without electronic regeneration. The various aspects of system design that we studied in this chapter apply to point-to-point links as well as all-optical networks, and we have attempted to consider several factors that affect networks more than point-to-point links. Designing networks is significantly harder than designing point-to-point links for the following reasons:

- The network is more susceptible to crosstalk, which is accumulated at each node along the path.

- Misalignment of multiplexers and demultiplexers along the path is more of a problem in networks than in links.

- Owing to bandwidth narrowing of cascaded multiplexers and demultiplexers, the requirements on laser wavelength stability and accuracy are much higher than in point-to-point links.

- The system designer must deal with the variation of signal powers and signal-to-noise ratios among different lightpaths traveling through different numbers of nodes and having different path lengths. This may require equalizing the powers of different lightpaths at each node.

- Rapid dynamic equalization of the amplifier gains will be needed to compensate for fluctuations in optical power as lightpaths are taken down or set up, or in the event of failures.

- Loss, dispersion, and nonlinearities do not get reset at each node.

5.10.5 Wavelength Planning

The International Telecommunications Union (ITU) has been active in trying to standardize a set of wavelengths for use in WDM networks. This is necessary to ensure eventual interoperability between systems from different vendors (although this is very far away). An important reason for setting these standards is to allow component vendors to manufacture to a fixed standard, which allows volume cost reductions, as opposed to producing custom designs for different system vendors.

The first decision to be made is whether to standardize channels at equal wavelength spacing or at equal frequency spacing. At $\lambda = 1550$ nm, $c = 3 \times 10^8$ m/s, a 1 nm wavelength spacing corresponds to approximately 120 GHz of frequency spacing. Equal frequency spacing results in somewhat unequal wavelength spacing. Certain components used in the network, such as AWGs and Mach-Zehnder filters naturally accept channels at equal frequency spacings, whereas other components, including other forms of gratings, accept channels more naturally at equal wavelength spacings. There appears to be no major technical reason to favor one or the other. The ITU has picked equal frequency spacing for their standard. The channels are to be placed in a 100 GHz grid (0.8 nm wavelength spacing) with a nominal center frequency of 193.1 THz (1552.52 nm) in the middle of the 1.55 μm fiber and EDFA passband, as shown in Figure 5.35. The usable EDFA band is from 1530 nm to 1564 nm, which allows us to place a maximum of 43 channels in the 100 GHz grid.

The choice of the 100 GHz frequency spacing is based on what is feasible with today's technology in terms of mux/demux resolutions, frequency stability of lasers and mux/demuxes, and so on. As the technology improves, and systems with more channels become practical, the grid spacing will have to be reduced. Moreover, in systems that must operate over dispersion-shifted fiber, it may be desirable to have

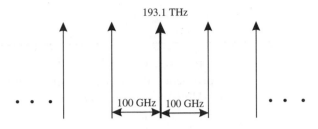

Figure 5.35   Wavelength grid selected by the ITU.

Table 5.3   Frequency deviation as a function of channel spacing specified by the ITU, from [ITU96b].

Channel Spacing (GHz)	Deviation (+ GHz)
100	TBD
200	40
300	60
400	80
500	100
600	120
$\Delta f > 600$	$\Delta f/6$

unequal channel spacings to alleviate the effects of four-wave mixing, which may also require a finer grid spacing.

That being said, a much more difficult decision is to pick a standard set of wavelengths for use in 4-, 8-, 16-, and 32-wavelength systems to ensure interoperability. This is because different manufacturers have different optimized channel configurations and different upgrade plans to go from a system with a small number of channels to a system with a larger number of channels. As of this writing, there is no agreement yet on these specific sets of wavelengths.

It is not enough to specify the nominal center frequencies of the channels alone. A maximum deviation must also be specified because of manufacturing tolerances and aging over the system's lifetime. The deviation should not be too large; otherwise, we would get significant penalties due to crosstalk, additional loss, chirp, and the like. The deviation is a function of the interchannel spacing. Table 5.3 lists the deviation values chosen by the ITU.

5.10.6 Transparency

Among the advantages touted for WDM systems is the fact that they are transparent to bit rate, protocol, and modulation formats. It is true to a large extent that a wavelength can carry arbitrary data protocols. Providing transparency to bit rate and modulation formats is much more difficult. For instance, analog transmission requires much higher signal-to-noise ratios and linearity in the system than digital transmission, and is much more susceptible to impairments. A WDM system can be designed to operate at a maximum bit rate per channel and can support all bit rates below that maximum. We cannot assume that the system is transparent to increases in the maximum bit rate. The maximum bit rate affects the choice of amplifier spacings, filter bandwidths, and dispersion management, among other parameters. Thus the system must be designed up front to support the maximum possible bit rate.

Summary

This chapter was devoted to studying the effect of various impairments on the design of the new generation of WDM and high-speed TDM transmission systems and networks. Although impairments due to amplifier cascades, dispersion, nonlinearities, and crosstalk may not be significant in lower-capacity systems, they play significant roles in the new generation of systems, particularly in networks, as opposed to point-to-point links. We learned how to compute the penalty due to each impairment and budget for the penalty in the overall system design. We also studied how to reduce the penalty due to each impairment. Transmission system design requires careful attention to each impairment because requirements on penalties usually translate into specifications on the components that the system is built out of, which in turn, translate to system cost.

Further Reading

We recommend the recent book by Kaminow and Koch [KK97] for an in-depth coverage of the advanced aspects of lightwave system design. For an authoritative treatment of EDFAs, see [Des94]. Gain equalization of amplifiers is an important problem, and several approaches have been proposed [Des94]. Amplifier cascades are discussed in several papers. See, for example, [Ols89, RL93]. Amplifier power transients are a relatively new phenomenon and are just beginning to be understood [Zys96].

Chromatic dispersion and modal dispersion are treated at length in the afore-mentioned books. The different types of single-mode fiber have been standard-ized; see [ITU93a, ITU93b, ITU96a]. Polarization-mode dispersion is studied in [PTCF91, CDdM90, BA94, ZO94].

Crosstalk is analyzed extensively in several papers. Intrachannel crosstalk is considered in [ZCC+96, GEE94, TOT96]. Interchannel crosstalk is analyzed in [ZCC+96, HH90]. Dilation in switches is discussed in [Jac96, PN87].

Good surveys of fiber nonlinearities appear in [Chr90, Agr95, Buc95, SNIA90]. See also [TCF+95, FTC95, SBW87, Chr84, OSYZ95].

The standards bodies have given a lot of thought in defining the system param-eters for WDM systems. The 100 GHz wavelength grid is specified in [ITU96b]. It is instructive to read this and other related standards [ITU96c, ITU96d, Bel96a, Bel95, Bel96b], which provide values for most of the system parameters used in this chapter.

Problems

5.1 In an experiment designed to measure the attenuation coefficient α of optical fiber, the output power from an optical source is coupled onto a length of the fiber and measured at the other end. If a 10-km long spool of fiber is used, the received optical power is -20 dBm. Under identical conditions but with a 20-km long spool of fiber (instead of the 10-km long spool), the received optical power is -23 dBm. What is the value of α (in dB/km)? If the source–fiber coupling loss is 3 dB, the fiber–detector coupling loss is 1 dB, and there are no other losses, what is the output power of the source (expressed in mW)?

5.2 The following problems relate to simple link designs. Assume that the bit rate on the link is 1 Gb/s, the dispersion at 1.55 μm is 17 ps/km-nm, and the attenuation is 0.25 dB/km, and at 1.3 μm, the dispersion is 0 and the attenuation is 0.5 dB/km. (Neglect all losses except the attenuation loss in the fiber.)

(a) You have a transmitter that operates at a wavelength of 1.55 μm, has a spectral width of 1 nm, and an output power of 0.5 mW. The receiver requires -30 dBm of input power in order to achieve the desired bit error rate. What is the length of the longest link that you can build?

(b) You have another transmitter that operates at a wavelength of 1.3 μm, has a spectral width of 2 nm, and an output power of 1 mW. Assume the same receiver as before. What is the length of the longest link that you can build?

(c) You have the same 1.3 μm transmitter as before, and you must achieve an SNR of 30 dB using an APD receiver with a responsivity of 8 A/W, a gain of

10, an excess noise factor of 5 dB, negligible dark current, a load resistance of 50 Ω, and an amplifier noise figure of 3 dB. Assume that a receiver bandwidth of $B/2$ Hz is sufficient to support a bit rate of B b/s. What is the length of the longest link you can build?

(d) Using the same 1.3 μm transmitter as before, you must achieve an SNR of 20 dB using a *pin* receiver with a responsivity of 0.8 A/W, a load resistance of 300 Ω, and an amplifier noise figure of 5 dB. Assume that a receiver bandwidth of $B/2$ Hz is sufficient to support a bit rate of B b/s. What is the length of the longest link you can build?

5.3 Compute the dispersion-limited transmission distance for links with standard single-mode fiber at 1550 nm as a function of the bit rate (100 Mb/s, 1 Gb/s, and 10 Gb/s) for the following transmitters: (a) a Fabry-Perot laser with spectral width of 10 nm, (b) a directly modulated DFB laser with a spectral width of 0.1 nm, and (c) an externally modulated DFB laser with a spectral width of 0.01 nm. Assume that the modulation bandwidth equals the bit rate and the dispersion penalty is 2 dB.

5.4 Repeat Problem 5.3 for nonzero dispersion fiber (NDF) assuming a dispersion parameter of 5 ps/nm-km.

5.5 Derive equation (5.4).

5.6 Show that the extinction ratio penalty in amplified systems limited by signal-spontaneous beat noise and spontaneous-spontaneous beat noise is

$$PP = -10 \log \left(\frac{r-1}{r+1} \frac{\sqrt{r+1}}{\sqrt{r}+1} \right).$$

Assume that other noise terms are negligible.

5.7 Consider the amplifier chain discussed in Section 5.5.3. Using equations (5.6) and (5.7), compute the steady-state values of $\overline{P}_{\text{out}}$ and $\overline{G}$ in a long chain of amplifiers. Assume $G_{\text{max}} = 35$ dB, $l = 120$ km, $\alpha = 0.25$ dB/km, $n_{\text{sp}} = 2$, $P^{\text{sat}} = 10$ mW, and $B_o = 50$ GHz. How do these values compare against the unsaturated gain G_{max} and the output saturation power of the amplifier $P_{\text{out}}^{\text{sat}}$? Plot the evolution of the signal power and optical signal-to-noise ratio as a function of distance along the link.

5.8 Derive equations (5.9), (5.10), (5.11), and (5.12) when there are N interfering signals rather than just one.

5.9 Consider the WDM link shown in Figure 5.1. Each multiplexer and demultiplexer introduces crosstalk from adjacent channels that is C dB below the desired channel.

(a) Compute the crosstalk at the output when N such stages are cascaded.

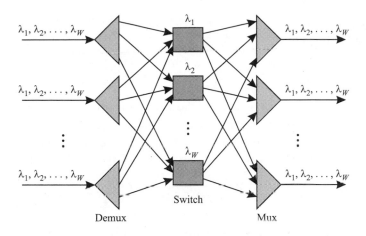

Figure 5.36 A node in a WDM network for Problem 5.11.

(b) What must C be so that the overall crosstalk penalty after five stages is less than 1 dB?

5.10 Consider a WDM system with W channels, each with average power P and extinction ratio, $P_1/P_0 = r$. Derive the interchannel crosstalk power penalty (5.11) for this system compared to a system with ideal extinction and no crosstalk. What should the crosstalk level be for a maximum 1-dB penalty if the extinction ratio is 10 dB?

5.11 Consider the WDM network node shown in Figure 5.36. Assume the node has two inputs and two outputs. The multiplexers/demultiplexers are ideal (no crosstalk) but each switch has a crosstalk level C dB below the desired channel. Assume that in the worst case, crosstalk in each stage adds coherently to the signal.
   (a) Compute the crosstalk level after N nodes.
   (b) What must C be so that the overall crosstalk penalty after five nodes is less than 1 dB?

5.12 Consider a node in a WDM network shown in Figure 5.36. Assume the node has two inputs and two outputs. The mux/demuxes have adjacent channel crosstalk suppressions of -25 dB, and crosstalk from other channels is negligible. The switches have a crosstalk specification of -40 dB. How many nodes can be cascaded in a network without incurring more than a 1-dB penalty due to crosstalk? Consider only intrachannel crosstalk from the switches and the multiplexers/demultiplexers.

5.13 Consider a WDM system with N nodes, each node being the one shown in Figure 5.36. The center wavelength λ_c' for each channel in a mux/demux has an accuracy of $\pm\Delta\lambda$ nm around the nominal center wavelength λ_c. Assume a Gaussian passband shape for each channel in a mux, that is, the ratio of output power to input power, called the transmittance, is given by

$$T_R(\lambda) = e^{-\frac{(\lambda - \lambda_c')^2}{2\sigma^2}},$$

where σ is a measure of the channel bandwidth and λ_c' is the center wavelength. This passband shape is typical for an arrayed waveguide grating.

    (a) Plot the worst-case and best-case peak transmittance in dB as a function of the number of nodes N for $\sigma = 0.2$ nm, $\Delta\lambda = 0.05$ nm. Assume that the laser is centered exactly at λ_c.

    (b) What should $\Delta\lambda$ be if we must have a worst-case transmittance of 3 dB after 10 nodes?

5.14   Consider a system with the same parameters as in Problem 5.13. Suppose the WDM channels are spaced 0.8 nm apart. Consider only crosstalk from the two adjacent channels. Compute the interchannel crosstalk power relative to the signal power in dB, as a function of N, assuming all channels are at equal power and exactly centered. Compute the crosstalk also for the case where the desired channel is exactly centered at λ_i, but the adjacent channels are centered at $\lambda_{i-1} + \Delta\lambda$ and $\lambda_{i+1} - \Delta\lambda$.

5.15   Consider the simple add/drop element shown in Figure 3.11(b). Suppose we use another circulator instead of the coupler shown in the figure to add the wavelength. This eliminates the loss due to the coupler. Let the input power on the wavelength to be dropped be -30 dBm and the transmitted power on the added wavelength be 0 dBm. Suppose the grating has a reflectivity of 99%. Compute the intrachannel crosstalk power arising from (a) leakage of the added wavelength into the dropped wavelength, and (b) leakage of the dropped wavelength into the added wavelength. Assume that each circulator has a loss of 1 dB. Will the element work?

5.16   Why is equation (5.16) an approximation? Derive a precise form of this equation.

5.17   Neglecting the depletion of the pump wave, solve (5.17) and (5.18) to obtain the evolution of the SBS pump and Stokes waves.

5.18   Compute the SBS threshold power for the following systems: (a) a single-channel system using a Fabry-Perot laser with 10 lines, each line having a modulated line width of 1 GHz, (b) a multichannel system with a DFB laser having a modulated line width of 1 GHz, (c) same as (b) except that the line width is 10 GHz.

5.19   You are required to design a four-wavelength transmission system operating over dispersion-shifted fiber. The four wavelengths are to be placed in a band from 193.1 THz to 194.1 THz. The possible slots are spaced 100 GHz apart in this band. Pick the four wavelengths carefully so that no four-wave mixing component falls on any of the chosen wavelengths.

5.20   Compute and plot the four-wave mixing limit on the transmit power per channel for a WDM system operating over nonzero dispersion fiber. Assume that the channels are equally spaced and transmitted with equal power, and the maximum allowable penalty due to FWM is 1 dB. For the fiber, assume the dispersion parameter $D = 3$ ps/km-nm in the middle of the transmitted band of channels, and the slope of the dispersion curve is $dD/d\lambda = 0.055$ ps/km-nm^2. Consider the same three cases as in Figure 5.33: (a) 8 channels spaced 100 GHz apart, (b) 32 channels spaced 100 GHz apart, and (c) 32 channels spaced 50 GHz apart.

5.21   Why do second-order nonlinearities typically not affect a lightwave system?

━━ References

[Agr92]   G. P. Agrawal. *Fiber-Optic Communication Systems*. John Wiley, New York, 1992.

[Agr95]   G. P. Agrawal. *Nonlinear Fiber Optics, 2nd edition*. Academic Press, San Diego, CA, 1995.

[BA94]   F. Bruyère and O. Audouin. Assessment of system penalties induced by polarization mode dispersion in a 5 Gb/s optically amplified transoceanic link. *IEEE Photon. Tech. Lett.*, 6(3):443–445, March 1994.

[Bel95]   Bellcore. *SONET transport systems: Common generic criteria*, 1995. GR-253-CORE.

[Bel96a]   Bellcore. *Generic criteria for SONET point-to-point wavelength division multiplexed systems in the 1550-nm region*, July 1996. GR-2918-CORE, Issue 1.

[Bel96b]   Bellcore. *SONET OC-192 transport system generic criteria*, Aug. 1996. GR-1377-CORE, Issue 3.

[Buc95]   J. A. Buck. *Fundamentals of Optical Fibers*. John Wiley, New York, 1995.

[CDdM90]   F. Curti, B. Daino, G. de Marchis, and F. Matera. Statistical treatment of the evolution of the principal states of polarization in single-mode fibers. *IEEE/OSA Journal on Lightwave Technology*, 8(8):1162–1166, Aug. 1990.

[Chr84]   A. R. Chraplyvy. Optical power limits in multichannel wavelength-division-multiplexed systems due to stimulated Raman scattering. *Electronics Letters*, 20:58, 1984.

[Chr90]   A. R. Chraplyvy. Limitations on lightwave communications imposed by optical-fiber nonlinearities. *IEEE/OSA Journal on Lightwave Technology*, 8(10):1548–1557, Oct. 1990.

[Des94]   E. Desurvire. *Erbium-Doped Fiber Amplifiers*. John Wiley, New York, 1994.

[FTC95]   F. Forghieri, R. W. Tkach, and A. R. Chraplyvy. WDM systems with unequally spaced channels. *IEEE/OSA Journal on Lightwave Technology*, 13(5):889–897, May 1995.

[FTCV96] F. Forghieri, R. W. Tkach, A. R. Chraplyvy, and A. M. Vengsarkar. Dispersion compensating fiber: Is there merit in the figure of merit? In *OFC'96 Technical Digest*, pages 255–257, 1996.

[GEE94]   E. L. Goldstein, L. Eskildsen, and A. F. Elrefaie. Performance implications of component crosstalk in transparent lightwave networks. *IEEE Photon. Tech. Lett.*, 6(5):657–670, May 1994.

[HH90]   P. A. Humblet and W. M. Hamdy. Crosstalk analysis and filter optimization of single- and double-cavity Fabry-Perot filters. *IEEE Journal of Selected Areas in Communications*, 8(6):1095–1107, Aug. 1990.

[ITU93a] ITU-T. *Recommendation G.652: Characteristics of a single-mode optical fiber cable*, 1993.

[ITU93b] ITU-T. *Recommendation G.653: Characteristics of a dispersion-shifted single-mode optical fiber cable*, 1993.

[ITU96a] ITU-T. *Recommendation G.655: Characteristics of a nonzero-dispersion shifted single-mode optical fiber cable*, 1996.

[ITU96b] ITU-T SG15/WP 4. *Draft Rec. G.mcs: Optical interfaces for multichannel systems with optical amplifiers*, June 1996.

[ITU96c] ITU-T SG15/WP 4. *Draft Rec. G.scs: Optical interfaces for single-channel SDH systems with optical amplifiers and STM-64 systems*, June 1996.

[ITU96d] ITU-T SG15/WP 4. *Rec. G.681: Functional characteristics of interoffice and long-haul line systems using optical amplifiers, including optical multiplexing*, 1996.

[Jac96]   J. L. Jackel et al. Acousto-optic tunable filters (AOTFs) for multiwavelength optical cross-connects: Crosstalk considerations. *IEEE/OSA JLT/JSAC Special Issue on Multiwavelength Optical Technology and Networks*, 14(6):1056–1066, June 1996.

[KK97]   I. P. Kaminow and T. L. Koch, editors. *Optical Fiber Telecommunications III*. Academic Press, San Diego, CA, 1997.

[Lam97]   R. I. Laming et al. Fiber gratings for dispersion compensation. In *OFC'97 Technical Digest*, pages 234–235, 1997.

[Ols89]   N. A. Olsson. Lightwave systems with optical amplifiers. *IEEE/OSA Journal on Lightwave Technology*, 7(7):1071–1082, July 1989.

[OSYZ95] M. J. O'Mahony, D. Simeonidou, A. Yu, and J. Zhou. The design of a European optical network. *IEEE/OSA Journal on Lightwave Technology*, 13(5):817–828, May 1995.

[PN87] K. Padmanabhan and A. N. Netravali. Dilated networks for photonic switching. *IEEE Transactions on Communications*, 35:1357–1365, 1987.

[PTCF91] C. D. Poole, R. W. Tkach, A. R. Chraplyvy, and D. A. Fishman. Fading in lightwave systems due to polarization-mode dispersion. *IEEE Photon. Tech. Lett.*, 3(1):68–70, Jan. 1991.

[RL93] R. Ramaswami and K. Liu. Analysis of effective power budget in optical bus and star networks using Erbium-doped fiber amplifiers. *IEEE/OSA Journal on Lightwave Technology*, 11(11):1863–1871, Nov. 1993.

[SBW87] N. Shibata, R. P. Braun, and R. G. Waarts. Phase-mismatch dependence of efficiency of wave generation through four-wave mixing in a single-mode optical fiber. *IEEE Journal of Quantum Electronics*, 23:1205–1210, 1987.

[Smi72] R. G. Smith. Optical power handling capacity of low loss optical fibers as determined by stimulated Raman and Brillouin scattering. *Applied Optics*, 11(11):2489–2160, Nov. 1972.

[SNIA90] N. Shibata, K. Nosu, K. Iwashita, and Y. Azuma. Transmission limitations due to fiber nonlinearities in optical FDM systems. *IEEE Journal of Selected Areas in Communications*, 8(6):1068–1077, Aug. 1990.

[TCF+95] R. W. Tkach, A. R. Chraplyvy, F. Forghieri, A. H. Gnauck, and R. M. Derosier. Four-photon mixing and high-speed WDM systems. *IEEE/OSA Journal on Lightwave Technology*, 13(5):841–849, May 1995.

[TOT96] H. Takahashi, K. Oda, and H. Toba. Impact of crosstalk in an arrayed-waveguide multiplexer on $n \times n$ optical interconnection. *IEEE/OSA JLT/JSAC Special Issue on Multiwavelength Optical Technology and Networks*, 14(6):1097–1105, June 1996.

[ZCC+96] J. Zhou, R. Cadeddu, E. Casaccia, C. Cavazzoni, and M. J. O'Mahony. Crosstalk in multiwavelength optical cross-connect networks. *IEEE/OSA JLT/JSAC Special Issue on Multiwavelength Optical Technology and Networks*, 14(6):1423–1435, June 1996.

[ZO94] J. Zhou and M. J. O'Mahony. Optical transmission system penalties due to fiber polarization mode dispersion. *IEEE Photon. Tech. Lett.*, 6(10):1265–1267, Oct. 1994.

[Zys96] J. L. Zyskind et al. Fast power transients in optically amplified multiwavelength optical networks. In *OFC'96 Technical Digest*, 1996. Postdeadline paper PD31.

Networks

chapter 6

First-Generation Optical Networks

THIS CHAPTER DESCRIBES several types of first-generation optical networks. All of them use fiber as a transmission medium, but do all switching, processing, and routing electronically. All of them are single-wavelength networks as well. We will study the architecture and the link and physical layers of these networks.

First-generation optical networks are widely deployed today. We will study optical networks that are part of the public telecommunications infrastructure. We will also study a variety of networks used to interconnect computers to their peripherals, as well as local-area and metropolitan-area networks.

An interesting feature of second-generation optical networks, which we will be studying in future chapters, is that in many cases they carry traffic belonging to first-generation optical networks and protocols. Each of these protocols will require specific functions to be provided by second-generation optical networks. The fact that all these different protocols exist, and are in fact quite widespread, motivates the need for transparent second-generation networks.

6.1 SONET/SDH

SONET (Synchronous Optical Network) is the current transmission and multiplexing standard for high-speed signals within the carrier infrastructure in North America. A closely related standard, SDH (Synchronous Digital Hierarchy), has been adopted in Europe and Japan.

In order to understand the factors underlying the evolution and standardization of SONET and SDH, we need to look back in time and understand how multiplexing

Table 6.1   Transmission rates for PDH, adapted from [SS96].

Level	North America	Europe	Japan
0	0.064 Mb/s	0.064 Mb/s	0.064 Mb/s
1	1.544 Mb/s	2.048 Mb/s	1.544 Mb/s
2	6.312 Mb/s	8.448 Mb/s	6.312 Mb/s
3	44.736 Mb/s	34.368 Mb/s	32.064 Mb/s
4	139.264 Mb/s	139.264 Mb/s	97.728 Mb/s

was done in the public network. Prior to SONET and SDH, the existing infrastructure was based on the *plesiochronous digital hierarchy* (PDH) dating back to the mid-1960s. (North American operators refer to PDH as the asynchronous digital hierarchy.) At that time the primary focus was on multiplexing digital voice circuits. An analog voice circuit with a bandwidth of 4 kHz could be sampled at 8 kHz, and quantized at 8 bits per sample, leading to a bit rate of 64 kb/s for a digital voice circuit. This became the widely accepted standard. Higher-speed streams were defined as multiples of this basic 64 kb/s stream. Different sets of standards emerged in different parts of the world for these higher-speed streams, as shown in Table 6.1. In North America, the 64 kb/s signal is called DS0 (digital signal-0), the 1.544 Mb/s signal is DS1, the 44.736 Mb/s is DS3, and so on. In Europe, the hierarchy is labeled E1, E2, E3, and so on. These rates are widely prevalent today in carrier networks and are widely offered as leased-line services by carriers to customers, more often than not to carry data rather than voice traffic.

PDH suffered from several problems, which led carriers and vendors alike to seek a new transmission and multiplexing standard in the late 1980s.

1. **Multiplexing:** In PDH it is very difficult to pick out a low bit rate stream, say, at 2 Mb/s, from a high-speed stream passing through, say, at 140 Mb/s, without significant processing of the high-speed signal. This is because of the way these low-speed streams are multiplexed. Notice that the bit rates in the plesiochronous hierarchy are not integral multiples of the basic 64 kb/s rate. For instance, a DS1 signal is designed to carry 24 64 kb/s signals, but its bit rate (1.544 Mb/s) is slightly higher than 24 × 64 kb/s. This is because the clocks of the lower-speed streams are not perfectly *synchronized* and extra bits may need to be stuffed in the multiplexed stream to accommodate delays between the different clocks. This makes PDH multiplexers and demultiplexers significantly complicated. SONET/SDH defines explicit multiplexing methods that make it easy to extract low-speed streams from a high-speed stream, as will be seen in Section 6.1.1. All the clocks in the network are perfectly synchronized to a single

master clock, and as a consequence, the rates defined in SONET/SDH are integral multiples of the basic rate. This makes the design of SONET multiplexers and demultiplexers much easier than their PDH equivalents.

2. **Management:** The SONET and SDH standards incorporate extensive management information for monitoring the performance of traffic, unlike PDH.

3. **Interoperability:** Although PDH defined multiplexing methods, it did not define a standard format on the transmission link. Thus different vendors used different line coding, optical interfaces, and so forth to optimize their products, which made it very difficult to connect one vendor's equipment to another's via a transmission link. SONET and SDH avoid this problem by defining standard optical interfaces that enable interoperability between equipment from different vendors on the link. Unfortunately, there are still certain aspects of SONET and SDH that were not standardized, such as the data communication channel for the purposes of network management, which makes it difficult to interconnect multivendor equipment.

4. **Networking:** The SONET and SDH standards have evolved to incorporate specific network topologies and specific optical protection schemes on these topologies to provide high-availability services. As a consequence, the service restoration time after a failure with SONET and SDH is much smaller—less than 60 ms—than the restoration time in PDH networks, which typically took several seconds to minutes.

6.1.1 Multiplexing

A PDH multiplexer simply interleaves the *bits* from the individual lower-speed streams into the higher-speed aggregate stream. We saw earlier that because the clocks of the lower-speed streams may not be synchronized, the design of PDH multiplexers and demultiplexers is quite complicated.

SONET and SDH employ a much more sophisticated multiplexing scheme, which can, however, be easily implemented in today's very large-scale integrated (VLSI) circuits, as shown in Figure 6.1. Although SONET and SDH are basically similar, the terms used in SONET and SDH are different, and we will use the SONET version in what follows. A lower-speed PDH stream is mapped into a *synchronous payload envelope,* or SPE (called *synchronous container* in SDH). A set of overhead bytes called the *path overhead* is added to this SPE. The path overhead remains unchanged until the SPE arrives at its destination and the PDH stream is extracted from it. This overhead allows a carrier to monitor the PDH stream end-to-end and measure important parameters such as the bit error rate—something that was quite difficult to do in a PDH system. The SPE container along with its path overhead is called

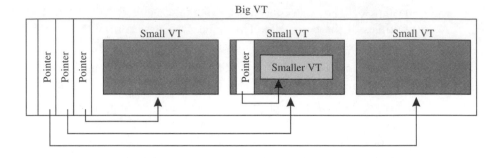

Figure 6.1   The hierarchical multiplexing structure employed in SONET and SDH.

a *virtual tributary* (VT) in SONET and *virtual container* (VC) in SDH. The term *virtual* applies because the overhead and SPE container may be placed at different points within a *frame*. A frame is 125 μs in duration. This time is set by the 8 kHz sampling rate of a voice circuit.

Many small VTs can be multiplexed into a larger VT. This hierarchical multiplexing structure is illustrated in Figure 6.1. Each VT consists of an overhead followed by a payload. The overhead includes a pointer to each smaller VT that is multiplexed into the larger VT in its payload portion. The small VT may in turn contain a number of even smaller VTs, with pointers to each of them. This structure makes it particularly easy to extract a low-speed stream from a higher-speed stream.

VTs and VCs have been defined in the standards to carry a variety of payloads. The detailed mapping of PDH as well as *asynchronous transfer mode* (ATM) streams into VTs is shown in Figure 6.2. (We will study ATM in Section 6.3.2.) Each VT is designed to have sufficient bandwidth to carry its payload. In SONET, VTs have been defined in four sizes: VT1.5, VT2, VT3, and VT6. These VTs are designed to carry 1.5, 2, 3, and 6 Mb/s PDH streams, as shown in Figure 6.2. At the next level in the hierarchy, a VT group consists of either four VT1.5s, three VT2s, two VT3s, or a single VT6. Seven such VT groups are *byte* interleaved to create a *basic* SONET SPE. For SONET, the basic rate is 51.84 Mb/s, called the synchronous transport signal level-1 (STS-1). Higher-rate signals (STS-N) are obtained by interleaving the bytes from N STS-1s, all of whose frames are aligned. Sometimes it is necessary to map higher-speed non-SONET signals, such as a 150 Mb/s ATM signal, into an SPE. For this purpose, an STS-Nc signal with a *locked* payload is also defined in the standards. The locked payload implies that this signal cannot be demultiplexed into lower-speed streams. For example, a 150 Mb/s ATM signal is mapped into an STS-3c signal. Mappings have been defined in the standards for a variety of signals, including ATM and FDDI (fiber distributed data interface).

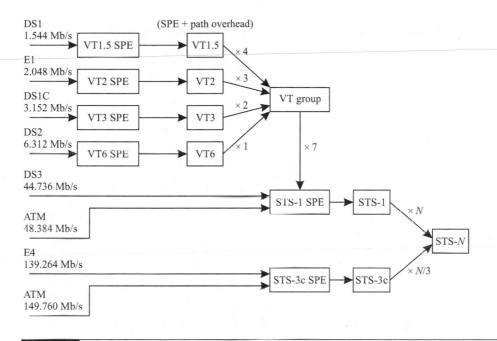

Figure 6.2   The mapping of lower-speed PDH streams into virtual tributaries in SONET.

The currently defined SONET and SDH rates are shown in Table 6.2. Note that an STS signal is an electrical signal and in many cases (particularly at the higher speeds) may never be surfaced out of the SONET equipment. The interface to other equipment is usually optical and is essentially a scrambled version of the STS signal in optical form. Scrambling is used to prevent long runs of 0s or 1s in the data stream. (See Section 4.1.1 for a more detailed explanation of scrambling.) The optical interface corresponding to the STS-3 rate is called OC-3 (optical carrier-3), and similar optical interfaces have been defined for OC-12, OC-48, and OC-192, corresponding to the STS-12, STS-48, and STS-192 signals.

For SDH, the basic rate is 155 Mb/s, and is called STM-1 (synchronous transport module-1). Higher bit rate signals are defined analogous to SONET, as shown in Table 6.2.

6.1.2   Elements of a SONET/SDH Infrastructure

Figure 6.3 shows different types of SONET equipment deployed in a network. SONET is deployed in three types of network configurations: rings, linear configurations, and point-to-point links. The early deployments were in the form of

Table 6.2 Transmission rates for SONET/SDH, adapted from [SS96].

SONET Signal	SDH Signal	Bit Rate (Mb/s)
STS-1		51.84
STS-3	STM-1	155.52
STS-12	STM-4	622.08
STS-24		1244.16
STS-48	STM-16	2488.32
STS-192	STM-64	9953.28

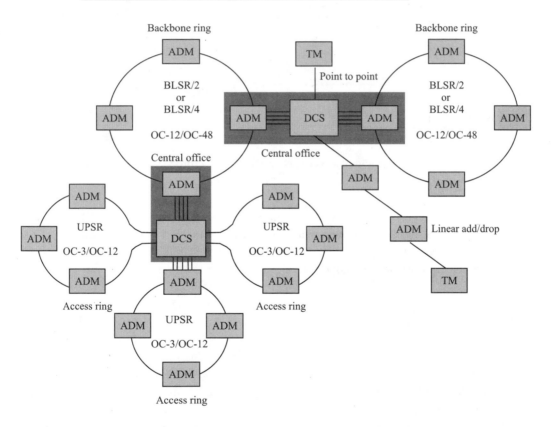

Figure 6.3 Elements of a SONET infrastructure. Several different SONET configurations are shown, including point-to-point, linear add/drop, and ring configurations. Both access and interoffice (backbone) rings are shown. The figure also explains the role of a DCS in the SONET infrastructure, to crossconnect lower-speed streams, to interconnect multiple rings, and to serve as a node on rings by itself.

point-to-point links, and this topology is still used today for many applications. In this case, the nodes at the ends of the link are called *terminal multiplexers* (TMs). TMs are also sometimes called *line terminating equipment* (LTE). In many cases, it is necessary to pick out one or more low-speed streams from a high-speed stream and, likewise, add one or more low-speed streams to a high-speed stream. This function is performed by an *add/drop multiplexer* (ADM). For example, an OC-48 ADM may be able to drop and add OC-12 or OC-3 streams from/to an OC-48 stream. Similarly, an OC-3 ADM may be able to drop DS3 streams from/to an OC-3 stream. ADMs are now widely used in the SONET infrastructure. ADMs can be inserted in the middle of a point-to-point link between TMs to yield a linear configuration.

An added function that has become a key driver in SONET deployment is that of service availability even in the presence of failures such as fiber cuts and transmission equipment failures. The most common topology used for this purpose is a ring. Rings offer a high degree of availability in the presence of failures while being topologically simple. The rings are made up of ADMs, which in addition to performing the multiplexing and demultiplexing operations, incorporate the protection mechanisms needed to handle failures. Usually, SONET equipment can be configured to work in any of these three configurations: ring ADM, linear ADM, or as a terminal multiplexer.

Rings are used both in the access part of the network and in the backbone (interoffice) part of the network to interconnect central offices. Today, most access rings run at OC-3/OC-12 speeds, and interoffice rings at OC-12/OC-48/OC-192 speeds. Clearly these ring speeds will increase in the future. Two types of ring architectures are used: *unidirectional path-switched rings* (UPSRs) and *bidirectional line-switched rings* (BLSRs). The BLSRs can use either two fibers (BLSR/2) or four fibers (BLSR/4). We will discuss these architectures and the protection mechanisms that they incorporate in detail in Chapter 10. In general, UPSRs are used in the access part of the network to connect multiple nodes to a hub node residing in a central office, and BLSRs are used in the interoffice part of the network to interconnect multiple central offices.

Another major component in the SONET infrastructure is a *digital crossconnect* (DCS). A DCS is used to manage all the transmission facilities in the central office. Before DCSs arrived, the individual DS1s and DS3s in a central office were manually patched together using a patch panel. Although this worked fine for a small number of traffic streams, it is quite impossible to manage today's central offices, which handle thousands of such streams, using this approach. A DCS automates this process and replaces such a patch panel by crossconnecting these individual streams under software control. It also does performance monitoring and has grown to incorporate multiplexing as well. DCSs started out handling only PDH streams but have evolved to handle SONET streams as well. They can handle a large number of ports, for example, up to 2048 DS3 ports. Today's DCSs are capable of switching individual traffic streams at DS1 or DS3 levels. A DCS switching data at DS1 speeds is called *wideband,* and a DCS switching data at DS3 speeds is termed *broadband.* Today's DCSs have OC-3 and OC-12 ports and will no doubt soon have higher-speed ports. DCSs are used to interconnect SONET rings. They have also grown to incorporate the ADM functions. Thus DCSs can be connected to ADMs to provide connectivity between rings as well as be part of the rings themselves.

Grooming is the term used to describe how different traffic streams are switched and packed into higher-speed streams. The SONET layer usually does grooming at higher speeds, from OC-3 and upwards, and sometimes including the lower-speed DS1 streams. Lower-level grooming at DS1 and DS3 is done primarily by a DCS.

6.1.3 SONET/SDH Physical Layer

A variety of physical layer interfaces are defined for SONET/SDH, depending on the bit rates and distances involved, as shown in Table 6.3. The range varies from LEDs or multilongitudinal mode (MLM) Fabry-Perot lasers at 1310 nm for short distances

Table 6.3 Different physical interfaces for SONET, adapted from [Bel95]. In terms of loss, the systems are classified as short reach (SR), intermediate reach (IR), or long reach (LR). The transmitters include multilongitudinal mode (MLM) Fabry-Perot lasers and single-longitudinal mode (SLM) DFB lasers, as well as light-emitting diodes (LEDs). Almost all the interfaces use standard single-mode fiber (SMF). Although multimode fiber (MMF) interfaces have been defined for the low-speed signals, they are not used much in practice.

Bit Rate	Loss	Wavelength	Fiber Type	Transmitter
OC-3	SR	1310 nm	MMF	LED
			SMF	LED/MLM
	IR	1310 nm	SMF	MLM
		1550 nm	SMF	MLM/SLM
	LR	1310/1550 nm	SMF	MLM/SLM
OC-12	SR	1310 nm	SMF	LED/MLM
	IR	1310 nm	SMF	MLM
		1550 nm	SMF	SLM
	LR	1310 nm	SMF	MLM/SLM
		1550 nm	SMF	SLM
OC-48	SR	1310 nm	SMF	MLM
	IR/LR	1310/1550 nm	SMF	SLM

at the lower bit rates to 1550 nm single-longitudinal mode (SLM) DFB lasers for the higher bit rates and longer distances. The physical layer uses scrambling to prevent long runs of 1s or 0s in the data (see Section 4.1.1). The systems are classified as *short reach* (SR), *intermediate reach* (IR), or *long reach* (LR). SR systems have a loss of less than 7 dB, IR systems have a loss of less than 12 dB, and LR systems have a loss between 10 and 28 dB at OC-3 bit rates and between 10 and 24 dB at OC-12 and OC-48 bit rates. These are specified in terms of loss rather than distance because the loss includes both fiber attenuation and other losses in the paths, due to connectors, splices, and so forth. We can obtain an approximate equivalent distance by assuming a loss of 0.25 dB/km at 1550 nm and 0.5 dB/km at 1310 nm. So an OC-48 LR system would range in distance between 20 and 48 km at 1310 nm, and between 40 and 96 km at 1550 nm. These standards were defined before optical amplifiers arrived on the scene. With optical amplifiers, we are now seeing spans without regeneration well in excess of the LR limits specified here, and these systems are sometimes called *ultra long reach* (ULR) systems.

6.2   Computer Interconnects

Note that although SONET/SDH is prevalent mostly within the carrier infrastructure today, most of the following networks are found within enterprise networks. Unlike SONET/SDH, most of them do not incorporate protection mechanisms and would thus depend on the optical layer to provide protection against failures. The common characteristics of all these networks is that they tend to use low-cost optical components and operate at modest bit rates.

The three networks described next are all primarily used for interconnecting computers to other computers or peripheral systems such as disks, tapes, and printers. The fourth, FDDI, is a widely deployed metropolitan-area network. The key attributes of these networks are summarized in Table 6.4. Along with FDDI, we also briefly describe two other networking technologies: ATM and IP.

6.2.1   ESCON

ESCON™ (Enterprise Serial Connection) was developed by IBM to replace the cumbersome, low-speed, and limited number of copper-based I/O interfaces on mainframe computers. It is widely deployed in large mainframe installations. The overall architecture of an ESCON network is shown in Figure 6.4. A mainframe computer can have hundreds of ESCON I/O channels. These channels may be connected to other mainframes or to peripheral devices. The ESCON architecture includes an

Table 6.4 Different first-generation networks used in enterprise networks.

Network	Topology	Baud Rate (Mbaud)	Transmitter
ESCON	Mesh	200	LED/MMF
			MLM/SMF
FDDI	Ring	125	LED/MMF
			MLM/SMF
HIPPI (serialized)	Mesh	1,200	MLM/SMF
Fiber Channel	Mesh	1,062.5	MLM/SMF
		531.25	
		265.625	

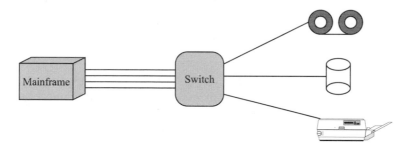

Figure 6.4 The ESCON architecture.

electronic circuit switch called the ESCON *director*, which allows ESCON devices to be interconnected in a flexible manner.

In early installations, the entire network was located within a building or campus, but increasingly, the network is being distributed over a wider metropolitan area for a variety of reasons, to be discussed in Section 13.2.4.

The bit rate per ESCON channel is 200 Mb/s. LEDs at 1.3 μm are used over multimode fiber if the link length is less than 3 km. Longer distances, up to 20 km, are supported by using 1.3 μm MLM lasers over single-mode fiber.

ESCON uses an (8, 10), line code (see Section 4.1.1) to avoid long runs of 0s or 1s and to achieve DC balance, that is, equal numbers of transmitted 0 and 1 bits.

6.2.2   Fiber Channel

Fiber Channel is a recently developed standard used for the same set of applications as ESCON. The standard allows payload (useful data) bit rates of either 200, 400, or 800 Mb/s. The last bit rate is expected to be the most prevalent. At the highest bit rate, MLM 1.3 μm lasers are used over single-mode fiber, even over short distances. As of this writing, Fiber Channel is just beginning to be deployed. Like ESCON, the Fiber Channel architecture includes I/O ports on computers and peripherals, as well as an electronic switch.

Fiber Channel uses the (8, 10), line code (see Section 4.1.1) as ESCON. This along with some other overhead means that the actual rates of transmission over the optical fiber corresponding to the payload bit rates of 200, 400, and 800 Mb/s are 265.625, 531.25, and 1062.5 Mb/s, respectively. The rates obtained after line coding are usually referred to as the *baud rates;* thus we say the transmission rate is 1062.5 Mbaud rather than 1062.5 Mb/s.

6.2.3   HIPPI

HIPPI (high-performance parallel interface) is an 800 Mb/s parallel electrical I/O interface standard. Owing to clock skew, the maximum distance is limited to 25 m. For longer distances, HIPPI is serialized and transmitted over single-mode fiber. A new standard called Serial HIPPI, which includes an optical interface at 1.2 Gbaud, has been defined recently for this purpose. HIPPI predates Fiber Channel, and is widely deployed in supercomputer installations. Like ESCON and Fiber Channel, a HIPPI network consists of hosts and peripherals connected via HIPPI switches and, in many cases, serial fiber-optic links.

6.3   Metropolitan-Area Networks

6.3.1   FDDI

FDDI (fiber distributed data interface) is a metropolitan-area standard, operating at 100 Mb/s over multimode or single-mode fiber. It is commonly deployed in the form of two-fiber rings, similar to SONET BLSR/2s, and incorporates a similar protection mechanism as well. It is an extension to a higher speed, and optical fiber, of the widely deployed token ring local-area network standard. The maximum length between two stations on an FDDI ring is limited to 2 km when multimode fiber is used. The FDDI standard was developed specifically with a low-cost implementation in mind, and thus the standards specifications are designed to be met by LED transmitters operating in the 1.3 μm band over multimode fiber using a *pin* diode receiver. However, lasers and single-mode fiber can be used, and in this case, the distance between two stations can go up to 40 km. The minimum average output power specified for the transmitter is −20 dBm, and the minimum average receiver input power is −31 dBm so that a loss of 11 dB is permitted. Since the link length is at most 2 km, the attenuation loss is no more than 5 dB (even at 2.5 dB/km) so that a considerable margin has been allocated for losses arising from splicing, connectors, and such.

FDDI uses a (4, 5), line code (see Section 4.1.1) to avoid long runs of 0s or 1s and to achieve some measure of DC balance. Thus the actual rate of transmission over the optical fiber is 125 Mbaud. Unlike the (8, 10), line code used in Fiber Channel, the (4, 5), line code used in FDDI does not achieve perfect DC balance; there are input data sequences that can cause a worst-case DC unbalance of 10%. This results in a power penalty of 1 dB that must be allowed for in the link budget calculations.

6.3.2 ATM

Voice and data networks have traditionally been separate even though almost the entire telephone network is digital. ATM (asynchronous transfer mode) is a networking standard that was developed with many goals, one of which was the integration of voice and data networks. An ATM network uses packets or *cells* with a fixed size of 53 bytes; this packet size is a compromise between the conflicting requirements of voice and data applications. A small packet size is preferable for voice since the packets must be delivered with only a short delay. A large packet size is preferable for data since the overheads involved in large packets are smaller. Of the 53 bytes in an ATM packet, at least 5 bytes constitute the header, which is the overhead required to carry information such as the destination of the packet. ATM networks span the whole gamut from local-area networks (LANs) to metropolitan-area networks (MANs) to wide-area networks (WANs).

One of the key advantages of ATM is its ability to provide quality-of-service guarantees, such as bandwidth and delay, to applications even while using statistical multiplexing of packets to make efficient use of the link bandwidth (see Chapter 1). ATM achieves this by using *a priori* information about the characteristics of a connection (say, a virtual circuit), for example, the peak and average bandwidth required by it. ATM uses *admission control* to block new connections when necessary to satisfy the guaranteed quality-of-service requirements.

Another advantage of ATM is that it employs switching even in a local-area environment unlike other LAN technologies like ethernets, token rings, and FDDI, which use a shared medium such as a bus or a ring. This enables it to provide quality-of-service guarantees more easily than these other technologies. The fixed size of the packets used in an ATM network is particularly advantageous for the development of low-cost, high-speed switches.

Various lower or *physical layer* standards are specified for ATM. These range from 25.6 Mb/s over twisted-pair copper cable to 622.08 Mb/s over single-mode optical fiber. Among the optical interfaces is a 100 Mb/s interface whose specifications such as transmit power, maximum allowed attenuation, and line coding, are identical to that of FDDI, which we have described. A 155.52 Mb/s optical interface that operates over distances up to 2 km using LEDs over multimode fiber in the 1300 nm band is also defined. Using the specified minimum transmit and receive powers, the loss budget for this interface is 9 dB. The line code used in this case is the (8, 10), line code specified by the Fiber Channel standard.

These two interfaces are called *private user–network interfaces* in ATM terminology, since they are meant for interconnecting ATM users and switches in networks that are owned and managed by private enterprises. A number of *public user–network interfaces,* which are meant for connecting ATM users and switches to the public or carrier network, are also defined. In these latter interfaces, ATM uses either PDH or SONET/SDH as the immediately lower layer. These interfaces are defined at many of the standard PDH and SONET/SDH rates shown in Tables 6.1 and 6.2, respectively. Among these are a 44.736 Mb/s DS3 interface, a 155.52 Mb/s STS-3c interface, and a 622.08 Mb/s STS-12c interface. In the terminology of the ATM standards, the layer below ATM is called the physical layer so that these interfaces to PDH and SONET/SDH are called *physical layer interfaces.* On the other hand, in the classical layered view of networks, which we discuss in Section 6.4, PDH and SONET/SDH must be viewed as *data link layers* when ATM is viewed as a network layer.

The deployment of ATM is proving to be slower than expected for several reasons. One reason is that the venerable internet protocol (IP), which we will study next, continues to be sufficient for many applications and is also evolving to provide the same kind of functionality as ATM. Another reason is the relatively slow development of standards. In the LAN arena, ATM is facing competition from other emerging LANs such as the 100 Mb/s and 1 Gb/s versions of the ethernet.

6.3.3   IP

IP (internet protocol) is by far the most widely used wide-area networking technology today. There are probably very few readers of this book who haven't used the Internet for e-mail or web browsing. IP is a networking technology, or protocol, that is designed to work over a wide variety of lower layers, which are termed *data link layers* in the classical layered view of networks (Section 6.4). This is one of the important reasons for its widespread success. Some traditional data link layers over which IP operates are those associated with popular local-area networks such as ethernet and token ring. IP also operates over metropolitan-area networks such as FDDI. IP can use well-known data link layer protocols—for example, *high-level data link control* (HDLC)—when operating over leased lines from carriers.

Compared to ATM, traditional IP provides only a simple datagram service to its higher layers—there is no notion of a connection. It also does not provide any quality-of-service guarantees unlike ATM. Nevertheless, ATM has not succeeded in displacing IP to even a moderate extent at the time of this writing. In fact, the ATM standards define interfaces so that IP can operate using ATM as its immediately lower layer. Since it was developed solely by the data networking community, IP was not designed with support for voice applications in mind. One consequence of this is that IP uses variable size packets unlike ATM. When IP packets are transmitted over an ATM network, these variable size packets are segmented into fixed size ATM packets or cells at the transmitting end, and reassembled into IP packets at the receiving end.

One of the most common higher (transport) layer protocols used on top of IP is TCP (transmission control protocol). For this reason, such networks are commonly referred to as TCP/IP networks.

With the explosive growth in traffic for Internet services, both users and network operators are increasingly feeling the need for some quality-of-service guarantees. This has generated a considerable amount of effort within the IP standards community toward providing support for quality-of-service guarantees in IP. Protocols such as RSVP (resource reservation protocol) have been developed for this purpose. Of course, a simpler alternative is to retain the same protocol but increase the bandwidth available and the processing speeds of the routers to keep up with the bandwidth. This may well be what happens in practice as bandwidth gets cheaper and routers become more powerful. The impact of these efforts on the deployment of ATM networking will be interesting to watch.

6.4   Layered Architecture

We now introduce the notion of a layered architecture. Networks are complicated entities with a variety of different functions being performed by different components of the network, with equipment from different vendors all interoperating together. A component of the network is called a *network element* (NE). For instance, nodes, amplifiers, and regenerators are all network elements. In order to simplify our view of the network, it is desirable to break up the functions of the network into different layers, as shown in Figure 6.5. Each layer performs a certain set of functions and provides a certain set of services to the next higher layer. In turn, each layer expects the layer below it to deliver a certain set of services to it. The service interface between

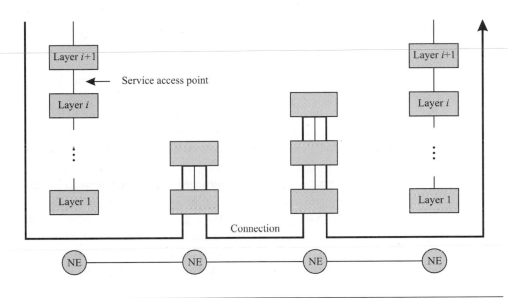

Figure 6.5 Layered hierarchy of a network.

two adjacent layers is called a *service access point* (SAP), and there can be multiple SAPs between layers corresponding to different types of services offered.

In most cases, the network provides *connections* to the user. A connection is established between a source and a destination node. Setting up, taking down, and managing the state of a connection is the job of a separate network control and management entity (not shown in Figure 6.5), which may control each individual layer in the network. There are also examples where the network provides *connectionless* services to the user. These services are suitable for transmitting short messages across a network, without having to pay the overhead of setting up and taking down a connection for this purpose. We will confine our discussion to the connection-oriented model.

Within a node, data belonging to a connection flows between the layers. Each layer multiplexes a number of higher-layer connections and may add some additional overheads to data coming from the higher layer. Each intermediate node and network element along the path of a connection embodies a set of layers starting from the lowest layer up to a certain layer in the hierarchy. Within a node, data flows between the layers.

It is important to define the functions of each layer and the interfaces between layers. This is essential because it allows vendors to manufacture a variety of hardware and software products performing the functions of some but not all of the layers, and provide the appropriate interfaces to communicate with other products performing the functions of other layers.

Note that there are many possible implementations and standards for each layer. A given layer may work together with a variety of lower or higher layers. Each of the different types of optical networks that we will study constitutes a layer. Each layer itself can in turn be partitioned into several layers. As we study these networks, we will explore this layered hierarchy further.

Figure 6.6 shows a classical breakdown of the different layers in a network that was proposed by the International Standards Organization in the early 1980s. The lowest layer in the hierarchy is the *physical layer*, which provides a "pipe" with a certain amount of bandwidth to the layer above it. In our case, the physical layer is optical fiber with different types of physical interfaces (single-mode, multimode, and so on) possible. The next layer above is the *data link layer*, which is responsible for framing, multiplexing, and demultiplexing data sent over the physical layer. The data link layer may or may not incorporate some techniques to handle link errors. Included in the data link layer is the *media-access control layer* (MAC), which coordinates the transmissions of different nodes when they all share common bandwidth, as is the case in many local-area networks, such as ethernets or token rings. Above the data link layer resides the *network layer*. The network layer usually provides *virtual circuits* or *datagram* services to the higher layer. A virtual circuit (VC) represents an end-to-end connection with a certain set of quality-of-service parameters associated with it, such as bandwidth and error rate. Data transmitted by the source over a VC is delivered in sequence at its destination. Datagrams, on the other hand, are short messages transmitted end to end, with no notion of a connection. The network layer performs the end-to-end routing function of taking a message at its source and

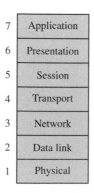

Figure 6.6   The classical layered hierarchy.

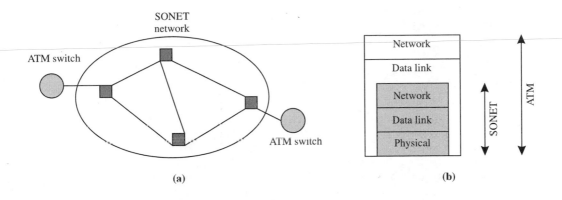

Figure 6.7 An ATM over SONET network. (a) The network has ATM switches with SONET adaptors that are connected to a SONET network. (b) The layered view of this network.

delivering it to its destination. The *transport layer* resides on top of the network layer and is responsible for ensuring the end-to-end, in-sequence, and error-free delivery of the transmitted messages. Above the transport layer reside other layers such as the *session*, *presentation*, and *application* layers, but we will not be concerned with these layers in this book.

This classical layered view of networks needs some embellishment to handle the variety of networks and protocols that are proliferating today. Many of the first- and second-generation optical networks provide functions that might be thought of as falling primarily within the physical or data link layer. However, many of them incorporate several sublayers, which in turn, correspond to the link and network layer functions in the classical layered view. A more realistic layered model for today's networks would employ multiple protocol stacks residing one on top of the other. To provide some concrete examples of this, consider an ATM over SONET network shown in Figure 6.7. In this case, the ATM network treats the SONET network as its link layer. The ATM switches in the network have SONET adaptor cards that connect them into the SONET network. From the ATM network's point of view, the SONET layer is used to provide point-to-point connections between ATM switches. Note, however, that the SONET layer itself incorporates its own link, physical, and network layer.

Yet another example of this sort of layering is an IP over ATM network, shown in Figure 6.8. Again the story is very similar to the case of the ATM over SONET network that we just studied. The vision of the service providers is to deploy an ATM infrastructure and have IP packets converted to ATM cells at the periphery of their network. Again, the IP network treats the ATM network as its link layer.

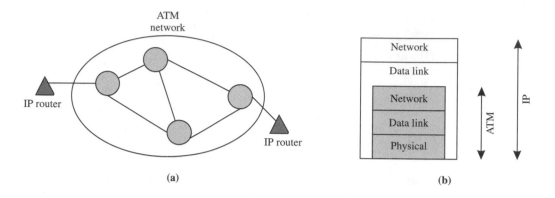

(a)   **(b)**

Figure 6.8   An IP over ATM network. (a) The network has IP routers connected to an ATM network. The IP packets are converted into ATM cells, transported over the ATM network, and converted back to IP packets at their destination. (b) The layered view of this network.

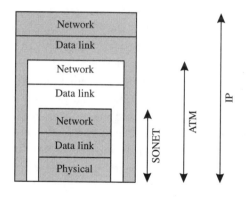

Figure 6.9   The layered view of an IP over ATM over SONET network.

More complex layering structures are possible as well. For example, Figure 6.9 shows the layered view of an IP over ATM over SONET network. The IP network then treats the ATM layer as its link layer, and the ATM layer in turn treats the SONET layer as its link layer.

The introduction of second-generation optical networks introduces yet another layer in the protocol hierarchy—the so-called *optical* layer. We will see in later chapters that this second-generation optical layer provides lightpaths to a variety of

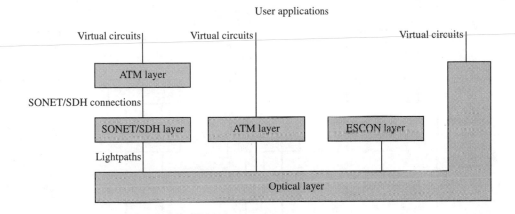

Figure 6.10 A layered view of a network consisting of a second-generation optical network layer that supports a variety of first-generation network layers above it.

first-generation optical layers, as shown in Figure 6.10. Examples of layers residing above a second-generation optical network layer include all the first-generation networks that we studied in this chapter. As second-generation optical networks evolve, they may provide other services besides lightpaths, such as packet-switched virtual circuit or datagram services. These services may directly interface with user applications, as shown in Figure 6.10.

Many issues are involved in supporting first-generation networks over the lightpaths provided by second-generation networks. We will discuss these issues in detail in Chapter 10.

6.4.1 SONET/SDH Layers

The SONET layer consists of four sublayers, as shown in Figure 6.11. The *path* layer is responsible for end-to-end connections between nodes and is needed only at the ends of a SONET connection. It is responsible for monitoring and tracking the status of a connection. Each connection traverses a set of links and intermediate nodes in the network. The path layer may be thought of as being equivalent to the network layer in the classical protocol hierarchy of Figure 6.6. The *line* layer multiplexes a number of path-layer connections onto a single link between two nodes. Thus the line layer is present at each intermediate node along the route of a SONET connection. The line layer is also responsible for performing certain types of protection switching to restore service in the event of a line failure, as will be seen in Section 10.4. Each link consists of a number of *sections*, corresponding to

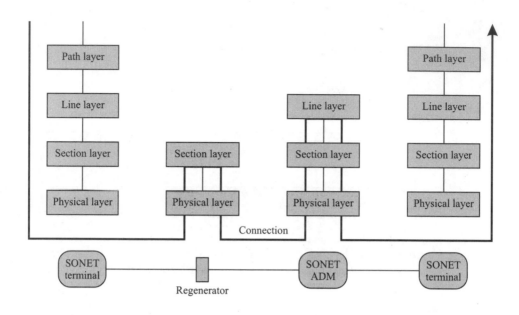

Figure 6.11 SONET/SDH layers. The path layer handles end-to-end SONET connections and is present at the ends of a connection. Multiple path-layer connections are multiplexed together by the line layer, which is present at each SONET terminal. The section layer resides below the line layer and is present at each regenerator and terminal in the network. The thick line indicates a SONET connection.

link segments between regenerators. The *section* layer is present at each regenerator in the network. The line and section layers correspond to the data link layer in the classical protocol hierarchy of Figure 6.6. Finally, the *physical* layer is responsible for actual transmission of bits across the fiber.

6.4.2 Second-Generation Optical Network Layers

Before we study the different types of second-generation network architectures, let us see where these networks fit into the layered hierarchy. This is illustrated in Figure 6.10. In first-generation optical networks, the physical layer was essentially a point-to-point optical fiber link and provided a full wavelength's worth of bandwidth to the layer above it. In second-generation networks, the physical layer incorporates more sophisticated mechanisms that can provide variable amounts of bandwidth between pairs of nodes.

The International Telecommunications Union (ITU) has defined a new layer called the *optical layer*. This definition is particularly appropriate to describe WDM

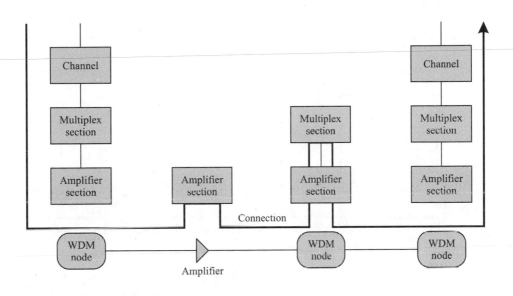

Figure 6.12 The optical layer, which consists of the channel, multiplex section, and amplifier section sublayers. The thick line indicates an optical layer connection.

networks. The optical layer provides lightpaths to the higher layer. A *lightpath* is an end-to-end connection established across the optical network, and uses a wavelength on each link in a path between the source and destination. A lightpath provides a full wavelength's worth of bandwidth to the higher layer.

Analogous to the SONET layer, the optical layer itself consists of three sublayers, as shown in Figure 6.12. At the top is the *lightpath layer*, also called the *optical channel* (OC) layer by the ITU. This layer takes care of end-to-end routing of the lightpaths. Each lightpath traverses a number of links in the network, and each of these links carries multiple wavelengths. The *optical multiplex section* (OMS) layer is used to represent a point-to-point link along the route of a lightpath. Each OMS in turn consists of several link segments, each segment being the portion of the link between two optical amplifier stages. Each link segment belongs to the *optical amplifier section* (OAS) layer. Thus in principle, once the interfaces between the different layers are defined, it is possible for vendors to provide standardized equipment ranging from just optical amplifiers to WDM links to entire WDM networks.

The preceding definition of an optical layer does not include second-generation networks that can provide more sophisticated packet-switched services, such as virtual circuits or datagrams. For example, the broadcast and select networks that we will study in Chapter 7 and the photonic packet-switched networks of Chapter 14

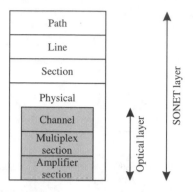

Figure 6.13   A SONET network with an underlying optical layer. The physical layer of SONET is replaced by the optical layer.

both provide such services, and are not adequately described using this layering approach. In the case of a broadcast and select network, the packet-switching function is performed by a media-access control (MAC) layer, and in the case of a mesh photonic packet-switched network, a true additional network layer must also be included within the optical layer.

Just as we had ATM networks running over the SONET layer in Figure 6.7, we can have SONET networks on top of the optical layer, as shown in Figure 6.13. The physical layer of SONET is now replaced by the optical layer. We will study the optical layer in great detail in the remaining chapters of the book.

Summary

First-generation optical networks have been deployed widely in public telecommunications networks as well as private enterprise networks. The public network infrastructure in North America is dominated by SONET, and European networks are all evolving to SDH, a similar standard. We studied the reasons that drove the standardization of SONET and SDH and examined their basic principles. We also studied optical networks such as ESCON, FDDI, HIPPI, and Fiber Channel, all of which are used in enterprise networks, and a little bit of ATM and IP. Then we described the principles underlying the layered network architecture and examined how different networks fit into this layered model. We saw how the layered model has become more complicated as a result of a variety of networks working with one another and looked at several such examples, such as SONET over the optical layer and ATM over the SONET layer.

Further Reading

There is an extensive body of literature dealing with SONET/SDH. A comprehensive set of papers that cover the multiplexing standards, network topologies, and performance and management is collected in [SS96]. See also the book by Sexton and Reid for an advanced treatment of the subject [SR92]. SONET/SDH has been extensively standardized by the ANSI and the ITU. In addition, Bellcore publishes generic criteria for equipment vendors. A list of the standards documents may be obtained on the World Wide Web at *http://www.itu.ch*, *http://www.ansi.org*, and *http://www.bellcore.com*.

Many references are devoted to one of the other protocols described in this chapter; see [CdLS92, FS92] for ESCON, [Ame89] for HIPPI, [Ame94, Ben96, SV96] for Fiber Channel, [SR94, Ros86, Bur86] for FDDI, [dP93, MS95, For95] for ATM, and [Com94, Ste94] for IP. There is an ongoing attempt to establish an ANSI standard for ESCON, called SBCON; see *http://www.amdahl.com/ext/CARP/SBCON/SBCON.html*. ANSI standards have been established for HIPPI, Fiber Channel, and FDDI. A list of the ATM standards and copies of many of them can be obtained from *http://www.atmforum.com*.

The concept of a layered architecture is well known and quite fundamental to our understanding of networks. The classical layering hierarchy is covered well in several books [Tan88, BG92, PD96]. The SONET sublayers are described in [Wu92, SS96]. The breakdown of the optical layer into its various layers is described in ITU recommendation G.681 [ITU96].

A good general reference on first-generation and other networks is the book by Walrand and Varaiya [WV97].

Problems

6.1 Which sublayer within the SONET or optical layer would be responsible for handling the following functions:

    (a) A SONET path fails and the traffic must be switched over to another path.

    (b) Many SONET streams are to be multiplexed onto a higher-speed stream and transmitted over a SONET link.

    (c) The error rate on a SONET link between regenerators is to be monitored.

6.2 In Table 6.3, calculate the equivalent distance limitations of the different types of SONET systems. Assume a loss of 0.25 dB/km at 1550 nm and 0.5 dB/km at 1310 nm.

6.3 Which sublayer within the optical layer would be responsible for handling the following functions:

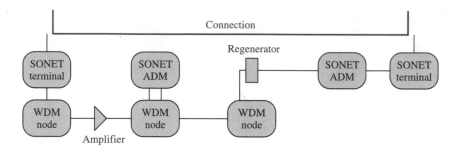

Figure 6.14   A combined SONET/WDM optical network for Problem 6.4.

(a) WDM optical networks usually use an additional supervisory channel over each link in addition to the data channels. This channel must be multiplexed and demultiplexed at each amplifier and at the ends of each link.

(b) Setting up and taking down lightpaths in the network.

(c) Rerouting all the lightpaths on a failed link onto another link.

6.4   Consider the SONET network operating over the optical layer shown in Figure 6.14. Trace the path of the connection through the network, and show the termination of different layers at each network element, as was done in Figure 6.11.

References

[Ame89]   American National Standards Institute, X3T9.3. *High-performance parallel interface*, Nov. 1989. Rev. 6.9.

[Ame94]   American National Standards Institute, X3T9.3. *Fibre channel: Signalling protocol (FC-2)*, Nov. 1994. Rev. 4.2.

[Bel95]   Bellcore. *SONET transport systems: Common generic criteria*, 1995. GR-253-CORE.

[Ben96]   A. F. Benner. *Fiber Channel*. McGraw-Hill, New York, 1996.

[BG92]   D. Bertsekas and R. G. Gallager. *Data Networks*. Prentice Hall, Englewood Cliffs, NJ, 1992.

[Bur86]   W. E. Burr. The FDDI optical data link. *IEEE Communications Magazine*, 24(5):18–23, May 1986.

[CdLS92]   S. A. Calta, S. A. deVeer, E. Loizides, and R. N. Strangewayes. Enterprise systems connection (ESCON) architecture—system overview. *IBM Journal of Research and Development*, 36(4):535–551, July 1992.

[Com94]   D. E. Comer. *Internetworking with TCP/IP: Vol. II: Design, Implementation and Internals*. Prentice Hall, Englewood Cliffs, NJ, 1994.

[dP93]   M. de Prycker. *Asynchronous Transfer Mode: Solution for Broadband ISDN*. Ellis Horwood, New York, 1993.

[ES92]   J. C. Elliott and M. W. Sachs. The IBM enterprise systems connection architecture. *IBM Journal of Research and Development*, 36(4):577–591, July 1992.

[For95]   The ATM Forum. *ATM User-Network Interface (UNI) Specification Version 3.1*. PTR Prentice Hall, Englewood Cliffs, NJ, 1995.

[ITU96]   ITU-T SG15/WP 4. *Rec. G.681: Functional characteristics of interoffice and long-haul line systems using optical amplifiers, including optical multiplexing*, 1996.

[MS95]   D. E. McDysan and D. L. Spohn. *ATM: Theory and Application*. McGraw-Hill, New York, 1995.

[PD96]   L. L. Peterson and B. S. Davie. *Computer Networks: A Systems Approach*. Morgan Kaufmann, San Francisco, 1996.

[Ros86]   F. E. Ross. FDDI—a tutorial. *IEEE Communications Magazine*, 24(5):10–17, May 1986.

[SR92]   M. Sexton and A. Reid. *Transmission Networking: SONET and the Synchronous Digital Hierarchy*. Artech House, Boston, 1992.

[SR94]   A. Shah and G. Ramakrishnan. *FDDI: A High Speed Network*. PTR Prentice Hall, Englewood Cliffs, NJ, 1994.

[SS96]   C. A. Siller and M. Shafi, editors. *SONET/SDH: A Sourcebook of Synchronous Networking*. IEEE Press, Los Alamitos, CA, 1996.

[Ste94]   W. R. Stevens. *TCP/IP Illustrated, Volume 1*. Addison-Wesley, Reading, MA, 1994.

[SV96]   M. W. Sachs and A. Varma. Fibre channel and related standards. *IEEE Communications Magazine*, 34(8):40–49, Aug. 1996.

[Tan88]   A. Tanenbaum. *Computer Networks*. Prentice Hall, Englewood Cliffs, NJ, 1988.

[Wu92]   T. H. Wu. *Fiber Network Service Survivability*. Artech House, Boston, 1992.

[WV97]   J. Walrand and P. Varaiya. *High-Performance Communication Networks*. Morgan Kaufmann, San Francisco, 1997.

chapter 7

Broadcast and Select Networks

WITH THIS CHAPTER, we begin our study of second-generation optical networks. The fundamental purpose of any communication network is to provide *connectivity* between pairs of nodes that desire to communicate with each other. Broadly speaking, there are two kinds of communication network architectures (optical or not) based on how this connectivity is provided. In networks based on a broadcast architecture, the connectivity is provided in an almost trivial fashion: the network sends the signal received from each node to all the nodes. Thus *no routing* function is provided by the network. Most local-area networks today belong to this category, for example, ethernets, token rings, FDDI networks. The other network architecture is one that selectively transmits the signals received from a node over a part of the network based on information received from the source node. Most wide-area networks today belong to this category and consist of nodes interconnected by point-to-point links. Signals are routed over a subset of these links chosen to include the intended recipient node(s). In the case of WDM optical networks, such networks are called *wavelength routing networks* and are the subject of Chapter 8. In this chapter, we study networks based on a broadcast architecture, focusing primarily on WDM networks. Optical TDM broadcast networks will be explored in Chapter 14.

7.1 Topologies for Broadcast Networks

The two most popular topologies for broadcast and select networks are the *star* and the *bus* topologies. (To be precise, one must say *single-folded bus*; another kind of

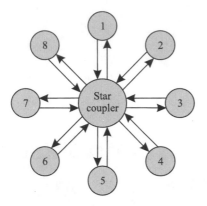

Figure 7.1   A network using a broadcast star topology.

bus is discussed in Problem 7.4.) Examples of these are shown in Figures 7.1 and 7.2, respectively. Both the star and the bus networks use optical couplers. The star coupler in Figure 7.1 can be made out of the 2×2 couplers that we studied in Section 3.1, or as a single integrated-optics device. An 8×8 star coupler made out of 2×2 couplers is shown in Figure 7.3.

In the bus topology shown in Figure 7.2, nodes transmit into the bus through a coupler and receive from the bus via another coupler. On the transmit coupler, only one of the output ports is used, and on the receive coupler, only one of the input ports is used, and the unused ports are not shown in the figure. The two topologies differ in the number and manner in which the couplers are used. A bus network with n nodes uses $2n$ 2×2 couplers. In contrast, a star network with n nodes uses a single $n \times n$ star coupler, which can be made out of $\frac{n}{2} \log_2 n$ 2×2 couplers (assuming n is a power of 2). However, though each signal passes through an average of n couplers in the case of the bus ($2n - 1$ in the worst case), it passes through only $\log_2 n$ couplers in the case of the star. This factor plays a significant role in determining the link budget performance of these topologies.

Recall from Section 3.1, equation (3.1), that the output electric fields of a 2×2 directional coupler can be written in terms of the input electric fields as follows:

$$\begin{pmatrix} E_{o1}(f) \\ E_{o2}(f) \end{pmatrix} = e^{-i\beta l} \begin{pmatrix} \cos(\kappa l) & i\sin(\kappa l) \\ i\sin(\kappa l) & \cos(\kappa l) \end{pmatrix} \begin{pmatrix} E_{i1}(f) \\ E_{i2}(f) \end{pmatrix}.$$

Here, κ is the coupling coefficient, l is the coupling length, and β is the propagation constant. This equation assumes that the couplers are ideal and no power is lost. If we assume that a fraction γ of the power from each input is lost (doesn't appear at

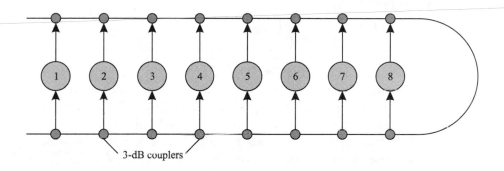

3-dB couplers

Figure 7.2 A network using a bus topology.

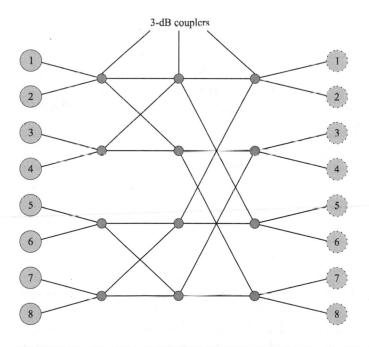

3-dB couplers

Figure 7.3 The internal structure of a star coupler.

either output) and denote $\alpha = \sin^2(\kappa l)$, this equation can be written in terms of the optical powers as

$$\begin{pmatrix} P_{o1}(f) \\ P_{o2}(f) \end{pmatrix} = (1 - \gamma) \begin{pmatrix} 1 - \alpha & \alpha \\ \alpha & 1 - \alpha \end{pmatrix} \begin{pmatrix} P_{i1}(f) \\ P_{i2}(f) \end{pmatrix}. \tag{7.1}$$

The derivation of this equation is left as an exercise (Problem 7.1). Thus a fraction γ of the power from each input is lost, and of the remainder, a fraction $1 - \alpha$ of the power from input 1 (resp. 2) appears at output 1 (resp. 1) and a fraction α at output 2 (resp. 1). α is called the *splitting loss* ratio, and γ the *excess loss* ratio.

In the case of the star, we set $\alpha = 1/2$ so that all outputs receive the same fraction of the power from each input. As can be seen from Figure 7.3, each output receives a fraction $(\gamma/2)^{\log_2 n}$ of the power transmitted from each input. In other words, the loss in dB between each input–output pair, neglecting the propagation loss, is

$$L_{\text{star}} = 10 \log_{10} n - (\log_2 n) 10 \log_{10} \gamma. \tag{7.2}$$

Since we are distributing the power from each input to n outputs, the splitting loss of $10 \log_{10} n$ is unavoidable; the key point to note is that the *excess loss grows logarithmically with n* in the case of the star.

For the bus topology, we assume that all $2n$ couplers are identical and that input 1 and output 1 are connected to the bus. Thus a fraction α of the power from the bus is coupled into each node in the bottom or receiver half of the bus, and a fraction α of the power from each node is coupled onto the bus in the top or transmit half. The worst-case loss occurs when node 1 transmits to node 2 and equals

$$L_{\text{bus}} = \alpha^2 (1 - \alpha)^{2n-3} \gamma^{2n-1}.$$

The optimum value of α that minimizes L_{bus} is $\alpha^{\text{opt}} = 2/(2n - 1)$ and the corresponding L_{bus} is

$$L_{\text{bus}}^{\text{opt}} \approx e^{-2} \gamma^{2n-1} / n^2,$$

for large n. Expressed in dB,

$$L_{\text{bus}}^{\text{opt}} \approx 8.7 + 20 \log_{10} n - (2n - 1) 10 \log_{10} \gamma. \tag{7.3}$$

Not only is the splitting loss greater, but more important, *the excess loss increases linearly with n* in the case of the bus.

The preceding analysis applies to the case when amplifiers are not used in the network. The situation is much more complex when amplifiers are used and we must consider carefully the issue of amplifier gain saturation, particularly in the case of WDM (or multichannel) networks. This has been studied in detail in [RL93]. The conclusion is that the star topology is the better choice for many of the kinds of networks we have considered. There are a few cases where the bus topology outperforms the star, but even here it is not by much.

7.1.1   Interconnected Stars

In many cases, it is infeasible to have a single broadcast star for the entire network. This may be because the number of nodes, and thus the splitting loss, becomes large, or because the nodes are not geographically close together. In such cases, a number of broadcast stars can be interconnected in a suitable fashion. To motivate this interconnection, let us look at how the same problem is tackled in electronic local-area networks.

The local-area networks of today, such as ethernets, are interconnected by *bridges*. Since the whole interconnected network is also called an ethernet, we use the term *ethernet segment* for each of the networks that are so interconnected. The interconnected network is no longer a single broadcast medium. Transmissions within each ethernet segment are broadcast only on that segment. The bridge selectively transmits packets from other segments that are intended for a specific segment; for this reason, a bridge is also called a *selective repeater*. When the interconnection between networks is at the network layer (see Section 6.4), the entity performing this interconnection is called a *router*.

Figure 7.4 shows how a similar function can be accomplished in a network comprising four broadcast stars interconnected by a *wavelength router*. In this figure, four stars are interconnected using four wavelengths $\lambda_1, \ldots, \lambda_4$. Each star uses a unique wavelength for transmitting to each other star and a unique wavelength for receiving from each other star. For example, star 1 is connected to star 3 using λ_3. Packets from nodes in star 1 to nodes in star 3 must thus be transmitted on λ_3. One possible device that can be used as a wavelength router is the arrayed waveguide grating (AWG) that we studied in Section 3.3.7.

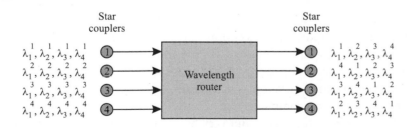

Figure 7.4   Four broadcast stars interconnected by a wavelength router.

Note that each broadcast star can reuse the same set of wavelengths for communication within that star, provided that this set of wavelengths is different from that used for interstar communication.

The AON testbed is an example of a network that uses this architecture of broadcast stars interconnected by a wavelength router. This testbed is described in Chapter 11. We will study wavelength routing networks further in Chapter 8.

7.2   Media-Access Control (MAC) Protocols

In a broadcast and select network, any signal transmitted by a node is *broadcast* to all the nodes. Also each node must *select* the desired signal(s) for reception from the set of signals transmitted simultaneously. We will now consider the problems of "when to broadcast" and "what to select." The discussion is applicable to any broadcast topology; the star and bus topologies studied in the last section are examples. We assume that each node (or station) has a pair of fibers—one for transmission and the other for reception—connecting it to the network and that the network broadcasts every signal it receives from a node to all the nodes (including the transmitting node). We also assume that each signal is carried on one of W wavelengths, the specific values of which have been agreed upon by all the nodes in the network, perhaps adhering to the ITU standard discussed in Section 5.10.5. If two nodes transmit simultaneously on the same wavelength, because of the broadcast nature of the network, the signals *collide* and both signals will be lost or corrupted. Consider the case where two nodes transmit simultaneously on different wavelengths and these transmissions are intended for the same receiving node. If the receiving node has only a single tunable receiver, it can tune to—or select—only one of the transmissions. In this case, we say that the two transmissions *contend*. To resolve contentions and avoid, or minimize, wasteful collisions, some coordination is required between the various nodes in the network. A mechanism that provides this coordination is called a *media-access control (MAC)* protocol.

MAC protocols are designed depending on the needs of the application, the hardware capabilities at the nodes, and the level of performance required. Some applications may require that the entire bandwidth available on a single wavelength (which can range from a few hundred Mb/s to well over a Gb/s) be dedicated to them. In this case, we must set up a "circuit" between the source node and the destination node of that application. Examples of such applications include high-speed interconnections between supercomputers and between supercomputers and high-resolution graphic visualization terminals, and very high-quality (and possibly uncompressed) video like that required in film production studios or for medical imaging. The Rainbow-I network [JRS93] to be discussed in Section 7.3 was designed for such applications. We will briefly discuss the "circular search" protocol that Rainbow-I uses for the purpose of setting up circuits in that section. Other applications do not need the entire bandwidth of a wavelength. Thus the bandwidth available on a single wavelength can be shared among several applications with the same source node or the same destination node, or even with different sources and destinations. We will assume that this sharing is done using some form of time division multiplexing and that each wavelength channel is divided into time slots for this purpose. The applications transmit data in the form of packets, each of which fits into a time slot.

The hardware capabilities at a single node can range from having multiple tunable transmitters and multiple tunable receivers to having a single transmitter and a single receiver, one of which may be fixed-tuned to a predetermined wavelength and the other, tunable. With today's optical technology, a tunable transmitter or receiver is much more expensive than its fixed-tuned counterpart. This has motivated the design of protocols that operate with at least some components being fixed-tuned. Supporting packet switching requires the transmitter or receiver to tune between time slots in a small fraction of the duration of the time slot itself. For example, a 1000-bit packet at 1 Gb/s lasts 1 μs, and so in order to make use of the bandwidth efficiently, the tunable transmitter or receiver must be capable of tuning between wavelengths in a small fraction of a μs. This is not easy to do with today's components, which is one of the reasons that such networks are not yet commercially feasible.

Note that if each node has a single fixed-tuned transmitter and a single fixed-tuned receiver, it will be able to communicate only with a limited set of other nodes unless, of course, all the nodes are tuned to the same wavelength, in which case, we have only a single (wavelength) channel. MAC protocols for single-channel networks have been widely studied for several decades and the most popular ones are ethernet, token ring, and FDDI (Section 6.3.1), the last of which is specifically designed for use on optical fiber. The case where each node has a small number of fixed-tuned transmitters and fixed-tuned receivers has been widely studied under the name of "multihop" networks. In these networks, there is direct connectivity from a node x only to those nodes, say, Y, that have a receiver tuned to the same wavelength as a transmitter of node x, and packets intended for other nodes must be routed through the nodes in Y. We will study such multihop networks in Chapter 9, particularly in Section 9.4. In this chapter, we will consider only multichannel MAC protocols for star networks. We also assume that a node has either a tunable transmitter or a tunable receiver so that direct connectivity can be achieved between all pairs of nodes in the network.

The level of performance is measured by the packet delays and *throughput* of the network. In any broadcast network, some of the transmitted data is lost owing to collisions or contentions. The *throughput* of a network is the fraction of the transmission capacity of the network that carries useful data, that is, data that are successfully received by their intended destinations. We will give a more precise description later. As is usually the case, there is a tradeoff between the performance of a protocol and its implementation complexity, including the hardware capabilities that have to be provided at each node. We will study the design and performance of protocols designed for a range of hardware capabilities.

All the packet-switching protocols we describe will use a separate channel (or channels), termed the *control channel(s)*, to send information about the packets that are transmitted on the data channels. It is best to think of a control channel as occupying a separate wavelength, though in many cases, control channels can be made to share the same wavelengths as the data channels in a time-multiplexed fashion.

7.2.1   Synchronization

Assume the network has a star topology. In any practical network, the propagation delay from each node to the star will, in general, be different. We denote the maximum propagation delay permitted by the system between any pair of nodes (including from a node to itself) by d_{prop}. (Thus the maximum propagation delay from any node to the star is $d_{\text{prop}}/2$.) This value determines the maximum permitted geographical extent of the network. For example, $d_{\text{prop}} = \underline{1 \text{ ms}}$ corresponds to a maximum permitted geographical extent of about $\underline{200 \text{ km}}$. In many of the protocols we consider, the value of d_{prop} is assumed to be known to all the nodes.

All the packet-switching protocols that we will describe assume that there is *slot synchronization* among all the network nodes. There are protocols that work without synchronization, but their performance in general is poorer than protocols of comparable complexity that make use of synchronized nodes. This means that all nodes have a suitable time reference so that signals transmitted in different slots do not collide anywhere in the network. There are several possible ways to achieve slot synchronization. We explain one method that is applicable to a star topology. This method is illustrated in Figure 7.5. Three nodes A, B, and C whose propagation delays to the star are 1, 1.5, and 2 units of time, respectively, are shown. There is also a *synchronizer* node, denoted by O, that is located at the star coupler. This node transmits a pulse called the *sync pulse* at periodic intervals. The period of the sync pulses is some known integral number of slots. In the case of many protocols, a fixed number of slots are grouped into a frame; in these cases, we can assume that the pulses are transmitted once per frame. We will make this assumption for the rest of this discussion. These pulses are transmitted on a well-known wavelength, possibly the control wavelength that is used in most of the protocols we consider. The time of reception of these pulses at each node will be taken by those nodes as

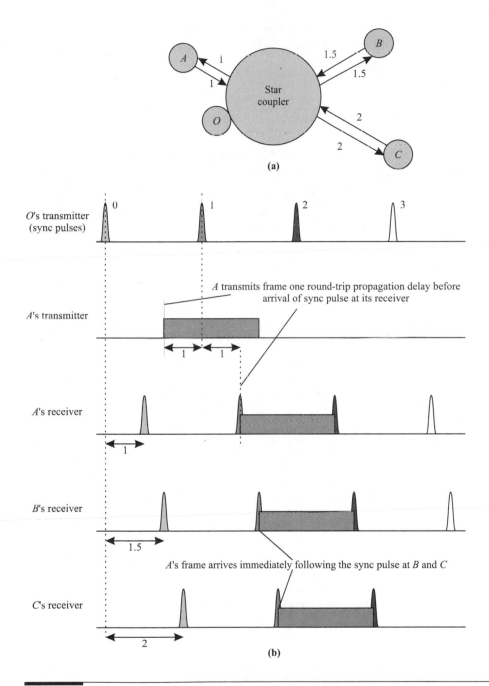

Figure 7.5 Achieving frame/slot synchronization in a network.

the *start of frame* in their *receivers*. The algorithm that each node uses to achieve frame synchronization is as follows.

Algorithm 7.1

1. Each node estimates, or predicts, the time of arrival of the next sync pulse at its receiver. The periodicity of the sync pulses is used in making this prediction quite accurate.

2. Each node estimates its round-trip delay to the star using the fact that the signals sent by it are broadcast by the star to it. For example, a node can measure its propagation delay to the star by transmitting a known pulse and measuring the elapsed time interval before its reception from the star.

3. A node transmits the information for a specific frame, say, frame x, one round-trip delay prior to the estimated time of arrival of the sync pulse at the start of frame x. This is illustrated in Figure 7.5, where node A transmits a frame $1 + 1$ time units before it receives a start-of-frame pulse from node O.

We leave it as an exercise (Problem 7.6) to the reader to show that Algorithm 7.1 achieves frame synchronization. Figure 7.5 illustrates how the frame transmitted by node A is received by all the nodes immediately following the reception of the start-of-frame pulse for that frame. In practice, we also need to worry about what happens when the synchronizer node fails, and must incorporate a mechanism by which the function is taken over by another node.

Once frame synchronization is achieved, since the number of slots per frame is known, each node can compute the slot times by dividing the known frame transmission interval suitably. The periodic transmission of the start-of-frame pulses from node O ensures that any drifts in the individual clocks of the nodes are compensated. Each node must also estimate its round-trip delay to the star at not too infrequent intervals in order to compensate for changes due to temperature, aging, and similar factors.

We will also assume that the tuning time of the transmitters and receivers is negligible compared to a slot duration (or that this tuning time is included in the slot length) so that a transmitter or receiver can be tuned to a particular wavelength in one slot and to any other wavelength in the next slot, if necessary. There are several papers dealing with protocols that are designed for operation with transmitters and receivers with nonnegligible tuning times [ABM96, PS94, ABC+94, RS97], but we do not describe them here.

7.2.2   *Slotted Aloha/Slotted Aloha*

We describe only one of a family of protocols [HKS87, Meh90] that are designed on the assumption that the number of wavelengths or channels, W, that are used

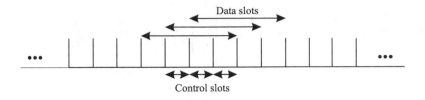

Figure 7.6 Control slots and data slots for the Slotted Aloha/Slotted Aloha protocols.

to transmit data is much smaller than the number of nodes, n. In addition, there is a $(W + 1)$st control wavelength. The protocol requires each node to be equipped with a tunable transmitter and a tunable receiver for data. In addition, each node must have a fixed-tuned transmitter and fixed-tuned receiver operating at the control wavelength.

We first briefly describe the Aloha and Slotted Aloha protocols used in single-channel broadcast networks. These were some of the earliest media-access control protocols devised for a single-channel network [Abr70]. In the Aloha protocol, any node that has a packet to send transmits it immediately. In the Slotted Aloha protocol, time is divided into slots whose length is equal to that of a maximum-sized packet. A node that has a packet to transmit sends it in the immediately following slot. If no other transmission overlaps with this transmission, the transmission is received successfully; otherwise, there is a *collision*, and the nodes involved in the collision retransmit their packets after a random time interval. We will now see how this protocol can be generalized to the multichannel case.

On the data channels as well as the control channel, time is divided into slots, but the size of a data slot is L times that of a control slot. The motivation behind this assumption is that control packets are likely to be much smaller than data packets. The effect of L on the performance of the protocol is illustrated in Problem 7.10. We arbitrarily choose the size of the control slot to be unity and assume that the control slots are $\ldots, [-1, 0), [0, 1), [1, 2), \ldots$, where $[x, y]$ denotes the time interval from epoch x to epoch y (including the epoch x but not the epoch y). Then the data slots are $\ldots, [-1, L-1), [0, L), [1, L+1), \ldots$. This is illustrated in Figure 7.6. Note that each data slot overlaps in time with the $L - 1$ data slots that precede it and the $L - 1$ data slots that follow it.

The *basic* Slotted Aloha/Slotted Aloha (SA/SA) protocol [HKS87] operates as follows. Whenever a node, say, x, has a data packet to send, it sends a control packet in a control slot and the data packet in the data slot immediately following it. For example, if the control packet is sent in slot $[0, 1)$, the data packet will be sent in slot $[1, L + 1)$. This is illustrated in Figure 7.7.

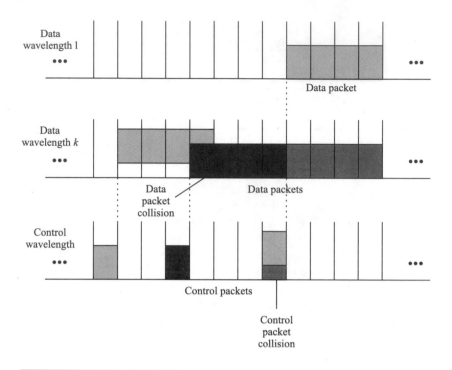

Figure 7.7   The operation of the basic Slotted Aloha/Slotted Aloha protocol.

Thus the protocol used on the control wavelength is the Slotted Aloha protocol. The protocol used on each one of the data wavelengths is also the Slotted Aloha protocol for $L = 1$; hence the name Slotted Aloha/Slotted Aloha for this protocol. For large L, the protocol on the data wavelength is very much like the unslotted Aloha protocol; nevertheless, we will continue to use the name Slotted Aloha/Slotted Aloha for this protocol, regardless of the value of L.

The control packet is sent on the control wavelength $(W + 1)$, and the data packet on one of the data wavelengths $1, \ldots, W$. The control packet carries the identity of the intended receiving node, say, node y, for the corresponding data packet, and the identity of the wavelength on which the data packet will be transmitted, say, λ_k. Each node continuously monitors the control channel. Thus, *provided no other node transmits a control packet in slot* $[0, 1)$, node y will receive the control packet sent by node x in the interval $[d_{\mathrm{prop}}, d_{\mathrm{prop}} + 1)$ and know that in the next data slot, a data packet intended for it has been transmitted on wavelength λ_k, and this has to be received in the interval $[d_{\mathrm{prop}} + 1, d_{\mathrm{prop}} + L + 1)$. Node y then tunes its data receiver to wavelength λ_k by time $d_{\mathrm{prop}} + 1$ and *attempts* to receive the data packet. (Recall the assumption of negligible tuning times.) It will receive the data packet successfully provided that no other data packet collides or contends with it.

Note that once a packet is available for transmission at a node, that node simply "tells" the other nodes about this packet in a control slot and "goes" ahead and transmits the packet in the next data slot. We refer to this feature of the protocol as *tell-and-go*. The *access delay* is defined as the delay between the time at which a packet is available for transmission at a node and the time at which it is *first transmitted*. Thus a protocol has the *tell-and-go* feature if it has zero or very low access delay. It is desirable to have low access delay for two reasons. The first is that some applications may not be able to tolerate large delays. The second is that because the transmission speeds in optical networks are very high, a large access delay will result in large buffer requirements at the transmitting nodes.

In the preceding discussion, if node z also transmits a control packet in slot $[0, 1)$ (intended for some node in the network), node y will not be able to receive the control packet from node x. Therefore, even if the data packet transmitted by node x does not collide with any other packet, node y will not be aware of the transmission of this packet. Thus in order for a data packet to be received successfully, *both* the data packet and the associated control packet must be free of collisions.

Node x becomes aware of the collision of the control packet it sent in slot $[0, 1)$ after time $d_{\mathrm{prop}} + 1$ since all nodes are continuously monitoring the control channel. If d_{prop} were zero (or negligible compared to the slot length), node x could abstain from the wasteful transmission of the corresponding data packet in slot $[1, L+1)$. However, even for arbitrary d_{prop}, node x can avoid the wasteful transmission of the data packet *if we modify the protocol* so that the data packet is transmitted after the transmitting node has received feedback that the associated control packet was successful. In our discussion, node x would transmit the data packet in slot $[d_{\mathrm{prop}} + 1, d_{\mathrm{prop}} + L + 1)$ instead of in slot $[1, L+1)$ (assuming d_{prop} is an integer; otherwise, it can be rounded up to the next integer). This modification of the basic SA/SA protocol, which we will call the *wait-and-see* modification, was introduced in [Meh90]. Its operation is illustrated in Figure 7.8. We will see later that the wait-and-see modification results in an increased throughput. However, we have given up the tell-and-go feature of the protocol. This is a recurring theme in the study of MAC protocols; we can trade increased access delay for increased throughput. We will see further examples in the following section.

Throughput Analysis

We now analyze the throughput of both the basic and the modified SA/SA protocols. In order to make the analysis tractable, we make a few assumptions.

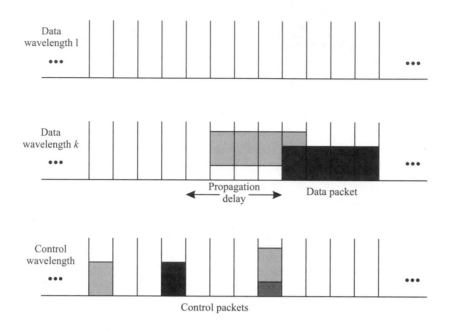

Figure 7.8   The operation of the modified Slotted Aloha/Slotted Aloha protocol.

Independent transmissions. The first assumption is that in any slot and for any node, the probability that the node has a packet for transmission is p, *independent* of all other slots and all other nodes. This assumption clearly cannot hold exactly in a practical network. For example, the retransmission of packets that suffer collisions induces a correlation between the transmission of packets from the same node (though we attempt to reduce this correlation by waiting for a random number of slots before retransmission).

Large n. The second assumption is that the number of nodes in the network n is very large compared to W and that the traffic (data packets) to or from each individual node is negligible. More precisely, we will assume that W is fixed, but $n \rightarrow \infty$ and $p \rightarrow 0$ while $np \rightarrow G$. (If $n \rightarrow \infty$ and p is fixed, the expected number of packets in the network in each slot, np, $\rightarrow \infty$, and cannot be handled by a finite number of wavelengths.) Thus G is the expected number of data packets that are available for transmission in each slot. G is also the expected number of control packets that will be transmitted in each control slot. It is a well-known result in probability theory that under these assumptions, G is a Poisson random variable and thus

$$\text{Prob}(G = k) = e^{-G} \frac{G^k}{k!}, \qquad k \geq 0.$$

Another consequence of the infinite-node assumption is that any particular receiver is free with probability 1. (Or, equivalently, the probability that two data packets are transmitted for the same receiving node in overlapping data slots is negligible.) Thus the analysis neglects the effect of contentions.

Uniform traffic. The last assumption is that each data packet is equally likely to be transmitted on any one of the W data channels, independent of all other data packets.

Consider an arbitrary data slot in an arbitrary data channel. We first find the expected number of data packets that are transmitted in this slot and that will be successfully received. Without loss of generality, we take the data channel to be 1 and the data slot to be $[1, L + 1)$. At most, one data packet can be successfully transmitted in this data slot. So the expected number of data packets that are successfully transmitted in data slot $[1, L + 1)$ is simply the probability that a data packet is successfully transmitted in this slot. In order for a data packet to be successfully transmitted in data slot $[1, L + 1)$, the following independent events must occur:

- Exactly one control packet must have been transmitted in control slot $[0, 1)$. This has probability Ge^{-G} by the assumption of Poisson arrivals of control packets in a control slot.

- This control packet must choose data channel 1. This occurs with probability $1/W$ since we assume that the data slots are chosen with uniform probability.

- No data packet must be transmitted in data slots $[-L+2, 2), \ldots, [L, 2L)$, excluding the data slot $[1, L + 1)$. Each of these $2(L - 1)$ events is independent and has probability $e^{-G/W}$ in the case of the basic protocol [HKS87] and $1 - Ge^{-G}/W$ in the case of the modified protocol [Meh90]. To see this, for the basic protocol, observe that since the arrival of control packets in each control slot is Poisson with rate G, the traffic is uniform, and there is a one-to-one correspondence between the control and data slots, the arrival of data packets in each data slot on a given wavelength is Poisson with rate G/W. Hence the probability that no data packet is transmitted in any data slot is $e^{-G/W}$. The reasoning for the modified protocol is slightly different and is left as an exercise (Problem 7.7).

Thus the expected number of data packets that are successful in any data slot is

$$Ge^{-G} \cdot \frac{1}{W} \cdot (e^{-G/W})^{2(L-1)}$$

for the basic SA/SA protocol and

$$Ge^{-G} \cdot \frac{1}{W} \cdot (1 - Ge^{-G}/W)^{2(L-1)}$$

for the modified SA/SA protocol.

We define the *throughput per data channel* as the expected number of data packets carried by a data channel at an arbitrary point in time that will be successfully received. Note that by this definition, the throughput corresponds to the fraction of time a given data channel is carrying successful data packets and is thus the *effective utilization* of the data channel. Without loss of generality, we can take this epoch to lie in $[1, 2)$. The expected number of successful data packets carried at any epoch in the interval $[1, 2)$ is the sum of the expected number of successful data packets carried in the data slots $[-L + 2, 2), \ldots, [1, L + 1)$, and this is L times the expected number of successful data packets in any specific data slot, say, $[1, L + 1)$. Thus the throughput of the basic SA/SA protocol is

$$\frac{LGe^{-G}}{W}(e^{-G/W})^{2(L-1)}$$

and that of the modified SA/SA protocol is

$$\frac{LGe^{-G}}{W}(1 - Ge^{-G}/W)^{2(L-1)}.$$

These throughputs are plotted versus G in Figure 7.9 for $L = 10$ and $W = 16$. It can be seen that the modified SA/SA protocol has a higher throughput than the basic SA/SA protocol for all values of G considered in this example. We note that the maximum throughput is 0.11 for the basic SA/SA protocol and 0.15 for the modified SA/SA protocol. These values are typical of these protocols. Further properties of the

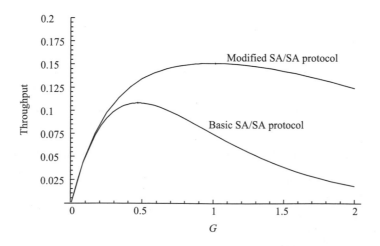

Figure 7.9   Throughputs of the basic and modified SA/SA protocols versus G for $L = 10$ and $W = 16$.

throughputs of these two protocols, and in particular the dependence of the throughputs on L, W, and G, are explored in Problems 7.9, 7.10, and 7.11. Problem 7.8 discusses the comparative performance of these two protocols.

The most important observation to be made from all these results is that the throughput of the basic SA/SA protocol is quite low under almost all circumstances. The performance of the modified SA/SA protocol is somewhat improved but not by very much. Moreover, we have given up the tell-and-go property. We will now discuss another protocol that has a significantly higher throughput but still retains the tell-and-go feature.

7.2.3   DT-WDMA

Among the MAC protocols designed specifically for multiwavelength optical networks, DT-WDMA [CDR90] has perhaps been the most influential one and has spurred a number of research papers on modified and improved versions.

In contrast to the SA/SA protocols, this protocol assumes that the number of nodes n *equals* the number of wavelengths W that are used to transmit data. In addition, there is a $(W + 1)$st control wavelength. The protocol requires each node to be equipped with a fixed-tuned data transmitter, tuned to a unique wavelength at each node, and a tunable data receiver. Without loss of generality, we may assume that node x_i, $i = 0, 1, \ldots, n - 1$, is assigned wavelength λ_i for data transmission. In addition, each node must have a fixed-tuned control transmitter and fixed-tuned control receiver operating at the control wavelength.

On the data channels as well as the control channel, time is divided into slots, but the size of a data slot is n (or W) times that of a control slot. However, unlike the SA/SA protocols, the data slots do not overlap in time and if we assume the control slots are $\ldots, [-1, 0), [0, 1), [1, 2), \ldots$, the data slots can be taken to be $\ldots, [-n, 0), [0, n), [n, 2n), \ldots$. Thus we can associate the n control slots $[kn, kn + 1), [kn + 1, kn + 2), \ldots, [2kn - 1, 2kn)$ with the data slot $[kn, 2kn)$. This is illustrated in Figure 7.10. In each data slot, one of these n control slots is assigned to

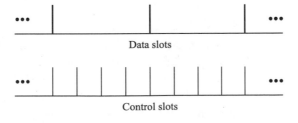

Figure 7.10   The data and control slots for the DT-WDMA protocol.

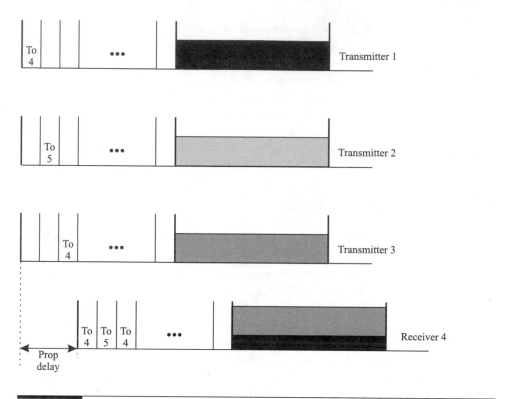

Figure 7.11   The operation of the DT-WDMA protocol.

each node in the network, and a node transmits its control packets only in the control slots assigned to it. Without loss of generality, we may assume that the control slots $kn + i$ are assigned to node i. The protocol operates as follows.

Whenever a node, say, x_i, has a data packet to send, it sends a control packet in a control slot and the data packet in the data slot immediately following it. For example, if the control packet is sent in slot $[i, i + 1)$, the data packet will be sent in slot $[n, 2n)$. This is illustrated in Figure 7.11.

The control packet is sent on the control wavelength $(W + 1)$ and the data packet on the wavelength assigned to node i's fixed-tuned transmitter, namely, wavelength λ_i. The control packet carries the identity of the intended receiving node, say, node x_j, and the control slot in which this packet is transmitted implicitly identifies the wavelength on which the data packet will be transmitted, namely, λ_i. Each node continuously monitors the control channel. Thus node x_j will receive the control packet sent by node x_i in the interval $[d_{\mathrm{prop}} + i, d_{\mathrm{prop}} + i + 1)$ and know that in the next data slot, a data packet intended for it has been transmitted on wavelength λ_i, and this has to be received in the interval $[d_{prop} + n, d_{prop} + 2n)$. Node x_j then tunes its data receiver to wavelength λ_i by time $d_{prop} + n$ and receives the data packet.

Note that since each node transmits its data packets on a different wavelength, *data packets never collide*. Also since each node transmits its control packets on different control slots, *control packets never collide*. However, two or more nodes may transmit data packets intended for the same receiver simultaneously, and the receiver will be able to receive only one of these *contending* data packets. Since all the nodes monitor the control channel, the transmitting nodes involved in a data packet contention will become aware of this at the same time as the receiving node. The algorithm used by a receiving node to *resolve a contention*—determine the data packet to be received among the contending packets—is known to all the nodes. Thus the transmitting nodes that *lost the contention*—whose packets were not chosen by the receiving node—can transmit the data packets again.

Throughput Analysis

We make the independence assumption again: in any slot and for any node, the probability that the node has a packet for transmission is p, *independent* of all other slots and all other nodes. We also make the assumption of uniform traffic: each data packet is equally likely to be destined for any one of the $n - 1$ nodes other than the transmitting one, independent of all other data packets.

Recall that the *throughput per data channel* is the expected number of data packets carried by a data channel at an arbitrary point in time (epoch) that will be successfully received. Since data slots do not overlap, the throughput per data channel is also the expected number of data packets that are successfully received in an arbitrary data slot, in an arbitrary data channel. Equivalently, we may also compute the throughput as the expected number of data packets that are successfully received in an arbitrary data slot, by an arbitrary receiver. Therefore, consider an arbitrary receiver, say, receiver 1 without loss of generality, and an arbitrary data slot, say, $[n, 2n)$. One data packet will be successfully received if *at least one* data packet intended for receiver 1 is transmitted in data slot $[n, 2n)$. A data packet intended for receiver 1 is transmitted in data slot $[n, 2n)$ by transmitter i, $i = 2, \ldots, n$ with probability $p/(n-1)$. Thus no such packet is transmitted with probability $1 - p/(n-1)$. Since the transmission of data packets and the choice of their destinations are independent at each node, the probability that no data packet intended for receiver 1 is transmitted in data slot $[n, 2n)$ is $(1 - p/(n - 1))^{n-1}$ and the throughput of the protocol is

$$1 - (1 - p/(n - 1))^{n-1} \quad \overset{n \to \infty}{\Longrightarrow} \quad 1 - e^{-p}.$$

If every node has a data packet for transmission in every slot (all the nodes are saturated), $p = 1$, and the throughput of the DT-WDMA protocol is $1 - e^{-1} \approx 0.632$. In practice, when the correlations between data packets in different slots are taken into account, the throughput of the protocol has been estimated to be around 0.6 for large n, using simulations. Note that these throughput values are much higher than what could be obtained with the SA/SA protocol even with the wait-and-see modification.

7.2.4   Scheduling Protocols

The DT-WDMA protocol also has the tell-and-go property like the basic SA/SA protocol. Again, if we are willing to give up this property, we can achieve a higher throughput. Many protocols do this. Among the early ones were [CY91, CZA92]. All of them make the same assumptions as DT-WDMA on the hardware available at each node, namely, a fixed-tuned transmitter and tunable receiver for data in addition to a control transmitter and receiver operating at the common control wavelength. The control and data slot structures are also the same as that of DT-WDMA (Figure 7.10). The basic idea behind all these scheduling protocols is as follows.

A node sends a control packet in its assigned control slot as soon as it has a new packet available for transmission announcing the destination node for this packet but *does not send* the data packet immediately. Instead, it waits for a time d_{prop} so that it can learn which other nodes have packets to transmit to the same destination node. With this knowledge and working together in cooperation, all nodes that have packets to transmit to the same destination node *schedule their transmissions in different data slots* so that they never contend with each other.

The protocol can be more precisely described as follows. We first make precise the notion of a *frame*, which we introduced earlier. A *frame* is a group of (one or more) consecutive slots on the data and control channels. In the case of DT-WDMA, a frame consists of a single data slot on the data channel and n control slots on the control channel. Frame k consists of the data slot $[kn, (k+1)n)$ and the control slots $[kn, kn+1), [kn+1, kn+2), \ldots, [kn+n-1, kn+n)$.

Assume that in each frame, a node has at most one new packet that arrives. A node transmits the destination address of the new packet, if any, in its assigned control slot in the next frame, say, k. Assume d_{prop} is a multiple of n and let $d = d_{\mathrm{prop}}/n$. Then, all nodes will receive frame k when they are transmitting frame $k + d$. When a node completes the reception of a frame, it becomes aware of the destinations of *all* the data packets that had arrived at their respective transmitting nodes before the transmission of that frame. This information may be conveniently represented in the form of a *backlog matrix*, $B(k) = (b_{ij}(k))_{i,j=1}^{n}$, where $b_{ij}(k)$ represents the number of data packets at node i that are destined for node j just before the transmission of frame k. All the nodes use a common *matching algorithm* on the matrix $B(k)$ to determine the data packet that each of them must transmit, if any, in frame $k + d + 1$. A *matching algorithm* on the matrix $B(k)$ picks a set of packets among those represented in $B(k)$ such that no two packets in the set have the same source node or destination node. More precisely, a matching algorithm on $B(k)$ finds a matrix $M = (m_{ij})_{i,j=1}^n$ such that $m_{ij} = 1$ only if $b_{ij} \geq 1$, and each row and column of M contains at most a single 1. (Thus if $m_{ij} = 1$, $m_{i'j} = 0$, $i' \neq i$, and $m_{ij'} = 0$, $j' \neq j$.) Thus the simultaneous transmission of the set of packets picked by a matching algorithm results in *no contentions*.

Summarizing, in any such protocol, in each frame k, every node executes the following four steps:

1. (control transmitter) transmission of a control packet disseminating the destination address of a new packet arrival, if any, during the transmission of frame $k - 1$

2. (control receiver) reception of the control packets transmitted in frame $k - d$, computation of the matrix $B(k - d)$, and a matching in that matrix to determine the data packet, if any, that must be transmitted in the next frame $(k + 1)$

3. (data transmitter) transmission of the data packet, if any, determined by running the matching algorithm on matrix $B(k - d - 1)$

4. (data receiver) reception of the data packet destined to this node, if any, and transmitted in frame $k - d$

Using these protocols, each packet suffers an access delay of at least d frames, but this enables us to increase the maximum throughput beyond the value of $1 - e^{-1}$ that is achieved by DT-WDMA (for large n). How much beyond? That depends on the complexity of the matching algorithm that we use, as we briefly discuss next.

Recall that given a set of packets with specified sources and destinations (matrix $B(k)$ in our earlier discussion), a matching is a subset of packets such that no two packets in the subset have the same source node or destination node. Clearly, there are many possible matchings but two kinds of matchings will be of interest in the following discussions. A *maximum matching* is a matching of largest size (measured in number of packets). A *maximal matching* is a matching that cannot be enlarged further; that is, all packets not included in the matching have either a source or a destination in common with one of the packets included in the matching. As is to be expected, finding a maximum matching is much harder than finding a maximal matching.

If a scheduling algorithm computes a maximum matching in every slot, it can achieve a maximum throughput of 1. Several researchers have shown, however, that the loss in throughput is fairly small when less complex matching algorithms such as maximal matching are used [CY91].

Throughput Analysis

To calculate the throughput of the scheduling DT-WDMA protocol using a maximum matching in each slot, we make the same two assumptions as we have made so far: (i) the independence assumption, which states that in any slot and for any node, the probability that the node has a packet for transmission is p, *independent* of all other slots and all other nodes, and (ii) the uniform traffic assumption, which states that each data packet is equally likely to be destined for any one of the $n - 1$ nodes other than the transmitting one, independent of all other data packets. Under these assumptions, it can be shown, using techniques beyond the scope of this book [Tas97, MAW96], that all packets are successfully transmitted, provided $p < 1$. Thus the throughput of this protocol—the expected number of packets successfully transmitted in an arbitrary data slot—is simply p. If the uniform traffic assumption is relaxed but instead we assume that a packet arriving at transmitter i is destined for receiver j with probability p_{ij} and p_{ij} satisfy $\sum_i p_{ij} = \sum_j p_{ij} = 1$, we can still transmit all packets successfully, provided we use an appropriate maximum matching algorithm that preferentially transmits older packets. This algorithm is discussed in [MAW96].

We can gain an intuitive understanding of these results as follows. The sum of all the entries in the backlog matrix $B(k)$ is the number of packets that are waiting in the system before the transmission of frame k. If every entry of $B(k)$ is nonzero—so we have backlogged packets at every transmitter for every receiver—clearly we can transmit n packets in frame $k + d + 1$ by using *any* maximum matching. On average, we have $pn < n$ packet arrivals into the system in every frame. This *suggests* that if all the backlogs build up at the same rate, we can "catch up" by using *any maximum matching*. This is the case for uniform traffic. However, when the traffic is nonuniform, some backlogs build up faster than others and have to cleared faster. So we cannot use an arbitrary maximum matching, but must use a maximum matching algorithm that preferentially transmits older packets.

Delay versus Throughput

In considering the performance of various MAC protocols, we have discussed only the throughput of these protocols though we have alluded several times to the trade-off between delay, particularly access delay, and throughput. Thus the scheduling algorithms we discussed previously achieve a throughput close to 1 compared to the throughput value of 0.632 achieved by DT-WDMA, but the price to be paid is a larger delay. The analysis of the delay performance of MAC protocols is considerably more complex, but qualitatively the delay performance of DT-WDMA and

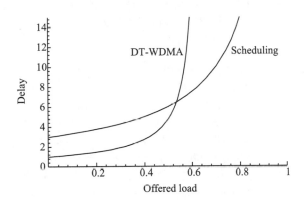

Figure 7.12   Delay versus the offered load for the DT-WDMA and (maximum matching) scheduling protocols. (The delay values are not accurate, and the plot is meant only to illustrate the qualitative behavior of the two protocols.)

(maximum matching) scheduling protocols is as shown in Figure 7.12. Here we plot the delay in units of the one-way propagation time between nodes (assumed to be constant) versus the offered load to the network. The minimum delay suffered by a packet from the time it is transmitted to the time it is received by the destination is thus one unit. The offered load is the average number of packet arrivals per data slot per wavelength. For low offered loads, the DT-WDMA protocol achieves this delay since packets are rarely retransmitted because of contentions. As the offered load gets closer to the throughput value of 0.632, the delay increases substantially since a larger number of packets will now have to be retransmitted owing to receiver contentions. In the case of scheduling protocols, the minimum delay is three units since it takes one round-trip propagation time to gather the scheduling information before the packet is transmitted. However, as the offered load increases close to and beyond the DT-WDMA throughput, the delays in the scheduling protocol become lower than that of DT-WDMA.

7.2.5   Scheduling Deterministic Traffic

So far, we have assumed a stochastic model for the traffic: each slot has a packet with probability p and so on. A set of protocols with several interesting properties have been devised for the case when the input traffic satisfies the following deterministic model, also called the (α, S) constraint [WH94, HW95]:

In every set of S consecutive data slots, at most αS packets arrive for transmission at each node and at most αS packets, among packets arriving at all n nodes, are destined for any particular destination.

The parameter α is thus an upper bound on the average number of packets per slot per node, which we call the *average packet arrival rate*. The parameter S represents the time interval (number of slots) over which this upper bound α on the average arrival rate is to be met. Traffic satisfying this constraint can be quite bursty, and the parameter S controls the degree of burstiness. For example, αS packets destined for a single receiver can arrive in a single slot. But if αS packets do arrive in this fashion, no packets must arrive for that receiver in the next $S - 1$ slots, and no packets must have arrived for that receiver in the previous $S - 1$ slots. Thus, heuristically, we can interpret the parameter S as controlling the burstiness of the traffic; the larger the value of S, the larger the allowed burstiness. The parameter α controls the average packet arrival rate. Both parameters are assumed to be known to all the nodes.

The main virtue of these protocols is that they provide delay guarantees provided the traffic satisfies an (α, S) constraint. Both the *maximum* and *average* access delay can be bounded for certain ranges of values of α. In addition to delay, another consideration in the implementation of scheduling protocols is the storage required while the packets are waiting for transmission. Recall that the entries of the backlog matrix $B(k)$ represent the number of packets waiting for transmission at each node for each destination node in the network, just before the transmission of frame k. The sum of all the entries in row i of the backlog matrix is the number of packets waiting for transmission at node i for all destinations. Thus a measure of the storage required is the maximum rowsum of the backlog matrix. This quantity is called the *backlog*. Another useful property of these scheduling protocols is that their maximum backlog over all frames is bounded.

We do not discuss these protocols here but refer the interested reader to [WH94] and [HW95] for detailed discussions of these protocols and their properties.

7.2.6   Scalability and Traffic Classes

A significant drawback of all the protocols we have considered is that the control information is broadcast to all the nodes. This results in an unnecessary computational burden because every node has to process *all* the control packets. This can be a severe bottleneck in a large network (when n is large). In other words, these protocols *do not scale* from a computation viewpoint with the network size.

Another drawback is related to the notion of traffic classes. We can think of the network as supporting three different traffic classes:

- Class 1 traffic: connection oriented with guaranteed bandwidth. Traffic from applications that are very delay sensitive and thus cannot tolerate retransmissions will belong to this class. A typical example is videoconferencing.

- Class 2 traffic: connection oriented with no bandwidth guarantees. Traffic from applications that have the notion of a connection but are not delay sensitive will belong to this class. A typical example is file transfer.

- Class 3 traffic: connectionless. This corresponds to traffic from applications like e-mail or control messages. This kind of traffic is usually called *datagram traffic*.

All the protocols we have considered so far have been designed to support datagram traffic only. DT-WDMA can also support one circuit-switched connection per node [CDR90] but not multiple connections. In a computer network, a node typically has a number of connections that it has set up with other nodes but that may not be continuously active and thus may not require dedicated bandwidth. It has usually been true in most networks to date that the underlying network or MAC layers have supported only connectionless service and the notion of connection has been imposed at the transport layer. It is time to reexamine this issue in the context of high-speed networking. With the broadcast topologies that we are considering, the network layer is essentially absent (since there is no routing function). Thus the task of the transport layer would be considerably simplified if the MAC layer provided some support for connection-oriented traffic.

A protocol that is scalable computationally and provides support for the three classes of traffic we defined is described in [HRS92]. We do not describe this protocol here since it is quite complex but just state its main features. The computational scalability is achieved by having n control channels for a network of n nodes and suitably designing the protocol so that each node looks at the packets on only one control channel. There are n data channels, one per node in the network, as in DT-WDMA. If the n control channels are implemented on separate wavelengths, the protocol requires $2n$ wavelengths for a network of n nodes. The n control channels can also be time multiplexed with the n data channels so that only n wavelengths are necessary. This would result in a reduction in the utilization of the data channels.

Another media-access protocol that is also computationally scalable is described in [LCT93]. Unlike the protocol in [HRS92], this does not require slot synchronization. The tradeoff is that there is no support for different traffic classes.

$\underline{7.3}$ Testbeds

A number of broadcast and select testbeds have been developed by various research laboratories. Primarily, these demonstrate circuit switching and not packet switching,

Table 7.1 A summary of the broadcast and select testbeds described in this section. The number of wavelengths that was actually demonstrated is listed first, and the number of wavelengths the system was designed to accommodate is listed in parentheses. The Lightning and Supercomputer Supernet testbeds, which are not listed, were under construction at the time of this writing.

Testbed	Topology	Number of Wavelengths	Wavelength Spacing	Bit Rate per Wavelength
Lambdanet	Star	18 (18)	2 nm	1.5 Gb/s
NTT	Star	100 (100)	10 GHz	622 Mb/s
Rainbow-I	Star	12 (32)	1 nm	300 Mb/s
Rainbow-II	Star	4 (32)	1 nm	1 Gb/s
STARNET-I	Star	2 (80)	10 GHz (at 1.25 Gb/s)	1.25/2.5 Gb/s
BBC	Interconnected stars	– (16)	4 nm	2.5 Gb/s

because of the current state of the technology. A brief description of some of the important ones follows. The salient features of these testbeds are listed in Table 7.1.

7.3.1 Lambdanet

Bellcore's Lambdanet was one of the early broadcast and select network demonstrations [GKV$^+$90]. Each node used a fixed-tuned transmitter. On the receiving side, each node used a grating demultiplexer to separate the wavelengths and an array of receivers, one for each wavelength. Experiments demonstrated transmission of 18 wavelengths spaced 2 nm apart, each at 1.5 Gb/s over 57 km.

7.3.2 NTT's Testbed

NTT's experiment [NTIO93] used 100 wavelengths, spaced 10 GHz apart, each carrying data at 622 Mb/s. Only one receiver was used in the experiment. It consisted of a tunable Mach-Zehnder interferometric filter made using silica waveguide technology with an optical preamplifier. (See Section 3.3.6 for a description of this device.) The filter is tuned by varying the temperature.

7.3.3 Rainbow

The Rainbow-I and Rainbow-II networks of IBM [DGL$^+$90, JRS93, Hal96] were designed to support 32 wavelengths, 1 nm apart, in a star configuration. Each

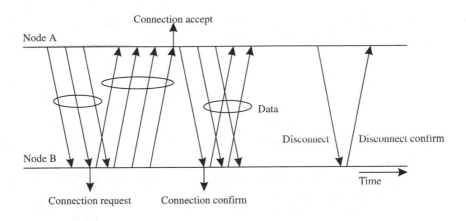

Figure 7.13 The connection setup protocol used in Rainbow-I.

node transmits using a fixed-tuned transmitter at a unique wavelength and uses a piezo-tuned fiber Fabry-Perot filter to select the desired channel. The filter tunes between wavelengths in about 25 ms. A Rainbow-I network node consists of a PC with a Rainbow adaptor card that contains the laser and receiver along with the tunable filter, as well as hardware to implement a connection setup protocol. A connection setup protocol was implemented in the testbed, which at one time consisted of seven such nodes. After a connection is set up, external data can be transmitted at bit rates up to 300 Mb/s on each wavelength.

The connection setup protocol used in Rainbow-I is a simple polling protocol that works as follows (see Figure 7.13). Suppose we wish to establish a full-duplex connection between nodes A and B. Assume that node A initiates the connection setup process. Node A transmits a *connection request* message on its assigned wavelength λ_A for a certain time duration τ_r. (If A does not receive any message from B within this period, the connection setup is aborted.) If node B is idle, it continuously scans its tunable filter across all the wavelengths looking for a connection request message from another node. Upon seeing node A's connection request message, node B locks its tunable filter on to λ_A. It then transmits back a *connection accept* message on its assigned wavelength λ_B for a duration τ_a. (If B does not receive any message from A within this period, the connection setup is aborted.) Node A meanwhile scans its tunable filter across all the wavelengths looking for a connection accept message. Upon receiving the connection accept message from node B, node A locks its filter on to λ_B and transmits back a *connection confirm* message. At this point, the connection is established and A can start transmitting data to B. Once B receives the connection confirm message, it can start transmitting data to A.

One of the advantages of this protocol is that it does not require nodes to know the wavelengths of other nodes or be able to tune to specific wavelengths directly. This requirement was dictated by the hysteresis of the tunable filter used in the testbed.

In Rainbow-II, the bit rate per channel was upgraded to 1 Gb/s. Rainbow-II was primarily built to tackle the problem of developing suitable higher-layer software/hardware to handle the high bit rates offered by the physical layer. Transport protocols such as TCP/IP were designed at a time where communication bandwidths were low, links were error prone, and protocol processing speed was not a limitation. The situation today is just the opposite: bandwidths are high, links are relatively error free, and protocol processing has become a severe bottleneck as more and more packets have to be processed each second. The result is that even if the links run at gigabit/second rates, a user application may see only a few megabits/second owing to the processing bottlenecks in the higher-layer protocols. Another consequence is that the host computer may spend most of its processor cycles on protocol processing and will not be able to run other useful applications. One solution to this problem is to improve the specific protocols themselves, and the other solution is to off-load the protocol processing work from the host computer onto suitable hardware platforms. In Rainbow-II, the latter approach was chosen, and application throughputs of several hundred megabits/second were realized.

7.3.4   STARNET

The STARNET architecture [Cha96] is similar to that of Rainbow. The unique feature here is that each node transmits data on two channels using a single laser at a unique wavelength, as shown in Figure 7.14. One channel runs at 2.5 Gb/s, and the other at 100 Mb/s. The high-speed channel is used to establish circuit-switched connections with other nodes as in Rainbow. The low-speed channel is treated differently. Node i has a receiver that receives the low-speed channel from node $(i - 1) \mod N$, N being the number of nodes. Thus the low-speed channels are used to establish a logical ring network at 100 Mb/s. Two forms of transmitters and receivers were used. In an early version called STARNET-I, the 2.5 Gb/s data was phase modulated and the 100 Mb/s data was amplitude modulated, using an external modulator. The receiver used coherent detection. The high-speed receiver used a thermally tuned laser as a local oscillator to select the desired channel. The low-speed receiver used a small fraction of the power from its transmitter as its local oscillator.

In the later version, called STARNET-II, the high-speed channel was at 1.25 Gb/s. This data was baseband modulated and the 100 Mb/s data was sent on a subcarrier channel, using an external modulator. At the receiver, a low-pass filter was used to

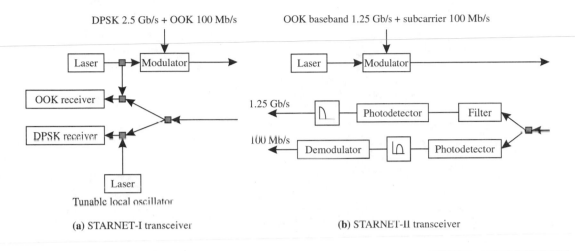

Figure 7.14 Combined modulation of two channels using a single laser in STARNET. The corresponding receivers are also shown.

extract the baseband data, and a band-pass filter was used to extract the subcarrier multiplexed data.

7.3.5 BBC Television Studio Testbed

This testbed was developed under the Research and Technology Development in Advanced Communication Technologies in Europe (RACE) program [Hoo93]. The topology of the testbed is shown in Figure 7.15. Each node in the network is a *local routing center* (LRC) connected with up to 16 signal sources and destinations. Up to 16 such LRCs are interconnected using a star coupler. Each LRC transmits on a unique wavelength and receives all 16 wavelengths from the star coupler. The LRC uses a Stimax grating (see Section 3.3.1) to demultiplex the wavelengths. The bit rate on each wavelength is the STM-16 rate of 2.5 Gb/s. Thus each signal source can transmit an STM-1 channel (155 Mb/s), and each LRC has access to all the data on 16 STM-16 (or 256 STM-1) channels. The data received by an LRC is switched by a 16 × 16 electronic switch operating at 2.5 Gb/s per port to the signal destinations attached to it.

In addition to the single-star topology shown in Figure 7.15, topologies consisting of multiple interconnected stars have also been proposed; we refer to [Hoo93] for the description of these topologies.

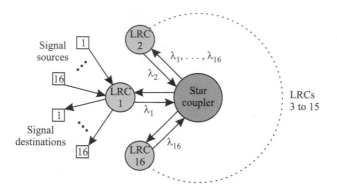

Figure 7.15   The topology of the BBC television studio testbed.

7.3.6   Lightning

The Lightning testbed is under development jointly by the State University of New York at Buffalo, the University of Maryland (College Park and Baltimore County), the Laboratory for Physical Sciences (College Park), the Center for Computing Sciences (Bowie), and David Sarnoff Research Center (Princeton) [Dow96]. It is a hierarchical WDM network primarily intended for processor interconnection. The network can have an arbitrary tree structure; a symmetric example with three levels is shown in Figure 7.16. The processors are located at the leaves of the tree, and the internal nodes of the tree nodes represent *wavelength partitioners*. The function of the wavelength partitioner is shown in Figure 7.17. These devices provide wavelength routing capability within the network and increase wavelength reuse—just as the wavelength router does in the case of interconnected stars (Section 7.1.1).

Before we discuss the architecture of the testbed, it is helpful to understand the function of the wavelength partitioners. The wavelength partitioner is a 2-input, 2-output router and also has a partition wavelength associated with it. In the Lightning tree network, the inputs from the nodes below a wavelength partitioner are combined and connected to input 1. The input from the node above it is considered to be input 2. Similarly, output 1 is split and distributed to the nodes below it in the tree, and output 2 is sent to the node above. Assume the incoming wavelengths on each input are $\lambda_1, \ldots, \lambda_N$ and the partition wavelength is λ_i. Then, wavelengths $\lambda_1, \ldots, \lambda_i$ are routed from input 1 to output 1, and input 2 to output 2, as illustrated in Figure 7.17. Wavelengths $\lambda_{i+1}, \ldots, \lambda_N$ are routed from input 1 to output 2, and input 2 to output 1.

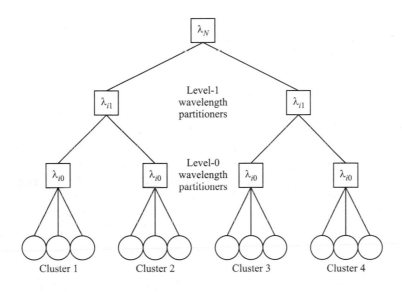

Figure 7.16 The hierarchical tree structure of the Lightning testbed. Processors are represented by the leaves of the tree, and wavelength partitioners by the internal nodes. Each link interconnecting a pair of nodes represents a pair of fibers, one for each direction of transmission.

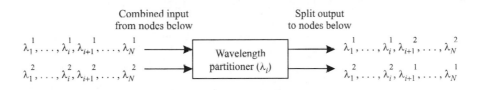

Figure 7.17 The wavelength partitioner used in the Lightning testbed.

The tree structure of the network specifies the hierarchical grouping of the processors. In the example of Figure 7.16, there are four clusters of processors at the lowest level (say, level 0), which are labeled cluster 1 to cluster 4. A set of wavelengths is used for communication within each cluster in a broadcast manner; the same set of wavelengths can be used for this purpose in all four clusters. Clusters 1 and 2 at level 0 are grouped into a single cluster at level 1, and similarly, clusters 3 and 4. A set of wavelengths (distinct from those used in level-0 clusters) is used for communication within a level-1 cluster, for example, between clusters 1 and 2, in a broadcast manner. The same set of wavelengths can be used in all other level-1 clusters, for example, between clusters 3 and 4. The broadcast and routing of the wavelengths within and between clusters is accomplished by the wavelength partitioners, as we will now explain.

If the set of wavelengths $\lambda_1, \ldots, \lambda_{i0}$ is to be used for communication within each level-0 cluster, the partition wavelengths of all the wavelength partitioners at level 0 are set to λ_{i0}. This results in the wavelengths $\lambda_1, \ldots, \lambda_{i0}$ being broadcast within each level-0 cluster. If the set of wavelengths $\lambda_{i0+1}, \ldots, \lambda_{i1}$ is used for communication between level-0 clusters in the same level-1 cluster, the partition wavelength of the wavelength partitioners at level 1 is set at λ_{i1}. As a result of this setting, all packets sent on wavelengths $\lambda_{i0+1}, \ldots, \lambda_{i1}$ from the nodes in cluster 1 are broadcast to the nodes in cluster 2, and vice versa. The remaining wavelengths $\lambda_{i1}, \ldots, \lambda_N$ are used for communication between processors in different level-1 clusters.

The Lightning network proposes to use a scheduling protocol to obtain collision-less transmission. Since the network is meant for processor interconnection, propagation times, and thus access delays, are negligible. The control channels are not on a separate wavelength but are time division multiplexed with the data channels. Furthermore, the control data is proposed to be broadcast on all the wavelengths using an arrayed transmitter. Thus all channels are used for control packet transmission for part of the time. Fast tunable receivers will be required in this testbed.

7.3.7   Supercomputer Supernet Testbed

The Supercomputer Supernet Testbed is being developed jointly by the University of California (Los Angeles), Jet Propulsion Laboratory and the Aerospace Corporation, under ARPA support [Kle96]. The principal application is the interconnection of supercomputers geographically separated by several km. A backbone broadcast WDM network using a star coupler enables circuit-switched connections using the bandwidth of a full wavelength to be established to demand, much like in the Rainbow-I network described earlier. These circuit-switched connections can be used to establish a multihop virtual topology over which packet switching can be implemented electronically, as we will describe in Chapter 9.

Summary

The WDM broadcast and select networks that we explored were primarily realized using a star topology because of its superiority over other topologies in distributing the transmitted power equally to all the stations without inducing much excess loss. These networks can provide circuit-switched lightpath service as well as packet-switched virtual circuit or datagram services. The circuit-switched lightpath service is feasible using today's technology and has been demonstrated in several testbeds. We studied several protocols for packet switching. Packet switching will become feasible when rapidly tunable components become available.

The various testbeds indicate that it is possible to build such networks and provide circuit-switched services. However, the reason they are not being deployed widely today is many other approaches, notably electronic packet switching, can provide better services (virtual circuits/datagrams) at lower cost for bit rates less than 1 Gb/s per node. Eventually, as local-area networks start needing very high per-node bandwidths, these broadcast and select networks may find their niche.

Further Reading

There was some early work on bus physical topologies for broadcast and select networks, but the star topology soon became the preferred choice. See [RL93] for a comparison of the two topologies from the link budget point of view. There is a vast amount of literature on media-access protocols and scheduling. See [Muk92, Ram93] for an overview and detailed references, in addition to the ones at the end of this chapter. MAC protocols that avoid receiver collisions are discussed in [JM92, Jos97]. A unified framework encompassing several media-access protocols as well as a unified analysis of their throughput and delay performance is described in [Jos97].

Problems

7.1 Derive (7.1), the relation between the input and output powers of a 2×2 directional coupler.

7.2 Neglecting propagation losses, prove that the choice $\alpha = 3$ dB minimizes the worst-case loss between any pair of nodes in the star network, when all 2×2 couplers used are identical.

7.3 Derive (7.3) for the optimum worst-case loss in dB for the bus topology.

7.4 There are many different bus networks; the bus network shown in Figure 7.2 should strictly be termed a single-folded (or reentrant) bus. Consider the *double bus* shown in Figure 7.18. This topology uses two transmitters and two receivers per node. Each node transmits to the nodes on its right on the top bus and to the nodes on its left on the bottom bus. Assume that no amplifiers are used. Assuming identical 2×2 couplers are used throughout the network, find the value of the splitting loss ratio α

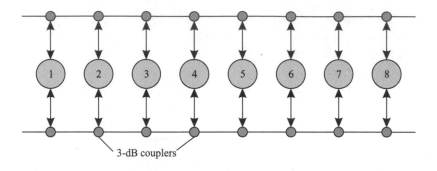

Figure 7.18   A network using a double-bus topology.

of these couplers to minimize the worst-case loss between any pair of nodes. (Neglect propagation losses.)

7.5   Consider the bus network of Figure 7.2, but now assume that we are free to choose all the $2n$ couplers to be different if necessary. How should these couplers be chosen to minimize the worst-case loss? Assume that the excess loss ratio of each coupler is fixed (say, γ) and is independent of the splitting loss. Compare this minimum loss with that obtained by using identical couplers (with optimized α) for $n = 8, 16, 64, 256,$ and 1024. Assume $\gamma = 0.2$ dB.

7.6   Prove that the protocol described by Algorithm 7.1 and illustrated in Figure 7.5 achieves frame synchronization.

7.7   Prove that in the modified SA/SA protocol the probability that no data packet is transmitted on a given data slot and given wavelength is $1 - Ge^{-G}/W$, where G is the arrival rate of control packets in each control slot. Assume the traffic is uniform.

7.8   Prove that for all values of W, L, and G, the modified SA/SA protocol has a throughput at least as high as that of the basic SA/SA protocol.

7.9   For fixed W and L, what is the value of G that maximizes the throughput of the basic SA/SA protocol? Repeat for the modified SA/SA protocol.

7.10   For fixed W and G, what is the value of L that maximizes the throughput of the basic SA/SA protocol? Repeat for the modified SA/SA protocol. What do you infer about the choice of control and data packet sizes?

7.11   Consider the expression for the throughput of the modified SA/SA protocol. Consider the limit as $W \to \infty$, and let $\lim_{W \to \infty} L/W = \alpha > 0$.

(a) Find an expression for $\gamma(\alpha)$, which is defined as the maximum achievable throughput of the protocol in this limit (that is, α is fixed, and we maximize over all values of G).

(b) Plot $\gamma(\alpha)$ versus α.

(c) What is the maximum value of γ? Compare this with the maximum achievable throughput for DT-WDMA of $1 - e^{-1} \approx 0.632$, which was calculated in a similar limit (infinite number of data channels).

(d) What is the minimum value of α for which this maximum value of γ is achieved?

(e) If you were employing this protocol and had the freedom to choose the size of the data packets, what value would you choose? (Assume you have a large number of nodes n and a moderately large number of wavelengths W.)

(f) Repeat (a)–(e) for the basic SA/SA protocol.

7.12 Consider the following *tell-and-go* MAC protocol for a broadcast optical network. There are W data channels and a $(W + 1)$st control channel. Time is divided into frames. Each frame on the data channel consists of a single data slot but on the control channel consists of x control slots. The number of network nodes n is very large so that the number of packet arrivals in any control slot can be modelled as a Poisson random variable with mean G. The arrivals in each control slot are independent of the arrivals in other control slots. Each packet announces the data channel selected and its destination in its control packet, and transmits the data packet on the selected data channel in the following frame. Every data channel is equally likely to be chosen by a packet. Neglecting retransmissions and receiver contentions, derive an expression for the *throughput*, $\gamma(G, x, W)$, of this protocol. For fixed x and W, what is the value of G that maximizes the throughput? If we denote this maximizing value by G_*, let $\gamma_*(x, W) = \gamma(G_*, x, W)$. For fixed W, how would you choose x to maximize γ_*, and what is the maximum value of γ_* that you can achieve?

Now let $x = W$ and impose the added constraint on the protocol that if control slot i, $1 \leq i \leq W$, is chosen, the corresponding data packet *must* be transmitted in data channel i of the next frame. What is the throughput of this new protocol? For fixed W, what is the maximum throughput achievable, and for what value of G is this achieved? Compare the performance of the two protocols. What do you conclude?

7.13 For fixed n, what is the value of p that maximizes the throughput of the DT-WDMA protocol?

7.14 Consider a modification of the DT-WDMA protocol where the Slotted Aloha protocol is used on the common control channel instead of TDM. Let the number of nodes in the system be n. (Thus there are n data channels, and each node has a fixed-tuned transmitter tuned to a unique data channel and a tunable receiver for data.) Assume that each frame consists of L control slots on the control channel and one data slot on the data channels. Each node simply transmits a newly generated control packet in the first control slot after the packet generation time, and transmits the corresponding data packet in the next frame. Assume $L \ll n$ so that the arrival of packets on the control channel (new plus retransmissions) can be assumed to be Poisson with rate, say, G. Assume that the packet destinations are chosen uniformly among the n nodes. (All unspecified aspects of the protocol are the same as in DT-WDMA.)

Find the throughput of this protocol. (This will be a function of G, L, and n.) What value of G maximizes the throughput?

References

[ABC+94] A. Aggarwal, A. Bar-Noy, D. Coppersmith, R. Ramaswami, B. Schieber, and M. Sudan. Efficient routing and scheduling algorithms for optical networks. In *Proceedings of 5th Annual ACM-SIAM Symposium on Discrete Algorithms*, pages 412–423, Jan. 1994.

[ABM96] M. Azizoglu, R. A. Barry, and A. Mokhtar. Impact of tuning delay on the performance of bandwidth-limited optical broadcast networks with uniform traffic. *IEEE JSAC/JLT Special Issue on Optical Networks*, pages 935–944, June 1996. An earlier version appeared in *Proc. Infocom'95*.

[Abr70] N. Abramson. The Aloha system—another alternative for computer communications. In *Proceedings of Fall Joint Computing Conference*, page 37, 1970.

[CDR90] M. S. Chen, N. R. Dono, and R. Ramaswami. A media-access protocol for packet-switched wavelength-division metropolitan area networks. *IEEE Journal of Selected Areas in Communications*, 8(6):1048–1057, Aug. 1990.

[Cha96] T. K. Chang et al. Implementation of STARNET: A WDM computer communications network. *IEEE JSAC/JLT Special Issue on Optical Networks*, 14(6):824–839, June 1996.

[CY91] M. Chen and T-S. Yum. A conflict-free protocol for optical WDMA networks. *Proceedings of IEEE Globecom*, pages 1276–1281, 1991.

[CZA92] R. Chipalkatti, Z. Zhang, and A. S. Acampora. High-speed communication protocols for optical star networks using WDM. *Proceedings of IEEE Infocom*, 1992.

[DGL+90] N. R. Dono, P. E. Green, K. Liu, R. Ramaswami, and F. F. Tong. A wavelength division multiple access network for computer communication. *IEEE Journal of Selected Areas in Communications*, 8(6):983–994, Aug. 1990.

[Dow96] P. Dowd et al. Lightning network and systems architecture. *IEEE/OSA JLT/JSAC Special Issue on Multiwavelength Optical Technology and Networks*, 14(6):1371–1387, June 1996.

[GKV+90] M. S. Goodman, H. Kobrinski, M. Vecchi, R. M. Bulley, and J. M. Gimlett. The LAMBDANET multiwavelength network: Architecture, applications and demonstrations. *IEEE Journal of Selected Areas in Communications*, 8 issue(6):995–1004, Aug. 1990.

[Hal96] W. E. Hall et al. The Rainbow-II gigabit optical network. *IEEE JSAC/JLT Special Issue on Optical Networks*, 14(6):814–823, June 1996.

[HKS87] I. M. I. Habbab, M. Kavehrad, and C-E. W. Sundberg. Protocols for very high speed optical fiber local area networks using a passive star topology. *IEEE/OSA Journal on Lightwave Technology*, LT-5(12):1782–1794, Dec. 1987.

[Hoo93] K. J. Hood et al. Optical distribution systems for television studio applications. *IEEE/OSA Journal on Lightwave Technology*, 11(5/6):680–687, May/June 1993.

[HRS92] P. A. Humblet, R. Ramaswami, and K. N. Sivarajan. An efficient communication protocol for high-speed packet-switched multichannel networks. *Proceedings of ACM SIGCOMM*, pages 2–13, 1992.

[HW95] B. Hajek and T. Weller. Scheduling nonuniform traffic in a packet switching system with large propagation delay. *IEEE Transactions on Information Theory*, 41(2):358–365, March 1995.

[JM92] F. Jia and B. Mukherjee. The receiver collision avoidance (RCA) protocol for a single-hop WDM lightwave network. *Proceedings of IEEE International Conference on Communication*, pages 6–10, 1992.

[Jos97] A. S. Joshi. Media access control protocols for broadcast all-optical networks. Technical report, Indian Institute of Science, Bangalore, Jan. 1997.

[JRS93] F. J. Janniello, R. Ramaswami, and D. G. Steinberg. A prototype circuit-switched multi-wavelength optical metropolitan-area network. *IEEE/OSA Journal on Lightwave Technology*, 11:777–782, May/June 1993.

[Kle96] L. Kleinrock et al. The Supercomputer Supernet Testbed: A WDM-based supercomputer interconnect. *IEEE/OSA JLT/JSAC Special Issue on Multiwavelength Optical Technology and Networks*, 14(6):1388–1399, June 1996.

[LCT93] C.-S. Li, M.-S. Chen, and F. F. Tong. POPSMAC: A medium access control strategy for high speed WDM multiaccess networks. *IEEE/OSA Journal on Lightwave Technology*, 11(5/6):1066–1077, May/June 1993.

[MAW96]   N. McKeown, V. Ananthram, and J. Walrand. Achieving 100% throughput in an input-queued switch. In *Proceedings of IEEE Infocom*, pages 296–302, 1996.

[Meh90]   N. Mehravari. Performance and protocol improvements for very high speed optical fiber local area networks using a passive star topology. *IEEE/OSA Journal on Lightwave Technology*, LT-8:520–530, April 1990.

[Muk92]   B. Mukherjee. WDM-based local lightwave networks—Part I: Single-hop systems. *IEEE Network*, 6(3):12–27, May 1992.

[NTIO93] K. Nosu, H. Toba, K. Inoue, and K. Oda. 100 channel optical FDM technology and its applications to optical FDM channel-based networks. *IEEE/OSA Journal on Lightwave Technology*, 11:764–776, May/June 1993.

[PS94]   G. R. Pieris and G. H. Sasaki. Scheduling transmissions in WDM broadcast and select networks. *IEEE/ACM Transactions on Networking*, pages 105–110, April 1994.

[Ram93]   R. Ramaswami. Multi-wavelength lightwave networks for computer communication. *IEEE Communications Magazine*, 31(2):78–88, Feb. 1993.

[RL93]   R. Ramaswami and K. Liu. Analysis of effective power budget in optical bus and star networks using Erbium-doped fiber amplifiers. *IEEE/OSA Journal on Lightwave Technology*, 11(11):1863–1871, Nov. 1993.

[RS97]   G. Rouskas and V. Sivaraman. Packet scheduling in broadcast WDM networks with arbitrary transceiver tuning latencies. *IEEE/ACM Transactions on Networking*, 5(3):359–370, June 1997.

[Tas97]   L. Tassiulas. Scheduling and performance limits of networks with constantly changing topologies. *IEEE Transactions on Information Theory*, 43:1067–1073, May 1997.

[WH94]   T. Weller and B. Hajek. Scheduling non-uniform traffic in a packet switching system with small propagation delay. *Proceedings of IEEE Infocom*, 1994.

8 chapter

Wavelength Routing Networks

W<small>E HAVE ALREADY EXPLORED</small> some of the motivations for deploying WDM point-to-point links in Chapter 5 and will go back to this issue in Chapter 13. In Chapter 7, we explored simple second-generation WDM networks employing a broadcast topology. In this chapter, we will explore more general WDM network architectures that provide significant advantages by *routing* and *switching* optical signals based on their wavelengths.

Example 8.1 To illustrate some of the advantages to be gained by routing and switching wavelengths, let us consider a typical telephone carrier's first-generation interoffice network shown in Figure 8.1 and its evolution. As we saw in Chapter 6, the major telephone carriers in the world have all deployed SONET/SDH networks. These networks usually take the form of rings, and the highest speed they operate at today is typically 2.5 Gb/s (OC-48/STM-16). As described in Chapter 6, the nodes in the network have *add/drop multiplexers* (ADMs). An ADM drops and adds a few lower-speed streams from the line signal. Typically, with an OC-48 line signal, these lower-speed streams are OC-12 (622 Mb/s) or OC-3 (155 Mb/s) streams, and sometimes still lower-speed streams. Thus they provide *grooming* of the signals at these latter bit rates. In many cases, it is necessary to extract and switch a large number of lower-speed streams at the nodes. This function is provided by a *digital crossconnect* (DCS), which provides grooming at DS3 (45 Mb/s) and DS1 (1.5 Mb/s) rates.

We will assume full-duplex links and full-duplex connections. This is the case for our public network infrastructure today. Thus, the ring in Figure 8.1 actually consists of a pair of optical fibers carrying traffic in opposite directions. This

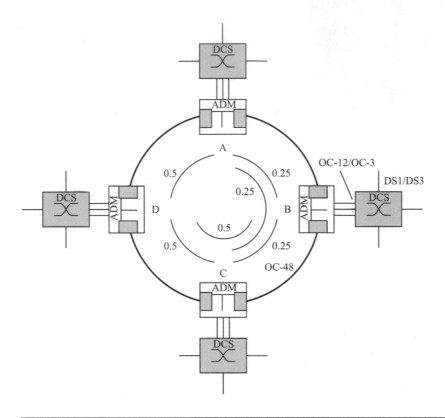

Figure 8.1   A typical high-speed interoffice carrier network. The routing of traffic is shown in the inner arcs.

network can support a total of 2.5 Gb/s traffic on its links. For example, it can support the following traffic demand (in units of OC-48 trunks) between the nodes in the ring:

	A	B	C	D
A	–	0.25	0.25	0.5
B	0.25	–	0.25	0.5
C	0.25	0.25	–	0.5
D	0.5	0.5	0.5	–

The routing of this traffic demand is shown in Figure 8.1.

As traffic demands increase, the carrier must upgrade its network. Suppose the new traffic demands, in units of OC-48 trunks, between the nodes are as follows:

	A	B	C	D
A	–	1	2	1
B	1	–	1	2
C	2	1	–	1
D	1	2	1	–

To increase the transmission capacity on the fiber links, the carrier now uses WDM as shown in Figure 8.2. At each node, the WDM signal is demultiplexed and converted into electronic form. The switching is handled electronically by the ADMs and the DCS. Each node is the source/sink of a total of four OC-48 streams. Suppose we route the traffic as shown on the next page.

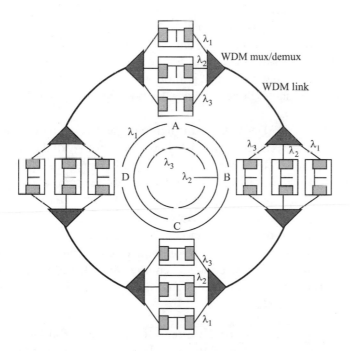

Figure 8.2 Upgrading the carrier network with WDM links. The ADMs at each node are connected to a DCS, not shown in the figure. The routing of traffic is shown by the inner arcs.

Traffic Stream	Wavelength	Number of OC-48s
AB	λ_1	1
BD	λ_1	1
AD	λ_1	1
AC	λ_2	2
BC	λ_3	1
BD	λ_3	1
CD	λ_3	1

This routing is illustrated in Figure 8.2. Note that three wavelengths are sufficient to support this traffic pattern (we do not consider any protection requirements here). As the table shows, wavelength λ_1 can be used to support three lightpaths AB, BD, and AD. Likewise, λ_2 can be used to establish two lightpaths between A and C on disjoint paths along the ring. Further, λ_3 can be used to support three lightpaths BC, BD, and CD. However, each node requires three ADMs, of which one is used solely to handle pass-through traffic. For example, at node A, all the traffic on λ_3 must be passed through. Similarly, at node B, all the traffic on λ_2 must be passed through.

Consider, instead, what can be achieved by providing some routing at the optical level itself. As shown in Figure 8.3, now the nodes directly route the wavelengths that must be passed through, without terminating them at the ADMs. In order to support the same traffic as before, we now need only two ADMs at each node.

As for the SONET ADMs, they treat lightpaths as replacements for physical links that interconnect ADMs. Figure 8.4 shows the topology of the network from the viewpoint of the SONET layer. Each link actually represents a lightpath. This topology is called the *virtual topology* to distinguish it from the topology of the underlying network (a ring in this instance). We will study several aspects related to the design of such topologies in Chapter 9.

The optical part of the network in Figure 8.3 is essentially a fixed network. Going one step further, in order to accommodate changing traffic patterns, as well as provide automatic protection switching to handle failures, switches can be included in this part, as shown in Figure 8.5. We will discuss the protection switching aspect in Chapter 10.

This example brings out a major advantage of wavelength routing: by allowing pass-through traffic to be routed within a lower layer, significant costs can be saved at the next layer, in terms of added regenerator, switch port, and processing costs. By providing switching within the optical network, different traffic configurations can be supported, effectively "future-proofing" the network. We will quantify these cost savings further in Section 8.4.

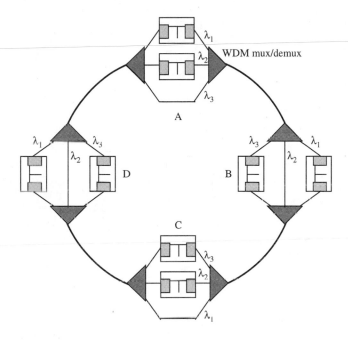

Figure 8.3 A better solution for upgrading the carrier network using fixed wavelength routing. The ADMs at each node are connected to a DCS, not shown in the figure.

The same arguments would apply if we were instead to consider a private network, where, say, ATM traffic is directly sent over the optical wavelengths. In this case, the savings are obtained in ATM processing and ATM switch ports.

8.1 The Optical Layer

In general, the topology of a wavelength routing network may be an arbitrary mesh, as shown in Figure 8.6. It consists of *wavelength crossconnect* (WXC) nodes interconnected by fiber links. The network provides *lightpaths* between pairs of network nodes. A lightpath is simply a high-bandwidth pipe, carrying data at up to several gigabits per second. It is realized by allocating a wavelength on each link on the path between the two nodes. Clearly, we cannot assign the same wavelength to two lightpaths on any given link.

Each link can support a certain number of wavelengths. The number of wavelengths that can be supported depends on the component- and transmission-imposed

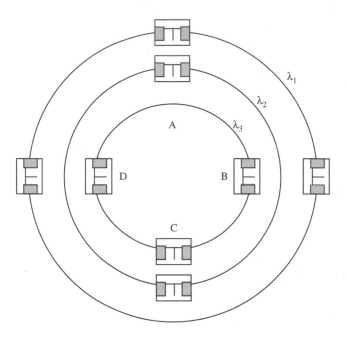

Figure 8.4   The topology seen by the SONET layer corresponding to the lightpaths in Figure 8.3.

limitations that we studied in Chapters 2, 3, and 5. Typical numbers today range from 4 to 32 wavelengths but will increase as the technology improves.

We can think of this network as constituting an *optical layer*, in the layered hierarchy of networks described in Section 6.4. The optical layer provides lightpaths to the higher layers. In addition to the pass-through capability provided by the optical layer, several other features are worth discussing:

Transparency.   Transparency refers to the fact that the lightpaths can carry data at a variety of bit rates, protocols, and so forth, and can, in effect, be made protocol insensitive. This enables the optical layer to support a variety of higher layers *concurrently*, as shown in Figure 6.12 in Chapter 6. Some lightpaths could carry SONET data, whereas others could carry ATM cells directly or ESCON mainframe traffic, all at different bit rates.

Wavelength Reuse.   Although the number of wavelengths available may be limited, the network can still provide enormous capacities, since wavelengths can be spatially reused in the network. This is illustrated in Figure 8.6, where two separate lightpaths are both carried at the same wavelength λ_1. Thus the number

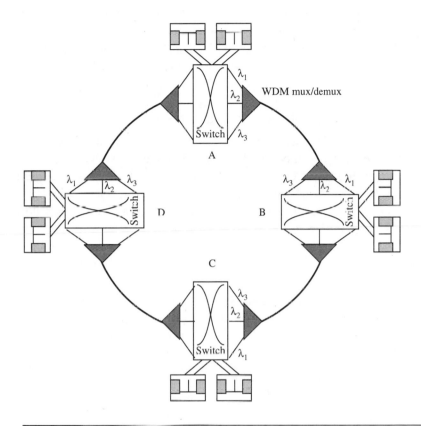

Figure 8.5 A more flexible solution using reconfigurable wavelength routing. The ADMs at each node are connected to a DCS, not shown in the figure.

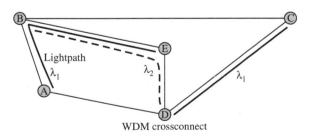

Figure 8.6 A wavelength routing mesh network.

of lightpaths that the network can support can be much larger than the number of wavelengths available.

Reliability. The network can be configured such that in the event of failures, light-paths can be rerouted over alternative paths automatically. This provides a high degree of reliability in the network. Also many optical components such as grating multiplexers and demultiplexers are passive (unpowered) and therefore inherently very reliable. We will study this aspect further in Chapter 10.

Virtual Topology. The *virtual topology* is the graph consisting of the network nodes, with an edge between two nodes if there is a lightpath between them. The virtual topology thus refers to the topology seen by the higher layers using the optical layer. To an ATM network residing above the optical layer, the lightpaths look like links between ATM switches. The set of lightpaths can be tailored to meet the traffic requirements of the higher layers. This topic will be explored further in Chapter 9.

Circuit Switching. The lightpaths provided by the optical layer can be set up and taken down upon demand. These are analogous to setting up and taking down circuits in circuit-switched networks, except that the rate at which the setup and take-down actions occur is likely to be much slower than, say, the rate for telephone networks with voice circuits. No packet switching is provided within the optical layer. It is left to the higher layer, for example, ATM, to do any packet-switching functions needed.

8.2   Node Designs

The key element in the network is the *wavelength crossconnect* (WXC). Figure 8.7 shows a functional block diagram of a WXC. The node has *trunk ports* that connect it to other nodes. Each trunk port is attached to an optical fiber-pair. We assume that all ports are bidirectional. The WXC also has *tributary ports*, or *local ports*. These ports form a local source and sink of traffic. Local ports may be electrical or optical. Lightpaths start and end at a local port. In addition, a *network element manager* is associated with the node to control and manage it; we will study its functions in Chapter 10. For the case where there are exactly two trunk ports (excluding any protection fibers), the node is called a *wavelength add/drop multiplexer* (WADM) node.

The key elements required to realize these nodes are passive wavelength multi-plexers and demultiplexers, switches, and/or wavelength converters. A wavelength converter is a device that takes in data at one wavelength and outputs it on a different wavelength.

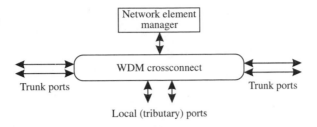

Figure 8.7 Block diagram of a wavelength crossconnect node.

Depending on the functionality available at the nodes, these networks can be classified as either *static* or *reconfigurable*. A *static* network does not have any switches or dynamic wavelength converters in it. In other words, the routing pattern at the nodes is fixed and cannot be changed. A *reconfigurable* network, on the other hand, contains switches and/or dynamic wavelength converters, giving it the capability to change the routing patterns at the nodes.

8.2.1 Degree of Wavelength Conversion

Wavelength conversion can play a significant role in improving the utilization of the available wavelengths in the network, or reducing the blocking rate for lightpath requests. It can also be helpful when we need to set up a lightpath across multiple domains administered by different operators who do not coordinate their wavelength assignment, or when we need to interconnect equipment from different vendors that use incompatible wavelengths. In the absence of wavelength conversion, a lightpath must be assigned the same wavelength on all the links along its route. With wavelength conversion, it may be assigned different wavelengths on different links along its route. To see why wavelength conversion can help improve the utilization of wavelengths, let us look at the mesh network shown in Figure 8.6. Suppose only two wavelengths, λ_1 and λ_2, are available in the network and we wish to set up an additional lightpath between nodes C and E, along the route CDE. Observe that link CD and DE both have a wavelength available, but they are not the same wavelength. So without wavelength conversion at node D, we cannot set up this new lightpath, even though free wavelengths are available on both the links along its route. With wavelength conversion at node D, we can set up the desired lightpath using wavelength λ_2 on link CD and wavelength λ_1 on link DE.

Figure 8.8 shows the different types of wavelength conversion that may be realized in a node. To illustrate the concept, only one direction of a WADM is shown in the figure, with the wavelength conversion happening for the traffic that passes

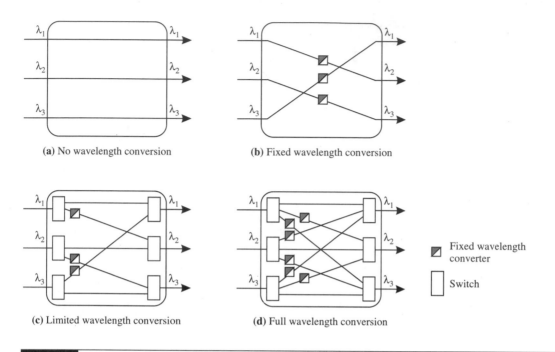

(a) No wavelength conversion   **(b)** Fixed wavelength conversion

(c) Limited wavelength conversion   **(d)** Full wavelength conversion

Figure 8.8   Different types of wavelength conversion illustrated in a wavelength add/drop multiplexer. The local ports are not shown.

through the WADM. (The add/drop local ports are not shown.) The architecture uses *fixed-input, fixed-output* wavelength converters that take in a signal at a given fixed wavelength and convert it to a given fixed, output wavelength. It is also possible to build the node using a smaller number of *variable-input, fixed-output* wavelength converters. Such a device accepts signals at arbitrary input wavelengths and converts them to a fixed, output wavelength.

The conversion capability of a node can be characterized by a conversion degree $d, 1 \leq d \leq W$. An incoming wavelength can be converted to d different outgoing wavelengths at the node. The most flexible situation is when a node has *full* conversion capabilities, in which case, any wavelength can be converted to any other wavelength. In this case, $d = W$. If $d = 1$, the node has a *fixed* wavelength conversion capability, in which case, the input–output wavelength mapping is fixed; that is, an incoming wavelength is always converted to a fixed outgoing wavelength. An important special case of $d = 1$ is when we have *no* wavelength conversion—in this case, the incoming and outgoing wavelengths must be the same. If all the nodes in the network have no wavelength conversion capability, a lightpath must be carried on the same wavelength from its source to its destination. A more flexible situation occurs when the nodes have *limited* dynamic conversion capability—the ability to convert an input wavelength to a subset of the available wavelengths in the network. More precisely:

- With *fixed* wavelength conversion, a signal entering the node on wavelength λ_i must always leave the node on wavelength λ_j, regardless of its input or output ports. With *no* wavelength conversion, $\lambda_i = \lambda_j$.

- With *full* wavelength conversion, a signal entering the node on λ_i can leave the node on any wavelength λ_j.

- With *limited* wavelength conversion, a signal entering the node on λ_i may leave the node at any wavelength $\lambda \in S(\lambda_i)$, where $S(\lambda_i)$ is the subset of wavelengths that it can be converted to.

Note that a network could be built out of different types of nodes.

In terms of implementation complexity, no conversion is the simplest to implement, followed by fixed, limited, and full conversion in that order. For the case where the conversion is done all-optically, full wavelength conversion is particularly difficult to implement, whereas limited conversion can be implemented more easily. For example, in some all-optical conversion techniques (see Section 3.8), the conversion efficiency for a wavelength is high only when it is converted to a small set of adjacent wavelengths. Thus limited conversion becomes very important in this case.

Note that there is a close correlation between the amount of switching required and the degree of wavelength conversion. In general, a certain degree of wavelength conversion is achieved by using a combination of switches and wavelength converters. Thus limited conversion allows us to reduce the number of switches and converters required, compared to full conversion. Problem 8.4 quantifies this savings. Note further that though limited conversion reduces the hardware complexity of the nodes, it increases the complexity of the network control software, which must keep track of a larger set of constraints for routing, compared to full wavelength conversion.

8.2.2 Multiple Fiber Networks

In many situations, networks may use multiple fiber-pairs between nodes to provide higher capacities. We will now see that having multiple fiber-pairs is equivalent to having a single fiber-pair but with some limited wavelength conversion capabilities at the nodes. Figure 8.9(a) shows a network with two fiber-pairs between nodes,

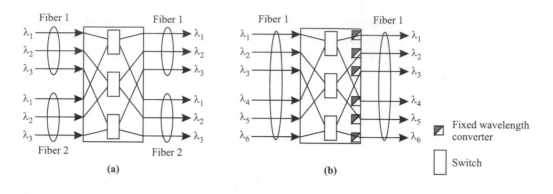

Figure 8.9   The equivalence between multiple fiber networks and single fiber networks.

and no wavelength conversion at the nodes. Each fiber-pair carries W wavelengths. At each node, signals from one fiber-pair can be switched to the other fiber-pair. Figure 8.9(b) shows a network with one fiber-pair between nodes, with that pair carrying $2W$ wavelengths. The nodes have limited conversion of degree 2. These two networks are equivalent in terms of their traffic-carrying capacity. Any set of lightpaths supported by one network can be supported by the other network as well. The proof of this is left as an exercise (Problem 8.5). Therefore, we can characterize multiple fiber networks with no conversion by equivalent single fiber networks with limited degree wavelength conversion at the nodes. For this reason, we will not consider multiple fiber networks separately in this chapter.

8.2.3   Degree of Transparency

The level of transparency offered by the node may vary. A fully optical implementation may yield a high degree of transparency, namely, insensitivity to digital/analog data, bit rate, and modulation format. At the other extreme, an implementation consisting of an electronic SONET digital crossconnect switch may offer no transparency at all.

The degree of transparency offered by an electronic implementation depends on the type of signal regeneration employed within the node. If the implementation is completely analog, it can offer almost the same level of transparency as the optical one (aside from being able to support only amplitude-based modulation formats). If the implementation is digital, it clearly cannot support analog traffic.

There are three types of regeneration techniques for digital data. The standard one is called regeneration *with* retiming and reshaping, also called 3R. Here the bit clock is extracted from the signal, and the signal is reclocked. This technique essentially produces a "fresh" copy of the signal at each regeneration step, allowing the signal to go through a very large number of regenerators. However, it completely eliminates transparency to bit rates and frame formats, since acquiring the clock usually requires knowledge of both of these. Some limited form of bit rate transparency may be possible by making use of programmable clock recovery chips that can work at a set of bit rates that are multiples of each other. For example, it is possible to buy chipsets that provide clock recovery at OC-48 or OC-12 bit rates.

A second method of regenerating the optical signal is to reshape the signal *without* retiming. This is also called 2R, and may offer transparency to bit rate without supporting analog data or different modulation formats [GJR96]. However, this approach limits the number of regeneration steps allowed, particularly at higher bit rates, over a few hundred Mb/s. The limitation is due to jitter that accumulates at each regeneration step.

The final form of regeneration is 1R, where the signal is simply received and retransmitted without retiming or reshaping. This form of regeneration can handle analog data as well, but its performance is significantly poorer than the other two forms of regeneration.

8.2.4   Realizations

Let us now see how different types of WXC nodes can be realized. First, let us consider the optical WXC, shown in Figure 8.10. The WXC has M incoming fiber links and M outgoing fiber links, each link carrying W wavelengths. The incoming signal on a link is demultiplexed by a wavelength demultiplexer. For each wavelength, there is a dedicated $M \times M$ optical switch, that is, the signals on wavelength λ_1 from each input link are sent to an optical switch dedicated to switching only signals on λ_1. For each outgoing link, a wavelength multiplexer combines all the different wavelengths from the switches into the outgoing fiber. This configuration allows a wavelength on an incoming link to be switched to any outgoing link, independent of the other wavelengths. Note that this WXC requires M wavelength demultiplexers, M wavelength multiplexers, and W $M \times M$ optical switches. Note also that this WXC does not allow a wavelength to be converted to any other wavelength. The local ports and trunk ports are not explicitly shown in the figure. In practice, some of the ports may be trunk ports and others local ports. Other implementations may realize these ports differently.

Now let us consider an optical WXC that allows full wavelength conversion, shown in Figure 8.11. This WXC has the same set of demultiplexers and multiplexers as in the WXC without wavelength conversion, but uses an $MW \times MW$ optical switch, along with MW wavelength converters. It is capable of taking an incoming wavelength and switching it to any output port on any wavelength. However, it is

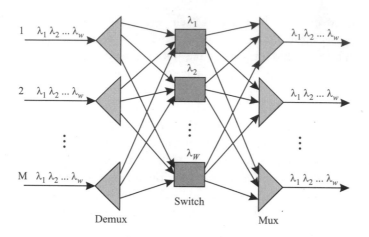

Figure 8.10   An all-optical WXC with no wavelength conversion.

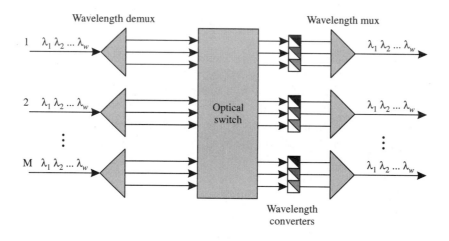

Figure 8.11   An all-optical WXC with wavelength conversion.

vastly more complicated to implement than an optical WXC without wavelength conversion.

So far we have looked only at optical WXCs. A WXC does not necessarily have to be realized entirely in optical form. A WXC can also be realized using a combination of optics and electronics. One possible generic realization is shown in Figure 8.12. Again, this WXC uses optical wavelength demultiplexers and multiplexers. After

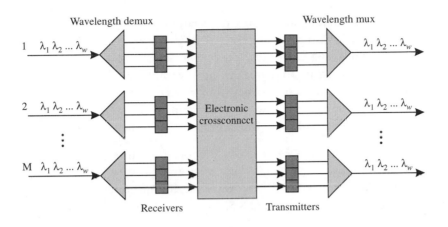

Figure 8.12 A WXC with electronic switching.

Table 8.1 Comparison of optical and electronic WXCs.

	Optical WXC	Electronic WXC
Transparency	Yes	Difficult
Wavelength conversion	Difficult	Easier
Bit rates	> 10 Gb/s	$\leq$ 2.5 Gb/s
Crossconnect size	Small	Large
Physical layer design	Difficult	Easier
Monitoring	Limited	Extensive
Components needed:		
Mux/demux	Yes	Yes
Optical switches	Yes	No
Electrical switches	No	Yes
Transmitters/receivers	No	Yes
Wavelength converters	Maybe	No

Scalability
Cost
# of components

demultiplexing the wavelengths, the signal at each wavelength is converted to electronic form and switched to another port by an electronic switch. At each output port of the switch, a laser is needed to convert the signal back to optical form. The switch itself is a simple circuit switch (crossconnect), and no buffering is needed.

A comparison of this hybrid electronic/optical approach with a purely optical approach appears in Table 8.1.

- The optical WXC can be fully transparent to the bit rate, modulation format, and protocol used by the signals, whereas it is very difficult to achieve this with the electronic WXC. For high-speed signals beyond a few hundred Mb/s, it will usually be necessary to retime the signal within the switch. Regeneration without retiming preserves transparency to bit rates but imposes additional penalties due to jitter accumulation. If we have to retime the signal, the circuitry becomes bit rate dependent, and so we lose bit rate transparency.

- With electronic WXCs, it is much easier to realize wavelength conversion, if needed. Optical wavelength converters are still very much a research curiosity today. Whether we will need wavelength converters or not will be explored further in Sections 8.3.2 and 8.5.

- To first order, the optical WXC does not care about the bit rate. Thus it can handle signals at very high bit rates, even beyond 10 Gb/s. Designing electronic switches at higher bit rates is quite difficult. The per-port speed of today's electronic crosspoint switches is limited to about 2.5 Gb/s. In practice, bit rate dependencies do arise in optical WXCs, for example, owing to filter bandwidth limitations, polarization-mode dispersion of the components, and so on, but they are relatively easier to deal with than making electronic crossconnects bit rate independent.

- Electronic switches are cheaper than optical ones and can be integrated to realize larger switches. Optical switches are yet to attain such levels of integration.

- Perhaps the most significant impact of optical WXCs is that they make the transmission system design much harder. With electronic WXCs, the transmission system consists essentially of point-to-point links with full regeneration at each intermediate node. With optical WXCs, lightpaths remain in optical form from their source to their destination, passing through several intermediate nodes. The consequences of this on the design of the transmission system are discussed in detail in Section 5.10.4.

- Once the signal is converted to electronic form at a node, it is possible to have extensive monitoring by looking at the bits, provided one is willing to lose transparency. This is not an option available with optical WXCs.

- Reliability of optical switches needs to be established since many of these are relatively new components.

- The question of cost is still open. It is likely that optical WXCs will end up being cheaper than electronic ones, particularly at high bit rates, mostly because the electronic version requires a large number of receivers and transmitters.

8.3 Network Design and Operation

The previous sections have no doubt stimulated some questions in the reader's mind. Listed here are some of the key questions for which we will attempt to provide detailed answers.

1. What is the role of the optical layer in providing grooming of signals at high bit rates, and how much can this save equipment costs at the higher layer?

2. How many wavelengths are required to build a "reasonable" network? The number of wavelengths that can be provided is determined primarily by component and other physical layer limitations, and the cost of the network will increase with the number of wavelengths that it must support. For a given number of wavelengths, we would like to support as much traffic as possible and as many nodes as possible in the network.

3. How much do wavelength converters help in improving the capacity of a network? Optical wavelength converters are being researched actively, but at this time are still laboratory curiosities. Thus we would like to avoid using them if possible. Another way to convert between wavelengths is to receive the data, convert it to electronic form, and retransmit it on a different wavelength. Although this approach is practical today, we would still like to limit the amount of wavelength conversion needed in the network from a cost point of view.

4. What are good techniques for routing and assigning wavelengths to lightpaths? The answer to this question will directly influence the answers to the previous two questions.

5. How does one combine SONET and WDM networks? How does one combine ATM and WDM networks? The optical layer provides a transport mechanism to the higher layers, such as SONET or ATM. We must determine how these layers will best operate together.

6. How are these networks controlled and managed?

We will attempt to provide answers to the first four questions in this chapter. The last two questions we will deal with in Chapter 10.

8.3.1 Traffic Models and Performance Criteria

One of the first steps in network design is to understand the type of traffic that must be supported by the network. From the point of view of the optical layer, the traffic demands are for *lightpaths* between pairs of nodes. In the case of a carrier's inter-office network, these lightpaths will be trunks (running at typically OC-48 speeds) between nodes, as we saw in Example 8.1. In the case of an ATM network, the lightpaths could provide the links between the ATM switches.

Many different models have been used to describe the traffic demands for lightpaths. These models are quite different and reflect different modes of operation of the network, and can lead to substantially different performance optimization criteria for the network. Each of these models has its pros and cons, and unfortunately, none of them provides an entirely realistic model. This is because, historically, it has been difficult to model network traffic exactly even when the traffic characteristics of the sources are known, and in our case, even the traffic characteristics of the sources aren't quite known yet. In the near-term scenario, lightpaths are likely to be set up and retained for a fairly long time (days or months). The lightpath setup may take place all at once or over a period of time to reflect growing traffic demands. Lightpaths may be taken down to reconfigure the network in the event of failures or significant traffic changes. We will discuss the relative pros and cons of the different traffic models toward the end of this section.

Depending on the temporal nature of the demand for lightpaths, we can classify the lightpath requests into two categories: *offline* and *online*. In the *online* case, the demands for lightpaths arise one at a time, and each lightpath must be provided on demand without waiting for future lightpath demands to become known. Existing lightpaths cannot be rerouted to accommodate the new lightpath request. In the *offline* case, we are given the entire set of lightpaths that are to be routed up front. The offline case is equivalent to the online case with the additional freedom of rerouting existing lightpaths when new demands for lightpaths arise. As is to be expected, designing networks to handle online lightpath requests is harder than offline requests.

There is another dimension to the temporal nature of demand for lightpaths. The demand could be for a *permanent* lightpath—the lightpath will not be taken down—or *nonpermanent*—the lightpath will be released sometime later. (Typically, the time of release of the lightpath will be unknown at the time of demand.) Note that in the case of offline demands, we implicitly assume that the lightpaths are permanent.

Another important question is whether we are allowed to block some lightpaths (the *blocking* model) or whether the network must support all requested lightpaths (the *nonblocking* model). For example, the telephone network is designed to support the majority of call requests, but some call requests may be blocked owing to insufficient capacity in the network. The goal is to design the network to keep the *blocking probability* within an acceptable limit. These models will be compared toward the end of this section.

It is impossible to design a network to meet arbitrary demands with limited resources. So we usually assume some properties for the lightpath demands that may arise. Depending on the properties assumed, the model may reflect an offline or online mode of operation, with or without blocking. The traffic models commonly employed to study optical networks are the following:

1. **Fixed traffic matrix.** In this case, the set of lightpaths to be set up is given in the form of a traffic matrix $T = (t(i, j))$, where $t(i, j)$ denotes the number of lightpaths to be set up between nodes i and j. The entire traffic demand is known up front. This may reflect a situation where the network is being provisioned at the time of initial deployment, but will not reflect the situation where lightpaths get set up or taken down during network operation. In this case, the desired optimization objective is to minimize the number of wavelengths and/or other equipment-related parameters (for example, the number of switches or wavelength converters) needed to support this traffic. This is an offline, nonblocking model.

2. **Permutations.** In this traffic model, each pair of nodes is allowed to have at most one lightpath between them, and each node is allowed to source/sink at most one lightpath. Thus, when all nodes source and sink exactly one lightpath, the set of lightpath destinations is a *permutation* of the set of lightpath sources. This model is appropriate to characterize the traffic in an $N \times N$ switch (N is the number of inputs/outputs). The idea behind this model is that it covers a wide range of "traffic states" (note that there are $N!$ different possible traffic matrices). It is not a realistic model to describe lightpath demands, but can be used to derive some fundamental requirements on important parameters, such as the number of wavelengths, switches, and wavelength converters needed in the network. This model applies both to the offline and online cases. Both blocking and nonblocking models have been studied in this context. In this case, a blocking model might imply that the network is designed to support a majority of the possible permutations, but that some lightpaths in some permutations may be blocked.

3. **Maximum load.** Here the traffic is characterized by a parameter called the *load*. The load is defined as the maximum number of concurrent lightpaths that can be present on any link in the network. This is an important parameter because the load that can be supported will be at most the number of wavelengths that are available on a link. The load is also a measure of the utilization of the links. If the load that can be supported is small compared to the number of wavelengths, the network is not being utilized efficiently.

    This is typically a nonblocking model. The objective here is to maximize the load that can be supported, given the number of wavelengths available, as well as the number and location of available wavelength converters and switches.

Equivalently, we may seek to minimize the number of wavelengths required to support a given load.

This model applies to both the online and offline cases. However, it assumes that the routing of the lightpaths is already specified—otherwise, we would be unable to determine the load. The advantage of this model is that it requires hardly any knowledge or characterization of the traffic demands, but provides either a measure of network utilization as a function of the resources available, or, equivalently, quantifies the resources needed to achieve a certain network utilization.

4. **Statistical model.** In the statistical model, we have some knowledge of the statistics of both requests for lightpath establishment and release. For example, we may assume that the requests for lightpaths between each node pair forms a Poisson process with a *known* rate, and that the holding time (the time between establishment and release of a lightpath) has an exponential distribution with a *known* mean. This kind of statistical model for the demand has been used for nearly a century in the design of telephone networks. For optical networks, it is too early to predict the statistics of the lightpath arrivals and holding times, which limits the validity of this model. Most of the work using this model assumes Poisson traffic, although there has been some recent work on non-Poisson traffic [SSAB97]. This is usually an online, blocking model.

The blocking model is an appropriate model for the telephone network. It allows network operators to obtain substantial cost savings in the network infrastructure. We would need a much more expensive telephone network infrastructure if we wanted to support all possible call requests without blocking. Moreover, this expensive infrastructure would be underused most of the time because the actual traffic would be less than the worst-case traffic that the network was designed for.

The blocking model has been applied to analyzing the performance of optical networks as well, but the appropriateness of this model is in doubt, given that lightpaths carry data at high bit rates and are typically set up on a provisioning basis. Rather than block a lightpath request, an operator is likely to add more capacity in his or her network to support the request.

When we consider nonblocking models for the demand, we usually design the network to meet all demands conforming to the assumed model. This is appropriate for the fixed traffic model considered earlier, but is not necessarily appropriate for the other models described. Moreover, as pointed out earlier, we may have to overdesign the network significantly, if *all* possible permutations, or *all* possible traffic demands with a given load, must be supported without blocking. Although the majority of this large set of possible traffic demands may be "well behaved" in that they require only moderate resources from the network, a few pathological cases may require an

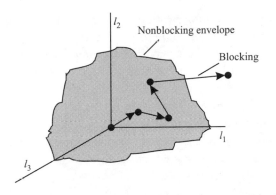

Figure 8.13   The state space of the network. Each axis represents the number of light-paths established between a different node pair.

enormous amount of network resources if they are to be supported without blocking. An example that illustrates this point will be given in Section 8.5 in the context of ring networks.

To understand this issue better, it is useful to consider a simplified graphical representation of the state space of the network, shown in Figure 8.13. Suppose there are P node pairs in the network, and l_i denotes the number of lightpaths set up between node pair i. The state space of the network is the P-tuple $l_1, l_2, \ldots, l_P$. The axes in Figure 8.13 represent the number of lightpaths between each node pair. The network is designed to support a set of allowed states indicated by the (arbitrary-shaped) envelope in the figure. The envelope depends on the traffic model used. For the maximum load model, the envelope denotes the set of all lightpath patterns that conform to a given maximum load. For the statistical model, the envelope denotes the set of all lightpath patterns that can be supported without blocking. Note that the envelope and the state space depend on the history of the network (the order in which lightpaths are set up and taken down) as well as the specific algorithms used to assign routes and wavelengths for the lightpaths. The history is not needed if we are allowed to rearrange existing lightpaths to support a new lightpath—which is, however, unlikely to be the case.

The operation of the network over time can be traced by a set of connected points in the state space through which the network evolves as setup and take-down requests for lightpaths arrive. If a new setup request will cause the network state to go outside the allowed envelope, then that request must be blocked, as shown in Figure 8.13. The *blocking probability* is simply the number of requests that are blocked over a long period, divided by the total number of requests in that time. Rather than design the network to achieve a certain blocking probability, it may be more appropriate in our case to design it to maximize the time before the first blocking event occurs, that is, the first time a request causes the network state to go outside the allowed envelope. In statistical terms, this is called the *first passage time*. This may be an appropriate metric because this is the time at which the network operator must add more capacity in the network. Unfortunately, computing the first passage time is not an easy task under most traffic models; for now, we must pick between a worst-case nonblocking model and a blocking model that uses the blocking probability as the performance metric. Both types of models will be discussed in this chapter.

8.3.2   Network Types: Static or Reconfigurable

There are two kinds of wavelength routing networks, *static* and *reconfigurable*. Both networks support lightpaths between their *users*. A *static* network uses no switches inside the wavelength crossconnect nodes. It may use fixed or static wavelength converters, but may not use dynamic wavelength converters. Nothing inside the network can change state. *Reconfigurable* networks, on the other hand, use switches (optical or electronic) within the wavelength crossconnect nodes and/or dynamic wavelength converters. Note that networks with switches and static converters are considered reconfigurable networks, as are networks without switches but with dynamic wavelength converters.

The main difference between the two types of networks is that the set of lightpaths that can be established between users is fixed for a *static* network, whereas it can be changed, by changing the states of the switches or wavelength converters at the WXC nodes, for a *reconfigurable* network. Figure 8.14 is an example of a static WXC. Figures 8.10, 8.11, and 8.12 are examples of reconfigurable WXC nodes.

We expect that a static network will be more economical than a reconfigurable one. Such a network could be built entirely out of passive components, thus being more reliable than a reconfigurable network, which would need to have active components inside it. The network in itself is fixed. In other words, a signal entering the network at some input port on some wavelength is always routed to a specific output port(s) at a specific wavelength(s). The port(s) and wavelength(s) are determined at the time the network is built. The user gets to pick among the available routes by choosing the wavelength that he inputs to a port in the network. Similarly, he can choose the wavelength at which he receives from a network port.

As we have already seen, a static network design is appropriate if we are given a fixed set of lightpath requests that we need to support. However, in most networks, the set of lightpath requests either is not known *a priori* or changes with time. The question is whether static networks can handle such requests or whether switches

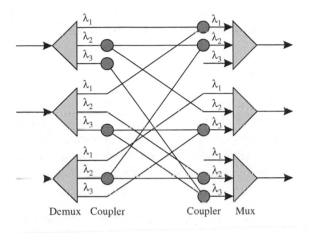

Figure 8.14 A static WXC.

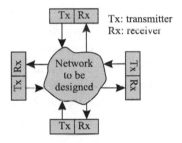

Figure 8.15 The network design problem.

will be needed inside the network for this purpose. We will explore this subject in the rest of this section. We will see that the best known static networks require a large number of wavelengths to support even traffic patterns with limited variability, and see how the number of wavelengths can be reduced by incorporating switches in the network.

We will use the model illustrated in Figure 8.15 for both static and reconfigurable networks in the rest of this section. We are allowed to design the topology of the network, which consists of wavelength crossconnect nodes interconnected by fiber links. The users are connected to the network, and each user has a tunable transmitter and a tunable receiver. To determine the capabilities of these networks to handle varying traffic patterns, we will use permutation routing as an example. We will determine the number of wavelengths needed to establish permutations of lightpaths between users in the network.

Static Networks

As we discussed earlier, in a static network, the only choice available to the users is to select the wavelength at which to transmit and the wavelength at which to receive. Such a network can be characterized by a *connectivity matrix*, which is defined as follows. If the network has n users, the *connectivity matrix* is the $n \times n$ matrix, $\mathbf{C} = (C_{ij})_{i,j=0}^{n-1}$, where C_{ij} represents the *set of wavelengths* that can be used by user i to transmit to user j.

Example 8.2   Consider the static network consisting of the single static WXC shown in Figure 8.14. The connectivity matrix of this network is

$$
\begin{pmatrix}
\{1,2\} & \{2\} & \{3\} \\
\{1\} & \{3\} & \{2,3\} \\
\{2\} & \{1,3\} & \{2\}
\end{pmatrix}.
$$

The same static network can also be represented as a *bipartite (multi)graph*. (A bipartite graph is one whose vertices can be divided into two classes such that all the edges of the graph have one vertex in each class. A multigraph is a graph that can have more than one edge between the same pair of vertices.) The graph has $2n$ vertices—n vertices correspond to the transmitters and n vertices to the receivers. There are $|C_{ij}|$ edges from transmitter i to receiver j, each edge labeled with one of the wavelengths in C_{ij}. Figure 8.16 shows the equivalent bipartite graph representation.

It is straightforward to construct a static wavelength routing network from its connectivity matrix or bipartite multigraph representation. If the connectivity matrix $\mathbf{C}$ is an $n \times n$ matrix and the union of the sets of wavelengths used in $\mathbf{C}$ is (without loss of generality) $\{\lambda_1, \lambda_2, \ldots, \lambda_W\}$, we can construct the following static wavelength routing network whose connectivity matrix will be given by $\mathbf{C}$. The network has n users interconnected by a single WXC like the one shown in Figure 8.14. The WXC node has one fiber link from and to each of the n users. Each link carries all W wavelengths. The W wavelengths on each link are first demultiplexed in the WXC, and each wavelength in the set C_{ij} from the output of the ith demux is routed by the crossconnect to the jth demux. Of course, this construction is not unique, and there could be other static networks with the same connectivity matrix.

Now let us look at the constraints imposed by the connectivity matrix on how users can communicate. Consider the example shown in Figure 8.16. Since the network is static, if user i transmits on some wavelength λ, all users j such that $\lambda \in C_{ij}$

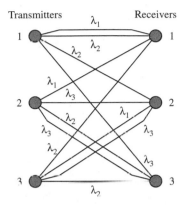

Transmitters λ_1 Receivers

Figure 8.16 The bipartite graph representation of the static network of Example 8.2. The numbers on the links represent wavelengths.

will receive the transmission. This is illustrated in Figure 8.17, which shows the subgraph associated with wavelength λ_2 from the example in Figure 8.16. Thus the lightpaths using a wavelength λ and originating from user i form a "multicast light-tree," and (since we are considering only unicast connections) only one of these lightpaths can be used at a given time. Figure 8.17 shows the three light-trees originating at each of the transmitters for wavelength λ_2. Observe that transmitter 1 can transmit to receiver 2 at λ_2 at the same time that transmitter 3 is transmitting to receiver 3 on λ_2. However, we cannot have transmitter 1 sending to receiver 1 at λ_2, and transmitter 3 sending to receiver 3 at λ_2, concurrently. This is because transmitter 3's transmission also reaches receiver 1 and will collide with the other transmission from transmitter 1, and neither will be received successfully.

This raises the following question: given the connectivity matrix of a static network, what are the lightpaths *on the same wavelength* that can be concurrently used to transmit successfully? The answer is given by the following lemma.

Lemma 8.1 *Two lightpaths (i_1, j_1) and (i_2, j_2), $i_1 \neq i_2$, $j_1 \neq j_2$, can be concurrently used to transmit successfully on the same wavelength $\lambda \in C_{i_1,j_1} \cap C_{i_2,j_2}$ if and only if $\lambda \notin C_{i_1,j_2} \cup C_{i_2,j_1}$.*

Proof. In other words, this lemma states that in order to concurrently use the lightpaths (i_1, j_1) and (i_2, j_2) on λ, λ should be an element of both C_{i_1,j_1} and C_{i_2,j_2} but not an element of either C_{i_1,j_2} or C_{i_2,j_1}. The lemma may be obvious, particularly from the bipartite graph representation, but we prove it anyway.

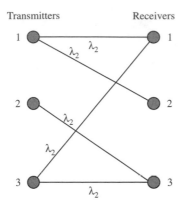

Transmitters   Receivers

Figure 8.17   The subgraph associated with wavelength λ_2 from the example of Figure 8.16.

If the two lightpaths (i_1, j_1) and (i_2, j_2) are used concurrently on λ, and $\lambda \in C_{i_1, j_2}$ ($\lambda \in C_{i_2, j_1}$), then the transmissions from both user i_1 and i_2 collide at user j_2 (j_1). If $\lambda \notin C_{i_1, j_2}$ and $\lambda \notin C_{i_2, j_1}$, only the transmission from i_1 (resp. i_2) is received at j_1 (resp. j_2), and both lightpaths (i_1, j_1) and (i_2, j_2) can be used concurrently.   ■

We now consider the problem of designing static networks to support online permutation routing and wavelength assignment; that is, we constrain the demands for lightpaths at any point in time to form a permutation. Note that in a static network the routing is determined by the choice of the wavelength.

Theorem 8.2   [BH92, BH94] *At least $(n!)^{1/2n} \geq \sqrt{n/e}$ wavelengths are necessary for permutation routing in a static network with n users.*

Proof.   We define a *tuning state* of a static network as an assignment of one wavelength to each of the transmitters and receivers. A static network with n users and W wavelengths has W^{2n} tuning states. We leave it as an exercise to the reader (Problem 8.14) to prove that each tuning state can support at most one permutation. Since there are $n!$ permutations, for any static network that supports permutation routing, we must have, $W^{2n} \geq n!$, or $W \geq (n!)^{1/2n}$. By Stirling's formula [AS72], $n! \geq (n/e)^n$.   ■

Note that the result holds for both online and offline routing. When deriving this lower bound, we have assumed that for each tuning state, the transmitter and receiver could be using different wavelengths. This is equivalent to assuming fixed wavelength converters inside the network. It may appear that we should be able to improve this lower bound in the case when no wavelength converters are used. However, the improvement that can be obtained by a more careful argument that accounts for the lack of wavelength converters is negligible [BH94].

This theorem is encouraging. For example, it suggests that to construct a network of 1000 users, we may require only $\lceil \sqrt{1000/e} \rceil = 20$ wavelengths. However, we do not know that there are any static networks that are as good as this, nor do we know how to improve this lower bound. The best known static networks today that are capable of routing permutations are summarized by the following theorems.

Theorem 8.3   [Bar93] *If $W \geq 2\sqrt{n \log_2(\sqrt{2}n)}$ and $W^2/2n$ is an integer, there exists a static network with n users for which W wavelengths are sufficient for offline (online rearrangeably nonblocking) routing of every permutation.*

The reader can verify that this theorem implies that there exists a static network with 1024 users for which 256 wavelengths are sufficient for offline routing of permutations. A similar result ($W \geq 4\sqrt{n \log_2 n}$ wavelengths) was proved in [ABC+94].

If we require online routing with wide-sense nonblocking, the best known result is the following.

Theorem 8.4   [ABC+94] *If $b \geq \sqrt{n/\log_2 n}$ and $k \geq 32 \log_2 n$ are integers, there exists a static network with n users for which $W = bk$ wavelengths are sufficient for online routing of permutations with wide-sense nonblocking.*

These two results are proved using probabilistic arguments that only show the existence of a network with the required property without giving an explicit construction. For practical values of n (say, less than a few thousand users), the best known explicit construction is the following construction based on *oblivious routing*. In oblivious routing, the wavelength assignment for a lightpath is done without any knowledge of the wavelengths being used by other lightpaths in the network. Clearly, this property makes network control easier since we do not need to know all the other lightpaths that are currently set up in order to set up a new one. In an oblivious routing network, *for every permutation*, and every lightpath (i, j) in that permutation, the condition in Lemma 8.1 would be satisfied for every wavelength in C_{ij}. Thus, while operating the network, we need not explicitly check before routing a connection (assigning a wavelength to a lightpath) that this condition is satisfied. It also follows that since only one connection can be established from and to a user at a given time, we may as well design the network so that $|C_{ij}| = 1$, for all i, j; that is, such that a connection from user i to user j will always be established on a fixed wavelength.

Theorem 8.5   [BH92, BH94] *A static network with n users can be constructed for which $\lceil \frac{n}{2} \rceil + 2$ wavelengths are sufficient for oblivious permutation routing.*

Proof.   We state the construction of the connectivity matrix (with one wavelength for each element) for the two cases: n odd and n even. To show that these connectivity matrices correspond to networks that are capable of oblivious permutation routing, we have to show that these matrices satisfy the condition of Lemma 8.1, that is, if $\lambda = C_{i_1, j_1} = C_{i_2, j_2}$ $i_1 \neq i_2$ and $j_1 \neq j_2$, then $C_{i_2, j_1} \neq \lambda$ and $C_{i_1, j_2} \neq \lambda$. We leave this as an exercise (Problem 8.13).

For n even, say, $n = 2k$, the matrix **C** is of the form

$$\mathbf{C}(n) = \begin{pmatrix} A & B \\ B & A \end{pmatrix},$$

where $A = (a_{ij})$ and $B = (b_{ij})$ are $k \times k$ matrices with $a_{ij} = i$, for $i + j < k - 1$, $a_{ij} = k - 1 - j$, for $i + j > k - 1$ and $a_{i,k-1-i} = k + 1$, and $b_{ij} = k - 1 - j$, for $i + j < k - 1$, $b_{ij} = i$, for $i + j > k - 1$ and $b_{i,k-1-i} = k$. Note that this construction uses the $n/2 + 2 = k + 2$ wavelengths $0, 1, \ldots, k + 1$.

For n odd, say, $n = 2k+1$, note that we have $k+3$ wavelengths, $0, 1, \ldots, k+2$. The $n - 1 \times n - 1$ submatrix of **C** obtained by omitting first row and last column is the connectivity matrix $\mathbf{C}(n - 1)$ stated earlier for the even case ($n - 1$ is even), and does not use the wavelength $k + 2$. We use this wavelength in the first row and last column for all but one entry: $C_{0,j} = C_{i,n-1} = k+2$, for $i = 0, 1, \ldots, n-2$, and $C_{n-1,n-1} = k$.   ∎

We now illustrate this construction for the case $n = 10$ and $n = 11$.

$$\mathbf{C}(10) = \left(\begin{array}{ccccc|ccccc} 0 & 0 & 0 & 0 & 6 & 4 & 3 & 2 & 1 & 5 \\ 1 & 1 & 1 & 6 & 0 & 4 & 3 & 2 & 5 & 1 \\ 2 & 2 & 6 & 1 & 0 & 4 & 3 & 5 & 2 & 2 \\ 3 & 6 & 2 & 1 & 0 & 4 & 5 & 3 & 3 & 3 \\ 6 & 3 & 2 & 1 & 0 & 5 & 4 & 4 & 4 & 4 \\ \hline 4 & 3 & 2 & 1 & 5 & 0 & 0 & 0 & 0 & 6 \\ 4 & 3 & 2 & 5 & 1 & 1 & 1 & 1 & 6 & 0 \\ 4 & 3 & 5 & 2 & 2 & 2 & 2 & 6 & 1 & 0 \\ 4 & 5 & 3 & 3 & 3 & 3 & 6 & 2 & 1 & 0 \\ 5 & 4 & 4 & 4 & 4 & 6 & 3 & 2 & 1 & 0 \end{array} \right)$$

and

$$
\mathbf{C}(11) = \left(
\begin{array}{ccccc|ccccc|c}
7 & 7 & 7 & 7 & 7 & 7 & 7 & 7 & 7 & 7 & 5 \\
\hline
0 & 0 & 0 & 0 & 6 & 4 & 3 & 2 & 1 & 5 & 7 \\
1 & 1 & 1 & 6 & 0 & 4 & 3 & 2 & 5 & 1 & 7 \\
2 & 2 & 6 & 1 & 0 & 4 & 3 & 5 & 2 & 2 & 7 \\
3 & 6 & 2 & 1 & 0 & 4 & 5 & 3 & 3 & 3 & 7 \\
6 & 3 & 2 & 1 & 0 & 5 & 4 & 4 & 4 & 4 & 7 \\
\hline
4 & 3 & 2 & 1 & 5 & 0 & 0 & 0 & 0 & 6 & 7 \\
4 & 3 & 2 & 5 & 1 & 1 & 1 & 1 & 6 & 0 & 7 \\
4 & 3 & 5 & 2 & 2 & 2 & 2 & 6 & 1 & 0 & 7 \\
4 & 5 & 3 & 3 & 3 & 3 & 6 & 2 & 1 & 0 & 7 \\
5 & 4 & 4 & 4 & 4 & 6 & 3 & 2 & 1 & 0 & 7
\end{array}
\right) .
$$

We leave it as an exercise (Problem 8.15) to show that this construction requires fewer wavelengths than what is needed for the network of Theorem 8.3, even for networks with a few thousand users. It is also shown in [BH94, ABC+94] by deriving a lower bound that this is the best possible construction for oblivious permutation routing.

Note that we can support oblivious permutation routing on a broadcast network topology using n wavelengths, for example, by assigning a unique wavelength to each transmitter or to each receiver. This is only about twice the number required by the preceding construction. Moreover, in the broadcast case, either the transmitter or the receiver can be fixed-tuned, whereas both must be tunable here.

The results show that the best known static networks are not adequately *scalable* for reasonable values of n; that is, they require a number of wavelengths that is a large fraction of n. Clearly, this implies that switches and/or dynamic wavelength converters will be necessary to realize scalable networks.

Reconfigurable Networks

In the rest of this chapter, we will deal with several aspects of reconfigurable wavelength routing networks. In this section, we derive a lower bound on the number of switches (or switching states) or, equivalently, the number of wavelengths that will be required by any such network. This result is a generalization of Theorem 8.2.

We define a *traffic* τ as a set of connections that have to be routed concurrently. A *traffic set* T is a set of traffics. In the permutation routing problems we considered earlier, T is the set of all connections of the form $\{(0, d_0), (1, d_1), \ldots, (n - 1, d_{n-1})\}$, where $(d_0, d_1, \ldots, d_{n-1})$ is a permutation of $(0, 1, \ldots, n - 1)$. Theorem 8.2 can be generalized to the following.

Lemma 8.6 [BH94] *A static network that supports a traffic set T must use at least $W \geq |T|^{1/2n}$ wavelengths if T is a subset of the permutation traffic set.*

The proof is along the same lines as that of Theorem 8.2 and is left as an exercise (Problem 8.17).

Note that for the permutation traffic set $|T| = n!$. This result can be further generalized to reconfigurable networks as follows.

Theorem 8.7 [BH94] *A (reconfigurable) wavelength routing network of n users that supports offline (rearrangeably nonblocking) routing of a traffic set T that is a subset of the permutation traffic set, has S switching states, and uses W wavelengths must satisfy*

$$SW^{2n} \geq |T|.$$

Equivalently,

$$W \geq \left(\frac{|T|}{S}\right)^{1/2n}$$

or

$$S \geq \frac{|T|}{W^{2n}}.$$

Proof.   A switching state is any configuration (setting) of the switches and wavelength converters used in the network. For example, if the network uses k 2×2 switches and no wavelength converters, $|S| = 2^k$. In any switching state, a reconfigurable network behaves like a static network. Since the network supports $|T|$ traffics in all using S switching states, it must support at least $|T|/S$ traffics in at least one switching state. The theorem follows by applying Lemma 8.6 to the static network corresponding to any one such switching state.   ■

Note that given the number of wavelengths, Theorem 8.7 gives us a lower bound on the number of switching states and vice versa. Just as in the case of static networks, a number of attempts have been made to construct or prove the existence of reconfigurable networks that satisfy these lower bounds as tightly as possible. We refer to [BH94, ABC$^+$94, FFP88] for the details. Although the order of growth of these theoretical networks approaches the lower bound, they are not efficient constructions for most reasonable network sizes; moreover, these networks have highly specialized (and usually centralized) topologies that may be difficult to implement in practice. Therefore, in the remainder of the chapter, we will consider reconfigurable wavelength routing networks where we are not allowed to choose the network topology.

8.4   Optical Layer Cost Tradeoffs

Example 8.1 showed that we could reduce the number of SONET ADMs required in a SONET network by employing optical wavelength routing. Essentially, we are providing an additional level of grooming in the network by adding this new optical layer. Traffic that is to be passed through can be routed directly within the optical layer instead of having the higher layer handle it. This allows us to save on equipment costs for the higher layers while adding some equipment cost for the additional optical layer. In this section, we will quantify these costs.

Note that ideally we would like to have all the pass-through traffic handled by the optical layer. However, a problem arises because the optical layer cannot perform any grooming at bit rates lower than the capacity of a wavelength. Suppose we have a total of, say, 16 wavelengths, of which 15 wavelengths worth of traffic needs to be passed through and 1 wavelength worth needs to be dropped. If all the traffic that is to be dropped happens to be on a single wavelength, then the optical layer can drop that wavelength and route the remaining 15 wavelengths through. However, if we need to drop, say, a 155 Mb/s stream from each of the 16 2.5 Gb/s streams, with the remaining traffic being passed through, then the optical layer cannot help. Each of the 16 wavelengths must be received, and the low-speed extraction must be done by the SONET ADMs. Thus designing the network so that the local traffic is concentrated onto as few wavelengths as possible becomes important.

We will study a ring network with a set of given offline uniform traffic demands. Let t denote the traffic sourced/sunk at each node in a network of N nodes (for simplicity, we will also assume that N is even), with $t/(N-1)$ being the traffic between each pair of nodes. The traffic is measured in units corresponding to the capacity of a lightpath. Thus $t = 1$ would mean a total traffic requirement of 1 lightpath per node (or, say, 2.5 Gb/s of traffic if each lightpath carries OC-48 traffic). This number need not be an integer (to reflect real-world requirements). For instance, if 20 OC-3 streams are to be sunk at a node, and each lightpath carries an OC-48 stream (1 OC-48 = 16 OC-3s), then $t = 1.25$.

Example 8.3   Let us start by considering how we would implement a network with only point-to-point WDM links and no wavelength routing or switching, called a *PWDM ring*. The network shown in Figure 8.2 is a PWDM ring. At each node, all the wavelengths are received and sent to SONET ADMs, which are connected to a DCS. For this network, all lightpaths are "single-hop" lightpaths between adjacent nodes in the ring. If W denotes the number of wavelengths, then we can set up W lightpaths between each pair of adjacent nodes.

Rather than count the number of ADMs, we will count the number of SONET line terminals (LTs). Each ADM can be thought of as being the equivalent of two

LTs. The number of LTs needed will depend on the algorithm used to route the traffic. Suppose we route each traffic stream along the shortest path between its source and destination. We can calculate the traffic load (in units of lightpaths) on each link to be

$$
L = \frac{N + 1 + \frac{1}{N-1}}{8} t.
\tag{8.1}
$$

In this case, since all lightpaths are single-hop lightpaths, the number of wavelengths needed to support this traffic is simply

$$
W = \lceil L \rceil = \left\lceil \frac{N + 1 + \frac{1}{N-1}}{8} t \right\rceil.
\tag{8.2}
$$

Since all the wavelengths are received and retransmitted at each node, the number of LTs required per node, Q, is

$$
Q = 2W.
\tag{8.3}
$$

This example has illustrated the following set of design parameters that need to be considered in determining the cost of the network:

LTs. Clearly, we would like to use the minimum possible number of SONET line terminals to support the given traffic. Note that since a lightpath is established between two LTs, minimizing the number of LTs is the same as minimizing the number of lightpaths that must be set up to support the traffic.

Wavelengths. At the same time, we would also like to use the minimum possible number of wavelengths since using more wavelengths incurs additional equipment cost in the optical layer.

Hops. This parameter refers to the maximum number of hops taken up by a lightpath. For the PWDM ring, each lightpath takes up exactly one hop. The reason this parameter becomes important is that it becomes more difficult to design the transmission system as the number of hops increases—see Chapter 5—which again increases the cost of optical layer equipment.

In general, we will see that there is a tradeoff between these different parameters. For example, we will see that the PWDM ring uses a large number of LTs, but the smallest possible number of wavelengths. Next, we show examples of two other designs that use fewer LTs at the cost of requiring more wavelengths.

Example 8.4 Here, we will consider the hubbed network architecture shown in Figure 8.18. An additional hub node is added to the ring. At the hub node, all

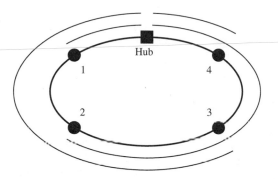

Figure 8.18 A hubbed WDM ring architecture. The lightpaths and their wavelength assignment are shown in the figure for the case $\lceil t \rceil = 1$.

the wavelengths are received and switched by a combination of LTs and a DCS. This node is identical to a PWDM ring node. The other N nodes are simpler nodes that contain just enough LTs to source and sink the traffic at that node. (To keep the example simple, we will assume that the hub node itself does not source or sink any traffic. This is, of course, not true in practice. In fact, the hub node could serve as a gateway node to the rest of the network.) Lightpaths are established between each node and the hub node h. Traffic from a nonhub node i to another nonhub node j is routed on two lightpaths—one from i to h and another from h to j. To support this traffic, we will set up $\lceil t \rceil$ lightpaths from each node to the hub node. Thus the number of LTs needed per node for this configuration is

$$Q = 2 \lceil t \rceil . \tag{8.4}$$

Two adjacent nodes can use different paths along the ring and thus reuse the same set of wavelengths, as shown in Figure 8.18. The number of wavelengths required can be calculated to be

$$W = \frac{N}{2} \lceil t \rceil . \tag{8.5}$$

The worst-case hop length is

$$H = N - 1. \tag{8.6}$$

Example 8.5 The final example will be a *fully optical* design shown in Figure 8.19, where data is transmitted on a single lightpath between its source and

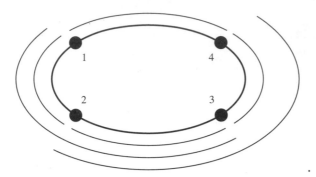

Figure 8.19 A fully optical four-node network configuration. The lightpaths and their wavelength assignment are shown in the figure for the case $\lceil t/3 \rceil = 1$.

destination and never sent through a SONET ADM or DCS enroute. In this case, we must set up $\lceil t/(N - 1) \rceil$ lightpaths between each pair of nodes to handle the $t/(N - 1)$ units of traffic between each node pair. The number of LTs per node is therefore

$$Q = (N - 1) \left\lceil \frac{t}{N - 1} \right\rceil . \tag{8.7}$$

The number of wavelengths will depend on how the lightpaths are routed and assigned wavelengths—see Problem 8.9. It is possible to obtain a suitable routing and wavelength assignment such that

$$W = \left\lceil \frac{t}{N - 1} \right\rceil \left(\frac{N^2}{8} + \frac{N}{4} \right) . \tag{8.8}$$

To understand the quality of the designs produced by the three preceding examples, we can compare them to some simple lower bounds on the number of LTs and wavelengths required for any design. Clearly, any design requires $Q \geq \lceil t \rceil$. We next derive a lower bound on the number of wavelengths required as follows. Let h_{ij} denote the minimum distance between nodes i and j in the network measured in number of hops. Define the minimum average number of hops between nodes as

$$H_{\min} = \frac{\sum_{i=1}^{N} \sum_{j=1}^{N} h_{ij}}{N(N - 1)} .$$

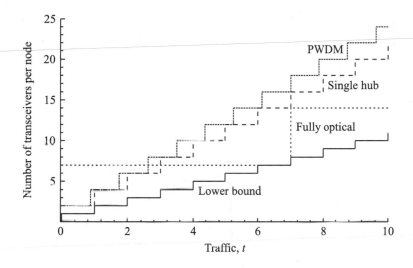

Figure 8.20 Number of SONET line terminals (LTs) required for the different designs of Examples 8.3–8.5, for a ring with $N = 8$ nodes. The lower bound of $\lceil t \rceil$ is also shown in the figure.

For a ring network, we can derive the following equation on $H_{\min}$ (N even):

$$H_{\min} = \frac{N+1}{4} + \frac{1}{4(N-1)}. \tag{8.9}$$

Note that the maximum traffic load on any link is greater than the average traffic load, which is given by the equation

$$L \geq L_{\mathrm{avg}} = \frac{H_{\min} \times \text{Total traffic}}{\text{Number of links}} = \frac{H_{\min} \times \frac{1}{2} Nt}{N}$$

$$= \left(\frac{N+1}{8} + \frac{1}{8(N-1)} \right) t. \tag{8.10}$$

Clearly, we need to have the number of wavelengths $W \geq L$.

Figure 8.20 plots the number of line terminals required for the three different designs, as well as the lower bound, for a network with eight nodes. Observe that for small amounts of traffic, the hubbed network requires the smallest number of LTs. The PWDM design requires the largest number of LTs. This clearly demonstrates the value of routing signals within the optical layer, as opposed to having just point-to-point WDM links.

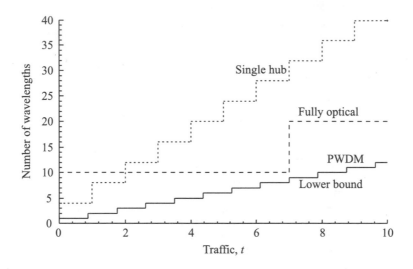

Figure 8.21   Number of wavelengths required for the different designs of Examples 8.3–8.5, for a ring with $N = 8$ nodes. The lower bound from (8.10) is also shown in the figure.

Unfortunately, the reduction in LTs is achieved at the expense of requiring a larger number of wavelengths to support the same traffic load. Figure 8.21 plots the number of wavelengths required for the three different designs, along with the lower bound derived earlier. The PWDM ring uses the smallest number of wavelengths—it achieves the lower bound and is the best possible design from this point of view. The hubbed architecture uses a relatively large number of wavelengths to support the same traffic load.

The fully optical design is a good design provided t is slightly less than or equal to $N - 1$ (or some multiple of $N - 1$). This is because, in these cases, an integral number of lightpaths is needed between each pair of nodes, which is best realized by having dedicated lightpaths between the node pairs without terminating any traffic in intermediate nodes. This brings out an important point: denote the traffic between a pair of nodes by $m + t'$, where m is a nonnegative integer and $0 \leq t' < 1$. Then the best solution is to set up m lightpaths between that node pair to route m units of traffic, and to handle the residual t' units by some other methods such as the hubbed or PWDM architectures. If t' is close to one unit, then the best solution may be to have another direct lightpath between them.

Overall, we have learned that it is possible to save significantly in LT equipment costs and associated DCS port costs by providing networking functions (routing and switching of wavelengths) within the optical layer.

8.5   Routing and Wavelength Assignment

In Section 8.3.2, we considered the case where we are allowed to design a network topology that tries to minimize the number of wavelengths required to support some given traffic patterns. The more practical case is when the network topology itself is given. We will assume a network wherein each node is a reconfigurable WXC of the form shown in Figure 8.10 or 8.11, depending on whether wavelength converters are used or not. Users are assumed to be connected to and associated with the WXCs, and we are interested in establishing lightpaths between nodes in the network.

In the previous section, we saw that the overall design problem involves a tradeoff between optical layer equipment (essentially, number of wavelengths) and higher-layer equipment (for example, SONET line terminals). We will study this problem further in Chapter 9. Here we focus on an important subproblem that is part of the overall network design problem: the *routing and wavelength assignment* (RWA) problem, which is defined as follows. Given a network topology, a set of end-to-end lightpath requests, determine a route and wavelength(s) for the requests, using the minimum possible number of wavelengths.

In this chapter, we assume that the network as well as the lightpaths are *undirected*. Different combinations of types of lightpaths and types of networks are possible as shown in Table 8.2. The combination that we explore here corresponds to a network that has a pair of unidirectional fiber links in opposite directions between nodes, and assumes that all lightpaths are bidirectional, with the same route and wavelength chosen for both directions of the lightpath. From an operational

Table 8.2   Different combinations of types of light-paths and network edges. We study the case of networks with undirected edges that support undirected lightpaths.

Undirected lightpaths, Undirected edges	Directed lightpaths, Undirected edges
Undirected lightpaths, Directed edges	Directed lightpaths, Directed edges

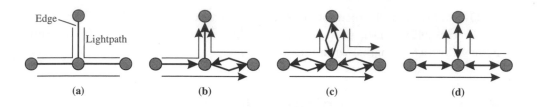

Figure 8.22 Different network models corresponding to undirected/directed edges and undirected/directed lightpaths. (a) Undirected edges, undirected lightpaths. (b) Directed edges, directed lightpaths. (c) and (d) show two different cases of undirected edges and directed lightpaths.

viewpoint, most lightpaths will be full duplex, as the higher-level traffic streams that they carry (for example, SONET streams) are full duplex. Moreover, network operators would prefer to assign the same route and wavelength to both directions for operational simplicity. Note, however, that it is possible to reduce the number of wavelengths needed in some cases by assigning different wavelengths to different directions of the lightpath. This is treated in Problem 8.29.

An undirected edge can also represent a bidirectional fiber link with transmission in both directions over a single fiber. We consider this case in the example below. While our assumption is valid for most current systems, we are also seeing an increasing number of bidirectional connections that require vastly different bandwidths in each direction. This could eventually cause operators to deploy networks with directed links and to support directed connections at the physical layer.

The routing and wavelength problem can be also be studied in the context of the other combinations shown in Table 8.2. There has been a fair amount of theoretical work devoted to solving the routing and wavelength assignment problem on networks with directed edges and directed lightpaths, which the reader can find in the references at the end of this chapter. This is the most general case, and all the other three cases are special subsets of this general problem.

Example 8.6   In this example, we will illustrate the differences between the different network models considered in Table 8.2, using an example. Assume that no wavelength conversion is available. Consider a simple four-node star network shown in Figure 8.22. In Figure 8.22(a), we have a network with undirected edges that must support three lightpaths. Note that although the load on the links is only 2, we need three wavelengths to support this traffic pattern.

Next consider a network with directed edges and directed lightpaths shown in Figure 8.22(b). Note that the load is again 2, but only two wavelengths are required in this instance.

Figure 8.22(c) and (d) show two cases, both with undirected edges and directed lightpaths. In Figure 8.22(c), we represent the undirected edge by two unidirectional edges. This corresponds to having a fiber in each direction in the real network and having W wavelengths on each fiber. In this case, note that only two wavelengths are required to support this traffic pattern.

The final case is Figure 8.22(d), where we represent the undirected edge by a bidirectional edge. This corresponds to having a single fiber over which transmission takes place in both directions. There is a fixed total number of wavelengths; some wavelengths are transmitted in one direction, and the remaining ones in the opposite direction. We may assume that this assignment can be done in a flexible manner as required for the traffic pattern. In this case the wavelength assignment constraint is somewhat different. If a wavelength is used in one direction of the link, it cannot be used in the other direction. Note that in this case, the direction of a lightpath does not affect the wavelength assignment. In practice, bidirectional systems have a fixed set of wavelengths in each direction, which further constrains this case, as we will see in Problem 8.19.

Sometimes we are already given the routing, in which case, we are concerned only with the *wavelength assignment* (WA) problem. The wavelength assignment for a network with undirected lightpaths and undirected edges must obey the following constraints:

1. Two lightpaths must not be assigned the same wavelength on a given link.

2. If no wavelength conversion is available, then a lightpath must be assigned the same wavelength on all the links in its route.

We will use the suffixes NC, FC, C, and LC to denote no wavelength conversion, fixed conversion, full conversion, and limited conversion, respectively (see Figure 8.8).

Given a set of lightpath requests and a routing, let l_i denote the number of lightpaths on link i. Then we define the *load* of a request to be $L = \max_i l_i$. Clearly, from the first constraint, we need at least L wavelengths to accommodate this set of lightpath requests. If we have full wavelength conversion in the network, then the problem of wavelength assignment becomes trivial because it no longer matters what wavelength we assign to a lightpath on a given link. As long as no more than L lightpaths use this link, L wavelengths will clearly be sufficient to accommodate this request. However, without wavelength conversion, the number of wavelengths required could be much larger. The important question is: how much larger?

Example 8.7   Consider the network shown in Figure 8.23. The set of lightpath requests is shown in the figure to be the following. Transmitter t_i must be connected to receiver r_{n-i+1}, where n is the number of transmitters or receivers.

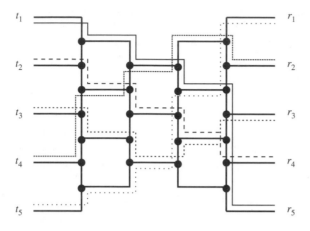

Figure 8.23   An example to illustrate the difference between having and not having wavelength conversion.

Clearly, there are many routes for each lightpath. Interestingly, however, regardless of how we route each lightpath, any two lightpaths belonging to this set of requests must share a common link. Thus each lightpath must be assigned a different wavelength, requiring a total of n wavelengths to satisfy this set of requests.

If we are clever about how we route these lightpaths, we can arrange matters so that at most two lightpaths use a given link, as shown in the figure. This means that the load is 2. Thus two wavelengths are sufficient to satisfy this set of requests, if full wavelength conversion is available at each node in the network.

Does this mean that full wavelength conversion is absolutely needed? Luckily for us, the example shown here is a worst-case scenario. We will quantify the benefit due to wavelength conversion in the following sections.

8.5.1   Relationship to Graph Coloring

It turns out that the WA problem described earlier is closely related to the problem of coloring the nodes in a graph. To understand this better, consider a graph representation of the network G, where the vertices of the graph represent nodes in the network, with an undirected edge between two vertices corresponding to an optical fiber link between the corresponding nodes. Figure 8.24(a) is an example. The route for each lightpath corresponds to a path in G, and thus the set of routes that have

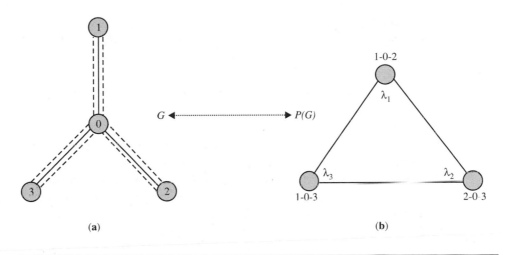

Figure 8.24   Illustrating the relationship to graph coloring.

been specified for the lightpaths corresponds to a set of paths, say, P. Now consider another graph, the *path graph* of G, denoted by $P(G)$, which is constructed as follows. Each path in P corresponds to a node in $P(G)$, and two nodes in $P(G)$ are connected by an (undirected) edge if the corresponding paths in P share a common edge in G. Figure 8.24(b) shows the path graph of the graph in Figure 8.24(a).

Solving the WA problem is then equivalent to solving the classical graph coloring problem on $P(G)$; that is, we have to assign a color to each node of $P(G)$ such that adjacent nodes are assigned distinct colors and the total number of colors is minimized. These colors correspond to wavelengths used on the paths in G. The minimum number of colors needed to color the nodes of a graph in this manner is called the *chromatic number* of the graph. Thus the minimum number of wavelengths required to solve the WA problem is the chromatic number of $P(G)$.

Example 8.8   Let the graph G depicting the network be as shown in Figure 8.24. Since there is only one path between any pair of nodes in G, given the set of node pairs to be connected by lightpaths, the routes are uniquely determined. So we have only to solve the WA problem. Suppose we need to set up lightpaths between nodes 1 and 2, 2 and 3, and 1 and 3. The resulting path graph, $P(G)$, is also shown in the same figure. The chromatic number of $P(G)$ is 3 and a coloring of $P(G)$ in 3 colors is also shown. Thus we need three wavelengths to solve the WA problem in this example.

Coloring an arbitrary graph is a hard problem that has been intensively studied for several decades. In fact, it is an NP-complete problem [GJ79]. However, there are several special classes of graphs for which fast coloring algorithms have been found. If the $P(G)$ we are interested in belongs to one of these special classes, then we can find an exact solution to the WA problem. Otherwise, unless $P(G)$ has only a few nodes, we have to content ourselves with finding an approximate solution to the WA problem. Many fast but approximate (heuristic) algorithms have been devised for the general graph coloring problem (see, for example, [Big90, dW90]), and these algorithms can be used to find good but approximate solutions to the WA problem.

Although this transformation illustrates the relationship to graph coloring, it does not prove that the WA problem is in itself hard or, specifically, NP complete. To show this, one needs to perform the transformation in the opposite direction, namely, take an instance of a graph coloring problem and convert it into an instance of the WA problem. This has been done in [CGK92], which proves that WA is indeed NP complete. However, it is still possible to obtain useful bounds for this problem, as well as develop algorithms for several specific and important topologies such as ring networks, as we will see next.

8.5.2   Offline RWA: Maximum Load Model

Theorem 8.8   [ABC+94] *Given a routing of a set of lightpaths with load L in a network G with M edges, with the maximum number of hops in a lightpath being D, the number of wavelengths sufficient to satisfy this request is $W \leq \min[(L-1)D + 1, (2L-1)\sqrt{M} - L + 2]$.*

Proof.   Observe that each lightpath can intersect with at most $(L-1)D$ other lightpaths. Thus the maximum degree of the path graph $P(G)$ is $(L-1)D$. Any graph with maximum degree Δ can be colored using $\Delta + 1$ colors by a simple greedy coloring algorithm, and hence the path graph can be colored using $(L-1)D + 1$ colors. So $W \leq (L-1)D + 1$.

To prove the remainder of the theorem, suppose there are K lightpaths of length $\geq \sqrt{M}$ hops. The average load due to these lightpaths on an edge is

$$\frac{K\sqrt{M}}{M} \leq L$$

so that $K \leq L\sqrt{M}$. Assign $L\sqrt{M}$ separate wavelengths to these lightpaths. Next consider the lightpaths of length $\leq \sqrt{M} - 1$ hops. Each of these intersects with at most $(L-1)(\sqrt{M} - 1)$ other such lightpaths, and so will need at most $(L-1)(\sqrt{M} - 1) + 1$ additional wavelengths. So we have

$$W \leq L\sqrt{M} + (L-1)(\sqrt{M} - 1) + 1 = (2L-1)\sqrt{M} - L + 2,$$

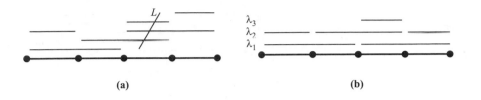

Figure 8.25   (a) A line network with a set of lightpaths, also called an interval graph. (b) Wavelength assignment done by Algorithm 8.1.

which proves the theorem.   ■

A line network, shown in Figure 8.25, is simply a network of nodes interconnected in a line. A sample set of lightpath requests is also shown in the figure. In this case, there is no routing aspect; only the wavelength assignment problem remains. We study this topology because the results will be useful in analyzing ring networks, which are practically important.

Our WA-NC problem is equivalent to the problem of coloring intervals on a line. The following *greedy* algorithm accomplishes the coloring using L wavelengths. The algorithm is greedy in the sense that it never backtracks and changes a color that it has already assigned when assigning a color to a new interval.

Algorithm 8.1   [Ber76, Sec. 16.5]

1. Number the wavelengths from 1 to L. Start with the first lightpath from the left and assign to it wavelength 1.

2. Go to the next lightpath starting from the left and assign to it the least numbered wavelength possible, until all lightpaths are colored.

Rings are perhaps the most important specific topology to consider. A ring is the simplest two-connected topology and has been adopted by numerous standards (FDDI, SONET) as the topology of choice. We expect WDM networks to be first deployed as rings.

In a ring, we have two possible routes for each lightpath. Given a set of lightpath requests, there is an algorithm [FNS+92] that does the routing with the minimum possible load $L_{\min}$. A simpler alternative is to use shortest-path routing, which, however, yields a higher load, as shown next.

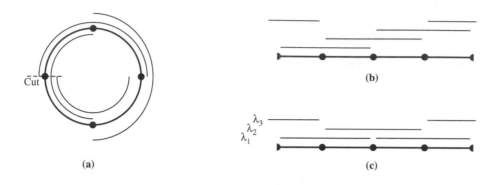

Figure 8.26 Wavelength assignment in a ring network. (a) A ring network and a set of lightpaths. (b) The ring is cut at a node that has a minimum number of lightpaths passing through it to yield a line network. (c) The lightpaths in the line network are assigned wavelengths according to Algorithm 8.1. The lightpaths going across the cut node are assigned separate additional wavelengths.

Lemma 8.9 [RS97] *Suppose we are given a request of source–destination pairs and the minimum possible load for satisfying this request is L_{min}. Then shortest-path routing yields a load of at most $2L_{min}$.*

Proof. Suppose shortest-path routing yields a load L_{sp}. Consider a link i with load L_{sp}. Rerouting k connections using link i on their longer routes on the ring can reduce the load on link i to at most $L_{sp} - k$. Note that since all these connections are routed on paths on length $\leq \lfloor N/2 \rfloor$ initially, their longer routes on the ring will all use the link $\lfloor N/2 \rfloor + i$, increasing its load by k. Therefore, the load L_{min} of the optimal routing algorithm must satisfy $L_{min} \geq \min_k \max(L_{sp} - k, k)$, or $L_{min} \geq \lceil L_{sp}/2 \rceil$. ■

It turns out that the joint RWA-NC problem is hard, even in rings. However, we can get good bounds on how many wavelengths are needed.

Theorem 8.10 [Tuc75] *Given a set of lightpath requests and a routing on a ring with load L, WA-NC can be done with $2L - 1$ wavelengths.*

Proof. Determine the node in the ring with a minimum number l of lightpaths passing through it (do not count lightpaths starting or terminating at the node). Cut the ring at this point (see Figure 8.26). Now we have an interval graph with a maximum load of L, which we can color with L wavelengths, using Algorithm 8.1. However, we still have to deal with the l lightpaths that may wrap around the edge of the line. In the worst case, we can always assign wavelengths to these lightpaths using l additional wavelengths, requiring a total of $L + l$ wavelengths.

Now with any routing, there is a node in the ring where $l \leq L - 1$. To see this, suppose all nodes have at least L paths flowing through them. There exists a node, say, node x, where a path terminates. Let y be the node adjacent to x on this path. Then link xy must have a load of at least $L + 1$, a contradiction. ■

It is possible to construct an example of a traffic pattern consisting of $2L - 1$ lightpaths, with each pair of lightpaths sharing at least one common link. This implies that all of them have to be assigned different wavelengths regardless of the algorithm used, showing that there are examples for which $2L - 1$ wavelengths will be required. However, this is not a scenario that occurs very commonly. In fact, it has been shown in [Tuc75] that if no three lightpaths in a given traffic pattern cover the entire ring, then $\frac{3}{2}L$ wavelengths are sufficient to perform the wavelength assignment. This is an example where the worst-case nonblocking model results in overdesigning the network. In order to support a few pathological patterns, we end up using approximately $\frac{L}{2}$ additional wavelengths.

Let us see what can be gained by having wavelength conversion capabilities in a ring network. Clearly, if we have full conversion capabilities at all the nodes, then we can support all lightpath requests with load $L \leq W$. However, the same result can be achieved by providing much less conversion capabilities, as shown by the following results.

Theorem 8.11 [RS97] *Consider the ring network that has full wavelength conversion at one node and no wavelength conversion at the other nodes. This network can support all lightpath requests with load $L \leq W$.*

The proof of this result is left as an exercise (Problem 8.26).

Limited wavelength conversion can help significantly in improving the load that can be supported in many network configurations. The detailed derivations of the results for this case are beyond the scope of this book. We summarize the key results here.

Theorem 8.12 [RS97] *Consider the ring network shown in Figure 8.27, which has fixed wavelength conversion at one node where wavelength i is converted to wavelength $(i + 1)$ mod W, and no wavelength conversion at the other nodes. This network can support all lightpath requests with load $L \leq W - 1$.*

By having $d = 2$ limited conversion at two nodes and no conversion at the others, it is possible to improve this result to $L \leq W$ [RS97], making such a network as good as a network with full wavelength conversion at each node. Note that according to Section 8.2.2, this network with $d = 2$ limited conversion is also equivalent to a

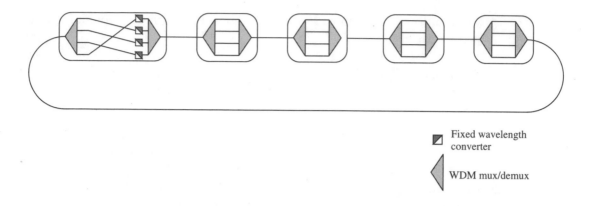

Fixed wavelength converter

WDM mux/demux

Figure 8.27   A ring network with fixed wavelength conversion at one node and no conversion at the others that is able to support lightpath requests with load $L \leq W - 1$. One of the nodes is configured to convert wavelength i to wavelength $(i + 1) \bmod W$, and the other nodes provide no wavelength conversion.

network with two fibers between some of the nodes and no wavelength conversion at any of the nodes.

Other topologies such as star networks and tree networks have also been considered in the literature. In star and tree networks, $\frac{3}{2}L$ wavelengths are sufficient to do WA-NC [RU94]. In star networks, L wavelengths are sufficient for WA-FC [RS97]. The same result can be extended to arbitrary networks where lightpaths are at most two hops long. Table 8.3 summarizes the results to date on this problem. It is still a topic of intense research.

8.5.3   Online RWA in Rings: Maximum Load Model

We next consider the online wavelength assignment problem in rings. Assume that the routing of the lightpaths is already given and that lightpaths are set up as well as taken down, that is, the lightpaths are nonpermanent. Here, it becomes much more difficult to come up with smart algorithms that maximize the load that can be supported for networks without full wavelength conversion. (With full wavelength conversion at all the nodes, an algorithm that assigns an arbitrary free wavelength can support all lightpath requests with load up to W.) We describe an algorithm that provides efficient wavelength assignment for line and ring networks without wavelength conversion.

Table 8.3 Number of wavelengths required to perform offline wavelength assignment as a function of the load L with and without wavelength converters. The fixed conversion result for arbitrary topologies applies only to one- and two-hop lightpaths.

Network	None	Conversion Type		
		Fixed	Full	Limited
Arbitrary	$\min[(L-1)D+1,$ $(2L-1)\sqrt{M}-L+2]$	L	L	
Ring	$2L-1$	$L+1$	L	L
Star	$\frac{3}{2}L$	L	L	
Tree	$\frac{3}{2}L$		L	L

Lemma 8.13 [GSKR97] *Let $W(N,L)$ denote the number of wavelengths required to support all online lightpath requests with load L in a network with N nodes without wavelength conversion. In a line network, $W(N,L) \leq L + W(N/2, L)$, when N is even.*

Proof. Break the line network in the middle to realize two disjoint subline networks, each with $N/2$ nodes. Break the set of lightpath requests into two groups: one group consisting of lightpaths that lie entirely within the subline networks, and the other group consisting of lightpaths that go across between the two subline networks. The former group of lightpaths can be supported with at most $W(N/2, L)$ wavelengths (the same set of wavelengths can be used in both subline networks). The latter group of lightpaths can have a load of at most L. Dedicate L additional wavelengths to serving this group. This proves the lemma. ∎

The following theorem follows immediately from Lemma 8.13, with the added condition that $W(1, L) = 0$ (or $W(2, L) = L$).

Theorem 8.14 [GSKR97] *In a line network with N nodes, all online lightpath requests with load L can be supported using at most $L \lceil \log_2 N \rceil$ wavelengths without requiring wavelength conversion.*

The algorithm implied by this theorem is quite efficient since it is possible to come up with lightpath traffic patterns for which any algorithm will require at least $0.5L \log_2 N$ wavelengths [GSKR97].

Theorem 8.15 [GSKR97] *In a ring network with N nodes, all online lightpath requests with load L can be supported using at most $L\lceil\log_2 N\rceil + L$ wavelengths. without requiring wavelength conversion.*

The proof of this theorem is left as an exercise (Problem 8.28).

When we have permanent lightpaths being set up, it is possible to obtain somewhat better wavelength assignments, as given by the following theorem, the proof of which is beyond the scope of this book.

Theorem 8.16 [GSKR97] *In a ring network with N nodes, all online permanent lightpath requests with load L can be supported using (a) at most 2L wavelengths without wavelength conversion, and (b) with at most $\max(0, L - d) + L$ wavelengths with degree-d $(d \geq 2)$ limited wavelength conversion.*

Table 8.4 summarizes the results to date on the offline and online RWA problem for ring networks, with the deterministic traffic model characterized by the maximum link load. For this model, observe that significant increases in the traffic load can be achieved by having wavelength converters in the network. For the offline case, very limited conversion provides almost as much benefit as full wavelength conversion. For the online cases, the loads that can be supported are much less than the offline case. The caveat is that, as mentioned in Section 8.3.1, this model represents worst-case scenarios, and a majority of traffic patterns could perhaps be supported efficiently without requiring as many wavelengths, or as many wavelength converters. In fact, we will see that this conclusion is borne out by the statistical model studied next.

8.5.4 Online RWA: Statistical Model

The results discussed so far have assumed a deterministic model for the lightpath requests. In other words, we have dealt with worst-case scenarios. In many cases, we are interested in the average-case scenario. This corresponds to the situation where we assume that lightpath arrival and termination requests follow a statistical pattern. We may allow some lightpath requests to be blocked, and are interested therefore in minimizing the blocking probability. In this case, a measure of the lightpath traffic is the *offered load*, which is defined as the arrival rate of lightpath requests multiplied by the average lightpath duration.

In practice, the maximum blocking probability is specified, say, 1%. We are then interested in determining the maximum offered load that the network can support. A more convenient metric is the wavelength *reuse factor*, R, which we define as the offered load per wavelength in the network. Clearly, R could depend on (a) the

Table 8.4 Maximum loads that can be supported in a WDM ring network for different traffic scenarios, from [GRS97, GSKR97]. W denotes the number of wavelengths available and d the degree of wavelength conversion. The upper bound indicates that there are some traffic patterns for which no algorithm can achieve a higher load. The lower bound indicates that there is a known algorithm that can support this load for any traffic pattern. For the online traffic model, we consider two cases, one where lightpaths are set up over time but never taken down, and another, where lightpaths are both set up and taken down over time.

Conversion Degree	Lower Bound on Load	Upper Bound on Load
Offline traffic model		
No conversion	$\lfloor (W+1)/2 \rfloor$	$\lfloor (W+1)/2 \rfloor$
Fixed conversion	$W-1$	$W-1$
≥ 2	W	W
Online model without lightpath terminations		
No conversion	$\lfloor W/3 \rfloor$	$\lfloor W/3 \rfloor$
Fixed conversion	$\lfloor W/3 \rfloor$	W
$2 \leq d < W$	$\lfloor (W+d)/2 \rfloor$	W
W	W	W
Online model with lightpath terminations		
$d < W$	$\max(d, \lfloor (W/\log_2 N) \rfloor)$	W
W	W	W

network topology, (b) the traffic distribution in the network, (c) the actual RWA algorithm used, and (d) the number of wavelengths available.

In principle, if we are given (a)–(d), we can determine the reuse factor R. However, this problem is analytically intractable, and in practice, the only way to estimate R even for small networks is by simulation. It is possible to calculate the maximum value of R when the number of wavelengths is very large for small networks; this has been done in [RS95]. When the number of wavelengths is small, simulation techniques can be used to compute the reuse factor. To this end, we summarize some of the simulation results from [RS95]. We will also compare the analytical result discussed earlier with the simulation results. We will use randomly chosen graphs to model the network, assume a Poisson arrival process with exponential holding times, assume a uniform traffic distribution, and use the following RWA algorithm.

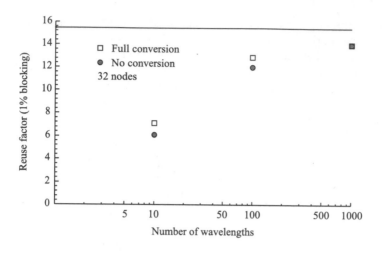

Figure 8.28   Reuse factor plotted against the number of wavelengths for a 32-node random graph with average degree 4, with full wavelength conversion and no wavelength conversion, from [RS95]. The horizontal line indicates the value of the reuse factor that can be achieved with an infinite number of wavelengths with full wavelength conversion, which can be calculated analytically.

Algorithm 8.2

1. Number the W available wavelengths from 1 to W.

2. For a lightpath request between two nodes, assign to it the first available wavelength on a fixed shortest path between the two nodes.

Figure 8.28 shows the reuse factor plotted against the number of wavelengths for a 32-node random graph with average node degree 4. The figure also shows the value of the blocking probability that can be achieved with an infinite number of wavelengths, which can be calculated analytically as mentioned before [RS95]. The reuse factor is slightly higher with full conversion. The interesting point to be noted is that the reuse factor improves as the number of wavelengths increases. This is due to a phenomenon known as *trunking efficiency*, which is familiar to designers of telephone networks. Essentially, the blocking probability is reduced if one scales up both traffic and link capacities by the same factor. To illustrate this phenomenon, consider a single link with Poisson arrivals with offered load ρ with W wavelengths. The blocking probability on this link is given by the famous Erlang-B formula

$$P_b(\rho, W) = \frac{\frac{\rho^W}{W!}}{\sum_{i=0}^{W} \frac{\rho^i}{i!}}.$$

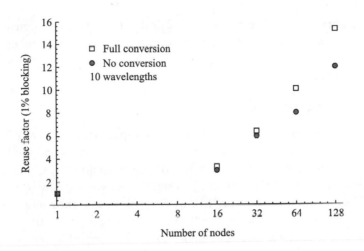

Figure 8.29 Reuse factor plotted against the number of nodes for random graphs with average degree 4, with full wavelength conversion and no wavelength conversion, from [RS95].

The reader can verify that if both the offered traffic and the number of wavelengths are scaled by a factor $\alpha > 1$, then

$$P_b(\alpha\rho, \alpha W) < P_b(\rho, W)$$

and

$$P_b(\alpha\rho, \alpha W) \to 0 \text{ as } \alpha \to \infty \text{ if } \rho \leq W.$$

Figure 8.29 shows the reuse factor plotted against the number of nodes n. The value of R for each n is obtained by averaging the simulated results over three different random graphs, each of average degree 4. The figure shows that (a) R increases with n, and (b) the difference between not having conversion and having it also increases with n. Note that (a) is to be expected because the average lightpath length (in number of hops) in the network grows as $\log n$, whereas the number of links in the network grows as n. Thus we would expect the reuse factor to increase roughly as $n/\log n$. The reason for (b) is that the average path length (or hops) of a lightpath in the network increases with n. We will see next that wavelength converters are more effective when the network has longer paths.

A similar simulation has been performed in [KA96] for ring networks. In general, the increase in reuse factor obtained after using wavelength conversion was found to be very small. This may seem counterintuitive initially because hop lengths in rings are quite large compared to mesh networks. We will see next that hop length alone is not the sole criterion for determining the gain due to wavelength conversion. In rings, lightpaths that overlap tend to do so over a relatively large number of links, compared to mesh networks. We will see that the larger this overlap, the less the gain due to wavelength conversion.

Factors Governing Wavelength Reuse

We will next quantify the impact of the number of hops and the "overlap" between lightpaths on the wavelength conversion gain. We assume a statistical model for the lightpath requests and make a highly simplified comparison of the probability that a lightpath request will be denied (blocked) when the network uses wavelength converters and when it does not, based on [BH96]. We assume that the route through the network for each lightpath is specified. When the network does not use wavelength converters, the wavelength assignment algorithm assigns an arbitrary but identical wavelength on every link of the route when one such wavelength is free (not assigned to any other lightpath) on every link of the path. When the network uses wavelength converters, the wavelength assignment algorithm assigns an arbitrary free wavelength on every link in the route to the lightpath; thus we assume full wavelength conversion. In both cases, if the wavelength assignment algorithm is unable to find a suitable wavelength, the lightpath request is blocked.

In order to compute the blocking probability for lightpath requests, we make the simplifying assumption that the probability that a wavelength is used on a link is π and that this event is independent of the use of other wavelengths on the same link and the use of (the same and other) wavelengths on other links. If the network has W wavelengths on every link and a lightpath request chooses a route with H links, the probability that it is blocked is given by

$$P_{b,nc} = \left(1 - (1 - \pi)^H\right)^W \tag{8.11}$$

when the network does not use wavelength converters. To see this, note that the probability that a given wavelength is free on any given link is $(1 - \pi)$, and thus the probability that it is *free on all the H links* in the route is $(1 - \pi)^H$ by the assumed independence of the use of a wavelength on each link. Therefore, $(1 - (1 - \pi)^H)$ is the probability that a given wavelength is *not free on some link* of the route and, since the use of each wavelength is assumed to be independent of the use of other wavelengths, $(1 - (1 - \pi)^H)^W$ is the probability that all W wavelengths are not free on some link of the route, that is, $P_{b,nc}$.

When the network uses full wavelength conversion, the probability that a lightpath request is blocked is given by

$$P_{b,fc} = 1 - \left(1 - \pi^W\right)^H. \tag{8.12}$$

The derivation of this equation using reasoning similar to that used in the derivation of (8.11) is left as an exercise (Problem 8.30).

Given the blocking probability, we denote the solution of (8.11) and (8.12) for π by π_{nc} and π_{fc} respectively. Thus π_{nc} (resp. π_{fc}) represents the achievable link utilization for a given blocking probability when wavelength converters are not used (resp. used). It is easily seen that

$$\pi_{nc} = 1 - \left(1 - P_{b,nc}^{1/W}\right)^{1/H} \tag{8.13}$$

and

$$\pi_{fc} = \left(1 - (1 - P_{b,fc})^{1/H}\right)^{1/W}. \tag{8.14}$$

For small values of $P_{b,.}$ (which is the case of practical interest) and sufficiently small values of W such that $P_{b,.}^{1/W}$ is not too close to 1, π_{nc} and π_{fc} can be approximated by

$$\pi_{nc} = P_{b,nc}^{1/W}/H \tag{8.15}$$

and

$$\pi_{fc} = \left(P_{b,fc}/H\right)^{1/W}. \tag{8.16}$$

Thus for the same blocking probability, the ratio π_{fc}/π_{nc} can be approximated by $H^{1-1/W}$. Therefore, this simplified analysis predicts that even for moderately large values of W the achievable link utilization is lower by approximately a factor of H when wavelength converters are not used in the network.

Although the preceding analysis is highly simplified, ignores several important effects, and overestimates the efficacy of wavelength converters in improving the link utilization, it does predict correctly that the achievable link utilization is more sensitive to the path length (H) when wavelength converters are not used than otherwise.

We now remove the assumption that the probability of a wavelength being used on a link is independent of the use of the same wavelength on other links. However, we will continue to assume that the events on one wavelength are independent of the events on all other wavelengths. We first consider networks with no wavelength conversion and calculate the probability that a lightpath request that chooses a route with H links is blocked. Any lightpath that has already been established and uses one of these H links is termed an *interfering* lightpath. We assume that an interfering lightpath that uses one of these H links, say, link i, will *not use the next link $i + 1$* with probability π_l. (So with probability π_l a lightpath that interferes on link i of the route chosen by the lightpath request leaves after that link.) For any wavelength λ, we also assume that a *new* lightpath request (one that does not interfere on link

$i - 1$) would interfere on link i of the route chosen by the lightpath request with probability π_n. This gives us the following conditional probabilities for the use of wavelength λ on link i:

Prob(λ used on link $i|\lambda$ not used on link $i - 1$) $= \pi_n$,

and

Prob(λ used on link $i|\lambda$ used on link $i - 1$) $= (1 - \pi_l) + \pi_l\pi_n$.

Note that under the assumption of independent use of the same wavelength on the links, both these conditional probabilities must equal π; thus this assumption corresponds to setting $\pi_l = 1$ and $\pi = \pi_n$.

Using the same reasoning as that used to derive (8.11), we can show that now

$$P_{b,nc} = \left(1 - (1 - \pi_n)^H\right)^W. \tag{8.17}$$

For networks with full wavelength conversion, the following expression for blocking probability can be derived under a set of assumptions that are similar to that used to derive (8.17):

$$P_{b,fc} = 1 - \prod_{i=1}^{H}\left(1 - \frac{\pi_i^W - (1 - \pi_l + \pi_l\pi_n)^W\pi_i^W}{1 - \pi_{i-1}^W}\right), \tag{8.18}$$

where

$$\pi_i = \frac{\pi_n}{\pi_n + \pi_l - \pi_n\pi_l}\left(1 - (1 - (\pi_l + \pi_n - \pi_l\pi_n))^i\right).$$

For a given blocking probability, we can solve (8.17) and (8.18) for π_{nc} and π_{fc}, respectively. Then we can approximate the *conversion gain* π_{fc}/π_{nc} for small blocking probabilities and $H \gg 1/\pi_l$ by

$$\frac{\pi_{fc}}{\pi_{nc}} \approx H^{1-1/W}(\pi_n + \pi_l - \pi_l\pi_n). \tag{8.19}$$

Define the *interference length* $L_i = 1/\pi_l$. L_i is an approximation to the expected number of links that an interfering lightpath uses on the route chosen by a lightpath request. The assumption $H \gg 1/\pi_l = L_i$ is thus equivalent to assuming that the number of hops in the path chosen by a lightpath request is much larger than the average number of hops that it shares with an interfering lightpath. This assumption is a good one when the network is well connected, but it is a poorer approximation to the behavior in, say, rings.

The conversion gain under the assumption of independent use of a wavelength on each link ($\pi_l = 1$) is approximately $H^{1-1/W}$. Thus the conversion gain given by

(8.19) is lower than this by the factor $(\pi_n + \pi_l - \pi_l\pi_n)$. This factor is the *mixing probability*: the probability that at a node along the route chosen by a lightpath request, an interfering lightpath leaves or a new interfering lightpath joins. Thus the conversion gain is more in networks where there is more mixing, for example, in dense mesh networks where the node degrees (switch sizes) are large, as opposed to ring networks where the mixing is small and the interference length is large.

In summary, path length is only one of the factors governing the amount of reuse we get by using wavelength conversion; interference length and switch sizes are other important factors.

Wavelength Assignment and Alternate Routes

So far, while studying the online RWA problem using a statistical model for the traffic, we have assumed a fixed route between each source–destination pair. We will now present some simulation results to show the effect of using alternate routes. We will also consider two different ways of assigning wavelengths once the route has been selected. Thus we consider the following four RWA algorithms.

Random-1. For a lightpath request between two nodes, choose at random one of the available wavelengths on a fixed shortest path between the two nodes.

Random-2. Fix two shortest paths between every pair of nodes. For a lightpath request between two nodes, choose at random one of the available wavelengths on the first shortest path between the two nodes. If no such wavelength is available, choose a random one of the available wavelengths on the second shortest path.

Max-used-1. For a lightpath request between two nodes, among the available wavelengths on a fixed shortest path between the two nodes, choose the one that is used the most number of times in the network at that point of time.

Max-used-2. Fix two shortest paths between every pair of nodes. For a lightpath request between two nodes, among the available wavelengths on the first shortest path between the two nodes, choose the one that is used the most number of times in the network at that point of time. If no such wavelength is available, among the available wavelengths on the second shortest path between the two nodes, choose the one that is used the most number of times in the network at that point of time.

The topology we consider is the 20-node, 39-link network from [RS95]. We assume 32 wavelengths are available on each link and that the traffic is uniform (same for every pair of nodes). The reuse factor obtained by using each of the above four RWA algorithms for a blocking probability of 1% is shown in Table 8.5. Observe that the reuse factor improves substantially when an alternate path is considered.

Table 8.5 Reuse factor for 1% blocking for different RWA algorithms for the 20-node network considered in [RS95].

RWA Algorithm	Reuse Factor
Random-1	6.9
Random-2	7.8
Max-used-1	7.5
Max-used-2	8.3

Ideally we would like to have more alternate routes for longer routes and less for shorter routes. This will help reduce the blocking probability on longer routes, and ensure better fairness overall. Otherwise, short routes tend to have much less blocking than long routes. Having more routes to consider usually increases the control traffic in the network and leads to an additional compuational burden on the network nodes, but this is not significant in networks with a moderate number of nodes where lightpaths are set up and taken down slowly.

In addition to the choice of routes, the wavelength assignment algorithm also plays an important role in determining the reuse factor. Note that for the same number of available paths, the max-used algorithms have a distinct advantage over the random algorithms. The intuitive reason for this phenonmenon is that the max-used strategy provides a higher likelihood of finding the same free wavelength on all the links along a particular route. A drawback of the max-used algorithm is that it requires a knowledge of the wavelengths in use by all other connections in the network. When the routing and wavelength assignment is performed in a distributed manner, such information typically has to be obtained by means of periodic updates broadcast by each node. This again increases the control traffic load on the network.

8.6 Architectural Variations

In the wavelength routing networks that we have studied so far, the nodes are able to route signals based on their wavelength. A variation of this architecture arises when the nodes are able to route signals but the routing is independent of the wavelength. These networks are called *linear lightwave networks* (LLNs) [Ste90, SBJS93, BSSLB95]. The motivation for this is that the wavelength-independent routers are likely to be easier to build and cheaper. An LLN is shown in Figure 8.30. The nodes in the network have so-called *linear splitters and combiners* (LSCs). A simple LSC with three inputs and three outputs is

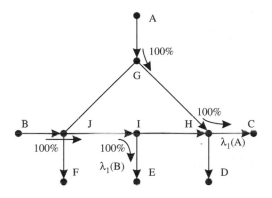

Figure 8.30   A linear lightwave network with two lightpaths set up using the same wavelength λ_1.

shown in Figure 8.31. It is made up of splitters and combiners, with switches in the middle. Depending on the switch settings, the power coming into an input port can be transmitted on a subset of the output ports. The switch settings determine the specific set of output ports. For example, in Figure 8.31, the switches are set so that signal S_1 at the first input port is transmitted out on the first and second output ports but not on the third output port. Note that since the LSC is not sensitive to the wavelength, *all wavelengths* present in the input signal S_1 are transmitted out on the first and second output ports. Similarly, S_2 is transmitted out on the first and third output ports.

In this sense, as explained earlier, an LLN can be thought of as a wavelength routing network where the routing nodes are not wavelength selective. LLNs provide a limited amount of wavelength reuse capability. For example, by setting the LSCs at nodes as indicated in Figure 8.30, we can realize two simultaneous lightpaths using wavelength λ_1, one from B to E, and another from A to C.

However, LLNs also impose a number of additional constraints on how light-paths can be routed. Suppose we wish to set up another lightpath from B to C, along the route BJIHC in the network of Figure 8.30. Clearly, this cannot use λ_1 since it is already in use on links along the route of the lightpath. So we must set up this lightpath on another wavelength λ_2, as shown in Figure 8.32. In order to set up this lightpath, we must change the switch settings at node I so that power is transmitted on link IH in addition to link IE. Unfortunately, this results in creating *unwanted* lightpaths. In addition to λ_2, link IH will carry some power at λ_1, also originating at B. The result is that node C would now receive signals at λ_1 from two different

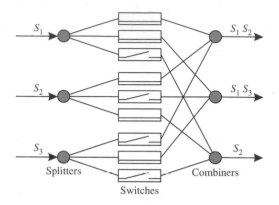

Figure 8.31   A linear splitter and combiner node. The switch settings control the distribution of signal power from each input port onto the output ports.

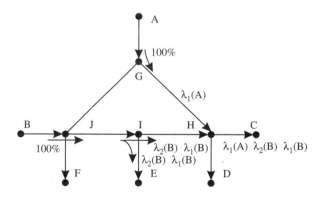

Figure 8.32   Illustrating the creation of unwanted lightpaths in a linear lightwave network.

nodes, A and B. Clearly, these signals would interfere with each other. So we cannot set up another lightpath from B to C!

Other forms of interference also can occur in an LLN. Suppose we have set up a lightpath from A to C on λ_1 and a lightpath from B to C on λ_2, as shown in Figure 8.33(a). Now suppose we wish to set up another lightpath from A to E on λ_3 using the path AGJIE. This would result in wavelength λ_1 from A arriving on two different paths to the two inputs at node H, resulting in undesirable interference

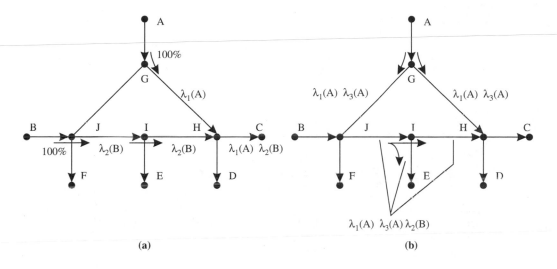

Figure 8.33 Multipath interference in a linear lightwave network.

again. Such conditions must be prevented by the routing algorithm. Several routing algorithms have been devised for this purpose [BSSLB95].

The advantage of an LLN is that it makes multicasting very easy. In fact, in order to understand the concept of routing in an LLN, we must think in terms of *multicast trees*. A multicast tree is a tree consisting of a subset of the links in the network, on which a signal is broadcast. For example, a multicast tree from node A to nodes C, F, G, H, and J is shown in Figure 8.34. Each time we establish a connection in the network, we are actually setting up a multicast tree. Multiple multicast trees can be set up as long as they are *edge-disjoint*, that is, they do not share any common edges. Another multicast tree is also shown in Figure 8.34. The edge-disjoint property is needed to ensure that there is no interference between the multiple signals being multicasted.

The LLN concept has also been extended to work in cases where the LSCs in the network are partially wavelength selective; that is, they can separately switch groups of wavelengths, called wavebands, but cannot distinguish between wavelengths within a waveband. Within each waveband, we can establish edge-disjoint multicast trees. Overall, the added complexity of routing, along with the splitting and combining losses present at the nodes, is preventing this concept from becoming practical. LLNs may still play a role when multicasting capabilities must be incorporated within a wavelength routing network. An efficient way to support multicasting

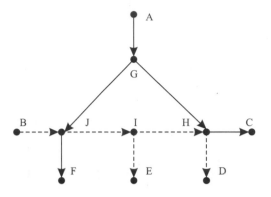

Figure 8.34   Multicasting in an LLN. Two multicast trees are shown.

in a regular wavelength routing network is to use an LSC on the desired multicast wavelength instead of the switch shown in Figure 8.10.

Summary

We explored wavelength routing networks in this chapter. We saw that there is a clear benefit to building wavelength routing networks, as opposed to simple point-to-point WDM links. The main benefit is that traffic that is not to be terminated within a node can be passed through by the node, resulting in significant savings in higher-layer terminating equipment. However, the traffic must be carefully groomed so that the traffic to be dropped is packed onto as few wavelengths as possible.

Next, we explored the fundamental capabilities of these networks and showed that switching must be provided within the network if we are to realize scalable networks capable of supporting a variety of traffic patterns.

Given a network, the problem of routing and assigning wavelengths to lightpaths is a complex and important one, and clever algorithms are needed to ensure that this function is performed using a minimum number of wavelengths. We saw that the increase in traffic carrying capacity obtained in the network due to wavelength converters depends strongly on the traffic model. For a worst-case nonblocking-type model, we saw that significant gains can be obtained by using some amount of wavelength conversion. On the other hand, for the statistical blocking model, the achievable gains do not appear to be very large for most of the cases studied in the literature. Determining the right traffic model to use thus becomes very important.

Finally, we explored some architectural variants of wavelength routing networks suitable for supporting multicast connections.

Further Reading

Tutorials on wavelength routing networks appear in [Ram93a, Ram93b]. The various wavelength routing testbeds are covered in [Ale93, Kam96, Bra93, Cha94, CEG+96, Hil93, Joh95, Joh96, HH96, ACT, WASG96, Der95]. These papers, and also [RS95] describe different types of node architectures. The use of regeneration without retiming and its impact on transparency is addressed in [GJR96, BCG95].

The issue of how much cost savings is afforded by providing networking functions within the optical layer is only beginning to be understood. For some more insights into this issue, see [RLB95, Bal96, GRS98]. The material in this chapter is based on [GRS98].

The design of optimal network topologies that minimize the number of wavelengths required is addressed in [BH94, Bar93, ABC+94, Pan92, PS93, BCB96, Lin96]. Several papers [ABC+94, RU94, RS95, CGK92, RS97, MKR95, KS97, KPEJ97, ACKP97] study the offline routing and wavelength assignment problem. The online statistical model is analyzed in [BK95, RS95, KA96, SAS96, YLES96, BH96]. Very little work [GK97] exists on the worst-case analysis of the online deterministic model. There is also a vast body of literature describing routing and wavelength assignment heuristics. See, for example, [CGK92, SBJS93, RS95, Bir96, WD96, SOW95].

For more on linear lightwave networks, see [Ste90, SBJS93, BSSLB95, KG95, BPS93].

Problems

8.1 Consider the network design approach using fixed wavelength routing shown in Example 8.1. Suppose the traffic requirements are as follows:

	A	B	C	D
A	–	3	–	3
B	3	–	2	3
C	–	2	–	2
D	3	3	2	–

(a) Do a careful routing of traffic onto each wavelength so as to minimize the number of wavelengths needed.

(b) How do you know that your solution uses the minimum possible number of wavelengths required to do this routing for any algorithm?

(c) How many ADMs are required at each node to support this traffic?

(d) How many ADMs are required at each node if instead of fixed wavelength routing, you decided to use point-to-point WDM links and receive and retransmit all the wavelengths at each node? How many ADMs does wavelength routing eliminate?

8.2   Redraw Figure 8.8(d) using variable-input, fixed-output wavelength converters.

8.3   Draw block diagrams of one or more node architectures similar to Figure 8.11 that allow full wavelength conversion.

8.4   Consider the implementation of a node shown in Figure 8.8 using limited conversion (Figure 8.8(c)) and full conversion (Figure 8.8(d)).

(a) What is the number and size of the optical switches and wavelength converters required for each case?

(b) The preceding node has one input fiber port carrying three wavelengths and one output fiber port carrying three wavelengths (the WDM demux and mux units are not shown in the figure). Draw a block diagram of a node with two input fiber ports and two output fiber ports, showing limited conversion of degree 2 and full conversion (of degree 3), using fixed-output wavelength converters. What is the number and size of the optical switches and wavelength converters required for each case?

8.5   Show that a network having P fiber-pairs between nodes and W wavelengths on each fiber with no wavelength conversion is equivalent to a network with 1 fiber-pair between nodes with PW wavelengths, and degree P wavelength conversion capability at the nodes.

8.6   Consider the example discussed in Section 8.2.2. Suppose the multifiber network there itself had degree 2 limited wavelength conversion. What is the equivalent single fiber network with limited wavelength conversion?

8.7   Derive (8.1). What is the value when N is odd?

8.8   Derive (8.5). What is the value when N is odd?

8.9   Derive (8.8) for the case where there is one full duplex lightpath between each pair of nodes. *Hint:* Use induction. Start with two nodes on the ring, and determine the number of wavelengths required. Add two more nodes so that they are diametrically opposite to each other on the ring, and continue.

8.10   Show that when N is odd, (8.8) is modified to

$$W = \left\lceil \frac{t}{N-1} \right\rceil \frac{N^2 - 1}{8}.$$

8.11   Derive (8.9). What is the value when N is odd?

8.12   Develop other network designs besides the ones shown in Examples 8.3, 8.4, and 8.5, and compare the number of LTs and wavelengths required for these designs against these three examples.

8.13   Complete the proof of Theorem 8.5. (*Hint*: Consider the entries of C that use wavelength 0.)

8.14   Show that in any static network, each tuning state (see Theorem 8.2) can support at most one permutation. (*Hint*: Use Lemma 8.1.)

8.15   Compute the smallest value of W for each value of n of the form $n = 2^\alpha$, where α is a positive integer, for which the conditions of Theorem 8.3 are satisfied. What is the least value of α for which $W < n/2$?

8.16   Compute the smallest value of W for each value of n of the form $n = 2^\alpha$, where α is a positive integer, for which the conditions of Theorem 8.4 are satisfied. What is the least value of α for which $W < n/2$?

8.17   Prove Lemma 8.6. Where, in your proof, did you use the condition that T is a subset of the permutation traffic set?

8.18   Consider the design of a static network with $n = k^2$ users, where the users are partitioned into k disjoint groups, each with k users. Consider a traffic set that consists of all traffics with exactly one transmitter (resp. receiver) in each group connected to a receiver (resp. transmitter) in the same, or another, group. Apply Lemma 8.6 to prove that $W \geq \sqrt{n}/e$ wavelengths are required to support this traffic set in any static network. Design a static network that uses only $\sqrt{n}$ wavelengths and supports this traffic set. This problem shows that the lower bound of Lemma 8.6 can be quite tight.

8.19   This problem illustrates the complexity of wavelength assignment in networks where the transmission is bidirectional over each fiber. Consider the two networks shown in Figure 8.35. In Figure 8.35(a), the network uses two fibers on each link, with two wavelengths on each fiber, with unidirectional transmission on each fiber. In Figure 8.35(b), the network uses one fiber on each link, with four wavelengths. Transmission is bidirectional on each fiber, with two wavelengths in one direction and two in the other, as shown in the figure. No wavelength conversion is allowed in either network. Both networks have the same nominal capacity (4 wavelengths/link). Which network utilizes the capacity more efficiently?

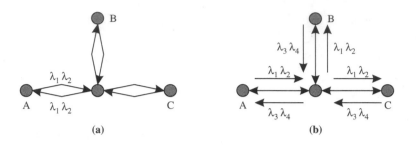

Figure 8.35   Two different scenarios of wavelength assignment in networks with bidirectional links.

8.20   Generalize the example of Figure 8.23 to the case when the number of nodes is arbitrary, say, N. Compare the number of wavelengths required in this general case to the upper bound given by Theorem 8.8.

8.21   Show that Algorithm 8.1 always does the wavelength assignment using L wavelengths. *Hint:* Use induction on the number of nodes.

8.22   Consider the following modified version of Algorithm 8.1. In step 2, the algorithm is permitted to assign any free wavelength from a fixed set of L wavelengths, instead of the least numbered wavelength. Show that this algorithm always succeeds in performing the wavelength assignment.

8.23   Prove that Theorem 8.10 can be tight in some cases. In other words, give an example of a ring network and a set of lightpath requests and routing with load L that requires $2L - 1$ wavelengths. *Hint:* First, give an example that requires $2L - 2$ wavelengths and then modify it by adding an additional lightpath without increasing the load. Note that the example in Figure 8.26 shows such an example for the case $L = 2$. Obtain an example for the case $L > 2$.

8.24   Consider a ring network with a lightpath request set of one lightpath between each source–destination pair. Compute the number of wavelengths sufficient to support this set with full wavelength conversion and without wavelength conversion. What do you conclude from this?

8.25   Give an example of a star network without wavelength conversion where $\frac{3}{2}L$ wavelengths are necessary to perform the wavelength assignment.

8.26   Prove Theorem 8.11.

8.27   Prove Theorem 8.14. Based on this proof, write pseudo-code for an algorithm to perform wavelength assignment.

8.28   Prove Theorem 8.15.

8.29   This problem relates to the wavelength assignment problem in networks without wavelength conversion. Let us assume that the links in the network are duplex, that is, consist of two unidirectional links in opposite directions. A set of duplex lightpath requests and their routing is given. In practice, each request between two nodes A and B is for a lightpath l from A to B and another lightpath l' from B to A, which we will assume are both routed along the same path in the network.

One wavelength assignment scheme (scheme 1) is to assign the same wavelength to both l and l'. Give an example to show that it is possible to do a better wavelength assignment (using fewer wavelengths) by assigning different wavelengths to l and l' (scheme 2). Show using this example that scheme 1 can need up to $\frac{3}{2}W$ wavelengths, where W is the number of wavelengths required for scheme 2. *Hint:* Consider a representation of the path graph corresponding to directed lightpaths.

8.30   Derive the expression (8.12) for the probability that a lightpath request is blocked when the network uses full wavelength conversion.

8.31   Derive the approximate expressions for π_{nc} and π_{fc} given by (8.15) and (8.16). Plot these approximations and the exact values given by (8.13) versus W for $P_b = 10^{-3}$, 10^{-4}, and 10^{-5}, and $H = 5$, 10, and 20 hops to study the behavior of π_{nc} and π_{fc}, and to verify the range of accuracy of these approximations.

8.32   Derive (8.17).

▬ References

[ABC+94]   A. Aggarwal, A. Bar-Noy, D. Coppersmith, R. Ramaswami, B. Schieber, and M. Sudan. Efficient routing and scheduling algorithms for optical networks. In *Proceedings of 5th Annual ACM-SIAM Symposium on Discrete Algorithms*, pages 412–423, Jan. 1994.

[ACKP97]   V. Auletta, I. Caragiannis, C. Kaklamanis, and P. Persiano. Bandwidth allocation algorithms on tree-shaped all-optical networks with wavelength converters. In *Proceedings of the 4th International Colloquium on Structural Information and Communication Complexity*, 1997.

[ACT]   *ACTS web site. http://www.analysys.co.uk/acts/cec/.*

[Ale93]   S. B. Alexander et al. A precompetitive consortium on wide-band all-optical networks. *IEEE/OSA Journal on Lightwave Technology*, 11:714–735, May/June 1993.

[AS72]   M. Abramovitz and I. A. Stegun, editors. *Handbook of Mathematical Functions*. Dover Press, Mineola, NY, 1972.

[Bal96]   K. Bala et al. WDM network economics. In *Proceedings of National Fiber Optic Engineers Conference*, pages 163–174, 1996.

[Bar93]   R. A. Barry. An all-optical non-blocking $M \times M$ switchless connector with $O(\sqrt{M \log M})$ wavelengths and without wavelength changers. *Electronics Letters*, 29(14):1252–1254, July 1993.

[BCB96]   K. Bala, F. R. K. Chung, and C. A. Brackett. Optical wavelength routing, translation and packet/cell switched networks. *IEEE/OSA Journal on Lightwave Technology*, 14(3):336–343, March 1996.

[BCG95]   K. Bala, R. R. Cordell, and E. L. Goldstein. The case for opaque multiwavelength optical networks. In *IEEE LEOS Summer Topical Meetings*, Keystone, Colorado, Aug. 1995.

[Ber76]   C. Berge. *Graphs and Hypergraphs*. North Holland, Amsterdam, 1976.

[BH92]   R. A. Barry and P. A. Humblet. Bounds on the number of wavelengths needed in WDM networks. In *LEOS'92 Summer Topical Meeting Digest*, pages 21–22, 1992.

[BH94]   R. A. Barry and P. A. Humblet. On the number of wavelengths and switches in all-optical networks. *IEEE Transactions on Communications*, 42(2/3/4):583–591, Feb./March/April 1994.

[BH96]   R. A. Barry and P. A. Humblet. Models of blocking probability in all-optical networks with and without wavelength changers. *IEEE JSAC/JLT Special Issue on Optical Networks*, 14(5):858–867, June 1996.

[Big90]   N. Biggs. Some heuristics for graph colouring. In R. Nelson and R. J. Wilson, editors, *Graph Colourings*, Pitman Research Notes in Mathematics Series, pages 87–96. Longman Scientific & Technical, Burnt Mill, Harlow, Essex, UK, 1990.

[Bir96]   A. Birman. Computing approximate blocking probabilities for a class of optical networks. *IEEE JSAC/JLT Special Issue on Optical Networks*, 14(5):852–857, June 1996.

[BK95]   A. Birman and A. Kershenbaum. Routing and wavelength assignment methods in single-hop all-optical networks with blocking. In *Proceedings of IEEE Infocom*, pages 431–438, 1995.

[BPS93]   K. Bala, K. Petropoulos, and T. E. Stern. Multicasting in a linear lightwave network. In *Proceedings of IEEE Infocom*, pages 1350–1358, 1993.

[Bra93]   C. A. Brackett et al. A scalable multiwavelength multihop optical network: A proposal for research on all-optical networks. *IEEE/OSA Journal on Lightwave Technology*, 11:736–753, May/June 1993.

[BSSLB95] K. Bala, T. E. Stern, D. Simchi-Levi, and K. Bala. Routing in a linear lightwave network. *IEEE/ACM Transactions on Networking*, 3(4):459–469, Aug. 1995.

[CEG+96] G. K. Chang, G. Ellinas, J. K. Gamelin, M. Z. Iqbal, and C. A. Brackett. Multiwavelength reconfigurable WDM/ATM/SONET network testbed. *IEEE/OSA JLT/JSAC Special Issue on Multiwavelength Optical Technology and Networks*, 14(6):1320–1340, June 1996.

[CGK92] I. Chlamtac, A. Ganz, and G. Karmi. Lightpath communications: An approach to high-bandwidth optical WAN's. *IEEE Transactions on Communications*, 40(7):1171–1182, July 1992.

[Cha94] G. K. Chang et al. Experimental demonstration of a reconfigurable WDM/ATM/SONET multiwavelength network testbed. In *OFC'94 Technical Digest*, 1994. Postdeadline paper PD9.

[Der95] F. Derr. Design of an 8x8 optical cross-connect switch: Results on subsystems and first measurements. In *ECOC'95 Optical Networking Workshop*, 1995. Paper S2.2.

[dW90] D. de Werra. Heuristics for graph coloring. In G. Tinhofer, E. Mayr, and H. Noltemeier, editors, *Computational Graph Theory*, volume 7 of *Computing, Supplement*, pages 191–208. Springer-Verlag, Berlin, 1990.

[FFP88] P. Feldman, J. Friedman, and N. Pippenger. Wide-sense nonblocking networks. *SIAM Journal on Discrete Mathematics*, 1(2):158–173, May 1988.

[FNS+92] A. Frank, T. Nishizeki, N. Saito, H. Suzuki, and E. Tardos. Algorithms for routing around a rectangle. *Discrete Applied Mathematics*, 40:363–378, 1992.

[GJ79] M. R. Garey and D. S. Johnson. *Computers and Intractibility—A Guide to the Theory of NP Completeness*. W. H. Freeman, San Francisco, 1979.

[GJR96] P. E. Green, F. J. Janniello, and R. Ramaswami. Multichannel protocol-transparent WDM distance extension using remodulation. *IEEE JSAC/JLT Special Issue on Optical Networks*, 14(6):962–967, June 1996.

[GK97] O. Gerstel and S. Kutten. Dynamic wavelengh allocation in all-optical ring networks. In *Proceedings of IEEE International Conference on Communication*, 1997.

[GRS97] O. Gerstel, R. Ramaswami, and G. H. Sasaki. Benefits of limited wavelength conversion in WDM ring networks. In *OFC'97 Technical Digest*, pages 119–120, 1997.

[GRS98] O. Gerstel, R. Ramaswami, and G. H. Sasaki. Cost effective traffic grooming in WDM rings. In *Proceedings of IEEE Infocom*, 1998.

[GSKR97] O. Gerstel, G. H. Sasaki, S. Kutten, and R. Ramaswami. Worst-case dynamic wavelength allocation in optical networks. Technical Report RC 20717, IBM Research Division, Feb. 1997.

[HH96]   A. M. Hill and A. J. N. Houghton. Optical networking in the European ACTS programme. In *OFC'96 Technical Digest*, pages 238–239, San Jose, Feb. 1996.

[Hil93]   G. R. Hill et al. A transport network layer based on optical network elements. *IEEE/OSA Journal on Lightwave Technology*, 11:667–679, May/June 1993.

[Joh95]   S. Johansson. A field demonstration of a manageable optical network. In *Proceedings of European Conference on Optical Communication*, pages 851–854, 1995.

[Joh96]   S. Johansson et al. A transport network involving a reconfigurable WDM network layer—a European demonstration. *IEEE/OSA JLT/JSAC Special Issue on Multiwavelength Optical Technology and Networks*, 14(6):1341–1348, June 1996.

[KA96]   M. Kovacevic and A. S. Acampora. On the benefits of wavelength translation in all optical clear-channel networks. *IEEE JSAC/JLT Special Issue on Optical Networks*, 14(6):868–880, June 1996.

[Kam96]   I. P. Kaminow et al. A wideband all-optical WDM network. *IEEE JSAC/JLT Special Issue on Optical Networks*, 14(5):780–799, June 1996.

[KG95]   M. Kovacevic and M. Gerla. A new optical signal routing scheme for linear lightwave networks. *IEEE Transactions on Communications*, 43(12):3004–3014, Dec. 1995.

[KPEJ97]   C. Kaklamanis, P. Persiano, T. Erlebach, and K. Jansen. Constrained bipartite edge coloring with applications to wavelength routing in all-optical networks. In *International Colloquium on Automata, Languages, and Programming*, 1997.

[KS97]   V. Kumar and E. Schwabe. Improved access to optical bandwidth in trees. In *Proceedings of the ACM Symposium on Distributed Algorithms*, 1997.

[Lin96]   P. J. Lin. *Wide area optical backbone networks*. PhD thesis, Massachusetts Institute of Technology, 1996.

[MKR95]   M. Mihail, C. Kaklamanis, and S. Rao. Efficient access to optical bandwidth. In *IEEE Symposium on Foundations of Computer Science*, pages 548–557, 1995.

[Pan92]   R. K. Pankaj. *Architectures for linear lightwave networks*. PhD thesis, Massachusetts Institute of Technology, 1992.

[PS93]   G. R. Pieris and G. H. Sasaki. A linear lightwave Beneš network. *IEEE/ACM Transactions on Networking*, pages 441–445, Aug. 1993.

[Ram93a]   R. Ramaswami. Multi-wavelength lightwave networks for computer communication. *IEEE Communications Magazine*, 31(2):78–88, Feb. 1993.

[Ram93b]   R. Ramaswami. Systems issues in multi-wavelength optical networks. In *Proceedings of 31st Annual Allerton Conference on Communications, Control and Computing*, Sept. 1993.

[RLB95]   P. Roorda, C-Y. Lu, and T. Boutlier. Benefits of all-optical routing in transport networks. In *OFC'95 Technical Digest*, pages 164–165, 1995.

[RS95]   R. Ramaswami and K. N. Sivarajan. Routing and wavelength assignment in all-optical networks. *IEEE/ACM Transactions on Networking*, pages 489–500, Oct. 1995. An earlier version appeared in *Prof. Infocom'94*.

[RS97]   R. Ramaswami and G. H. Sasaki. Multiwavelength optical networks with limited wavelength conversion. In *Proceedings of IEEE Infocom*, pages 490–499, 1997.

[RU94]   P. Raghavan and E. Upfal. Efficient routing in all-optical networks. In *Proceedings of 26th ACM Symposium on Theory of Computing*, pages 134–143, May 1994.

[SAS96]   S. Subramaniam, M. Azizoglu, and A. K. Somani. Connectivity and sparse wavelength conversion in wavelength-routing networks. In *Proceedings of IEEE Infocom*, pages 148–155, 1996.

[SBJS93]   T. E. Stern, K. Bala, S. Jiang, and J. Sharony. Linear lightwave networks: Performance issues. *IEEE/OSA Journal on Lightwave Technology*, 11:937–950, May/June 1993.

[SOW95]   K-I. Sato, S. Okamoto, and A. Watanabe. Photonic transport networks based on optical paths. *International Journal of Communication Systems (UK)*, 8(6):377–389, Nov./Dec. 1995.

[SSAB97]   S. Subramaniam, A. K. Somani, M. Azizoglu, and R. A. Barry. A performance model for wavelength conversion with non-Poisson traffic. In *Proceedings of IEEE Infocom*, pages 500–507, 1997.

[Ste90]   T. E. Stern. Linear lightwave networks : How far can they go? In *Proceedings of IEEE Globecom*, pages 1866–1872, 1990.

[Tuc75]   A. Tucker. Coloring a family of circular arcs. *SIAM Journal on Applied Mathematics*, 29(3):493–502, 1975.

[WASG96]   R. E. Wagner, R. C. Alferness, A. A. M. Saleh, and M. S. Goodman. MONET: Multiwavelength optical networking. *IEEE/OSA JLT/JSAC Special Issue on Multiwavelength Optical Technology and Networks*, 14(6):1349–1355, June 1996.

[WD96]   N. Wauters and P. Demeester. Design of the optical path layer in multiwavelength cross-connected networks. *IEEE JSAC/JLT Special Issue on Optical Networks*, 14(6):881–892, June 1996.

[YLES96]   J. Yates, J. Lacey, D. Everitt, and M. Summerfield. Limited-range wavelength translation in all-optical networks. In *Proceedings of IEEE Infocom*, pages 954–961, 1996.

9
chapter

Virtual Topology Design

IN CHAPTER 8, we focused mainly on the provision of lightpaths by the optical layer to the *higher layer*—the layer operating immediately above it. In this chapter, we will study how the higher layer uses these lightpaths. Examples of higher layers are SONET and ATM. The higher layer itself receives requests for *connections* between nodes that it must try and establish. The higher layer can use the optical layer to establish connections in two ways. One way is for it to map each connection onto a (unique) lightpath. So a lightpath is established when a connection request arrives and taken down when the connection is released. This would be done if the connection requests received by the higher layer are "circuit-switched" in nature; that is, the connection must be assigned a dedicated bit rate, and the bit rate required by the connection is the entire bit rate of a lightpath. Lightpaths can be operated at bit rates in excess of 2 Gb/s, and most applications today do not require a dedicated bit rate of this magnitude. Thus, at this time, we do not feel that this is the most appropriate way of using the optical layer.

Another way in which a higher layer can use the optical layer is to simply treat each lightpath like a physical link between two of its nodes. In this case, the lightpaths are relatively static (permanent lightpaths). For example, a lightpath could serve as a link between SONET terminating equipment, or ATM switches. We consider only this case in the remainder of this chapter.

To discuss this concept further, we introduce the notions of *physical* and *virtual topologies*. The physical topology of a network is the network topology seen by the optical layer. Therefore, the nodes in this topology correspond to the WXCs and two nodes are connected by a link if the corresponding WXCs are connected by an

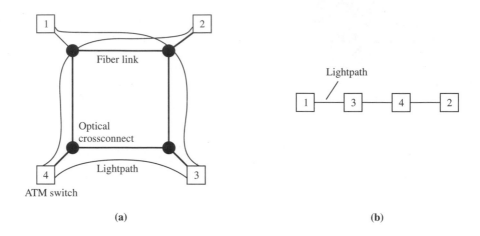

Figure 9.1   Physical and virtual topologies for an ATM network operating over the optical layer. (a) The physical topology, which consists of the optical wavelength cross-connects and the fiber links, along with a set of lightpaths to carry the higher-layer traffic. (b) The virtual topology, with the nodes being the ATM switches and the links corresponding to the lightpaths in the physical topology.

optical fiber link. The virtual topology is the network topology seen by the higher layer. The nodes in this topology correspond to nodes of the higher layer, and a link in this topology represents a lightpath that has been established between the corresponding nodes. This concept is illustrated in Figure 9.1. Note that the higher layer will route and multiplex its connections over the links in the virtual topology. The virtual topology is also sometimes called the *logical topology*; we will use the terms interchangeably.

Let us look at a few examples to help clarify the notion of a connection and its mapping to lightpaths.

Example 9.1   *SONET over the Optical Layer:* We have already seen examples of the optical layer providing lightpaths to support SONET traffic in Chapters 6 and 8. The lightpaths provided by the optical layer usually carry traffic at high data rates. In the case of SONET, lightpaths may carry data at OC-48 (2.488 Gb/s) speeds. The SONET layer residing above the optical layer has to provide its users with lower-level SONET pipes, say, at OC-3 (155 Mb/s) speeds. Thus the connection requests received by the SONET layer are for OC-3 SONET pipes. An OC-3 SONET connection is carried from its source to its destination through a sequence of lightpaths, as shown in Figure 9.2. At the termination point of each lightpath, the OC-48 signal on the lightpath must be received and

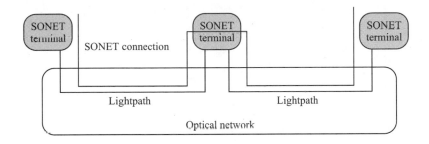

Figure 9.2 Mapping lower-speed SONET connections onto lightpaths.

converted to electronic form. It must then be demultiplexed, the OC-3 signal extracted and switched to the appropriate output port, and multiplexed onto the next lightpath in the sequence. This function is accomplished by SONET line terminating equipment, in conjunction with a SONET digital crossconnect (DCS), if needed.

Example 9.2 *ATM over the Optical Layer:* Analogous to the SONET case, the ATM connections (virtual circuits) are carried end to end through a sequence of lightpaths. Between two adjacent lightpaths in a sequence, the optical signal is received and switched electronically by an ATM switch.

In some cases, routing of connections at the higher layer may require setting up or taking down lightpaths in the optical layer. In fact, this is one of the advantages obtained by having the optical layer. Without the optical layer, the links between the higher-layer equipment would be nailed-down physical links that cannot be changed easily. On the other hand, with the optical layer, it may be possible to change the set of lightpaths in response to changes in the traffic demands at the higher layer. This is one of the important reasons for providing switching inside the optical layer, so that a variety of different sets of lightpaths can be supported. However, taking down lightpaths will disrupt the traffic in the higher layer, and therefore, the process of reconfiguring the lightpaths needs to be coordinated carefully and will depend on the requirements of the higher layer. This problem still has no good solutions and is an active area of research today.

9.1 The Virtual Topology Design Problem

Before describing the topology design problem in optical networks, it is worthwhile to understand the general topology design problem in networks. Usually, the network

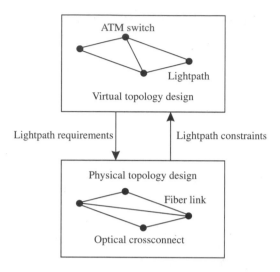

Figure 9.3   The two-level topology design problem.

designer is given the nodes in the network and has some idea about the projected traffic between the different pairs of nodes. (Sometimes the designer may even have to pick the locations for the nodes, based on the overall traffic distribution.) She also has estimates about the cost of putting in links between each node pair. Given these inputs, she must determine the topology of the network, that is, the set of links in the network, as well as how traffic must be routed over this topology. This problem has been very well studied in the literature and is known to be a hard problem. Accordingly, several heuristic design algorithms have been developed [Ker93, Cah98] for this purpose.

With this background, the topology design problem in optical networks can be viewed as a combined two-level design problem, as shown in Figure 9.3. At the bottom level is the design of the physical topology of the optical network, which is somewhat analogous to the classical network design problem. On top of it is the design of the virtual topologies that are to be supported by this physical topology. The two problems are coupled to each other. The physical topology must ideally be designed with some knowledge about the traffic (lightpaths) that are to be supported over it. This in turn depends on what the virtual topology is. Likewise, the virtual topology ideally is not designed independent of the physical topology because the physical topology may impose constraints on the set of lightpaths that can be provided to realize the virtual topology.

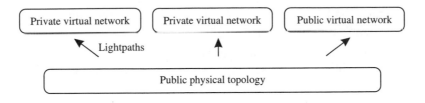

Figure 9.4   Different scenarios for the virtual topology design problem.

In practice, the two-level topology design problem may end up being decomposed into two independent problems: the virtual topology design problem and the physical topology design problem, for the reasons we will discuss shortly. Note that once the virtual topology is designed, the set of lightpaths to be supported by the physical topology is known. In this case, the physical topology design problem becomes akin to the classical topology design problem in that the designer must determine the links in the physical topology and solve the *routing and wavelength assignment* for the lightpaths discussed in Section 8.5. Note that the higher layer wants the virtual topology to be optimized to suit its needs. The optical layer, on the other hand, wants to see its infrastructure used in the most efficient manner.

The decomposition of the two-level topology design problem arises because of the following scenarios, depicted in Figure 9.4:

1. **Private network over a public infrastructure:** A likely scenario is that the physical topology (optical layer) is owned and controlled by a service provider, such as a telephone company. The service provider would provide ATM or SONET service using lightpaths to private customers. Note that these private customers may in some cases even be other service providers who are leasing capacity from this service provider. In this case, the private ATM or SONET network would specify the source–destination pairs and the number of lightpaths required between them. The service provider would provide the lightpaths. We will examine the network design problem that the private customer faces—the virtual topology design problem—in detail in Section 9.3. Since the service provider is likely to support many independent private networks, all requesting different sets of lightpaths, he must design his network infrastructure or physical topology (wavelength cross-connects and the fiber links interconnecting them) and a routing and wavelength assignment algorithm, so as to meet all these lightpath demands simultaneously while minimizing his cost. The cost of the service provider's network consists of the cost of the WXC nodes and the optical fiber links interconnecting them, and we considered several special cases of this network design problem (usually

assuming that the network cost is proportional to the number of wavelengths used in the network) in Chapter 8.

2. **Public network over a public infrastructure:** The service provider may deploy his own public ATM or SONET network over his physical topology. Here the service provider typically has an idea of the traffic requirements (in terms of, say, Mb/s) between nodes in the network and must decide for himself what lightpaths he needs. In this case, he must formulate and solve the combined two-level design problem. Since each problem by itself is hard, he may choose to solve the individual problems separately, but this may not necessarily be optimal.

We will consider the first model, that is, a private network over a public infrastructure, and examine the network design problem that the private customer faces. The physical topology of the network is assumed to be already given. In simple terms, the virtual topology design problem is the problem of deciding what lightpaths to set up so as to optimize the performance/cost of the virtual topology. The actual measure to be optimized varies depending on the situation as we saw earlier.

From the private customer's viewpoint, network design is the determination of the set of lightpaths that must be set up, that is, the virtual topology. Therefore, we call this the *virtual topology design* problem. In general, the private customer tries to design a virtual topology that either meets his traffic requirements and minimizes his cost, or optimizes the performance seen by his connections while meeting his cost budget. The cost of a lightpath is the tariff charged by the public network (utility). The utility could provide different tariffs for lightpaths between the same pair of nodes depending on the *quality of service* (QOS) provided on those paths. QOS parameters might include, for example, the propagation delay of those paths, and are discussed in Section 10.6. We saw in Examples 9.1 and 9.2 that the customer uses SONET crossconnects or ATM switches in order to route connections that use more than one lightpath. While designing the virtual topology, the private customer has to consider not only the lightpath cost but also the cost of these "switching" components: the *switching cost*. The performance measure used depends on the specific higher layer and the model for the connection requests. We illustrate this with the SONET and ATM examples.

Example 9.3   *SONET over the Optical Layer (cont'd.):* In this case, the desired goal is to reduce the cost of the SONET-layer equipment needed. Minimizing the number of SONET line terminals is the same as minimizing the number of lightpaths that must be set up to support the SONET traffic, since each lightpath terminates in a pair of SONET line terminals. We studied several examples of this problem in Section 8.4, and we will examine this problem in more detail in Section 9.2.

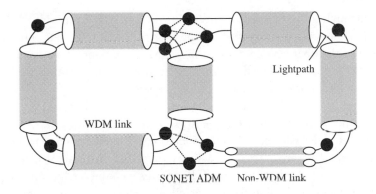

Figure 9.5   The combined SONET/WDM network design problem.

Example 9.4   *ATM over the Optical Layer (cont'd.):* The ATM network receives connection requests for virtual circuits that are used to send ATM packets (or cells) in a statistically multiplexed fashion. Here, we usually seek to optimize the performance of the ATM network, measured in terms of its throughput or average delay. Another related measure that is used sometimes is the congestion in the network, that is, the maximum utilization of any (virtual) link, which we seek to minimize. However, we do so subject to constraints on the number and sizes of the ATM switches that can be used in the network.

9.2   Combined SONET/WDM Network Design

We will give a general framework for designing SONET networks that use WDM links, based on the examples that we have considered so far. There are many variants of this problem, but we consider a typical one here. Assume that the service provider is interested in deploying SONET in the form of rings for reasons of fault tolerance. Some of these rings use WDM links, as shown in Figure 9.5, whereas other links may be physical fiber links without any WDM.

We are given the locations of the nodes, and the traffic between nodes, in units of, say, Mb/s. The problem is to determine a set of interconnected SONET rings, say, each running at OC-48 speeds, that can carry this traffic. The links of the SONET rings are realized by lightpaths, routed over existing fiber links. The rings are made up of SONET ADMs. At each node location, multiple ADMs may be present. The ADMs at any given location are interconnected so that traffic can be switched between rings at that location. This may be done by interconnecting them directly or through a digital crossconnect. Our objective is to minimize the cost of the network, which is a combination of the cost of the SONET equipment, WDM equipment, and the fiber links between the WDM equipment. If we were to assume that the WDM equipment and fiber links, as well as the interconnections between the ADMs at a node location, are free (which is never the case), then this statement would translate into simply minimizing the number of SONET ADMs required to handle the traffic, as we saw in Example 9.3.

The problem consists of several interrelated tasks. First we need to find a set of lightpaths to carry the traffic. Then we will have to group the lightpaths into rings. To do so, we may need to add some dummy lightpaths to complete certain rings. Then we route the traffic onto the lightpaths. We will also need to assign wavelengths to all the lightpaths. All these steps depend on one another. Of course, we could perform one step at a time, but that would lead to a suboptimal solution.

The problem is further complicated by several factors. There may be existing rings that will have to be supported as is. We could also have different rings running at different bit rates (OC-12, OC-48, and so on). There may be some links where we prefer not to use WDM, owing to cost or other reasons. Finally, it may not be very easy to capture all the costs involved in a realistic manner.

As of today, this problem is just beginning to be addressed [GRS98, GLS98]. We saw examples of some simple cases of this problem earlier in Chapter 8, and related problems have been solved for other scenarios. For example, network design tools are available for designing other SONET, ATM, and IP networks. These tools can be modified to design WDM networks by incorporating the new constraints imposed by WDM networks.

9.3 An Integer Linear Programming Formulation

We now consider a specific, though rather simplified, virtual topology design problem and examine how it can be solved. We will assume that no constraints are imposed by the underlying physical topology. Consider the ATM network case we discussed in Examples 9.2 and 9.4. We will assume, in this instance, that the lightpaths are *simplex;* that is, a private network may use a lightpath from node i to node j but need not necessarily use a lightpath from node j to node i. Such cases can occur in practice since the higher-layer traffic may be quite asymmetrical in the case of many applications. Although ATM today assumes that the links are full duplex, the simplex mode is more general than assuming full-duplex links, and by adding additional constraints, we can constrain the virtual topology to use full-duplex links if needed.

One constraint is that at each node we can use only a single $(\Delta + 1) \times (\Delta + 1)$ ATM switch; this constrains the switching component of the cost. Here, Δ is the number of trunk ports on the switch that connect it to other switches. The remaining pair of switch ports is used at each node for routing ATM packets originating from, and destined to, that node. A second constraint is that we can set up only one lightpath per port at each node for a total of Δ lightpaths from and to each node, and $n\Delta$ lightpaths in the network, where n is the number of nodes in the network. This constraint is equivalent to a constraint on the lightpath costs, if we assume that the tariff for a lightpath is the same regardless of its end points. This is an assumption that would clearly not hold in a wide-area environment where we expect longer lightpaths to be more expensive than shorter ones. However, it may hold in a regional network. (Many phone companies offer a single rate for all calls made within their region. So it is not inconceivable that we could have a single tariff for all lightpaths within a region.) The main reason for the assumption, of course, is that it simplifies the problem.

Recall that in Chapter 8, when we considered the network design problem from the optical layer viewpoint, we also had to solve the routing and wavelength assignment problem. Similarly, when we design the virtual topology, we also have to solve the problem of routing connections over the virtual topology in conjunction. This is because the performance depends on both the topology itself and the routing algorithm that is used.

To formulate the problem in mathematical terms, we need to introduce a number of definitions. We assume a statistical model for the ATM traffic: the arrival rate for packets for source–destination (s–d) pair (s, d) is λ^{sd} (in packets/second), $s, d = 1, \ldots, n$. $b_{ij}, i, j = 1, \ldots, n, i \neq j$, are n^2 binary valued (0 or 1) variables, one for each possible virtual link. $b_{ij} = 1$ if the designed virtual topology has a link from node i to node j; otherwise, $b_{ij} = 0$. The solution to the virtual topology design problem will specify which of the b_{ij} are 1 and which are 0. We assume that we can arbitrarily split the traffic between the same pair of nodes over different paths through the network. Since all packets belonging to a virtual circuit must be routed on the same path (by definition of a virtual circuit!), this is tantamount to assuming that the traffic between nodes consists of a large number of virtual circuits. Let the fraction of the traffic between s–d pair (s, d) that is routed over link (i, j) (if it exists) be a_{ij}^{sd}. Then $\lambda_{ij}^{sd} = a_{ij}^{sd} \lambda^{sd}$ is the traffic (in packets/second) between s–d pair (s, d) that is routed over link (i, j). The total traffic from all s–d pairs that is routed over link (i, j) is thus $\lambda_{ij} = \sum_{sd} \lambda_{ij}^{sd}$. We define a parameter called the *congestion*, as $\lambda_{\max} = \max_{ij} \lambda_{ij}$. Note that the λ_{ij}^{sd} (and thus the λ_{ij} and $\lambda_{\max}$) are variables that we have to determine. Determining their values amounts to finding a routing algorithm.

To understand why the congestion is an important parameter, let us consider the case where the packet arrivals follow a Poisson process and the packet transmission times are exponentially distributed with mean time given by $1/\mu$ seconds. Making the standard assumption that the traffic offered to a (virtual) link in the network is independent of the traffic offered to other links, each link can be modeled as an M/M/1 queue. The average queuing delay on link (i, j) is then given by [BG92, Sec. 3.6.1]

$$d_{ij} = \frac{1}{\mu - \lambda_{ij}}. \tag{9.1}$$

The *throughput* can be defined as the minimum value of the offered load for which the delay on any link becomes infinite. This happens when $\lambda_{max} = \max_{i,j} \lambda_{ij} = \mu$. Thus our performance objective will be to minimize the congestion λ_{max}. Note that in the case of an ATM network, the packets are of fixed length and are not exponentially distributed, and therefore, the congestion implied by (9.1) is only an approximate metric.

We are now ready to state the problem formally as a *mathematical program*:

Objective function:

min λ_{max}

subject to

Flow conservation at each node:

$$\sum_j \lambda_{ij}^{sd} - \sum_j \lambda_{ji}^{sd} = \begin{cases} \lambda^{sd} & \text{if } s = i, \\ -\lambda^{sd} & \text{if } d = i, \\ 0 & \text{otherwise}, \end{cases} \qquad \text{for all } s, d, i,$$

Total flow on a logical link:

$$\begin{aligned} \lambda_{ij} &= \sum_{s,d} \lambda_{ij}^{sd}, & \text{for all } i, j, \\ \lambda_{ij} &\leq \lambda_{max}, & \text{for all } i, j, \\ \lambda_{ij}^{sd} &\leq b_{ij}\lambda^{sd}, & \text{for all } i, j, s, d, \end{aligned}$$

Degree constraints:

$$\sum_i b_{ij} \leq \Delta, \qquad \text{for all } j,$$

$$\sum_j b_{ij} \leq \Delta, \qquad \text{for all } i,$$

Nonnegativity and integer constraints:

$$\lambda_{ij}^{sd}, \lambda_{ij}, \lambda_{max} \geq 0, \qquad \text{for all } i, j, s, d,$$

$$b_{ij} \in \{0, 1\}, \qquad \text{for all } i, j.$$

We identify the packets to be routed between each s–d pair with the *flow* of a commodity. The left-hand side of the flow conservation constraint at node i in the network computes the *net* flow out of a node i for one commodity (sd). The net flow is the difference between the outgoing flow and the incoming flow. The right-hand side is 0 if that node is neither the source nor the destination for that commodity ($i \neq s, d$). If node i is the source of the flow ($i = s$), the net flow equals λ^{sd}, the arrival rate for those packets, and if node i is the destination, $i = d$, the net flow equals $-\lambda^{sd}$.

The constraint $\lambda_{ij} = \sum_{s,d} \lambda_{ij}^{sd}$ is just the definition of λ_{ij}. The constraint $\lambda_{ij} \leq \lambda_{\max}$ together with the fact that we are minimizing $\lambda_{\max}$ ensures that the minimum value of $\lambda_{\max}$ is the congestion. The constraint $\lambda_{ij}^{sd} \leq b_{ij}\lambda^{sd}$ ensures that if $b_{ij} = 0$, $\lambda_{ij}^{sd} = 0$ for all values of s and d. So if the link (i, j) doesn't exist in the topology, no packets can be routed on that link. If the link (i, j) exists in the topology ($b_{ij} = 1$), this constraint simply states that $\lambda_{ij}^{sd} \leq \lambda^{sd}$, which is always true; thus it imposes no constraint on the values of λ_{ij}^{sd} in this case.

The degree constraints ensure that the designed topology has no more than Δ links into and out of each node. The constraints $b_{ij} \in \{0, 1\}$ restrict the b_{ij} to take on only the values 0 or 1. But for these constraints, the problem would have been easy to solve! Note that the objective function and the constraints are linear functions of the variables (λ_{ij}^{sd}, λ_{ij}, $\lambda_{\max}$, b_{ij}). A mathematical program with this property is called a *linear program* or LP if, in addition, all the variables are real. It is called an *integer linear program* or ILP if all the variables are restricted to take integer values. In our case, some of the variables, for instance, the b_{ij}, are restricted to integer values. So our program is an example of a *mixed integer linear program* or MILP. We call it the VTD-MILP. Although many efficient algorithms are known for solving even very large LPs, no efficient algorithms are known for the solution of arbitrary ILPs and MILPs. In fact, a general ILP or MILP is an example of an NP-hard problem [GJ79].

Using the fact the LPs are easy to solve, we can obtain an approximate solution to this mathematical program by using the techniques of *LP-relaxation* and *rounding*. First, we need to define a few terms used in mathematical programming.

A *feasible solution of a mathematical program* is any set of values of the variables that satisfy all the constraints. An *optimal solution*, or simply *solution*, of a mathematical program is a feasible solution that optimizes (minimizes or maximizes, as the case may be) the objective function. The *value* of a mathematical program is the value of the objective function achieved by any optimal solution.

Note that if we replace the constraints $b_{ij} \in \{0, 1\}$ by the constraints $0 \leq b_{ij} \leq 1$, the VTD-MILP reduces to an LP, which we will call the VTD-LP. Moreover, any feasible solution of the VTD-MILP is also a feasible solution of the VTD-LP, but the VTD-LP may (and usually will) have other feasible solutions. If some optimal solution of the VTD-LP happens to be a feasible solution of the VTD-MILP (that is, the b_{ij}s are 0 or 1), the values of the VTD-MILP and VTD-LP will be equal. Otherwise, the value of the VTD-LP will be a lower bound on the value of the VTD-MILP. We call this lower bound the *LP-relaxation* bound.

Note that if the values of the b_{ij} are fixed at 0 or 1 such that the degree constraints are satisfied, the VTD-MILP again reduces to an LP. Fixing the values of the b_{ij} fixes the virtual topology; the remaining problem is to route the packets over this virtual topology to minimize the congestion. So we call the LP obtained in this manner the routing-LP. The value of any routing-LP is an upper bound on the value of the VTD-MILP. If we are clever (or lucky) in fixing the values of the b_{ij} so that the degree constraints are satisfied, this will be a good upper bound. For clues on how to fix the values of the b_{ij}, we turn again to the VTD-LP.

Consider any optimal solution of the VTD-LP. Intuitively, we expect that b_{ij}s that are close to 1 (resp. close to 0) must be equal to 1 (resp. 0) in the VTD-MILP. So we could try a heuristic approach to determine the values of b_{ij} in the VTD-MILP from the values of b_{ij} in the VTD-LP: *round* the b_{ij} in the VTD-LP to the closest integer. However, we have to be careful not to violate the degree constraints on the b_{ij}. So we modify the rounding approach to incorporate this in the following *rounding algorithm*.

Algorithm 9.1

1. Arrange the values of the b_{ij} obtained in an optimal solution of the VTD-LP in decreasing order.

2. Starting at the top of the list, set each $b_{ij} = 1$ if the degree constraints would not be violated. Otherwise, set the $b_{ij} = 0$.

3. Stop when all the degree constraints are satisfied or the b_{ij}s are exhausted.

If the LP-relaxation lower bound and the upper bound obtained by using the rounding algorithm and solving the routing-LP are close to each other, then we have a good approximation to the value of the MILP. We can then use the topology and routing algorithm obtained by the rounding algorithm and routing-LP as approximations to the optimal topology and routing algorithm. A modified version of this approach has been used in [RS96, Jai96] to solve the VTD-MILP approximately in a few examples. Table 9.1 shows the congestion as a function of the degree for one such example, which is a 14-node network with a sample traffic matrix given in [RS96]. The three columns correspond to the LP-relaxation lower bound, an exact value obtained by solving the MILP, and the value obtained by the rounding algorithm. Note that the rounding algorithm yields a value that is quite close to the optimum value and in fact achieves the optimum value as the degree increases.

Table 9.1 Congestion versus node degree for a virtual topology designed over a 14-node sample network with a given traffic pattern from [RS96]. Observe that the LP rounding algorithm yields very good results in this example.

Degree	LP-Relaxation	MILP	LP Rounding
2	282.51	297.98	305.39
3	189.62	189.78	189.78
4	142.32	142.33	142.33
5	113.87	113.87	113.87
6	94.89	94.89	94.89

The problem we have considered is a very special case of the general problem, and even it is hard! Not unexpectedly, network design problems have been studied for many years [Ker93] and are known to be hard. In many cases, even formulating the problem becomes hard because of a large number of parameters to be optimized and a large number of constraints to be dealt with. We illustrated one heuristic method for solving such an ILP, but several other techniques exist that can be used—see, for example, [MBRM96, BG95, ZA95, JBM95, GW94, CGK93, LA91].

9.4   Regular Virtual Topologies

Although a number of heuristics have been proposed to design virtual topologies, another approach taken by researchers has been to ignore the traffic demands and simply design *regular* virtual topologies that have some nice structural properties. The topology is regular in the sense that all the nodes in the virtual topology have the same degree. These regular topologies make routing of traffic very simple, and in general provide high throughputs and low delays, provided the traffic is uniform. Such virtual topologies may make sense in cases where the traffic demand is entirely unknown, or when the traffic demand is known to be uniform, as is frequently assumed to be the case in designing multiprocessor interconnection networks. Their usefulness as virtual topologies for metropolitan- and wide-area networks is somewhat questionable.

Let us see next what are the important parameters that determine the performance of regular topologies. For uniform traffic, let $\lambda = \lambda^{sd}$ and let l_{ij} denote the number of source–destination pairs whose traffic is routed over link (i, j). (In this section, for simplicity, we will assume that traffic between a source–destination pair is not split across multiple routes.) We will call l_{ij} the *loading* on link (i, j). Then (9.1) can be rewritten as

$$d_{ij} = \frac{1}{\mu - l_{ij}\lambda}. \tag{9.2}$$

The average queuing delay for a packet through a network of N nodes over all source–destination pairs is given by

$$d_q(\lambda) = \frac{1}{N(N-1)} \sum_{i,j} \frac{l_{ij}}{\mu - l_{ij}\lambda}. \tag{9.3}$$

In this case, our earlier objective function of minimizing $\lambda_{\max}$ is equivalent to minimizing $l_{\max} = \max_{i,j} l_{ij}$. The *average* link loading in the network is given by

$$\bar{l} = \frac{1}{M} \sum_{i,j} l_{ij}, \tag{9.4}$$

where M denotes the number of links in the virtual topology. Note that $\bar{l} \leq l_{\max}$.

We define the length of a path to be the number of edges in that path. The *diameter*, D, of the virtual topology is the maximum over all node pairs of the length of the shortest path between a pair of nodes. Let $n(i)$ denote the number of node pairs in the virtual topology between whom the shortest path has length i. Then, the average number of hops between a source–destination pair, $\overline{H}$ (for shortest-path routing), is defined as

$$\overline{H} = \frac{1}{N(N-1)} \sum_{i=0}^{D} i\, n(i). \tag{9.5}$$

$\overline{H}$ is the average number of links used in the virtual topology to communicate between a source–destination pair. It depends on the routing scheme that is used. We first prove the following relation between $\overline{H}$ and $\bar{l}$:

$$N(N-1)\overline{H} = \sum_{i,j} l_{ij} = M\bar{l}. \tag{9.6}$$

To see this, assume that one packet has to be sent for every source–destination pair in the network. Let us count the total number of edges traversed by all these packets in two ways. First, since every packet goes through $\overline{H}$ hops on average and the total number of source–destination pairs is $N(N-1)$, the total number of edges traversed is $N(N-1)\overline{H}$. But by the definition of the loading on an edge, this is also equal to $\sum l_{ij} = M\bar{l}$. Equating the two, we get (9.6).

The reason $\overline{H}$ is an important parameter will become clear from the following theorem.

Theorem 9.1 [SR94] *For a given topology with N nodes, M (directed) edges, and in- and out-degree $\leq \Delta$, the average queuing delay under any routing scheme satisfies*

$$d_q(\lambda) \geq \frac{\overline{H}\Delta}{\mu\Delta - (N-1)\overline{H}\lambda}, \qquad for\ 0 \leq \lambda \leq 1/l_{\max}. \tag{9.7}$$

Proof. Note that the function

$$f(x) = \frac{x}{\mu - x}$$

is a convex $\cup$ function of x; that is,

$$\frac{1}{M} \sum_{i,j} f(l_{ij}) \geq f\left(\frac{\sum_{i,j} l_{ij}}{M}\right). \tag{9.8}$$

Using this property, from (9.3), we have

$$d_q(\lambda) > \frac{1}{N(N-1)} \frac{\sum_{i,j} l_{ij}}{\mu - \frac{\sum_{i,j} l_{ij}}{M}\lambda}.$$

Substituting for $\sum_{i,j} l_{ij}$ from (9.6) in the preceding equation, and using the fact that $M \leq N\Delta$, we obtain the desired result. ∎

Note that an equality is obtained in Theorem 9.1 when the load is the same on every link in the network, that is, $l_{ij} = \bar{l}$, and $M = N\Delta$ (which is true for a regular topology). Note also that $d_q(\lambda)$ is a monotonically increasing function of $\overline{H}$. Thus an important property of a regular topology is that it must have a small value of $\overline{H}$. Note, additionally, that if each link has a propagation delay of d_{prop}, then the average propagation delay in the network is $\overline{H}d_{\mathrm{prop}}$, and is also minimized by minimizing $\overline{H}$. Thus the best possible routing scheme is a shortest-path routing scheme that also equalizes the load on all the links.

The following theorem, stated without proof, establishes a minimum possible value for $\overline{H}$.

Theorem 9.2 [SR94] *Let*

$$\overline{H}_{\min}(N, \Delta) = \begin{cases} \frac{\Delta - \Delta^{m+1} + Nm(\Delta-1)^2 + m(\Delta-1)}{(N-1)(\Delta-1)^2}, & \Delta \geq 2, \\ N/2, & \Delta = 1, \end{cases} \tag{9.9}$$

where m is the largest integer that satisfies

$$N \geq 1 + \Delta + \Delta^2 + \cdots + \Delta^{m-1} = \frac{\Delta^m - 1}{\Delta - 1}. \tag{9.10}$$

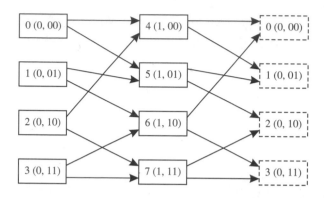

Figure 9.6   A (2, 2) shufflenet.

Then for any directed graph with N nodes, maximum out-degree Δ, and any routing algorithm, $\overline{H} \geq \overline{H}_{\min}(N, \Delta)$.

Note that for the case $\Delta = 1$, a ring with N vertices satisfies $\overline{H} = N/2$.

9.4.1   Shufflenets

We will next study a popular regular virtual topology called the shufflenet. A shufflenet is characterized by two parameters, Δ and k. A (Δ, k) shufflenet consists of $k\Delta^k$ nodes, arranged in k columns, each with Δ^k nodes. Adjacent columns are connected by a *perfect shuffle* as described later. We can think of a (Δ, k) shufflenet in terms of the state transition diagram of a k-digit shift register, with each digit in $\{0, 1, \ldots, \Delta - 1\}$. Each node $(c, a_0 a_1 \ldots a_{k-1})$ is labeled by its column index $c \in \{0, 1, 2, \ldots, k - 1\}$ along with a k-digit string $a_0 a_1 \ldots a_{k-1}$, $a_i \in \{0, 1, \ldots, \Delta - 1\}$, $0 \leq i \leq k - 1$. There is an edge from a node i to another node j in the following column if node j's string can be obtained from node i's string by one shift. In other words, there is an edge from node $(c, a_0 a_1 \ldots a_{k-1})$ to a node $((c + 1) \bmod k, a_1 a_2 \ldots a_{k-1}*)$, where $* \in \{0, 1, \ldots, \Delta - 1\}$. The in- and out-degree of each node in the (Δ, k) shufflenet is Δ, and its diameter $D = 2k - 1$ (see Problem 9.3). The (2, 2) shufflenet is shown in Figure 9.6.

The average number of hops for shortest-path routing in a shufflenet is given by (see Problem 9.4)

$$\overline{H} = \frac{k\Delta^k(\Delta - 1)(3k - 1) - 2k(\Delta^k - 1)}{2(\Delta - 1)(k\Delta^k - 1)}. \tag{9.11}$$

We can use $\overline{l}$ (9.4) as a lower bound on $\lambda_{\max}$ for shortest-path routing. For the (4, 4) 1024-node shufflenet, we have $\overline{H} = 5.1730$ and $\lambda_{\max} \geq \overline{l} = 1323$.

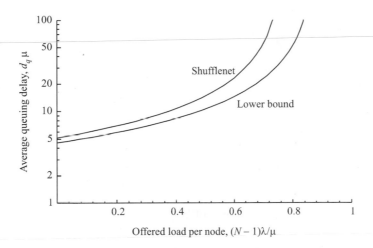

Figure 9.7 Average queuing delay versus offered load for a (4, 4) shufflenet. The lower bound indicates the best possible delay that can be obtained in any virtual topology with the same degree and number of nodes.

Figure 9.7 shows the normalized average queuing delay $d_q\mu$ versus normalized offered load per node $(N - 1)\lambda/\mu$ for the (4, 4) shufflenet with 1024 nodes. We use Theorem 9.1 with $\overline{H}$ given by (9.11). It turns out that the shortest-path routing scheme in the shufflenet almost exactly equalizes the load on all the links, and so the plotted curve is close to actual delay. We also plot a lower bound on the delay that can be realized by any topology, by using Theorem 9.1 where $\overline{H}$ is given by $\overline{H}_{min}$ from Theorem 9.2. Note that the two curves are fairly close to each other, indicating that the shufflenet in this case is a very good virtual topology.

In addition to shufflenets, a large number of other regular topologies have been explored in the literature that have similar properties and, in some cases, certain advantages. For example, the de Bruijn graph [SR94] has slightly higher throughputs for the same degree and number of nodes. Many of these regular topologies don't exist for all values of N and specific topologies, for example, GEMNET [IBM95] have been devised that exist for all values of N.

9.5 Implementation in Broadcast and Select Networks

So far we have studied designing virtual topologies over wavelength-routed optical networks. However, virtual topologies were originally proposed in [Aca87] for use over a WDM broadcast and select physical topology to avoid the need for having rapidly tunable WDM transmitters/receivers needed to realize the single-hop packet-switched networks that we studied in Chapter 7. As an example, let us see

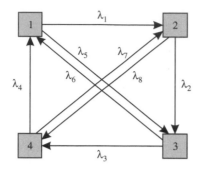

Figure 9.8   A regular virtual topology with degree 2.

how we can implement a regular topology of degree Δ over a star network. Each node is provided with Δ transmitters and Δ receivers. Each transmitter in the network is tuned to a different wavelength. Likewise, each receiver is tuned to a different wavelength. The virtual topology is dictated by the tuning state of the transmitters and receivers. To illustrate this, consider the virtual topology shown in Figure 9.8. Figure 9.9 shows the assignment of wavelengths to the transmitters and receivers to obtain this virtual topology over a four-node broadcast and select WDM network using eight wavelengths. In general, we would need $N\Delta$ wavelengths to implement a virtual topology with degree Δ. This does not compare favorably with the N wavelengths that are required for the single-hop packet-switched WDM star networks that we studied in Chapter 7. Of course, the number of wavelengths in both cases can be reduced by time-sharing each wavelength between multiple nodes.

Note that by tuning the transmitters and/or receivers to different wavelengths, the virtual topology can be changed. If this feature is not desired, much simpler implementations are possible. One such implementation of the virtual topology of Figure 9.8 is shown in Figure 9.10. Each node has two (non-WDM) transmitters and two receivers. The links in the virtual topology are established by using direct point-to-point optical fiber links. If desired, all the fibers can be brought to a hub where the interconnections are made as shown in the figure. This option is much less expensive than the WDM implementation because of the cheaper nonwavelength-specific lasers, avoidance of splitting losses, and the fact that the receivers need not care about the wavelength as well.

However, there may still be circumstances under which it would make sense to deploy such a virtual topology over a broadcast network. For example, there may be a scenario where a broadcast network is already deployed to provide circuit-switched

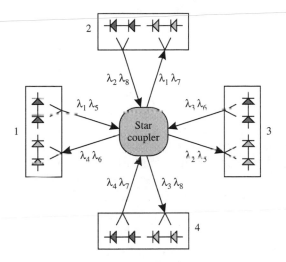

Figure 9.9   Implementation of the virtual topology of Figure 9.8 over a broadcast and select WDM physical topology.

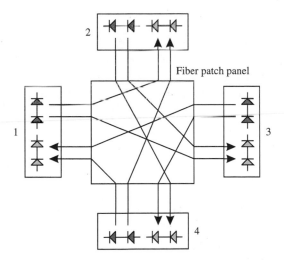

Figure 9.10   A simpler implementation of the virtual topology of Figure 9.8.

lightpath services, in which case, packet switching can be supported efficiently by overlaying such a virtual topology at different wavelengths over the existing network.

Summary

This chapter explored the design of virtual topologies over an optical layer that constitutes the physical topology. Instead of using physical links to interconnect higher-level SONET or ATM equipment, the interconnection is done via lightpaths. This feature enables the interconnection pattern to be changed if desired, a flexibility that is not found when conventional point-to-point links are used for the interconnection. The classical network design problem now becomes a two-level design problem, although it is still solved in many scenarios as two separate design problems: that of designing the virtual topology, and that of designing the physical topology. These problems are hard and solved using heuristic algorithms. Finally, we looked at regular virtual topologies, which are good at supporting uniform traffic.

A major advantage of virtual topologies is that the topology can be reconfigured if needed. This may be desirable to support changes in traffic patterns or to respond to failures in the network. This is an area that requires further study.

Further Reading

There is a lot of ongoing research in the area of designing good virtual topologies. For some recent work, see [KS98, RS96, MBRM96, BG95, ZA95, JBM95, GW94, CGK93, LA91]. Reconfiguring virtual topologies is a relatively open problem, and good techniques are yet to be developed; see [LAH92, AP95]. In contrast, there is a vast body of literature available on various kinds of regular virtual topologies and their properties, following the original paper by Acampora [Aca87]. See, for example, [HK91, SR94, RS94] and the surveys in [Siv92, Muk92].

Problems

9.1   Consider a wavelength routing network that consists of six wavelength routing nodes connected in a ring as follows: 1–2–3–4–5–6–1. Each link consists of a pair of fibers carrying WDM signals in opposite directions. Assume the wavelength routing nodes are of the type shown in Figure 8.9 of the text. Specifically, no wavelength conversion is employed.

   (a) You are required to realize a SONET network consisting of the following duplex links: 1–3, 3–6, and 2–5. Each SONET link is to be realized as a lightpath in the optical layer. Assume both halves of the duplex SONET link use the same route and wavelength in the optical layer. Find W_S, the minimum number of wavelengths required to realize this SONET network. (First find a lower bound, W_{Sl} on W_S. Then to show that this lower bound is tight, find a routing and wavelength assignment for all the SONET links using W_{Sl} wavelengths.)

(b) Instead of a SONET network as in part (a), you must now realize an ATM network consisting of the following duplex links: 1–4, 2–4, and 1–5. Each ATM link is to be realized as a lightpath in the optical layer. Assume both halves of the duplex ATM link use the same route and wavelength in the optical layer. Find W_A, the minimum number of wavelengths required to realize this ATM network.

(c) If both networks are to be realized *simultaneously*, what is the minimum number of wavelengths required, W_{S+A}? Compare W_{S+A} and $W_S + W_A$.

9.2 Consider a directed graph with diameter D and each node having maximum out-degree Δ. Show that the maximum number of nodes in this graph is given by

$$N_{\max} = \frac{\Delta^{D+1} - 1}{\Delta - 1}.$$

This bound is called the Moore bound.

9.3 Show that the diameter of a (Δ, k) shufflenet is $2k - 1$.

9.4 Show that the average number of hops for shortest-path routing in a (Δ, k) shufflenet is given by

$$\overline{H} = \frac{k\Delta^k(\Delta - 1)(3k - 1) - 2k(\Delta^k - 1)}{2(\Delta - 1)(k\Delta^k - 1)}.$$

9.5 The hypercube of order n is a graph on 2^n vertices with the vertices corresponding to the 2^n n-bit (binary, 0–1) sequences. Two vertices are connected by an edge if the corresponding n-bit sequences differ in exactly 1 bit. For example, in the hypercube of order 3, the vertex corresponding to the sequence 010 is connected by an edge to each of the vertices corresponding to 110, 000, and 011.

To obtain a directed network topology from a hypercube, we replace each (undirected) edge by two oppositely directed edges. Consider the topology obtained in this manner from a hypercube of order n. What is the in- and out-degree of each vertex? What is its diameter? Assuming one unit of traffic is routed on the shortest path between each s–d pair in this topology, find the average number of hops traversed by a packet. What is the average load on the edges of this topology?

━━━ References

[Aca87] A. S. Acampora. A multi-channel multihop local lightwave network. *Proceedings of IEEE Globecom*, pages 37.5.1–9, 1987.

[AP95] J. S. Auerbach and R. K. Pankaj. Use of delegated tuning and forwarding in WDMA networks. *IEEE Transactions on Communications*, 43(1):52–63, Jan. 1995.

[BG92] D. Bertsekas and R. G. Gallager. *Data Networks*. Prentice Hall, Englewood Cliffs, NJ, 1992.

[BG95] D. Bienstock and O. Gunluk. Computational experience with a difficult mixed-integer multicommodity flow problem. *Mathematical Programming*, 68:213–237, 1995.

[Cah98] R. Cahn. *The Art of Network Design*. Morgan Kaufmann, San Francisco, 1998.

[CGK93] I. Chlamtac, A. Ganz, and G. Karmi. Lightnets: Topologies for high-speed optical networks. *IEEE/OSA Journal on Lightwave Technology*, 11(5/6):951–961, May/June 1993.

[GJ79] M. R. Garey and D. S. Johnson. *Computers and Intractibility—A Guide to the Theory of NP Completeness*. W. H. Freeman, San Francisco, 1979.

[GLS98] O. Gerstel, P. Lin, and G. H. Sasaki. A new angle on wavelength assignment in WDM rings: Minimize system cost, not number of wavelengths. In *Proceedings of IEEE Infocom*, 1998.

[GRS98] O. Gerstel, R. Ramaswami, and G. H. Sasaki. Cost effective traffic grooming in WDM rings. In *Proceedings of IEEE Infocom*, 1998.

[GW94] A. Ganz and X. Wang. Efficient algorithm for virtual topology design in multihop lightwave networks. *IEEE/ACM Transactions on Networking*, 2(3):217–225, June 1994.

[HK91] M. G. Hluchyj and M. J. Karol. Shufflenet: An application of generalized perfect shuffles to multihop lightwave networks. *IEEE/OSA Journal on Lightwave Technology*, 9(10):1386–1397, 1991.

[IBM95] J. Iness, S. Banerjee, and B. Mukherjee. GEMNET: A generalized, shuffle-exchange-based, regular, scalable, modular, multihop, WDM lightwave network. *IEEE/ACM Transactions on Networking*, 3(4):470–476, Aug. 1995.

[Jai96] M. Jain. Topology designs for wavelength routed optical networks. Technical report, Indian Institute of Science, Bangalore, Jan. 1996.

[JBM95] S. V. Jagannath, K. Bala, and M. Mihail. Hierarchical design of WDM optical networks for ATM transport. In *Proceedings of IEEE Globecom*, pages 2188–2194, 1995.

[Ker93]   A. Kershenbaum. *Telecommunications Network Design Algorithms*. McGraw-Hill, New York, 1993.

[KS98]   R. M. Krishnaswamy and K. N. Sivarajan. Design of logical topologies: A linear formulation for wavelength routed optical networks with no wavelength changers. In *Proceedings of IEEE Infocom*, 1998.

[LA91]   J.-F. P. Labourdette and A. S. Acampora. Logically rearrangeable multihop lightwave networks. *IEEE Transactions on Communications*, 39(8):1223–1230, Aug. 1991.

[LAH92]   J.-F. P. Labourdette, A. S. Acampora, and G. W. Hart. Reconfiguration algorithms for rearrangeable lightwave networks. In *Proceedings of IEEE Infocom*, pages 2205–2214, 1992.

[MBRM96] B. Mukherjee, D. Banerjee, S. Ramamurthy, and A. Mukherjee. Some principles for designing a wide-area optical network. *IEEE/ACM Transactions on Networking*, 4(5):684–696, 1996.

[Muk92]   B. Mukherjee. WDM-based local lightwave networks—Part II: Multihop systems. *IEEE Network*, 6(4):20–32, July 1992.

[RS94]   R. Ramaswami and K. N. Sivarajan. A packet-switched multihop lightwave network using subcarrier and wavelength-division multiplexing. *IEEE Transactions on Communications*, March 1994.

[RS96]   R. Ramaswami and K. N. Sivarajan. Design of logical topologies for wavelength-routed optical networks. *IEEE JSAC/JLT Special Issue on Optical Networks*, 14(5):840–851, June 1996.

[Siv92]   K. N. Sivarajan. Multihop logical topologies in gigabit lightwave networks. *IEEE Lightwave Telecommunication Systems Magazine*, Aug. 1992.

[SR94]   K. N. Sivarajan and R. Ramaswami. Lightwave networks based on de Bruijn graphs. *IEEE/ACM Transactions on Networking*, 2(1):70–79, Feb. 1994.

[ZA95]   Z. Zhang and A. S. Acampora. A heuristic wavelength assignment algorithm for multihop WDM networks with wavelength routing and wavelength reuse. *IEEE/ACM Transactions on Networking*, 3(3):281–288, June 1995.

10 chapter

![10 chapter logo]

Control and Management

N ETWORK MANAGEMENT is an important part of any network. However attractive a specific technology might be, it can be deployed in a network only if it can be managed. The cost of managing a large network in many cases dominates the cost of the equipment deployed in the network. Our goal in this chapter is to provide a brief introduction to network management concepts and describe specifically how optical networks can be managed.

10.1 Network Management Functions

Classically, network management consists of several functions:

1. *Configuration management* deals with the set of functions associated with managing orderly changes in a network. For example, this could include setting up and taking down connections in a network, provided that these events do not occur very frequently or the network is very large and complex. In the latter cases, this function may be handled by a separate distributed *network control* entity that is capable of handling events rapidly. Other functions include tracking the equipment in the network and managing the addition/removal of equipment, including any rerouting of traffic this may involve. Configuration management is discussed further in Section 10.2.

2. *Performance management* deals with monitoring and managing the various parameters that measure the performance of the network. Performance management is an essential function that enables network operators to provide

quality-of-service guarantees to their clients and to ensure that clients comply with the requirements imposed by the operator. It is also needed to provide input to other network management functions, in particular fault management, when anomalous conditions are detected in the network. This function is discussed further in Section 10.3.

3. *Fault management* is the function responsible for detecting failures when they happen, isolating the failed component, and restoring traffic that may be disrupted due to the failure. We will study fault management extensively in Section 10.4.

4. *Security management* involves protecting data belonging to network users from being tapped or corrupted by unauthorized entities. It includes administrative functions such as authentication of users as well. For example, the broadcast and select networks of Chapters 7 and 12 are particularly vulnerable to this problem. For now, security aspects of optical networks appear to be similar to those of other networks. For instance, data can be encrypted before transmission. This prevents unauthorized tapping and allows the recipient to detect any corrupted data.

5. *Accounting management* is the function responsible for billing and for developing lifetime histories of the network components. Again, this function doesn't appear to be much different for optical networks, compared to other networks, and we will not be discussing this topic further.

For optical networks, an additional consideration is *safety management*, which is needed to ensure that optical radiation conforms to limits imposed for ensuring eye safety. This subject is treated in Section 10.5.

Most functions of network management are implemented in a centralized manner by a *network management center*. However, this method of implementation is rather slow, and it can take several tens of milliseconds to seconds to communicate between the network management center and different parts of the network owing to the large software path overheads usually involved in this process. Therefore, certain management functions that require rapid action may have to be decentralized, such as responding to failures and setting up and taking down connections if these must be done rapidly. Decentralized methods are usually much faster than centralized methods, even in small networks with only a few nodes. For example, a SONET ring can restore failures within 60 ms, and this is possible only because this process is completely decentralized. Another reason for decentralizing some of the functions is if the network becomes very large. In this case, it becomes difficult for a single central manager to manage the entire network. Further, networks could include multiple

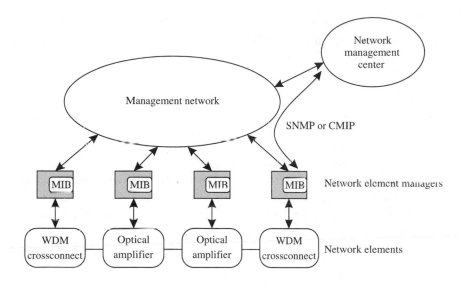

Figure 10.1   Overview of network management in a typical optical network.

domains administered by different managers. The managers of each domain will need to communicate with each other to perform certain functions in a coordinated manner.

Figure 10.1 provides an overview of how network management functions are implemented on a typical network. The individual components to be managed are called *network elements*. Network elements include optical amplifiers, crossconnects, and add/drop multiplexers. Each element is managed by its *network element manager*. The element itself has a built-in *agent*, which communicates with its element manager. The agent is implemented in software, usually in a microprocessor in the network element. The element managers communicate with a *network management center* through a management network. The actual communication between an agent and its manager may use an out-of-band network, or it may use one of the wavelengths in the network as a supervisory channel.

The information to be managed for each network element is represented in the form of a *management information base* (MIB). The MIB contains a set of variables representing the information to be managed. These will include various operating parameters to be monitored by the agent and the manager, as well as several parameters that are set by the manager to control the network element. An example of a MIB for a simple point-to-point WDM system is provided in Appendix H.

Most network management systems use a master–slave sort of relationship between a manager and the agents managed by the manager. The manager queries the agent to obtain the status of variables in the MIB (called the *get* operation). For example, the manager may query the agent periodically for performance information. The manager can also change the values of variables in the MIB (called the *set* operation), and uses this method to effect changes within the network element. For example, the manager may use this method to change the configuration of the switches inside a network element such as a wavelength router. In addition to these methods, it is necessary for the agent sometimes to initiate a message to its manager. This is essential if the agent detects problems in the network element and wants to alert its manager. The agent then sends a *trap* or *alarm* to its manager.

The agent–manager relationship described here is a simplified picture. In reality, there is a hierarchy of managers. For example, an *element management system* (EMS) is used to manage a set of common network elements, such as ADMs on a SONET ring. This EMS communicates with the individual network element managers for each element in the ring. Likewise, there may be another EMS for managing digital crossconnects in the network. The two EMSs in turn are managed by another network management system. To the network management system, the EMSs are the agents, and to the EMSs, the network management system is their manager.

There are two primary standards relating to network management and perhaps two thousand acronyms describing them. Here is a brief summary. The Internet world uses a management framework based on the *simple network management protocol* (SNMP). SNMP is an application protocol that runs over a standard TCP/IP protocol stack (see Section 6.3.3). The manager communicates with the agents using SNMP.

The carrier world uses a variety of protocols today and in fact uses multiple management systems to implement the different components of network management. It is converging toward a management framework called the *telecommunications management network* (TMN). In TMN, the network element managers usually communicate with the manager using a protocol called the *common management information protocol* (CMIP), which usually runs over an *open systems interconnection* (OSI) protocol stack. The format of the MIB is also different. The MIB has an object-oriented structure and is based on a standard called *guidelines for description of managed objects* (GDMO).

10.2 Configuration Management

We can break down configuration management functions into two parts: managing the equipment in the network and managing the connections in the network.

10.2.1   Equipment Management

In general, the principles of managing optical networking equipment are no different from those of managing other high-speed networking equipment. We must be able to keep track of the actual equipment in the system (for example, number of optical line amplifiers) as well as the equipment in each network element and its capabilities. For example, in a terminal of a point-to-point WDM system, we may want to keep track of the maximum number of wavelengths and the number of wavelengths currently equipped, whether there are optical pre- and power amplifiers or not, and so forth. Appendix H provides an example of some of the variables that are present for this purpose in the MIB.

Among the considerations are that we should be able to add to existing equipment in a modular fashion. For instance, we should be able to add additional wavelengths (up to a designed maximum number) without disrupting the operation of the existing wavelengths. An issue that comes up in this regard is the use of arrayed multiwavelength components versus separate components for individual wavelengths, such as multiwavelength laser arrays instead of individual lasers for each wavelength. It is likely that the arrayed version may be significantly cheaper than having several individual components. However, if one element in the array fails, the entire array will have to be replaced. This may be more expensive than replacing just a single failed element for the case without arrays. Moreover, replacing the array will involve disrupting the operation of all the wavelengths, not just the failed wavelength.

We may also want to start out by deploying the equipment in the form of a point-to-point link and later upgrade it to handle ring or other network configurations. We may also desire flexibility in associating specific port cards in the equipment with specific wavelengths. For example, it is better to have a system where we can choose the wavelength transmitted out of a port card independently of what slot it is located in.

On the other hand, allowing users to choose their transmit wavelengths in a flexible manner may pose some security concerns. For instance, a user may unwittingly (or maliciously!) choose a transmit wavelength that interferes with other wavelengths in the network. Such actions can be prevented by assigning a specific band of wavelengths to each user and providing a filtering function at the input to the network that prevents other wavelengths from entering the network.

Another related problem in WDM systems is the need to maintain an inventory of wavelength-specific spare cards. For example, each channel may be realized by using a card with a wavelength-specific laser in it. Thus one would need to stock spare cards for each wavelength. This can be avoided by using a wavelength-selectable (or tunable) laser on each card instead of a wavelength-specific laser; however, such devices are not yet commercially available at reasonable cost.

10.2.2 Connection Management

An important configuration management function deals with setting up connections, keeping track of them, and taking them down when they are not needed anymore and freeing up the resources associated with them for other connections. In a WDM network, these connections correspond to lightpaths. If the network is small, and if requests for setting up and taking down lightpaths occur somewhat infrequently (minutes to hours), then this function can be performed by a centralized manager. In a large network, or in a network where these events happen more frequently, distributed control methods are called for. Distributed methods may also have to be invoked when setting up lightpaths across network domain boundaries administered by different managers. With distributed methods, we need to worry about two additional complications: (a) dealing with contention for wavelengths when multiple parties attempt to simultaneously set up a lightpath, and (b) maintaining consistency of the network topology and lightpaths in the presence of failures of parts of the network or the distributed controllers. Distributed protocols have been used for connection setup purposes in other networks and have been proposed for use in optical networks as well [RS96].

The process of taking down a lightpath must be executed carefully. For example, if the lightpath is simply taken down by the source and destination, then the intermediate nodes may sense the loss of light on the lightpath as a failure condition and trigger unwanted alarms. This can be avoided by suitable coordination among the nodes along the route of the lightpath.

Another concern is that during the operation of the network, inadvertent loops may be formed on specific wavelengths. Inadvertent loops can be prevented by careful network control. In some cases, as we will see in Section 10.4 (see Figure 10.16 in that section), we may actually set this loop deliberately for the purposes of protection switching. Such loops may have optical amplifiers in them and may create lasing if the gain in the loop is not properly controlled.

10.3 Performance Management

As we stated earlier, the goal of performance management is to enable network operators to provide guaranteed quality of service to the users of their network. This usually requires monitoring of the performance parameters for all the connections supported in the network and taking any actions necessary to ensure that the desired performance goals are met.

The parameters to be monitored depend very much on the types of connections provided by the network. In the context of a transparent optical network providing lightpaths, performance primarily implies bandwidth and bit error rate. In this case, bandwidth simply corresponds to the bandwidth of a wavelength and is thus not a major parameter to monitor. The story is quite different if bandwidth is characterized in statistical terms, for example, average bandwidth over time, as is the case in networks that make use of statistical multiplexing. In this case, characterizing and monitoring bandwidth is in itself a major challenge.

In a transparent optical network, the management mechanism may have no prior knowledge of the protocols or bit rates being used in the network. Therefore, it is not possible to access overhead bits in the transmitted data to obtain performance-related measures. This makes it very difficult, for example, to monitor the bit error rate. However, transmission-related parameters that can be monitored include optical power levels, optical signal to noise ratios, temperature, and various parameters associated with the electronics that is necessarily present at the transmitters and receivers. Based on these parameters, the network management system must be able to provide a guaranteed bit error rate performance to the users of the optical network.

Performance management is also necessary to ensure that the users of the network comply with requirements that were negotiated between them and the network operator. For example, one function may be to monitor the wavelength and power levels of signals being input to the network to ensure that they meet the requirements imposed by the network. Another more important function may be to monitor the actual service being utilized by the user. For example, the network operator may choose to provide two services, say, an FDDI service and an OC-3 service, by renting a transparent lightpath to the user. The two services may be tariffed differently. However, with a transparent network, it is difficult to prevent a user who opts for the FDDI service from sending OC-3 traffic. It is the job of the monitoring system to detect such infringements.

Another problem related to transparency is in determining the threshold values for the various parameters at which alarms must be set off. These values depend on the bit rate on the channel and should ideally be set depending on the bit rate. However, in a truly transparent network, one may have to set the alarms to correspond to the highest possible bit rate that can be present on the channel. In addition, since the signal is not terminated at an intermediate node, if a wavelength fails, all nodes along the path downstream of the failed wavelength trigger an alarm. This can lead to a large number of alarms for a single failure, and makes it somewhat more complicated to determine the cause of the alarm. This is not a problem in conventional networks because each intermediate node regenerates the signal, and therefore, the alarm is issued only by the node just downstream of the failure.

Another desirable function might be to track the origin of each optical signal that is monitored. This can be done by adding a *pilot tone* to each optical signal that contains relevant information such as the address of the source originating that signal. Additional network-related parameters include the status of available wavelengths on all the links and the set of lightpaths that are currently set up in the network.

10.4 Fault Management

Providing resilience against failures is an important requirement for many high-speed networks. As these networks carry more and more data, the amount of disruption caused by a network-related outage becomes more and more significant. Several techniques exist to ensure that networks can continue to provide reliable services even in the presence of failures. These *protection* techniques all involve providing some redundant capacity within the network that is used to reroute traffic in the presence of failures. Moreover, in most cases, they are all implemented in a distributed manner without requiring coordination between all the nodes in the network. The latter feature is necessary to ensure fast restoration of service after a failure.

The term *survivability* refers to a network's ability to continue to provide service in the presence of failures. Survivability can be addressed within many layers in the network. For instance, consider a typical ATM network operating over SONET links, which in turn, are provided by optical layer lightpaths. Here all three layers—ATM, SONET, and the optical layer—may have their own protection mechanisms. We will see how protection mechanisms in different layers can work together in Section 10.4.5.

We will be concerned with failures of network links, nodes, and individual channels (in the case of a WDM network). Links can fail because of a fiber cut. Nodes may fail because of power outages or equipment failures. Individual channel failures may be caused by the failure of a component associated with that channel, such as a transmitter or a receiver. In almost all cases, protection mechanisms are designed to protect against a single failure event. This assumes that the network is designed well enough that simultaneous multiple failures are very rare. Alternatively, we may assume that it is unlikely that we will have a failure event occur while we are trying to restore service from another earlier failure event.

The restoration times required depend on the application/type of data being carried. For SONET/SDH networks, the maximum allowed restoration time is 60 ms; see Section 6.1.

10.4.1 Protection Concepts

We will start by describing the different types of protection mechanisms that are used for simple point-to-point links, and then discuss how these can be applied for networks. Two fundamental types of protection mechanisms are used in point-to-point

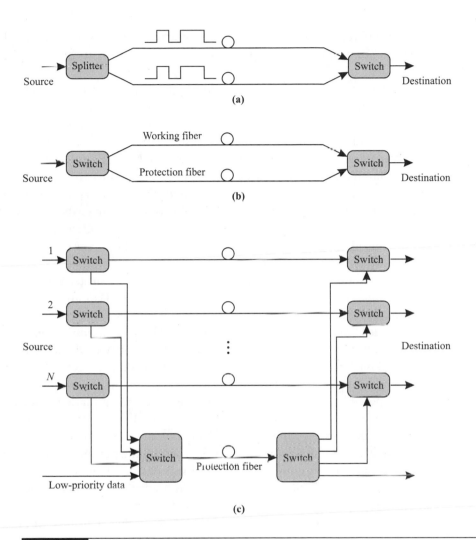

Figure 10.2   Different types of protection techniques for point-to-point links: (a) $1 + 1$ protection, (b) 1:1 protection, and (c) 1:N protection.

links: $1 + 1$ protection and 1:1 or, more generally, 1:N protection, as shown in Figure 10.2.

In $1 + 1$ protection, traffic is transmitted simultaneously on two separate fibers (usually over disjoint routes) from the source to the destination. We will call one fiber the *working* fiber and the other the *protection* fiber. The destination selects one of the two fibers for reception. If that fiber is cut, the destination simply switches over to the other fiber and continues to receive data. This form of protection is very fast and requires no signaling protocol between the two ends. In an all-optical implementation, this may require the signal to be split up at the transmitting end, resulting in 3 dB of additional loss.

In 1:1 protection, there are still two fibers from the source to the destination. However, traffic is transmitted over only one fiber at a time, say, the working fiber. If that fiber is cut, the source and destination both switch over to the other protection fiber. In a unidirectional communication system, where traffic is transmitted in only one direction over a fiber, a fiber cut will be detected by the destination and not by the source. Thus the destination must tell the source to switch over to the protection fiber. This requires a signaling protocol, called an *automatic protection switching* (APS) protocol. The APS protocol used in SONET networks is described in [Wu92]. In a bidirectional communication system, where traffic is transmitted in both directions over a single fiber, a fiber cut will be detected by both the source and the destination. Thus no APS protocol is required.

Clearly, in unidirectional communication systems, 1:1 protection is not as quick as $1+1$ protection in restoring traffic because of the added communication overhead involved. However, it offers two main advantages over $1+1$ protection. The first is that under normal operation, the protection fiber is unused. Therefore, it can be used to transmit lower-priority traffic. This lower-priority traffic must be discarded if the working fiber is cut. Note that this advantage disappears if no extra transmitter or receiver is available to handle this lower-priority traffic. The second advantage is that it is possible to share a single protection fiber among many working fibers. In a more general 1:N protection scheme, N working fibers share a single protection fiber. This arrangement can handle the failure of any single working fiber. Note that in the event of multiple failures, the APS protocol must ensure that only traffic on one of the failed fibers is switched over to the protection fiber.

Once protection switching has been employed, what happens when the original working fiber cut has been repaired? In $1+1$ protection, no action is needed since the repaired fiber now becomes the protection fiber. This type of protection is termed *nonreverting*. In 1:N protection, however, it is desirable to have the traffic switched back onto the original working fiber so that new failures can be handled and low-priority traffic may continue to use the protection fiber. This type of protection, called *reverting,* can be done automatically or by manual intervention.

In a network, each link carries traffic from different sources intended for different destinations. There are two ways of protecting this traffic: *path switching* and *line switching*, as shown in Figure 10.3. In path switching, which is also called *path protection*, the restoration of traffic is handled by the source and destination of each individual traffic stream. Traffic is rerouted at the source and destination nodes in the event of a failure somewhere along the route between the two nodes. In line

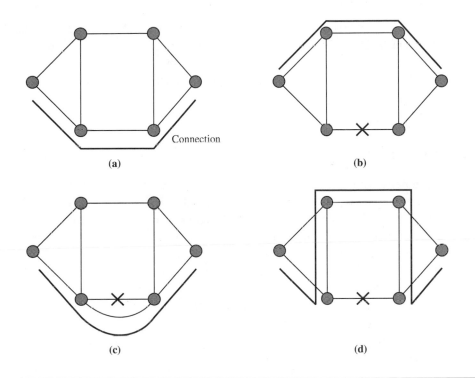

Figure 10.3   Path and line switching in a mesh network. (a) Normal operation. (b) Path-switched restoration after a link failure. (c) Span protection, a form of line switching. (d) Line protection, another form of line switching.

switching, the restoration of traffic is handled by the nodes at the ends of a failed link, rather than the sources and destinations.

There are two ways of implementing line switching: *span protection* and *line protection* (note the distinction between line switching and line protection). In span protection, if a fiber is cut between two nodes, traffic is switched to another fiber between the same two nodes, as shown in Figure 10.3. In line protection, the traffic is switched to another route through the network between the same two nodes, as shown in Figure 10.3. In a ring network, for example, line protection involves routing the traffic all the way around the ring in case a link fails.

As in point-to-point links, path protection can be implemented in a $1 + 1$ or a $1:N$ arrangement. $1 + 1$ path protection is inefficient because twice as much bandwidth is needed for each connection. In a $1:N$ arrangement, N paths can share an additional single spare path for protection, which is more efficient.

1:1 path protection requires less bandwidth for traffic restoration than does line protection. This is because path protection uses shorter-hop routes in the network to reroute traffic compared to line protection. However, in a worst-case traffic scenario (see Problem 10.1), path protection will require the same amount of bandwidth as line protection.

10.4.2   Ring Networks

Ring networks have become very popular in the carrier world as well as in enterprise networks. A ring is the simplest topology that is *two-connected,* that is, provides two separate paths between any pair of nodes that do not have any nodes or links in common except the source and destination nodes. This allows a ring network to be resilient to failures. Much of the carrier infrastructure today uses SONET/SDH rings. These rings are called *self-healing* since they incorporate protection mechanisms that detect failures and reroute traffic away from failed links and nodes onto other routes rapidly. The protection concepts described here apply to second-generation WDM ring networks as well.

The different types of ring architectures differ in two aspects: the directionality of traffic, and in the protection mechanisms used. A *unidirectional* ring carries working traffic in only one direction of the ring (say, clockwise), as shown in Figure 10.4. Working traffic from node A to node B is carried clockwise along the ring, and working traffic from B to A is also carried clockwise, on a different set of links in the ring. A *bidirectional* ring carries working traffic in both directions. Figure 10.5 shows a four-fiber bidirectional ring. Working traffic from A to B is carried clockwise, and working traffic from B to A is carried counterclockwise along the ring. Note that in both unidirectional and bidirectional SONET/SDH rings, all connections are bidirectional and use up the same amount of bandwidth in both directions. The two directions of a connection are routed differently based on the type of ring, as we discussed earlier.

The SONET/SDH standards dictate that in SONET/SDH rings, service must be restored within 60 ms after a failure. This number includes the failure detection time, a hold-off time, switching time, the time to reacquire the SONET frame synchronization, and the propagation delay in the system. This time is set by the requirement that the lower-speed streams, such as DS1 streams at 1.5 Mb/s, and DS3 streams at 45 Mb/s that are multiplexed into the high-speed traffic stream must not lose frame synchronization at their receivers.

Three ring architectures have become popular: two-fiber unidirectional path-switched rings (UPSR), four-fiber bidirectional line-switched rings (BLSR/4), and two-fiber bidirectional line-switched rings (BLSR/2). These are also called USHR,

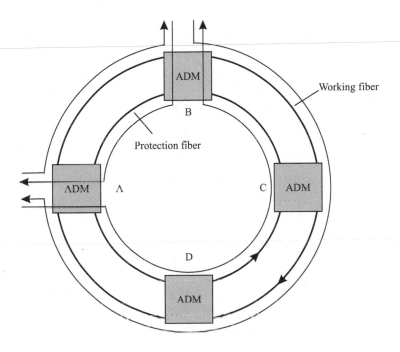

Figure 10.4   A unidirectional path-switched ring (UPSR). One of the fibers is considered the working fiber and the other the protection fiber. Traffic is transmitted simultaneously on the working fiber in the clockwise direction and on the protection fiber in the counter-clockwise direction.

BSHR/4, and BSHR/2, respectively, where SH stands for *self-healing*. Table 10.1 compares the key features in the different ring architectures.

Unidirectional Path-Switched Rings

Figure 10.4 shows a UPSR. One fiber is used as a working fiber and the other as the protection fiber. Traffic from node A to node B is sent simultaneously on the working fiber in the clockwise direction, and on the protection fiber in the counterclockwise direction. Node B continuously monitors both the working and protection fiber and selects the better signal between the two. Under normal operation, suppose node B receives traffic from the working fiber. If there is a link failure, say, of link AB, then B will switch over to the protection fiber and continue to receive the data. This is essentially like the 1 + 1 protection concept that we studied earlier in the context of point-to-point links. The same protection scheme applies in the case of node failures as well. Note that the capacity required for protection purposes is equal to

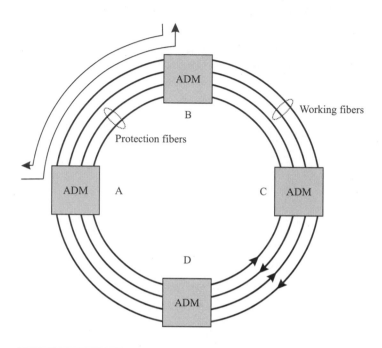

Figure 10.5 A four-fiber bidirectional line-switched ring (BLSR/4). The ring has two working fibers and two protection fibers. Traffic between two nodes is transmitted normally on the shortest path between them, and both span and line protection are used to restore service after a failure.

Table 10.1 Comparison of different types of self-healing rings.

Parameter	UPSR	BLSR/4	BLSR/2
Fiber-pairs	1	2	1
TX/RX pairs/node	2	4	2
Spatial reuse	None	Yes	Yes
Protection capacity	= Working capacity	= Working capacity	= Working capacity
Link failure	Path protection	Span/line protection	Line protection
Node failure	Path protection	Line protection	Line protection
Restoration speed	Faster	Slower	Slower
Node complexity	Low	High	High

the working capacity. This will turn out to be the case for the other ring architectures as well.

The main drawback with the UPSR is that it does not spatially reuse the fiber capacity. This is because each (bidirectional) SONET connection uses up capacity on every link in the ring. In other words, a 1.5 Mb/s SONET connection would use up 1.5 Mb/s of capacity on each fiber in the ring. Thus, if the transmission rate on the links is, say, 622 Mb/s, then the total traffic that the UPSR ring can handle is exactly 622 Mb/s. We will study other architectures that do incorporate spatial reuse and can support aggregate traffic capacities higher than the transmission rate.

UPSRs are popular topologies in lower-speed local exchange and access networks, particularly where the traffic is primarily point to multipoint, that is, from each node to a hub node and vice versa. In this case, we will see that the traffic capacity that a UPSR can support is the same as what the more complicated ring architectures incorporating spatial reuse can support. This makes the UPSR an attractive option for such applications due to its simplicity, and thus, lower cost. Typical ring speeds today are OC-3 (STM-1) and OC-12 (STM-4). There is no specified limit on the number of nodes in a UPSR, or on the ring length. In practice, the ring length will be limited by the fact that the clockwise and counterclockwise path taken by a signal will have different delays associated with them, which in turn, will affect the restoration time in the event of a failure. UPSRs are also fairly easy to implement because their protection scheme is very simple, requiring action only at the receiver, without any complicated signaling protocols.

Bidirectional Line-Switched Rings

BLSRs provide spatial reuse capabilities and incorporate additional protection mechanisms, compared to UPSRs. Figure 10.5 shows a four-fiber BLSR. Two fibers are used as working fibers, and two are used for protection. Unlike a UPSR, working traffic in a BLSR can be carried on both directions along the ring. For example, traffic between nodes A and B is carried clockwise along the ring on the working fiber, whereas traffic from B to A is carried counterclockwise along the ring. In general, traffic belonging to both directions of a connection is routed on the shortest path between the two nodes in the ring. Note that this maximizes the amount of spatial reuse obtained.

A BLSR can support up to 16 nodes, and this number is limited by the 4-bit addressing field used for the node identifier. The maximum ring length is limited to 1200 km (6 ms propagation delay) owing to the requirements on the restoration time in the case of a failure. For longer rings, particularly for undersea applications, the 60 ms restoration time has been relaxed.

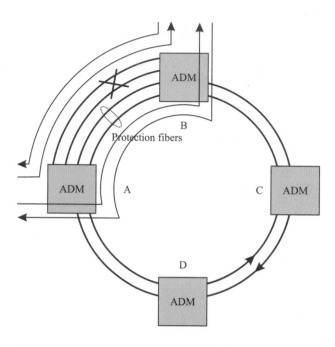

Figure 10.6   Illustrating span protection in a BLSR/4.

A BLSR/4 employs two types of protection mechanisms: *span protection* and *line protection*. In span protection, if a transmitter or receiver on a working fiber fails, the traffic is routed onto the protection fiber between the two nodes on the same link, as shown in Figure 10.6. If the protection fibers are routed separately from the working fibers, they are unlikely to get cut simultaneously. In this case, span protection can also be used to handle a cut of a working fiber. In any case, if the protection fibers also get cut along with the working fibers, service is restored by line protection, as illustrated in Figure 10.7. Suppose link AB fails. The traffic on the failed link is then rerouted by nodes A and B around the ring on the protection fibers. Line protection also works in the case of a node failure.

A BLSR/2, shown in Figure 10.8, can be thought of as a BLSR/4 with the protection fibers "embedded" within the working fibers. In a BLSR/2, both of the fibers are used to carry working traffic, but half the capacity on each fiber is reserved for protection purposes. Unlike a BLSR/4, span protection is not possible here, but line protection works in much the same way as in a BLSR/4. In the event of a link failure, the traffic on the failed link is rerouted along the other part of the ring using the protection capacity available in the two fibers. As with 1:1 protection on point-to-point

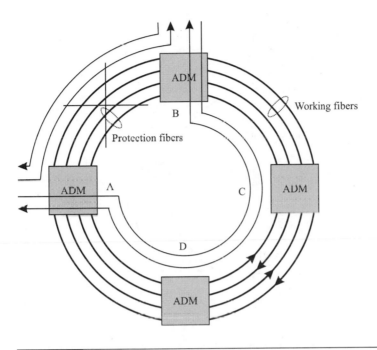

Figure 10.7   Illustrating line protection in a BLSR/4.

links, an advantage of the line protection in BLSRs is that the protection bandwidth can be used to carry low-priority traffic during normal operation. This traffic is preempted if the bandwidth is needed for service restoration.

BLSRs are more efficient than UPSRs in supported distributed traffic patterns, as opposed to the hubbed traffic pattern that we studied above. Their efficiency comes from the fact that the protection capacity in the ring is shared among all the connections. For instance, consider a BLSR/2 ring with 10 nodes. Suppose we have a 1.5 Mb/s connection between each adjacent pair of nodes. All these connections would together share 1.5 Mb/s of protection capacity on each fiber in the ring. Thus only 1.5 Mb/s of protection capacity is required to support a total connection bandwidth of 15 Mb/s. In contrast, the UPSR architecture requires dedicated protection capacity for each connection. For the example considered here, a UPSR would require 15 Mb/s of protection capacity on each fiber in the ring.

For this reason, BLSRs are widely deployed in long-haul and interoffice networks, where the traffic pattern is more distributed than in access networks. Today, these rings operate at OC-48 (STM-16) and OC-12 (STM-4) speeds, and OC-192 (STM-64) rings are just being introduced. Most of the deployed networks today

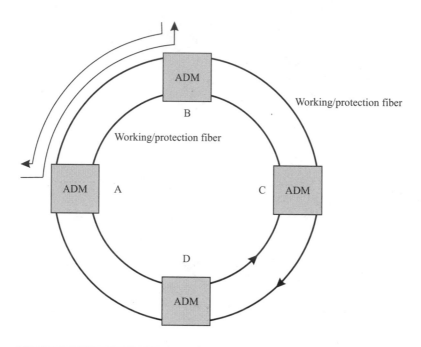

Figure 10.8   A two-fiber bidirectional line-switched ring (BLSR/2). The ring has two fibers and half the bandwidth. Line protection is used to restore service after a failure.

are two-fiber rings, although some carriers, notably Sprint, have deployed four-fiber rings. BLSR/4s can handle more failures than BLSR/2s. For example, a BLSR/4 can simultaneously handle one transmitter failure on each span in the ring. It is also easier to service than a BLSR/2 ring because multiple spans can be serviced independently without taking down the ring. However, ring management in a BLSR/4 is more complicated than in a BLSR/2 because multiple protection mechanisms have to be coordinated.

Dual Homing

The ring architectures described suffer from the problem that if a node fails, all traffic sourced or sunk at the node is lost. This may be a significant problem if the node in question happens to be a major hub node or central office that sources or sinks a large amount of traffic. A way to deal with this problem is to use *dual homing*, which is being deployed increasingly in business access networks. Dual homing makes use of two hub nodes, instead of the one normally employed in UPSRs, as shown in

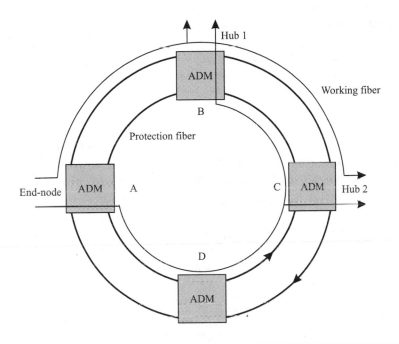

Figure 10.9   Dual homing to handle hub node failures. Each end-node is connected to two hub nodes so as to be able to recover from the failure of a hub node. The ADMs in the nodes have a "drop and continue" feature that allows them to drop a traffic stream as well as have it continue onto the next ADM.

Figure 10.9. Connections are set up between each nonhub node and both the hub nodes. Thus if one of the hub nodes fails, the other node can take over, and the end user does not see any disruption to traffic. As in a UPSR, $1 + 1$ path protection is employed. Working traffic is sent in one direction of the ring, and protection traffic is transmitted simultaneously along the other direction. Rather than set up two separate connections between a node and the two hub nodes, the architecture uses a multicasting feature present in the ADMs. Consider the connection between node A and the two hub nodes Hub 1 and Hub 2 in Figure 10.9. In the clockwise direction of the ring, the ADM at Hub 1 drops the traffic associated with the connection between node A and Hub 1 but also simultaneously allows this traffic to continue along the ring, where it is again dropped at Hub 2. Likewise, along the counterclockwise direction, the ADM at Hub 2 uses its "drop and continue" feature to multicast the traffic from node A.

10.4.3   Mesh Networks

Service restoration in mesh networks is somewhat more complicated than in point-to-point links or in ring networks. A simple protection technique is to establish two edge- or node-disjoint paths for each connection, and handle failures by using $1 + 1$ path protection. As in rings, this is a very inefficient approach because the bandwidth needed for protection is not shared among multiple connections.

A better approach is to use line protection, which will enable sharing of protection resources between connections. If a link fails, all the connections on that link are rerouted along another path between the nodes at the ends of the failed link. The problem is to do this without requiring coordination among the nodes along this path.

We now describe such a line protection scheme that can be executed locally by the nodes at the ends of a failed link, without requiring any coordination whatsoever [Gar94, ES96]. Note that restoration is possible only if the graph is *two edge connected*, that is, there are at least two *edge-disjoint* paths between any pair of nodes so that no single edge failure can disconnect the network.

Consider a two edge connected mesh network whose links have four fibers, with a working fiber and a protection fiber in each direction. The fibers can all be routed together. If one fiber is cut, it is therefore likely that others along the route may be cut as well. Note that in a BLSR/4, the span protection is effective against fiber cuts only if the protection and working fibers are routed separately, but line protection is effective even if both pairs of fibers are routed together. The line protection scheme here works in a similar fashion. The main problem to be solved is to find a way to implement such a scheme without requiring the nodes in the network to communicate with each other so that the restoration can be accomplished quickly.

To start with, we will consider only two protection fibers on each link. Let us represent the network by a directed graph, as shown in Figure 10.10. Each link in the network is represented by two directed edges in opposite directions in the graph. Assume that the graph is *planar*.

We will now construct a partition of the protection edges in the graph into cycles. Each edge belongs to exactly one cycle, and all edges are included in the partition. To do so, we make use of the following theorem from graph theory, the proof of which is included in Appendix G.

Theorem 10.1   *Given a two-connected planar directed graph $G(V, E)$, with bidirectional edges, the edges in G can be partitioned into a set of cycles of edges $C_1, C_2, \ldots, C_K$, such that each edge belongs to exactly one cycle and all edges are included in the partition.*

Figure 10.10 shows the decomposition of the protection edges into cycles for this sample network. Let $C(e_p)$ denote the cycle of protection edges associated with

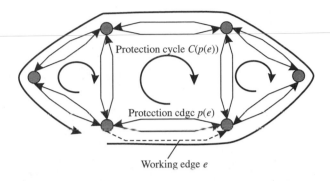

Protection cycle $C(p(e))$

Protection edge $p(e)$

Working edge e

Figure 10.10 Protection cycles in a mesh network.

protection edge e_p. Consider a particular working edge e, and let $p(e)$ denote the edge between the same two nodes as e, but in the opposite direction. Then we will call $C(p(e))$ the *protection* cycle for e. The figure shows an example of a working edge e, its protection edge $p(e)$, and its protection cycle $C(p(e))$.

The implementation of the line protection scheme based on this concept is illustrated in Figures 10.11 and 10.12. Figure 10.11 shows the network of Figure 10.10 with both the protection and working fibers, with the protection fibers connected according to the protection cycles. Figure 10.12(a) shows a unidirectional lightpath from node A to node D going through nodes B, C, and E, respectively. For simplicity, we do not show the other direction. The nodes have switches inside them to make the connections required to connect the various protection and working fibers. Figure 10.12(b) illustrates what happens when link BC fails. Node B switches the lightpath onto the protection cycle BFEC, and node C switches the lightpath from the protection cycle back onto link CE. The important thing to note is that only nodes B and C are involved in the restoration. Just as in a ring, line protection can make somewhat inefficient use of the bandwidth in some cases. In this example, the restored lightpath uses link EC and then link CE. Path protection could avoid this scenario. The problem is that there is no easy way to implement this form of path protection without requiring coordination between nodes. In a simple form of path protection, we would establish a redundant lightpath *a priori* at the time the original lightpath is established. As we mentioned at the beginning of this section, this would be even more wasteful than line protection in utilizing bandwidth.

There is only one problem with this approach. Theorem 10.1 applies only to two-connected planar graphs. However, there is a well-known conjecture in graph theory called the *orientable cycle double cover conjecture* that says that it is possible to construct these cycles for two-connected nonplanar graphs as well, and several

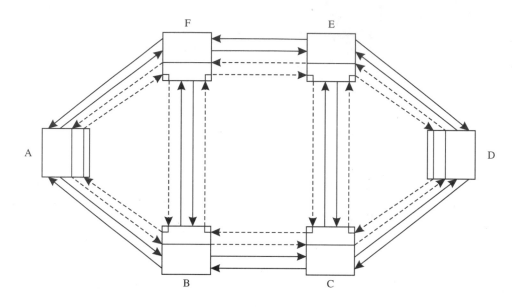

Figure 10.11   The mesh network of Figure 10.10 redrawn with both protection and working fibers. The working fibers are shown using solid lines, and the protection fibers are shown using dashed lines. The protection fibers are connected in protection cycles.

heuristic algorithms have been proposed to construct them [Gar94]. So far, no example of a two-connected network exists where such a construction is not possible. Note that the protection cycles are constructed at the time the network is deployed, and so this is a one-time computation.

10.4.4   Handling Node Failures

So far, we have dealt primarily with how to handle failures of links, such as those occurring from a fiber cut. Failures of nodes are usually less likely because, in many cases, redundant configurations (such as dual power supplies and switch fabrics) are used. However, nodes may still fail owing to some catastrophic events. Restoration mechanisms that must handle both node and link failures are significantly more complicated than those that must handle only link failures. The failure of a node is seen by all its adjacent nodes as failures of the links that connect them to the failed node. If each of these adjacent nodes performs restoration assuming that it is a single link failure, there can be undesirable consequences. One example is shown in Figure 10.13. Here, when node 1 fails, nodes 6 and 2 assume it is a link failure and attempt to reroute the traffic around the ring (line protection) to restore service.

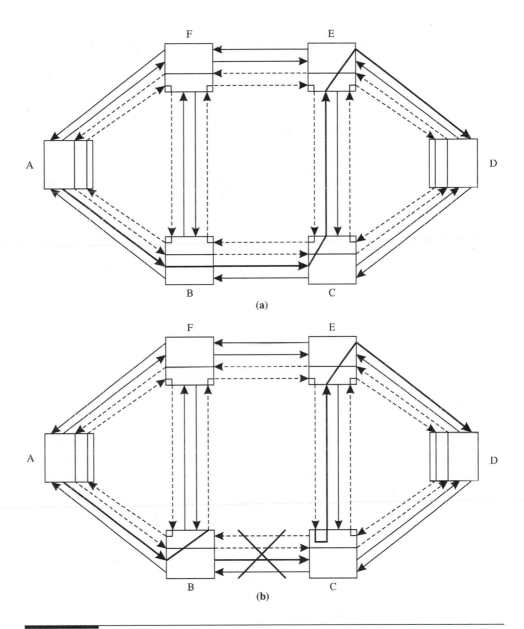

Figure 10.12   Line protection in a mesh network using protection cycles. The working fibers are shown using solid lines, and the protection fibers are shown using dashed lines. (a) A unidirectional lightpath from node A to node D going through nodes B, C, and E is shown. (b) After link BC fails, the lightpath is rerouted by nodes B and C along the route ABFECED.

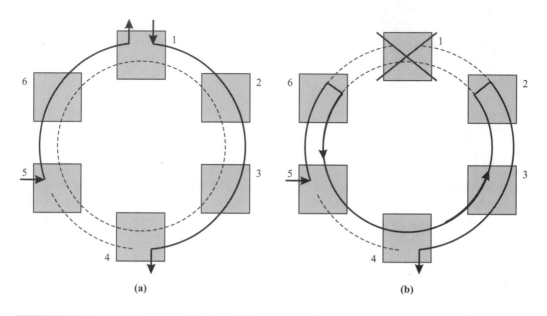

Figure 10.13   Erroneous connections due to the failure of a node being treated by its adjacent nodes as link failures: (a) Normal operation, with a connection from node 5 to node 1 and another connection from node 1 to node 4. (b) After node 1 fails, node 5 gets connected to node 4 after nodes 6 and 2 invoke line protection independently.

This causes erroneous connections, as shown in the figure. The only way to prevent such occurrences is to ensure that the nodes performing the restoration determine the type of failure before invoking their restoration mechanisms. This would require exchanging messages between the nodes in the network. In the preceding example, nodes 6 and 2 could first try to exchange messages around the ring to determine if they have both recorded link failures and, if so, invoke the appropriate restoration procedure. This restoration procedure can avoid these misconnections by not attempting to restore any traffic that originates or terminates at the failed node. This is called *squelching*. The price paid for this is a slower restoration time owing to the coordination required between the nodes to determine the appropriate restoration mechanism to be invoked.

10.4.5   Interworking Between Layers

Different protection schemes belong to different layers in the layered hierarchy considered in Section 6.4. For example, in a SONET network, path protection belongs to the SONET *path* layer, whereas line and span protection belong to the SONET *line* layer. Likewise, in an optical WDM network, path protection belongs to the *optical channel layer*, whereas line and span protection belong to the *optical multiplex section* layer.

What complicates matters is that a network consists of many layers, and each layer may have its own protection mechanisms built in, independent of the other layers. Unfortunately, in developing these protection mechanisms, no thought is usually given to how these would work with protection mechanisms present in other layers. This is because each layer is assumed to work with a variety of other layers above and below it, and also because each layer is usually developed and standardized by a separate group of people.

In general, having protection mechanisms in different layers can provide two distinct advantages. First, we do not know *a priori* what layers are going to be present above and below a given layer in the network. In some cases, these other layers may not have built-in protection mechanisms and may thus rely on this particular layer to provide the protection.

Second, different types of faults are best handled by different layers, and protection resources may be more efficiently utilized by having certain types of failures dealt with in the lower layers. To illustrate this point, we consider two examples. The first is shown in Figure 10.14. This is an example of a SONET network running over WDM links. Consider two network configuration options. Figure 10.14(a) shows two SONET rings (with two ADMs each) with two diversely routed WDM links connecting the SONET ADMs. In this case, no protection is provided by the optical layer, and the protection against fiber cuts as well as equipment failures (for example, ADM laser failure) is handled completely by the SONET layer. Two separate fibers are used to interconnect the ADMs. Note that the configuration shown requires four ADMs and two sets of WDM equipment.

Figure 10.14(b) shows a better way of realizing a network with the same capabilities, by making use of protection within the optical layer. In this case, the two SONET ADMs are replaced by simpler line terminals (LTEs). Note that the optical layer cannot handle failures within SONET equipment. For this purpose, a third SONET LTE is added along with 1:2 protection. If a laser inside one of the working LTEs fails, the traffic is routed onto the spare LTE. However, fiber cuts are handled by the optical layer. A simple bridge and switch arrangement is used to connect two diversely routed fibers in a single WDM system. In general, it is more efficient to have fiber cuts handled by the optical layer, since a single switch then takes care of the restoration, instead of having each individual SONET link running over the WDM link take care of the restoration by itself. More important, this arrangement can result in a significant savings in equipment cost. In contrast with the previous configuration, this configuration requires six LTEs and only one set of WDM equipment.

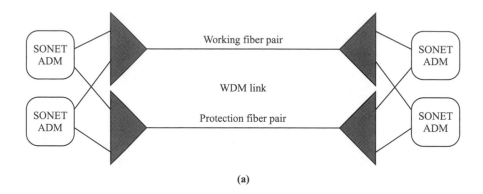

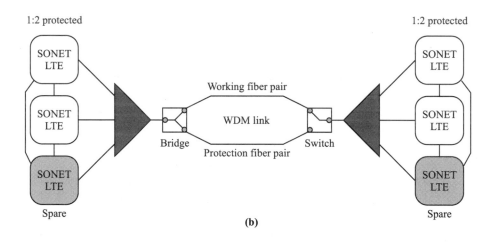

Figure 10.14   A WDM network carrying SONET traffic. (a) Both fiber cuts and equipment failures are handled by the SONET layer. (b) Fiber cuts are handled by the optical layer and equipment failures by the SONET layer.

Consider another example of a WDM ring network with lightpaths carrying higher-layer traffic. Figure 10.15 illustrates an example where there is no optical layer protection. Two pairs of SONET line terminal equipment (LTE) are connected via the WDM ring. A unidirectional connection is to be established from LTE A to LTE B, and another such connection from LTE C to LTE D. The SONET LTEs use $1 + 1$ protection. To support this, two lightpaths are required for each pair of LTEs. The working connection from LTE A to LTE B is established on wavelength λ_1 along the shortest path in the ring, and the other protection connection is established,

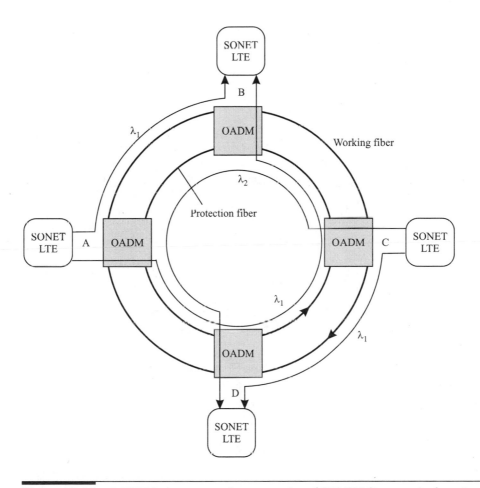

Figure 10.15   A WDM ring supporting two pairs of SONET line terminal equipment
(LTE) with 1 + 1 protection provided by the SONET layer.

say, on the same wavelength λ_1 around the ring. Likewise, the working connection
from LTE C to LTE D may be established on λ_1 on the shortest path. However,
the protection connection from LTE C to LTE D, which needs to be routed around
the ring, must be allocated another wavelength, say, λ_2. Thus two wavelengths are
required to support this configuration.

Figure 10.16 shows what can be gained by having the optical layer do the protection instead. Now we can eliminate the individual 1 + 1 protection for each LTE
pair and make them share a common protection wavelength around the ring. Only
a single wavelength is required to support this configuration. Note, however, that

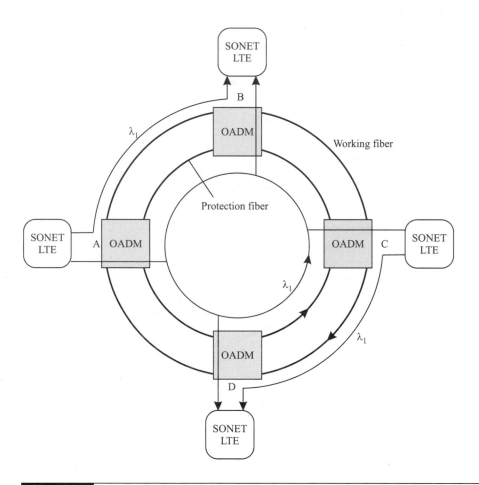

Figure 10.16   Benefit of optical layer protection. The configuration is the same as that of Figure 10.15. However the SONET LTEs now share a common wavelength around the ring for protection.

only a single link cut can be handled by this arrangement, whereas the earlier arrangement of Figure 10.15 can handle some combinations of multiple fiber cuts (see Problem 10.14). Likewise, the arrangement of Figure 10.15 can support two simultaneous transmitter failures, whereas the arrangement of Figure 10.16 can support only a single such failure. Nevertheless, if we are primarily interested in handling one failure at any given time, the optical layer protection scheme of Figure 10.16 offers a clear savings in capacity.

Consider what would happen if we had to support N such pairs of LTEs (N being the number of links in the ring) with each of them being adjacent on the ring. Without optical layer protection, N protection wavelengths would be required. With optical layer protection, only one wavelength would be needed.

Unfortunately, having protection mechanisms in different layers can also have some disadvantages. By default, the protection mechanisms in different layers will work independently. In fact, a single failure might trigger multiple protection mechanisms, all trying to restore service simultaneously, which would result in a large number of unnecessary alarms flooding the management center.

It is thus desirable to have some sort of coordination between protection mechanisms in different layers. This may not always be possible. For example, the protection mechanisms in different layers may actually be activated by different nodes. This would be the case if there is line protection in one layer and path protection in the layer above. In some cases, it may be possible to add a priority mechanism where one layer attempts to restore service first, and only afterwards does the second layer try. One automatic way to ensure this is to have the restoration in one layer happen so quickly that the other layer doesn't even sense that a failure has occurred. For example, consider a WDM network carrying SONET traffic. SONET can initiate protection switching only 2.3 μs after a failure occurs. If the optical layer can restore traffic within this time, the SONET layer will not even sense the failure. However, it is very difficult to achieve the restoration within this time scale. Another way to implement this would be to impose an additional *hold-off* time in the SONET layer before it attempts restoration so as to provide sufficient time for the optical layer to do its restoration. In general, it would make sense to have the priorities arranged such that the layer that can provide the fastest restoration tries first.

10.5 Optical Safety

The semiconductor lasers used in optical communication systems are relatively low-power devices; nevertheless, their emissions can cause serious damage to the human eye, including permanent blindness and burns. The closer the laser wavelength is to the visible range, the more damage it can do, since the cornea is more transparent to these wavelengths. For this reason, systems with lasers must obey certain safety standards. Systems with lasers are classified according to their emission levels, and the relevant classes for communication systems are described next.

A *Class I* system cannot emit damaging radiation. The laser itself may be a high-power laser, but it is prevented from causing damage by enclosing it in a suitably interlocking enclosure. The maximum power limit in a fiber for a Class I system is about 10 mW (10 dBm) at 1.55 μm and 1 mW (0 dBm) at 1.3 μm. Moreover, the power must not exceed this level even under a single failure condition within the equipment. A typical home CD player, for example, is a Class I system. A *Class IIIa* system allows higher emission powers—up to 17 dBm in the 1.55 μm wavelength range—but access must be restricted to trained service personnel.

Under normal operation, optical communication systems are completely "enclosed" systems in that laser radiation is confined to within the system and not seen outside. The problem arises during servicing or installation, or when there is a fiber cut, in which case the system is no longer completely enclosed and emission powers must be kept below the levels recommended for that particular system class. Communication systems deployed in the enterprise world must generally conform to Class I standards since untrained users are likely to be using them. Systems deployed within carrier networks, on the other hand, may likely be Class IIIa systems, since access to these systems is typically restricted to trained service personnel.

The safety issue thus limits the maximum power that can be launched into a fiber. For single-channel systems without optical power amplifiers using semiconductor lasers, the emission levels are small enough (−3 to 0 dBm typically) that we do not have to worry much about laser safety. However, with WDM systems, or with systems using optical power amplifiers, we must be careful to regulate the total power into the fiber at all times.

In order to conform to Class I standards, communication systems typically employ an *open fiber control* (OFC) protocol that (a) detects fiber cuts and turns off the lasers, (b) maintains subsequent laser emissions on the cut fiber below the levels specified for the safety Class, and (c) allows the link to be brought back up once the cut is restored. Here, we describe a particular protocol that has been chosen for the Fiber Channel standard.

10.5.1 Open Fiber Control Protocol

Figure 10.17 shows a block diagram of a system with two nodes A and B using the OFC protocol. Figure 10.18 shows the finite state machine of the protocol.

The protocol works as follows:

1. Under normal operating conditions, A and B are in the ACTIVE state. If the link from A to B fails, receiver B detects a loss of light and turns off laser B, and B enters the DISCONNECT state. Receiver A subsequently detects a loss of light and turns off its laser and also enters the DISCONNECT state. Similarly, if the link from B to A fails, or if both links fail simultaneously, A and B both enter the DISCONNECT state.

2. In the DISCONNECT state, A transmits a pulse of duration τ every T seconds. B does the same. If A detects light while it is transmitting a pulse, it enters the

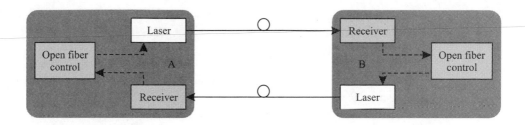

Figure 10.17   Open fiber control protocol in the Fiber Channel standard.

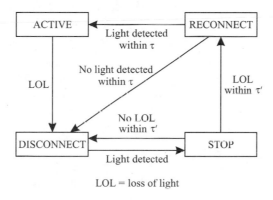

Figure 10.18   State machine for the open fiber control protocol in Fiber Channel standard.

STOP state and is called the *master*. If A detects light while it is not transmitting a pulse, it transmits a pulse for τ seconds and then enters the STOP state, and is called the *slave*; likewise for B.

3. Upon entering the STOP state, the node turns off its laser for a period of τ' seconds. It remains in this state until a loss of light condition is detected on the incoming link. If this happens within the τ' seconds, it moves into the RECONNECT state. Otherwise, it moves back into the DISCONNECT state.

4. Upon entering the RECONNECT state, if the node is the master, it sends out a pulse of duration τ. If light is detected on the incoming link within this time period, the node enters the ACTIVE state. Otherwise, it shuts off its transmitter and enters the DISCONNECT state. If the node is the slave, it monitors the link

for a period of τ seconds, and if light is detected on the incoming link within this period, it turns on its laser and enters the ACTIVE state. Otherwise, it goes back to the DISCONNECT state.

This is a fairly complex protocol. A simpler version of this protocol would not have the STOP and RECONNECT states. Instead, the nodes would directly enter the ACTIVE state from the DISCONNECT state upon detecting light. The reason for having the other states is to try to ensure that both nodes have functioning safety circuitry. If one of the nodes does not turn off its laser during the STOP period, it is assumed that the safety circuitry is not working and the other node goes back to the DISCONNECT state.

In order for the protocol to work, τ, τ', and T must be chosen carefully. In the DISCONNECT state, the average power transmitted is $\tau P/T$, where P is the transmitted power when the laser is turned on. This must be less than the allowed emission limits for the safety class. The values chosen for τ and τ' depend on the link propagation delay (see Problem 10.15).

Since the Class I safety standard also specifies that emission limits must be maintained during single fault conditions, the open fiber control circuitry at each node is duplicated for redundancy.

10.5.2 Systems with Optical Amplifiers

In a link with optical amplifiers, it is not sufficient to simply turn off the lasers at the ends of the link upon detecting a loss of signal condition. This is because the spontaneous emission noise from an amplifier can by itself cause eye damage. To prevent this from happening, the amplifiers must be turned off upon detecting a line cut. This can be done by turning off the pump laser(s) within the amplifiers. In this case, the amplifier actually absorbs any input signal. If an amplifier is turned off, it must be turned back on upon detecting a signal at its input.

Consider a chain of amplifiers shown in Figure 10.19. Suppose that a link segment AB fails. All receivers affected by this link cut, and not just the receiver at node B, will detect a loss of light and execute the usual open fiber control protocol. The only question is whether to turn off the amplifiers on the entire link or only on the link segment.

Turning off all the amplifiers results in a longer restoration time after the failure has been repaired, and disrupts traffic on the entire link, as opposed to traffic on just the link segment where the failure occurs. For example, the link in Figure 10.19 includes an optical add/drop multiplexer (OADM) at point C where a wavelength is added and dropped. If link segment AB fails, and all the amplifiers between A and D are turned off, it will affect the wavelength from C to the end point D.

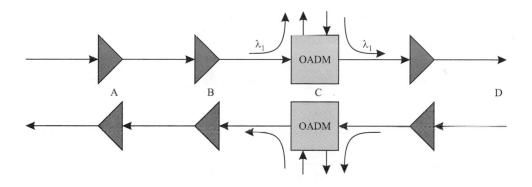

Figure 10.19   Open fiber control in a system with line amplifiers.

10.6 Service Interface

The WDM optical layer provides lightpaths to the higher layer. The question that we will address next is how these lightpaths interface with the network "users." This involves defining interfaces for data communication as well as for control and management purposes. To simplify our treatment, we will look as these two interfaces separately.

10.6.1 Data Communication Interface

Figure 10.20 shows the different possible data communication interfaces. The WDM network must support different types of interfaces to accommodate a variety of different users requiring different functions. Typical interfaces are the following:

1. *Fiber interface:* At one extreme, the network may simply provide a fiber connection to the user. The user would then be expected to send in the appropriate set of wavelengths, and conform to a variety of transmission-related criteria set by the network, such as power levels and signal-to-noise ratios.

2. *Compliant wavelength interface:* Another interface might be to allow the user to send in light at a wavelength that is supported in the network. Again, the user would be expected to comply with a variety of criteria set by the network. These wavelengths may be regarded as *compliant* wavelengths. In this case, the interface might be a purely optical interface, with no optoelectronic conversions required (a significant cost savings). For example, one might envision that SONET equipment must incorporate WDM-capable lasers at wavelengths suitable for

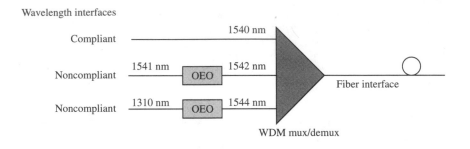

Figure 10.20   Different types of data communication interfaces between a WDM optical network and its "users."

the WDM network. Likewise, it would be possible to directly send a wavelength from the WDM network into SONET equipment. Here the user complies to the requirements imposed by the network.

3. *Noncompliant wavelength interface:* This is likely to be a popular interface and encompasses a variety of different types of attached user equipment that use optical transmitters and/or receivers not compatible with the WDM network. For example, this would include SONET equipment using 1.3 μm lasers. Here unless optical wavelength conversion (and perhaps optical regeneration) become feasible, optoelectronic conversion must be used, along with possibly regeneration, to convert the signal to a form suitable for the WDM network. This is likely to be the interface as well when we need to interconnect WDM equipment from different vendors adhering to different specifications, as we will discuss in Section 10.6.3. In contrast to the compliant interface, we may view this interface as providing a function where the network adapts to the requirements imposed by the user.

10.6.2 Control and Management Interface

In order to enable the optical layer to set up and take down lightpaths, we must establish a control interface over which the users of the network communicate with the network to instruct it to perform these functions. This requires the optical layer to provide the following functions to its users, namely, the higher layers:

- *Addressing.* Nodes in the network must have an address in the optical layer that the higher layer can use to request lightpaths.
- *Multicast* capability. This feature is optional.

- *Unidirectional or bidirectional* lightpaths. Depending on traffic requirements, the optical layer may be required to set up either of these. In the case of bidirectional lightpaths, network control is considerably simplified if both directions are established on the same route in the network and the same wavelengths on each link in that route.

- *Quality-of-service* (QOS) parameters. This feature enables the higher layer to negotiate with the optical layer to establish lightpaths satisfying mutually acceptable criteria. This negotiation occurs at the time the lightpath is set up. These parameters vary depending on the type of service offered by the optical layer. Thus the network elements must be programmable so as to be able to provide different sets of QOS requirements based on the application. For the optical layer, the relevant QOS parameters include the following:

  - *Degree of transparency.* This parameter determines the level of transparency of the lightpath that is to be set up. For instance, a truly transparent lightpath will be able to carry analog or digital data with arbitrary modulation formats up to a certain maximum bandwidth. At the other extreme, the lightpath might be able to carry only OC-48 SONET data, if it includes OC-48-specific regenerators in its path. In between these two extremes are various other possible levels of transparency.

  - *Level of protection.* The optical layer may incorporate protection techniques so as to be able to restore service in the event of failures inside the network. As we saw in Section 10.4, the application determines whether a lightpath must be protected, must not be protected, or must be protected if possible. This parameter must be negotiated at the time of establishing a lightpath.

  - *Required bit error rate/signal-to-noise ratio.* Different types of traffic may have different requirements for these parameters. Analog signals have a much higher signal-to-noise ratio requirement than digital signals.

  - *End-to-end delay* on the lightpath and its backup lightpath (if any). Since there is no buffering in the optical layer, this is essentially the end-to-end propagation delay. This parameter again is application specific. Certain higher-layer protocols, such as ESCON (see Chapter 6), are very sensitive to the delay, whereas other protocols (for example, SONET) are not as sensitive.

  - *Jitter* requirements, particularly for SONET/SDH. SONET/SDH equipment must comply with a certain specified requirement on the jitter in the bit stream. If the optical layer does not have any regeneration in it, or has only 2R regeneration, it can only increase any jitter that is already present in the input traffic stream. The only way to reduce jitter is to use 3R regeneration.

10.6.3   WDM Multivendor Interoperability

Service providers like to deploy equipment from multiple vendors that operate together in a single network. This is desirable to reduce the dependence on any single vendor as well as to drive down costs, and is one of the driving factors behind network standards.

However, interoperability is easier said than done. The SONET standards were established in the late 1980s and only recently have we been able to achieve interoperability between equipment from different vendors. In the case of WDM, achieving interoperability at the optical level is a rather difficult task. At this time, standards are just beginning to be developed. The set of parameters that we would need to standardize to achieve interoperability include optical wavelength, optical power, signal-to-noise ratio, bit rate, and the supervisory channel wavelength, bit rate, and its contents. Note that many of these are analog in nature, as is the design of the entire optical path. This makes it difficult to guarantee quality of service and localize faults in a multivendor environment.

In the near term, a limited form of interoperability can be accomplished by demultiplexing the wavelengths and converting the wavelengths coming out of one vendor's equipment from optical to electronic form and then back into an optical form suitable for use in the other vendor's equipment. This allows the service provider to divide the network into different domains, each domain consisting of a single vendor's equipment. Within a given domain, the service provider can obtain the benefits of all-optical networking. While this is an expensive approach, it does make it possible to provide quality-of-service guarantees and localize faults by establishing clear boundaries between the different vendor equipment.

Summary

Network management is essential to operate and maintain any network. In the case of optical networks, certain factors such as transparency limit the number of parameters that can be monitored and create some problems in setting alarm thresholds. The story on what network operators are willing to accept is not entirely clear yet.

Fault management is crucial in these networks because of the vast amount of data carried on each link. Service restoration can be performed in a variety of methods and across different layers. The problem of coordinating the restoration procedure between layers is a difficult one, and no easy solution appears to be in sight.

Eye safety considerations are a unique feature of optical fiber communication systems and are particularly important in systems deployed in areas that are accessed by untrained users. These considerations set an upper limit on the power that can be emitted from an open fiber, and these limits make it harder to design WDM systems, since they apply to the total power and not to the power per channel.

Further Reading

Network management is a vast subject, and several books have been written on the subject—see, for instance, [Bla95, AP94] for good introductions to the field, including descriptions of the various standards.

Distributed protocols for connection management are commonly used in many types of networks; see, for example, [CGS93]. [RS96] gives a set of protocols for optical networks.

For a detailed treatment of network survivability, particularly as it applies to SONET/SDH, we refer the reader to the book by Wu [Wu92]. Optical layer protection mechanisms are explored in [GR96, MB96, GRS97]. The mesh network line-switched restoration scheme described here is from [ES96], and another scheme is described in [FMB97]. The interworking of protection schemes between different layers is just beginning to be addressed [MB96, GR96].

Laser safety is covered by several standards, including ANSI, IEC, and the U.S. FDA [Ame88, Int93, U.S86]. Safety issues in amplified systems are discussed in [ITU96].

Problems

10.1   Consider a ring network. Give an example of a traffic pattern where path protection uses less ring bandwidth than line protection. Give another example where the two require the same amount of bandwidth.

10.2   Show that in a ring architecture, if the protection capacity is less than the working capacity, then service cannot be restored under certain single failure conditions.

10.3   Compare the performance of UPSRs and BLSR/2s in cases where all the traffic is between a hub node and the other nodes. Assume the same ring speed in both cases. Is a BLSR/2 any more efficient than a UPSR in traffic carrying capacity in this scenario?

10.4   Construct a traffic distribution for which the traffic carrying capacity of a BLSR/4 is maximized. What is this capacity as a multiple of the bit rate on the working fibers?

10.5   Assuming a uniform traffic distribution, compute the traffic carrying capacity of a BLSR/4 as a multiple of the bit rate on the working fibers.

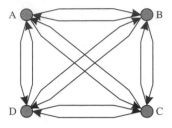

Figure 10.21   Mesh network for Problem 10.10.

10.6   The UPSR, BLSR/4, and BLSR/2 are designed primarily to handle single failures. However, they can handle some cases of simultaneous multiple failures as well. Carefully characterize the types of multiple link/node failure combinations that these different architectures can handle.

10.7   The $1+1$ protection in a UPSR is not implemented at a fiber level but at an individual SONET connection level: for each connection, the receiver picks the better of the two paths. An alternative and simpler approach would be to have the receiver simply pick the better of the two fiber lines coming in, say, based on the bit error rate. In this case, the receiver would not have to look at the individual connections in order to make its decision, but rather would look at the error rate of the composite signal on the fiber. Why doesn't this work?

10.8   Suppose you had only two fibers but could use two wavelengths, say, 1.3 μm and 1.55 μm, over each fiber. This can be used to deploy a BLSR/4 ring in three different ways: (1) the two working fibers could be multiplexed over one fiber and the two protection fibers over the other, (2) a working fiber and a protection fiber in the same direction could be multiplexed over one fiber, or (3) a working fiber and a protection fiber in the opposite direction could be multiplexed over one fiber. Which option would you choose?

10.9   Consider a four-fiber BLSR that uses both span and line protection. What are the functions required in network management to (a) coordinate span and line protection mechanisms, (b) allow multiple failures to be restored?

10.10   Obtain the protection cycles (enumerate the edges in each cycle) for the mesh network shown in Figure 10.21.

10.11   Consider the example shown in Figure 10.12. Consider a unidirectional lightpath from node D to node A (the reverse of the example), going through nodes E, C, and B, respectively. Show how it is restored if link BC is cut.

10.12 Consider the mesh network protection scheme described in Section 10.4.3. Can it handle more than one concurrent link failure? If so, characterize what set of concurrent failures it can handle as a function of the number of *faces* in the graph (see Appendix G for the definition of faces). Consider only bidirectional lightpaths.

10.13 Consider the mesh network protection scheme described in Section 10.4.3. How would you extend it to work in WDM networks where the edges are two fibers between nodes, with each fiber carrying half the wavelengths in one direction and the remaining half in the opposite direction? Specifically, how would you assign wavelengths to bidirectional lightpaths, and how would you configure the switches at each node so that no wavelength conversion is required for protection purposes?

10.14 Consider the example shown in Figure 10.15. Carefully characterize the set of simultaneous multiple fiber cuts that can be handled by this arrangement.

10.15 Consider the open fiber control protocol in the Fiber Channel standard.
  (a) How would you choose the parameters τ and τ' as a function of the maximum link propagation delay d_{prop}?
  (b) What is the time taken for a node to go from the DISCONNECT state to the ACTIVE state, assuming a successful reconnection attempt, that is, it never has to go back to the DISCONNECT state?

━━ References

[Ame88] American National Standards Institute, Z136.2. *Safe use of optical fiber communication systems utilizing laser diodes and LED sources*, 1988.

[AP94] S. Aidarus and T. Plevyak, editors. *Telecommunications Network Management into the 21st Century*. IEEE Press, Los Alamitos, CA, 1994.

[Bla95] U. Black. *Network Management Standards*. McGraw-Hill, New York, 1995.

[CGS93] I. Cidon, I. S. Gopal, and A. Segall. Connection establishment in high-speed networks. *IEEE/ACM Transactions on Networking*, 1(4):469–482, Aug. 1993.

[ES96] G. Ellinas and T. E. Stern. Automatic protection switching for link failures in optical networks with bidirectional links. In *Proceedings of IEEE Globecom*, 1996.

[FMB97] S. Finn, M. M. Medard, and R. A. Barry. A novel approach to automatic protection switching using trees. In *Proceedings of IEEE International Conference on Communication*, 1997.

[Gar94] L. M. Gardner et al. Techniques for finding ring covers in survivable networks. In *Proceedings of IEEE Globecom*, pages 1862–1866, 1994.

[GR96]   O. Gerstel and R. Ramaswami. Multiwavelength optical network architectures and protection schemes. In *Proc. Tirrenia Workshop on Optical Networks*, pages 42–51, 1996.

[GRS97]   O. Gerstel, R. Ramaswami, and G. H. Sasaki. Fault tolerant WDM rings with limited wavelength conversion. In *Proceedings of IEEE Infocom*, pages 508–516, 1997.

[Int93]   International Electrotechnical Commission. *825-1: Safety of laser products*, 1993.

[ITU96]   ITU-T SG15/WP 4. *Rec. G.681: Functional characteristics of interoffice and long-haul line systems using optical amplifiers, including optical multiplexing*, 1996.

[MB96]   J. Manchester and P. Bonenfant. Fiber optic network survivability: SONET/optical protection layer interworking. In *Proceedings of National Fiber Optic Engineers Conference*, pages 907–918, 1996.

[RS96]   R. Ramaswami and A. Segall. Distributed network control for wavelength-routed optical networks. In *Proceedings of IEEE Infocom*, pages 138–147, 1996.

[U.S86]   U.S. Food and Drug Administration, Department of Radiological Health. *Requirements of 21 CFR Chap. J for Class 1 Laser Products*, Jan. 1986.

[Wu92]   T. H. Wu. *Fiber Network Service Survivability*. Artech House, Boston, 1992.

11 chapter

Wavelength Routing Testbeds

$\mathbf{T}$HE LAST FEW YEARS have witnessed a flurry of activity leading toward building several significant wavelength routing testbeds. Many of these testbeds have been realized because of cooperative efforts involving several companies, both network operators and network equipment suppliers. These efforts have received a significant boost from funding in part by the Defense Advanced Research Projects Agency (DARPA) in the United States and by the European Commission's RACE (Research and Development in Advanced Communication Technologies in Europe) and ACTS (Advanced Communications Technologies and Services) programs. The RACE program on optical networks started in the late 1980s and stimulated the development and feasibility demonstrations of some key component technologies. In the United States, DARPA started a similar program in the early 1990s. In the mid-1990s, we saw a second wave of funding in Europe (under the ACTS umbrella) and in the United States to focus on integrating the technology into field-ready networks and consider operational and economic issues. These testbeds have shown that it is possible to build operational networks based on existing components and have brought up a number of issues that need to be solved before these networks can be commercialized. Table 11.1 summarizes the key features of some testbeds that have been demonstrated and others that are being constructed currently.

Table 11.1 Summary of demonstrated and planned wavelength routing testbeds. The testbeds in the first grouping (MWTN–NTONC) have been demonstrated and those in the second grouping (COBNET–METON) are under construction. (OWXC = all-optically implemented wavelength crossconnects; EWXC = electronically implemented wavelength crossconnects; OADM = optical add/drop multiplexer; OEADM = optoelectronic add/drop multiplexer (includes regeneration).)

Name	Architecture	Topology	Router Ports	Wave-lengths	Channel Spacing (nm)	Bit Rate	Distance (km)
MWTN	OWXC	Ring/mesh	4	4	4	622 Mb/s	230
AON	Static	Star	8	20	0.4	2.5 Gb/s	100
ONTC	OWXC	Linked rings	2	4	4	155 Mb/s	150
NTT	OADM	Ring	2	15	0.8	622 Mb/s	120
Alcatel	OEADM	Ring	2	4	1.6	2.5 Gb/s	160
MONET	OWXC	Mesh/ring	4	8	1.6	10 Gb/s	2000
NTONC	OADM	Dual ring	2	4	4	2.5 Gb/s	700
COBNET	EWXC/ OWXC	Ring	Many/2	12	1.6		
PHOTON	OWXC	Mesh	2	8	3.2	2.5 Gb/s, 10 Gb/s	500
METON	OWXC	Mesh/ring	4	6	3.2	622 Mb/s, 2.5 Gb/s	230

Name	Architects
MWTN	BT, Ericsson, Pirelli, Ellemtel, Televerket, Italel, CSELT, CNET, U. Essex, U. Paderborn
AON	AT&T, MIT, Digital Equipment Corp. (DEC)
ONTC	Bellcore, Columbia U., Hewlett-Packard, Hughes, Northern Telecom, Rockwell, United Tech.
MONET	AT&T, Bellcore, Bell Atlantic, Bell South, Pacific Telesis
NTONC	LLNL, Columbia, Hewlett-Packard, Hughes, Northern Telecom, Rockwell, United Tech.
COBNET	BNR Europe, BT, EPF Lausanne, ETH Zurich, GEC Marconi, IBM France, IBM Zurich, Italtel Sit, Siemens AG, Siemens ATEA, U. Dortmund
PHOTON	Siemens, Centro de Estudos Telecom., Deutsche Telekom, Heinrich Hertz, Interuniv. Microelectron. Ctr, Austria PTT, Philips, TU, BBC, Telecom Australia
METON	Ericsson, Thomson, Telia, CNET, Tech. U. Denmark, Heinrich Hertz, CSELT, Deutsche Telekom, Royal Inst. of Tech., Nat. Microelectron. Res. Ctr.

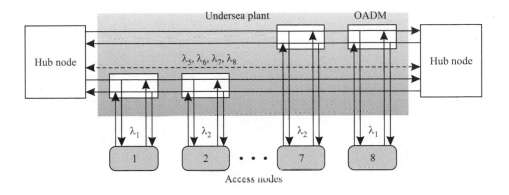

Figure 11.1   Architecture of Africa ONE.

11.1 Africa ONE/Sea Me We-3

Before describing the various testbeds, we start with a program that is focused on actual deployment of a wavelength routing network under fairly demanding conditions. The Africa Optical Network (Africa ONE) [MS96] is an ambitious project being planned by AT&T Submarine Systems and Alcatel Submarine Networks to deploy an undersea WDM/SDH ring around the African continent. The same architecture is used in the Sea Me We-3 regional network [MR97], which will be deployed between more than a dozen countries in Europe, the Middle East, and Asia in 1998. The architecture is an interesting combination of WDM links with OADMs, along with SDH ADMs. The overall ring length is 40,000 km with nodes located in about 40 countries.

The network consists of *hub* nodes (called central offices in Africa ONE terminology) and *access nodes* (called cable stations). The hub nodes are interconnected by two fiber-pairs to form a ring. A link between two hub nodes is shown in Figure 11.1. Each fiber carries eight wavelengths of STM-16 data at 2.5 Gb/s. The undersea link between hub nodes is all-optical and can be up to 5000 km in length, with optical amplifiers deployed at periodic intervals. Up to eight OADMs (called branching units) can be placed along this link. Each OADM drops and adds one predetermined wavelength from a fiber-pair. The OADMs are connected to the access nodes located in the shore countries by two fiber-pairs. Most of the fiber span, along with the amplifiers and OADMs, is under water, as shown in Figure 11.1. The reason for using OADMs is that they are very simple, passive, and thus more reliable than electronic ADMs. Note also that an access node cannot tap or otherwise interfere with the traffic destined for other access nodes. This was a key architectural requirement for the network.

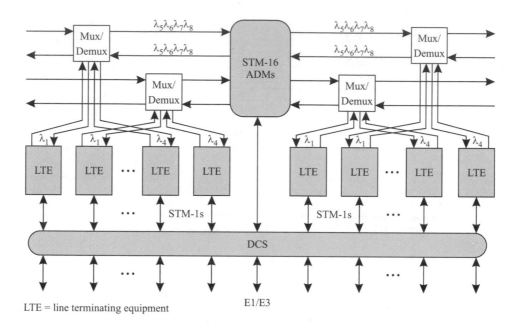

Figure 11.2   Architecture of a hub node in Africa ONE.

Each access node is connected to its two adjacent hub nodes by a lightpath. Thus each access node can source and sink two STM-16 streams. Four access nodes are connected via OADMs to one fiber-pair, and four more access nodes are connected to the other fiber-pair. This takes up four wavelengths on each fiber-pair. The remaining four wavelengths are used to establish lightpaths between the hub nodes to carry interhub traffic.

A hub node is shown in Figure 11.2. All the eight wavelengths on each fiber are demultiplexed and received. The four wavelengths from the access nodes are received and demultiplexed into lower-speed STM-1 streams and sent to a digital crossconnect (DCS). The four wavelengths used for interhub traffic are sent to STM-16 ADMs. The ADMs drop and add STM-1 streams, which are then sent into the DCS. The DCS is responsible for grooming the lower-speed streams and suitably interconnecting the traffic between the access nodes and the hub-to-hub links.

The network incorporates several types of protection mechanisms. If there is a fiber cut on the link between the two hub nodes, the access nodes between the two hubs can still reach one of the hub nodes. This is similar to the dual homing concept that we discussed in Chapter 10. Moreover, the traffic on this failed link can be rerouted by the STM-16 ADMs around the ring (line protection). For this purpose, half the bandwidth on the hub-to-hub links is reserved for protection. This bandwidth can be used to carry nonessential data that can be preempted, if needed, for restoring service in the event of a failure. Note that there is no protection against the failure of a link between an access node and its OADM.

11.2 AON

The AON (All-Optical Network Consortium) testbed [Kam96, Ale93] is an example of a static wavelength routing testbed. The testbed has a two-level hierarchy, as shown in Figure 11.3. Level 0 corresponds to a local-area network (LAN) and uses a broadcast star architecture. However, some of the wavelengths are tapped off (not broadcast) and sent to the level-1 network. Level 1 corresponds to a metropolitan-area network (MAN) and uses a single static wavelength crossconnect consisting of an integrated-optic arrayed waveguide grating (AWG) router.

The testbed is currently deployed in the Boston area between MIT's Lincoln Laboratories, the MIT campus, and DEC, as shown in Figure 11.3. The level-1 AWG is at Lincoln, along with two level-0 networks, one of them having three end-nodes and the other having two end-nodes. The other two locations each have a level-0 network with one or two end-nodes each.

The testbed uses 20 wavelengths, spaced 50 GHz (0.4 nm) apart. The odd-numbered wavelengths are used within the level-0 networks, and the even-numbered ones are sent to the level-1 network. This allocation is determined by the bypass filter, in this case, a fixed integrated-optic Mach-Zehnder filter. Thus the allocation has to be determined at the time the network is built.

Each end-node has a tunable transmitter and a tunable receiver. The tunable transmitter is an externally modulated distributed Bragg grating (DBR) laser that can tune between wavelengths in 10 ns. Two types of receiver structures are used depending on the type of service provided.

The AON provides three types of service. The A-service provides simple circuit-switched lightpaths that can be set up or taken down by tuning the transmitters and receivers at the end-nodes. The A-service can be a transparent service. The A-service receiver uses a tunable fiber Fabry-Perot filter (10 ms tuning time between channels). The A-service was demonstrated at both 2.5 Gb/s and 10 Gb/s.

The B-service is a circuit-switched service that provides preassigned time slots on a lightpath. This is appropriate if the end-node needs only a small fraction of the bandwidth available on a lightpath. It is also possible in principle for the B-service to support packet switching and provide datagram services. The B-service requires the receivers to tune between wavelengths in a short fraction of the slot duration.

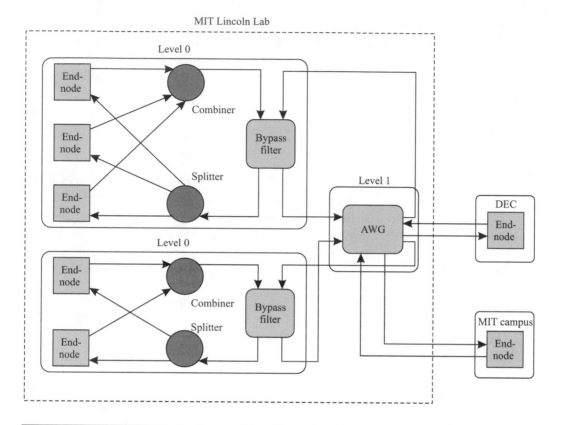

Figure 11.3   The AON testbed.

The B-service uses a coherent optical receiver consisting of a DBR laser as the local oscillator followed by a photodetector, with polarization diversity incorporated. The time required to switch between wavelengths is the sum of the laser tuning time and the time taken to acquire the bit clock—around 200 ns in the testbed receiver. The B-service also requires all nodes in the network to be synchronized to a common clock, which was accomplished in the testbed. Although this may be possible in a small network with a single "hub," it becomes very difficult to achieve in a larger network with many interconnected routers. The B-service was demonstrated at 1 Gb/s.

The C-service is a datagram service and runs out-of-band at the 1310 nm band as a broadband ethernet. It is used primarily to set up and take down A- and B-service connections. Each level-0 and level-1 network has a centralized scheduler connected via the C-service to each other and the end-nodes. The scheduler is responsible for allocating wavelengths/time slots to connection requests.

Among the unique features of the AON are the support of multiple traffic classes, particularly the B-service. The AON also demonstrates the value of a hierarchical architecture.

11.3   NTT Ring

NTT's testbed [TOI⁺96] consists of a unidirectional ring, with one working fiber and one protection fiber, as shown in Figure 11.4. This is similar to a unidirectional path-switched SONET ring (UPSR). The network has one hub node (called the center node) and many access nodes (called remote nodes). In this architecture, the hub node sends out signals at N different wavelengths, all multiplexed into the working fiber. There can be up to N access nodes. At access node i, wavelength i is dropped and added. The hub node communicates with access node i on wavelength i, and access node i communicates with the hub node also on wavelength i along the ring. An access node is shown in Figure 11.5. It uses an AWG to drop and add a fixed wavelength. It also incorporates hardware to support two types of protection mechanisms, as we discuss next.

Two mechanisms were implemented in the testbed to protect against link failures. Only one method can be employed at a time. The first approach uses line protection

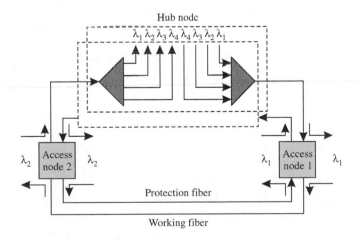

Figure 11.4   The NTT ring testbed.

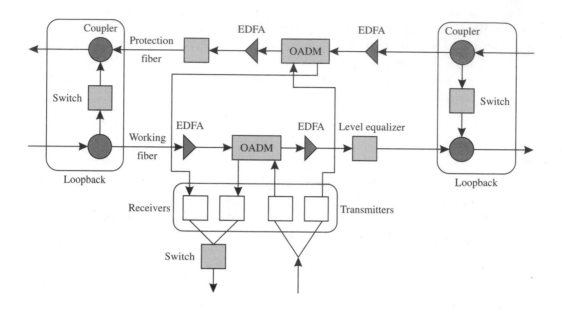

Figure 11.5   The node architecture in the NTT testbed.

(see Section 10.4). Here, the protection fiber does not carry any traffic normally. In the event of a fiber cut, restoration is accomplished by looping the traffic on the working fiber onto the protection fiber around the ring. The second restoration method is $1 + 1$ path protection, where the same traffic is sent on both the working and the protection fibers in opposite directions. The receiver in the access node selects one of them.

The testbed had six wavelengths, spaced 100 GHz apart, running over dispersion-shifted fiber with a distance of 40 km between nodes at 622 Mb/s (STM-4), with a hub node and two access nodes. Each access node included optical fiber amplifiers to compensate for losses and a multichannel power equalizer to equalize the channel power variations due to different component losses at different wavelengths and due to the nonflatness of the amplifiers. The testbed distance was limited primarily by four-wave mixing. In order to reduce the four-wave mixing penalty, at each node, after demultiplexing the wavelengths, each wavelength was delayed by a different value. This randomizes the phase relationship between the different wavelengths at each node. Effectively, this means that the FWM powers introduced at each transmission stage between the nodes are summed, rather than the electric fields being summed in phase, which would be the case if no delays were introduced.

The major accomplishments of this testbed were the demonstration of WDM transmission over dispersion-shifted fiber, along with the demonstration of different protection mechanisms.

11.4 MWTN

MWTN (Multi-Wavelength Transport Network) was one of the earliest reconfigurable wavelength routing testbeds [Joh96, Hil93]. It was developed in the RACE program. Both optical crossconnects and add/drop multiplexers were developed during this program. The optical crossconnect (OXC) is shown in Figure 11.6, and the add/drop multiplexer (OADM) is shown in Figure 11.7. Several types of optical switches were tried out, including lithium niobate switches, semiconductor optical amplifier switches, and optomechanical switches. Channel selection was done by using dielectric thin film–based filters. Within each node, the channel powers were equalized using separate attenuators for each channel.

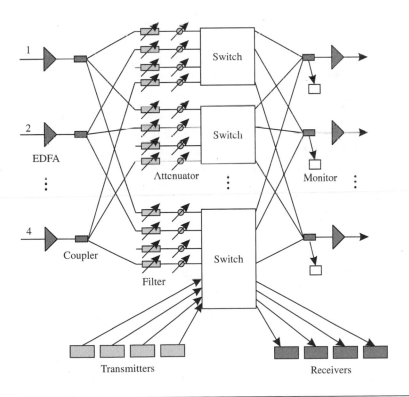

Figure 11.6 The MWTN optical crossconnect.

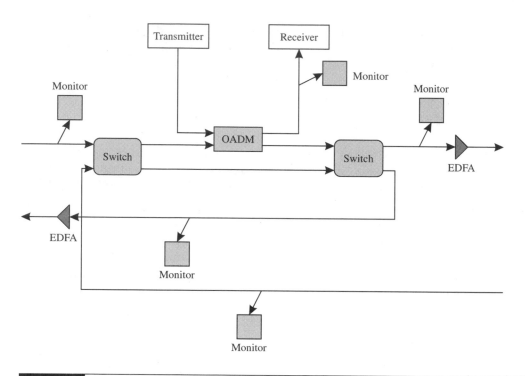

Figure 11.7   The MWTN optical add/drop multiplexer.

The testbed used four wavelengths spaced 4 nm apart, with each wavelength carrying SDH data at 622 Mb/s or 2.5 Gb/s, in a field trial in Stockholm. At various times, the testbed consisted of two OXCs, an OXC and an OADM, or two OADMs. Each wavelength carried a superimposed pilot tone, and this pilot tone was monitored within the nodes. This feature can be used to detect and isolate failures. A full TMN-based management system was also implemented.

This early testbed demonstrated the feasibility of all-optical wavelength routing, along with several key technologies for the crossconnects. Another accomplishment was the demonstration of the pilot tone approach and the TMN-based management framework for the network.

11.5 ONTC

The ONTC (Optical Network Technology Consortium) testbed [CEG+96, Bra93] uses a reconfigurable wavelength routing architecture. The testbed consisted of two interconnected unidirectional rings. Each ring had two nodes with one additional common node, as shown in Figure 11.8.

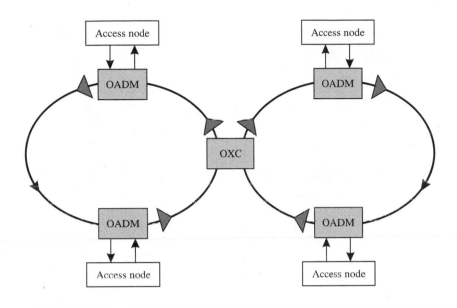

Figure 11.8 The ONTC network testbed.

The testbed had four wavelengths, spaced 4 nm apart, running over standard single-mode fiber with a total distance of 150 km, at 155 Mb/s (OC-3), carrying ATM traffic. One of the wavelengths was also used to carry four analog subcarrier multiplexed video channels. The testbed used an EDFA after each optical node to compensate for fiber and component losses, as shown in Figure 11.8.

An OADM and access node are shown in Figure 11.9. The wavelength crossconnects and add/drop multiplexers were made by combining wavelength mux/demuxes with optical switches, as in Figure 8.10. The mux/demux units were made with dielectric thin film–based filters, and the switches were relay-activated mechanical switches. Each end-node had a four-wavelength DFB laser array as a transmitter and a four-wavelength integrated receiver.

The switches within the nodes were controlled by a central controller. The central controller communicated to the controllers within the nodes via in-band ATM connections. Each node had a 10-dB coupler at its output. A small portion of the power was tapped off, and the wavelength and power of each channel were monitored by a wavelength/power meter. A major emphasis in ONTC was to develop commercial-quality acousto-optic filters (AOTFs) for wavelength routers, but the AOTFs developed were found to have many problems, in particular, excessive crosstalk.

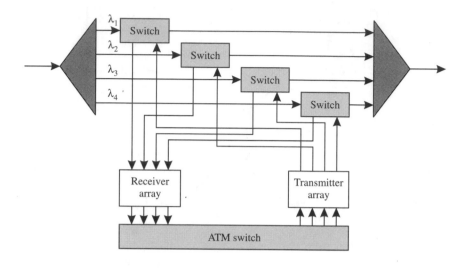

Figure 11.9   An OADM and an access node in the ONTC network testbed.

Like MWTN, ONTC demonstrated several key technologies. It also demonstrated the use of an ATM virtual topology over the optical layer, and demonstrated the transparency aspect of WDM by transmitting several forms of data over different lightpaths concurrently. The ONTC work was followed by the NTONC (National Transparent Optical Network Consortium), which deployed the ONTC-developed technologies, including the improved-upon AOTFs, in a testbed network in the San Francisco Bay Area.

11.6 Alcatel's WDM Ring

Alcatel has demonstrated a two-fiber ring network with OADMs [Ber96a, Ber96b]. Their OADM architecture (see Figure 11.10) is an interesting mix of optical switching and electronic regenerators. The regenerators provide wavelength conversion and also retime the signal from link to link. The demultiplexing was done by using a splitter followed by fiber Fabry-Perot filters. The switches were optomechanical switches.

Note that since the signals are received and retimed anyway, an alternative OADM architecture could be the one shown in Figure 11.11. Here the signals are

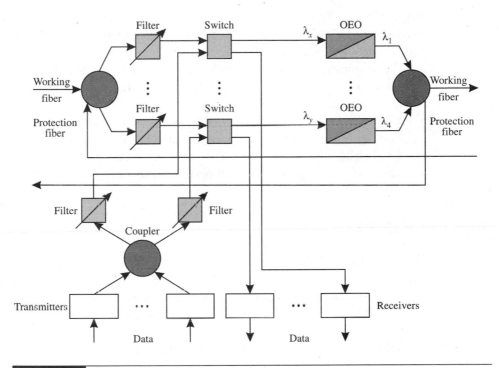

Figure 11.10 Alcatel's OADM.

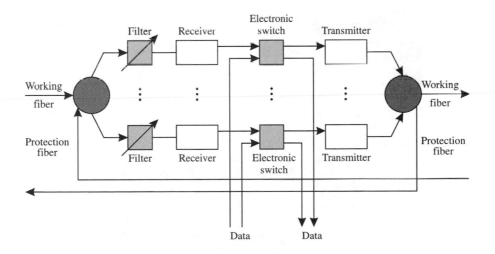

Figure 11.11 An alternative architecture for Alcatel's OADM using electronic switching.

received first and then switched electronically, rather than optically. However, an additional set of transmitters and receivers may be required if the signal to be dropped and added is needed in optical form.

The demonstration had three nodes and used four wavelengths spaced 200 GHz apart, each carrying SDH data at 2.5 Gb/s. Because the signal is regenerated at each node, the physical layer design is considerably simplified, since it consists only of point-to-point links. The network used line switching to recover from fiber cuts.

Since the signal is electronically regenerated at each node, the number of nodes that can be cascaded is very large. This approach might prove to be more practical in the near term, compared to the all-optical approach.

11.7 MONET

The goal of the MONET program [WASG96, Vod97] is to develop field-hardened testbeds of wavelength-routed networks to bring them closer to commercial deployment. The field trial consists of a local ring network with OADMs interconnected to a long-distance network via an OXC. The testbed uses eight wavelengths spaced 200 GHz apart, with data being transmitted over it at 2.5 Gb/s per wavelength. The testbed is shown in Figure 11.12. As of this writing, the program has demonstrated

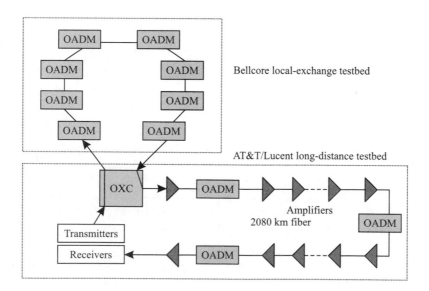

Figure 11.12   The MONET testbed.

transmission of eight wavelengths at 10 Gb/s over 2000 km of dispersion-managed fiber consisting of standard single-mode fiber along with dispersion compensating fiber at appropriate intervals. The demonstration also includes a local ring network with several OADMs in it and a 4 × 4 OXC to interconnect the local ring network to the long-distance testbed.

Among the advances made in the MONET program relative to earlier programs are a thorough understanding of operational issues associated with actual network deployment, such as handling monitoring and management, being robust against outages, developing field-ready optical components such as lithium niobate–based optical crossconnects, and understanding the economics of WDM networks versus other alternatives—the subject of Chapter 13.

Summary

In the near term, networks with WDM point-to-point links and electronic regeneration at each node, such as Alcatel's ring network, are quite practical. However, electronic regeneration can be quite expensive, and in the longer term, the all-optical approach is likely to reduce the node cost significantly.

As we have seen, the all-optical testbed demonstrations were mostly transmission oriented and concerned with the physical layer issues discussed in Chapter 5. They also focused on demonstrating the use of specific types of switches, mux/demuxes, filters, and amplifiers. This is where the major problems are today.

These testbeds have shown that dielectric thin film–based filters in combination with splitters and combiners are good mux/demuxes. They have flat passbands, low loss, and are polarization insensitive. Optomechanical switches have slow switching times (tens of ms) but have low loss, and more important, very low crosstalk. The other types of switches, based on newer technologies, have several problems and are much more expensive today. AOTFs, which can simultaneously switch many channels, were found to have high crosstalk and loss. The same goes for lithium niobate switches and semiconductor amplifier-based switches. The good news is that these switches can switch much faster than optomechanical switches, in the μs to ns time scale, and are more amenable to integration than optomechanical switches. All the OXC and OADM nodes suffer from fairly large losses overall (over 10 dB) and need EDFAs to compensate for them.

In terms of transmission-related issues, losses, amplifier gain equalization, power equalization of channels, and crosstalk were all seen to be major issues. Most of the testbeds could not successfully transmit data all optically through more than a few nodes. However, they give a good indication of the types of networks that will become commercially feasible in the next few years.

Further Reading

In addition to the references given in the text, the periodic special issues of the *Journal of Selected Areas in Communication* and *Journal of Lightwave Technology,* and other magazines [HSS98, CHK+96, FGO+96, HD97, Bar96, NO94, KLHN93, CNW90, Pru89, Bra89] provide good summaries of recent testbeds. See also [Gre93] for a description of some of the early testbeds.

Problems

11.1 In the AON approach, the B-service attempts to allocate slots on wavelengths for end-nodes to communicate with each other. What problems do you foresee in implementing the B-service?

11.2 Consider the ONTC testbed node shown in Figure 11.9. It has a four-wavelength transmitter array and receiver array. Suppose the node wants to terminate only two lightpaths, but these lightpaths can be at any of the four wavelengths. Draw a node architecture that can realize this, assuming the availability of tunable transmitters and tunable receivers.

11.3 Compare the optical crossconnect and ADM architectures in the ONTC, MWTN, Alcatel, and NTT testbeds.

References

[Ale93]   S. B. Alexander et al. A precompetitive consortium on wide-band all-optical networks. *IEEE/OSA Journal on Lightwave Technology*, 11:714–735, May/June 1993.

[Bar96]   R. A. Barry, editor. *IEEE Network: Special Issue on Optical Networks*, volume 10, Nov. 1996.

[Ber96a] L. Berthelon et al. Experimental assessment of node cascadability in a reconfigurable survivable WDM ring network. In *Proceedings of Topical Meeting on Broadband Optical Networks*, 1996.

[Ber96b] L. Berthelon et al. Over 40,000 km across a layered network by recirculation through an experimental WDM ring network. In *Proceedings of European Conference on Optical Communication*, 1996.

[Bra89]   C. A. Brackett, editor. *IEEE Communications Magazine: Special Issue on Lightwave Systems and Components*, volume 27, Oct. 1989.

[Bra93] C. A. Brackett et al. A scalable multiwavelength multihop optical network: A proposal for research on all-optical networks. *IEEE/OSA Journal on Lightwave Technology*, 11:736–753, May/June 1993.

[CEG+96] G. K. Chang, G. Ellinas, J. K. Gamelin, M. Z. Iqbal, and C. A. Brackett. Multiwavelength reconfigurable WDM/ATM/SONET network testbed. *IEEE/OSA JLT/JSAC Special Issue on Multiwavelength Optical Technology and Networks*, 14(6):1320–1340, June 1996.

[CHK+96] R. L. Cruz, G. R. Hill, A. L. Kellner, R. Ramaswami, and G. H. Sasaki, editors. *IEEE JSAC/JLT Special Issue on Optical Networks*, volume 14, June 1996.

[CNW90] N. K. Cheung, G. Nosu, and G. Winzer, editors. *IEEE JSAC: Special Issue on Dense WDM Networks*, volume 8, Aug. 1990.

[FGO+96] M. Fujiwara, M. S. Goodman, M. J. O'Mahony, O. K. Tonguez, and A. E. Willner, editors. *IEEE/OSA JLT/JSAC Special Issue on Multiwavelength Optical Technology and Networks*, volume 14, June 1996.

[Gre93] P. E. Green. *Fiber-Optic Networks*. Prentice Hall, Englewood Cliffs, NJ, 1993.

[HD97] G. R. Hill and P. Diemeester, editors. *IEEE Communications Magazine: Special Issue on Photonic Networks in Europe*, volume 35, April 1997.

[Hil93] G. R. Hill et al. A transport network layer based on optical network elements. *IEEE/OSA Journal on Lightwave Technology*, 11:667–679, May/June 1993.

[HSS98] A. M. Hill, A. A. M. Saleh, and K. Sato, editors. *IEEE JSAC: Special Issue on High-Capacity Optical Transport Networks*, 1998. To appear.

[Joh96] S. Johansson et al. A transport network involving a reconfigurable WDM network layer—a European demonstration. *IEEE/OSA JLT/JSAC Special Issue on Multiwavelength Optical Technology and Networks*, 14(6):1341–1348, June 1996.

[Kam96] I. P. Kaminow et al. A wideband all-optical WDM network. *IEEE JSAC/JLT Special Issue on Optical Networks*, 14(5):780–799, June 1996.

[KLHN93] M. J. Karol, C. Lin, G. Hill, and K. Nosu, editors. *IEEE/OSA Journal of Lightwave Technology: Special Issue on Broadband Optical Networks*, May/June 1993.

[MR97] W. C. Marra and D. G. Ross. The impact that Erbium doped fiber amplifier and WDM technologies have had on undersea fiber optic networks. In *Proceedings of National Fiber Optic Engineers Conference*, pages 243–254, 1997.

[MS96] W. C. Marra and J. Schesser. Africa ONE: The Africa optical network. *IEEE Communications Magazine*, 34(2):50–57, Feb. 1996.

[NO94] K. Nosu and M. J. O'Mahony, editors. *IEEE Communications Magazine: Special Issue on Optically Multiplexed Networks*, volume 32, Dec. 1994.

[Pru89]   P. R. Prucnal, editor. *IEEE Network: Special Issue on Optical Multiaccess Networks*, volume 3, March 1989.

[TOI+96]   H. Toba, K. Oda, K. Inoue, K. Nosu, and T. Kitoh. An optical FDM based self-healing ring network employing arrayed-waveguide-grating ADM filters and EDFAs with level equalizers. *IEEE JSAC/JLT Special Issue on Optical Networks*, 14(6):800–813, June 1996.

[Vod97]   R. S. Vodhanel et al. National-scale WDM networking demonstration by the MONET consortium. In *OFC'97 Technical Digest*, 1997. Postdeadline paper PD27.

[WASG96]   R. E. Wagner, R. C. Alferness, A. A. M. Saleh, and M. S. Goodman. MONET: Multiwavelength optical networking. *IEEE/OSA JLT/JSAC Special Issue on Multiwavelength Optical Technology and Networks*, 14(6):1349–1355, June 1996.

12
chapter

Access Networks

IN PREVIOUS CHAPTERS, we have explored the use of optical networks for interoffice and backbone network applications, as well as private local-area and metropolitan-area network applications. The telephone and cable companies are placing a major emphasis on the development of networks that will allow them to provide a variety of services to individual homes and businesses. The "last leg" of such a network that runs from the service provider's facility to the home or business is called the *access* network.

Today, homes get essentially two types of services: plain old telephony service (POTS) over the telephone network, and broadcast analog video over the cable network. Businesses are already used to being provided with high-capacity connections, including SONET/SDH connections. Early efforts on developing high-capacity access networks were devoted to developing networks that would accommodate various forms of video, such as video-on-demand and high-definition TV. However, the range of services that users are expected to demand in the future is vast and unpredictable. Today's list of services includes Internet access, telecommuting, distance learning, and other high-speed data access, in addition to other video applications such as teleconferencing. The term *full service* encompasses the variety of services that are expected to be delivered via access networks. A sampling of the different services and their characteristics is given in Table 12.1. Both telephone and cable companies are striving to become full-service providers.

At a broad level, these services can be classified based on three major criteria. The first is the bandwidth requirement, which can vary from a few kHz for telephony to several MHz per video stream. The second is whether this requirement is *symmetric*

Table 12.1 Different types of services that must be supported by an access network. The bandwidth requirements are given for each individual stream.

Service	Type	Downstream Bandwidth	Upstream Bandwidth
Telephony	Switched	4 kHz	4 kHz
ISDN	Switched	144 kb/s	144 kb/s
Broadcast video	Broadcast	Analog or 6 Mb/s	0
Interactive video	Switched	6 Mb/s	Small
Internet access	Switched	A few Mb/s	Small initially
Videoconferencing	Switched	6 Mb/s	6 Mb/s
Business services	Switched	1.5–622 Mb/s	1.5–622 Mb/s

(two way), for example, videoconferencing, or *asymmetric* (one way), for example, broadcast video. Today, the consensus appears to be that it is mostly asymmetric, with more bandwidth needed from the service provider to the user (the downstream direction) than from the user to the service provider (the upstream direction). The last criterion is whether the service is inherently broadcast, where every user gets the same information, for example, broadcast video, or whether the service is switched, where different users get different information, as is the case with Internet access.

12.1 Network Architecture Overview

Let us now look at how the access network should be architected to provide the services described. In broad terms, an access network consists of a hub, remote nodes (RNs), and network interface units (NIUs), as shown in Figure 12.1. In the case of a telephone company, the hub is a *central office*, and in the case of a cable company, it is called a *head end*. Each hub serves several homes via the NIUs. An NIU either may be located in a home or may itself serve several homes. The hub itself may be part of a larger network, but for our purposes, we can think of the hub as being the source of data to the NIUs and the sink of data from the NIUs. In many cases, rather than running cables from the hub to each individual NIU, another hierarchical level is introduced between the hub and the NIUs. Each hub may be connected to several RNs deployed in the field, with each RN in turn serving a separate set of NIUs. The network between the hub and the RN is called the *feeder* network, and the network between the RN and the NIUs is called the *distribution* network.

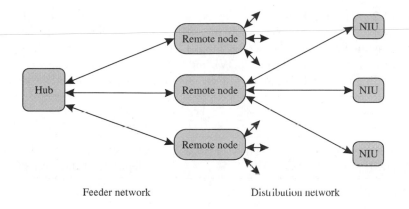

Figure 12.1   Architecture of an access network. It consists of a hub, which is a telephone company central office (CO) or cable company head end, remote nodes deployed in the field, and network interface units (NIUs) that serve one or more individual subscribers.

We saw that services could be either broadcast or switched. In the same way, the distribution network could also either be broadcast or switched. Different combinations of the two are possible—a broadcast service may be supported by a broadcast or a switched network, and a switched service may be supported by a broadcast or a switched network. In a broadcast network, an RN broadcasts the data it receives from the feeder network to all its NIUs. In a switched network, the RN processes the data coming in and sends possibly separate data streams to different NIUs. The telephone network that we will study in Section 12.2 is a switched network, whereas the cable television network is a broadcast network. Broadcast networks may be cheaper than switched networks, are well suited for delivering broadcast services, and have the advantage that all the NIUs are identical, making them easier to deploy. Switched networks, as their name suggests, are well suited for delivering switched services and provide more security. For example, it is not possible for one subscriber to tap into another subscriber's data, and it is more difficult for one subscriber to corrupt the entire network. Fault location is generally easier in a switched network than in a broadcast network. In broadcast networks, the "intelligence" is all at the NIUs, whereas in switched networks, it is in the network. Thus NIUs in switched networks may be simpler than in broadcast networks.

Another way of classifying access networks is based on the type of feeder network. In one scenario, the feeder network could assign each NIU its own *dedicated* bandwidth. In another scenario, the feeder network could have a total bandwidth that is *shared* by all the NIUs. In this case, each NIU could potentially access the

Table 12.2 Classification of different types of access networks, from [FRI96]. The acronyms refer to the following: HFC—hybrid fiber coax network; ADSL—asymmetric digital subscriber loop; FTTC—fiber to the curb, also sometimes called switched digital video (SDV); and PON—passive optical network, with the T standing for telephony, W for wavelength, and WR for wavelength routed.

| Distribution | Feeder Network | |
Network	Shared	Dedicated
Broadcast	Cable TV (HFC), TPON	WPON
Switched	FTTC (SDV)	Telephone, ADSL, WRPON

entire bandwidth for short periods. However, some form of media-access control will be required to coordinate access to the shared bandwidth by the NIUs. If the traffic from/to the NIUs is bursty, it is more efficient to share a large total amount of bandwidth among many NIUs rather than assign each NIU its own dedicated bandwidth. On the other hand, with dedicated bandwidth, each NIU can be guaranteed a certain quality of service, which is more difficult to do with shared bandwidth. A disadvantage of the shared bandwidth approach is that each NIU must have optics/electronics that operate at the total bandwidth of the network as opposed to the bandwidth needed by the NIU.

Table 12.2 classifies the different types of access networks that we will be studying in this chapter according to whether their distribution network is broadcast or switched, and whether they use dedicated or shared bandwidth in the feeder network. For example, the telephone network is a switched network with each NIU getting its own dedicated bandwidth of 4 kHz. The cable network is a broadcast network with all NIUs sharing the total cable bandwidth. A broadcast star WDM passive optical network (WPON), with each NIU assigned a separate wavelength, is an example of a broadcast network but with dedicated bandwidth to each NIU.

12.2 Today's Access Networks

Today, two kinds of access networks reach our homes: the telephone network and the cable network. The telephone network runs over twisted-pair copper cable. It consists of point-to-point copper pairs between the telco central office and the individual home. The two wires in a pair are twisted together to reduce the crosstalk between them, hence the name *twisted pair*. This plant was designed to provide 4 kHz bandwidth to each home. Wires from individual homes are aggregated in a

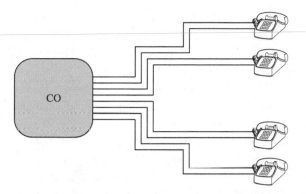

Figure 12.2   The twisted-pair telephone access network, which consists of individual twisted pairs routed from the central office (CO) to the individual subscribers.

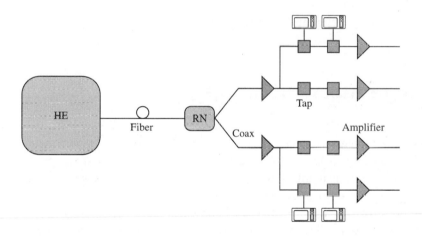

Figure 12.3   The hybrid fiber coax cable television network. The head end broadcasts signals over fiber to the remote node, which then distributes it to individual subscribers via coaxial cable drops.

hierarchical manner, as shown in Figure 12.2. The telephone network is a switched network that provides dedicated bandwidth to each user.

A typical cable network is shown in Figure 12.3. It consists of fibers between the cable company head end (analogous to a telco central office) and remote (fiber) nodes. Usually, the channels from the head end are broadcast to the remote nodes by using subcarrier multiplexing (SCM) on a linear laser. From the remote node, coaxial cables go to each home. A remote node serves between 500 and 2000 homes. Such a network is called a hybrid fiber coax (HFC) network. The entire architecture today is a broadcast architecture. The same set of signals from the head end is delivered to all the homes. The cable bandwidth used is between 50 and 550 MHz, and the cable carries AM-VSB (amplitude-modulated vestigial sideband) television signals in channels placed 6 MHz apart in the American NTSC (National Television System Committee) standard. The cable network is a broadcast network where all users share a common total bandwidth. Some cable companies are deploying cable modems over their cable infrastructure to support Internet access. These modems provide a total downstream bandwidth of up to 30 Mb/s, which is shared among all the users.

The telephone and cable networks are vastly different. The telephone network provides very little bandwidth per home but incorporates sophisticated switching equipment and operations and management systems. The cable network provides a lot of bandwidth to each home, but it is all unidirectional and broadcast, with no switching and very simple management.

12.3 Future Access Networks

Several approaches have been proposed to upgrade the access network infrastructure to support the emerging set of new services. The *integrated services digital network* (ISDN) today provides 128 kb/s of bandwidth over the existing twisted-pair infrastructure and is available in many metropolitan areas. *Asymmetric digital subscriber loop* (ADSL) is another technique that works over the existing twisted-pair infrastructure but provides significantly more bandwidth than ISDN. ADSL uses sophisticated modulation and coding techniques to realize a capacity of a few Mb/s over twisted pair, which is sufficient to transmit compressed video. This requires the central office (CO) and the home to each have an ADSL modem. However, ADSL has several limitations. The realizable bandwidth is inversely proportional to the distance between the CO and the home, and with today's technology, we can achieve a few Mb/s (up to 9 Mb/s depending on distance and line conditions) over this infrastructure. The existing twisted-pair infrastructure incorporates several 4 kHz filters that must be removed. The bandwidth on the upstream (return) path is severely limited to a few hundred kb/s (up to 800 kb/s depending on distance and line conditions). Many variations of ADSL have been proposed. As in the conventional telephone network, ISDN and ADSL can be classified as switched networks with dedicated bandwidth per NIU.

Another approach that is popular today is to use satellites. The direct broadcast satellite system uses a geosynchronous satellite to broadcast a few hundred channels to individual homes. A satellite may provide more bandwidth than a terrestrial coaxial cable system. However, the main problem is that unlike terrestrial systems, the amount of spatial reuse of bandwidth possible is quite limited, since a single satellite has a wide coverage area within which it broadcasts the signals. Also there is no easy way to handle the upstream traffic. Wireless access is yet another viable option. Although it suffers from limited bandwidth and range, it can be deployed rapidly and allows providers without an existing infrastructure to enter the market. Among the variants are the *multichannel multipoint distribution service* (MMDS), which is a terrestrial line-of-sight system with 33 6 MHz channels in the 2–3 GHz band, and the *local multipoint distribution service* (LMDS), which operates in the nonline-of-sight 28 GHz band with 1.3 GHz of bandwidth, and is suitable for short-range deployment in dense metropolitan areas.

The two main architectures being considered today, however, are the so-called hybrid fiber coax (HFC) approach and the fiber-to-the-curb (FTTC) approach. The HFC approach is still a broadcast architecture, whereas the FTTC approach incorporates switching.

12.3.1   HFC

Although we have used the term *HFC* to describe the existing cable infrastructure, HFC is also the term used to describe an upgraded version of this architecture. A better term to describe this is *subcarrier modulated fiber coax bus* (SMFCB). The network architecture is essentially the same as that shown in Figure 12.3. Like the existing cable network, downstream data is broadcast from the head end to remote (fiber) nodes by using a passive optical star coupler. From a remote node, several coax trees branch out to the network interface units (NIUs). An NIU may serve one or more homes. Its function is to separate the signals into telephone signals and broadcast video signals, and send the telephone signal on twisted pair and the video signal on coax to each home that it serves. Each coax leg serves about 100–500 homes. Logically, the architecture is a broadcast bus, although it is implemented as a combination of optical stars and coax trees/buses. Downstream broadcast video to the home would be sent on analog subcarrier channels. Video signals could be sent as analog AM-VSB streams, compatible with existing equipment inside homes. Digital video, as well as telephony and data services, can be carried over the same infrastructure. In addition, upstream channels can be provided in the 5–40 MHz band, which is not used for downstream traffic.

Clearly, HFC is the natural evolution path for the cable service providers. It maintains compatibility with existing analog equipment and is an efficient approach

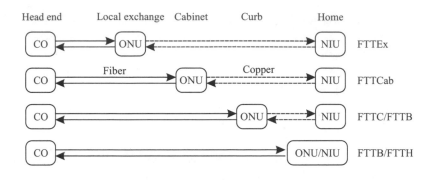

Figure 12.4   Different types of fiber access networks.

to deliver broadcast services. On the other hand, it has the disadvantages of a coax-based solution, such as limited upstream bandwidth, reliability, and powering needed for the many amplifiers in the path.

12.3.2 FTTC

In contrast to HFC, in FTTC, data is transmitted digitally over optical fiber from the hub to remote terminating nodes that are called *optical network units* (ONUs). The expectation is the fiber would get much closer to the home with this architecture. Depending on how close the fiber gets to an individual home, different terms are employed to describe this architecture (see Figure 12.4). In the most optimistic scenario, fiber would go to each home, in which case this architecture is called *fiber to the home* (FTTH), and the ONUs would perform the function of the network interface units (NIUs). For the case where ONUs serve a few homes, say 8–64, this can be thought of as *fiber to the curb* (FTTC) or *fiber to the building* (FTTB). In this case, there is an additional distribution network from the ONUs to the NIUs. In many architectures, the remote node (RN) may be a simple passive device such as an optical star coupler, and it may sometimes be colocated in the central office itself rather than in the field.

Although many different architectural alternatives can be used for FTTC, the term *FTTC* is usually used to describe a version where the signals are broadcast from the central office to the ONUs, and the ONUs share a common total bandwidth in time division multiplexed fashion, using either conventional TDM techniques or statistical multiplexing methods such as asynchronous transfer mode (ATM).

In FTTC, the feeder network is the portion of the network between the central office and the ONUs, and the distribution network is between the ONUs and the

NIUs. With this qualification, FTTC is a switched network with shared bandwidth, according to our classification of Table 12.2. We will describe this architecture and other variations in more detail in the following section.

Practically speaking, it is quite expensive today to transmit analog video signals over an all-fiber infrastructure; this may necessitate an analog hybrid fiber coax overlay that carries the analog video signals. The FTTC architecture is sometimes also called *baseband modulated fiber coax bus* (BMFCB) or *switched digital video* (SDV).

12.4 Optical Access Network Architectures

In what follows, we shall concentrate on different alternatives for realizing the portion of the access network that is optical. Optical access network architectures must be simple, and the network must be easy to operate and service. This means that passive architectures, where the network itself does not have any switching in it and does not need to be controlled, are preferable to active ones. This is analogous to the static network architectures considered in Chapter 8. Moreover, the ONU itself must be kept very simple in order to reduce cost and improve reliability. This rules out using sophisticated lasers and other optical components within the ONU. Preferably, the components used in the ONU must be capable of operating without any temperature control. The CO equipment can be somewhat more sophisticated, since it resides in a controlled environment, and its cost can be amortized over the many subscribers served out of a single CO.

The optical networks proposed for this application are commonly called PONs (passive optical networks)—all of them use passive architectures. They use some form of passive component, such as an optical star coupler or static wavelength router, as the remote node. The main advantages of using passive architectures in this case come from their reliability, ease of maintenance, and the fact that the field-deployed network does not need to be powered. Moreover, the fiber infrastructure itself is transparent to bit rates and modulation formats, and the overall network can be upgraded in the future without changing the infrastructure itself. Table 12.3 compares the different architectures.

The simplest PON architecture, shown in Figure 12.5(a), uses a separate fiber-pair from the CO to each ONU. The main problem with this approach is that the cost of CO equipment scales with the number of ONUs. Moreover, one needs to install and maintain all these fiber-pairs. This approach is being implemented on a limited scale today, primarily to provide high-speed services to businesses. In Japan, NTT is operating such a system at bit rates from 8–32 Mb/s over each fiber. Although, logically, there is a separate fiber-pair to each ONU, physically, the fibers could be

Table 12.3   Comparison of different PON architectures. N denotes the number of optical network units (ONUs) in the network. An ONU bit rate of 1 indicates that the ONU operates at the bit rate corresponding to the traffic it terminates rather than the aggregate traffic of N. Node sync. refers to whether the nodes in the network must be synchronized to a common clock or not.

Architecture	Fiber Sharing	Power Splitting	ONU Bit Rate	Node Sync.	CO Sharing
All fiber	No	None	1	No	No
TPON	Yes	$1/N$	N	Yes	Yes
WPON	Yes	$1/N$	1	Yes	No
WRPON	Yes	None	1	Yes	Yes

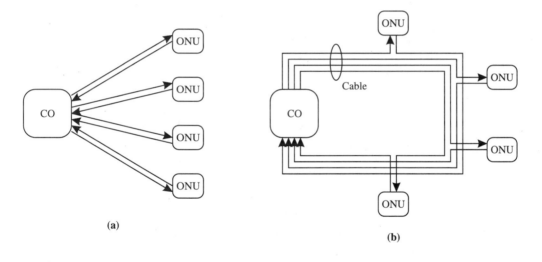

Figure 12.5   (a) The point-to-point fiber approach. (b) In practice the fibers could be laid in the form of a ring.

laid in a ring configuration, as shown in Figure 12.5. Similar architectures are also being deployed in the United States in the form of SONET rings running at OC-3 and OC-12 speeds to provide businesses with high-speed leased-line services. In this case, an ONU is a SONET ADM, and multiple ONUs can be present on the same ring.

Instead of providing a fiber-pair to each ONU, a single fiber can be used with bidirectional transmission. However, the same wavelength cannot be used to transmit data simultaneously in both directions because of uncontrolled reflections in the fiber. One way is to use time division multiplexing so that both ends don't transmit simultaneously. Another is to use different wavelengths (1310 and 1550 nm, for example) for the different directions.

Another simple architecture is the TPON (PON for telephony) architecture [Ste87] shown in Figure 12.6. The downstream traffic is broadcast by a transmitter at the CO to all the ONUs by a passive star coupler, similar to the broadcast and select networks we studied in Chapter 7. Though the architecture is a broadcast architecture, switched services can be supported by assigning specific time slots to individual ONUs based on their bandwidth demands. For the upstream channel, the ONUs share a channel that is combined using a coupler, again via fixed time division multiplexing, or some other multiaccess protocol.

This architecture allows the CO equipment to be shared among all the ONUs and makes use of fairly mature low-cost optical components. The CO transmitter can be an LED or a Fabry-Perot laser, and cheap, uncooled pinFET receivers and

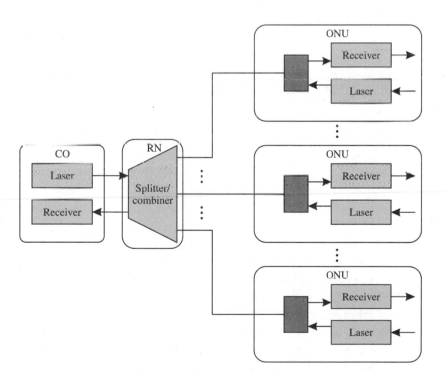

Figure 12.6   A broadcast and select PON.

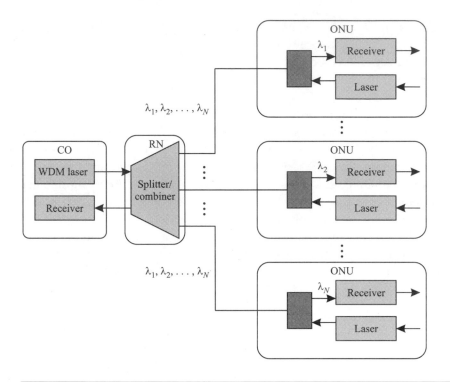

Figure 12.7   A broadcast and select WDM PON.

LEDs/Fabry-Perot lasers can be used within the ONUs. The number of ONUs that can be supported is limited by the splitting loss in the star coupler. Each ONU must have electronics that runs at the *aggregate* bit rate of all the ONUs. A few hundred Mb/s total bandwidth can be supported by this architecture.

The next step, shown in Figure 12.7, is to replace the single transceiver at the CO with a WDM array of transmitters or a single tunable transmitter to yield a WDM PON. This approach allows each ONU to have electronics running only at the rate it receives data, and not at the aggregate bit rate. However, it is still limited by the power splitting at the star coupler.

Introducing wavelength routing solves the splitting loss problem while retaining all the other advantages of the WDM PON. In addition, it allows point-to-point dedicated services to be provided to ONUs. This leads to the WRPON architecture shown in Figure 12.8.

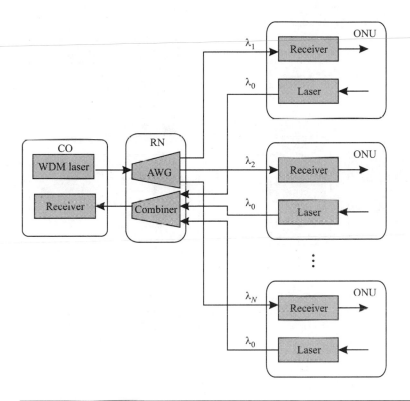

Figure 12.8   WRPON.

Several types of WRPONs have been proposed and demonstrated. They all use a wavelength router, typically an arrayed waveguide grating (AWG) for the downstream traffic, but vary in the type of equipment located at the CO and ONUs, and in how the upstream traffic is supported. The router directs different wavelengths to different ONUs. The earliest demonstration was the so-called passive photonics loop (PPL) [WKR+88, WL88]. It used 16 channels in the 1310 nm band for downstream transmission and 16 additional channels in the 1550 nm band for upstream transmission. However, this approach is not economical because we need two expensive lasers for each ONU—one inside the ONU and one at the central office. We describe several variants of this architecture that provide more economical sharing of resources at the CO and ONUs.

The RITENET architecture [Fri94] (see Figure 12.9) uses a tunable laser at the CO. A frame sent to each ONU from the CO consists of two parts: a *data* part,

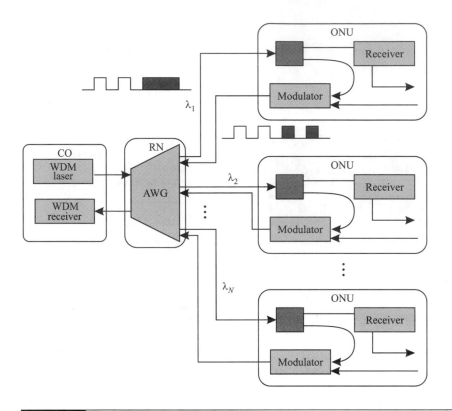

Figure 12.9   The RITENET WRPON architecture.

wherein data is transmitted by the CO, and a *return traffic* part, wherein no data is transmitted but the CO laser is left turned on. Each ONU is provided with an external modulator. During the return traffic part of the frame, the ONU uses the modulator to modulate the light signal from the CO. This avoids the need for having a laser at the ONU. The upstream traffic from the ONUs is also sent to the router. The router combines all the different wavelengths and sends them out on a common port to a receiver in the CO. This architecture allows a single laser to be shared among all the ONUs but requires each ONU to have an external modulator.

A lower-cost alternative to RITENET is the LARNET architecture [ZJS+95] (see Figure 12.10), which uses an LED at the ONU instead of an external modulator. The LED emits a broadband signal that gets "sliced" upon going through the wavelength router, as shown in Figure 12.11. Only the power in the part of the LED spectrum corresponding to the passband of the wavelength router is transmitted through. Note,

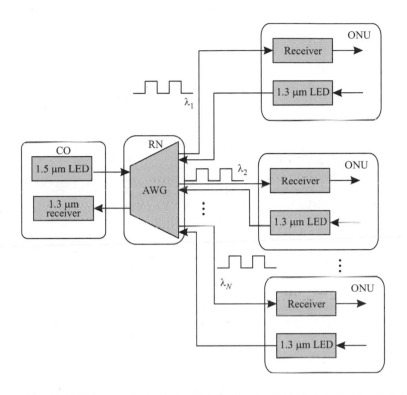

Figure 12.10 The LARNET WRPON architecture.

however, that with N ONUs, this imposes a splitting loss of at least $1/N$—only a small fraction of the total power falls within the passband of the router.

More important, an LED can be used at the CO as well [IFD95]. In this case, the signal sent by the CO LED effectively gets broadcast to all the ONUs. It is in fact possible to have two transmitters within the CO: an LED, say, at 1.3 μm, broadcasting to all the ONUs, and a tunable laser at 1.5 μm selectively transmitting to the ONUs. This is an important way to carry broadcast analog video signals over the digital switched fiber infrastructure at low cost without having to use a separate overlay network for this purpose.

WDM components for PONs are not yet mature and are more expensive than the components required for simple broadcast PONs. However, WRPONs offer much higher capacities than the simple broadcast PONs and offer a nice upgrade path over the same infrastructure.

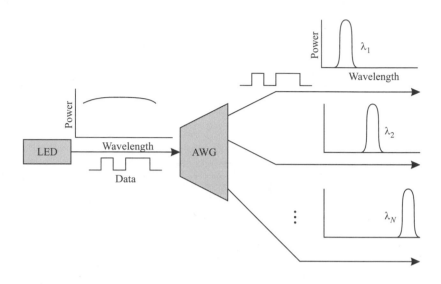

Figure 12.11   Spectral slicing: if a broadband LED signal is sent through a filter, only the portion of the LED spectrum that is passed by the filter comes out.

As for PONs, we will consider the part of the network between the CO and the RN as the feeder network, and the part of the network between the RN and the ONU as the distribution network. Note that this is different from what we adopted for FTTC, where we assumed that the feeder network is the part of the network from the CO to the ONU. We adopt this classification here since it is better suited to describing the properties of the various PONs that we will study.

Based on this classification, the upgrade scenario for PONs could go as follows. The operator can start by deploying a simple broadcast TPON, which is a broadcast star network with shared bandwidth, according to the classification of Table 12.2. If more ONUs need to be supported, the operator can upgrade the network to a WDM broadcast PON, which is a broadcast network with dedicated bandwidth provided to each ONU. This can be done by upgrading the transmitters at the hub to WDM transmitters, and the operator may be able reuse the existing ONUs. If higher capacities per ONU are needed, the operator can further upgrade the network to a wavelength-routed PON, which is a switched network with dedicated bandwidth. Moreover, this wavelength-routed PON can also support broadcast services efficiently using the spectral slicing technique described earlier. Thus there is a nice upgrade path starting from a broadcast network with shared bandwidth to a broadcast network with dedicated bandwidth and eventually to a switched network with dedicated bandwidth.

Summary

Service providers, both telephone operators and cable companies, are actively looking to deploy broadband access networks to provide a variety of new services. The FTTC approach has a higher initial cost, but provides bandwidth deeper in the network and may prove to be a better longer-term solution. Although FTTC refers to a simple broadcast TDM star architecture, we also explored several upgrade options of the FTTC approach that provide higher capacities by making clever use of wavelength division multiplexing techniques.

The HFC approach, on the other hand, is attractive in places where coaxial cable is already deployed to the home, such as the United States. FTTC is attractive in places where coaxial cable is not already deployed, which is the case in many countries other than the United States. In Japan and parts of Europe, such as Germany, fiber is being deployed to reach buildings. The choice between these different approaches will be dictated by deployment and operational costs, bandwidths that can be provided, and the number of users that can be serviced out of a central office or head end.

The cable companies with their existing coaxial cable infrastructure are seriously considering hybrid fiber coax (HFC) architectures, whereas the telephone operators, lacking this infrastructure, are leaning toward FTTC architectures. As of this writing, a number of major telephone carriers and manufacturers in the world have gotten together to arrive at a consensus toward defining the requirements for an FTTC-based architecture to enable them to deploy the full-service access network [FSA97]. Thus it is clear that optical fiber will play a major role in these access networks—the question is how close will it get to our homes?

Further Reading

There is a vast body of literature on access networks, and several conferences have sessions devoted to it. There is an informative Web page maintained by the ADSL forum (*http://www.adsl.com*). The papers in [SKY89, Aar95, Kob94] describe plans for deploying fiber in the access network and compare different architectural approaches. TDM PONs were first proposed in [Ste87]. A variety of WDM PONs are described in [WKR+88, WL88, Fri94, ZJS+95, IFD95, IRF96]. At this time, a major initiative is underway from a group of telephone carriers and manufacturers toward deploying a fiber-based access architecture, called the full-service access network initiative. Details may be found on the Web at *http://btlabs1.labs.bt.com/profsoc/access/* and in [FSA97].

Problems

12.1 Do a power budget calculation for the different types of PON architectures considered in this chapter and determine the number of ONUs that can be supported in each case, assuming the following parameters:

Laser output power	−3 dBm
LED output power	−20 dBm
Transmit bit rate	155 Mb/s
Receiver sensitivity	−40 dBm
Fiber loss, incl. connectors	10 dB
1 × 8 wavelength router loss	5 dB
1 × 32 wavelength router loss	9 dB
1 × 64 wavelength router loss	12 dB
Excess splitter loss	1 dB

Assume that with spectral slicing we get only $1/2N$ of the transmitted power in each channel, where N is the number of ONUs.

12.2 Consider the RITENET architecture shown in Figure 12.9. Suppose the laser speed at the CO is limited to 155 Mb/s. The network needs to support 20 ONUs, and provide each ONU with 10 Mb/s bandwidth from the CO to the ONU and 2 Mb/s from the ONU to the CO. How could you modify the architecture to support this requirement?

References

[Aar95]   R. Aaron, editor. *IEEE Communications Magazine: Special Issue on Access to Broadband Services*, volume 33, Aug. 1995.

[Fri94]   N. J. Frigo et al. A wavelength-division-multiplexed passive optical network with cost-shared components. *IEEE Photonics Technology Letters*, 6(11):1365–1367, 1994.

[FRI96]   N. J. Frigo, K. C. Reichmann, and P. P. Iannone. WDM passive optical networks: A robust and flexible infrastructure for local access. In *Proceedings of International Workshop on Photonic Networks and Technologies*, pages 201–212, 1996.

[FSA97] *Full Services Access Network Requirements Specification*, 1997. Available on the Web at *http://btlabs1.labs.bt.com/profsoc/access/*.

[IFD95] P. P. Iannone, N. J. Frigo, and T. E. Darcie. WDM passive optical network architecture with bidirectional optical spectral slicing. In *OFC'95 Technical Digest*, pages 51–53, 1995. Paper TuK2.

[IRF96] P. P. Iannone, K. C. Reichmann, and N. J. Frigo. Broadcast digital video delivered over WDM passive optical networks. *IEEE Photonics Technology Letters*, 8(7):930–932, 1996.

[Kob94] I. Kobayashi, editor. *IEEE Communications Magazine: Special Issue on Fiber-Optic Subscriber Loops*, volume 32, Feb. 1994.

[SKY89] P. W. Shumate, O. Krumpholz, and K. Yamaguchi, editors. *IEEE/OSA JLT/JSAC Special Issue on Subscriber Loop Technology*, volume 7, Nov. 1989.

[Ste87] J. Stern et al. Passive optical local networks for telephony applications. *Electronics Letters*, 23:1255–1257, 1987.

[WKR⁺88] S. S. Wagner, H. Kobrinski, T. J. Robe, H. L. Lemberg, and L. S. Smoot. Experimental demonstration of a passive optical subscriber loop architecture. *Electronics Letters*, 24:344–346, 1988.

[WL88] S. S. Wagner and H. L. Lemberg. Technology and system issues for the WDM-based fiber loop architecture. *IEEE/OSA Journal on Lightwave Technology*, 7(11):1759–1768, 1988.

[ZJS⁺95] M. Zirngibl, C. H. Joyner, L. W. Stulz, C. Dragone, H. M. Presby, and I. P. Kaminow. LARnet, a local access router network. *IEEE Photonics Technology Letters*, 7(2):1041–1135, Feb. 1995.

13 chapter

Deployment Considerations

IN THIS CHAPTER, we will study some of the issues facing network operators as they upgrade their networks to higher and higher capacities. We will also try to understand the role of TDM and WDM technologies in different types of networks.

13.1 Upgrading Transmission Capacity

Today's first-generation optical fiber links operate typically at a bit rate of 2.5 Gb/s or less in the 1550 nm low-loss window of the fiber. When network operators upgrade their links, as a rough rule of thumb, they usually look for at least a fourfold increase in capacity but at only twice the cost. In other words, they expect 10 Gb/s transmission equipment to cost about twice as much as 2.5 Gb/s transmission equipment.

There are essentially three approaches toward increasing the transmission capacity on a link:

1. The *space division multiplexing* (SDM) approach: keep the bit rate the same but use more fibers.

2. The TDM approach: increase the transmission bit rate on the fiber.

3. The WDM approach: keep the bit rate the same but add more wavelengths, each operating at the original bit rate over the same fiber.

Of course, it is possible to employ a combination of all three approaches as well since they are complementary, and this will most likely be the case in practice.

501

13.1.1 The SDM Approach

The SDM approach is the most straightforward upgrade alternative. However, it has two main drawbacks. It requires more fibers, which may not be available along the desired route. The cost of laying new fiber varies widely. If there is space in existing conduits, fiber can be pulled through relatively inexpensively. However, if new conduits must be laid, the cost can be very expensive, even over short distances. If there are no fibers along the desired route whatsoever, there is no alternative but to build the link from scratch, in which case, the new link is built with a large number of fibers in the bundle. Today's fiber bundles come with hundreds of fibers.

The second drawback of SDM is that even if the fibers are available, a separate set of optical amplifiers or repeaters must be installed for each fiber, which becomes a significant expense over long distances. The TDM and WDM approaches allow the amplifiers/repeaters to be shared among many channels. Thus SDM is a competitive alternative when fibers are available and distances are relatively short so that no repeaters or amplifiers are needed.

13.1.2 The TDM Approach

The TDM approach requires the bit rate on the fiber to be increased to 10 Gb/s or beyond. The two major system impairments that these systems face are chromatic dispersion and polarization-mode dispersion (PMD). Chromatic dispersion is not a problem if the link uses dispersion-shifted fiber. With standard single-mode fiber, from Figure 2.10, the chromatic dispersion limit is about 60 km at 10 Gb/s and about 1000 km at 2.5 Gb/s. With practical transmitters, the distances are even smaller. The 10 Gb/s limit can be further reduced in the presence of self-phase modulation. Beyond these distances, the signal must be electronically regenerated, or some form of chromatic dispersion compensation must be employed.

As we saw in Section 5.7.4, the distance limit due to PMD at 10 Gb/s is 16 times less than that at 2.5 Gb/s. On old fiber links, the PMD value can be as high as $2 \text{ ps}/\sqrt{\text{km}}$. For this value, assuming a 1-dB penalty requirement, the distance limit calculated from (5.15) is about 25 km at 10 Gb/s. Electronic regeneration is required for longer distances. The PMD-induced distance limit may be even lower because of additional PMD caused by splices, connectors, and other components along the transmission path. PMD does not pose a problem in newly constructed links where the PMD value can be kept as low as $0.1 \text{ ps}/\sqrt{\text{km}}$.

Eventually, TDM is limited by the speeds that can be achieved by electronics. Although optical TDM is an option that may be used at some point in the future to push bit rates beyond the electronic limit, WDM is the more practical option today.

As we saw in Chapter 5, about 90% of the installed base of fiber in the United States and in Europe is standard single-mode fiber. Japan has a significant installed base of dispersion-shifted fiber. TDM is a competitive approach for short- to medium-distance links, or for links operating over dispersion-shifted fiber.

An additional factor that may influence network operators' decisions to deploy TDM or SDM is the fact that both of these approaches are compatible with the standard network management techniques that operators are familiar with and require no additional learning on the part of those dealing with installing and managing the links. 10 Gb/s TDM systems are becoming commercially available from a number of vendors today, and there is ongoing research to develop 20 Gb/s and 40 Gb/s TDM systems.

13.1.3 The WDM Approach

The WDM approach is to keep the bit rate the same, say, at 2.5 Gb/s, and add more wavelengths, each carrying data at this bit rate. The advantages of WDM over TDM are the following:

1. Because of the lower bit rates, the distance limit due to chromatic dispersion is much larger for WDM systems than for equivalent TDM systems. Likewise, PMD does not impose a significant distance limitation at bit rates of 2.5 Gb/s or lower in most links.

2. The transmission capacity can be increased in a modular manner by adding additional wavelengths as and when capacity increases are required, as opposed to a large up-front installation in the case of TDM. For example, in a four-channel WDM system, the capacity can be modularly increased from 2.5 Gb/s all the way to 10 Gb/s in steps of 2.5 Gb/s. On the other hand, a 10 Gb/s TDM system must be installed all at once and may not be as modular.

3. WDM systems can be designed to be transparent systems. This allows different wavelengths to carry data at different bit rates and protocol formats. This can be a major advantage in some cases.

4. WDM may be preferred to TDM in designing more complicated networks. For example, if there is a network node at which most of the traffic is to be passed through and a small fraction is to be dropped and added, it may be more cost effective to use a WDM optical add/drop element than a full-blown set of TDM terminals (or WDM terminals).

On the other hand, WDM does suffer some disadvantages as well relative to TDM:

1. WDM systems are generally not suitable for deployment over dispersion-shifted fiber because of the limitations imposed by four-wave mixing (see Chapter 5).

2. WDM systems require specially designed optical amplifiers that provide flat gain profiles. Moreover, their gain must be independent of the number of wavelengths in the system so as to make upgrades easy and, more important, prevent a failure in one channel from causing an outage in another channel.

3. As in the SDM approach, WDM systems require separate terminating equipment for each channel, including an expensive laser and a receiver. A TDM system, on the other hand, requires one piece of terminating equipment. However, this equipment must include the electronics necessary to multiplex and demultiplex the lower-speed streams.

4. Transparent WDM systems offer less monitoring and network management capability than TDM systems because they are unaware of the actual format and data rate on the individual channels. Thus they cannot monitor parameters such as the bit error rate or frame errors in the data. Of course, the other equipment attached to the WDM equipment, which actually terminates the data, can perform all these functions. However, this makes fault isolation somewhat tricky. In some cases, it may be difficult to determine whether a fault is in the WDM equipment or in the attached equipment.

WDM systems with 4–20 wavelengths at bit rates of 1–10 Gb/s per channel are commercially available today from several vendors, and systems with 32 and 40 wavelengths will arrive soon.

Based on the preceding discussion, the interesting question is not whether to use TDM or WDM—both alternatives will be pursued—but to determine the combination of bit rates and number of wavelengths that makes most sense. For example, to get a total capacity of 80 Gb/s, should we deploy a network with 32 wavelengths at 2.5 Gb/s each, or a network with 8 wavelengths and 10 Gb/s each? This is a complicated question with many parameters affecting the right choice. From the transmission system viewpoint, 10 Gb/s systems are more limited by dispersion (both chromatic and polarization-mode dispersion) and self-phase modulation, but fewer channels implies higher output powers per channel from the optical amplifiers, less stringent constraints on amplifier gain flatness, and fewer losses through optical wavelength add/drop multiplexers. These factors, along with operational issues (management, inventory, problem determination, and tracking), determine the cost of these different types of systems and hence their relative competitive positions. The problems at the end of the chapter provide a partial insight into some of the issues.

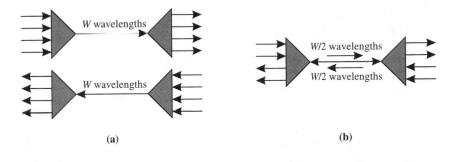

Figure 13.1   (a) Unidirectional and (b) bidirectional transmission systems.

Unidirectional versus Bidirectional Systems

A unidirectional WDM system uses two fibers, one for each direction of traffic, as shown in Figure 13.1(a). A bidirectional system, on the other hand, requires only one fiber, and typically uses half the wavelengths for transmitting data in one direction and the other half for transmitting data in the opposite direction on the same fiber. Both types of systems are being developed and have their pros and cons. We will compare the two types of systems, assuming that technology limits us to having a fixed number of wavelengths, say, W per fiber, in both cases.

1. A unidirectional system is capable of handling W full-duplex channels over two fibers. A bidirectional system handles $W/2$ full-duplex channels over one fiber. The bidirectional system, therefore, has half the total capacity, but allows a user to build capacity more gradually than a unidirectional system. For instance, the user can buy a second bidirectional system with $W/2$ full-duplex channels at a later point when he needs more capacity.

2. If only one fiber (not two) is available, then there is no alternative but to deploy bidirectional systems.

3. Consider two equivalent all-optical networks in terms of capacity. One network uses a bidirectional link between nodes with a total of W wavelengths per link. Another network uses two unidirectional links between nodes, with a total of $W/2$ wavelengths on each unidirectional link. Problem 8.19 in Chapter 8 shows that the bidirectional network is less efficient at utilizing the available capacity than the unidirectional network.

4. As we saw in Chapter 10, if optical layer protection is required, unlike unidirectional systems, bidirectional systems do not require an automatic protection

switching (APS) protocol between the two ends of the link, since both ends detect a fiber cut simultaneously.

5. BLSR/4 four-fiber SONET rings are better supported using bidirectional systems than unidirectional systems, as shown in Figure 13.2. A BLSR/4 requires four lightpaths between ADMs. It can be supported using two bidirectional WDM systems over two fibers, without compromising on the protection features of the BLSR. Alternatively, it takes two unidirectional WDM systems over four fibers to support a BLSR/4. Using a single unidirectional WDM system (with two wavelengths per fiber) will not allow the BLSR span protection to respond to fiber cuts. However, span protection can still handle transmitter/receiver failures in this case.

6. Bidirectional systems also provide better support for deploying point-to-point SONET systems in $1 + 1$ or 1:1 configurations. These configurations can be supported with two fibers instead of four fibers with bidirectional WDM systems.

7. Bidirectional systems can be configured to handle asymmetric traffic. For example, a large number of wavelengths could be used in one direction and a smaller number in the other direction.

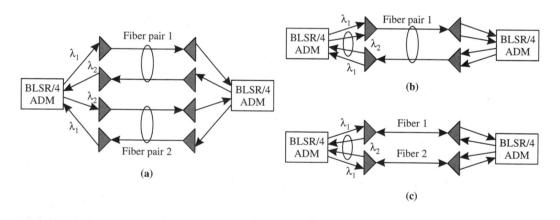

Figure 13.2 Supporting BLSR/4 rings with unidirectional and bidirectional transmission systems: (a) two unidirectional systems using four fibers, (b) one unidirectional system using two fibers with two wavelengths used for the BLSR connections, and (c) two bidirectional systems using two fibers and two wavelengths per fiber.

8. In general, it is more difficult to design the transmission system in bidirectional systems since more impairments must be taken into account, in particular, reflections, as discussed in Section 5.6.4.

9. Although amplifiers for bidirectional systems may employ more complicated structures than unidirectional systems, they need to handle only half as many channels as unidirectional systems, which means that they can produce higher output powers per channel and provide more gain flatness.

10. Bidirectional systems usually require a guard band between the two sets of wavelengths traveling in opposite directions to avoid crosstalk penalties, which may not be needed for unidirectional systems.

11. Finally, note that a bidirectional system can also be operated as a unidirectional system by simply reversing the direction of propagation of half the wavelengths and the corresponding amplifiers.

13.1.4   Trading SONET Against WDM

As we start planning networks rather than links, the planning options become more complicated. As we saw in Chapters 8 and 9, WDM ADMs can be used to bypass through traffic without terminating them in SONET equipment. This reduces the number of SONET ADMs needed in the network and can help reduce the overall network cost significantly. This is the single most important factor driving the need for WDM optical networks, rather than just point-to-point links. We saw several examples of this in Chapter 8, and one more example appears in Problem 13.2.

13.2 Application Areas

We will now explore the considerations underlying the deployment of the preceding approaches in different types of networks. Access networks were considered in Chapter 12. In general, it is a difficult decision to choose between the different technologies, and network operators often employ sophisticated network design tools to help them understand the cost tradeoffs between different approaches. The problems at the end of this chapter will help the reader gain a better understanding of these tradeoffs.

13.2.1   Interexchange Networks

The interexchange carriers in the United States have links spanning several hundred to a few thousand km. Among the major carriers, AT&T and Sprint have primarily installed standard single-mode fiber. Thus WDM is an attractive option for them, and they are actively deploying WDM systems on many of their routes. Another major carrier, MCI, has a number of links using dispersion-shifted fiber and is looking to deploy high-speed TDM systems on these routes and WDM systems on other routes that use standard single-mode fiber. Meanwhile, some of the new links being installed use nonzero dispersion fiber, which allows both types of systems to be considered for deployment.

In Europe and Japan, the links tend to be shorter. As of this writing, several European carriers are considering the deployment of WDM.

13.2.2 Undersea Networks

The economics of undersea links is somewhat similar to that of the interexchange links. Undersea links tend to be even longer and may span distances of several thousand km. Shorter-distance repeaterless undersea links are also being deployed in many places. In long links, the case for WDM over standard single-mode fiber becomes quite strong. However, many new undersea links are constructed from scratch and can choose the type of fiber to be installed. Thus they can use the dispersion management technique described in Section 5.8.5 by having alternating spans with positive and negative dispersion fiber to realize a total dispersion of zero but at the same time have finite dispersion at all points along the link.

Reliability is a very important consideration for undersea links, which are usually designed to operate over a 25-year period. Passive WDM multiplexing and demultiplexing technology, combined with 2.5 Gb/s systems whose reliability characteristics are well understood, give WDM an edge over higher-speed TDM systems whose reliability has not yet been quantified.

WDM also allows segregation of traffic between channels. This turned out to be a useful feature in the Africa ONE undersea network that we studied in Section 11.1.

13.2.3 Local-Exchange Networks

These networks tend to operate over shorter distances, typically, a few tens of km between major sites. This makes the case for WDM less compelling than the interexchange networks and makes both TDM and SDM more viable options.

On the other hand, reasons other than pure capacity growth may drive the deployment of WDM in these networks. Local-exchange carriers will need to provide high-capacity connections to their customers such as large enterprises. These customers may want to transmit different types of protocols at different bit rates. The bit rates tend to be somewhat lower compared to interexchange networks, typically, a few hundred to several hundred Mb/s lower. Thus it may be useful to have several lower-speed channels than a few high-speed channels in the network. Moreover, the carrier may want to rearrange the network capacity as the traffic distribution changes. This happens on a more frequent time scale in these networks than in interexchange networks.

Another factor favoring WDM is that carriers typically end up deploying multiple networks, either because their different service offerings tend to be segregated or because certain customers require dedicated private networks. These two factors may motivate local exchange carriers to deploy wavelength routing networks as opposed to just point-to-point links.

As of this writing, several carriers in the Unisted States are considering the deployment of WDM on selected routes where they need higher capacities; they are also studying the economic value of deploying wavelength routing networks.

13.2.4 Enterprise Links

Large enterprises face an increasing need for a number of high-bandwidth connections between their sites. Many enterprises, for example, maintain two data centers that are separated by a few tens of km. All transactions are mirrored at both sites. This allows the enterprise to recover quickly from a disaster where one of the centers fails. There may be other reasons for this as well, such as lower real estate costs at one location than at the other. This allows peripheral equipment to be placed at the cheaper site. The large mainframes at these data centers need to be interconnected by several hundred channels, each at up to a few hundred Mb/s. For example, IBM mainframes communicate using hundreds of ESCON channels, discussed in Chapter 6, running at 200 Mb/s each. Typically, these data centers tend to be located in dense metropolitan areas where most of the installed fiber is already in use. Moreover, these networks use a large variety of protocols and bit rates. These two factors make WDM an attractive option for these types of networks. WDM systems are being installed in large enterprise networks in the United States and all over Europe as well.

Since the links tend to be short, there is usually no need to use optical amplifiers or regenerators. This makes the SDM option highly competitive provided multiple fibers are available, or when the fiber is being installed from scratch. Given the variety of protocols and bit rates, the TDM option becomes complicated to implement. Even if a TDM solution is provided, it cannot be adapted easily to handle another new protocol or bit rate that comes along in the future.

<u>13.3</u> Equipment Design Requirements

So far, we have explored the factors driving the deployment of different TDM and WDM technologies in different types of high-capacity networks. The equipment that is deployed in these different networks may use the same set of underlying technologies but must conform to very different design requirements, some of which we explored earlier in this chapter.

1. Equipment deployed in interexchange and local-exchange carrier networks usually operates at much higher bit rates than equipment deployed in enterprise networks. The maximum bit rate per enterprise channel is usually around 1 Gb/s, whereas bit rates in the carrier world can be as high as 10 Gb/s per channel today.

2. A large variety of protocols and bit rates are used in the enterprise world. This number is much less in the carrier world, where high-speed connections are usually SONET/SDH, along with some remaining PDH connections.

3. The transmission links in carrier networks tend to be much longer than in enterprise networks. Undersea links can span distances of around 10,000 km. High-speed enterprise links tend to be much shorter—less than 100 km typically, partly because of the lack of fiber availability to enterprises over long routes.

4. As we saw in Chapter 10, network management in enterprise networks is SNMP based and usually fairly simple. The management requirements in carrier networks are far more stringent, and the carriers are moving to the telecommunications management network (TMN) framework and the open-system interconnection (OSI) common management information (CMI) standards [AP94].

5. An interesting difference arises with regard to laser eye safety. Enterprise networks have much more stringent standards in this regard and must conform to Class I safety specifications. Carrier networks can operate on a less stringent Class IIIa safety specification. We discussed these safety issues in Section 10.5.

6. Equipment deployed in carrier premises must conform to a set of physical packaging and environmental specifications called NEBS (Network Equipment Building System) [Bel95]. This imposes stringent requirements on packaging and robustness that are not needed in the enterprise world. For example, the required temperature range for central office equipment is −10 to 60°C, whereas it is 0 to 40°C for equipment in enterprise buildings.

Summary

The topic of whether to upgrade the network using TDM, WDM, or SDM has been debated in many circles, and the conclusion is that all types of systems will be deployed, depending on the individual circumstances. Obtaining the exact combination of WDM, TDM, and SDM is complicated even for simple point-to-point links and becomes even more complicated for networks that employ add/drop elements and crossconnects. The exact combination of equipment to use depends strongly on the traffic demands and their distribution, the distances involved, the cost and features of the available equipment, and the need to support legacy equipment already installed. The problems at the end of this chapter will give the reader an inkling of what such a comparison might involve. Network planners need to make their own analysis of the different alternatives, perhaps with the aid of some network planning and design tools, to decide which way to go.

Further Reading

Although the topic of this chapter is intensely debated in the industry and the tradeoffs are not completely understood, relatively little has been published on this topic so far. However, there is no doubt that we will see a number of economic comparisons of different architectural alternatives in the future. See, for instance, [Bal96, SC96, DEM96, Car97, Red97, MP97, Sle97], all of which are economic analyses, mostly by vendors in support of their products. Each of these studies makes its own assumptions about the equipment cost and network models.

Problems

13.1 Imagine that you are a network planner for a major carrier that is interested in deploying a 20 Gb/s link. You must choose between the following options:
  (a) An SDM approach using eight fiber-pairs, each operating at 2.5 Gb/s.
  (b) A TDM approach using two 10 Gb/s transmission systems over two fiber-pairs.
  (c) A WDM approach using eight wavelengths over a fiber-pair.

  Do an economic analysis to determine the costs of installing each type of system for a link of length (a) 600 km, (b) 240 km, and (c) 40 km. Use a spreadsheet or a computer program so that you can vary the parameters and see how they affect your system choice.

Assume the following costs:

Equipment	Cost (U.S. $)
2.5 Gb/s terminal	100,000
10 Gb/s terminal	300,000
8-WDM terminal equipment	100,000
Optical amplifier pair	100,000
10 Gb/s regenerator pair	150,000

The WDM terminal equipment includes only the multiplexing and demultiplexing equipment and any amplifiers needed, but it does not include the 2.5 Gb/s terminal equipment that must be paid for separately.

Assume that the chromatic dispersion limit is 600 km at 2.5 Gb/s and 120 km at 10 Gb/s, and that the PMD limit at 10 Gb/s is 600 km. Regeneration is required beyond these limits. An optical amplifier is required every 120 km, unless the link is terminated at that point, and the same type of amplifier can be used in all the systems. Instead of an amplifier, you can opt to use a regenerator, but one is required every 80 km. Assume that standard single-mode fibers are already installed and available for free.

What do you conclude from your study? How would your conclusions change if the cost of the 10 Gb/s terminal equipment drops 25%, the 2.5 Gb/s 40%, and the WDM terminal equipment by 25%?

13.2   This is similar to the previous problem, except that now you have to design a linear network with three nodes A, B, and C. 17.5 Gb/s of traffic is to be routed between A and C, and 2.5 Gb/s of traffic between A and B, and B and C. Now you have an additional element that you can use at B if you choose: an optical add/drop that drops one wavelength and passes the others through, which costs $20,000. Compare the costs of the following approaches:

(a) Two WDM point-to-point links AB and BC.
(b) Two TDM point-to-point links AB and BC.
(c) One WDM link between A and C with an optical add/drop at B.

Assume that distances are short and hence that no amplifiers or regenerators are required.

References

[AP94]   S. Aidarus and T. Plevyak, editors. *Telecommunications Network Management into the 21st Century*. IEEE Press, Los Alamitos, CA, 1994.

[Bal96]   K. Bala et al. WDM network economics. In *Proceedings of National Fiber Optic Engineers Conference*, pages 163–174, 1996.

[Bel95]   Bellcore. *Network equipment-building system (NEBS) generic equipment requirements*, 1995. GR-63-CORE.

[Car97]   R. Cardwell et al. WDM network economic sensitivities. In *Proceedings of National Fiber Optic Engineers Conference*, pages 105–116, 1997.

[DEM96]   F. Diner, H. Escobar, and K. Min. Optimum protection schemes for the multi-wavelength inter-office network: A comparative analysis. In *Proceedings of National Fiber Optic Engineers Conference*, pages 291–298, 1996.

[MP97]   S. Melle and M. Page. WDM planning and deployment considerations for optimizing network evolution. In *Proceedings of National Fiber Optic Engineers Conference*, pages 137–147, 1997.

[Red97]   G. B. Redifer. DWDM versus TDM in metro and long-haul applications. In *Proceedings of National Fiber Optic Engineers Conference*, pages 117–124, 1997.

[SC96]   L. Steinhorst and H. Calhoun. Alternatives for next-generation high-capacity networks. In *Proceedings of National Fiber Optic Engineers Conference*, pages 271–282, 1996.

[Sle97]   C. Sleath. Wavelength division multiplexing targets add/drop multiplexers and digital cross-connects. In *Proceedings of National Fiber Optic Engineers Conference*, pages 259–270, 1997.

14 chapter

Photonic Packet Switching

IN THIS CHAPTER, we study second-generation optical networks that are capable of providing *packet-switched service at the optical layer.* We call these networks *photonic packet-switching networks.* By this definition, note that we have already studied some types of networks that are capable of providing packet-switched services. For instance, the WDM broadcast and select networks of Chapter 7 can provide packet-switched services if either fast-tunable transmitters or receivers are present. Of course, packet-switched services are provided using electronic switches today by many networks, including the Internet and ATM networks. We are interested in networks where the switching functions are performed *optically.* As we discussed in Chapter 1, the goal of photonic packet-switched networks is to provide the same services that electronic packet-switched networks provide, but at much higher speeds.

In contrast, the WDM broadcast and select networks, in the absence of fast-tunable transmitters and receivers, provide circuit-switched services. Likewise, the WDM wavelength routing networks of Chapter 8 also provide circuit-switched services. There we assumed that the switches inside the network route signals based only on the wavelength of the signals, and not based on any other information carried in the signal. Providing packet-switched services in these networks would require us to set up and take down a lightpath for each packet. For reasonable packet sizes, network bit rates and network geographical extents, a packet transmission time is much shorter than the time to set up a lightpath. Thus provisioning packet-switched services by means of lightpaths is an extremely inefficient way of utilizing network resources.

In this chapter, we will consider optical time division multiplexing (OTDM) photonic packet-switching networks. An example of such a network is one where the switches inside the network optically route packets based on information carried in the packet, such as its destination address. We will see as we explore further that, owing to various technological constraints, OTDM networks are at this time still in research laboratories and have not yet entered the commercial marketplace. For the near future, we envision that packet-switched service will be provided by electronic networks that may in turn use the (circuit-switched) lightpath service provided by WDM networks.

14.1 OTDM

OTDM is illustrated in Figure 14.1. Optical signals representing data streams from multiple sources are interleaved in time to produce a single data stream. The interleaving can be done on a bit-by-bit basis as shown in Figure 14.1(a). Assuming the data is sent in the form of packets, it can also be done on a packet-by-packet basis, as shown in Figure 14.1(b). If the packets are of fixed length, the recognition of packet boundaries is much simpler. In what follows, we will assume that fixed-length packets are used.

In both the bit-interleaved and the packet-interleaved case, *framing pulses* can be used. In the packet-interleaved case, framing pulses mark the boundary between packets. In the bit-interleaved case, if n input data streams are to be multiplexed, a framing pulse is used every n bits. As we will see later, these framing pulses will turn out to be very useful for demultiplexing individual packets from a multiplexed stream of packets.

Just like their WDM counterparts, OTDM networks can be based on a broadcast topology or incorporate optical switching. In the case of *broadcast OTDM networks*, the topology used is either a star or a bus. Those photonic packet-switching networks that incorporate photonic switching and routing will be referred to as *switch-based networks*.

In broadcast networks, there is no routing or switching within the network. Switching occurs only at the periphery of the network by means of tunable transmitters and receivers. Note that tunability in the case of TDM networks refers to the ability to select one of several time multiplexed streams. For example, in the case of bit-interleaved multiplexing, a tunable receiver, in each tuning state, will be able to receive a fixed time slot in every frame. The switch-based networks perform routing and switching functions *optically* within the network in order to provide packet-switched service at very high bit rates. The goal of photonic packet-switching networks is to provide packet-switched service at rates that would be infeasible

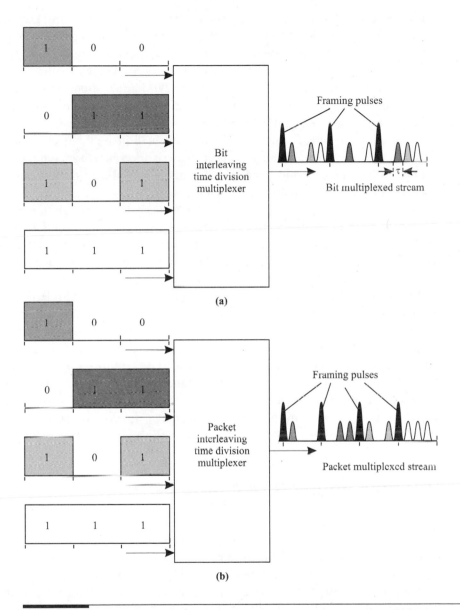

Figure 14.1 (a) Function of a bit-interleaved optical multiplexer. (b) Function of a packet-interleaved optical multiplexer. The same four data streams are multiplexed in both cases. In (b), the packet size is shown as 3 bits for illustration purposes only; in practice, packets are much larger. Note that the data must be compressed in time in both cases.

with electronic packet-switched networks. The tradeoffs between broadcast and switch-based photonic packet-switching networks are similar to the case of WDM networks. The broadcast networks suffer from large splitting losses, are not scalable, and are generally suitable only for LAN applications. The switch-based networks, on the other hand, are scalable and suited for WDM applications. However, they are also significantly more complex since they have to perform many more tasks—and all of them optically—than the broadcast networks.

The outline of this chapter is as follows. We will first study techniques that are common to both broadcast and switch-based networks. First, both types of networks require techniques for optical multiplexing and demultiplexing data streams. We will consider both bit interleaving and packet interleaving. Both types of interleaving may be used in broadcast photonic packet-switching networks although, for reasons that will become clear later, bit interleaving is the preferred choice. Switch-based networks must use packet interleaving. Next, we will study *synchronization* techniques. Synchronization can be broadly defined as the process of aligning two signal streams. In photonic packet-switching networks, it refers either to the alignment of an incoming pulse stream and a locally available *clock* pulse stream or to the relative alignment of two incoming pulse streams. The first situation is more common in broadcast networks, and the second in switch-based networks. Synchronization can be achieved by delaying one stream with respect to the other. In this context, we will also study how tunable optical delays can be realized. After a brief description of broadcast networks, we will study in some detail the problems and techniques specific to switch-based networks. These include packet header recognition and deflection routing. Finally, we will survey the photonic packet-switching network testbed experiments that have been performed to date.

14.2 Multiplexing and Demultiplexing

At the inputs to the network, lower-speed data streams are multiplexed optically into a higher-speed stream, and at the outputs of the network, the lower-speed streams must be extracted from the higher-speed stream optically by means of a demultiplexing function. Functionally, optical TDM is identical to electronic TDM. The only difference is that the multiplexing and demultiplexing operations are performed entirely optically at high speeds. The typical aggregate rate in OTDM systems is of the order of 100 Gb/s, as we will see in Section 14.6.

Note from Figure 14.1 that very short pulses—much shorter than the bit interval of each of the multiplexed streams—must be used in OTDM systems. A periodic train of very short pulses with widths of the order of a few ps can be generated using a mode-locked laser, as described in Section 3.5.1. Since the pulses are very short, their frequency spectrum will be large. Therefore, unless some special care is taken, there will be significant pulse broadening due to the effects of chromatic dispersion. For this purpose, the *soliton pulses* we studied in Section 2.5 are usually used in OTDM systems.

As we have already seen, solitons can propagate for long distances without dispersion-induced broadening. But how do we shape the output of the mode-locked laser into the precise sech($\cdot$) shape of the soliton? It turns out that precise pulse shaping is not required to launch soliton pulses; almost any pulse shape gets transformed into the soliton pulse shape after propagating some distance through optical fiber. The only requirement is that the pulse should have the right peak power. The required peak power is inversely proportional to the pulse width and thus directly proportional to the bit rate of operation. Another interesting property of soliton pulses is that their shape-maintenance properties are true only if the soliton pulses are sufficiently isolated from each other. If this is not the case, soliton pulses interact with each other in an undesirable manner. In a digital communication system, the soliton pulse must occupy only a small fraction of the bit interval so that it is sufficiently isolated from the pulse, if any, in the adjacent bit interval. Thus soliton communication systems use the short pulse format discussed in Section 4.1.1.

Assume that n data streams are to be multiplexed and the bit period of each of these streams is T. Also assume that framing pulses are used. Then the interpulse width is $\tau = T/(n+1)$, because $n+1$ pulses (including the framing pulse) must be transmitted in each bit period. Thus the temporal width τ_p of each (soliton) pulse must satisfy $\tau_p \le \tau$. Note that usually $\tau_p < \tau$ so that there is some guard time between successive pulses. One purpose of this guard time is to provide for some tolerance in the multiplexing and demultiplexing operations. Another reason is to prevent the undesirable interaction between adjacent soliton pulses that we discussed earlier.

14.2.1   Bit Interleaving

We will first study how the bit interleaving multiplexing illustrated in Figure 14.1(a) can be performed optically. This operation is illustrated in Figure 14.2. The periodic pulse train generated by a mode-locked laser is split, and one copy is created for each data stream to be multiplexed. The pulse train for the ith data stream, $i = 1, 2, \ldots, n$ is delayed by $i\tau$. This delay can be achieved by passing the pulse train through the appropriate length of optical fiber. Since the velocity of light in silica fiber is about 2×10^8 m/s, one meter of fiber provides a delay of about 5 ns. Thus the delayed pulse streams are nonoverlapping in time. The undelayed pulse stream is used for the framing pulses. Each data stream is used to externally modulate the appropriately delayed periodic pulse stream. The outputs of the external modulator and the framing

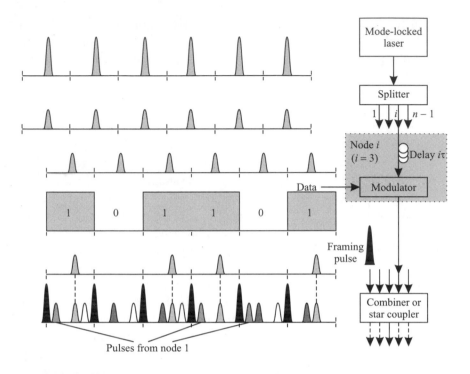

Figure 14.2   An optical multiplexer to create the bit-interleaved TDM stream shown in Figure 14.1(a). Only the operations at one node (node 3) are shown (after [Mid93], Chapter 6).

pulse stream are combined to obtain the bit-interleaved optical TDM stream. The power level of the framing pulses is chosen to be distinctly higher than that of the data pulses. This will turn out to be useful in demultiplexing, as we will see. In the case of broadcast networks with a star topology, the combining operation is naturally performed by the star coupler.

The corresponding demultiplexing operation is illustrated in Figure 14.3. The multiplexed input is split into two streams using, say, a 3-dB coupler. If the jth stream from the multiplexed stream is to be extracted, one of these streams is delayed by $j\tau$. A thresholding operation is performed on the delayed stream to extract the framing pulses. The reason the framing pulses were multiplexed with higher power than the other pulses was to facilitate this thresholding operation. Note that owing to the induced delay the extracted framing pulses coincide with the pulses in the undelayed stream that correspond to the data stream to be demultiplexed. A logical AND operation between the framing pulse stream and the multiplexed pulse stream

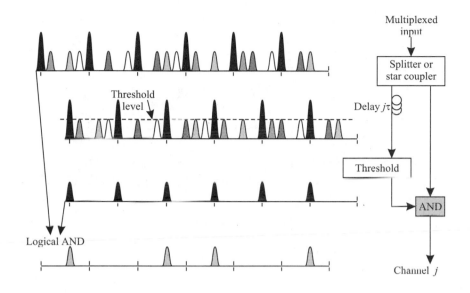

Figure 14.3   An optical demultiplexer to extract one of the multiplexed channels from a bit-interleaved TDM stream (after [Mid93], Chapter 6).

is used to extract the jth stream. The output of the *logical AND gate* is a pulse if, during a pulse interval, both inputs have pulses; the output has no pulse otherwise. We will discuss two devices to perform the logical AND operation in Section 14.2.3: a *nonlinear optical loop mirror (NOLM)* and a *soliton trapping gate.*

14.2.2   Packet Interleaving

We next consider how the packet interleaving operation shown in Figure 14.1(b) can be performed. This operation is illustrated in Figure 14.4(a). As in the case of bit interleaving, a periodic stream of narrow pulses is externally modulated by the data stream. If the bit interval is T, the separation between successive pulses is also T. We must somehow devise a scheme to reduce the interval between successive pulses to τ, corresponding to the higher-rate multiplexed signal. This can done by passing the output of the external modulator through a series of compression stages. If the size of each packet is l bits, the output goes through $k = \lceil \log_2 l \rceil$ compression stages. In the first compression stage, bits $1, 3, 5, 7, \ldots$, are delayed by $T - \tau$. In the second compression stage, the pairs of bits $(1, 2), (5, 6), (9, 10), \ldots$, are delayed by $2(T - \tau)$. In the third compression stage, the bits $(1, 2, 3, 4), (9, 10, 11, 12), \ldots$, are delayed by $4(T - \tau)$. The jth compression stage is shown in Figure 14.4(b). Each

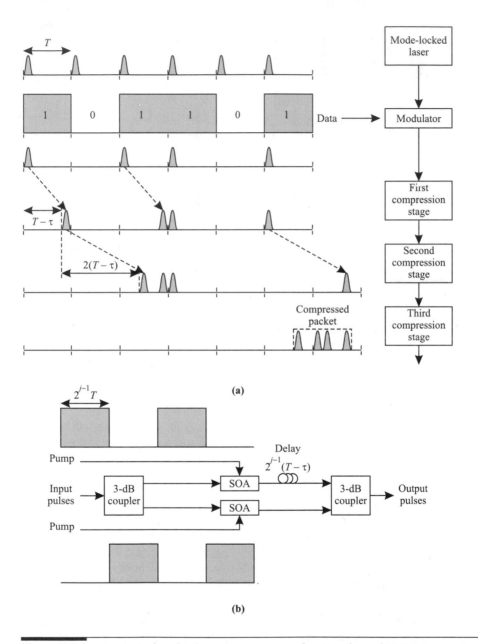

Figure 14.4   An optical multiplexer to create a packet-interleaved TDM stream. (a) The packet passes through k compression stages, where 2^k is the smallest power of two that is not smaller than the packet length l in bits. (b) Detailed view of compression stage j (after [SBP96]).

compression stage consists of a pair of 3-dB couplers, two semiconductor optical amplifiers (SOAs) used as on–off switches, and a delay line. The jth compression stage has a delay line of value $2^{j-1}(T - \tau)$. It is left as an exercise (Problem 14.1) to show that the delay encountered by pulse i, $i = 1, 2, \ldots, l$, on passing through the kth compression stage is $(2^k - i)(T - \tau)$. Combined with the fact that the input pulses are separated by time T, this implies that pulse i occurs at the output at time $(2^k - 1)(T - \tau) + (i - 1)\tau$. Thus the output pulses are separated by a time interval of τ.

The demultiplexing operation is equivalent to "decompressing" the packet. In principle, this can be accomplished by passing the compressed packet through a set of decompression stages that are similar to the compression stage shown in Figure 14.4(b). This approach is discussed in Problem 14.2. Again, the number of stages required would be $k = \log\lceil l \rceil$, where l is the packet length in bits. However, the on–off switches required in this approach must have switching times of the order of the pulse width τ, making this approach impractical for the small values of τ that are of interest in photonic packet-switching networks.

A more practical approach is to use a bank of AND gates, like the one used in Figure 14.3, and convert the single (serial) high-speed data stream into multiple (parallel) lower-speed data streams that can then be processed electronically. This approach is illustrated in Figure 14.5. In this figure, a bank of five AND gates is used to break up the incoming high-speed stream into five parallel streams each with five times the pulse spacing of the multiplexed stream. This procedure is identical to what would be used to receive five bit-interleaved data streams. One input to each AND gate is the incoming data stream, and the other input is a control pulse stream where the pulses are spaced five times apart. The control pulse streams to each AND gate are appropriately offset from each other so that they select different pulses. Thus the first parallel stream would contain bits $1, 6, 11, \ldots$, of the packet, the second would contain bits $2, 7, 12, \ldots$, and so on. This approach can also be used to demultiplex a portion of the packet, for example, the packet header. This is useful in switch-based networks for optical routing of packets at intermediate nodes in the network. We will discuss this issue further in Section 14.5.

14.2.3   Optical AND Gates

The logical AND operations shown in Figures 14.3 and 14.5 are performed optically at very high speeds. A number of mechanisms have been devised for this purpose. We describe two of them. Note that the logical AND operation between two signals can be performed by an on–off switch if one of the signals is input to the switch and the other is used to control it. This viewpoint will be useful in the following discussion.

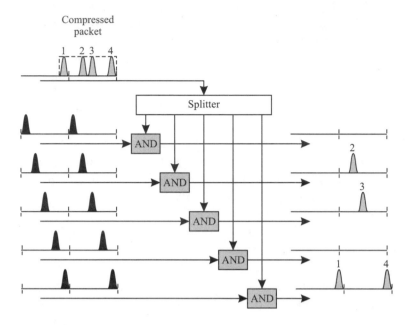

Figure 14.5   An optical demultiplexer to extract one of the multiplexed channels from a packet-interleaved TDM stream.

Nonlinear Optical Loop Mirror

The *nonlinear optical loop mirror* (NOLM) consists of a 3-dB directional coupler, a fiber loop connecting both outputs of the coupler, and a *nonlinear element* (NLE) located asymmetrically in the fiber loop, as shown in Figure 14.6(a). First, ignore the nonlinear element, and assume that a signal (pulse) is present at one of the inputs, shown as arm A of the directional coupler in Figure 14.6(a). Then, the two output signals are equal and undergo *exactly the same phase shift* on traversing the fiber loop. (Note that we are talking about the phase shift of the optical carrier here and not pulse delays.) We have seen in Problem 3.1 that in this case both the clockwise and the counterclockwise signals from the loop are completely reflected onto input A; specifically, no output pulse emerges from arm B in Figure 14.6(a). Hence the name fiber loop *mirror* for this configuration. However, if one of the signals were to undergo a different phase shift compared to the other, then an output pulse emerges from arm B in Figure 14.6(a). It is left as an exercise to show that the difference in the phase shifts should be π in order for all the energy to emerge from arm B (Problem 14.4).

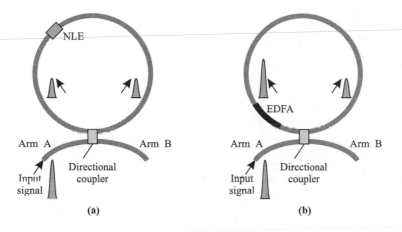

Figure 14.6   (a) A nonlinear optical loop mirror (NOLM). (b) A nonlinear amplifying loop mirror (NALM).

In many early experiments with the NOLM for the purpose of switching, there was no separate NLE; rather, the intensity-dependent phase (or refractive index) change induced by the silica fiber was itself used as the nonlinearity. This intensity-dependent refractive index change is described by (2.40) and is the basis for the cancellation of group velocity dispersion effects in the case of soliton pulses. We discussed this effect in Section 2.5. An example of such a configuration is shown in Figure 14.6(b), where the pulse traversing the fiber loop clockwise is amplified by an EDFA shortly after it leaves the directional coupler. Owing to the use of an amplifier within the loop, this configuration is called the *nonlinear amplifying loop mirror* (NALM). The amplified pulse has higher intensity and undergoes a larger phase shift on traversing the loop compared to the unamplified pulse.

However, these configurations are not convenient for using the NOLM as a high-speed demultiplexer. First, the intensity-dependent phase change in silica fiber is a weak nonlinearity, and typically, a few hundred meters of fiber are required in the loop to exploit this effect for pulse switching. It would be desirable to use a nonlinear effect that works with shorter lengths of fiber. Second, to realize an AND gate, we require an NLE whose nonlinear properties can be conveniently controlled by the use of control pulses. The configuration shown in Figure 14.7 has both these properties and is called the *terahertz optical asymmetric demultiplexer* (TOAD).

The principle of operation of the TOAD is as follows. The TOAD has another directional coupler spliced into the fiber loop for the purpose of injecting the control pulses. The control pulses carry sufficiently high power and energy so that the optical

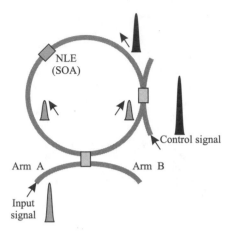

Figure 14.7   The terahertz optical asymmetric demultiplexer.

properties of the NLE are significantly altered by the control pulse for a short time interval after the control pulse passes through it. In particular, the phase shift undergone by another pulse passing through the NLE during this interval is altered. An example of a suitable NLE for this purpose is a semiconductor optical amplifier (SOA) that is driven into saturation by the control pulse. For proper operation of the TOAD as a demultiplexer, the timing between the control and signal pulses is critical. Assuming the NLE is located such that the clockwise signal pulse reaches it first, the control pulse must pass through the NLE *after* the clockwise signal pulse but *before* the counterclockwise signal pulse. If this happens, the clockwise signal pulse experiences the unsaturated gain of the amplifier, whereas the counterclockwise pulse sees the saturated gain. The latter also experiences an additional phase shift that arises due to gain saturation. Owing to this asymmetry, the two halves of the signal pulse do not completely destructively interfere with each other, and a part of the signal pulse emerges from arm B of the input coupler.

Note that along with the signal pulse, the control pulse will also be present at the output. This can be eliminated by using different wavelengths for the signal and control pulses and placing an optical filter at the output to select only the signal pulse. But both wavelengths must lie within the optical bandwidth of the SOA. Another option is to use orthogonal polarization states for the signal and control pulses, and discriminate between the pulses on this basis. Whether this is done or not, the polarization state of the signal pulse must be maintained while traversing the fiber loop; otherwise, the two halves of the pulse will not interfere at the directional coupler in the desired manner after traversing the fiber loop. Another advantage of the TOAD is that because of the short length of the fiber loop, the polarization state of the pulses is maintained even if standard single-mode fiber (nonpolarization maintaining) is used. If the fiber loop is long, it must be constructed using polarization-maintaining fiber.

Soliton-Trapping AND Gate

The soliton-trapping AND gate uses some properties of soliton pulses propagating in a birefringent fiber. In Chapter 2, we saw that in a normal fiber, the two orthogonally polarized degenerate modes propagate with the same group velocity. We also saw that in a birefringent fiber, these two modes propagate with different group velocities. As a result, if two pulses at the same wavelength but with orthogonal polarizations are launched in a birefringent fiber, they would *walk off*, or spread apart in time, owing to this difference in group velocities. However, soliton pulses are an exception to this walk-off phenomenon. Just as soliton pulses propagate in nonbirefringent silica fiber without pulse spreading due to group velocity dispersion (Section 2.5), a pair of orthogonally polarized soliton pulses propagate in birefringent fiber without walk-off. The quantitative analysis of this phenomenon is beyond the scope of this book, but qualitatively what occurs is that the two pulses undergo wavelength shifts in opposite directions so that the group velocity difference due to the wavelength shift exactly compensates the group velocity difference due to birefringence! Since the two soliton pulses travel together (don't walk off), this phenomenon is called *soliton trapping*.

The logical AND operation between two pulse streams can be achieved using this phenomenon if the two pulse streams correspond to orthogonally polarized soliton pulses. Most high-speed TDM systems use soliton pulses to minimize the effects of group velocity dispersion so that the soliton pulse shape requirement is not a problem. The orthogonal polarization of the two pulse streams can be achieved by appropriately using polarizers (see Section 3.2.1). The logical AND operation is achieved by using an optical filter at the output of the birefringent fiber.

Figure 14.8 shows the block diagram of such a soliton-trapping AND gate. It consists of a piece of birefringent fiber followed by an optical filter. Figure 14.9

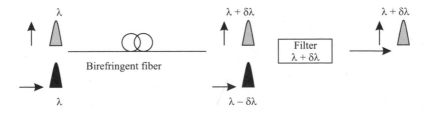

Figure 14.8 Block diagram of a soliton-trapping logical AND gate.

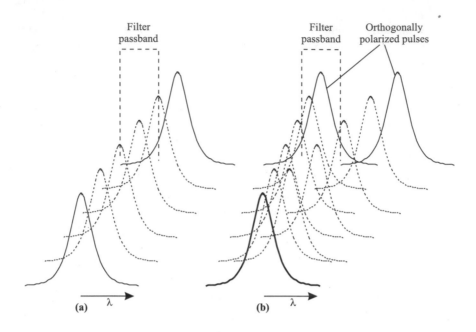

Figure 14.9 Illustration of the operation of a soliton-trapping logical AND gate. In (a) only one pulse is present, and very little energy passes through to the filter output. This state corresponds to a logical zero. In (b) both pulses are present, undergo wavelength shifts due to the soliton-trapping phenomenon, and most of the energy from one pulse passes through to the filter output. This state corresponds to a logical one.

illustrates the operation of this gate. When pulses of both polarizations are present at the wavelength λ, one of them gets shifted in wavelength to $\lambda + \delta\lambda$, and the other to $\lambda - \delta\lambda$. The filter is chosen so that it passes the signal at $\lambda + \delta\lambda$ and rejects the signal at λ. Thus the passband of the filter is such that one of the wavelength-shifted pulses lies within it. But the same pulse, if it does not undergo a wavelength shift, will not be selected by the filter. Thus the filter output has a pulse (logical one) only if both pulses are present at the input, and no pulse (logical zero), otherwise.

14.3 Synchronization

Synchronization is the process of aligning two pulse streams in time. In photonic packet-switching networks, it can refer either to the alignment of an incoming pulse stream and a locally available *clock* pulse stream or to the relative alignment of two incoming pulse streams. The function of a synchronizer can be understood

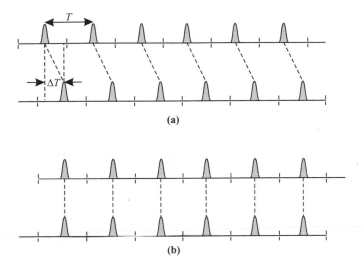

Figure 14.10 The function of a synchronizer. In (a), the two periodic pulse streams with period T are out of synchronization; the top stream is ahead by ΔT. In (b), the two periodic streams have been synchronized by introducing a delay ΔT in the top stream relative to the bottom stream.

from Figure 14.10. The two periodic pulse streams, with period T, shown in Figure 14.10(a) are not synchronized because the top stream is ahead in time by ΔT. In Figure 14.10(b), the two pulse streams are synchronized. Thus to achieve synchronization, the top stream must be delayed by ΔT with respect to the bottom stream. The delays we have hitherto considered, for example, while studying optical multiplexers and demultiplexers, have been *fixed* delays. A fixed delay can be achieved by using a fiber of the appropriate length. However, in the case of a synchronizer, and in some other applications in photonic packet-switching networks, a *tunable delay* element is required since the amount of delay that has to be introduced is not known *a priori*. Thus we will now study how tunable optical delays can be realized.

14.3.1 Tunable Delays

A tunable optical delay line capable of realizing any delay, in excess of a reference delay, from 0 to $T - 2^{-k}$, in steps of 2^{-k}, is shown in Figure 14.11. The parameter k controls the resolution of the delay achievable. The delay line consists of $k - 1$ fixed delays with values $T/2, T/4, \ldots, T/2^{k-1}$ interconnected by k 2×2 optical switches, as shown. By appropriately setting the switches in the cross or bar state, an input

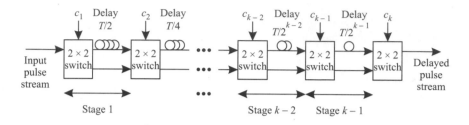

Figure 14.11 A tunable delay line capable of realizing any delay from 0 to $T - 2^{-k}$, in steps of 2^{-k}.

pulse stream can be made to encounter or avoid each of these fixed delays. If all the fixed delays are encountered, the total delay suffered by the input pulse stream is $T/2 + T/4 + \ldots + T/2^{k-1} = T - 2^{-k}$. This structure can be viewed as consisting of $k - 1$ stages followed by an output switch, as indicated in Figure 14.11. The output switch is used to ensure that the output pulse stream always exits the same output of this switch. The derivation of the control inputs $c_1, c_2, \ldots, c_k$ to the k switches is discussed in Problem 14.3.

With a tunable delay line like the one shown in Figure 14.11, two pulse streams can be synchronized to within a time interval of $T/2^k$. The value k, and thus the number of fixed delays and optical switches, must be chosen such that $2^{-k}T \ll \tau$, the pulse width.

Given a tunable delay, the synchronization problem reduces to one of determining the relative delay, or *phase*, between two pulse streams. A straightforward approach to this problem is to compare all shifted versions of one stream with respect to the other. The comparison can be performed by means of a logical AND operation. This is a somewhat expensive approach. An alternative approach is to use an optical *phase lock loop* to sense the relative delay between the two pulse streams. Just as more than one phenomenon can be used to build an optical AND gate, different mechanisms can be used to develop an optical phase lock loop. We discuss one such mechanism that is based on the NOLM that we studied in Section 14.2.3.

14.3.2 Optical Phase Lock Loop

Consider a NOLM that does not use a separate nonlinear element but rather uses the intensity-dependent refractive index of silica fiber itself as the nonlinearity. Thus if a low-power pulse stream, say, stream 1, is injected into the loop—from arm A of the directional coupler in Figure 14.6(a)—the fiber nonlinearity is not excited, and both the clockwise and the counterclockwise propagating pulses undergo the same phase shift in traversing the loop. As a consequence, no power emerges from the output (arm B) in this case. If a high-power pulse stream, say, stream 2, is injected *in phase* (no relative delay) with, say, the clockwise propagating pulse stream, owing to the intensity dependence of the refractive index of silica fiber, the refractive index seen by the clockwise pulse, and hence the phase shift undergone by it, is different from that of the counterclockwise pulse. This mismatch in the phase shift causes an output to emerge from arm B in Figure 14.6(a). Note that if the high-power pulse stream is not in phase (has a nonzero relative delay) with the clockwise propagating pulse stream, the clockwise and counterclockwise pulses undergo the same phase shift, and no output emerges from arm B of the directional coupler. To achieve synchronization between pulse streams 1 and 2, a tunable delay element can be used to adjust their relative delays till there is no output of stream 1 from the NOLM.

Note that the same problem of discriminating between the pulse streams 1 and 2 at the output of the directional coupler (arm B) as with the TOAD arises in this case as well. Since pulses from stream 2 will always be present at the output, in order to detect the absence of pulses from stream 1, the two streams must use different wavelengths or polarizations. When different wavelengths are used, owing to the chromatic dispersion of the fiber, the two pulses will tend to walk away from each other, and the effect of the nonlinearity (intensity-dependent refractive index) will be reduced. To overcome this effect, the two wavelengths can be chosen to lie symmetrically on either side of the zero dispersion wavelength of the fiber so that the group velocities of the two pulse streams are equal.

A phase lock loop can also be used to adjust the *frequency and phase* of a local clock source—a mode-locked laser—to those of an incoming periodic stream. We have seen in Section 3.5.1 that the repetition rate, or frequency, of a mode-locked laser can be determined by modulating the gain of the laser cavity. We assume that the modulation frequency of its gain medium, and hence the repetition rate of the pulses, is governed by the frequency of an electrical oscillator. The output of the NOLM can then be photodetected and used to control the frequency and phase of this electrical oscillator so that the pulses generated by the local mode-locked laser are at the same frequency and phase as that of the incoming pulse stream. We refer to [Bar96] and the references therein for the details.

14.4 Broadcast OTDM Networks

Although OTDM networks can be based on a star or a bus topology, in this section, we assume the topology is a star. In a star-based network, all the nodes are connected by a pair of optical fibers to a central star coupler, just like the networks in Chapter 7. First consider the case of bit interleaving. For a network of n nodes, assuming framing bits are used, each TDM frame consists of at least $n + 1$ bits: one bit for each node plus a framing bit. The operations performed at each node for transmission of data are as shown in Figure 14.2. The combining operation shown in this figure is now done by the star coupler. The demultiplexing operation performed at each receiver is as depicted in Figure 14.3, with the splitting operation being performed by the star coupler itself. Assuming each node has only one receiver, it can receive only one bit in each frame. Thus just like broadcast WDM networks, a multichannel media-access protocol will be required so that nodes can decide how to tune (among the bits in each frame) their transmitters and receivers. The need for a multichannel media-access protocol is eliminated if packet interleaving is used; however, a single-channel media-access protocol will still be required.

Although star networks have better link budget characteristics than bus networks, bus networks offer a natural ordering of the nodes that makes synchronization and designing a media-access control protocol at these high speeds somewhat easier. Broadcast networks were explored before switch-based networks, but they suffer from the same problems as WDM broadcast and select networks, including the splitting loss and the lack of spatial reuse of capacity. Most of the recent research has thus focused on developing switch-based networks.

14.5 Switch-Based Networks

The packet-switched networks of today are all electronic and one of two types. The first type of network is based on a broadcast topology, and a media-access protocol is required in order to share the bandwidth of the broadcast medium. Networks such as ethernets, token rings, and FDDI belong to this category. The broadcast and select networks we studied in Chapter 7 and the broadcast photonic packet-switching networks discussed in this chapter are the optical analogs of these networks. The second type of electronic packet-switched network is based on an arbitrary mesh topology and is called a *store and forward* network. The ATM and IP networks of today are of this type.

A generic example of a store and forward packet-switched network is shown in Figure 14.12. In this network, the nodes A–F are the switching/routing nodes; the *end-nodes* 1–6 are the sources and sinks of packet data. We will assume that all packets are of fixed length. Packets sent by an end-node will, in general, traverse multiple links and hence multiple routing nodes, before they reach their destination end-node. For example, if node 1 has to send a packet to node 6, there are several possible routes that it can take, all consisting of multiple links and routing nodes. If the route chosen for this packet is 1–A–B–D–F–6, this packet traverses the links 1–A, A–B, B–D, D–F, and F–6. The routing nodes traversed are A, B, D, and F.

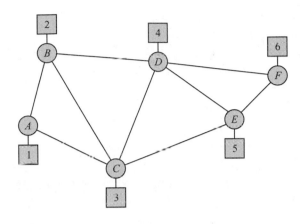

Figure 14.12 A generic store and forward network.

Note that the route chosen may be specified by the packet itself, or the packet may simply specify only the destination node and leave the choice of route to the routing nodes in its path. In the remainder of the discussion, we will assume that the route is chosen by the routing nodes based on the packet destination that is carried in the packet header.

Figure 14.12 is also the block diagram of a switch-based photonic packet-switching network. The major difference is that the links run at very high speeds (100s of Gb/s) and the signals are handled entirely optically within each routing node.

14.5.1 Functions of a Routing Node

Let us now understand how the routing and switching of signals is accomplished optically within a routing node. A block diagram depicting the functions of a routing node is shown in Figure 14.13. Only two inputs and outputs are shown for clarity. In general, there is one input from, and one output to, each other routing node and end-node that this routing node is connected to by a link. For example, in Figure 14.12, routing node A has three inputs and outputs: from/to routing node B, routing node C, and end-node 1. Similarly, routing node C has five inputs and outputs. We now study the functions performed by a routing node in the case of photonic packet-switching networks.

Synchronization

The two incoming packet streams must first be synchronized. Recall our assumption of fixed size packets. Thus if framing pulses are used to mark the packet boundaries,

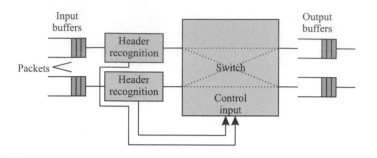

Figure 14.13   A two-input, two-output routing node in the network of Figure 14.12.

the framing pulses must occur periodically. Synchronization can be carried out by delaying one stream with respect to the other, as discussed in Section 14.3.

Header Recognition

For a header of fixed size, the time taken for demultiplexing and processing the header is fixed, and the remainder of the packet is buffered optically using a delay line of appropriate length. The processing of the header bits may be done electronically or optically, depending on the kind of control input required by the switch. Electrically controlled switches employing the electro-optic effect and fabricated in lithium niobate (see Section 3.7) are most commonly used in switch-based network experiments today. In this case, the header processing can be carried out electronically (after the header bits have been demultiplexed into a parallel stream). The packet destination information from the header is used to determine the outgoing link from the switch for this packet, using a look-up table. If the switch has two inputs and outputs, as shown in Figure 14.13, the look-up table determines, *for each input packet*, whether the switch should be set in the cross state or bar state. Of course, this leads to a conflict if both inputs have a packet destined for the same output. This is one of the reasons for having buffers in the routing node, as explained next.

If the destination address is carried in the packet header, it can be read by demultiplexing the header bits using a bank of AND gates, for example, TOADs, as shown in Figure 14.5. However, this is a relatively expensive way of reading the header, which is a task that is easier done with electronics than with optics. With this in mind, several techniques have been proposed to simplify the task of header recognition. One common technique is to transmit the header at a much lower bit rate than the packet itself, allowing the header to be received and processed relatively easily within the routing node. The packet header could also be transmitted on a wavelength that is different from the packet data. It could also be transmitted on a separate subcarrier channel on the same wavelength. All these methods allow the header to be carried at a lower bit rate than the high-speed data in the packet, allowing for easier header recognition.

Buffering

In general, a routing node contains buffers to *store* the packets from the incoming links before they can be transmitted or *forwarded* on the outgoing links. Hence the name *store and forward* for these networks. In a general store and forward network, electronic or optical, the buffers may be present at the inputs only, at the outputs only, or at both the inputs and the outputs, as shown in Figure 14.13. The buffers may also be integrated within the switch itself. This option is used quite often in the case of electronic networks where both the memory and switch fabric are fabricated on the same substrate, say, a silicon-integrated circuit. This is unlikely to be practical, or even feasible, in photonic packet-switching networks since the memory typically consists of relatively long lengths of fiber (20 cm/ns), whereas the switch fabric is made in an integrated-optics substrate such as lithium niobate.

There are at least three reasons for having to store or buffer a packet before it is forwarded on its outgoing link. First, the incoming packet must be buffered while the packet header is processed to determine how the packet must be routed. Second, the required switch input and/or output port may not be free, causing the packet to be queued at its input buffer. The switch input may not be free because other packets that arrived on the same link have to be served earlier. The switch output port may not be free because packets from other input ports are being switched to it. Third, after the packet has been switched to the required output port, the outgoing link from this port may be busy transmitting other packets, thus making this packet wait for its turn. In the case of photonic packet-switching networks, buffers are scarce resources. The best known way to construct an optical buffer is to use a piece of optical fiber and delay the signal within it. Thus usually very small buffers are used in photonic packet-switching networks. Note that unlike an electronic buffer, a packet cannot be accessed at an arbitrary point of time; it can exit the buffer only after a fixed time interval after entering it. This is the time taken for the packet to traverse the fiber length. This constraint must be incorporated into the design of photonic packet-switching networks. Of course, by repeated traversals of the same piece of fiber, packet delays that are multiples of this basic delay can be obtained. Buffering while processing the packet header is essential, and photonic packet-switching networks try to avoid buffers except for this purpose. We will now see how other buffers are avoided in photonic packet-switching networks.

In photonic packet-switching networks, the switch operates at the speed of the input and output links (assumed to be equal), but usually not faster. This means that the packets arrive to the output links from the switch no faster than the rate at which they can be transmitted on the output links. Thus the packets are transmitted immediately on arrival, and no buffering at the output links is necessary. Consider the 2×2 switch shown in Figure 14.13. At the same time, if both inputs have a packet for the same output, only one of them can be transmitted by the switch immediately since the switch runs at the same speed as the input links. There are three options in this case. The first option is for the packet to wait, which necessitates an input buffer beyond what is needed merely for packet header recognition. This is expensive. The second option is for the packet to be dropped. This is not attractive because such events will occur quite often unless the links are occupied by very few packets compared to their capacities. For each such event, the source must retransmit the packet causing the effective link utilization to drop even farther. The third option is for the packet to be *misrouted* by the switch, that is, transferred by the switch to the *wrong output*. This option, termed *deflection routing,* has received considerable study in the research literature on photonic packet-switching networks.

14.5.2 Deflection Routing

Deflection routing was invented by Baran in 1964 [Bar64]. It was studied and implemented in the context of processor interconnection networks in the 1980s [Hil85, Hil87, Smi81]. In these networks, just as in photonic packet-switching networks, buffers are expensive owing to the high transmission speeds involved, and deflection routing is used as an alternative to buffering. Deflection routing is also sometimes called *hot-potato* routing.

Intuitively, misrouting packets rather than storing them will cause packets to take longer paths on average to get to their destinations, and thus will lead to increased delays and lesser throughput in the network. This is the price paid for not having buffers at the switches. These tradeoffs have been analyzed in detail for regular network topologies such as the Manhattan Street network [GG93], an example of which is shown in Figure 14.14, or the shufflenet [KH90, AS92], which was discussed in Section 9.4.1, or both [Max89, FBP95]. Regular topologies are typically used for processor interconnections and may be feasible to implement in LANs. However, they are unlikely to be used in WANs, where the topologies used are usually arbitrary. We have already discussed this issue in the context of virtual topology design in Section 9.4. Nevertheless, these analyses shed considerable light on the issues involved in the implementation of deflection routing even in wide-area photonic packet-switching networks and the resulting performance degradation, compared to buffering in the event of a destination conflict.

Before we can discuss these results, we need to slightly modify the model of the routing node shown in Figure 14.13. While discussing this figure earlier, we said that the routing node has one input link and output link from/to every other routing node

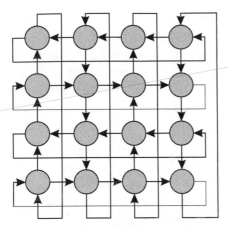

Figure 14.14 The Manhattan Street network with $4^2 = 16$ nodes. In a network with n^2 nodes, these nodes are arranged in a square grid with n rows and columns. Each node transmits to two nodes—one in the same row and another in the same column. Each node also receives from two other nodes—one in the same row and the other in the same column. Assuming n is even, the direction of transmission alternates in successive rows and columns.

and end-node to which it is connected. In many cases, the end-node is colocated with the routing node so that information regarding packets to be transmitted or received can be almost instantaneously exchanged between these nodes. In particular, this makes it possible for the end-node to inject a new packet into its associated routing node, *only when* no other packet is intended for the same output link. Thus this new injected packet neither gets deflected nor causes deflection of other packets. This is a reasonable assumption to make in practice.

Delay

The first consequence of deflection routing is that the average delay experienced by the packets in the network is larger than in store and forward networks. In this comparison, not only is the network topology fixed but the statistics of the packet arrivals between each source–destination pair is also fixed. In particular, the rate of injection of new packets into the network, which is called the *arrival rate,* for each source–destination pair must be fixed. The delay experienced by a packet consists of two components. The first is the *queuing delay,* which is the time spent waiting in the buffers at each routing node for transmission. There is no queuing delay in the case of deflection routing. The second component of the delay experienced by a packet is the *propagation delay,* which is the time taken for the packet to traverse all the links from the source node to the destination node. The propagation delay is often larger for deflection routing than for routing with buffers owing to the misdirection of packets away from their destinations. This increased propagation delay almost always more than compensates for the lack of queuing delay in deflection-routed networks so that the total average delay is higher for the same arrival rate.

Throughput

Another consequence of deflection routing is that the *throughput* of the network is decreased compared to routing with buffers. An informal definition of the throughput of these networks, which will suffice for our purposes here, is that it is the maximum rate at which *new* packets can be injected into the network from their sources. Clearly, this depends on the interconnection topology of the network and the data rates on the links. In addition, it depends on the *traffic pattern,* which must remain fixed in defining the throughput. The traffic pattern specifies the fraction of new packets for each source–destination pair. Typically, in all theoretical analyses of such networks, the throughput is evaluated for a *uniform traffic pattern,* which means that the arrival rates of new packets for all source–destination pairs in the network are equal. If all the links run at the same speed, the throughput can be conveniently expressed as a fraction of the link speed.

For Manhattan Street networks with sizes ranging from a few hundred to a few thousand nodes, deflection routing achieves 55–70% of the throughput achieved by routing with buffering [Max89]. For shufflenets in the same range of sizes, the value is only 20–30% of the throughput with buffers. However, since a shufflenet has a much higher throughput than a Manhattan Street network of the same size (for routing with buffers), the actual throughput of the Manhattan Street network in the case of deflection routing is lower than that of the shufflenet. All these results assume a uniform traffic pattern.

So what do these results imply for irregular networks? To discuss this, let us examine some of the differences in the properties of these two networks. One important property of any network is its *diameter,* which is the largest number of hops on the shortest path between any two nodes in the network. In other words, the diameter is the *maximum* number of hops between two nodes in the network. However, in most networks, the larger the diameter, the more the number of hops that a packet has to travel even *on average* to get to its destination. The Manhattan Street network has a diameter that is proportional to $\sqrt{n}$, where n is the number of nodes in the network. On the other hand, the shufflenet has a diameter that is proportional to $\log_2 n$. (We consider shufflenets of degree 2.) Thus if we consider a Manhattan Street network and a shufflenet with the same number of nodes and edges, the Manhattan Street network will have a lower throughput for routing with buffers than the shufflenet, since each packet has to traverse more edges, on the average. For arbitrary networks, we can generalize this and say that the smaller the diameter of the network, the larger the throughput for routing with buffers.

For deflection routing, a second property of the network that we must consider is its *deflection index*. This property was introduced in [Max89] though it was not called by this name. It was formally defined and discussed in greater detail in a later paper [GG93]. The *deflection index* is the largest number of hops that a single deflection adds to the shortest path between some two nodes in the network. In the Manhattan Street network, a single deflection adds at most four hops to the path length so that its deflection index is four. On the other hand, the shufflenet has a deflection index of $\log_2 n$ hops. This accounts for the fact that the Manhattan Street network has a significantly larger *relative* throughput—fraction of the store and forward throughput—than the shufflenet (55–70% versus 20–30%). For arbitrary networks, we can then say that the deflection index must be kept small so that the throughput remains high in the face of deflection routing.

Combining the two observations, we can conclude that network topologies with small diameters and small deflection indices are best suited for photonic packet-switching networks. A regular topology designed by combining the Manhattan Street and shufflenet topologies and having these properties is discussed in [GG93]. In addition to choosing a good network topology (not necessarily regular), the performance of deflection-routing networks can be further improved by using appropriate *deflection rules*. A *deflection rule* specifies the manner in which the packets to be deflected are chosen among the packets contending for the same switch output port. The results we have quoted assume that in the event of a conflict between two packets, both packets are equally likely to be deflected. This deflection rule is termed *random*. Another possible deflection rule, called *closest-to-finish* [GG93], states that when two packets are contending for the same output port, the packet that is farther away from its destination is deflected. This has the effect of reducing the average number of deflections suffered by a packet and thus increasing the throughput.

Small Buffers

Deflection routing, which uses no buffers except for packet header processing, is also called *hot-potato* routing. We leave it to the reader to guess the origin of this interesting term. We can also consider deflection routing with a very limited number of buffers, for example, buffers of one or two packets at each input port. If this limited buffer is full, the packet is again deflected. Such limited-buffer deflection-routing strategies achieve higher throughputs than hot-potato routing. We refer to [Max89, FBP95] for the quantitative details.

Livelock

When a network employs deflection routing, there is the possibility that a packet will be deflected forever and never reach its destination. This phenomenon has been called both *deadlock* [GG93] and *livelock* [LNGP96], but the term *livelock* seems to be more appropriate. Livelock can be eliminated by suitably designed deflection rules. However, proving that any particular deflection rule is livelock-free seems to be hard. We refer to [GG93, BDG95] for some further discussion of this issue (under the term *deadlock*). One way to eliminate livelocks is to simply drop packets that have exceeded a certain threshold on the hop-count.

14.5.3 Feed-Forward and Feedback Delay Lines

In our discussion of deflection routing, we remarked that the throughput and delay performance of a photonic packet-switching network can be significantly improved by the addition of a small number of buffers at each node. Although we will not undertake an evaluation of the achievable performance gains, we describe two principal ways in which the capability of buffering a few packets can be incorporated into an optical routing node. These two methods are illustrated in Figures 14.15 and 14.16, respectively. In both figures, a routing node with two inputs and two outputs is shown. We assume time is divided into slots where each slot holds one packet.

In the *feed-forward* architecture of Figure 14.15, a two-input, two-output routing node is constructed using three 2×2 switches interconnected by two delay lines. If each delay line can store one packet—that is, the propagation time through the delay line is equal to one slot—the routing node has a buffering capacity of two packets. If packets destined for the same output arrive simultaneously at both inputs, one packet will be routed to its correct output, and the other packet will be stored in delay line 1. This can be accomplished by setting switch 1 in the appropriate state. This packet then has the opportunity to be routed to its desired output in a subsequent slot. For example, if no packets arrive in the next slot, this stored packet can be routed to its desired output in the next slot by setting switches 2 and 3 appropriately.

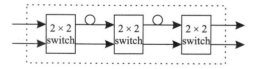

Figure 14.15   Example of a 2×2 routing node using a feed-forward delay line architecture.

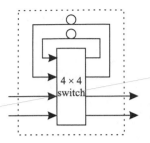

Figure 14.16   Example of a 2 × 2 routing node using a feedback delay line architecture.

In the *feedback* architecture of Figure 14.16, the delay lines connect the outputs of the switch to its inputs. With two delay lines, the switch is internally a 4 × 4 switch with two inputs from outside and two from the delay lines. Again, if two packets contend for a single output, one of them can be stored in a delay line. If the delay line has length equal to one slot, the stored packet has an opportunity to be routed to its desired output in the next slot. If there is contention again, it, or the contending packet, can be stored for another slot in a delay line.

In the feed-forward architecture, a packet has a fixed number of opportunities to reach its desired output. For example, in the routing node shown in Figure 14.15, the packet has at most three opportunities to be routed to its correct destination: in its arriving slot and the immediately next two slots. On the other hand, in the feedback architecture, it appears that a packet can be stored indefinitely. This is not true in practice since photonic switches have several dB of loss so that the same packet cannot be routed through a switch more than a few times. In practice, the feed-forward architecture is preferred to the feedback architecture since it attenuates the signals almost equally, regardless of the path taken through the routing node. This is because almost all the loss is in passing through the switches, and in this architecture, every packet passes through the same number of switches independent of the delay it experiences. This *low differential loss* characteristic is important in a network since it reduces the dynamic range of the signals that must be handled.

14.6 OTDM Testbeds

Several optical TDM testbeds have been built over the last few years, and many are being built today. The main focus of most of these testbeds is the demonstration of certain key optical TDM network functions such as multiplexing and demultiplexing, routing/switching, header recognition, optical clock recovery (synchronization or

Table 14.1 Key features of OTDM testbeds described in Section 14.6. Many of these testbeds are still under development at the time of this writing, and in a few cases, some of the functions listed are yet to be demonstrated.

Testbed	Topology	Bit Rate	Functions Demonstrated
ATMOS	Switch	2.5 Gb/s (per port)	4 × 4 routing node, subnanosecond switching, all-optical wavelength conversion
Synchrolan (BT Labs)	Bus	40 Gb/s (aggregate)	Bit-interleaved data transmission and reception
BT Labs	Switch	100 Gb/s (per port)	Routing in a 1 × 2 switch based on optical header recognition
Princeton	Switch	100 Gb/s (per port)	Packet compression, TOAD-based demultiplexing
AON	Helix (bus)	100 Gb/s (aggregate)	Optical phase lock loop, pulse generation, compression, storage
CORD	Star	2.5 Gb/s (per port)	Contention resolution
TBONE	Crossbar	(various) (plus analog)	Different control mechanisms

bit-phase alignment), pulse generation, pulse compression, and pulse storage. We will discuss some of these testbeds in the remainder of this section. The key features of these testbeds are summarized in Table 14.1.

14.6.1 ATMOS

The *asynchronous transfer mode optical switching* (ATMOS) project [Mas96] was jointly undertaken by 11 laboratories in Europe. The main goal of this project was to develop optical ATM switching capabilities so that the ATM network architecture we briefly discussed in Section 6.3.2 could be extended to very high speeds. Thus their aim was to demonstrate an optical store and forward routing node of the type discussed in Section 14.5. This testbed used a combination of WDM and TDM, and the switches inside the network routed packets based on their wavelength and other information carried in the packet, such as its destination address. Thus the routing nodes were somewhat different from the ones based only on optical TDM that we described in this chapter. Most of the cell-routing demonstrations were carried out at a bit rate of 2.5 Gb/s. At the functional level, routing nodes of size up to 4 × 4, based on a few different delay line architectures—both feed-forward and feedback—were fabricated and tested. At the component level, integrated-optic switches based on an

InP substrate and capable of switching at speeds of the order of 100–200 ps were fabricated. Among the switch types demonstrated were semiconductor optical amplifier gates, Mach-Zehnder interferometric switches, and directional coupler switches (see Section 3.7). Another significant achievement of this project was the development of all-optical wavelength converters based on carrier depletion in semiconductor optical amplifiers and lasers (see Section 3.8). Using these devices, wavelength conversion at a speed of 20 Gb/s was demonstrated.

14.6.2   BT Labs Testbeds

Recently, Researchers at British Telecom (BT) Laboratories demonstrated several aspects of both the broadcast and switch-based optical TDM networks [CLM97] that we discussed in this chapter. A prototype broadcast local-area network (LAN) based on a (single-folded) bus topology (see Figure 7.2) called *Synchrolan* [LGM+97, Gun97b] was demonstrated. Bit interleaving was used with each of the multiplexed channels operating at a bit rate of 2.5 Gb/s. The aggregate bit rate transmitted on the bus was 40 Gb/s. The clock signal (akin to a framing pulse) was distributed along with the bit-interleaved data channels. The availability of the clock signal meant that there was no need for optical clock recovery techniques. A separate time slot was not used for the clock signal, but rather it was transmitted with a polarization orthogonal to that of the data signals. This enabled the clock signal to be separated easily from the data. In a more recent demonstration [Gun97a], the data and clock signals were transmitted over two separate standard single-mode (nonpolarization-preserving) fibers, avoiding the need for expensive polarization-maintaining components.

A demonstration of a routing node in a switch-based photonic packet-switching network was also demonstrated separately at BT Labs [Cot95]. The optical header from an incoming packet was compared with the header—local address—corresponding to the routing node, using an optical AND gate (but of a different type than the ones we discussed). The rest of the packet was stored in a fiber delay line while the comparison was performed. The output of the AND gate was used to set a 1 × 2 switch so that the packet was delivered to one of two outputs based on a match, or lack of it, between the incoming packet header and the local address.

14.6.3   Princeton University Testbed

This testbed is currently being developed in the Lightwave Communications Laboratory at Princeton University, funded by DARPA [SBP96]. The goal is to demonstrate a single routing node in a network operating at a transmission rate of 100 Gb/s. Packet interleaving will be used, and packets from electronic sources at 1.25 Gb/s will be optically compressed to the 100 Gb/s rate using the techniques we described in Section 14.2. The limitations of the semiconductor optical amplifiers used in the packet compression process (Figure 14.4) require a 0.5 ns (50 bits at 100 Gb/s) guard band between successive packets. Optical demultiplexing of the compressed packet header is accomplished by a bank of AND gates, as described in Section 14.2. The TOAD architecture described in Section 14.2.3 is used for the AND gates. The number of TOADs to be used is equal to the length of the packet header. Thus the optically encoded *serial* packet header is converted to a parallel, electronic header by a bank of TOADs.

14.6.4 AON

This testbed is being developed by the All-Optical Network (AON) consortium consisting of AT&T Bell Laboratories, Digital Equipment Corporation, and the Massachusetts Institute of Technology, and is funded by DARPA [Bar96]. The aim is to develop an optical TDM LAN/MAN operating at an aggregate rate of 100 Gb/s using packet interleaving. Different classes of service, specifically *guaranteed bandwidth service* (class 1 traffic of Section 7.2.6) and *bandwidth-on-demand* service (class 3 traffic of Section 7.2.6) are proposed to be supported. The topology proposed to be used is shown in Figure 14.17. This is essentially a bus topology where users transmit in the top half of the bus and receive from the bottom half. One difference, however, is that each user is attached for transmission to two points on the bus such that the guaranteed bandwidth transmissions are always upstream from the bandwidth-on-demand transmissions. Thus the topology can be viewed as having the helical shape shown in Figure 14.17; hence the name *helical LAN* (HLAN) for this network.

Experiments that demonstrate an optical phase lock loop have been carried out. In these experiments, the frequency and phase of a 10 Gb/s electrically controlled

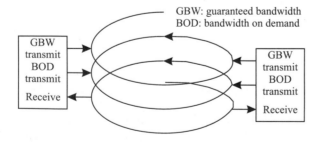

Figure 14.17   The helical LAN topology proposed to be used in the AON TDM testbed.

mode-locked laser were locked to those of an incoming 40 Gb/s stream. (Every fourth pulse in the 40 Gb/s stream coincides with a pulse from the 10 Gb/s stream.) Other demonstrated technologies include short pulse generation, pulse compression, pulse storage, and wavelength conversion.

14.6.5   CORD

The Contention Resolution by Delay Lines (CORD) testbed was developed by a consortium consisting of the University of Massachusetts, Stanford University, and GTE Laboratories [Chl96]. A block diagram of the testbed is shown in Figure 14.18. The testbed consisted of two nodes transmitting ATM-sized packets at 2.488 Gb/s using different transmit wavelengths (1310 nm and 1320 nm). A 3-dB coupler broadcasts all the packets to both the nodes. Thus this testbed is actually a WDM testbed using a broadcast architecture (networks we discussed in Chapter 7). We include this testbed here since it demonstrates some aspects of photonic packet switching that we discussed in this chapter. Each node generates packets destined to both itself and the other node. This gives rise to contentions at both the receivers. The headers of the packets from each node were carried on distinct subcarrier frequencies (3 GHz and 3.5 GHz) located outside the data bandwidth ($\approx$ 2.5 GHz). The subcarrier headers were received by tapping off a small portion of the power (10%) from the incoming signal.

Time was divided into slots with the slot size being equal to 250 ns. Since an ATM packet is only 424/2.488 $\approx$ 170 ns long, there was a fair amount of guard band in each slot. Slot synchronization between nodes was accomplished by a mechanism similar to that described in Section 7.2.1. However, a separate synchronizer node was not used, and one of the nodes itself acted as the synchronizer (called "master"

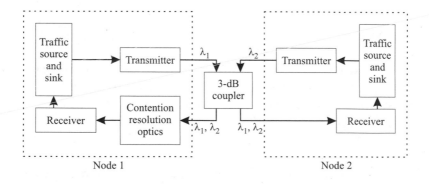

Figure 14.18   A block diagram of the CORD testbed.

in CORD) node. The data rate on the subcarrier channels was chosen to be 80 Mb/s so that a 20-bit header can be transmitted in the 250 ns slot.

In one of the nodes, a feed-forward delay line architecture similar to that shown in Figure 14.15 was used. Thus this node had greater opportunities to resolve contentions among packets destined to it. This is the origin of the name *contention resolution by delay lines* for this testbed. The current testbed is built using discrete components, including lithium niobate switches, semiconductor optical amplifiers (for loss compensation), and polarization-maintaining fiber for the delay lines. An integrated version of the *contention resolution optics* (CRO), which would integrate the three 2×2 switches and semiconductor amplifiers on a single InP substrate, is under development.

14.6.6 TBONE

The Testbed for Optical Networks (TBONE) being developed by Optivision, Mitre, and TASC is funded by DARPA [TBO]. It does not use WDM (for data), optical TDM, or photonic packet switching. Instead, it uses an optical crossbar switch to establish direct optical connections (lightpaths) between network nodes—on demand. This testbed is primarily intended for bandwidth-intensive applications such as image transfer and HIPPI host-to-host communications. The operating wavelength is 1310 nm, which is the zero-dispersion wavelength for standard single-mode fiber. This operating wavelength is chosen since analog services, which are also envisaged to be supported over this testbed, are very sensitive to dispersion. One interesting aspect of this testbed is the number of different control mechanisms being tested for requesting lightpaths. These include an in-band mechanism using HIPPI, an out-of-band mechanism using a separate ethernet, and an in-fiber but out-of-band mechanism operating at 1550 nm.

Summary

Photonic packet-switched networks offer the potential of realizing packet-switched networks with much higher capacities than may be possible with electronic packet-switched networks. However, significant advances in technology are needed to make them practical, and there are some significant roadblocks to overcome, such as the lack of economical optical buffering and the difficulty of propagating very high-speed signals at tens and hundreds of gigabits/second over any significant distances of optical fiber. There is a need for compact and economical soliton light sources. At this time, fast optical switches have relatively high losses, including polarization-dependent losses, and are not amenable to integration, which is essential to realize large switches. Temperature dependence of individual components can also be a significant problem when multiplexing, demultiplexing, or synchronizing signals at such high bit rates. All these topics are being explored in research laboratories today.

Further Reading

For an overview of OTDM, see [Mid93] or [Pru93].

The NOLM is described in [DW88], and its use for optical demultiplexing is described in [BDN90]. The NALM is described in [FHHH90]. The architecture of the TOAD is described in [SPGK93], and its operation is analyzed in [KGSP94]. Its use for packet header recognition is described in [GSP94]. Another nonlinear optical loop mirror structure, which uses a short loop length and an SOA within the loop, is described in [Eis92]. The soliton-trapping AND gate is described in [CHI+92].

For a recent summary of optical buffering techniques, see [Hal97b]. Optical buffering at 40 Gb/s is described in [Hal97a]. Packet compression and decompression can also be accomplished by a technique called *rate conversion*; see [PHR97].

For a recent overview of deflection routing, see [Bor95]. For an analysis of deflection routing on the hypercube topology, see [GH92]. Some other papers on deflection routing that may be of interest are [HC93, BP96].

The first experimental demonstration of a packet-switching photonic switch is described in [BCM+92]. [BPS94] is a review of photonic switch architectures and experimental implementations.

Most of the testbeds we have discussed, and some we haven't, are described in the two special issues on optical networks [CHK+96, FGO+96]. A design for a soliton ring network operating at 100 Gb/s and using soliton logic gates such as the soliton-trapping AND gate is described in [SID93].

A variant of OTDM networks that we haven't explored in this chapter is networks based on optical code division multiple access (OCDMA). Here different transmitters make use of different *codes* to *spread* their data, either in the time domain or in the frequency domain. The codes are carefully designed so that many transmitters can transmit simultaneously without interfering with one another, and the receiver can pick out a desired transmitter's signal from the others by suitably *despreading* the received signal. OCDMA networks were a popular research topic in the late 1980s and early 1990s, but they suffer from even more problems than OTDM networks. See [Sal89, SB89, PSF86, FV88] for a sampling of papers on this topic, and see [Gre93] for a good overview.

Problems

14.1 In the packet multiplexing illustrated in Figure 14.4, show that the delay encountered by pulse i, $i = 1, 2, \ldots, l$, on passing through the k compression stages is $(2^k - i)(T - \tau)$. Using the fact that the pulses are separated by time T at the input, now show that pulse i occurs at the output at time $(2^k - 1)(T - \tau) + (i - 1)\tau$. Thus the pulses are separated by a time interval of τ at the output.

14.2 Show that a compressed data packet of length l bits, obtained by the packet multiplexing technique illustrated in Figure 14.4, can be decompressed, in principle, by passing it through a series of $k = \log\lceil l \rceil$ expansion stages, where the jth expansion stage is as shown in Figure 14.19. What should be the switching time of the on–off switches used in this scheme?

14.3 Consider the tunable delay shown in Figure 14.11. Assume that a delay of $x2^{-k}$ is to be realized, where x is a k-bit integer. Consider the binary representation of x, and find an expression for the control inputs $c_1, \ldots, c_k$. Assume that if $c_i = 1$, switch i is set in the bar state, and if $c_i = 0$, switch i is set in the cross state.

14.4 Consider the fiber loop mirror shown in Figure 14.6, and show that the nonlinear element should introduce a phase shift of π between the clockwise and counterclockwise signals in order for all the energy entering the directional coupler from arm A to be transferred to arm B.

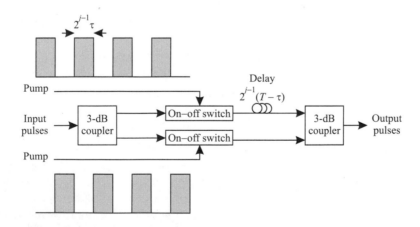

Figure 14.19 An optical packet demultiplexer can be built, in principle, by passing the compressed packet passes through k expansion stages, where 2^k is the smallest power of two that is not smaller than the packet length l in bits. The figure shows a detailed view of expansion stage j.

References

[AS92]   A. S. Acampora and S. I. A. Shah. Multihop lightwave networks: A comparison of store-and-forward and hot-potato routing. *IEEE Transactions on Communications*, 40(6):1082–1090, June 1992.

[Bar64]   P. Baran. On distributed communications networks. *IEEE Transactions on Communications*, pages 1–9, March 1964.

[Bar96]   R. A. Barry et al. All-optical network consortium—ultrafast TDM networks. *IEEE JSAC/JLT Special Issue on Optical Networks*, 14(5):999–1013, June 1996.

[BCM+92]   D. J. Blumenthal, K. Y. Chen, J. Ma, R. J. Feuerstein, and J. R. Sauer. Demonstration of a deflection routing 2 × 2 photonic switch for computer interconnects. *IEEE Photonics Technology Letters*, 4(2):169–173, Feb. 1992.

[BDG95]   C. Baransel, W. Dobosiewicz, and P. Gburzynski. Routing in multihop packet switching networks: Gb/s challange. *IEEE Network*, pages 38–61, May/June 1995.

[BDN90]   K. J. Blow, N. J. Doran, and B. P. Nelson. Demonstration of the nonlinear fibre loop mirror as an ultrafast all-optical demultiplexer. *Electronics Letters*, 26(14):962–964, July 1990.

[Bor95]   F. Borgonovo. Deflection routing. In M. Steenstrup, editor, *Routing in Communication Networks*. Prentice Hall, Englewood Cliffs, NJ, 1995.

[BP96]   A. Bononi and P. R. Prucnal. Analytical evaluation of improved access techniques in deflection routing networks. *IEEE/ACM Transactions on Networking*, 4(5):726–730, Oct. 1996.

[BPS94]   D. J. Blumenthal, P. R. Prucnal, and J. R. Sauer. Photonic packet switches: Architectures and experimental implementations. *Proceedings of IEEE*, 82:1650–1667, Nov. 1994.

[CHI+92]   M. W. Chbat, B. Hong, M. N. Islam, C. E. Soccolich, and P. R. Prucnal. Ultrafast soliton-trapping AND gate. *IEEE/OSA Journal on Lightwave Technology*, 10(12):2011–2016, Dec. 1992.

[CHK+96]   R. L. Cruz, G. R. Hill, A. L. Kellner, R. Ramaswami, and G. H. Sasaki, editors. *IEEE JSAC/JLT Special Issue on Optical Networks*, volume 14, June 1996.

[Chl96]   I. Chlamtac et al. CORD: Contention resolution by delay lines. *IEEE JSAC/JLT Special Issue on Optical Networks*, 14(5):1014–1029, June 1996.

[CLM97]   D. Cotter, J. K. Lucek, and D. D. Marcenac. Ultra-high bit-rate networking: From the transcontinental backbone to the desktop. *IEEE Communications Magazine*, 35(4):90–95, April 1997.

[Cot95]   D. Cotter et al. Self-routing of 100 Gbit/s packets using 6 bit 'keyword' address recognition. *Electronics Letters*, 31(25):2201–2202, Dec. 1995.

[DW88]   N. J. Doran and D. Wood. Nonlinear-optical loop mirror. *Optics Letters*, 13(1):56–58, Jan. 1988.

[Eis92]   M. Eiselt. Optical loop mirror with semiconductor laser amplifier. *Electronics Letters*, 28(16):1505–1506, July 1992.

[FBP95]   F. Forghieri, A. Bononi, and P. R. Prucnal. Analysis and comparison of hot-potato and single-buffer deflection routing in very high bit rate optical mesh networks. *IEEE Transactions on Communications*, 43(1):88–98, Jan. 1995.

[FGO⁺96]   M. Fujiwara, M. S. Goodman, M. J. O'Mahony, O. K. Tonguez, and A. E. Willner, editors. *IEEE/OSA JLT/JSAC Special Issue on Multiwavelength Optical Technology and Networks*, volume 14, June 1996.

[FHHH90]   M. E. Fermann, F. Haberl, M. Hofer, and H. Hochreiter. Nonlinear amplifying loop mirror. *Optics Letters*, 15(13):752–754, July 1990.

[FV88]   G. J. Foschini and G. Vannucci. Using spread spectrum in a high-capacity fiber-optic local network. *IEEE/OSA Journal on Lightwave Technology*, 6(3):370–379, March 1988.

[GG93]   A. G. Greenberg and J. Goodman. Sharp approximate models of deflection routing in mesh networks. *IEEE Transactions on Communications*, 41(1):210–223, Jan. 1993.

[GH92]   A. G. Greenberg and B. Hajek. Deflection routing in hypercube networks. *IEEE Transactions on Communications*, 40(6):1070–1081, June 1992.

[Gre93]   P. E. Green. *Fiber-Optic Networks*. Prentice Hall, Englewood Cliffs, NJ, 1993.

[GSP94]   I. Glesk, J. P. Sokoloff, and P. R. Prucnal. All-optical address recognition and self-routing in a 250 Gb/s packet-switched network. *Electronics Letters*, 30(16):1322–1323, Aug. 1994.

[Gun97a]   P. Gunning et al. 40 Gbit/s optical TDMA LAN over 300m of installed blown fibre. In *Proceedings of European Conference on Optical Communication*, volume 4, pages 61–64, Sept. 1997.

[Gun97b]   P. Gunning et al. Optical-TDMA LAN incorporating packaged integrated Mach-Zehnder interferometer channel selector. *Electronics Letters*, 33(16):1404–1406, July 1997.

[Hal97a]   K. L. Hall. 40 Gb/s optical packet buffering. In *OFC'97 Technical Digest*, page 250, 1997.

[Hal97b]   K. L. Hall. All-optical buffers for high-speed slotted TDM networks. In *IEEE/LEOS Summer Topical Meeting on Advanced Semiconductor Lasers and Applications*, page 15, 1997.

[HC93]   B. Hajek and R. L. Cruz. On the average delay for routing subject to independent deflections. *IEEE Transactions on Information Theory*, 39(1):84–91, Jan. 1993.

[Hil85]   W. D. Hillis. *The Connection Machine*. MIT Press, Cambridge, MA, 1985.

[Hil87]   W. D. Hillis. The connection machine. *Scientific American*, 256(6), June 1987.

[KGSP94]   M. G. Kane, I. Glesk, J. P. Sokoloff, and P. R. Prucnal. Asymmetric loop mirror: Analysis of an all-optical switch. *Applied Optics*, 33(29):6833–6842, Oct. 1994.

[KH90]   A. Krishna and B. Hajek. Performance of shuffle-like switching networks with deflection. In *Proceedings of IEEE Infocom*, pages 473–480, 1990.

[LGM+97]   J. K. Lucek, P. Gunning, D. G. Moodie, K. Smith, and D. Pitcher. Synchrolan: A 40 Gbit/s optical-TDMA LAN. *Electronics Letters*, 33(10):887–888, April 1997.

[LNGP96]   E. Leonardi, F. Neri, M. Gerla, and P. Palnati. Congestion control in asynchronous high-speed wormhole routing networks. *IEEE Communications Magazine*, pages 58–69, Nov. 1996.

[Mas96]   F. Masetti et al. High speed, high capacity ATM optical switches for future telecommunication transport networks. *IEEE JSAC/JLT Special Issue on Optical Networks*, 14(5):979–998, June 1996.

[Max89]   N. F. Maxemchuck. Comparison of deflection and store-and-forward techniques in the Manhattan Street and shuffle-exchange networks. In *Proceedings of IEEE Infocom*, pages 800–809, 1989.

[Mid93]   J. E. Midwinter, editor. *Photonics in Switching, Volume II: Systems*. Academic Press, San Diego, CA, 1993.

[PHR97]   N. S. Patel, K. L. Hall, and K. A. Rauschenbach. Optical rate conversion for high-speed TDM networks. *IEEE Photonics Technology Letters*, 9(9):1277, Sept. 1997.

[Pru93]   P. R. Prucnal. Optically processed self-routing, synchronization, and contention resolution for 1-d and 2-d photonic switching architectures. *IEEE Journal of Quantum Electronics*, 29(2):600–612, Feb. 1993.

[PSF86]   P. R. Prucnal, M. A. Santoro, and T. R. Fan. Spread spectrum fiber-optic local area network using optical processing. *IEEE/OSA Journal on Lightwave Technology*, LT-4(5):547–554, May 1986.

[Sal89]   J. A. Salehi. Code division multiple-access techniques in optical fiber networks—Part I: Fundamental principles. *IEEE Transactions on Communications*, 37(8):824–833, Aug. 1989.

[SB89]   J. A. Salehi and C. A. Brackett. Code division multiple-access techniques in optical fiber networks—Part II: Systems performance analysis. *IEEE Transactions on Communications*, 37(8):834–842, Aug. 1989.

[SBP96]   S-W. Seo, K. Bergman, and P. R. Prucnal. Transparent optical networks with time-division multiplexing. *IEEE JSAC/JLT Special Issue on Optical Networks*, 14(5):1039–1051, June 1996.

[SID93]   J. R. Sauer, M. N. Islam, and S. P. Dijaili. A soliton ring network. *IEEE/OSA Journal on Lightwave Technology*, 11(12):2182–2190, Dec. 1993.

[Smi81]   B. Smith. Architecture and applications of the HEP multiprocessor system. In *Real Time Signal Processing IV, Proceedings of SPIE*, pages 241–248, 1981.

[SPGK93]   J. P. Sokoloff, P. R. Prucnal, I. Glesk, and M. Kane. A terahertz optical asymmetric demultiplexer (TOAD). *IEEE Photonics Technology Letters*, 5(7):787–790, July 1993.

[TBO]   *Test Bed for All-Optical Networks (TBONE)*. *http://www.optivision.com/nsds/tbone.html*.

part III

Appendices

appendix A

Symbols and Parameters

Table A.1 Parameters and symbols used in Part I (dimensionless unless otherwise indicated).

Parameter	Symbol	Typical Value/Units
Effective area	A_e	50 μm^2
Pulse envelope	$A(z, t)$	
Fiber core radius	a	4 μm (SMF)
Bit rate	B	Mb/s or Gb/s
Electrical bandwidth	B_e	GHz
Optical bandwidth	B_o	GHz
Bit error rate	BER	10^9–10^{-15}
Normalized effective index	b	
Capacitance	C	μF (microfarad)
Speed of light in vacuum	c	3×10^8 m/s
Dispersion parameter	D	ps/nm-km
Electric flux density	$\mathbf{D}$	Coulombs/m^2
Material dispersion	D_M	ps/nm-km
Polarization mode dispersion	D_{PMD}	ps/$\sqrt{\text{km}}$
Waveguide dispersion	D_W	ps/nm-km
Dispersion-shifted fiber	DSF	$D = 0$ (1.55 μm)
Electric field	$\mathbf{E}$	V/m
Energy level	E	differences, ΔE, expressed in nm using $\Delta E = hc/\lambda$
Electronic charge	e	1.6×10^{-19} Coulombs
Amplifier noise figure	F	dB
Finesse	F	
Optical carrier frequency	f_c	THz

Table A.1   Parameters and symbols used in Part I (dimensionless unless otherwise indicated). (*Continued*)

Parameter	Symbol	Typical Value/Units
Pump frequency	f_p	THz
Signal frequency	f_s	THz
Amplifier gain	G	
Amplifier unsaturated gain	G_{max}	
Brillouin gain coefficient	g_B	4×10^{-11} m/W
Raman gain coefficient	g_R	6×10^{-14} m/W
Magnetic field	$\mathbf{H}$	A/m
Planck's constant	h	6.63×10^{-34} J/Hz
Photocurrent	I_p	μA or nA
Thermal noise current	I_{th}	3 pA/$\sqrt{\text{Hz}}$
Boltzmann's constant	k_B	1.38×10^{-23} J/°K
Dispersion length	L_D	km
Effective length	L_e	km
Link length	L	km
Nonlinear length	L_{NL}	km
Coupling length	l	μm
Distance between amplifiers	l	km
Average number of photons per 1 bit	M	
Real part of x	$\Re[x]$	
Nonzero dispersion fiber	NDF	$-6 \leq D \leq 6$ ps/nm-km (1.55 μm)
Effective index	n_{eff}	
Refractive index	n	
Spontaneous emission factor	n_{sp}	
Core refractive index	n_1	
Cladding refractive index	n_2	
Nonlinear index coefficient	$\bar{n}$	2.2–3.4 $\times 10^{-8}$ μm^2/W
Amplifier output saturation power	P_{out}^{sat}	mW
Amplifier saturation power	P^{sat}	mW
Electric polarization	$\mathbf{P}$	Coulombs/m^2
Linear polarization	$\mathcal{P}_L$	Coulombs/m^2
Local-oscillator power	P_{LO}	dBm
Nonlinear polarization	$\mathcal{P}_{NL}$	Coulombs/m^2
Power	P	W or mW
Power penalty	PP	dB
Penalty (signal dependent noise)	PP$_{sig-dep}$	dB
Penalty (signal independent noise)	PP$_{sig-indep}$	dB
Receiver sensitivity	$\bar{P}_{rec}$	dBm
Load resistance	R_L	Ω or kΩ
Photodetector responsivity	$\mathcal{R}$	A/W
Reflectivity	R	

Table A.1 Parameters and symbols used in Part I (dimensionless unless otherwise indicated). (*Continued*)

Parameter	Symbol	Typical Value/Units
Extinction ratio	r	
Standard single-mode fiber	SMF	$D = 17$ ps/nm-km (1.55 μm), $D = 0$ (1.3 μm)
Signal-to-noise ratio	SNR	dB or no units
Bit period	T	ns
Decision threshold	T_d	
V-number	V	
Optical frequency	ν	Hz
Number of wavelengths	W	
Absorption coefficient	α	1/cm
Fiber attenuation	α	0.22 dB/km at 1.55 μm
Propagation constant	β	1/μm
Group velocity	$1/\beta_1$	m/s
GVD parameter	β_2	s^2/m (or in terms of D)
Coupling ratio	γ	0–1
Nonlinear propagation coefficient	γ	2.6 /W-km
Fractional core–cladding refractive index difference	Δ	
Brillouin gain bandwidth	Δf_B	20 MHz at 1.55 μm
Interchannel spacing	$\Delta\lambda$	nm
Detector quantum efficiency	η	1 for pinFETs
Four-wave mixing efficiency	η	
Input coupling efficiency	η_i	
Output coupling efficiency	η_o	
Chirp factor	κ	
Coupling coefficient	κ	1/μm
Grating period	Λ	μm
Filter center wavelength	λ_0	μm
Wavelength	λ	μm or nm
Permeability of vacuum	μ_0	$4\pi \times 10^{-7}$ H/m
Permittivity of vacuum	ϵ_0	8.854×10^{-12} F/m
Shot noise power	σ_{shot}^2	
Thermal noise power	σ_{th}^2	
Signal-spontaneous noise power	$\sigma_{\text{sig-spont}}^2$	
Spontaneous-spontaneous noise power	$\sigma_{\text{spont-spont}}^2$	
Phase	ϕ	radians
Susceptibility	χ	
Third-order susceptibility	$\chi^{(3)}$	6×10^{-15} cm^3/erg
Angular frequency	ω, ω_0	

appendix B

Decibel Units

IN OPTICAL COMMUNICATION, it is quite common to use decibel units (dB) to measure power and signal levels, as opposed to conventional units. The reason for doing this is that powers can vary over several orders of magnitude in a system, and conveniently for us, calculations that involve multiplication in the conventional domain become additive operations in the decibel domain. To understand this system, let us consider an optical link with transmitted power P_t W and link loss γ. The received power $P_r = P_t \gamma$ W. In terms of dB units, we have

$$(P_t)_{\mathrm{dBW}} = 10 \log(P_t)_{\mathrm{W}}.$$

In many cases, it is more convenient to measure powers in mW, and we have an equivalent dBm value given as

$$(P_t)_{\mathrm{dBm}} = 10 \log(P_t)_{\mathrm{mW}}.$$

Decibel units are also used to indicate ratios. For example, we have the loss given as

$$\gamma = \frac{P_r}{P_t}.$$

In dB units, we would have

$$(\gamma)_{\mathrm{dB}} = 10 \log \gamma = (P_r)_{\mathrm{dBW}} - (P_t)_{\mathrm{dBW}}.$$

As an example, if $P_t = 1$ mW and $P_r = 1\ \mu$W, implying that $\gamma = 1000$, we would have, equivalently,

$(P_t)_{\mathrm{dB}} = 0$ dBm or -30 dBW,

$(P_r)_{\mathrm{dB}} = -30$ dBm or -60 dBW,

and

$(\gamma)_{\mathrm{dB}} = -30$ dB.

appendix C

Nonlinear Polarization

THE LINEAR EQUATION (2.6) for the relationship between the induced polarization **P** and the applied electric field **E** hold when the power levels and/or bit rates are moderate. When this is not the case, this must be generalized to include higher powers of $\mathbf{E}(\mathbf{r}, t)$. For an isotropic medium and an electric field polarized along one direction so that it has a single component $E(\mathbf{r}, t)$, this relationship can be written as follows:

$$
\begin{aligned}
\mathcal{P}(\mathbf{r}, t) \;=\; & \epsilon_0 \int_{-\infty}^{t} \chi^{(1)}(\mathbf{r}, t - t_1) E(\mathbf{r}, t_1)\, dt_1 \\
& + \epsilon_0 \int_{-\infty}^{t} \int_{-\infty}^{t} \chi^{(2)}(t - t_1, t - t_2) E(\mathbf{r}, t_1) E(\mathbf{r}, t_2)\, dt_1\, dt_2 \\
& + \epsilon_0 \int_{-\infty}^{t} \int_{-\infty}^{t} \int_{-\infty}^{t} \chi^{(3)}(t - t_1, t - t_2, t - t_3) E(\mathbf{r}, t_1) E(\mathbf{r}, t_2) E(\mathbf{r}, t_3)\, dt_1\, dt_2\, dt_3 \\
& + \cdots .
\end{aligned}
$$

(C.1)

Now $\chi^{(1)}(\mathbf{r}, t)$ is called the *linear susceptibility* to distinguish it from $\chi^{(i)}(\mathbf{r}, t)$, $i = 2, 3, \ldots$, which are termed the *higher-order nonlinear susceptibilities*. Owing to certain symmetry properties of the silica molecule, $\chi^{(2)}(\mathbf{r}, t) = 0$. The effect of the higher-order susceptibilities $\chi^{(4)}(,)$, $\chi^{(5)}(,)$, $\ldots$, is negligible in comparison with that of $\chi^{(3)}(,)$. Thus we can write (C.1) as

$$
\mathcal{P}(\mathbf{r}, t) = \mathcal{P}_L(\mathbf{r}, t) + \mathcal{P}_{NL}(\mathbf{r}, t).
$$

Here $\mathcal{P}_L(\mathbf{r}, t)$ is the *linear polarization* given by (2.35). The *nonlinear polarization* $\mathcal{P}_{NL}(\mathbf{r}, t)$ is given by

$$\mathcal{P}_{NL}(\mathbf{r}, t) = \epsilon_0 \int_{-\infty}^{t} \int_{-\infty}^{t} \int_{-\infty}^{t} \chi^{(3)}(t - t_1, t - t_2, t - t_3)$$

$$E(\mathbf{r}, t_1) E(\mathbf{r}, t_2) E(\mathbf{r}, t_3) \, dt_1 \, dt_2 \, dt_3 \,. \qquad \text{(C.2)}$$

The nonlinear response of the medium occurs on a very narrow time scale of $<$ 100 fs—much smaller than the time scale of the linear response—and thus can be assumed to be instantaneous for pulse widths > 1 ps. Note that even if the pulse occupies only a tenth of the bit interval, this assumption is satisfied for bit rates > 100 Gb/s. We will consider only this instantaneous nonlinear response case in this book. When this assumption is satisfied,

$$\chi^{(3)}(t - t_1, t - t_2, t - t_3) = \chi^{(3)} \delta(t - t_1) \delta(t - t_2) \delta(t - t_3),$$

where $\chi^{(3)}$ on the right-hand side is now a constant, independent of t. This assumption enables us to simplify (C.2) considerably since it now reduces to

$$\mathcal{P}_{NL}(\mathbf{r}, t) = \epsilon_0 \chi^{(3)} E^3(\mathbf{r}, t),$$

which is (2.36).

appendix D

Random Processes

IN MANY PLACES in the book, we use random variables and random processes to model noise, polarization, and network traffic. Understanding the statistical nature of these parameters is essential in predicting the performance of communication systems.

D.1 Random Variables

A random variable X is characterized by a probability distribution function

$$F_X(x) = P\{X \le x\}.$$

The derivative of $F_X(x)$ is the probability density function

$$f_X(x) = \frac{dF_X(x)}{dx}.$$

Note that

$$\int_{-\infty}^{\infty} f_X(x)dx = 1.$$

In many cases, we will be interested in obtaining the expectation, or ensemble average, associated with this probability function. The expectation of a function $g(x)$ is defined as

$$E[g(X)] = \int_{-\infty}^{\infty} f_X(x)g(x)dx.$$

563

The mean of X is defined to be

$$E[X] = \int_{-\infty}^{\infty} x f_X(x) dx,$$

and the mean square (second moment) of X is

$$E[X^2] = \int_{-\infty}^{\infty} x^2 f_X(x) dx.$$

The variance of X is defined as

$$\sigma_X^2 = E[X^2] - E[X].$$

In many cases, we are interested in determining the statistical properties of two or more random variables that are not independent of each other. The joint probability distribution function of two random variables X and Y is defined as

$$F_{X,Y}(x, y) = P\{X \leq x, Y \leq y\}.$$

Sometimes we are given some information about one of the random variables and must estimate the distribution of the other. The conditional distribution of X given Y is denoted as

$$F_{X|Y}(x|y) = P\{X \leq x | Y \leq y\}.$$

An important relation between these distributions is given by Bayes' theorem:

$$F_{X|Y}(x|y) = \frac{F(x, y)}{F_Y(y)}.$$

D.1.1   Gaussian Distribution

A random variable X is said to follow a Gaussian distribution if its probability density function

$$f_X(x) = \frac{1}{\sqrt{2\pi}\sigma} e^{(x-\mu)^2/\sigma^2}, \quad -\infty \leq x \leq \infty.$$

Here, μ is the mean and σ^2 the variance of X. In order to compute bit error rates, we will need to compute the probability that $X \geq v$, which is defined as the function

$$Q(v) = \int_{v}^{\infty} f_X(x) dx.$$

This function can be numerically evaluated. For example, $Q(v) = 10^{-9}$ if $v = 6$, and $Q(v) = 10^{-15}$ if $v = 8$.

Also if X and Y are jointly distributed Gaussian random variables, then it can be proved that

$$E[X^2Y^2] = E[X^2]E[Y^2] + 2(E[XY])^2. \tag{D.1}$$

D.1.2   Maxwell Distribution

The Maxwellian probability density function is useful to calculate penalties due to polarization-mode dispersion. A random variable X is said to follow a Maxwellian distribution if its probability density function

$$f_X(x) = \frac{\sqrt{2}}{\alpha^3\sqrt{\pi}}x^2 e^{-x^2/2\alpha^2}, \qquad x \geq 0,$$

where α is a parameter associated with the distribution. The mean and mean-square value of X can be computed as

$$E[X] = 2\alpha\sqrt{\frac{2}{\pi}}$$

and

$$E[X^2] = 3\alpha^2 = \frac{3}{8}\pi(E[X])^2.$$

Therefore, the variance

$$\sigma_X^2 = E[X^2] - (E[X])^2 = \alpha^2\left(3 - \frac{8}{\pi}\right).$$

It can also be shown that

$$P(X > 3E[X]) \approx 4 \times 10^{-5}.$$

D.1.3   Poisson Distribution

A discrete random variable X takes on values from a discrete but possibly infinite set $S = \{x_1, x_2, x_3, \ldots\}$. It is characterized by a probability mass function $P(x)$, which is the probability that X takes on a value x. The expectation of a function $g(X)$ is defined as

$$E[g(X)] = \sum_{i|x_i \in S} g(x_i)P(x_i).$$

X is a Poisson random variable if

$$P(i) = \frac{e^{-r}r^i}{i!}, \quad i = 0, 1, 2, \ldots,$$

where r is a parameter associated with the distribution. It is easily verified that $E[X] = r$ and $\sigma_X^2 = r$.

D.2   Random Processes

Random processes are useful to model time varying stochastic events. A random process $X(t)$ is simply a sequence of random variables $X(t_1)$, $X(t_2)$, ..., one for each instant of time. The first-order probability distribution function is given by

$$F(x, t) = P\{X(t) \leq x\},$$

and the first-order density function by

$$f(x, t) = \frac{\partial F(x, t)}{\partial x}.$$

The second-order distribution function is the joint distribution function

$$F(x_1, x_2, t_1, t_2) = P\{X(t_1) \leq x_1, X(t_2) \leq x_2\},$$

and the corresponding second-order density function is defined as

$$f(x_1, x_2, t_1, t_2) = \frac{\partial^2 F(x_1, x_2, t_1, t_2)}{\partial x_1 \partial x_2}.$$

The mean of the process is

$$\mu(t) = E[X(t)] = \int_{-\infty}^{\infty} x f(x, t) dx.$$

The autocorrelation of the process is

$$R_X(t_1, t_2) = E[X(t_1)X(t_2)] = \int \int x_1 x_2 f(x_1, x_2, t_1, t_2) dx_1 dx_2.$$

The autocovariance of the process is defined as

$$L_X(t_1, t_2) = R_X(t_1, t_2) - E[X(t_1)]E[X(t_2)].$$

The random process is *wide-sense stationary* if it has a constant mean

$$E[X(t)] = \mu,$$

and the autocorrelation (and autocovariance) depends only on $\tau = t_1 - t_2$, that is, $R_X(\tau) = E[X(t)X(t + \tau)]$ and $L_X(\tau) = R(\tau) - \mu^2$. For a wide-sense stationary random process, the *power spectral density* is the Fourier transform of the autocovariance and is given by

$$S_X(f) = \int_{-\infty}^{\infty} L_X(\tau)e^{-i2\pi f\tau}d\tau.$$

Note that the variance of the random process is given by

$$\sigma_X^2 = R_X(0) = \int_{-\infty}^{\infty} S_X(f)df.$$

In many cases, we will represent noise introduced in the system as a stationary random process. In this case, the spectral density is useful to represent the spectral distribution of the noise. For example, in a receiver, the noise $X(t)$ and signal are sent through a low pass filter with impulse response $h(t)$. The transfer function of the filter $H(f)$ is the Fourier transform of its impulse response. In this case, the spectral density of the output noise process $Y(t)$ can be expressed as

$$S_Y(f) = S_X(f)|H(f)|^2.$$

Suppose the filter is an ideal low pass filter with bandwidth B_e, that is, $H(f) = 1, -B_e \leq f \leq B_e$ and 0 otherwise. The variance of the noise process at its output is simply

$$\sigma_Y^2 = R_Y(0) = \int_{-B_e}^{B_e} S_X(f)df.$$

D.2.1   Poisson Random Process

Poisson random processes are used to model the arrival of photons in an optical communication system. They are also used widely to model the arrival of traffic in a communication network. The model is accurate primarily for voice calls, but it is used for other applications as well, without much real justification.

A Poisson process $X(t)$ is characterized by a rate parameter λ. For any two time instants t_1 and $t_2 > t_1$, $X(t_2) - X(t_1)$ is the number of arrivals during the time interval $(t_1, t_2]$. The number of arrivals during this interval follows a Poisson distribution, that is,

$$P\left(X(t_2) - X(t_1) = n\right) = e^{-\lambda(t_2-t_1)}\frac{(\lambda(t_2 - t_1))^n}{n!},$$

where n is a nonnegative integer. Therefore, the mean number of arrivals during this time interval is

$$E[X(t_2) - X(t_1)] = \lambda(t_2 - t_1).$$

A Poisson process has many important properties that make it easier to analyze systems with Poisson traffic than other forms of traffic. See [BG92] for a good summary.

D.2.2   Gaussian Random Process

In many cases, we model noise as a wide-sense stationary Gaussian random process $X(t)$. It is also common to assume that at any two instants of time $t_1 \neq t_2$ the random variables $X(t_1)$ and $X(t_2)$ are independent Gaussian variables with mean μ. For such a process, we can use (D.1) and write

$$E[X^2(t)X^2(t + \tau)] = (E[X^2(t)])^2 + 2(E[X(t)]E[X(t + \tau)])^2,$$

that is,

$$E[X^2(t)X^2(t + \tau)] = R_X^2(0) + 2R_X^2(\tau).$$

Further Reading

There are several good books on probability and random processes. See, for example, [Pap84, BG92].

References

[BG92]   D. Bertsekas and R. G. Gallager. *Data Networks*. Prentice Hall, Englewood Cliffs, NJ, 1992.

[Pap84]   A. Papoulis. *Probability, Random Variables, and Stochastic Processes*. McGraw-Hill, New York, 1984.

appendix E

Multilayer Thin-Film Filters

To UNDERSTAND THE PRINCIPLE of operation of dielectric thin-film multicavity filters, we need to digress and discuss some results from electromagnetic theory.

E.1 Wave Propagation at Dielectric Interfaces

A plane electromagnetic wave is one whose electric and magnetic fields vary only in the spatial coordinate along the direction of propagation. In other words, along any plane perpendicular to the direction of propagation, the electric and magnetic fields are constant. The ratio of the amplitude of the electric field to that of the magnetic field at any such plane is called the *impedance* at that plane. In a medium that supports only one propagating wave (so there is no reflected wave), this impedance is called the *intrinsic impedance* of the medium and denoted by η. If ϵ is the dielectric permittivity of the medium and μ is its magnetic permeability, $\eta = \sqrt{\mu/\epsilon}$. If we denote the *intrinsic impedance of vacuum* by η_0, for a nonmagnetic dielectric medium with refractive index n, the intrinsic impedance $\eta = \eta_0/n$. (A nonmagnetic dielectric material has the same permeability as that of vacuum. Since most commonly used dielectrics are nonmagnetic, in the rest of the discussion, we assume that the dielectrics considered are nonmagnetic.)

Consider the interface between two dielectrics with refractive indices n_1 and n_2, illustrated in Figure E.1(a). Assume that a plane electromagnetic wave is incident normal to this interface. The reflection coefficient at this interface is the ratio of the amplitude of the electric field in the reflected wave to that in the incident wave. From

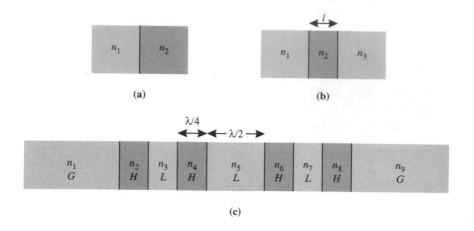

Figure E.1   (a) The interface between two dielectric media. (b) A dielectric slab or film placed between two other dielectric media. (c) Multiple dielectric slabs or films stacked together.

the principles of electromagnetics, [RWv84, section 6.7], it can be shown that the *reflection coefficient* at this interface (for normal incidence) is

$$\rho = \frac{\eta_2 - \eta_1}{\eta_2 + \eta_1} = \frac{n_1 - n_2}{n_1 + n_2}. \tag{E.1}$$

Thus the fraction of power transmitted through this interface is

$$1 - |\rho|^2 = 1 - \left| \frac{n_1 - n_2}{n_1 + n_2} \right|^2.$$

Here, as in the rest of the discussion, we assume that the dielectrics are lossless so that no power is absorbed by them.

Now consider a slab of a dielectric material of thickness l and refractive index n_2 (dielectric 2) that is placed between two dielectrics with refractive indices n_1 and n_3 (dielectrics 1 and 3, respectively). Assume that dielectrics 1 and 3 have very large, essentially infinite, thicknesses. This is illustrated in Figure E.1(b). A part of any signal incident from dielectric 1 will be reflected at the 1–2 interface and a part transmitted. Of the transmitted part, a fraction will be reflected at the 2–3 interface. Of this reflected signal, another fraction will be reflected at the 2–1 interface and the remaining transmitted to dielectric 1 and added to the first reflected signal, and so on. In principle, the *net* signal reflected at the 1–2 interface can be calculated by adding all the reflected signals calculated using the reflection coefficients given by

(E.1), with the proper phases. But the whole process can be simplified by using the concept of impedances and the following result concerning them.

If the impedance at some plane in a dielectric is Z_L, called the *load impedance,* the impedance at distance l in front of it, called the *input impedance* is given, as a function of the wavelength λ, by

$$Z_i = \eta \left(\frac{Z_L \cos(2\pi n l/\lambda) + i\eta \sin(2\pi n l/\lambda)}{\eta \cos(2\pi n l/\lambda) + iZ_L \sin(2\pi n l/\lambda)} \right). \tag{E.2}$$

Here, η is the intrinsic impedance of the dielectric, and n is its refractive index. Note that in a single dielectric medium, $Z_L = \eta$ and (E.2) yields $Z_i = \eta$ as well. This agrees with our earlier statement that the impedance at all planes in a single dielectric medium is η.

The reason that the concept of impedance is useful for us is that the reflection and transmission coefficients may be expressed in terms of impedances. Specifically, the reflection coefficient at an interface with load impedance Z_L, in a dielectric with intrinsic impedance η, is given by

$$\rho = \frac{Z_L - \eta}{Z_L + \eta}. \tag{E.3}$$

The transmission coefficient at the same interface is given by

$$\tau = 1 - \rho = \frac{2Z_L}{Z_L + \eta}. \tag{E.4}$$

Note that (E.1) is a special case of (E.3) obtained by setting $\eta = \eta_1$ and $Z_L = \eta_2$.

Now consider again the case of a single dielectric slab, placed between two other dielectrics, illustrated in Figure E.1(b). The impedance at the 2–3 interface is η_3. Thus the impedance at the 1–2 interface may be calculated using (E.2) as

$$Z_{12} = \eta_2 \left(\frac{\eta_3 \cos(2\pi n l/\lambda) + i\eta_2 \sin(2\pi n l/\lambda)}{\eta_2 \cos(2\pi n l/\lambda) + i\eta_3 \sin(2\pi n l/\lambda)} \right).$$

Using this, the reflection coefficient at the 1–2 interface can be obtained from (E.3) as

$$\rho = \frac{Z_{12} - \eta_1}{Z_{12} + \eta_1}.$$

If the slab of dielectric of thickness l shown in Figure E.1(b) is viewed as a filter, its power transfer function—the fraction of power transmitted by it—is given by

$$T(\lambda) = 1 - |\rho|^2.$$

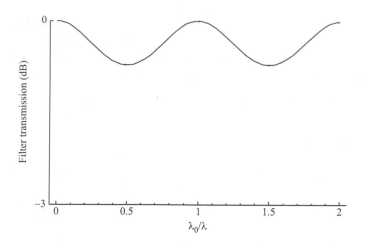

Figure E.2   Transfer function of the filter shown in Figure E.1(b) for $n_1 = n_3 = 1.52$, $n_2 = 2.3$, and $l = \lambda_0/2n_2$.

Let $\lambda_0 = 2nl$ so that the optical path length in the slab is a half wavelength. Note that $T(\lambda_0) = 1$. In Figure E.2, $T(\lambda)$ is plotted as a function of λ_0/λ, assuming $n_1 = n_3 = 1.5$ and $n_2 = 2.3$.

Note that for the case $n_1 = n_3$, this filter becomes a Fabry-Perot filter (see Problem 3.9).

This result can be generalized to an arbitrary number of dielectric slabs as follows. Consider a series of k dielectrics with refractive indices $n_1, n_2, \ldots, n_k$ (not necessarily distinct), and thicknesses $l_1, l_2, \ldots, l_k$, which are stacked together as shown in Figure E.1. We also assume that l_1 and l_k are very large, essentially infinite. This can be viewed as a filter of which a special case is the DTMF. We assume that the input signal is incident normal to the 1–2 interface. If we find the reflection coefficient, ρ, at the 1–2 interface, we can determine the power transfer function, $T(\lambda)$, of the filter, using $T(\lambda) = 1 - |\rho|^2$.

Using the impedance machinery, this is quite easy to do. If η_i is the intrinsic impedance of dielectric i, $i = 1, \ldots, k$, $\eta_i = \eta_0/n_i$. We start at the right end of the filter, at the $(k-1)$–(k) interface. The impedance at this plane is just the intrinsic impedance of medium k, namely, η_k. The intrinsic impedance at the $(k-2)$–$(k-1)$ interface can be calculated using (E.2) with $Z_L = \eta_k$, $\eta = \eta_{k-1}$, $n = n_{k-1}$, and $l = l_{k-1}$. Continuing in the same manner, we can recursively calculate the input impedances at the interfaces $(k-3)$–$(k-2), \ldots, 1$–2. From this, the reflection coefficient at the 1–2 interface can be calculated using (E.3), and the power transfer function of the filter can be determined.

$\underline{\text{E.2}}$ Filter Design

Although the power transfer function of any given stack of dielectrics can be determined using the preceding procedure, designing a filter of this type to meet a given filter requirement is a more typical problem encountered in practice. The multiple dielectric slab structure exemplified by Figure E.1(c) is quite versatile, and a number of well-known filter transfer functions such as the Butterworth and the Chebyshev may be synthesized using it [Kni76]. However, the synthesis of these filters calls for a variety of dielectric materials with different refractive indices. This may be a difficult requirement to meet in practice.

It turns out, however, that very useful filter transfer functions can be synthesized using just two different dielectric materials, a low index dielectric with refractive index n_L and a high index dielectric with refractive index n_H [Kni76]. Assume we want to synthesize a bandpass filter with center wavelength λ_0. Then, a general structure for doing this is to use alternate layers of high index and low index dielectrics with thicknesses equivalent to a quarter or a half wavelength at λ_0. (A quarter wavelength slab of the dielectric with refractive index n_L would have a thickness $\lambda_0/4n_L$.) Since these thicknesses at optical wavelengths are quite small, the term *thin film* is more appropriately used instead of *slab*. The dielectric thin films that are a half wavelength thick at λ_0 are called the *cavities* of the filter. A particularly useful filter structure consists of a few cavities separated by several quarter wavelength films. If H and L denote quarter wavelength films (at λ_0) of the high and low index dielectrics, respectively, then we can represent any such filter by a sequence of Hs and Ls. Two Ls or two Hs in succession would represent a half wavelength film. For example, if the lightly shaded dielectrics are of low index and the darker shaded are of high index, the filter consisting of the multiple dielectric films 2–8 shown in Figure E.1(c) can be represented by the sequence $HLHLLHLH$. If the surrounding dielectrics, 1 and 9, are denoted by G (for glass), the entire structure in Figure E.1(c) can be represented by the sequence $GHLHLLHLHG$. If we know the refractive indices n_G, n_L, and n_H of the G, L, and H dielectrics, respectively, the transfer function of the filter can be calculated using the procedure outlined. For $n_G = 1.52$, a typical value for the cover glass, $n_L = 1.46$, which is the refractive index of SiO_2 (a low index dielectric), and $n_H = 2.3$, which is the refractive index of TiO_2 (a high index dielectric), this transfer function is plotted in Figure E.3. From this figure, we see that the main lobe is quite

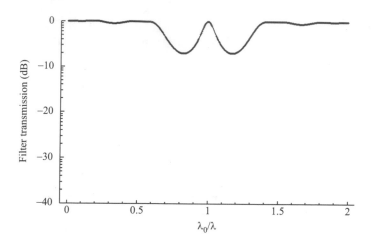

Figure E.3   Transfer function of the filter shown in Figure E.1(c) for $n_G = 1.52$, $n_L = 1.46$, and $n_H = 2.3$.

wide compared to the center wavelength, and the side lobe suppression is less than 10 dB. Clearly, a better transfer function is needed if the filter is to be useful.

A narrower passband and greater sidelobe suppression can be achieved by the use of more quarter wavelength films than just three. For example, the filter described by the sequence

$$G(HL)^9 HLL(HL)^9 HG$$

has the transfer function shown in Figure E.4. The notation $(HL)^k$ denotes the sequence $HL \cdot HL \cdot \ldots \cdot HL$, ($k$ times). Note that this filter is a single-cavity filter since it uses just one half wave film. However, it uses 38 quarter wave films; 19 on each side of the cavity.

The transfer function of a dielectric thin-film filter is periodic in frequency or in λ_0/λ, just like the Fabry-Perot filter. In Figure E.4(a), the transfer function of the filter for one complete period is shown. However, this figure hides the passband structure of the filter. Therefore, the transfer function of the filter is shown in Figure E.4(b) for a narrow spectral range around the center wavelength λ_0. The passband structure of the filter can now be clearly seen. The resemblance to the Fabry-Perot filter transfer function (Figure 3.14) is no accident; see Problem 3.9.

The use of multiple cavities leads to a flatter passband and a sharper transition from the passband to the stop band. Both effects are illustrated in Figure 3.16, where the filter transfer function, around the center wavelength λ_0, is plotted for a

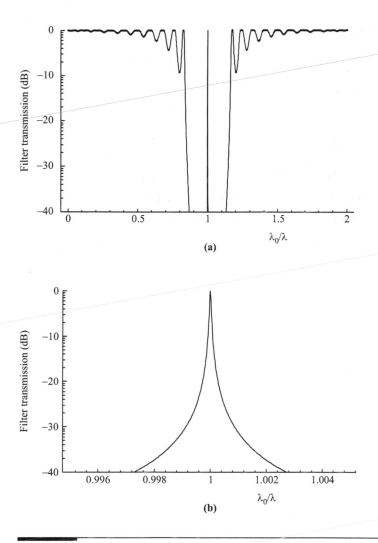

Figure E.4   Transfer function of a single-cavity dielectric thin-film filter. The sequence structure is $G(HL)^9HLL(HL)^9HG$. $n_G = 1.52$, $n_L = 1.46$, and $n_H = 2.3$.

single-cavity, two-cavity, and three-cavity dielectric thin-film filter. The single-cavity filter is the same as the one considered here. The two-cavity filter is described by the sequence

$$G(HL)^6HLL(HL)^{12}HLL(HL)^6HG.$$

The three-cavity filter is described by the sequence

$$G(HL)^5 HLL(HL)^{11} HLL(HL)^{11} HLL(HL)^5 HG.$$

Again, the values $n_G = 1.52$, $n_L = 1.46$, and $n_H = 2.3$ were used.

References

[Kni76] Z. Knittl. *Optics of Thin Films*. John Wiley, New York, 1976.

[RWv84] S. Ramo, J. R. Whinnery, and T. van Duzer. *Fields and Waves in Communication Electronics*. John Wiley, New York, 1984.

appendix F

Receiver Noise Statistics

WE START OUT BY DERIVING an expression for the statistics of the photocurrent in the *pin* receiver, along the lines of [BL90, RH90]. It is useful to think of the photodetection process in the following way. Each time a photon hits the receiver, the receiver generates a small current pulse. Let t_k denote the arrival times of photons at the receiver. Then the photocurrent generated can be expressed as

$$I(t) = \sum_{k=-\infty}^{\infty} eh(t - t_k), \qquad (F.1)$$

where e is the electronic charge and $eh(t - t_k)$ denotes the current impulse due to a photon arriving at time t_k. Note that since $eh(t - t_k)$ is the current due to a single electron, we must have

$$\int_{-\infty}^{\infty} eh(t - t_k)dt = e.$$

The arrival of photons may be described by a Poisson process, whose rate is given by $P(t)/hf_c$. Here, $P(t)$ is the instantaneous optical power, and hf_c is the photon energy. The rate of generation of electrons may then also be considered to be a Poisson process, with rate

$$\lambda(t) = \frac{\mathcal{R}}{e}P(t),$$

where $\mathcal{R} = \eta e/hf_c$ is the responsivity of the photodetector, η being the quantum efficiency.

To evaluate (F.1), let us break up the time axis into small intervals of length δt, with the k-th interval being $[(k - 1/2)\delta t, (k + 1/2)\delta t)$. Let N_k denote the number of electrons generated during the k-th interval. Using these notations, we can rewrite (F.1) as

$$I(t) = \sum_{k=-\infty}^{\infty} eN_k h(t - k\delta t).$$

Note that since the intervals are nonoverlapping, the N_k are independent Poisson random variables, with rate $\lambda(k\delta t)\delta t$.

We will first compute the mean value and autocorrelation functions of the photocurrent for a given optical power $P(.)$. The mean value of the photocurrent is

$$E[I(t)|P(.)] = \sum_{k=-\infty}^{\infty} eE[N_k]h(t - k\delta t) = \sum_{k=-\infty}^{\infty} e\lambda(k\delta t)\delta t \; h(t - k\delta t).$$

In the limit when $\delta t \to 0$, this can be rewritten as

$$E[I(t)|P(.)] = \int_{\infty}^{\infty} e\lambda(\tau)h(t - \tau)d\tau = \mathcal{R} \int_{\infty}^{\infty} P(\tau)h(t - \tau)d\tau.$$

Likewise, the autocorrelation of the photocurrent can be written as

$$
\begin{aligned}
E[I(t_1)I(t_2)|P(.)] &= \int_{\infty}^{\infty} e^2 \lambda(\tau)h(t_1 - \tau)h(t_2 - \tau)d\tau \\
&\quad + E[I(t_1)|P(.)]E[I(t_2)|P(.)] \\
&= e\mathcal{R} \int_{\infty}^{\infty} P(\tau)h(t_1 - \tau)h(t_2 - \tau)d\tau \\
&\quad + \mathcal{R}^2 \int_{\infty}^{\infty} P(\tau)h(t_1 - \tau)d\tau \int_{\infty}^{\infty} P(\tau)h(t_2 - \tau)d\tau.
\end{aligned}
$$

An ideal photodetector generates pure current impulses for each received photon. For such a detector $h(t) = \delta(t)$, where $\delta(t)$ is the impulse function with the properties that $\delta(t) = 0, t \neq 0$ and $\int_{\infty}^{\infty} \delta(t)dt = 1$. For this case, the mean photocurrent becomes

$$E[I(t)|P(.)] = \mathcal{R}P(t),$$

and its autocorrelation is

$$E[I(t_1)I(t_2)|P(.)] = e\mathcal{R}P(t_1)\delta(t_2 - t_1) + \mathcal{R}^2 P(t_1)P(t_2).$$

Removing the conditioning over $P(.)$ yields

$$E[I(t)] = \mathcal{R}E[P(t)], \tag{F.2}$$

and

$$E[I(t_1)I(t_2)] = e\mathcal{R}E[P(t_1)]\delta(t_2 - t_1) + \mathcal{R}^2 E[P(t_1)P(t_2)].$$

The autocovariance of $I(t)$ is then given as

$$
\begin{aligned}
L_I(t_1, t_2) &= E[I(t_1)I(t_2)] - E[I(t_1)]E[I(t_2)] \\
&= e\mathcal{R}E[P(t_1)]\delta(t_2 - t_1) + \mathcal{R}^2 L_P(t_1, t_2),
\end{aligned}
\tag{F.3}
$$

where L_P denotes the autocovariance of $P(t)$.

F.1   Shot Noise

First let us consider the simple case when there is a constant power P incident on the receiver. For this case, $E[P(t)] = P$ and $L_P(\tau) = 0$, and (F.2) and (F.3) can be written as

$$E[I(t)] = \mathcal{R}P$$

and

$$L_I(\tau) = e\mathcal{R}P\delta(\tau),$$

where $\tau = t_2 - t_1$. The power spectral density of the photocurrent is the Fourier transform of the autocovariance, and is given by

$$S_I(f) = \int_\infty^\infty L_I(\tau)e^{-i2\pi f\tau}d\tau = e\mathcal{R}P.$$

Thus the shot noise current can be thought of as being a white noise process with a flat spectral density as given here. Within a receiver bandwidth of B_e, the shot noise power is given by

$$\sigma_{\text{shot}}^2 = \int_{-B_e}^{B_e} S_I(f)df = 2e\mathcal{R}PB_e.$$

Therefore, the photocurrent can be written as

$$I = \overline{I} + i_s,$$

where $\overline{I} = \mathcal{R}P$, and i_s is the shot noise current with zero mean and variance $e\mathcal{R}PB_e$.

F.2   Amplifier Noise

An optical amplifier introduces spontaneous emission noise to the signal in addition to providing gain. Consider a system with an optical preamplifier shown in Figure 4.2. The electric field at the input to the receiver may be written as

$$E(t) = \sqrt{2P}\cos(2\pi f_c t + \Phi) + N(t).$$

Here, P is the signal power, f_c is the carrier frequency, and Φ is a random phase uniformly distributed in $[0, 2\pi]$. $N(t)$ represents the amplifier spontaneous emission noise. For our purposes, we will assume that this is a zero-mean Gaussian noise process with autocorrelation $R_N(\tau)$.

The received power is given by

$$P(t) = E^2(t) = 2P\cos^2(2\pi f_c t + \Phi) + 2\sqrt{2P}N(t)\cos(2\pi f_c t + \Phi) + N^2(t).$$

The mean power is

$$E[P(t)] = P + R_N(0). \tag{F.4}$$

To calculate the autocovariance, note that since $N(t)$ is a Gaussian process,

$$E[N^2(t)N^2(t+\tau)] = R_N^2(0) + 2R_N^2(\tau)$$

using the moment formula (D.1). Using this fact, the autocovariance of $P(.)$ can be calculated to be

$$L_P(\tau) = 2R_N^2(\tau) + 4PR_N(\tau)\cos(2\pi f_c\tau) + \frac{P^2}{2}\cos(4\pi f_c\tau). \tag{F.5}$$

The corresponding spectral density is given by

$$
\begin{aligned}
S_P(f) &= \int_\infty^\infty L_P(\tau)e^{-i2\pi f\tau}d\tau \\
&= 2S_N(f) * S_N(f) + 2P[S_N(f - f_c) + S_N(f + f_c)] \\
&\quad + \frac{P^2}{4}[\delta(f - 2f_c) + \delta(f + 2f_c)].
\end{aligned}
\tag{F.6}
$$

The $*$ denotes the convolution operator, where $f(x) * g(x) = \int_{-\infty}^\infty f(u)g(x - u)du$.

After photodetection, the last term in (F.5) and (F.6) can be omitted because the $2f_c$ components will be filtered out.

In order to derive the noise powers, we return to (F.3) and substitute for $E[P(.)]$ and $L_P(.)$ from (F.4) and (F.6), respectively, to obtain

$$L_I(\tau) = e\mathcal{R}[P + R_N(0)]\delta(\tau) + \mathcal{R}^2[4PR_N(\tau)\cos(2\pi f_c\tau)] + \mathcal{R}^2[2R_N^2(\tau)].$$

We also have

$$S_I(f) = e\mathcal{R}[P + R_N(0)] + \mathcal{R}^2 2P[S_N(f - f_c) + S_N(f + f_c)]$$
$$+ \mathcal{R}^2[2S_N(f) * S_N(f)]. \qquad (F.7)$$

The first term on the right-hand side represents the shot noise terms due to the signal and the amplifier noise. The second term represents the signal-spontaneous beat noise, and the last term is the spontaneous-spontaneous beat noise. Note that we have so far assumed that the amplifier noise is Gaussian but with an arbitrary spectral shape $S_N(f)$. In practice, it is appropriate to assume that the amplifier noise is centered at f_c and is white over an optical bandwidth $B_o < 2f_c$, with

$$S_N(f) = \begin{cases} \frac{P_n(G-1)}{2}, & |f \pm f_c| \le \frac{B_o}{2} \\ 0, & \text{otherwise.} \end{cases}$$

Here, P_n is given by $n_{sp}hf_c$, where n_{sp} is the spontaneous emission factor. Correspondingly, we have

$$R_N(0) = \int_{-\infty}^{\infty} S_N(f)df = P_n(G - 1)B_o.$$

The spectral density of the photocurrent $S_I(f)$ from (F.7) is plotted in Figure F.1 assuming the preceding value for $S_N(f)$. Note that, as before, the shot noise is white, but the signal-spontaneous beat noise spectrum has a rectangular shape, and the spontaneous-spontaneous beat noise a triangular shape. Moreover, the incident optical power P is given by GP_i, where P_i is the input power to the amplifier.

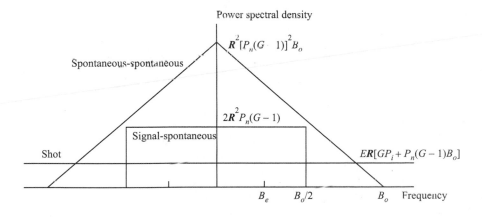

Figure F.1   Photocurrent spectral density.

Note that the photocurrent is passed through a low pass filter with bandwidth B_e. The noise power at the output of the filter is given by

$$\sigma^2 = \int_{-B_e}^{B_e} S_I(f)df = \sigma_{\text{shot}}^2 + \sigma_{\text{sig-spont}}^2 + \sigma_{\text{spont-spont}}^2,$$

where

$$\sigma_{\text{shot}}^2 = 2e\mathcal{R}[GP_i + P_n(G-1)B_o]B_e,$$

$$\sigma_{\text{sig-spont}}^2 = 4\mathcal{R}^2 GP_i P_n(G-1)B_e,$$

and

$$\sigma_{\text{spont-spont}}^2 = \mathcal{R}^2[P_n(G-1)]^2(2B_o - B_e)B_e.$$

References

[BL90]   J. R. Barry and E. A. Lee. Performance of coherent optical receivers. *Proceedings of IEEE*, 78(8):1369–1394, Aug. 1990.

[RH90]   R. Ramaswami and P. A. Humblet. Amplifier induced crosstalk in multi-channel optical networks. *IEEE/OSA Journal on Lightwave Technology*, 8(12):1882–1896, Dec. 1990.

appendix G

Graph Theory

A GRAPH $G(V, E)$ is a collection of vertices (or nodes) V and a collection of edges E that interconnect pairs of these vertices. In a directed graph $D(V, E)$, the edges are directed. We will use $p = |V|$ to denote the number of vertices, and $q = |E|$ to denote the number of edges.

G.1 Walks and Cycles

A *walk* is a path of edges between two nodes in the graph. A *cycle* is a closed walk, that is, a walk that starts and ends at the same node.

G.2 Planarity

A graph G is *planar* if it can be drawn on a plane such that no two edges intersect except possibly at a vertex. In Figure G.1, graphs G_1 and G_2 are planar, and G_3 is not planar. Observe that although G_2 looks as if it is not planar, it can be redrawn as a planar graph.

A *face* of a planar graph (see Figure G.2) is a maximal region in the plane such that any two points in this region can be connected by a curve that does not overlap or intersect with any edge or vertex of G. We can think of the faces as the disconnected pieces of the plane once the vertices and edges of G are removed from the plane. Each graph has one *outer* (or unbounded) face and one or more *inner* faces.

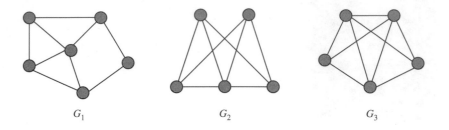

G_1　　　　　　G_2　　　　　　G_3

Figure G.1　Planar and nonplanar graphs.

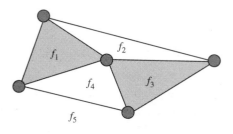

Figure G.2　Faces of a planar graph.

Theorem G.1　**Euler's formula:** *If G is a connected planar graph with p vertices, q edges, and f faces, then*

$$p - q + f = 2.$$

Theorem G.2　*Given a planar directed graph $G(V, E)$, with bidirectional edges, the edges in G can be partitioned into a set of cycles of edges $C_1, C_2, \ldots, C_K$, such that each edge belongs to exactly one cycle and all edges are included in the partition.*

　　Proof.　The partition is shown in Figure G.3. Set K to be the number of faces of G. For each face, there is a set of directed edges of the graph that form its boundaries. For each inner face, pick the set of directed edges to form a clockwise cycle. For the outer face, pick the set of directed edges to form a counterclockwise cycle. This yields the desired partition.　■

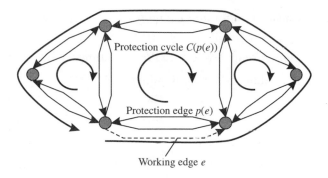

Figure G.3   Partition of a planar graph.

G.3   Connectivity

The vertex connectivity $\kappa_v(G)$ is the minimum number of vertices that must be removed from G to disconnect it. The edge connectivity $\kappa_e(G)$ is the minimum number of edges that must be removed from G to disconnect it. A graph G is k-edge connected if $\kappa_e(G) = k$.

Two paths are said to be *vertex-disjoint* if they do not share a common vertex (except for their end points). Let $r_v(i, j)$ denote the number of vertex-disjoint paths between vertices i and j. Likewise, let $r_e(i, j)$ denote the number of edge-disjoint paths between vertices i and j. Then

$$\kappa_v(G) = \min_{i,j} r_v(i, j),$$

and

$$\kappa_e(G) = \min_{i,j} r_e(i, j).$$

Further Reading

There are several excellent books on graph theory. See, for example, [Ber76, CL79, Har69, Eve79].

References

[Ber76]   C. Berge. *Graphs and Hypergraphs*. North Holland, Amsterdam, 1976.

[CL79]   G. Chartrand and L. Lesniak. *Graphs and Digraphs*. Wadsworth and Brooks/Cole, Monterey, CA, 1979.

[Eve79] S. Even. *Graph Algorithms*. Computer Science Press, Potomac, MD, 1979.

[Har69] F. Harary. *Graph Theory*. Addison-Wesley, Reading, MA, 1969.

appendix

WDM Link MIB

WE WILL GIVE AN EXAMPLE of an MIB for a point-to-point WDM link, along the lines of those used for commercial systems today. We will consider only the simple case where no line amplifiers are present in the system and only an optical preamplifier is present.

Each channel in the system has its wavelength-specific laser and a receiver, and has an input/output port interface from which it sources/sinks the data that is transmitted over the WDM link. The system uses a 1:1 optical protection technique to protect against fiber cuts, where traffic is switched from the working fiber to a protection fiber if the working fiber is cut. Redundant power supplies are commonly included in such systems.

The parameters that are monitored are described as follows in the form of MIB variables:

- For the entire unit:
  - **power_supply1:** an UP/DOWN variable representing the status of the first power supply in the unit.
  - **power_supply2:** an UP/DOWN variable representing the status of the second power supply in the unit. (Two power supplies are used for redundancy.)
  - **max_number_of_channels:** indicates the maximum number of channels that can be present in the unit.
  - **number_of_channels:** indicates the number of channels that the unit is currently configured for.
  - **number_of_active_channels:** indicates the number of channels currently active.

- **temperature:** indicates if the temperature inside the unit is within normal limits.
- **protection_type:** indicates whether 1:1 optical protection is to be used or not.

- For each channel:
  - **card_installed:** indicates whether the card containing the wavelength-specific laser and receiver for that channel is installed or not.
  - **traffic:** indicates the type of traffic being carried over that channel (OC-48, OC-192, ESCON, and so on).
  - **input_light:** indicates whether any light is present at the input on the port side. (This assumes an optical input. Electrical inputs may be supported as well.)
  - **link_light:** indicates whether light is being received on that channel from the WDM link.
  - **laser_current:** indicates the value of the laser drive current. Alarms can be set if it exceeds a given threshold.
  - **laser_output:** indicates the value of the laser output power. As the laser ages, the power goes down if the laser drive current is held constant, and a threshold can be set to indicate that it is time to replace the laser.
  - **optical_snr:** indicates the value of the optical signal-to-noise ratio on that channel.
  - **wavelength:** indicates the measured value of the wavelength and is used to keep track of wavelength drifts over time.

- For the protection switching:
  - **fiber_status:** indicates whether the link is using the working fiber or the protection fiber. This variable can be set by the network manager to cause the link to be deliberately switched over to the other fiber.
  - **protection_type:** indicates whether protection exists and, if so, whether the protection is reverting or nonreverting.

- For the optical preamplifier:
  - **amplifier_installed:** a YES/NO variable indicating whether the amplifier option is installed or not.
  - **pump_enable:** can be set to turn on or off one of two redundant pump lasers.
  - **pump_status:** indicates whether either pump is currently active or not.
  - **pump_power:** keeps track of the output power of each pump and senses any degradations.
  - **pump_temperature:** monitors the temperature of each laser.
  - **pump_voltage:** monitors the voltage across the pump laser and can be used to indicate open circuits in the drive circuitry for the laser.

Bibliography

[Aar95]   R. Aaron, editor. *IEEE Communications Magazine: Special Issue on Access to Broadband Services*, volume 33, Aug. 1995.

[ABC⁺94]   A. Aggarwal, A. Bar-Noy, D. Coppersmith, R. Ramaswami, B. Schieber, and M. Sudan. Efficient routing and scheduling algorithms for optical networks. In *Proceedings of 5th Annual ACM-SIAM Symposium on Discrete Algorithms*, pages 412–423, Jan. 1994.

[ABM96]   M. Azizoglu, R. A. Barry, and A. Mokhtar. Impact of tuning delay on the performance of bandwidth-limited optical broadcast networks with uniform traffic. *IEEE JSAC/JLT Special Issue on Optical Networks*, pages 935–944, June 1996. An earlier version appeared in *Proc. Infocom'95.*

[Abr70]   N. Abramson. The Aloha system—another alternative for computer communications. In *Proceedings of Fall Joint Computing Conference*, page 37, 1970.

[Aca87]   A. S. Acampora. A multi-channel multihop local lightwave network. *Proceedings of IEEE Globecom*, pages 37.5.1–9, 1987.

[ACKP97]   V. Auletta, I. Caragiannis, C. Kaklamanis, and P. Persiano. Bandwidth allocation algorithms on tree-shaped all-optical networks with wavelength converters. In *Proceedings of the 4th International Colloquium on Structural Information and Communication Complexity*, 1997.

[ACT]   *ACTS web site. http://www.analysys.co.uk/acts/cec/.*

[AD86]   G. P. Agrawal and N. K. Dutta. *Long-Wavelength Semiconductor Lasers.* Van Nostrand Reinhold, New York, 1986.

[Agr92]   G. P. Agrawal. *Fiber-Optic Communication Systems*. John Wiley, New York, 1992.

[Agr95]   G. P. Agrawal. *Nonlinear Fiber Optics, 2nd edition*. Academic Press, San Diego, CA, 1995.

[Ale93]   S. B. Alexander et al. A precompetitive consortium on wide-band all-optical networks. *IEEE/OSA Journal on Lightwave Technology*, 11:714–735, May/June 1993.

[Ame88]   American National Standards Institute, Z136.2. *Safe use of optical fiber communication systems utilizing laser diodes and LED sources*, 1988.

[Ame89]   American National Standards Institute, X3T9.3. *High-performance parallel interface*, Nov. 1989. Rev. 6.9.

[Ame94]   American National Standards Institute, X3T9.3. *Fibre channel: Signalling protocol (FC-2)*, Nov. 1994. Rev. 4.2.

[AP94]   S. Aidarus and T. Plevyak, editors. *Telecommunications Network Management into the 21st Century*. IEEE Press, Los Alamitos, CA, 1994.

[AP95]   J. S. Auerbach and R. K. Pankaj. Use of delegated tuning and forwarding in WDMA networks. *IEEE Transactions on Communications*, 43(1):52–63, Jan. 1995.

[AS72]   M. Abramovitz and I. A. Stegun, editors. *Handbook of Mathematical Functions*. Dover Press, Mineola, NY, 1972.

[AS92]   A. S. Acampora and S. I. A. Shah. Multihop lightwave networks: A comparison of store-and-forward and hot-potato routing. *IEEE Transactions on Communications*, 40(6):1082–1090, June 1992.

[AY86]   Y. Arakawa and A. Yariv. Quantum well lasers—gain, spectra, dynamics. *IEEE Journal of Quantum Electronics*, 22(9):1887–1899, Sept. 1986.

[BA94]   F. Bruyère and O. Audouin. Assessment of system penalties induced by polarization mode dispersion in a 5 Gb/s optically amplified transoceanic link. *IEEE Photon. Tech. Lett.*, 6(3):443–445, March 1994.

[Bal96]   K. Bala et al. WDM network economics. In *Proceedings of National Fiber Optic Engineers Conference*, pages 163–174, 1996.

[Bar64]   P. Baran. On distributed communications networks. *IEEE Transactions on Communications*, pages 1–9, March 1964.

[Bar93]   R. A. Barry. An all-optical non-blocking $M \times M$ switchless connector with $O(\sqrt{M \log M})$ wavelengths and without wavelength changers. *Electronics Letters*, 29(14):1252–1254, July 1993.

[Bar96a]   R. A. Barry, editor. *IEEE Network: Special Issue on Optical Networks*, volume 10, Nov. 1996.

[Bar96b] R. A. Barry et al. All-optical network consortium—ultrafast TDM networks. *IEEE JSAC/JLT Special Issue on Optical Networks*, 14(5):999–1013, June 1996.

[BC90] P. N. Butcher and D. Cotter. *The Elements of Nonlinear Optics*, volume 9 of *Cambridge Studies in Modern Optics*. Cambridge University Press, Cambridge, 1990.

[BCB96] K. Bala, F. R. K. Chung, and C. A. Brackett. Optical wavelength routing, translation and packet/cell switched networks. *IEEE/OSA Journal on Lightwave Technology*, 14(3):336–343, March 1996.

[BCG95] K. Bala, R. R. Cordell, and E. L. Goldstein. The case for opaque multiwavelength optical networks. In *IEEE LEOS Summer Topical Meetings*, Keystone, Colorado, Aug. 1995.

[BCM+92] D. J. Blumenthal, K. Y. Chen, J. Ma, R. J. Feuerstein, and J. R. Sauer. Demonstration of a deflection routing 2 × 2 photonic switch for computer interconnects. *IEEE Photonics Technology Letters*, 4(2):169–173, Feb. 1992.

[BDG95] C. Baransel, W. Dobosiewicz, and P. Gburzynski. Routing in multihop packet switching networks: Gb/s challange. *IEEE Network*, pages 38–61, May/June 1995.

[BDN90] K. J. Blow, N. J. Doran, and B. P. Nelson. Demonstration of the nonlinear fibre loop mirror as an ultrafast all-optical demultiplexer. *Electronics Letters*, 26(14):962–964, July 1990.

[Bel95a] Bellcore. *Network equipment-building system (NEBS) generic equipment requirements*, 1995. GR-63-CORE.

[Bel95b] Bellcore. *SONET transport systems: Common generic criteria*, 1995. GR-253-CORE.

[Bel96a] Bellcore. *Generic criteria for SONET point-to-point wavelength division multiplexed systems in the 1550-nm region*, July 1996. GR-2918-CORE, Issue 1.

[Bel96b] Bellcore. *SONET OC-192 transport system generic criteria*, Aug. 1996. GR-1377-CORE, Issue 3.

[Ben65] V. E. Beneš. *Mathematical Theory of Connecting Networks*. Academic Press, New York, 1965.

[Ben96a] A. F. Benner. *Fiber Channel*. McGraw-Hill, New York, 1996.

[Ben96b] I. Bennion et al. UV-written in-fibre Bragg gratings. *Optical Quantum Electronics*, 28(2):93–135, Feb. 1996.

[Ber76] C. Berge. *Graphs and Hypergraphs*. North Holland, Amsterdam, 1976.

[Ber96a] L. Berthelon et al. Experimental assessment of node cascadability in a reconfigurable survivable WDM ring network. In *Proceedings of Topical Meeting on Broadband Optical Networks*, 1996.

[Ber96b] L. Berthelon et al. Over 40,000 km across a layered network by recirculation through an experimental WDM ring network. In *Proceedings of European Conference on Optical Communication*, 1996.

[BG92] D. Bertsekas and R. G. Gallager. *Data Networks*. Prentice Hall, Englewood Cliffs, NJ, 1992.

[BG95] D. Bienstock and O. Gunluk. Computational experience with a difficult mixed-integer multicommodity flow problem. *Mathematical Programming*, 68:213–237, 1995.

[BH92] R. A. Barry and P. A. Humblet. Bounds on the number of wavelengths needed in WDM networks. In *LEOS'92 Summer Topical Meeting Digest*, pages 21–22, 1992.

[BH94] R. A. Barry and P. A. Humblet. On the number of wavelengths and switches in all-optical networks. *IEEE Transactions on Communications*, 42(2/3/4):583–591, Feb./March/April 1994.

[BH96] R. A. Barry and P. A. Humblet. Models of blocking probability in all-optical networks with and without wavelength changers. *IEEE JSAC/JLT Special Issue on Optical Networks*, 14(5):858–867, June 1996.

[Big90] N. Biggs. Some heuristics for graph colouring. In R. Nelson and R. J. Wilson, editors, *Graph Colourings*, Pitman Research Notes in Mathematics Series, pages 87–96. Longman Scientific & Technical, Burnt Mill, Harlow, Essex, UK, 1990.

[Big97] S. Bigo et al. Error-free 20-Gbit/s soliton transmission over 7150 km through all-optical synchronous phase modulation. In *OFC'97 Technical Digest*, pages 143–144, 1997.

[Bir96] A. Birman. Computing approximate blocking probabilities for a class of optical networks. *IEEE JSAC/JLT Special Issue on Optical Networks*, 14(5):852–857, June 1996.

[BK95] A. Birman and A. Kershenbaum. Routing and wavelength assignment methods in single-hop all-optical networks with blocking. In *Proceedings of IEEE Infocom*, pages 431–438, 1995.

[BL90] J. R. Barry and E. A. Lee. Performance of coherent optical receivers. *Proceedings of IEEE*, 78(8):1369–1394, Aug. 1990.

[Bla95] U. Black. *Network Management Standards*. McGraw-Hill, New York, 1995.

[Bor95] F. Borgonovo. Deflection routing. In M. Steenstrup, editor, *Routing in Communication Networks*. Prentice Hall, Englewood Cliffs, NJ, 1995.

[BP96] A. Bononi and P. R. Prucnal. Analytical evaluation of improved access techniques in deflection routing networks. *IEEE/ACM Transactions on Networking*, 4(5):726–730, Oct. 1996.

[BPS93] K. Bala, K. Petropoulos, and T. E. Stern. Multicasting in a linear lightwave network. In *Proceedings of IEEE Infocom*, pages 1350–1358, 1993.

[BPS94] D. J. Blumenthal, P. R. Prucnal, and J. R. Sauer. Photonic packet switches: Architectures and experimental implementations. *Proceedings of IEEE*, 82:1650–1667, Nov. 1994.

[Bra89] C. A. Brackett, editor. *IEEE Communications Magazine: Special Issue on Lightwave Systems and Components*, volume 27, Oct. 1989.

[Bra93] C. A. Brackett et al. A scalable multiwavelength multihop optical network: A proposal for research on all-optical networks. *IEEE/OSA Journal on Lightwave Technology*, 11:736–753, May/June 1993.

[BSSLB95] K. Bala, T. E. Stern, D. Simchi-Levi, and K. Bala. Routing in a linear lightwave network. *IEEE/ACM Transactions on Networking*, 3(4):459–469, Aug. 1995.

[Buc95] J. A. Buck. *Fundamentals of Optical Fibers*. John Wiley, New York, 1995.

[Bur86] W. E. Burr. The FDDI optical data link. *IEEE Communications Magazine*, 24(5):18–23, May 1986.

[BW80] M. Born and E. Wolf. *Principles of Optics*. Pergamon Press, Oxford, 1980.

[Cah98] R. Cahn. *The Art of Network Design*. Morgan Kaufmann, San Francisco, 1998.

[Car97] R. Cardwell et al. WDM network economic sensitivities. In *Proceedings of National Fiber Optic Engineers Conference*, pages 105–116, 1997.

[CDdM90] F. Curti, B. Daino, G. de Marchis, and F. Matera. Statistical treatment of the evolution of the principal states of polarization in single-mode fibers. *IEEE/OSA Journal on Lightwave Technology*, 8(8):1162–1166, Aug. 1990.

[CdLS92] S. A. Calta, S. A. deVeer, E. Loizides, and R. N. Strangewayes. Enterprise systems connection (ESCON) architecture—system overview. *IBM Journal of Research and Development*, 36(4):535–551, July 1992.

[CDR90] M. S. Chen, N. R. Dono, and R. Ramaswami. A media-access protocol for packet-switched wavelength-division metropolitan area networks. *IEEE Journal of Selected Areas in Communications*, 8(6):1048–1057, Aug. 1990.

[CEG+96] G. K. Chang, G. Ellinas, J. K. Gamelin, M. Z. Iqbal, and C. A. Brackett. Multiwavelength reconfigurable WDM/ATM/SONET network testbed. *IEEE/OSA JLT/JSAC Special Issue on Multiwavelength Optical Technology and Networks*, 14(6):1320–1340, June 1996.

[CGK92] I. Chlamtac, A. Ganz, and G. Karmi. Lightpath communications: An approach to high-bandwidth optical WAN's. *IEEE Transactions on Communications*, 40(7):1171–1182, July 1992.

[CGK93]   I. Chlamtac, A. Ganz, and G. Karmi. Lightnets: Topologies for high-speed optical networks. *IEEE/OSA Journal on Lightwave Technology*, 11(5/6):951–961, May/June 1993.

[CGS93]   I. Cidon, I. S. Gopal, and A. Segall. Connection establishment in high-speed networks. *IEEE/ACM Transactions on Networking*, 1(4):469–482, Aug. 1993.

[Cha94]   G. K. Chang et al. Experimental demonstration of a reconfigurable WDM/ATM/SONET multiwavelength network testbed. In *OFC'94 Technical Digest*, 1994. Postdeadline paper PD9.

[Cha96]   T. K. Chang et al. Implementation of STARNET: A WDM computer communications network. *IEEE JSAC/JLT Special Issue on Optical Networks*, 14(6):824–839, June 1996.

[Che90]   K-W. Cheung. Acoustooptic tunable filters in narrowband WDM networks: System issues and network applications. *IEEE Journal of Selected Areas in Communications*, 8(6):1015–1025, Aug. 1990.

[CHI+92]   M. W. Chbat, B. Hong, M. N. Islam, C. E. Soccolich, and P. R. Prucnal. Ultrafast soliton-trapping AND gate. *IEEE/OSA Journal on Lightwave Technology*, 10(12):2011–2016, Dec. 1992.

[CHK+96]   R. L. Cruz, G. R. Hill, A. L. Kellner, R. Ramaswami, and G. H. Sasaki, editors. *IEEE JSAC/JLT Special Issue on Optical Networks*, volume 14, June 1996.

[Chl96]   I. Chlamtac et al. CORD: Contention resolution by delay lines. *IEEE JSAC/JLT Special Issue on Optical Networks*, 14(5):1014–1029, June 1996.

[Chr84]   A. R. Chraplyvy. Optical power limits in multichannel wavelength-division-multiplexed systems due to stimulated Raman scattering. *Electronics Letters*, 20:58, 1984.

[Chr90]   A. R. Chraplyvy. Limitations on lightwave communications imposed by optical-fiber nonlinearities. *IEEE/OSA Journal on Lightwave Technology*, 8(10):1548–1557, Oct. 1990.

[CK94]   R. J. Campbell and R. Kashyap. The properties and applications of photosensitive germanosilicate fibre. *International Journal of Optoelectronics*, 9(1):33–57, 1994.

[CL79]   G. Chartrand and L. Lesniak. *Graphs and Digraphs*. Wadsworth and Brooks/Cole, Monterey, CA, 1979.

[Cle94]   B. Clesca et al. Gain flatness comparison between Erbium-doped fluoride and silica fiber amplifiers with wavelength-multiplexed signals. *IEEE Photonics Technology Letters*, 6(4):509–512, April 1994.

[CLM97]   D. Cotter, J. K. Lucek, and D. D. Marcenac. Ultra-high bit-rate networking: From the transcontinental backbone to the desktop. *IEEE Communications Magazine*, 35(4):90–95, April 1997.

[CNW90] N. K. Cheung, G. Nosu, and G. Winzer, editors. *IEEE JSAC: Special Issue on Dense WDM Networks*, volume 8, Aug. 1990.

[Com94] D. E. Comer. *Internetworking with TCP/IP: Vol. II: Design, Implementation and Internals*. Prentice Hall, Englewood Cliffs, NJ, 1994.

[Cot95] D. Cotter et al. Self-routing of 100 Gbit/s packets using 6 bit 'keyword' address recognition. *Electronics Letters*, 31(25):2201–2202, Dec. 1995.

[CY91] M. Chen and T-S. Yum. A conflict-free protocol for optical WDMA networks. *Proceedings of IEEE Globecom*, pages 1276–1281, 1991.

[CZA92] R. Chipalkatti, Z. Zhang, and A. S. Acampora. High-speed communication protocols for optical star networks using WDM. *Proceedings of IEEE Infocom*, 1992.

[Dan95] S. L. Danielsen et al. Detailed noise statistics for an optically preamplified direct detection receiver. *IEEE/OSA Journal on Lightwave Technology*, 13(5):977–981, 1995.

[Dar87] T. E. Darcie. Subcarrier multiplexing for multiple-access lightwave networks. *IEEE/OSA Journal on Lightwave Technology*, LT-5:1103–1110, 1987.

[DEK91] C. Dragone, C. A. Edwards, and R. C. Kistler. Integrated optics $N \times N$ multiplexer on silicon. *IEEE Photonics Technology Letters*, 3:896–899, Oct. 1991.

[DEM96] F. Diner, H. Escobar, and K. Min. Optimum protection schemes for the multi-wavelength inter-office network: A comparative analysis. In *Proceedings of National Fiber Optic Engineers Conference*, pages 291–298, 1996.

[Der95] F. Derr. Design of an 8x8 optical cross-connect switch: Results on subsystems and first measurements. In *ECOC'95 Optical Networking Workshop*, 1995. Paper S2.2.

[Des94] E. Desurvire. *Erbium-Doped Fiber Amplifiers*. John Wiley, New York, 1994.

[DGL+90] N. R. Dono, P. E. Green, K. Liu, R. Ramaswami, and F. F. Tong. A wavelength division multiple access network for computer communication. *IEEE Journal of Selected Areas in Communications*, 8(6):983–994, Aug. 1990.

[DMJ+96] T. Durhuus, B. Mikkelsen, C. Joergensen, S. Lykke Danielsen, and K. E. Stubkjaer. All optical wavelength conversion by semiconductor optical amplifiers. *IEEE/OSA JLT/JSAC Special Issue on Multiwavelength Optical Technology and Networks*, 14(6):942–954, June 1996.

[Dow96] P. Dowd et al. Lightning network and systems architecture. *IEEE/OSA JLT/JSAC Special Issue on Multiwavelength Optical Technology and Networks*, 14(6):1371–1387, June 1996.

[dP93]   M. de Prycker. *Asynchronous Transfer Mode: Solution for Broadband ISDN*. Ellis Horwood, New York, 1993.

[Dra89]   C. Dragone. Efficient $n \times n$ star couplers using Fourier optics. *IEEE/OSA Journal on Lightwave Technology*, 7(3):479–489, March 1989.

[DW88]   N. J. Doran and D. Wood. Nonlinear-optical loop mirror. *Optics Letters*, 13(1):56–58, Jan. 1988.

[dW90]   D. de Werra. Heuristics for graph coloring. In G. Tinhofer, E. Mayr, and H. Noltemeier, editors, *Computational Graph Theory*, volume 7 of *Computing, Supplement*, pages 191–208. Springer-Verlag, Berlin, 1990.

[Eis92]   M. Eiselt. Optical loop mirror with semiconductor laser amplifier. *Electronics Letters*, 28(16):1505–1506, July 1992.

[ES92]   J. C. Elliott and M. W. Sachs. The IBM enterprise systems connection architecture. *IBM Journal of Research and Development*, 36(4):577–591, July 1992.

[ES96]   G. Ellinas and T. E. Stern. Automatic protection switching for link failures in optical networks with bidirectional links. In *Proceedings of IEEE Globecom*, 1996.

[Eve79]   S. Even. *Graph Algorithms*. Computer Science Press, Potomac, MD, 1979.

[FBP95]   F. Forghieri, A. Bononi, and P. R. Prucnal. Analysis and comparison of hot-potato and single-buffer deflection routing in very high bit rate optical mesh networks. *IEEE Transactions on Communications*, 43(1):88–98, Jan. 1995.

[FFP88]   P. Feldman, J. Friedman, and N. Pippenger. Wide-sense nonblocking networks. *SIAM Journal on Discrete Mathematics*, 1(2):158–173, May 1988.

[FGO+96]   M. Fujiwara, M. S. Goodman, M. J. O'Mahony, O. K. Tonguez, and A. E. Willner, editors. *IEEE/OSA JLT/JSAC Special Issue on Multiwavelength Optical Technology and Networks*, volume 14, June 1996.

[FHHH90]   M. E. Fermann, F. Haberl, M. Hofer, and H. Hochreiter. Nonlinear amplifying loop mirror. *Optics Letters*, 15(13):752–754, July 1990.

[FMB97]   S. Finn, M. M. Medard, and R. A. Barry. A novel approach to automatic protection switching using trees. In *Proceedings of IEEE International Conference on Communication*, 1997.

[FNS+92]   A. Frank, T. Nishizeki, N. Saito, H. Suzuki, and E. Tardos. Algorithms for routing around a rectangle. *Discrete Applied Mathematics*, 40:363–378, 1992.

[For95]   The ATM Forum. *ATM User-Network Interface (UNI) Specification Version 3.1*. PTR Prentice Hall, Englewood Cliffs, NJ, 1995.

[Fra93]   A. G. Fraser. Banquet speech. In *Proceedings of Workshop on High-Performance Communication Subsystems*, Williamsburg, VA, Sept. 1993.

[Fri94]   N. J. Frigo et al. A wavelength-division-multiplexed passive optical network with cost-shared components. *IEEE Photonics Technology Letters*, 6(11):1365–1367, 1994.

[FRI96]   N. J. Frigo, K. C. Reichmann, and P. P. Iannone. WDM passive optical networks: A robust and flexible infrastructure for local access. In *Proceedings of International Workshop on Photonic Networks and Technologies*, pages 201–212, 1996.

[FSA97]   *Full Services Access Network Requirements Specification*, 1997. Available on the Web at *http://btlabs1.labs.bt.com/profsoc/access/*.

[FTC95]   F. Forghieri, R. W. Tkach, and A. R. Chraplyvy. WDM systems with unequally spaced channels. *IEEE/OSA Journal on Lightwave Technology*, 13(5):889–897, May 1995.

[FTCV96] F. Forghieri, R. W. Tkach, A. R. Chraplyvy, and A. M. Vengsarkar. Dispersion compensating fiber: Is there merit in the figure of merit? In *OFC'96 Technical Digest*, pages 255–257, 1996.

[FV88]   G. J. Foschini and G. Vannucci. Using spread spectrum in a high-capacity fiber-optic local network. *IEEE/OSA Journal on Lightwave Technology*, 6(3):370–379, March 1988.

[Gar94]   L. M. Gardner et al. Techniques for finding ring covers in survivable networks. In *Proceedings of IEEE Globecom*, pages 1862–1866, 1994.

[GEE94]   E. L. Goldstein, L. Eskildsen, and A. F. Elrefaie. Performance implications of component crosstalk in transparent lightwave networks. *IEEE Photon. Tech. Lett.*, 6(5):657–670, May 1994.

[GG93]   A. G. Greenberg and J. Goodman. Sharp approximate models of deflection routing in mesh networks. *IEEE Transactions on Communications*, 41(1):210–223, Jan. 1993.

[GH92]   A. G. Greenberg and B. Hajek. Deflection routing in hypercube networks. *IEEE Transactions on Communications*, 40(6):1070–1081, June 1992.

[GJ79]   M. R. Garey and D. S. Johnson. *Computers and Intractibility—A Guide to the Theory of NP Completeness*. W. H. Freeman, San Francisco, 1979.

[GJR96]   P. E. Green, F. J. Janniello, and R. Ramaswami. Multichannel protocol-transparent WDM distance extension using remodulation. *IEEE JSAC/JLT Special Issue on Optical Networks*, 14(6):962–967, June 1996.

[GK97]   O. Gerstel and S. Kutten. Dynamic wavelengh allocation in all-optical ring networks. In *Proceedings of IEEE International Conference on Communication*, 1997.

[GKV+90] M. S. Goodman, H. Kobrinski, M. Vecchi, R. M. Bulley, and J. M. Gimlett. The LAMBDANET multiwavelength network: Architecture, applications and demonstrations. *IEEE Journal of Selected Areas in Communications*, 8 issue(6):995–1004, Aug. 1990.

[GLS98]   O. Gerstel, P. Lin, and G. H. Sasaki. A new angle on wavelength assignment in WDM rings: Minimize system cost, not number of wavelengths. In *Proceedings of IEEE Infocom*, 1998.

[Gna96a]   A. H. Gnauck et al. 100 Gb/s × 10 channel OTDM/WDM transmission using a single supercontinuum WDM source. In *OFC'96 Technical Digest*, 1996. Postdeadline paper PD21.

[Gna96b]   A. H. Gnauck et al. One terabit/s transmission experiment. In *OFC'96 Technical Digest*, 1996. Postdeadline paper PD20.

[GR96]   O. Gerstel and R. Ramaswami. Multiwavelength optical network architectures and protection schemes. In *Proc. Tirrenia Workshop on Optical Networks*, pages 42–51, 1996.

[Gre91]   P. E. Green. The future of fiber-optic computer networks. *IEEE Computer*, 24(9):78–89, Sept. 1991.

[Gre93]   P. E. Green. *Fiber-Optic Networks*. Prentice Hall, Englewood Cliffs, NJ, 1993.

[GRS97a]   O. Gerstel, R. Ramaswami, and G. H. Sasaki. Benefits of limited wavelength conversion in WDM ring networks. In *OFC'97 Technical Digest*, pages 119–120, 1997.

[GRS97b]   O. Gerstel, R. Ramaswami, and G. H. Sasaki. Fault tolerant WDM rings with limited wavelength conversion. In *Proceedings of IEEE Infocom*, pages 508–516, 1997.

[GRS98]   O. Gerstel, R. Ramaswami, and G. H. Sasaki. Cost effective traffic grooming in WDM rings. In *Proceedings of IEEE Infocom*, 1998.

[GSKR97]   O. Gerstel, G. H. Sasaki, S. Kutten, and R. Ramaswami. Worst-case dynamic wavelength allocation in optical networks. Technical Report RC 20717, IBM Research Division, Feb. 1997.

[GSP94]   I. Glesk, J. P. Sokoloff, and P. R. Prucnal. All-optical address recognition and self-routing in a 250 Gb/s packet-switched network. *Electronics Letters*, 30(16):1322–1323, Aug. 1994.

[Gun97a]   P. Gunning et al. 40 Gbit/s optical TDMA LAN over 300m of installed blown fibre. In *Proceedings of European Conference on Optical Communication*, volume 4, pages 61–64, Sept. 1997.

[Gun97b]   P. Gunning et al. Optical-TDMA LAN incorporating packaged integrated Mach-Zehnder interferometer channel selector. *Electronics Letters*, 33(16):1404–1406, July 1997.

[GW94]   A. Ganz and X. Wang. Efficient algorithm for virtual topology design in multihop lightwave networks. *IEEE/ACM Transactions on Networking*, 2(3):217–225, June 1994.

[Hal96]   W. E. Hall et al. The Rainbow-II gigabit optical network. *IEEE JSAC/JLT Special Issue on Optical Networks*, 14(6):814–823, June 1996.

[Hal97a] K. L. Hall. 40 Gb/s optical packet buffering. In *OFC'97 Technical Digest*, page 250, 1997.

[Hal97b] K. L. Hall. All-optical buffers for high-speed slotted TDM networks. In *IEEE/LEOS Summer Topical Meeting on Advanced Semiconductor Lasers and Applications*, page 15, 1997.

[Har69]   F. Harary. *Graph Theory*. Addison-Wesley, Reading, MA, 1969.

[HC93]   B. Hajek and R. L. Cruz. On the average delay for routing subject to independent deflections. *IEEE Transactions on Information Theory*, 39(1):84–91, Jan. 1993.

[HD97]   G. R. Hill and P. Diemeester, editors. *IEEE Communications Magazine: Special Issue on Photonic Networks in Europe*, volume 35, April 1997.

[HH90]   P. A. Humblet and W. M. Hamdy. Crosstalk analysis and filter optimization of single- and double-cavity Fabry-Perot filters. *IEEE Journal of Selected Areas in Communications*, 8(6):1095–1107, Aug. 1990.

[HH96]   A. M. Hill and A. J. N. Houghton. Optical networking in the European ACTS programme. In *OFC'96 Technical Digest*, pages 238–239, San Jose, Feb. 1996.

[Hil85]   W. D. Hillis. *The Connection Machine*. MIT Press, Cambridge, MA, 1985.

[Hil87]   W. D. Hillis. The connection machine. *Scientific American*, 256(6), June 1987.

[Hil93]   G. R. Hill et al. A transport network layer based on optical network elements. *IEEE/OSA Journal on Lightwave Technology*, 11:667–679, May/June 1993.

[HJKM78] K. O. Hill, D. C. Johnson, B. S. Kawasaki, and R. I. MacDonald. CW three-wave mixing in single-mode optical fibers. *Journal of Applied Physics*, 49(10):5098–5106, Oct. 1978.

[HK91]   M. G. Hluchyj and M. J. Karol. Shufflenet: An application of generalized perfect shuffles to multihop lightwave networks. *IEEE/OSA Journal on Lightwave Technology*, 9(10):1386–1397, 1991.

[HKS87]   I. M. I. Habbab, M. Kavehrad, and C-E. W. Sundberg. Protocols for very high speed optical fiber local area networks using a passive star topology. *IEEE/OSA Journal on Lightwave Technology*, LT-5(12):1782–1794, Dec. 1987.

[Hoo93]   K. J. Hood et al. Optical distribution systems for television studio applications. *IEEE/OSA Journal on Lightwave Technology*, 11(5/6):680–687, May/June 1993.

[HRS92]   P. A. Humblet, R. Ramaswami, and K. N. Sivarajan. An efficient communication protocol for high-speed packet-switched multichannel networks. *Proceedings of ACM SIGCOMM*, pages 2–13, 1992.

[HSS98]   A. M. Hill, A. A. M. Saleh, and K. Sato, editors. *IEEE JSAC: Special Issue on High-Capacity Optical Transport Networks*, 1998. To appear.

[HW95]   B. Hajek and T. Weller. Scheduling nonuniform traffic in a packet switching system with large propagation delay. *IEEE Transactions on Information Theory*, 41(2):358–365, March 1995.

[IBM95]   J. Iness, S. Banerjee, and B. Mukherjee. GEMNET: A generalized, shuffle-exchange-based, regular, scalable, modular, multihop, WDM lightwave network. *IEEE/ACM Transactions on Networking*, 3(4):470–476, Aug. 1995.

[IFD95]   P. P. Iannone, N. J. Frigo, and T. E. Darcie. WDM passive optical network architecture with bidirectional optical spectral slicing. In *OFC'95 Technical Digest*, pages 51–53, 1995. Paper TuK2.

[Int93]   International Electrotechnical Commission. *825-1: Safety of laser products*, 1993.

[IRF96]   P. P. Iannone, K. C. Reichmann, and N. J. Frigo. Broadcast digital video delivered over WDM passive optical networks. *IEEE Photonics Technology Letters*, 8(7):930–932, 1996.

[ISSV96] E. Iannone, R. Sabella, L. De Stefano, and F. Valeri. All optical wavelength conversion in optical multicarrier networks. *IEEE Transactions on Communications*, 44(6):716–724, June 1996.

[ITU93a] ITU-T. *Recommendation G.652: Characteristics of a single-mode optical fiber cable*, 1993.

[ITU93b] ITU-T. *Recommendation G.653: Characteristics of a dispersion-shifted single-mode optical fiber cable*, 1993.

[ITU96a] ITU-T. *Recommendation G.655: Characteristics of a nonzero-dispersion shifted single-mode optical fiber cable*, 1996.

[ITU96b] ITU-T SG15/WP 4. *Draft Rec. G.mcs: Optical interfaces for multichannel systems with optical amplifiers*, June 1996.

[ITU96c] ITU-T SG15/WP 4. *Draft Rec. G.scs: Optical interfaces for single-channel SDH systems with optical amplifiers and STM-64 systems*, June 1996.

[ITU96d] ITU-T SG15/WP 4. *Rec. G.681: Functional characteristics of interoffice and long-haul line systems using optical amplifiers, including optical multiplexing*, 1996.

[Jac96] J. L. Jackel et al. Acousto-optic tunable filters (AOTFs) for multiwavelength optical cross-connects: Crosstalk considerations. *IEEE/OSA JLT/JSAC Special Issue on Multiwavelength Optical Technology and Networks*, 14(6):1056–1066, June 1996.

[Jai96] M. Jain. Topology designs for wavelength routed optical networks. Technical report, Indian Institute of Science, Bangalore, Jan. 1996.

[JBM95] S. V. Jagannath, K. Bala, and M. Mihail. Hierarchical design of WDM optical networks for ATM transport. In *Proceedings of IEEE Globecom*, pages 2188–2194, 1995.

[Jeu90] L. B. Jeunhomme. *Single-Mode Fiber Optics*. Marcel Dekker, New York, 1990.

[JM92] F. Jia and B. Mukherjee. The receiver collision avoidance (RCA) protocol for a single-hop WDM lightwave network. *Proceedings of IEEE International Conference on Communication*, pages 6–10, 1992.

[Joh95] S. Johansson. A field demonstration of a manageable optical network. In *Proceedings of European Conference on Optical Communication*, pages 851–854, 1995.

[Joh96] S. Johansson et al. A transport network involving a reconfigurable WDM network layer—a European demonstration. *IEEE/OSA JLT/JSAC Special Issue on Multiwavelength Optical Technology and Networks*, 14(6):1341–1348, June 1996.

[Jos97] A. S. Joshi. Media access control protocols for broadcast all-optical networks. Technical report, Indian Institute of Science, Bangalore, Jan. 1997.

[JQE91] *IEEE Journal of Quantum Electronics*, June 1991.

[JRS93] F. J. Janniello, R. Ramaswami, and D. G. Steinberg. A prototype circuit-switched multi-wavelength optical metropolitan-area network. *IEEE/OSA Journal on Lightwave Technology*, 11:777–782, May/June 1993.

[KA96] M. Kovacevic and A. S. Acampora. On the benefits of wavelength translation in all optical clear-channel networks. *IEEE JSAC/JLT Special Issue on Optical Networks*, 14(6):868–880, June 1996.

[Kam96] I. P. Kaminow et al. A wideband all-optical WDM network. *IEEE JSAC/JLT Special Issue on Optical Networks*, 14(5):780–799, June 1996.

[Kas95] N. Kashima. *Passive Optical Components for Optical Fiber Transmission*. Artech House, Boston, 1995.

[KBW96] L. G. Kazovsky, S. Benedetto, and A. E. Willner. *Optical Fiber Communication Systems*. Artech House, Boston, 1996.

[Ker93] A. Kershenbaum. *Telecommunications Network Design Algorithms*. McGraw-Hill, New York, 1993.

[KF86] M. V. Klein and T. E. Furtak. *Optics, 2nd edition*. John Wiley, New York, 1986.

[KG95]   M. Kovacevic and M. Gerla. A new optical signal routing scheme for linear lightwave networks. *IEEE Transactions on Communications*, 43(12):3004–3014, Dec. 1995.

[KGSP94]   M. G. Kane, I. Glesk, J. P. Sokoloff, and P. R. Prucnal. Asymmetric loop mirror: Analysis of an all-optical switch. *Applied Optics*, 33(29):6833–6842, Oct. 1994.

[KH90]   A. Krishna and B. Hajek. Performance of shuffle-like switching networks with deflection. In *Proceedings of IEEE Infocom*, pages 473–480, 1990.

[KK97]   I. P. Kaminow and T. L. Koch, editors. *Optical Fiber Telecommunications III*. Academic Press, San Diego, CA, 1997.

[Kle96]   L. Kleinrock et al. The Supercomputer Supernet Testbed: A WDM-based supercomputer interconnect. *IEEE/OSA JLT/JSAC Special Issue on Multiwavelength Optical Technology and Networks*, 14(6):1388–1399, June 1996.

[KLHN93]   M. J. Karol, C. Lin, G. Hill, and K. Nosu, editors. *IEEE/OSA Journal of Lightwave Technology: Special Issue on Broadband Optical Networks*, May/June 1993.

[KM88]   K. Kobayashi and I. Mito. Single frequency and tunable laser diodes. *IEEE/OSA Journal on Lightwave Technology*, 6(11):1623–1633, November 1988.

[Kni76]   Z. Knittl. *Optics of Thin Films*. John Wiley, New York, 1976.

[Kob94]   I. Kobayashi, editor. *IEEE Communications Magazine: Special Issue on Fiber-Optic Subscriber Loops*, volume 32, Feb. 1994.

[KPEJ97]   C. Kaklamanis, P. Persiano, T. Erlebach, and K. Jansen. Constrained bipartite edge coloring with applications to wavelength routing in all-optical networks. In *International Colloquium on Automata, Languages, and Programming*, 1997.

[Kra97]   J. M. Kraushaar. *Fiber Deployment Update*. Federal Communications Commission, Aug. 1997. Available from *http://www.fcc.gov*.

[KS97]   V. Kumar and E. Schwabe. Improved access to optical bandwidth in trees. In *Proceedings of the ACM Symposium on Distributed Algorithms*, 1997.

[KS98]   R. M. Krishnaswamy and K. N. Sivarajan. Design of logical topologies: A linear formulation for wavelength routed optical networks with no wavelength changers. In *Proceedings of IEEE Infocom*, 1998.

[LA91]   J.-F. P. Labourdette and A. S. Acampora. Logically rearrangeable multihop lightwave networks. *IEEE Transactions on Communications*, 39(8):1223–1230, Aug. 1991.

[LAH92]   J.-F. P. Labourdette, A. S. Acampora, and G. W. Hart. Reconfiguration algorithms for rearrangeable lightwave networks. In *Proceedings of IEEE Infocom*, pages 2205–2214, 1992.

[Lam97] R. I. Laming et al. Fiber gratings for dispersion compensation. In *OFC'97 Technical Digest*, pages 234–235, 1997.

[LCT93] C.-S. Li, M.-S. Chen, and F. F. Tong. POPSMAC: A medium access control strategy for high speed WDM multiaccess networks. *IEEE/OSA Journal on Lightwave Technology*, 11(5/6):1066–1077, May/June 1993.

[Lee91] T. P. Lee. Recent advances in long-wavelength semiconductor lasers for optical fiber communication. *Proceedings of IEEE*, 79(3):253–276, March 1991.

[LGM⁺97] J. K. Lucek, P. Gunning, D. G. Moodie, K. Smith, and D. Pitcher. Synchrolan: A 40 Gbit/s optical-TDMA LAN. *Electronics Letters*, 33(10):887–888, April 1997.

[Lin89] C. Lin, editor. *Optoelectronic Technology and Lightwave Communications Systems*. Van Nostrand Reinhold, New York, 1989.

[Lin96] P. J. Lin. *Wide area optical backbone networks*. PhD thesis, Massachusetts Institute of Technology, 1996.

[LL84] J. P. Laude and J. M. Lerner. Wavelength division multiplexing/demultiplexing (WDM) using diffraction gratings. *SPIE-Application, Theory and Fabrication of Periodic Structures*, 503:22–28, 1984.

[LM88] E. A. Lee and D. G. Messerschmitt. *Digital Communication*. Kluwer Academic Publishers, Boston, 1988.

[LNGP96] E. Leonardi, F. Neri, M. Gerla, and P. Palnati. Congestion control in asynchronous high-speed wormhole routing networks. *IEEE Communications Magazine*, pages 58–69, Nov. 1996.

[LZ89] T. P. Lee and C-N. Zah. Wavelength-tunable and single-frequency lasers for photonic communication networks. *IEEE Communications Magazine*, 27(10):42–52, Oct. 1989.

[Mar74] D. Marcuse. *Theory of Dielectric Optical Waveguides*. Academic Press, New York, 1974.

[Mas96] F. Masetti et al. High speed, high capacity ATM optical switches for future telecommunication transport networks. *IEEE JSAC/JLT Special Issue on Optical Networks*, 14(5):979–998, June 1996.

[MAW96] N. McKeown, V. Ananthram, and J. Walrand. Achieving 100% throughput in an input-queued switch. In *Proceedings of IEEE Infocom*, pages 296–302, 1996.

[Max89] N. F. Maxemchuck. Comparison of deflection and store-and-forward techniques in the Manhattan Street and shuffle-exchange networks. In *Proceedings of IEEE Infocom*, pages 800–809, 1989.

[MB96]   J. Manchester and P. Bonenfant. Fiber optic network survivability: SONET/optical protection layer interworking. In *Proceedings of National Fiber Optic Engineers Conference*, pages 907–918, 1996.

[MBRM96]   B. Mukherjee, D. Banerjee, S. Ramamurthy, and A. Mukherjee. Some principles for designing a wide-area optical network. *IEEE/ACM Transactions on Networking*, 4(5):684–696, 1996.

[Meh90]   N. Mehravari. Performance and protocol improvements for very high speed optical fiber local area networks using a passive star topology. *IEEE/OSA Journal on Lightwave Technology*, LT-8:520–530, April 1990.

[Mid93]   J. E. Midwinter, editor. *Photonics in Switching, Volume II: Systems*. Academic Press, San Diego, CA, 1993.

[MK88]   S. D. Miller and I. P. Kaminow, editors. *Optical Fiber Telecommunications II*. Academic Press, San Diego, CA, 1988.

[MKR95]   M. Mihail, C. Kaklamanis, and S. Rao. Efficient access to optical bandwidth. In *IEEE Symposium on Foundations of Computer Science*, pages 548–557, 1995.

[MP97]   S. Melle and M. Page. WDM planning and deployment considerations for optimizing network evolution. In *Proceedings of National Fiber Optic Engineers Conference*, pages 137–147, 1997.

[MR97]   W. C. Marra and D. G. Ross. The impact that Erbium doped fiber amplifier and WDM technologies have had on undersea fiber optic networks. In *Proceedings of National Fiber Optic Engineers Conference*, pages 243–254, 1997.

[MS88]   J. E. Midwinter and P. W. Smith, editors. *IEEE JSAC: Special Issue on Photonic Switching*, volume 6, Aug. 1988.

[MS95]   D. E. McDysan and D. L. Spohn. *ATM: Theory and Application*. McGraw-Hill, New York, 1995.

[MS96]   W. C. Marra and J. Schesser. Africa ONE: The Africa optical network. *IEEE Communications Magazine*, 34(2):50–57, Feb. 1996.

[Muk92a]   B. Mukherjee. WDM-based local lightwave networks—Part I: Single-hop systems. *IEEE Network*, 6(3):12–27, May 1992.

[Muk92b]   B. Mukherjee. WDM-based local lightwave networks—Part II: Multihop systems. *IEEE Network*, 6(4):20–32, July 1992.

[MYK82]   T. Mukai, Y. Yamamoto, and T. Kimura. S/N and error-rate performance of AlGaAs semiconductor laser preamplifier and linear repeater systems. *IEEE Transactions on Microwave Theory and Techniques*, 30(10):1548–1554, 1982.

[MZB97]   N. M. Margalit, S. Z. Zhang, and J. E. Bowers. Vertical cavity lasers for telecom applications. *IEEE Communications Magazine*, 35(5):164–170, May 1997.

[Neu88] E.-G. Neumann. *Single-Mode Fibers*. Springer-Verlag, Berlin, 1988.

[NO94] K. Nosu and M. J. O'Mahony, editors. *IEEE Communications Magazine: Special Issue on Optically Multiplexed Networks*, volume 32, Dec. 1994.

[NTIO93] K. Nosu, H. Toba, K. Inoue, and K. Oda. 100 channel optical FDM technology and its applications to optical FDM channel-based networks. *IEEE/OSA Journal on Lightwave Technology*, 11:764–776, May/June 1993.

[OLH89] R. Olshansky, V. A. Lanzisera, and P. M. Hill. Subcarrier multiplexed lightwave systems for broadband distribution. *IEEE/OSA Journal on Lightwave Technology*, 7(9):1329–1342, Sept. 1989.

[Ols89] N. A. Olsson. Lightwave systems with optical amplifiers. *IEEE/OSA Journal on Lightwave Technology*, 7(7):1071–1082, July 1989.

[O'M88] M. J. O'Mahony. Semiconductor laser amplifiers for future fiber systems. *IEEE/OSA Journal on Lightwave Technology*, 6(4):531–544, April 1988.

[Ona96] H. Onaka et al. 1.1 Tb/s WDM transmission over a 150 km 1.3 μm zero-dispersion single-mode fiber. In *OFC'96 Technical Digest*, 1996. Postdeadline paper PD19.

[Opt96] Optical Corporation of America. *16 Channel Dense Wavelength Division Multiplexer (DWDM)*, 1996. Specification available at *http://www.oca.com*.

[OSYZ95] M. J. O'Mahony, D. Simeonidou, A. Yu, and J. Zhou. The design of a European optical network. *IEEE/OSA Journal on Lightwave Technology*, 13(5):817–828, May 1995.

[Pan92] R. K. Pankaj. *Architectures for linear lightwave networks*. PhD thesis, Massachusetts Institute of Technology, 1992.

[Pap84] A. Papoulis. *Probability, Random Variables, and Stochastic Processes*. McGraw-Hill, New York, 1984.

[PAP86] M. J. Potasek, G. P. Agrawal, and S. C. Pinault. Analytic and numerical study of pulse broadening in nonlinear dispersive optical fibers. *Journal of Optical Society of America B*, 3(2):205–211, Feb. 1986.

[PD96] L. L. Peterson and B. S. Davie. *Computer Networks: A Systems Approach*. Morgan Kaufmann, San Francisco, 1996.

[Per73] S. D. Personick. Applications for quantum amplifiers in simple digital optical communication systems. *Bell System Technical Journal*, 52(1):117–133, Jan. 1973.

[PHR97] N. S. Patel, K. L. Hall, and K. A. Rauschenbach. Optical rate conversion for high-speed TDM networks. *IEEE Photonics Technology Letters*, 9(9):1277, Sept. 1997.

[PN87] K. Padmanabhan and A. N. Netravali. Dilated networks for photonic switching. *IEEE Transactions on Communications*, 35:1357–1365, 1987.

[Pru89] P. R. Prucnal, editor. *IEEE Network: Special Issue on Optical Multiaccess Networks*, volume 3, March 1989.

[Pru93] P. R. Prucnal. Optically processed self-routing, synchronization, and contention resolution for 1-d and 2-d photonic switching architectures. *IEEE Journal of Quantum Electronics*, 29(2):600–612, Feb. 1993.

[PS93] G. R. Pieris and G. H. Sasaki. A linear lightwave Beneš network. *IEEE/ACM Transactions on Networking*, pages 441–445, Aug. 1993.

[PS94] G. R. Pieris and G. H. Sasaki. Scheduling transmissions in WDM broadcast and select networks. *IEEE/ACM Transactions on Networking*, pages 105–110, April 1994.

[PSF86] P. R. Prucnal, M. A. Santoro, and T. R. Fan. Spread spectrum fiber-optic local area network using optical processing. *IEEE/OSA Journal on Lightwave Technology*, LT-4(5):547–554, May 1986.

[PTCF91] C. D. Poole, R. W. Tkach, A. R. Chraplyvy, and D. A. Fishman. Fading in lightwave systems due to polarization-mode dispersion. *IEEE Photon. Tech. Lett.*, 3(1):68–70, Jan. 1991.

[Ram93a] R. Ramaswami. Multi-wavelength lightwave networks for computer communication. *IEEE Communications Magazine*, 31(2):78–88, Feb. 1993.

[Ram93b] R. Ramaswami. Systems issues in multi-wavelength optical networks. In *Proceedings of 31st Annual Allerton Conference on Communications, Control and Computing*, Sept. 1993.

[Red97] G. B. Redifer. DWDM versus TDM in metro and long-haul applications. In *Proceedings of National Fiber Optic Engineers Conference*, pages 117–124, 1997.

[RH90] R. Ramaswami and P. A. Humblet. Amplifier induced crosstalk in multi-channel optical networks. *IEEE/OSA Journal on Lightwave Technology*, 8(12):1882–1896, Dec. 1990.

[RL93] R. Ramaswami and K. Liu. Analysis of effective power budget in optical bus and star networks using Erbium-doped fiber amplifiers. *IEEE/OSA Journal on Lightwave Technology*, 11(11):1863–1871, Nov. 1993.

[RLB95] P. Roorda, C-Y. Lu, and T. Boutlier. Benefits of all-optical routing in transport networks. In *OFC'95 Technical Digest*, pages 164–165, 1995.

[RN76] H.-D. Rudolph and E.-G. Neumann. Approximations for the eigenvalues of the fundamental mode of a step-index glass fiber waveguide. *Nachrichtentechnische Zeitschrift*, 29(14):328–329, 1976.

[Ros86] F. E. Ross. FDDI—a tutorial. *IEEE Communications Magazine*, 24(5):10–17, May 1986.

[RS94]   R. Ramaswami and K. N. Sivarajan. A packet-switched multihop lightwave network using subcarrier and wavelength-division multiplexing. *IEEE Transactions on Communications*, March 1994.

[RS95]   R. Ramaswami and K. N. Sivarajan. Routing and wavelength assignment in all-optical networks. *IEEE/ACM Transactions on Networking*, pages 489–500, Oct. 1995. An earlier version appeared in *Prof. Infocom'94*.

[RS96a]   R. Ramaswami and A. Segall. Distributed network control for wavelength-routed optical networks. In *Proceedings of IEEE Infocom*, pages 138–147, 1996.

[RS96b]   R. Ramaswami and K. N. Sivarajan. Design of logical topologies for wavelength-routed optical networks. *IEEE JSAC/JLT Special Issue on Optical Networks*, 14(5):840–851, June 1996.

[RS97a]   R. Ramaswami and G. H. Sasaki. Multiwavelength optical networks with limited wavelength conversion. In *Proceedings of IEEE Infocom*, pages 490–499, 1997.

[RS97b]   G. Rouskas and V. Sivaraman. Packet scheduling in broadcast WDM networks with arbitrary transceiver tuning latencies. *IEEE/ACM Transactions on Networking*, 5(3):359–370, June 1997.

[RU94]   P. Raghavan and E. Upfal. Efficient routing in all-optical networks. In *Proceedings of 26th ACM Symposium on Theory of Computing*, pages 134–143, May 1994.

[RWv84]   S. Ramo, J. R. Whinnery, and T. van Duzer. *Fields and Waves in Communication Electronics*. John Wiley, New York, 1984.

[Sal89]   J. A. Salehi. Code division multiple-access techniques in optical fiber networks—Part I: Fundamental principles. *IEEE Transactions on Communications*, 37(8):824–833, Aug. 1989.

[SAS96]   S. Subramaniam, M. Azizoglu, and A. K. Somani. Connectivity and sparse wavelength conversion in wavelength-routing networks. In *Proceedings of IEEE Infocom*, pages 148–155, 1996.

[SB87]   R. A. Spanke and V. E. Beneš. An *n*-stage planar optical permutation network. *Applied Optics*, 26, April 1987.

[SB89]   J. A. Salehi and C. A. Brackett. Code division multiple-access techniques in optical fiber networks—Part II: Systems performance analysis. *IEEE Transactions on Communications*, 37(8):834–842, Aug. 1989.

[SBJC90] D. A. Smith, J. E. Baran, J. J. Johnson, and K-W. Cheung. Integrated-optic acoustically-tunable filters for WDM networks. *IEEE Journal of Selected Areas in Communications*, 8(6):1151–1159, Aug. 1990.

[SBJS93] T. E. Stern, K. Bala, S. Jiang, and J. Sharony. Linear lightwave networks: Performance issues. *IEEE/OSA Journal on Lightwave Technology*, 11:937–950, May/June 1993.

[SBP96]   S-W. Seo, K. Bergman, and P. R. Prucnal. Transparent optical networks with time-division multiplexing. *IEEE JSAC/JLT Special Issue on Optical Networks*, 14(5):1039–1051, June 1996.

[SBW87]   N. Shibata, R. P. Braun, and R. G. Waarts. Phase-mismatch dependence of efficiency of wave generation through four-wave mixing in a single-mode optical fiber. *IEEE Journal of Quantum Electronics*, 23:1205–1210, 1987.

[SC96]   L. Steinhorst and H. Calhoun. Alternatives for next-generation high-capacity networks. In *Proceedings of National Fiber Optic Engineers Conference*, pages 271–282, 1996.

[SIA92]   Y. Suematsu, K. Iga, and S. Arai. Advanced semiconductor lasers. *Proceedings of IEEE*, 80:383–397, 1992.

[SID93]   J. R. Sauer, M. N. Islam, and S. P. Dijaili. A soliton ring network. *IEEE/OSA Journal on Lightwave Technology*, 11(12):2182–2190, Dec. 1993.

[Siv92]   K. N. Sivarajan. Multihop logical topologies in gigabit lightwave networks. *IEEE Lightwave Telecommunication Systems Magazine*, Aug. 1992.

[SKY89]   P. W. Shumate, O. Krumpholz, and K. Yamaguchi, editors. *IEEE/OSA JLT/JSAC Special Issue on Subscriber Loop Technology*, volume 7, Nov. 1989.

[Sle97]   C. Sleath. Wavelength division multiplexing targets add/drop multiplexers and digital cross-connects. In *Proceedings of National Fiber Optic Engineers Conference*, pages 259–270, 1997.

[Smi72]   R. G. Smith. Optical power handling capacity of low loss optical fibers as determined by stimulated Raman and Brillouin scattering. *Applied Optics*, 11(11):2489–2160, Nov. 1972.

[Smi81]   B. Smith. Architecture and applications of the HEP multiprocessor system. In *Real Time Signal Processing IV, Proceedings of SPIE*, pages 241–248, 1981.

[SNIA90]   N. Shibata, K. Nosu, K. Iwashita, and Y. Azuma. Transmission limitations due to fiber nonlinearities in optical FDM systems. *IEEE Journal of Selected Areas in Communications*, 8(6):1068–1077, Aug. 1990.

[Son95]   G. H. Song. Toward the ideal codirectional Bragg filter with an acousto-optic-filter design. *IEEE/OSA Journal on Lightwave Technology*, 13(3):470–480, March 1995.

[SOW95]   K-I. Sato, S. Okamoto, and A. Watanabe. Photonic transport networks based on optical paths. *International Journal of Communication Systems (UK)*, 8(6):377–389, Nov./Dec. 1995.

[Spa87]   R. A. Spanke. Architectures for guided-wave optical space switching systems. *IEEE Communications Magazine*, 25(5):42–48, May 1987.

[SPGK93] J. P. Sokoloff, P. R. Prucnal, I. Glesk, and M. Kane. A terahertz optical asymmetric demultiplexer (TOAD). *IEEE Photonics Technology Letters*, 5(7):787–790, July 1993.

[SR92] M. Sexton and A. Reid. *Transmission Networking: SONET and the Synchronous Digital Hierarchy*. Artech House, Boston, 1992.

[SR94a] A. Shah and G. Ramakrishnan. *FDDI: A High Speed Network*. PTR Prentice Hall, Englewood Cliffs, NJ, 1994.

[SR94b] K. N. Sivarajan and R. Ramaswami. Lightwave networks based on de Bruijn graphs. *IEEE/ACM Transactions on Networking*, 2(1):70–79, Feb. 1994.

[SS96a] M. A. Scobey and D. E. Spock. Passive DWDM components using microplasma optical interference filters. In *OFC'96 Technical Digest*, pages 242–243, San Jose, Feb. 1996.

[SS96b] C. A. Siller and M. Shafi, editors. *SONET/SDH: A Sourcebook of Synchronous Networking*. IEEE Press, Los Alamitos, CA, 1996.

[SSAB97] S. Subramaniam, A. K. Somani, M. Azizoglu, and R. A. Barry. A performance model for wavelength conversion with non-Poisson traffic. In *Proceedings of IEEE Infocom*, pages 500–507, 1997.

[Ste87] J. Stern et al. Passive optical local networks for telephony applications. *Electronics Letters*, 23:1255–1257, 1987.

[Ste90] T. E. Stern. Linear lightwave networks : How far can they go? In *Proceedings of IEEE Globecom*, pages 1866–1872, 1990.

[Ste94] W. R. Stevens. *TCP/IP Illustrated, Volume 1*. Addison-Wesley, Reading, MA, 1994.

[SV96] M. W. Sachs and A. Varma. Fibre channel and related standards. *IEEE Communications Magazine*, 34(8):40–49, Aug. 1996.

[Tan88] A. Tanenbaum. *Computer Networks*. Prentice Hall, Englewood Cliffs, NJ, 1988.

[Tas97] L. Tassiulas. Scheduling and performance limits of networks with constantly changing topologies. *IEEE Transactions on Information Theory*, 43:1067–1073, May 1997.

[TBO] *Test Bed for All-Optical Networks (TBONE)*. http://www.optivision.com/nsds/tbone.html.

[TCF+95] R. W. Tkach, A. R. Chraplyvy, F. Forghieri, A. H. Gnauck, and R. M. Derosier. Four-photon mixing and high-speed WDM systems. *IEEE/OSA Journal on Lightwave Technology*, 13(5):841–849, May 1995.

[TOI+96] H. Toba, K. Oda, K. Inoue, K. Nosu, and T. Kitoh. An optical FDM based self-healing ring network employing arrayed-waveguide-grating ADM filters and

EDFAs with level equalizers. *IEEE JSAC/JLT Special Issue on Optical Networks*, 14(6):800–813, June 1996.

[TOT96] H. Takahashi, K. Oda, and H. Toba. Impact of crosstalk in an arrayed-waveguide multiplexer on $n \times n$ optical interconnection. *IEEE/OSA JLT/JSAC Special Issue on Multiwavelength Optical Technology and Networks*, 14(6):1097–1105, June 1996.

[TOTI95] H. Takahashi, K. Oda, H. Toba, and Y. Inoue. Transmission characteristics of arrayed $n \times n$ wavelength multiplexer. *IEEE/OSA Journal on Lightwave Technology*, 13(3):447–455, March 1995.

[TSN94] H. Takahashi, S. Suzuki, and I. Nishi. Wavelength multiplexer based on SiO_2–Ta_2O_5 arrayed-waveguide grating. *IEEE/OSA Journal on Lightwave Technology*, 12(6):989–995, June 1994.

[Tuc75] A. Tucker. Coloring a family of circular arcs. *SIAM Journal on Applied Mathematics*, 29(3):493–502, 1975.

[U.S86] U.S. Food and Drug Administration, Department of Radiological Health. *Requirements of 21 CFR Chap. J for Class 1 Laser Products*, Jan. 1986.

[Ven96a] A. M. Vengsarkar et al. Long-period fiber-grating-based gain equalizers. *Optics Letters*, 21(5):336–338, 1996.

[Ven96b] A. M. Vengsarkar et al. Long-period gratings as band-rejection filters. *IEEE/OSA Journal on Lightwave Technology*, 14(1):58–64, Jan. 1996.

[Vod97] R. S. Vodhanel et al. National-scale WDM networking demonstration by the MONET consortium. In *OFC'97 Technical Digest*, 1997. Postdeadline paper PD27.

[VS91] A. R. Vellekoop and M. K. Smit. Four-channel integrated-optic wavelength demultiplexer with weak polarization dependence. *IEEE/OSA Journal on Lightwave Technology*, 9:310–314, 1991.

[vT68] H. L. van Trees. *Detection, Estimation, and Modulation Theory. Part I*. John Wiley, New York, 1968.

[WASG96] R. E. Wagner, R. C. Alferness, A. A. M. Saleh, and M. S. Goodman. MONET: Multiwavelength optical networking. *IEEE/OSA JLT/JSAC Special Issue on Multiwavelength Optical Technology and Networks*, 14(6):1349–1355, June 1996.

[WD96] N. Wauters and P. Demeester. Design of the optical path layer in multiwavelength cross-connected networks. *IEEE JSAC/JLT Special Issue on Optical Networks*, 14(6):881–892, June 1996.

[WF83] A. X. Widmer and P. A. Franaszek. A DC-balanced, partitioned-block, 8B-10B transmission code. *IBM Journal of Research and Development*, 27(5):440–451, Sept. 1983.

[WH94]   T. Weller and B. Hajek. Scheduling non-uniform traffic in a packet switching system with small propagation delay. *Proceedings of IEEE Infocom*, 1994.

[WKR+88]   S. S. Wagner, H. Kobrinski, T. J. Robe, H. L. Lemberg, and L. S. Smoot. Experimental demonstration of a passive optical subscriber loop architecture. *Electronics Letters*, 24:344–346, 1988.

[WL88]   S. S. Wagner and H. L. Lemberg. Technology and system issues for the WDM-based fiber loop architecture. *IEEE/OSA Journal on Lightwave Technology*, 7(11):1759–1768, 1988.

[WOe90]   W. I. Way, R. Olshansky, and K. Sato (editors). Special issue on applications of RF and microwave subcarriers to optical fiber transmission in present and future broadband networks. *IEEE Journal of Selected Areas in Communications*, 8(7), Sept. 1990.

[Wu92]   T. H. Wu. *Fiber Network Service Survivability*. Artech House, Boston, 1992.

[WV97]   J. Walrand and P. Varaiya. *High-Performance Communication Networks*. Morgan Kaufmann, San Francisco, 1997.

[Yam80]   Y. Yamamoto. Noise and error-rate performance of semiconductor laser amplifiers in PCM-IM transmission systems. *IEEE Journal of Quantum Electronics*, 16:1073–1081, 1980.

[Yan96]   Y. Yano et al. 2.6 Tb/s WDM transmission experiment using optical duobinary coding. In *ECOC'96 Technical Digest*, 1996. Postdeadline paper Th.B.3.1.

[Yar65]   A. Yariv. Internal modulation in multimode laser oscillators. *Journal of Applied Physics*, 36:388, 1965.

[Yar85]   A. Yariv. *Optical Electronics, 3rd Edition*. Holt, Rinehart and Winston, New York, 1985.

[Yar89]   A. Yariv. *Quantum Electronics, 3rd edition*. John Wiley, New York, 1989.

[YLES96]   J. Yates, J. Lacey, D. Everitt, and M. Summerfield. Limited-range wavelength translation in all-optical networks. In *Proceedings of IEEE Infocom*, pages 954–961, 1996.

[Yoo96]   S. J. B. Yoo. Wavelength conversion techniques for WDM network applications. *IEEE/OSA JLT/JSAC Special Issue on Multiwavelength Optical Technology and Networks*, 14(6):955–966, June 1996.

[ZA95]   Z. Zhang and A. S. Acampora. A heuristic wavelength assignment algorithm for multihop WDM networks with wavelength routing and wavelength reuse. *IEEE/ACM Transactions on Networking*, 3(3):281–288, June 1995.

[ZCC+96]   J. Zhou, R. Cadeddu, E. Casaccia, C. Cavazzoni, and M. J. O'Mahony. Crosstalk in multiwavelength optical cross-connect networks. *IEEE/OSA JLT/JSAC Special*

Issue on Multiwavelength Optical Technology and Networks, 14(6):1423–1435, June 1996.

[ZJS⁺95] M. Zirngibl, C. H. Joyner, L. W. Stulz, C. Dragone, H. M. Presby, and I. P. Kaminow. LARnet, a local access router network. *IEEE Photonics Technology Letters*, 7(2):1041–1135, Feb. 1995.

[ZO94] J. Zhou and M. J. O'Mahony. Optical transmission system penalties due to fiber polarization mode dispersion. *IEEE Photon. Tech. Lett.*, 6(10):1265–1267, Oct. 1994.

[Zys96] J. L. Zyskind et al. Fast power transients in optically amplified multiwavelength optical networks. In *OFC'96 Technical Digest*, 1996. Postdeadline paper PD31.

Index

Bold page numbers indicate principal occurrences of entries.

613